ROMANS 8

Other Puritan Commentaries published by the Trust

SERMONS

ON

THE EIGHTH CHAPTER

OF THE

EPISTLE TO THE ROMANS,

(VERSES 1-4.)

BY

THOMAS JACOMB, D.D.

THE BANNER OF TRUTH TRUST

THE BANNER OF TRUTH TRUST
3 Murrayfield Road, Edinburgh EH12 6EL
P.O. Box 621, Carlisle, Pennsylvania 17013, USA

*

This edition first published by James Nichol 1868
First Banner of Truth Trust reprint 1996
ISBN 0 85151 707 2

*

Printed in Great Britain by
The Bath Press, Bath

COUNCIL OF PUBLICATION.

W. LINDSAY ALEXANDER, D.D., Professor of Theology, Congregational Union, Edinburgh.

JAMES BEGG, D.D., Minister of Newington Free Church, Edinburgh.

THOMAS J. CRAWFORD, D.D., S.T.P., Professor of Divinity, University, Edinburgh.

D. T. K. DRUMMOND, M.A., Minister of St Thomas's Episcopal Church, Edinburgh.

WILLIAM H. GOOLD, D.D., Professor of Biblical Literature and Church History, Reformed
    Presbyterian Church, Edinburgh.

ANDREW THOMSON, D.D., Minister of Broughton Place United Presbyterian Church, Edinburgh.

General Editor.

THOMAS SMITH, D.D., EDINBURGH.

THOMAS JACOMB, D.D.

OF the many excellent works which we have had the privilege of making accessible to Christian readers by means of this series of reprints, there has been no one of which we have been led to form a higher estimate than we have formed of that reproduced in this volume. It might be supposed that a quarto volume occupied with the exposition of four verses would be tedious; but we do not think that the reader will find it so. Indeed, it may be said that while these four verses are formally the subject of the volume, its subject substantially is the gospel system of redemption and salvation;—salvation both in its procurement by the obedience and death of the incarnate Son of God, and in its application, in all its steps, from the *no-condemnation* with which the eighth chapter of the Epistle to the Romans begins, to the *no-separation* with which it closes. Dr Jacomb's exposition is at once learned and practical, the production of an erudite theologian and an earnest Christian. It deals with the controversies that have been raised respecting the great doctrines of the faith delivered to the saints—especially with some of the most important parts of the Socinian and Romish controversies—and it handles them with great ingenuity and dialectic skill. But it deals also with things pertaining more directly to practical matters of life and godliness; with the hopes and the fears, the encouragements and the trials, the duties and the destinies of the humble, earnest disciple of Christ. We know few books in which there is a finer blending of the doctrinal and the practical, a richer exhibition of the fulness of the grace that is in Christ, a more uncompromising demand of carefulness in maintaining good works on the part of those who have believed in Christ.

By way of introducing the author to such readers as may not be familiar with his name, we shall content ourselves with transcribing (1) the notice of him contained in Anthony à Wood's "Athenæ Oxonienses;" (2) the account that is given of him in Palmer's edition of Calamy's Nonconformist's Memorial; and (3) the estimate of his character given by Dr Bates in his funeral sermon; only omitting from the second of these the extracts borrowed into it from the third. To these we shall add (4) a few brief notes of our own.

(1) *From Wood's Athenæ.*

Thomas Jacomb, son of John Jacomb, was born at Burton Lazurs, near to Melton Mowbray, in Leicestershire, became either a batler or a commoner of Magdalen Hall, in Easter Term, anno 1640, aged eighteen years; left it upon the eruption of the civil wars; went to Cambridge, and taking the covenant, became Fellow of Trinity College there, in the place of a loyalist ejected; and having the degree of Master of Arts in that University conferred on him, became a person of high repute, (as one of his persuasion tells us,) for his good life, good learning, and excellent gravity, greatly beloved of the then master, who loved an honest man and a good scholar with all his heart. About that time, taking orders according to the Presbyterian way, he retired to London, and much about the same time that he became minister of St Martin's Church, joining to Ludgate, he became one of the assistants to the Commissioners of London for the ejecting of such whom the faction then called scandalous, ignorant, and insufficient ministers and schoolmasters. From that time to his silencing he was a very zealous person for promoting the cause, and in very great esteem by those of his persuasion, as the above said author tells us, " for his piety, parts, prudence, sound, judicious, practical, spiritual, substantial preaching;" yet another of a contrary persuasion, who lived afterwards, as now, in very great esteem for his loyalty and learning, represents him to have been the prettiest, nonsensical, trifling goose-cap that ever set pen to paper. On the 14th of March 1659, he was one of those zealots, who, by Act of Parliament, were appointed approvers of ministers according to the Presbyterian way, before they were to be settled in church livings; but that being soon after laid aside upon his Majesty's restoration, he himself was ejected from St Martin's, and laid aside also for non-conformity at Bartholomew-tide in 1662, he being about that time doctor of divinity. Afterwards he followed the trade of conventicling, for which he was brought several times into trouble, and at length became chaplain to the Countess of Exeter, in whose service he died.

After giving a list of his works, Wood continues :—

" Dr Jacomb also was one of the eight nonconforming ministers that undertook, in 1682, to finish the English Annotations on the Holy Scriptures, in two vols. in folio, begun by Matthew Poole, and by him carried on to the 58th chapter of Isaiah; and no doubt there is but that he did his share in that great work. At length he, giving way to fate in the house of Frances Countess of Exeter, situate and being in Little Britain, on the 27th of March (being then Easter Sunday) in sixteen hundred eighty and seven, was buried five days after in the church of St Anne, within, and near, Aldersgate, in the city of London, in the presence of very many, as well conformist as nonconformist divines."

(2) *From Palmer's Memorial.*

"THOMAS JACOMB, D.D., of Magdalene Hall, Oxford. Born near Melton Mowbray, in Leicestershire. When B.A. he removed to Emmanuel College, Cambridge. He was some time Fellow of Trinity, and much esteemed there. He came to London in 1647, and being received into the family of that excellent, pious, and devout lady, the Countess Dowager of Exeter, (daughter to the Earl of Bridgewater,) as her chaplain, he had the opportunity of preaching in the city, and was soon fixed in Ludgate parish, where his ministry was both acceptable and useful.

" He died at the Countess of Exeter's, March 27, 1687, leaving an incomparable library of the most valuable books, in all kinds of learning, which were sold by auction for £1300. Dr Bates preached his funeral sermon, from which the above account is principally extracted. No mention is made of Mr Jacomb's age, but from the introduction to this discourse it appears that he was much younger than Dr Bates, and that he had possessed a more vigorous constitution.

" Dr Jacomb's farewell sermon was on John viii. 29, ' He that sent me is with me : the Father hath not left me alone ; for I do always those things that please him.' The whole is so excellent and sententious that it is not easy to do justice to it by an analysis. Having treated on the words as they refer to Christ himself, he applies them to his people ; to whom he recommends it as their grand object—not to please themselves, not to please men—but in all things to please God. This he urges from what God is in himself, their relation to him, and their expectations from him. He that pleases God profits himself, particularly in the enjoyment of his presence. Please God and he will please you. He will never leave you; no, not in a time of distress and trouble, though all others forsake you. See that promise, Isa. xliii. 2. The saints in all ages have found he hath made it good. So Jacob under his sharp trials. 'Behold I am with thee.' So Joseph: his master threw him into prison, but the Lord was with Joseph. So Jeremiah, when cast into the dungeon. So the three children in the fiery furnace: there was a fourth with them, 'like the Son of God.' So Paul, when brought to his trial, all men forsook him, but 'the Lord stood by him.' So the first Christians: persecuted but not forsaken.

"*Directions:* Make conscience of those duties which are certainly pleasing to him. Be steadfast in his good ways in an apostatising age. Be not ashamed to own Christ before all the world. Reckon reproaches for his name better than the pleasures of sin. Assert the purity and spirituality of gospel-worship. Keep up religion in your families. Be good in bad times. Pray for and love those ministers that have been instrumental for your spiritual good, whatever dirt is now thrown in their faces, and though you never get more good by them. Forget not to distribute to the necessities of God's people. Be patient and meek towards them that wrong you. Do your duty to those in authority, and conduct yourselves, as Daniel did, against whom they had nothing, *save in the matter of his God.* In a word, walk as becometh the gospel. Phil. ii. 16. Use of comfort under sufferings: Pleasing God does not secure against suffering from men; sometimes it rather exposes to it; but it takes away the sting and venom of suffering. The presence of God in a time of affliction is exceedingly precious. Be not troubled in your thoughts about what you may undergo. If God be with you, all will be well. If God comes when the cross comes, the weight of it will never hurt you. What is a prison when God is there? We have more reason to be afraid of prosperity, with God's absence, than of adversity, with God's presence. A good God will make every condition to be good. It is not a prison, but a palace, where God is; and they that do the things that please him, may be assured whatever condition they may be in, the Father will not leave them alone. Ministers may leave you; ordinances may leave you; creature enjoyments may leave you; but God never will. O bless his holy name.

"Lastly:—Be tender of them that differ from you because they dare not displease God. Pass a charitable interpretation on our laying down the exercise of our ministry. There is a greater judge than you, who must judge us all at the last day; and to this judge we can appeal, before angels and men, that it is nothing but conscience toward God, and fear of offending him, that puts us upon this dissent. I censure none that differ from me, as though they displease God. But as to myself, should I do thus I should certainly violate the peace of my own conscience, and offend God; which I must not do, no, not to secure my ministry, though that is, or ought to be, dearer to me than my life. And dear it is, God knoweth. Do not add affliction to affliction; be not uncharitable in judging of us, as if through pride, faction, obstinacy, or devotedness to party, or (which is worse than all) opposition to authority, we dissent. The judge of all hearts knows that it is merely from these apprehensions which (after prayer and the use of all means) yet continue, that doing [otherwise] we should displease God. If we be mistaken, I pray God to convince us. But however things go, God will make good this truth to us, that *our Father will not leave us alone;* for it is the unfeigned desire of our soul in all things to *please God.*"

LIST OF HIS WORKS.

"A Commentary, or Sermons, on Rom. viii. 1–4. Treatise on holy Dedication, personal and domestic. Fun. Serm. for Mr M. Martin. Another for Mr Vines, with an account of his life. Another for Mr Case, with a narrative of his life and death. The life of Mr Whitaker. Two Sermons in Morn. Ex. Serm. at St Paul's, Oct. 26, 1656. Serm. before Lord Mayor, &c., at the Spittle. Wood is mistaken with respect to his concern in Pool's Contin."

(3) *From Dr Bates's Funeral Sermon.*

"I shall now address myself to the present occasion, which is to pay our last solemn respects to the memory of the Reverend Dr Thomas Jacomb, who was so universally known, esteemed, and beloved in this city, that his name is a noble and lasting elegy. I shall not give an account of the time he spent in Cambridge, where he was Fellow of Trinity College, and worthily esteemed in that flourishing society; but confine my discourse to his ministry in London. Here the divine providence disposed him into the family of a right honourable person, to whom he was deservedly very acceptable, and whose real and most noble favours conferred upon him, were only to be equalled by his grateful and high respects, and his constant care to promote serious religion in her family.

"He was a servant of Christ in the most peculiar and sacred relation; and he was true to his title, both in his doctrine and in his life. He was an excellent preacher of the gospel, and had a happy art of conveying saving truths into the minds and hearts of men.

"He did not entertain his hearers with curiosities, but with spiritual food. He dispensed the Bread of Life, whose vital sweetness and nourishing virtue is both productive and preservative of the life of souls. He preached Christ crucified, our only wisdom and righteousness, sanctification, and redemption. His great design was to convince sinners of their absolute want of Christ, that with flaming affections they might come to him, and from his fulness receive divine grace. This is to water the tree at the root, whereby it becomes flourishing and fruitful; whereas the laying down of moral rules for the exercise of virtue, and subduing vicious affections, without directing men to derive spiritual strength, by prayer, and in the use of divine ordinances, from the Mediator, the fountain of all grace, and without representing his love as the most powerful motive, and obligation to obedience, is but pure philosophy, and the highest effect of it is but unregenerate morality. In short, his sermons were clear, and solid, and affectionate. He dipped his words in his soul, in warm affections, and breathed a holy fire into the breasts of his hearers. Of this, many serious and judicious persons can give testimony, who so long attended upon his ministry with delight and profit.

"His constant diligence in the service of Christ was becoming his zeal for the glory of his Master, and his love to the souls of men. He preached thrice a week whilst he had opportunity and strength. He esteemed his labour in the sacred office both his highest honour and his pleasure.

"At the first appearance of an ulcer in his mouth, which he was told to be cancerous, he was observed to be not much concerned about it, than as it was likely to hinder his preaching, that was his delightful work. And when he enjoyed ease, and after wasting sickness, was restored to some degree of strength, he joyfully returned to his duty. Nay, when his pains were tolerable, preaching was his best anodyne when others failed. And, after his preaching, the reflection upon the divine goodness that enabled him for the discharge of the service, was great relief of his pains.

"His life was suitable to his holy profession. His sermons were printed in a fair and lively character in his conversation. He was an example to believers, in word, in conversation, in charity, in spirit, in faith, in purity.

" He was of a staid mind, and temperate passions, and moderate in counsels. In the managing of affairs of concernment he was not vehement and confident, not imposing and overbearing, but was receptive of advice, and yielding to reason.

" His compassionate charity and beneficence was very conspicuous amongst his other graces. His heart was given to God, and his relieving beneficent hand to the living images of God, whose pressing wants he resented with tender affections, and was very instrumental for their supplies.

" And as his life, so his death adorned the gospel, which was so exemplary to others, and so gracious and comfortable to himself. The words of men leaving the world make usually the deepest impressions, being spoken most feelingly, and with least affectation. Death reveals the secrets of men's hearts: and the testimony that dying saints give, how gracious a Master they have served, how sweet His service has been to their souls, has a mighty influence upon those about them. Now the deportment and expressions of this servant of Christ in his long languishing condition, were so holy and heavenly, that though his life had been very useful, yet he more glorified God dying than living.

" When he was summoned by painful sickness, his first work was to yield himself with resigned submission to the will of God. When a dear friend of his first visited him, he said, ' I am in the use of means, but I think my appointed time is come, that I must die. If my life might be serviceable to convert or build up one soul, I should be content to live; but if God hath no work for me to do, here I am, let him do with me as he pleaseth: but to be with Christ is best of all.' Another time he told the same person, ' That now it was visible it was a determined case. God would not hear the prayer, to bless the means of his recovery,' therefore desired his friend to be willing to resign him to God, saying, ' It will not be long before we meet in heaven, never to part more, and there we shall be perfectly happy; there neither your doubts and fears, nor my pains and sorrows shall follow us, nor our sins, which is best of all.' After a long continuance in his languishing condition without any sensible alteration, being asked how he did, he replied, ' I lie here, but get no ground for heaven or earth.' Upon which one said, ' Yes, in your preparations for heaven.' ' O yes,' said he, ' there I sensibly get ground, I bless God.'

" A humble submission to the divine pleasure was the habitual frame of his soul: like a die that, thrown high or low, always falls upon its square. Thus whether hope of his recovery was raised or sunk, he was content in every dispensation of Providence.

" His patience under sharp and continuing pains was admirable. The most difficult part of a Christian's duty, the sublimest degree of holiness upon earth, is to bear tormenting pains with a meek and quiet spirit. Then ' faith is made perfect in works:' and this was eminently verified in his long trial. His pains were very severe, proceeding from a cancerous humour, that spread itself in his joints, and preyed upon the tenderest membranes, the most sensible parts, yet his patience was invincible. How many restless nights did he pass through without the least murmuring or reluctancy of spirit.

" He patiently suffered very grievous things, ' through Christ that strengthened him:' and in his most afflicted condition was thankful.

" But what disease or death could disturb the blessed composure of his soul, which ' was kept by the peace of God that passes all understanding'? Such was the divine mercy, he had no anxieties about his future state, but a comfortable assurance of the favour of God, and his title to the eternal inheritance.

" He had a substantial double joy in the reflection upon his life spent in the faithful service of Christ, and the prospect of a blessed eternity ready to receive him. This made him long to be above. He said, with some regret, ' Death flies from me, I make no haste to my Father's house.' But the wise and gracious God, 'having tried His faithful servant, gave him the crown of life, which He hath promised to those that love Him.' His body, that poor relict of frailty, is committed in trust to the grave: his soul sees the face of God in righteousness, and is satisfied with His likeness.

"The hope of this should allay the sorrows of his dearest friends. When the persons we love and have lived with, are to be absent a few months, it is grievous; but at the last lamenting separation, all the springs of our tender affections are opened, and sorrows are ready to overwhelm us. But the steadfast belief of the divine world, and that our friends are safely arrived thither, is able to support our fainting spirits, and refresh all our sorrows. The truth is, we have reason to lay to heart the displeasure of God, and our own loss, when His faithful ministers are taken away. When the holy lights of heaven are eclipsed, it portends sad things. When the saints are removed from earth to heaven, and their souls freed from the interposition of their dark bodies, they truly live; but we that remain die, being deprived of their holy lives, and their examples, that are a preservative from the contagion of the world. A due sense of God's afflicting providence is becoming us; but always allayed with hope of our being shortly reunited with our dearest friends for ever in the better world. O that our serious preparations, our lively hopes, and the presence of the great Comforter in our souls, may encourage us most willingly to leave this lower world, so full of temptations and trouble, to ascend into the world above, where perfect peace, full joy, and the most excellent glory are in conjunction for ever."

(4.) *Notes.*

[1.] Mr Palmer was unable to ascertain the age at which Dr Jacomb died. He says that "from the introduction to Dr Bates's discourse, it appears that he was much younger than Dr Bates, and that he possessed a more vigorous constitution." This in his article on Jacomb. Then in that on Bates, he says: "It appears from Dr Bates's own account of himself, that he had for some years been remarkably infirm. In the beginning of his funeral sermon for Dr Jacomb, preached April 3, 1687, when he was about 62 years of age, he says—"Oh frail and faithless life of man! Who would have thought that Dr Jacomb, whose natural vigour and firm complexion promised a longer continuance here, should have a period put to his days, and that I should survive, whose life has been preserved for many years, like the weak light of a lamp in the open air." If, then, in 1687, Dr Bates was about 62, he must have been born about 1625; (in fact he was born in November of that year), and if Jacomb was "much younger" than he, it follows of course that he must have been born long after that date. But he came to London in 1627, after having taken his degree of B.A. in Oxford, and having been for some time Fellow of Trinity College in Cambridge. From these data it would appear that at this time he must have been "much less" than 22 years of age; which is altogether incredible. But it is curious to notice that Dr Bates says not a word about Dr Jacomb's being younger than himself; but only of his having possessed a more vigorous constitution. Now Wood, whom Palmer had read, states that on Jacomb's coming to Oxford in 1640, his age was 18. He was therefore born about 1622; he was not "much younger," but three years older than Dr Bates; at his coming to London he was 25, and at his death he was 65 years old.

[2]. From Palmer's account it would appear that he came to London as chaplain to the Countess of Exeter; and that his residence in her family was the means of his introduction to his parish. From Wood's account, it would appear that he did not get the chaplaincy till he was ejected from the parish, after fifteen years' ministry in it. The former account seems to us likely to be the correct one.

[3.] It may be safely presumed that readers are sufficiently acquainted with the history of the "Expurgators" and the "Triers," to put a right value on the reproach cast by Wood upon Jacomb, as having served upon these two courts.

[4.] We have not been able to ascertain who the divines were who finished "Poole's Annotations." In their own preface they give no hint of it. This appears to us to be a matter worthy of enquiry.   T. S.

TO THE RIGHT HONOURABLE

ELIZABETH, COUNTESS DOWAGER OF EXETER,

MY EVER HONOURED LADY.

MADAM,—Although I know beforehand how the prefixing of your name upon this account will be resented by your Ladyship, yet I am by so many reasons thereunto obliged, that I must venture to do it, and cast myself upon your goodness for my pardon. This volume of Sermons, which is but a forerunner to two or three more, I presume therefore humbly to dedicate to your Honour; which, though in itself, and in your Ladyship's esteem, it be a very insignificative thing, yet, however, it is a declaration to the world that I am sensible of my vast obligations to you, and that I would catch at everything wherein I might testify how much I am beholden to you. And I hope you will not be offended with me for the doing of that which all who know my circumstances would have wondered if I had omitted. Surely, madam, those extraordinary favours which, for above twenty years, you have been pleased to confer upon me and mine, deserve over and over all those little expressions of humble respect and gratitude which I can possibly make. This dedication, therefore, being designed for those ends, I beseech you that you will please to put a favourable interpretation upon it.

But besides this, your Ladyship may, upon several considerations, claim a special interest in this work, if there be anything of good either in it or by it; one of which I shall not conceal, the rest I must. When I had finished my preaching on the chapter

which I have gone over, you was pleased to desire me,—and your desires are, and ought to be, commands to me,—to publish to the world what I had done in a private auditory : which desire of yours, in concurrence with my own hopes of doing some good, did very much prevail with me to engage in this difficult and painful undertaking, which was before as much beside my intention as against my inclination. So that, madam, you are in a special manner to be owned in what is here done ; and the truth is, if any benefit shall thereby accrue to any, it must, under God, upon several accounts, in a great measure be ascribed to your Honour, you having been so instrumental in the promoting thereof.

Madam, that which once was preached to your ear is now presented to your eye ; and it is my hope, and shall be my prayer, that those heavenly truths, which in the hearing of them were not unto you, as well as others, without some considerable efficacy and sweetness, may not in the reading of them be unto you less efficacious and sweet. The chapter opened is a summary of evangelical duty and comfort ; through the rich grace of God you are, in a very eminent manner, a performer of the one, and through the same grace of God you are also a partaker of the other ; and shall, I trust, grow up daily yet more and more to a higher participation of it. I cannot wish you to be more holy than to do

A

what is here enjoined, nor more happy than to possess what is here promised.

It pleases the merciful God (the sovereign disposer of life and death, in whose hands yours and all our times are) as yet to continue you in the land of the living. When many, very many, of your dear relations are taken away and are not, you yourself are yet spared, with a small number of survivors. I beseech you give me leave (if you do not give it me I must take it) to pray for the long continuance of this mercy, that your days may still be prolonged on earth, and that you may arrive at a far greater age than what as yet you have arrived at. You are impatient, I fear a little too much, to be gone; partly from the dread you have of the infirmities which attend old age, and your weariness of the world; and partly from the pantings of your soul to be with Christ, and in the possessing of the heavenly glory. But, good madam, I beseech you not too much haste, no, not for heaven itself; you'll have it never the sooner for that. He that hath determined your days and months, and hath allotted you such work to do in your generation, will have you, let your own thoughts and desires be what they will, live out that time, and finish that work which he hath set you; be entreated, therefore, quietly and cheerfully to wait all the days of your appointed time, till your change shall come. Heaven will be the same twenty years hence that now it is; and the longer you are kept out of it upon the doing of God's work, the better it will be to you at last. It is one of the highest degrees of grace that here a saint is capable of, to be sure of heaven, and yet, in order to service, to be willing for a time to be kept out of heaven; here was the height of Paul's grace and the excellency of his spirit:[1] Phil. i. 23–25, 'For I am in a strait betwixt two, having a desire to depart, and to be with Christ; which is far better: nevertheless to abide in the flesh is more needful for you. And having this confidence, I know that I shall abide and continue with you all, for your furtherance and joy of faith.' It is a saying of Seneca, It argues a great and generous mind for one to be willing for the sake of another to return to life again;[2] surely that Christian discovers true greatness of spirit, who

[1] Θαυμάσαι ἄξιον τον θεῖον ἀπόστολον.—*Theodoret.*
[2] Ingentis animi est aliena causa ad vitam reverti.

for the good of others is willing to continue in this life, and to be kept out of that which is far better. Madam, your serviceableness is known to all but to yourself; many have cause to bless God for the good which they reap by your means, who can speak that which it is not convenient for me to write. It will be a rare piece of self-denial for you to submit, as to your own personal interest, to be a loser, if others may be gainers thereby. Assure yourself, many do earnestly beg of God the prolongation of your days; you pray for your death, but they for your life; I hope in this God will hear them, and not you. Your gracious Father hath given you a title to heaven, hath, in a great measure fitted you for heaven, and will in due time take you up into heaven; it being thus, as to the ordering of your passage thither, and the timing of your entrance into it, all that, good madam, you should wholly refer to his good pleasure.

Madam, the dedication of a book, I very well know, signifies but little to your Ladyship. Prayer is the thing which you desire and value; wherein should I be wanting, it being the only requital I can make you for all your favours, I should certainly be unworthy and ungrateful beyond all expressions. As God shall enable me, according to the many obligations which I lie under, I shall never cease to pray for you and yours. It hath pleased the sovereign and all-disposing God to cut off many branches which grew from your stock; yet one, and the principal one too, is hitherto spared; God grant he may be so long, and that all heavenly blessings as well as earthly may be multiplied upon him! And blessed be the Lord, you live to see others who are of you, though not immediately, yet but at one remove, whom God begins to bless with a hopeful issue; the best of his blessings be upon them also! That honourable family to which you are so nearly related, when so many great and ancient families are melted away like snow before the sun, yet keeps up in its pristine greatness and splendour; and may it so continue from generation to generation, till the world shall be no more! And for yourself, madam, the God of heaven bless you, and recompense into your bosom sevenfold all that kindness that ever you have shewn to any of his! He grant that you may bring forth fruit in your old age, and be fat and flourishing;

that you may come to your grave in a full age, like as a shock of corn cometh in its season ; that, as your outward man decays, your inward man may be renewed day by day ; that you may never want the light of his countenance ; that you may at the last arrive at that peace, comfort, assurance which you have so long been praying for ; that you may yet be a shining light in that more public orb wherein you are fixed, a pattern of humility and condescension, of all graces and virtues and good works to all who behold you ; and, finally, that when you have fought the good fight, and shall have finished your course, and kept the faith, you may receive that crown of righteousness, which the Lord, the righteous Judge, shall give you at that day. These are, have been, and ever shall be, the daily and ardent prayers of,

Madam, your Honour's most humble and ever obliged Servant and Chaplain,

THO. JACOMB.

September 18, 1672.

THE PREFACE TO THE READER.

———o———

CHRISTIAN READER,—That I may not be defective either in civility to thee, or in common prudence and justice to myself, it is necessary that I pre-advertise thee of some things convenient to be known about the ensuing work, the doing of which, therefore, is the design and business of this preface.

That which was the first rise and occasion of it was this : I having in my ministry gone over several of the most weighty points in divinity, relating both to faith and practice, and finding myself too often divided in my thoughts what text or subject next to insist upon ; upon this twofold consideration I resolved to fix upon some continued discourse in holy writ, where I might have my work cut out for me by the Spirit of God from time to time, by which being determined I might be freed from self-perplexing and time-wasting distractions. No sooner was I come to this resolution, but immediately it pleased God to bring to my thoughts the eighth chapter to the Romans, which, when I had a little surveyed in my mind, and taken a short view of the fulness and preciousness of its matter, without any further demur or hesitancy I resolved also that that should be the chapter which I would lay out my pains upon. Accordingly, I entered upon it ; and (for which I heartily bless the Lord) he who directed me to that undertaking was graciously pleased to assist me in it, and to carry me through it.

The excellency of this chapter being my great inducement to pitch upon it, it would have been requisite that I should here have endeavoured to have set forth that excellency, had I not in my first entrance upon the work itself said enough upon that account. To compare scripture with scripture, that one place may give light to another, is a thing very safe and good ; but to compare scripture before scripture is a thing that must be done with much tenderness and caution. I adore every part and parcel of sacred writ—all being given by inspiration of God, and admirably useful to that end for which it was appointed, 2 Tim. iii. 16—and would be very careful how I prefer one before another. Therefore, I do not say that Paul's epistles are the most excellent of all the New Testament writings, or that this Epistle to the Romans is the most excellent of all the other epistles, or that this chapter therein is the most excellent of all the other chapters, in which gradation some please themselves. Yet this I might safely say, that this epistle and this chapter, for sublimity of matter, variety of evangelical truths, admirable support and comfort to believers, are not inferior to any part whatsoever of the Holy Scriptures. Which, if so, I have then pitched upon a subject very well worthy of my best endeavours ; and none will blame me for attempting to open so rich a cabinet.

In digging into this mine I found it to be so full that it was a long time before I could get to the bottom of it ; for I was two years, and something more, in preaching over this chapter. In which time I preached very many sermons upon it, but the precise number I will not mention, because some from thence might take occasion to fasten that censure upon me which I hope I do not deserve; and others, seeing here but eighteen of so many published, might think I shall never come to the end of all. Well, though the work was long, yet it pleased God to spare me till I had finished it. I have now entered upon a work of another nature; whether he will also let me see the finishing of that, αὐτοῦ ἐν γούνασι κεῖται.

Wherein it fares with me much as it sometimes doth with seamen, who, after a long and tedious voyage, are no sooner arrived at shore but presently they are seized upon and sent to sea again, upon a voyage far more tedious and dangerous than the former. This is my case; when I had but just set my foot on land, and was got off from one service which was enough painful and troublesome, by the over-ruling providence of God I was commanded to sea again, and put upon another service far more difficult and dangerous than the former. But I must be at his dispose who may command me whither and about what he pleases; and it becomes me with all alacrity to go whithersoever he bids me go, and to do whatsoever he bids me do.

When I had finished my sermons on the whole chapter, several friends importuned me to print them; whose importunity, though I could not well withstand, yet surely had there been nothing more than that, I had not been drawn thereby to undertake such a task as I now have. And the truth is, when I consider my great averseness to printing, the vastness and difficulty of the present work, my great unfitness for it, (as upon other accounts, so in respect of my bodily infirmities, which daily grow upon me,) my sluggish, melancholy temper, the many divertisements I meet with by other employments; I say, when I consider these things, I cannot but stand and wonder how I came to be thus engaged. I must, upon the whole matter, resolve it mainly into the overpowering, all-determining will of God, and conclude he had appointed and cut out this work for me, and would have me do it. I write not this (I can appeal to the searcher of hearts) to heighten my fitness for this service, or the worth of anything that I have done; but only that I may declare the true ground of my engaging in the present business, duly acknowledge God in such an enterprise as this is, and also that I may animate my faith and hope

in him for assistance and success; as knowing that what he calls unto he will carry through, and what is of him shall be blessed by him.

As soon as my preaching work was off my hands, after a very short respite I set upon this of printing; wherein what progress I have made, this volume, which I publish as a *prodromus* to what is yet to come, will manifest. It contains what I preached upon the four first verses. Some, I assure myself, will be surprised, and think it strange that so few verses should make a volume of this bulk and bigness; but I would desire these, before they judge, to cast their eye upon the various heads discussed therein, to weigh the great latitude and importance of those heads; and I hope they will then be satisfied that in the due handling of so many and so material things less could not well be spoken. I did indeed design at first to have gone much farther; but afterwards I saw, the work growing so much upon me, these verses were as much as I could grasp in one book. And the apostle ending with them the first part of his discourse—viz., the confirmation of the predicate in the proposition, 'there is no condemnation,' &c.—I thought, without any unhandsome disjoining of the words, I might there break off. What comes after in the following verses, wherein there is the illustration of the subject, who 'walk not after the flesh,' &c., shall next be insisted upon, if God permit.

When I say that what I preached is here published, I would not be misunderstood, as if I had not varied in the latter from the former; for I acknowledge I have varied very much, and that too not only in words and expressions, but in several places even in the very method and matter; which alterations proceeded not only from my infelicity—that I cannot twice do the same thing in the same way—but also because I found, upon the review of what I had done, second thoughts to be necessary. Add to this too, there must be a difference when we have to do with the ear and when with the eye; for that style and method, yea, and matter too, which is proper for the one, is not always so for the other. I hope, therefore, none will be severe against me because of these variations; but if any will be so, let them be sure that they themselves do wear but the same clothes abroad which they do at home, which I think few do.

The matter in the first and second verses being, comparatively, more plain and practical, in going over them I have, to the best of my remembrance, varied but little ; but in the third and fourth verses, where the matter is more deep and controversial, there I have varied much more. They point me to Christ's natural sonship, incarnation, sacrifice for sin, &c., which excellent heads I did not pass over in preaching without some considerable enlargement upon them ; but had I then so fully handled them as here I do, I should but have tired and perplexed the generality of private auditors, and scarce have edified them. Indeed, these are points, especially if largely and thoroughly discussed, much more proper for a reader, whose thoughts may dwell upon them, he having them fixed before him, than for a hearer, who, through the constant succession of new matter, the slowness of understanding, the weakness of memory, is not so able to take them in or to judge aright of them. Upon this consideration I have here added and inserted many things which then I omitted, hoping that as what I then spake was not too little for hearers, so that what I now write will not be too much for readers.

Reader, I hope in the perusal of this book thou wilt find that things of a practical nature, such as concern faith, holy walking, deliverance from sin's dominion, and the like, have far the greatest room in it ; yet I am not ashamed to own that there are in it several things of another nature, I mean controversial, which I neither could, nor, in truth, did desire to avoid. As to controversies, more nice and curious than necessary and profitable, none delights in them less than myself, (who would love to walk in the midst of briers and thorns that hath pleasant meadows or gardens to walk in?) much less do I delight to trouble weak Christians with knotty and polemic matters. But the controversies which I handle are of such weight and importance, unto which, too, the texts I open did so unavoidably lead me, that I knew not, without falsehood to my trust as a minister of the gospel, how to shun them. Shall the natures, offices, sonship, incarnation, sacrifice, &c., of our dearest Lord and Saviour be assaulted by daring enemies, and shall not we, especially when they lie in our way, defend and vindicate them? And are these the great things upon which

the salvation and happiness of believers do depend, and shall not they understand how adversaries attempt to undermine them? yea, so to be able to answer such gainsayers as that they may stand firm and fixed upon these gospel foundations? That I might, therefore, heighten the knowledge and confirm the faith of such, I have been somewhat large upon these things ; in the managing whereof, if I have done too much for the unlearned and too little for the learned, I am sorry for it.

Of all the controversies with which the church is pestered, I have, as the texts did lead me, most concerned myself in those wherein we have to do with Papists and Socinians, but principally with the latter. These, not that I in other things acquit the former, are the great impugners of the Christian faith, in their denying Christ's Godhead, eternal Sonship, pre-existence before his nativity of the Virgin, (wherein they are worse than the old Arians,) satisfaction, his being a proper sacrifice for sin, the main ends of his death, &c. ; against whom, therefore, I have endeavoured to assert and maintain these high and glorious truths, which are indeed truths of the first magnitude. What thoughts others may have of Socinianism I know not—I know my own : and might I presume so far as to give advice to my reverend brethren in the ministry, I would humbly advise them to set themselves to their utmost against it ; for it doth not only strike at the whole platform of the gospel, but, of all other opinions, it gets nearest to the very vitals thereof. This cursed worm grows in the gospel's best fruit ; 'tis for the poisoning of those fountains from which the streams of life do most immediately flow. Whilst many other errors endanger but the remoter parts, this endangers the very heart of Christianity. Can we say or do too much to secure souls from it, and to defend the gospel against it? God prevent the growth of it in all the churches of Christ!

If, in the discussing of these points, I have said nothing but what the learned in their treatises about them have said before, yet however two things I have done : 1. According to my duty I have given my testimony to the great truths of God, let it signify what he pleases ; 2. I hope I have,—I am sure it hath been my endeavour,—made some things, in themselves dark and intricate, to be somewhat more plain and intelligible to weaker capacities ; and if I have done but that, though I have brought no new matter, my pains have not been ill-spent.   My soul's desire is that the professors of this age may be well-grounded in the articles of the Christian faith, and that they may attain to a clearer insight into gospel mysteries than what as yet they have attained to ; and if what is here done shall conduce to the promoting of these most desirable things, it will be a sufficient recompense to me for all the labour that I have been at.

I observe that many private Christians will read over those controversies in a sermon which they care not to read in treatises professedly penned about them.   The reason of which, I suppose, is this, they meet with that in a sermon which they do not in a treatise—viz., when the argumentative part is over, they come to something that is practical ; the bone being broken, they have marrow and sweetness to feed upon.   It hath been my care all along in this work to answer herein the expectation and desire of good souls, for at the close of every knotty subject I have always made thereof some plain and useful application, that so I might reach both the head and the heart too.

So long as the strife lay between an Israelite and an Egyptian, the matter was not very sad ; but when the Israelite and the Israelite strove one against the other, then it was sad indeed.   So here, so long as the contention was 'twixt Romanists and Socinians on one hand, and Protestants on the other, it was well enough ; but when Protestants divide and differ among themselves, that is matter of great sadness.   In the body of this work I have had occasion only to contend with the former, and there I had nothing but comfort ; but in the end I was necessitated to take notice of and to interest myself in a difference between the latter, concerning the imputation of Christ's active obedience, which some are for[1] and some against, and that afflicted me more than all that went before.   For though, in my own judgment, I am very well satisfied for the affirmative, yet it troubles me that I should therein dissent

[1] Amongst whom, in its proper place, had not my memory failed me, I should have cited that truly eminent person Bishop Reynolds on Ps. cx. p. 440, &c.

from those whose names, as to the dead, I highly honour, and whose persons, as to the living, I dearly love.   Well, these differences will be till heaven unite us all ; and, blessed be God, in this point we may differ *salvo fidei fundamento*.   I hope we shall make it to appear to the world that we can dissent and yet love ; that whereunto we have attained we shall walk by the same rule, and if in anything we be otherwise minded, God shall reveal even this unto us, according to that excellent decision of the apostle in cases of this nature.

But, reader, I must not detain thee longer in giving thee any further account of the particulars treated of in these sermons.   Do but thyself read over the contents of the several chapters, and they will, in short, give thee a prospect of the matter and method of the whole.   Thou seest already a great part of my way hitherto hath been somewhat rough and craggy ; I hope in what follows it will be more smooth and easy, bating those passages which some expositors conceive Peter referred unto when he spake of some things in Paul's epistles hard to be understood ; however, I must take it as it falls.

Two things as to the whole will be objected against me.   The one is overmuch prolixity.   As to which, all that I can say for myself is (1.) The subjects insisted upon are so various, lying so near the very heart of religion, bearing so high a place in evangelical faith, so necessary to be understood by all, and so desperately struck at by opposers, that truly for my part I thought (pardon me if I was mistaken) I could hardly be too full in the explication, confirmation, and application of them.   Good reader, please to read over the bare heads I go upon, as they will occur by and by, and then tell me whether so many and such fundamental truths could well have been crowded into a lesser room.   But (2.) If this will not satisfy such as are most judicious, it shall be mended in what is to follow.

The other is the unnecessariness of this undertaking, so many already having wrote upon this chapter.   *Answer*, So many ?   Who or where are those so many ?   I wish I could see them.   I deny not but that many, both ancients and moderns, have written commentaries upon it for the clearing up of the sense of the words (for whose labours I bless God, and shall in this work endeavour to make the best improvement of them); but having done that, there they leave off. I hope I go further than so, not satisfying myself barely to give the sense and meaning of the text, which is the proper work of an expositor; but also drawing out that sense, and making the best advantage of it for things doctrinal and practical, which is the work of a preacher. I acknowledge also that some have particularly and fully wrote upon it in the way which I take, as Mr Elton, Cowper, Parr, Streso, Philips, Binning, to the 15th verse; but not so but that there is yet room for the industry of others: there are good gleanings in this large field yet left for them that shall come after. I will not for my vindication fly to that common maxim, Good things we cannot hear (or read) too often—δὶς καὶ τρὶς τὰ καλὰ λέγειν καὶ ἐπισκοπεῖσθαι καλὸν; but I desire so much right may be done me as to compare what I have now done, with what others upon this chapter have done before. If I do no more than they, I deserve the severest censure; but if I do, the reader then, I hope, will be so candid, yea, so just, as to let me have his favourable sentence. I am conscious to myself of many weaknesses in the work; but as to the charge of but doing that which was done before, pardon me if in that I stand upon my vindication.

He gave good advice to them that will be printing, who counselled them to pitch upon such subjects which might not be above their strength, seriously to consider before they engaged whether they were able to go through with what they undertook.[1] I have duly weighed the mysteriousness and difficulties of the things which I am to write upon; and the more I look into them, the more I find them to be above me. Yet for all this I am not discouraged, because I trust I shall have a higher strength than mine own to help me, and to carry me through all of them, so that some benefit may accrue to souls. 'The way of the Lord is strength to the upright,' Prov. x. 29. He that hath God's call needs not to question God's help; and if he will help, the weakest instrument shall be strong enough for the highest and hardest work. Augustine, that great and blessed man, tells us of himself he had

begun a comment upon this Epistle to the Romans, but the difficulty of the matter he met with made him give over.[1] I have in what I have done encountered with some difficulties—more are before me as to what is yet to be done; but I bless the Lord I am not disheartened by them, so as to think of giving over the work. 'But David encouraged himself in the Lord his God,' (1 Sam. xxx. 6;) and in my present case I desire to do the same. Difficulties in the way of service should but quicken our diligence and heighten our dependence upon God, not take us off from doing our duty. Yea, further, I am not without some discouragement as to my eternal condition. The sun, as to bodily health, and some other considerations, is going off from me—few plants are so situated as to have the forenoon and afternoon sun too; but that doth not quite discourage me neither. May I but have the warm influences of the blessed Spirit, and the Sun of righteousness with his sweet beams yet shining upon me, I trust, though outwardly I decline and decay, I shall yet finish what I have begun.

The chapter being commonly divided into three parts, I hoped I should have finished one in each volume, and so have drawn the whole into three; but these four verses taking up so much room, I am forced to allot two volumes to the first part, hoping to grasp the two other parts in two more. So that, in my four days' journey, as it were, I have as yet gone but one of them; but he that hath been with me in that, will, I trust, be with me in the other also.

I must not be too bold with God in entitling him to what I do, yet I would fain hope that it is by his special providence that I am engaged in this undertaking; wherein I should be exceedingly confirmed might I see these first fruits, now published, owned and blessed by him to the profit of many; and with what cheerfulness should I go on if I might, in my first setting out, have such encouragement! Till I be able about this to pass a better judgment than as yet I can, it will be best for me for some little time to stay my hand, which accordingly I resolve upon. I am very loath to burden the world with unprofitable labours. May I do good! all that

---

[1] 'Sumite materiam vestris, qui scribitis, æquam,
Viribus, et versate diu, quid ferre recusent,
Quid valeant humeri.'—*Horat.*

[1] Retract. lib. i. cap. 25.

B

I shall do will be too little! but without that, that which I have already done is too much. Well, success and good issues must be expected only of God, and referred wholly to him. He hath enabled me to do something, which, if he please to bless it, shall prosper, but if he deny his blessing, I have laboured in vain. Now, reader, for the helping on so great a mercy I beg thy prayers, yea, thy best prayers. When thou art with God in secret remember me and the work in hand, I earnestly entreat thee; indeed, I need all thy praying help, wherein if thou beest wanting, thou thyself mayest be damnified thereby. If thou wilt forget me, I trust I shall not forget thee in my poor prayers, that God will bless thee in the clearer revealing of gospel mysteries to thee, the fuller illumination of thy understanding in spiritual things, the confirming and stablishing of thee in the great truths of God, the daily heightening and perfecting of thy graces, the sanctifying of all helps and means, public and private, to the furtherance of thy salvation; in a word, that thou mayest be the person in Christ Jesus, living the spiritual life, and thereby that the *no condemnation*, and all the other branches of the precious grace of God spoken of in these verses, yea, in the whole chapter, may be all thine. So for the present I leave thee, remaining

An unfeigned wisher of thy

Spiritual and eternal good,

THO. JACOMB.

THE

GRAND CHARTER OF BELIEVERS OPENED.

CHAPTER I.

OF BELIEVERS' EXEMPTION FROM CONDEMNATION.

There is therefore now no condemnation to them which are in Christ Jesus, who walk not after the flesh, but after the Spirit.—ROM. viii. 1.

The introduction to the work—The excellency of the chapter—Its main scope and parts—How this first verse comes in—Paul in the preceding chapter compared with himself in this—The proposition divided into its parts—The predicate in it, no condemnation, *first opened—Two observations raised from the words—The first spoken to—Seven things premised by way of explication: As,* 1. *It is not* no affliction, *or* no correction, *but* no condemnation *; 2. It is not* no matter of condemnation, *only* no condemnation de facto *; this enlarged upon against the Romanists; 3. It is God's condemnation only which is here excluded, not the condemnation of man, or of conscience, or of Satan ; 4. Of the import and significancy of the particle* now *in this place ; 5.* No condemnation *may be rendered* not one condemnation *; 6. Of the Indefiniteness of the proposition with respect to the subject ; 7. That the positive is included in the negative—The observation itself more closely handled—Condemnation opened as to the* quid nominis *and the* quid rei. *—It relates to guilt and punishment ; to the sentence and state—It is either virtual or actual—The point confirmed by parallel scriptures ; by a double argu-*

ment in the text—The first is couched in the illative, therefore, *which points to justification and sanctification, (both of which prove* no condemnation*)—The second is grounded upon union with Christ—Use 1. To shew the misery of such who are not in Christ Jesus—The dreadfulness of condemnation set forth in five particulars—Use 2. To exhort all to make sure of exemption from condemnation—Six directions touched upon about it—Use 3. To excite such as are in Christ to be very thankful—Use 4. Comfort to believers.*

I PURPOSE, with God's leave and gracious assistance, in the revolution of my ministerial labours, to go over this whole chapter. It is a very great undertaking, and I am very sensible how much it is above me ; I have only this encouragement, I serve a good master, one who both can, and I trust will, help me in it, and carry me through it, for he uses to give strength where he calls to work. And it is no matter what the instrument is, if he will be pleased to use it : the mighty God by weak means can effect great things : Mat. xxi. 16, ' Out of the mouths of babes and sucklings he can perfect praise to himself.' Here is indeed a rich and precious cabinet, full of grace, to be opened, yet a key of small value may open it, if God please to direct the hand. Therefore in all humble yet steady reliance upon him whose grace alone is sufficient for me, 2 Cor. xii. 9, I shall now enter upon this work, though it be vast and difficult.

And in the midst of all my discouragements, (which are very many, God knows,) yet I find myself under a strong inclination to engage in it, when I consider the transcendent excellency, preciousness, usefulness of that matter which the Spirit of God lays before us in this chapter. Who would not be willing to take pains in a mine that hath such treasures hid in it? Where the breast is so full, who would not be drawing from it? I think I should not hyperbolise should I say of it, Search all the Scriptures, (I will except none,) turn over the whole word of God, from the beginning of Genesis to the end of the Revelation, you will not find any one chapter into which more excellent, sublime, evangelical truths are crowded, than this which I am entering upon. The Holy Bible is the book of books; in some, though not in equal, respects, this chapter may be styled the chapter of chapters. From first to last it is high gospel, it is all gospel, (its matter being entirely evangelical,) and it is all the gospel, either directly or reductively, it having in it the very sum, marrow, pith of all gospel-revelation. It is indeed the epitome, abridgment, storehouse of all the saints' privileges and duties: you have in it the love of God and of Christ displayed to the utmost, and shining forth in its greatest splendour. Would any take a view of the *Magnalia Dei* with respect to his glorious grace? here they lie open before them. Paul in it speaks much of the blessed Spirit, and surely he was more than ordinarily full of this Spirit in the penning of it.[1] Blessed be God for every part and parcel of holy writ; and, in special, blessed be God for this eighth chapter to the Romans. Oh it is pity that it is not better understood through the dimness of our light, nor better improved through the weakness of our faith. May I in my poor endeavours be instrumental but in the least to further these two in any, I hope I shall own it as an abundant recompense for all my pains.

As to the scope and principal matter of it, it is consolatory. There is a vein of heavenly comfort running through the whole body of it; with this it begins, with this it ends, (for it begins with *no condemnation*, ver. 1, and ends with *no separation* from the love of God, vers. 38, 39,) and all the intermediate parts do exactly correspond with these extremes. The truth is, the sincere Christian here treads upon nothing but roses and violets; there is nothing but honey to be found in this hive; here is balm in every line for the healing of the wounded spirit. Let such as are in Christ—for that is the foundation of all—study, weigh, digest, believe, apply, what is laid down in this chapter, and let them walk dejectedly if they can.

Divines who write upon it commonly divide it into three parts. The first contains in it excellent supports and comforts for the people of God, as burdened under the relics and remainders of sin; and this reaches from the 1st ver. to the 17th. The second contains in it further supports and comforts in reference to the sufferings, afflictions which here are incident to the godly; this reaches from the 17th ver. to the 31st. The third contains in it those high and holy triumphs which the apostle, in his own person and in the person of all believers, makes over both sin and suffering; which reaches from the 31st ver. to the end. In this threefold channel the comforts of the whole chapter run. This division of it I shall follow, and accordingly divide my ensuing discourse into three parts.

For the first, The supporting and comforting the saints as burdened under the relics of sin; the apostle begins with that, because he very well knew that sin to such is their greatest burden. Oh nothing lies so sad and heavy upon their spirits as this! It was so with Paul himself, as you see chap. vii.; and it is so too with all that are gracious, they having the same Spirit which he had. All Paul's afflictions without, (though they were very many and very sharp, see his catalogue of them, 2 Cor. xi. 23, &c.,) were nothing to his corruptions within. The former never made him cry out, " O wretched man that I am," as the latter did, Rom. vii. 24. Oh this sin went to the heart of him, and almost overwhelmed him. And so, proportionably, it is with all who belong to God. For this reason, therefore, when the apostle would comfort himself and others, he first applies his discourse to that which might give ease as to what was and is most burdensome.

---

[1] Est caput aureum, et inter omnia hujus epistolæ illustrissimum; in quo cum de Spiritus muneribus disserere statuisset apostolus, Spiritus ipse divinus pleno numine in ejus pectus illapsus videtur; cujus ideo suavitate et fragrantia singulis verbis redolet, charismatibusque diffluit et exundat.—*Sott.*

In order to which he first lays down a notable faith-supporting and soul-reviving proposition; then, secondly, he amplifies and enlarges upon that proposition, which he doth chiefly with respect to the description of the subject of it. And all that is contained in this first part of the chapter will fall either under the one or the other of these two heads.

The proposition itself is this, ' There is therefore now no condemnation to them which are in Christ Jesus,' &c. In which the illative *therefore* shews that the words are an inference or conclusion drawn from what went before. Take but that away (though we must not so easily part with it) and they fall into a formal thesis or categorical proposition, ' There is no condemnation,' &c. I will by and by give you the force and strength of the illation, and shew what it is grounded upon; but at present we are only to consider the position itself. ' No condemnation to them which are in Christ Jesus.' Oh great and blessed words! How appositely, fully, and convincingly doth Paul speak to the thing in hand! What a basis and foundation doth he here lay for faith to build upon! Is the gracious heart burdened under the remainders of sin? What could be spoken more proper, more effectual for its relief, than to assure it, that though there may be much corruption, yet there is no condemnation? No condemnation to them which are in Christ? What a magnificent conclusion, what a faith-strengthening and heart-cheering consideration is this! Here is dainties and cordials at the very first. No sooner doth the apostle launch out, but immediately he is in the great deeps of the grace of God and of the happiness of believers.

By the way, I cannot but observe how the case is altered and mended with him. View him in the foregoing chapter; there you find him pensive, sad, cast down under the sense of sin, making sad complaints that he was ' carnal, sold under sin,' that ' in him (viz., in his flesh) there dwelt no good thing;' that ' the good he would, he did not; the evil he would not, that he did;' many such indictments he there draws up against himself, Rom. vii. 14, 18, 19. And thus it was with him in that chapter; but now follow him to this. Here he is another man, he speaks at another rate; now you have him rejoicing, yea, triumphing over sin and all.

From the depth of sorrow he is got up to the highest pinnacle of divine joy; that eye which but just now was fixed upon his own vileness, is now fixed upon his great blessedness in and through Christ. And indeed usually it is so with others too; after conviction comes consolation; a deep sense of sin, attended with brokenness of heart for it, doth commonly usher in the highest peace and comfort to the soul. After the dark night the day dawns; when the true penitent hath been most abased and cast down, then comes exalting and lifting up. See Job xxii. 29. There is, in this respect, *post nubila Phœbus*, a bright sun after the thick cloud, or a reaping in joy after a sowing in tears, Ps. cxxvi. 5. Penitential sorrow is τῆς χαρᾶς μητήρ, as Chrysostom expresses it, the mother, the precursor, of inward joy. God will heal where he thus wounds; he ' healeth the broken in heart,' Ps. cxlvii. 3. Such as thus mourn shall be comforted, Mat. v. 4; these waters Christ will turn into wine, John ii. 9. As joy in sin will end in sorrow, so sorrow for sin will end in joy. But to return to our apostle: he had, as to his outward state, his abasements and his advancements too, (and he knew how to carry himself under both: ' I know how to be abased, and I know how to abound,' Philip. iv. 12.) So as to his inward state he also had his abasements and his advancements. Sometimes it is, ' O wretched man that I am,' &c.; there it was abasement. Then presently is, ' There is no condemnation,' &c.; there it was advancement. And let me add, that Paul's comfort in this chapter had never been so high, so full as to himself, so encouraging as to others, if he had not in the former chapter first smarted under the cutting and piercing conviction of sin. Oh to have one who but even now was almost pressed down under soul-burdens, now saying, yet ' there is no condemnation to them,' &c. How may this animate and strengthen the faith of a poor Christian, whenever troubles of conscience, by reason of sin, shall be upon him!

This being the proposition, I will consider it in its parts; and so you have in it,

First, The predicate, or the privilege asserted, viz., exemption from condemnation; " There is therefore now no condemnation," &c.

Secondly, The subject, or the persons described, to whom, and to whom only, the privilege belongs.

And to take the most easy division of the words at present, they are described,

1. By their union with Christ in reference to their state; they are such who are ' in Christ Jesus.'

2. By their qualification or property in reference to their course : they ' walk not after the flesh but after the spirit.' I conceive this clause doth more immediately refer to the persons who are in Christ, and is properly descriptive of them; yet mediately they may refer to, and be descriptive of, the persons to whom there is no condemnation, as I shall hereafter shew.

If you take the words in the body of them, there is some, yet no very great, difference in the reading of them. The latter branch, ' but after the spirit,' is wholly left out by the Vulgate translation, and by those expositors who follow it. I know not why, unless it be because the Syriac version did the same,[1] which version in the reading of the words is not only defective as to this, but very harsh in the misplacing of them : ' There is therefore no condemnation to those who walk not after the flesh in Christ Jesus.' Some other such variations might be taken notice of, but I will pass them by.

The general proposition, being taken in pieces, will afford us these two observations :

1. That there is no condemnation to them who are in Christ Jesus.

2. That such who are in Christ Jesus, and so secured from condemnation, this is their property or course, ' they walk not after the flesh, but after the spirit.'

The discussing of these two points will take me up some time. I begin with the first, in the handling of which I will, 1. Chiefly speak to the privilege, and only in a general way join the description of the subject with it; 2. I will then more particularly speak to that, and shew what it is to be in Christ Jesus, or how persons may be said to be in Christ Jesus. Of the first at this time.

For the better opening of which I must premise these seven things :

1. First, The apostle doth not say, There is now no affliction or no correction to them who are in Christ; but there is no condemnation to them who

are in Christ. It is one thing to be afflicted, another thing to be condemned; God may, and will, afflict his children, but he will never condemn them; it may be much affliction, yet it is no condemnation; indeed God afflicts here that he may not condemn hereafter: 1 Cor. xi. 32, ' When we are judged we are chastened of the Lord, that we should not be condemned with the world.' God is so gracious that he will not condemn, yet withal so wise, so just, so holy, that he will afflict. Grace in the heart secures from eternal, not from temporal evils. God cannot condemn yet love, but he can chasten and yet love; nay, therefore he chastens because he loves : ' As many as I love, I rebuke and chasten ;' ' Whom the Lord loveth he chasteneth, and scourgeth every son whom he receiveth.' And it may be, even to them who are in Christ, not only bare affliction, but there may be something of the nature of punishment in that affliction,[1] though not in a vindictive way, or upon the account of satisfaction. The nearer a person is to Christ, and the dearer he is to God, the surer he is to be punished if he sin. ' You only have I known of all the families of the earth, therefore I will punish you for your iniquities,' Amos iii. 2. God may pardon and yet punish; temporal punishment is very consistent with pardoning mercy. Ps. xcix. 8, ' Thou answeredst them, O Lord our God; thou wast a God that forgavest them, though thou tookest vengeance of them for their iniquities.' God had put away David's sin, yet he shall smart for it; his own soul shall live, but his child shall die as a punishment for his sin. See 2 Sam. xii. 13, 14. The malefactor may not be condemned to die; as to his life he may be acquitted, yet he may be judged to be whipped or burned in the hand for his offence; so it is here. You must distinguish therefore betwixt no condemnation, and no affliction or no correction; saints are exempted from the former, but not from the latter.

2. Secondly, The apostle doth not say there is no matter of condemnation in them who are in Christ, only, as to fact, he saith, there is no actual con-

[1] Proinde nulla est condemnatio iis qui non ambulant secundum carnem in Jesu Christo.—*Vers. Syr.*

[1] Quamvis Deus absolvit vere pœnitentes ab omni pœna satisfactoria propter Christi mortem, non tamen illos liberat ab omni pœna medicinali et castigatoria.—*Davenant in Col.* i. 14. See of this Burg. of Justif., lect. 4, 5, 10; Baxt. Aphor., p. 68, &c.; Bolton's Bounds, &c., p. 163, &c.; Rutherf. Survey, part ii. ch. 31.

demnation to such. There is a vast difference betwixt what is deserved and what is actually inflicted; betwixt what is *de jure* and *ex merito*, and what is *de facto*. Take the very best of saints; there is enough and enough in them which deserves eternal condemnation; and, if God should proceed according to their merit, it would be condemnation over and over again; for even they have sin and commit sin, and wherever sin is there is matter of condemnation. There is not a man to be found on earth who, upon this account and in this sense, is not obnoxious and liable to a sentence and state of condemnation; for 'there is no man that sinneth not,' 1 Kings viii. 46; 'In many things we offend all,' James iii. 2; 'If we say we have no sin, we deceive ourselves, and the truth is not in us,' 1 John i. 8. Besides those actual sins which break forth in external acts, which are committed upon deliberation and with consent, of which all are more or less guilty—I say, besides these, there is in all a corrupt, wicked, depraved nature, which nature puts forth itself in evil motions, sinful propensions, strong inclinations to what is evil. Oh that *fomes peccati*, those *motus primo-primi*, as the schoolmen call them, those inward ebullitions of indwelling sin in impure and filthy desires, set forth in Scripture by concupiscence! What shall we say to these? Are not they sinful? Is there not in them matter of condemnation, if God should enter into judgment, and proceed according to the rigour of his justice, and the purity of his law? Surely yes! If it be proved that they are sinful, unquestionably then it follows that they expose a person to condemnation. Now how full are our divines in the proof of that! Concupiscence, the first risings and stirrings of corrupt nature, even in renewed and regenerate persons, are properly and formally sinful, whether they consent or not, for consent is not so of the essence of sin but that there may be sin without it; that may have some influence upon the degree, but not upon the nature of the thing itself. Those evil thoughts and motions in the heart, with which the best are so much pestered, are not mere infirmities attending the present state of imperfection, but they are plain iniquities; there is sin in them. The apostle, speaking of them, sets the black brand of sin upon them: Rom. vii. 7, 'What shall we say then? Is

the law sin? God forbid. Nay, I had not known sin, but by the law: for I had not known lust, except the law had said, Thou shalt not covet.' The holy law forbids these inward workings of the sinful nature as well as the exterior acts of sin, therefore they are ἀνομία, a breach of that law, and being so, therefore they are sinful. They flow from sin, they tend to sin, and yet are they not sin? 'When lust hath conceived it bringeth forth sin,' James i. 13. This is the doctrine of our church,[1] of the ancient fathers,[2] of the body of protestants;[3] and they make it good by several arguments of great strength.

The papists are wholly of another mind.[4] And whereas it is said here in the text, 'There is no condemnation,' &c., they carry it so high as to affirm that, in reference to original sin, the depravation of nature, concupiscence, the inward motions and inclinations of the heart to sin, after baptism, faith, regeneration, there is no matter of condemnation or nothing damnable in them who are in Christ. He that will please to cast his eye upon the citations here set down,[5] which are taken especially out of

[1] Art. ix.

[2] August., lib. i. contra duas Pelag. Ep., cap. 13, and lib. iii. contra Julian., cap. 3, with several others cited in Chamier, tom. iii. lib. x. cap. 10.

[3] *Vide* Cham., tom. iii. lib. x. cap. 4, &c.; Chemn. Exam. Decr., 5 sess. p. 93, &c.; Calv. Instit., lib. iii. cap. 3; Daven. Det., qu. 1; Ward. Determ. Theol., p. 136, &c.

[4] The Council of Trent anathematiseth all who hold concupiscence, in renewed persons and after baptism, to be sin, Sess. 5; *Bellarm. de Amiss. Grat.*, lib. v. cap. 7; *Valentia de Pec. Orig.*, cap. 7, 8; *Perer. Quæst.*, cap. 7, in Ep. ad Rom. Disput., 7–9.

[5] Non tam significat nullam esse condemnationem justificatis in Christo ob concupiscentiam, quam nihil esse in eis condemnatione dignum.—*Bellarm. de Am. Gr.*, lib. v. cap. 7. Tollitur damnatio quantum ad culpam et quantum ad poenam. Primus motus habet quod non sit peccatum mortale, ex eo quod rationem non attingit, in qua completur ratio peccati, &c.—*Aquin. in loc*, &c. Et consistit differentia in hoc, quod in illis, justificatis nempe in Christo, nihil committitur damnabile, propter donum Christi tam externum quam internum; intendit itaque per *nullam damnationem* nullum actum quo meremur damnari. Et dixit hoc ad differentiam primorum motuum, qui sunt etiam apud justificatos in Christo, ut intelligamus illos non esse materiam damnationis. Primi enim motus non reddunt sanctos damnabiles, tum ob eorum imperfectionem, tum quia absorbentur a copia sanctarum actionum continuarum.—*Cajet. in loc.* Hinc patet nec concupiscentiam, nec aliud quippiam in renatis esse peccatum damnatione

their expositors upon the text, may see that this is the interpretation which they put upon it.

What! No matter of condemnation? Nothing damnable in them who are in Christ? This is much too high. Our adversaries, I suppose, though they deny any merit of condemnation upon the forementioned things, yet surely they will not deny but that sin in its full act merits condemnation; if they will be so absurd, the apostle plainly determines it: 'Sin when it is finished brings forth death,' James i. 15. Now is there not too much of this to be found even in saints in Christ, and therefore are not they worthy of condemnation? True indeed sin, whether in the conception or in the finishing, is not imputed[1] or charged upon them, and so there is no condemnation; but yet, as considered in its own nature, it merits condemnation: it doth so *ex natura rei, ex judicio legis*, only it is not so in point of fact and in event, *ex indultu gratiæ*, as one expresses it. Sin is sin in the children of God, and it merits condemnation in them as well as in others; whence is it then that there is no condemnation to them? Merely from the grace of God, who doth not impute this sin to them. As Solomon told Abiathar he was worthy of death, yet he would not, for some considerations, put him to death, 1 Kings ii. 26; so here the highest in grace have that in them which renders them worthy of condemnation, but yet, they being in Christ, and thereupon sin not being imputed, they shall not actually be condemned. This is the true and genuine sense of the words, 'There is therefore now no condemnation to them,' &c.; and thus our protestant expositors open them,[2]

wherein their opinions are so far from being *ex orco excitatæ*, fetched from hell, as Pererius,[1] with virulency and malice truly *ex orco excitata*, is pleased to say, that they are from heaven, from the God of truth, and fully consonant to the word of truth.

3. I premise, thirdly, That it is God's condemnation only from which such as are in Christ are exempted: the universal negative, no condemnation, reaches no further than the supreme, final, irreversible, condemnatory sentence of the great God. As to this all in Christ are safe; but there is other condemnations which they do lie under. Take a threefold instance of this.

(1.) Men condemn them. I mean the wicked, who are, and always have been, condemners of the righteous. The saints, as assessors with Christ, shall judge the world hereafter, 1 Cor. vi. 2, and the world will be judging the saints here: the saints condemn sinners by their holy conversation, as, Heb. xi. 7, it is said of Noah, 'he prepared an ark by which he condemned the world;' and they will be condemning the saints in that false judgment, those sharp censures which they are pleased to pass upon them. What more common than for the godly to have their persons, practices, strict walking, condemned by a mistaken and malicious world! Oh they are hypocrites, factious, seditious, Ezra iv. 15, turbulent, troublers of kingdoms, 1 Kings xviii. 17, unnecessarily scrupulous, proud, selfish, false, covetous, and indeed what not! Sometimes the condemnation is only verbal, going no further than bitter words, wherein their names are aspersed, the innocency of their persons sullied, the goodness of their cause blackened. Sometimes it rises higher; men condemn God's people even to the taking away of their lives, as James v. 6, 'You have condemned and killed the just,' &c.; this is the 'condemning of the soul of the poor,' Ps. cix. 31: though possibly there may be something more in this expression than striking at the bare natural life; for such is the inveterate malice of the wicked against the godly,

---

diginum.—*A Lap.* Non quod volo, ago, &c., ex iis sequitur involuntarios esse concupiscentiæ motus in renatis ac justis, quibus proinde ad pœnam imputari non possint.—*Est.* Quamvis caro contra spiritum insultans molestias exhibeat iis qui sunt in Christo Jesu, nihil tamen est in iis damnationis, quia dum non consentiunt, non ipsi operantur illud, sed peccatum quod per concupiscentiam habitat in corde.—*Soto.*

[1] Ad hæc respondetur, dimitti concupiscentiam carnis in baptismo, non ut non sit, sed ut in peccatum non imputetur. —*Aug. de Nup. et Conc.*, lib. i. cap. 25.

[2] Non dicit non esse peccatum, &c., sed remitti propter fidem in Christum.—*Melanct. in Dispos. Orat. ad Ep. ad Rom.*, p. 18. Credentibus nulla est condemnatio, non per se quidem sed ex accidenti, *h.e.*, ex Dei misericordia non imputantis eis peccata ad condemnationem.—*Pareus in Resp. ad Dub.*, i. Notandum est quod non dicit, nihil condemnabile, aut οὐδὲν

ἁμάρτημα sed οὐδὲν κατάκριμα. Non dicit in Christianis nihil esse amplius peccatorum, &c., sed esse illos condemnationi quæ peccato competit exemptos. Habent quidem et sancti reliquias peccati, verum extra condemnationem sunt, propter gratiam Christi, &c.—*Muscul.*

[1] Disput. i. in cap. 8 ad Rom.

that they will be condemning of them even as to their final and everlasting state; they condemn the soul of the poor even to hell itself: thus the condemned world is a condemning world. But yet God condemns not, neither here nor hereafter: all this is but man's day and man's judgment, 1 Cor. iv. 3; the righteous God judges otherwise of his people. He is so far from condemning them, that he will openly vindicate them against all the groundless accusations and condemnations of their enemies. It was David's prayer to God, 'Let my sentence come forth from thy presence,' Ps. xvii. 2, q.d., Lord, man doth thus and thus pass sentence upon my person, cause, actions; but, Lord, do thou thyself pass séntence upon me; that, I am sure, will be as just and righteous as the sentence of my enemies is false and malicious; and do not keep thy sentence about me to thyself, but let it come forth from thy presence, that the world may see and know what I am, and what thoughts thou hast of me. It is a very gracious promise that in Ps. xxxvii. 32, 33, 'The wicked watcheth the righteous, and seeketh to slay him. The Lord will not leave him in his hand, nor condemn him when he is judged;' i.e., though man condemn, God will not. He will not always let such as are upright with him lie under the world's condemnation; he will clear up their innocency as the light of the noonday; probably he may do this for them here, but certainly he will do it at the great day; and certainly too, which is more close to my business, though men are very free in their condemning of them as to their present concerns, yet God will not condemn them as to their state for eternity.

(2.) Sometimes conscience condemns them; for this conscience bears the place and office of a judge in the soul, and therefore it will be passing sentence with respect to men's state and actions; and its sentence often is in a condemnatory way. 'If our heart condemn us not, then have we confidence towards God,' 1 John iii. 21. Ay! and it is so even with God's own children, upon the commission of some great sin, or under some great darkness of spirit in time of conviction or desertion. Oh how forward is conscience then to condemn and to give in sad judgment upon them! And truly a condemning conscience is a very dreadful thing; be

they saints or sinners who lie under it, they will all find it to be bad enough. It is a little hell, or an anticipation of hell. There is no pain in the body comparable to the torment of a condemning conscience. A man had better be condemned of all the world than of his own conscience. Yet the people of God have this to comfort them; though conscience condemns below, yet God doth not condemn above. To the wicked, it is a condemning conscience, and a condemning God too. Oh there is the very height of misery! To the godly, it is sometimes a condemning conscience, but never a condemning God; even when that speaks nothing but guilt and wrath, then God designs nothing but grace and mercy. The inferior judge condemns in the court below, but the supreme judge acquits and justifies in the court above.

(3.) Satan, too, he will be condemning such as are in Christ. He is a proud creature, and loves to be upon the bench, and to assume that authority and judicial power which doth not belong to him. Oh it greatly pleases him to be judging of the spiritual and eternal state of believers! He that is but God's executioner, he will take upon him to be a judge. And as his pride puts him upon judging, so his malice puts him upon condemning; there is not an upright person in the world, upon whom he either doth not, or would not, pronounce a black sentence of condemnation. He is condemned himself, and he is altogether for the condemning of others too. Especially when he meets with a poor troubled soul, how doth he bestir himself with his dreadful judgings to discourage and overwhelm that soul! What! *thou* a child of God? no, thou art a child of wrath. What! *thou* look for salvation? no, hell and damnation shall be thy portion for ever. What! *thou* pretend to grace? no, there is not one drachm of true grace in thee; thou art a hypocrite, a castaway—one that must perish for ever. The word *condemn*[1] in classical authors, Greek and Latin, signifies to accuse also. The devil is a great accuser; he accused Job to God; he is styled 'The accuser of the brethren,' Rev. xii.

---

[1] Extenditur interdum condemnandi verbum etiam ad accusatorem, ut idem sit quod reum peragere, vel efficere ut quis damnetur.—*Calepin.* Ego hoc uno crimine illum condemnem necesse est.—*Cic. in Ver.* Δολαβέλλαν ἔκρινε κακώσεως ἐπαρχίς. —*Plutarch in Vit. Cæs.*

C

10. But this will not satisfy him; he must condemn too, in the higher and stricter notion of the word; he is for absolute, decisive, irrepealable judgment upon and against the repenting sinner, but God will not let him proceed so far; this is his own prerogative, and he will keep it to himself. Well, condemn he doth, and very busy he is, in special, to condemn those who belong to Christ. Where God condemns least, there Satan condemns most; but his condemnation signifies nothing, for God condemns not. Who will regard the condemnatory sentence of the jailer, if he stand acquitted by the judge? so here. But I am too long upon this head. You see here is a great deal of condemnation, yet the *no condemnation* in the text is true; for though men and conscience and Satan condemn, yet God condemns not, and it is his condemnation only which is here denied.

4. Fourthly, The particle *now* is to be taken notice of. 'There is therefore *now* no condemnation.' &c. Beza looks upon this as so emphatical, that he blames the Syriac translation for the omitting it.[1] What then is the import and significancy of it in this place? *Answer*, I suppose the apostle doth not intend by it to point to any circumstance of time, as, namely, the present time of life, or the present time of the gospel. Cajetan applies it to the present time of life.[2] The apostle, saith he, says, *now*, that we may understand that he speaks of the present life, and that we may not think that he excludes all condemnation only in respect of the state of the future blessedness. Then the meaning must be this, that the saints are secure against condemnation, not only when they shall actually be instated in the heavenly blessedness, or only upon the account of that blessed estate, but even here whilst they are but in the way, and with respect to the present state of grace. *Now* there is no condemnation to them. There is a truth in this interpretation, yet I shall not close with it.

Others apply it to the time of the gospel. *Now*,

that is, when Christ is come. Now when the gospel dispensation takes place, and the gospel grace is advanced, '*Now* there is no condemnation.' A great truth! but it must be taken with some caution, or else it may be the occasion of a great and dangerous error. What! is there no condemnation now in the times of the gospel? Yes, surely there is! Yea, the highest and sorest condemnation is now under the gospel. 'This is the condemnation,' &c., by way of eminency, John iii. 19. No condemnation like to gospel condemnation; this is double condemnation, as the prophet imprecates double destruction, Jer. xvii. 18. And again, was there no exemption from this till the time of the gospel? Doth the apostle by this particle confine and limit this privilege to those only who now live under the gospel? God forbid! Believers under the law were justified and saved as well as believers now under the gospel. The Scriptures are exceeding clear in this matter. It is therefore a false and venomous gloss which a great Socinian gives upon the words.[1] He brings in Paul as setting the times of the gospel against the times of the law, under which, he saith, all, speaking of them in common, were liable to damnation; but now, under the gospel, to many there is no damnation, and, if all would, there should be none to any. Here is a complication of errors, but I must not engage in the refuting of them. To many now there is no damnation; and was it not so even under the law? Oh let us neither make the time of the law worse than indeed it was, nor the time of the gospel better than indeed it is! There was salvation then, and there is damnation now.

In short, with Pareus, I make this *now* to be only *particula αἰτιολογιχή*, a causal particle; it is as much as *cum hæc ita sint*, since things are so, as the apostle had made out in his preceding discourse. There is *now*, or *upon all this*, no condemnation, &c. It is the very basis or foundation upon which all is bottomed. The *therefore* in the text points to this *now*, and derives all its strength from it. The apostle crowds

[1] Magnum est pondus particulæ universaliter negantis, et adverbii præsentis temporis a Syro interprete male prætermissi.

[2] Dicit *nunc* ut intelligamus quod de præsentis vitæ statu loquitur, ne intelligeres quod ratione status futuræ beatitudinis excludit omnem damnationem.

[1] Nunc, *i.e.*, his temporibus; opponit hæc tempora allati et publicati evangelii anteactis temporibus, præsertim sub lege, quibus omnes in commune loquendo damnationi subjecti erant. Nunc autem multis hominibus nulla est damnatio, et (si omnes vellent) nulla esset omnibus.—*Slichting in loc.*

the force of all that he had said by way of argument into this little word, and lays the whole stress of his conclusion upon it: 'There is *now* no condemnation,' &c.

5. Fifthly, We read it *no condemnation;* the original will bear it if we read it *not one condemnation.* οὐδὲν κατάκριμα is as much as οὐδὲ ἓν κατάκριμα. Such is the grace of God to believers, and such is their safety in their justified estate, that there is no condemnation—no, not so much as one condemnation to be passed upon them. Suppose a condemnatory sentence for every sin, (I am sure every sin deserves such a sentence, and in point of merit it is so many sins, so many condemnations,) yet the pardon being plenary and full, every way adequate to the sinner's guilt, the exemption of the pardoned person from condemnation must be plenary and full too; so that if there be not one sin unpardoned, there is not one condemnation to be feared: Jer. l. 20, 'In those days the iniquity of Israel shall be sought for, and there shall be none.' It is an allusion to one that turns over all his bonds, searches into all his debt-books, to see if he can find any debt due to him from such or such a person; but upon all his searching he cannot find so much as one debt to charge upon him. So it is with the pardoned, justified sinner. Imagine that God should be inquisitive to find out some guilt as lying upon him, he might indeed find out enough, as he is in himself; but as he is in Christ, as he is pardoned and justified through Christ, so there is nothing to be found against him, and therefore not one condemnation. How doth this tend to the comfort and encouragement of God's people! This makes the proposition to be very emphatical and highly consolatory; there is not one condemnation for them who are in Christ. Œcumenius opens the words with this emphasis, οὐδὲ μία διὰ ἁμαρτίαν καταδίκη.

6. Sixthly, The apostle speaks indefinitely with respect to the subject: 'There is no condemnation *to them* which are in Christ Jesus.' He takes all such into the privilege, for the indefinite here is equipollent to a universal. Paul doth not narrow or confine or impropriate this non-condemnation to himself; it is not there is now no condemnation *to me;* but he extends it to all who have an interest in Christ. And herein he discovers much of wisdom, as Peter

Martyr observes;[1] for had he spoken in the singular number, *to me,* many poor weak Christians would have been afraid to have applied this blessedness to themselves; they would have been ready to object, Ah blessed Paul, thou art high in faith, eminent in grace, therefore thou mayest say there is no condemnation to thee; but it is not so with us, we are but poor shrubs, mere dwarfs in grace, it is not for us to lay hold upon so high a privilege. To obviate this discouragement, saith the apostle, I tell you there is no condemnation to any who are in Christ, let them be who they will; this belongs to all such, to you as well as to myself. True, I am an apostle, you are not so; but then I am a believer, and so are you: true, I may have more of grace than you, but yet you are in Christ as well as I, and the union being common the non-condemnation is common too, for that is the ground of this. It is the same righteousness 'to all and upon all that believe,' Rom. iii. 22; it is the same faith for substance in the highest and in the lowest, 'to them that have obtained like precious faith with us,' 2 Peter i. 1. It is the same head, and the same union with this head, in all, and therefore it must be the same exemption from condemnation.

The difference in Paul's expressing himself, according to the difference of the subject he was upon, is very observable. Take him in the former chapter, where he is bewailing sin; there he speaks altogether in the first person singular, and goes no further than himself; read from the seventh verse to the end, and you will find *I* and *me* in every verse. But now in this eighth chapter, where he is treating of privileges, there he speaks altogether in the plural number, as taking in the whole body of believers. Run over it all, and except but one verse, in which it is true he particularises himself—'The law of the spirit of life in Christ Jesus, hath made *me* free from the law of sin and death,'—I say, do but except this one verse, and in all the rest you will find the ob-

[1] Mirabilis sane est apostoli prudentia, qui cum de vi peccati scriberet, eam expressit in persona sua, ut intelligeremus, &c. Postea vero, cum agitur de auxilio Spiritus Christi, inducit personam aliorum, ne cuiquam in mentem veniret, non quoslibet Christianos frui hoc auxilio Dei, sed tantum primarios quosdam et eximios, quales fuerunt apostoli.—*Pet. Martyr.*

servation to be true ; but this will be further cleared up hereafter. And elsewhere too you find him very careful not to engross or confine happiness to himself, but to extend it to all who belonged to God as well as he himself did : as take but that one instance, 2 Tim. iv. 8, 'Henceforth there is laid up for me a crown of righteousness, which the Lord the righteous judge shall give me at that day,'—thus far he himself is concerned ; but doth he stop here and not take in others? No, it is not enough to him to be sure of this happiness himself, but he will let others know it shall be just so with them too, therefore he adds, 'and not to me only, but unto all them also that love his appearing.' In the great blessings of the gospel—justification, adoption, eternal life—all the saints shall fare alike ; they are all God's children, and therefore all shall have their portion, and the same portion too. Jude calls it 'common salvation,' (ver. 3 ;) and the same may be said of all other blessings, it is common justification, common adoption, &c.

7. Seventhly, The positive is included in the negative. There is no condemnation, &c. ; is this all that the apostle drives at or hath in his eye, viz., to hold forth that such who are in Christ shall not be condemned? no ; he aims at something more, namely at this, that such are fully justified, and shall be most certainly saved ; they shall not only, upon their being in Christ, be looked upon as not guilty, or barely kept out of hell, but they shall be judged completely righteous, and they shall also be admitted into heaven and eternally glorified. There is a *meiosis* in the words, more is to be understood than what is expressed ; the privative and the positive part of the blessedness are to be linked together, and blessed be God for both ! Had it been only freedom from condemnation, that would have been rich and glorious mercy ; but when it is not only that, but justification and salvation too, oh here is mercy in the very height and zenith of it ! Some inquire why the apostle expresseth it in the negative rather than in the positive ? they answer, Because men generally are more sensible of the goodness of God, in the freeing of them from evil, than in the collating or bestowing of good. No condemnation more affects than positive justification or salvation. It may be further added, the apostle

thus expresses it because negatives usually intend and heighten the thing spoken of. As in the commandments, such as are negative carry a higher obligation in them than those which are positive, for they oblige both *semper* and *ad semper* too ; and as in the promises, when they are negatively expressed, this makes them to rise the higher in the matter contained in them ; as take that promise, which is made up of so many negatives, Heb. xiii. 5, 'I will never leave thee nor forsake thee ;' this is more than if God had said, I will always be with thee. So here as to propositions, when they are laid down in the negative, this form of expression doth add both greatness and certainty, at leastwise as to us, to the matter of them. And therefore Paul designing here to set forth the safety and happiness of believers with the greatest advantage, he chooses to express it in the negative rather than in the positive.

These things being premised, I come now to the more close handling of the point : 'There is no condemnation to them who are in Christ Jesus.'

Here I will shew, 1. What this condemnation is, which the persons spoken of are secured from. 2. I will make out the truth of the assertion, and give you the grounds of it.

1. First it is requisite I should a little open the condemnation here mentioned. The word is κατάκριμα : here in this verse it is the substantive ; you have the verb, ver. 3, 'and for sin condemned,' &c., κατέκρινε ; and the participle, ver. 34, 'who is he that condemneth,' τίς ὁ κατακρίνων? Sometimes it is set forth by κρῖμα, as Mat. xxiii. 14 ; 1 Tim. iii. 6 ; 2 Peter ii. 3 ; Rom. iii. 8 : sometimes by κρίσις, as John iii. 19, and v. 24 ; sometimes by κατάκρισις, as 2 Cor. iii. 9. These several words are promiscuously used to signify one and the same thing. That here in the text commonly carries a very black and dreadful sense with it. I do not deny but that sometimes it is used to set forth temporal evils and punishments, as condemnation to a temporal death, so Mat. xx. 18, and xxvii. 3 ; but usually it, as the verb in this composition, is expressive of spiritual and eternal evils of everlasting death : so Rom. v. 16, 18 ; Mark xvi. 16 ; 1 Cor. xi. 32. As to its direct and proper notation it signifies *judgment against one*, that is, κατάκριμα : it is a forensic word relating to what is in use amongst men in their courts of judi-

cature. To condemn, *Proprie judicis est cum mulctam reo vel pœnam per sententiam erogat ;* it is the sentence of a judge decreeing a mulct or penalty to be inflicted upon the guilty person. Amongst men, for the parallel will illustrate that which I am upon, the malefactor or guilty person is indicted, arraigned before the judge, judicial process is formed against him, his offence is proved, upon this the judge passes sentence upon him ; that he is guilty of that which is charged upon him, and then that he must undergo the penalty or penalties which are answerable to the nature and quality of his crime—if that be the capital he must die for it. So here the impenitent unbelieving sinner is indicted, arraigned at God's bar ; process is made against him, he is found, guilty of the violation of the holy law, and, which is worse, of the contempt of the gospel too ; whereupon God judges him to be guilty, and upon that guilt adjudges him to everlasting death : this is God's condemning or condemnation, in allusion to that condemnation which is amongst men. Pareus makes it to be the damnatory sentence of the law, that curse which it denounceth upon all and against all because of sin, Gal. iii. 10 ; Grotius makes it to be that eternal death spoken of, Rom. vi. 23 : several such glosses there are upon it, but all tend to one and the same thing.

Condemnation is either *respectu culpæ et reatus,* or *pœnæ,* in respect of guilt or punishment ; for both of these are included in it. God condemns the sinner ; how ? why, first he judges him to be ἔνοχος, guilty of that which the law charges him with. O, saith the law, sinner ! thus and thus thou hast offended ; such duties have been omitted, such sins have been committed, such Sabbaths have been profaned, such mercies have been abused, such tenders of grace have been slighted ; here the gospel law comes in as an accuser too, &c. Well now, saith God, sinner ! what dost thou say to this charge ? is it true or false ? canst thou deny it ? what defence or plea canst thou make for thyself ? Alas ! he is speechless, Mat. xxii. 12, hath not one word to say for himself ; he can neither deny nor excuse or extenuate what is charged upon him. Why then, saith God the righteous judge, I must pronounce, and I do here pronounce thee to be guilty. And is this all ? no, upon this guilt the law pleads for a

further sentence, for the decreeing and inflicting of the penalty, threatened by God himself, and incurred by the sinner. Ah, saith God, and I cannot deny it, I must be just and righteous, and therefore, sinner, I here adjudge thee to die eternally. This is *condemnation* in the extensive notion of it : if you consider it with respect to guilt, so it is opposed to justification ; if you consider it with respect to punishment, so it is opposed to salvation. In the former notion you have it, Rom. v. 16, 18, 'And not as it was by one that sinned, so is the gift : for the judgment was by one to condemnation, but the free gift is of many offences to justification. Therefore as by the offence of one judgment came upon all men to condemnation ; even so by the righteousness of one the free gift came upon all men unto justification of life.' In the second notion you have it, Mark xvi. 16, 'He that believeth and is baptized, shall be saved, but he that believeth not, καταχριθήσεται, shall be condemned.' These are the two things which make up the condemnation in the text, guilt and death ; from both of which such as are in Christ are secured : they shall neither be judged guilty, their guilt being done away by Christ, and the sentence proceeding according to what they are in Christ, and not according to what they are in themselves ; nor shall a sentence of eternal death pass upon them, for guilt being taken off, that would not be righteous. There is therefore none of this condemnation to believers.

There is the *sentence* of condemnation and the *state* of condemnation ; the former, actively considered, refers to God, and is his act ; the latter refers to the sinner, and is consequential upon the former. The sentence hath been already opened. The state of condemnation is the sinner's undergoing of the utmost of vindictive justice, in his eternal separation from God and enduring of everlasting torments in hell, of which you will hear more in what follows. Neither of these do belong to them who are in Christ Jesus : not the former, they being now justified ; not the latter, they being sure to be glorified. I shall take in both, yet mainly freedom from the state of condemnation ; the apostle, I conceive, had this chiefly in his eye when he here said, 'There is now no condemnation,' &c. Justification and no condemnation with respect to the sentence are all one, only the one notes what is positive, the other what is negative : now the apostle in the words inferring no condemnation from justification, (as you will see he doth by and by,) it appears that his eye was upon something distinct from, and consequential upon, justification ; and that must be exemption from the state of condemnation. 'There is no condemnation,' &c. ; it is as if he had said, Such shall not be condemned hereafter, or lie under that damnation in hell which will be the portion of unbelievers : to this therefore I shall chiefly speak.

Further, as some distinguish of justification, it is either virtual or actual ; either in title as to the sentence of the word here, or full and complete in the sentence which shall solemnly be pronounced by God at the great day. So we may also distinguish of condemnation: it is either virtual, that which is now, in the sentence of the law or gospel ; or actual, that which is to come, when God by Christ will in a public and solemn way pass a condemnatory upon men according to the word ; and this shall be at the last and great judgment. You read of the first, John iii. 18, 'He that believeth on him is not condemned ; he that believeth not (ἤδη κέκριται) is condemned already :' so ver. 26 of that chapter. Of the second, Mark xvi. 16, and in divers other places. In both of these senses also God's people are exempted from condemnation ; take it virtually or actually, in title here or in the final sentence of the judge hereafter, it belongs not to them. And this I am now to make good, which was the second head that I propounded to speak to.

2. The negation in the text is so express, so absolute and peremptory, that there cannot be the least . doubt of the truth of it ; indeed, as to the application of this to a man's self *in hypothesi*, so there may be many doubts arising in the soul concerning it ; but as to the thing itself *in thesi*, nothing more sure and certain than it is. You have it asserted not only in this single scripture, but in divers others also : John iii. 18, 'He that believeth on him is not condemned,' neither is nor ever shall be. John v. 24, 'Verily, verily, I say unto you, (Christ would have believers fully settled in the belief of this precious truth, and therefore he premises asseveration upon asseveration, and gives you his own authority for it,) he that heareth my word, and believeth on him that

sent me, hath everlasting life, and shall not come into condemnation, but is passed from death to life.' Read John iii. 16, 36 ; Mark xvi. 16 ; 1 Thes. i. 10.

If you look into the text, (for I will go no further,) you will find a double argument, or ground, for the non-condemnation of believers.

(1.) The first lies couched in the illative particle, 'There is *therefore* now no condemnation,' &c. What doth this *therefore* point to ? when that is found out, we must then inquire what there is of strength in it to prove and bottom non-condemnation upon.

For answer to this, expositors do somewhat differ about it. Some make it to refer to all that goes before from the 16th ver. of the 1st chap. *Est conclusio totius superioris disputationis a ver.* 16, *primi capitis.*— *Beza.* It is a conclusion drawn from all that hath been taught hitherto.—*Deodate.* Others limit it to some special part of the apostle's foregoing discourse in this epistle. And so some apply it to what he had laid down in chap. iii., iv., and v., where he insists upon justification, and proves at large that believers are justified, and that through the righteousness of Christ ; which being so, from this their blessed state and this gracious act of God upon them, he here infers 'there is therefore now no condemnation,' &c. Others again make the springhead of the inference to lie in the 7th chap., especially in the close of it : Paul there thanks God, who had delivered him from the body of sin through Christ ; he says with his mind, his renewed and sanctified part, he served the law of God, though with the flesh, the carnal and unregenerate part, he served the law of sin. Now from this he draws the conclusion, 'There is therefore now no condemnation,' &c.[1]

I, for my part, will not limit the inference to the one or to the other, but I will take in all ; yet I will consider the whole in its main parts, viz., justifica-

[1] Thus Bucer : Infert ad illud in proxima sectione, Gratias ago, &c. Thus Pareus : Illatio est valde vehemens ex præcedenti querela et gratulatione. Thus Musculus : Nulla condemnatio, &c. Quare ? referendum est istud exordium ad gratiarum actionem capitis præcedentis, qua dixit, Gratias ago, &c. Thus Tolet : Connexa est hæc sententia ultimis præcedentis capitis verbis, et ex ipsis deducitur. Pendet initium hoc tam faustum et fælix, ex hoc quod ultimo dictum est in fine præcedentis.—*Corn. Mussus.*

tion and sanctification. The non-condemnation then of persons in Christ may be proved by, or is grounded upon,

(1.) Their justification. He that is a justified man cannot be a condemned man, for these two are contrary and incompatible. If it be justifying, it cannot be condemning; if it be condemning, it cannot be justifying. There being in justification an acquitting, absolving, discharging from guilt, how can this consist with the condemning of one as guilty, or because guilty? this would be a plain contradiction, *oppositum in apposito*. It is with law-contraries as it is with physical-contraries, upon the position of the one there needs must be the exclusion or negation of the other; now justification and condemnation are law-contraries, *ergo*, &c. The apostle argues upon this, ver. 33, 'Who shall lay anything to the charge of God's elect?' and surely there must be charging before there can be condemning; but there can be none of that; why? because 'it is God that justifieth.' The believer being justified, and justified by God too, he must needs be exempted from condemnation. He that will not acquit the guilty will not condemn the righteous, 'for both are equally an abomination to the Lord,' Prov. xvii. 15. Now the justified person is a righteous person, for else what doth his justification signify? and will the righteous judge condemn a righteous person?

Pray, that you may the better perceive how the deduction in the text is grounded, look back a little into the epistle, and see what the apostle there lays down concerning justification. He says, and this is the main position, upon which he doth but enlarge in all his following discourse, 'Therein is the righteousness of God revealed from faith to faith,' chap. i. 17: 'Even the righteousness of God, which is by faith of Jesus Christ unto all and upon all them that believe,' chap. iii. 22: 'Being justified freely by his grace through the redemption that is in Jesus Christ; whom God hath set forth to be a propitiation through faith in his blood,' &c., ver. 24–26: 'Abraham believed God, and it was counted to him for righteousness,' chap. iv. 3: 'Now it was not written for his sake alone that it was imputed to him; but for us also, to whom it shall be imputed, if we believe on him that raised up the Lord Jesus from the dead; who was delivered for our offences,

and was raised again for our justification,' ver. 23–25: 'Therefore being justified by faith, we have peace with God through our Lord Jesus Christ,' chap. v. 1. Especially read what the apostle writes in drawing up the parallel betwixt the two Adams, chap. v. 15 to the end. I say, read and consider what is before asserted over and over concerning justification, and then tell me whether the apostle might not well thus infer, 'There is therefore,' &c.; and whether there be not strength enough in these premises to bear the weight of the conclusion, 'There is therefore now no condemnation,' &c.: for unquestionably the illative, *therefore*, upon which the proposition is bottomed, like the handle in the dial, points to all that the apostle had been speaking of concerning justifying grace.

(2.) The privilege is farther sure upon sanctification. Such as are in Christ are always sanctified; wherever the union is with the Son there is sanctification by the Spirit: now such as are sanctified shall never be condemned. Rev. xx. 6, 'Blessed and holy is he that hath part in the first resurrection: on such the second death, or condemnation, hath no power.' Sanctification doth not carry in it such a direct and intrinsic opposition to condemnation as justification doth, nor is it any meritorious ground of non-condemnation. Yet where there is sanctification there shall be no condemnation: for upon this the power and dominion of sin is taken away, vigorous resistance is made against it, the bent of the heart is for God, there is the participation of the divine nature;[1] the image of God is renewed in the soul; the creature, in part, is restored to that original rectitude which was before the fall, with many suchlike considerations, upon all which the sanctified person is secured from condemnation. God hath such a love to grace, it being the work of his own Spirit, and to gracious persons, they in sanctification being made after himself, as it is ex-

---

[1] Dum non essent in Christo et consentirent concupiscentiæ, erat illis damnatio. Nunc autem cum sint in Christo, et repugnent concupiscentiæ, nihil damnationis est illis, quamquam ex carne concupiscant; quia non pugnatores sed victi damnantur; nec est damnabile si existant desideria carnalia, sed si eis ad peccatum obediatur.—*Anselm.* (This must be understood of condemnation in event, and that too as grounded upon the mere grace of God.)

pressed Eph. iv. 24, that he will never suffer such to perish eternally. Grace *merits* nothing, yet it *secures* from the greatest evils, and entitles to the greatest good. Nothing shall save where grace is not, nothing shall damn where grace is. The sinner shall not live, the saint shall not die. Oh this sanctification! though it be imperfect, yet how great good doth result from it! Paul had sad remainders of sin in him, but withal grace was in him; he had his double self, (as the moralist expresses it, ἕκαστος ἡμῶν δίττος ἐστιν,) his renewed self and his unrenewed self: 'the law was spiritual, but he was carnal, sold under sin;' 'what he would not, that he did; what he would, that he did not;' he was 'led captive by the law of sin and death;' here was his unrenewed self. Yet where he complains most of sin, even there he discovers much, if not most, of grace: he had a sinning nature, but he allowed not himself in sin; he 'consented to the law that it was good;' it was not he that did so and so, but 'sin that dwelt in him:' 'to will was present with him, though how to perform, he did not find:' he 'delighted in the law of God in the inward man:' 'with his mind he served the law of God,' &c., here was his renewed self. Do not these things evidence grace? was all this spoken *in persona irregeniti*, as some tell us? No, doubtless the apostle here speaks as a gracious man, and in the person of gracious men.[1] And what doth he infer from all this? 'There is therefore now no condemnation,' &c. Oh, saith Paul, I have sin enough to humble me, but yet sin shall not damn me; there is too much of it in me, but yet it hath not my heart: 'With my mind I serve the law of God;' the main bent of my heart is for holiness; the corrupt nature is very strong in me, but yet it hath not its full strength, its entire unbroken power and dominion over me; that, through grace, I am freed from. I am, though but imperfectly, yet truly sanctified; and hereupon, though I may lie under much trouble here, yet I am safe as to my eternal

state; there is therefore now no condemnation to me. I desire it may be observed, that he doth not only infer non-condemnation from the work of grace in him, spoken of in the closure of the former chapter, but as soon as he had laid down in common this great happiness of persons in Christ, he presently confirms it, as to himself, from his sanctification, and the dethroning of sin in him by the regenerating Spirit: 'For the law of the spirit of life in Christ Jesus hath made me free from the law of sin and death.' And with respect to others he much enlarges upon it, Rom. vi. 5–8, 21–23. Well, then, persons in Christ, they being justified and sanctified, are above the danger of condemnation; and these are the two great pillars upon which the *therefore* in the words is built.

The text affords us another argument or ground of non-condemnation, and that lies in the subject itself: 'There is no condemnation to them who are in Christ Jesus.' Why so? Because they are in Christ Jesus; for these words are not only descriptive of the persons to whom the privilege belongs, but they are also argumentative, and contain a reason or proof of the thing spoken of. The expression, as shall be hereafter opened, notes that near and intimate union which is betwixt Christ and believers. Now shall there be condemnation where there is such a union? What! in Christ, and yet under condemnation? Those that are so near to Christ here, shall they be set at an eternal distance from him hereafter? Will the head be so severed from his members? When Christ is in heaven, shall a part of him lie in hell? Oh, no! A limb of Christ shall not perish. Besides, upon this union there is interest in all that Christ hath done and suffered. He that is in Christ hath a right to all of Christ—the obedience, righteousness, merits, satisfaction, the life, death, resurrection, intercession of Christ. All are his who are in Christ. It being so, how can this person miscarry? The apostle upon this triumphs over condemnation: ver. 34, 'Who is he that condemneth? it is Christ that died; yea, rather that is risen again, who is even at the right hand of God, who also maketh intercession for us.' What there is in each of these heads—the death, resurrection, exaltation, intercession of Christ—to secure those who are in him from condemnation,

---

[1] With my mind I serve the law of God. Ego, qui in me significo quemlibet justum sub gratia constitutum.—*Anselm*. Quod meo judicio tantam vim, tantam emphasin habet, ut illi plane humanæ naturæ corruptionem ignorare videantur, si qui sint, qui eam cum tali animi constitutione consistere posse putant, nisi aliunde sit aliquatenus immutata.—*Amyral, Consid.*, cap. sept. Ep. ad Rom. p. 16. (He might have gone higher than *aliquatenus immutata*.)

shall in due time, if God please, be fully made out; but that is not now to be done. Only, for the further confirming of the truth in hand, let me a little descant upon the question which the apostle here doth so triumphantly propound, 'Who is he that condemneth?' He seems to challenge all inferior accusers, and bid them do their worst; he hangs out a flag of defiance to all. Who, saith he, will attempt, or in case they should attempt, would be able, to carry on such a thing as the condemning of those who are in Christ? For God himself, who must be spoken of with all reverence, he will not, for he justifies, and he cannot justify and condemn too. His justice is satisfied; he hath declared that he hath accepted of Christ's satisfaction made in the sinner's stead, and he will not be satisfied and yet condemn. Then, to be sure, Christ will not; for his great design was to prevent and keep off this condemnation. This was the very thing which he had in his eye in his great and most blessed undertaking. He is so far from doing this himself, that he will not suffer it to be done by any other. Come to sin, that shall not, for that is pardoned, expiated by the blood of Christ; that is condemned itself, Rom. viii. 3, and a condemned thing shall never be a condemning thing. The law cannot, for that is fulfilled by the surety, and that is appealed from as not a proper judge, and believers are not under it—i.e., as to its vis damnatrix—but under grace, Rom. vi. 14. The gospel too will not, because its conditions are performed, though imperfectly, yet sincerely, which it accepts of. It appears, then, by this induction, that there is, there shall be, no condemnation to them who are in Christ Jesus. So much for the proofs or grounds of the truth in hand. Observe that I have only instanced in those which the text leads me to; for divers others might have been produced, as God's eternal electing love, the covenant of grace, the earnest of the Spirit, &c., but these I pass by. Nothing remains but the application.

Use 1. And, first, This proclaims the misery of all who are not in Christ Jesus. The cloud is not so bright towards Israel, but it is as dark towards the Egyptians; the point is not so full of comfort to believers, but it is as full of terror to unbelievers. Here is the very marrow and sweetness of the gospel for the one, and yet withal here is the bitterest gall

and wormwood of the law for the other. There is no condemnation to them who are in Christ; what more sweet? But there is nothing but condemnation to them who are out of Christ; what more dreadful? Art thou a Christless, graceless, unbelieving, impenitent person? Do not deceive thyself; this exemption from condemnation belongs not to thee. The apostle doth not say there is no condemnation, and so break off; but, that none may flatter themselves, and presumptuously apply that to themselves which belongs not to them, he puts down the subject which only is concerned in the privilege. Oh you who are out of Christ, know it and be assured of it, there is condemnation to you; you are condemned already in the sentence of the law, John iii. 18; and it will not be long before you be actually, solemnly condemned by the sentence of the Judge; so many unbelievers, so many condemned persons. And if so, is it nothing to you to be condemned? What a dreadful word is condemnation! How should we all fear and tremble at the hearing of it! All the evils of the present life are a mere nothing, mere trifles to this. Put all afflictions, calamities, miseries together, one condemnation outweighs them all. Sickness, pain, poverty, sufferings, all are light, inconsiderable things in comparison of this. I cannot but stand and wonder, and be filled even with amazement, at the woeful stupidity and security of sinners out of Christ. The condemnation of God hangs over them; wherever they are or go they are no better than condemned men; and yet how merry, jovial, unconcerned are they! Good God! what shall we say to this! Amongst us, what a sad spectacle is it to see a poor malefactor that is condemned by man, and to be executed within a few days, altogether unaffected with his condition! He spends that span of time which he hath to live in feasting, drinking, trimming, and dressing of himself, and considers not that he is a condemned man, and must die within a day or two. Ah sinners, this is your state! Nay, yours is much worse, for you are under a far worser condemnation, even the condemnation of the great God, and that too to die eternally. And yet how do you carry it? You please the flesh, take your fill of sensual pleasures; you 'chant to the sound of the viol, drink wine in bowls,' Amos vi. 5, 6; live a merry life, nothing troubles you; no, though the dreadful sentence of God be passed upon you, and is ready to be executed every moment, yet all is well in your thoughts. What prodigious security is this! Belshazzar in his cups, and height of mirth, when he saw the handwriting upon the wall, this made him tremble, Dan. v. 5, 6. Sinner, thou art at ease, sporting thyself in thy worldly delights, look but into the word; there is a dreadful handwriting against thee, there is condemnation written over and over in broad and legible characters as thy portion, wilt not thou fear? Surely it is sad dancing over the mouth of hell. There is but a breath betwixt thee and everlasting flames, and yet art thou secure? Is eternal misery a thing to be dallied with or slighted? If men were not downright atheists, this condemnation would affright and startle them.[1] Now do I speak to any here of you as being under this woeful security? If it be possible to reach your consciences, and to stir up fear in you, I would desire you to consider these four or five things.

1. It is God himself who will be your judge, and who will pass the condemnatory sentence upon you. It is somewhat terrible to be arraigned and condemned at the bar of man, but how much more terrible will it be to be arraigned and condemned at the bar of God! What a vast disproportion is here betwixt the crimes, the judge, the sentence, the execution! &c. O sinners, when you must stand before such a judge, in order to the receiving of such a sentence, for crimes so high and heinous, will you not tremble? Methinks the majesty, omnisciency, omnipotency, righteousness of this judge should strike us all with fear and dread. There is no standing before him, such is his majesty; no hiding of anything from him, such is his omnisciency; no resisting of him, such is his omnipotency; no corrupting of him, such is his infinite righteousness. What, then, will become of you who are in your sins, but out of Christ? At the tribunal of this God you must hold up your hands, be tried, and so condemned. Is this nothing to you? And because he will not himself immediately judge the world, but mediately by Christ—that man whom he hath ordained to this office, Acts xvii. 31—therefore

[1] Hæc cura omnes non omnino atheos necessario excruciat, et est tristis conscientiarum tortura.—*Pareus in loc.*

Christ in his own person shall appear and ride his great circuit as the universal judge, and every one of you shall be summoned before him to be judged by him: 2 Cor. v. 10, 'We must all appear before the judgment-seat of Christ; that every one,' &c. And may not the consideration of this very much heighten your fear? You not being in Christ, how will you be able to stand before Christ? Where he is not a gracious head, will he not be a severe judge? You must be judged by him whom you so often, so scornfully have rejected. He will be your judge, whom you would not have to be your King and Saviour; what favour can you expect from him whom you have so basely used? In what glory will this judge appear when you shall stand before him? Now you know the glory and solemnity of the bench adds to the terror of the malefactor at the bar: Mat. xxv. 31, 'When the Son of man shall come in his glory, and all the holy angels with him, then shall he sit upon the throne of his glory.' Oh to be tried, cast, and sentenced by so glorious a judge, in so solemn a manner, this must needs be terrible to sinners when they see it and hear it, though now they make nothing of it! Rev. vi. 15–17, 'And the kings of the earth, and the great men, and the rich men, and the chief captains, and the mighty men, and every bond man, and every free man, hid themselves in the dens, and in the rocks of the mountains; and said to the mountains and rocks, Fall on us, and hide us from the face of him that sitteth on the throne, and from the wrath of the Lamb: for the great day of his wrath is come; and who shall be able to stand?'

2. Think with yourselves what this condemnation is. Men are fearless because they are thoughtless. Did they but weigh and ponder what the things of another world are, what it is to be everlastingly condemned, they would not be so secure as they are. Condemnation, what is it? It is, in short, to be adjudged to eternal death. Men condemn their guilty persons to die a temporal death, and that is as high as they can go; but God, being a higher judge, and greater offences being committed against him than what are committed by man against man, he inflicts a greater penalty, and his sentence is to die eternally. He doth not condemn to a prison, to an axe, or gallows, just to die, and then there is an end

of all; oh no! he sentences to death, and eternal death too. And this is no less than the loss of God's love and favour and presence, which is the *pœna damni;* and the undergoing of endless, ceaseless, remediless torments in hell, which is the *pœna sensus.* Both are very sad, but divines generally give the pre-eminence to the first.[1] The hell of hell is the loss of heaven and of God's love. But both put together must needs make the sinner extremely miserable; and he that is out of Christ shall feel both of them. Would you know what this condemnation is? You have a sad draught or description of it, Mat. xxv. 41, 'Depart from me, ye cursed, into everlasting fire, prepared for the devil and his angels.' Every word here, if I could speak to it, is thunder and lightning. To be thrust from Christ and thrown into fire, into everlasting fire, into that very fire which is prepared for the devil and his angels, oh, here is misery indeed! Hear me, therefore, you who are out of Christ; if you so live and so die, you shall never see God; and this is not all, for you shall also feel those torments, in comparison of which stone, gout, strangury, racking by men, the most exquisite pains here, are in a manner perfect ease, or at least very inconsiderable pain.[2] And this, too, you must lie under to all eternity. Oh this is worst of all! this puts an accent, indeed, upon this condemnation: it is eternal condemnation! This eternity fills up the measure of the unbeliever's misery, and makes it to run over. In heaven it is eternity of joy; in hell it is eternity of woe. To be miserable as long as God shall be blessed; to be always dying, and yet always to live; to be always drinking, and yet the cup still to continue full; to launch out into a boundless ocean of eternal wrath; to lie under evils, and to see no end of them; that when millions of millions of years are over, all is, as it were, to begin again, and the poor creature is—but after the efflux of so much time— just where he was at the first; to pass from dying comforts to never-dying sorrows;—what tongue can express, what heart can conceive the greatness of this misery! It is 'everlasting destruction from the presence of the Lord,' 2 Thes. i. 9; it is 'everlasting punishment,' Mat. xxv. 46; it is 'everlasting fire,' Mat. xxv. 41; it is 'the worm that never dies,' Mark ix. 44; it is 'everlasting chains,' Jude 6; 'the blackness of darkness for ever,' Jude 13. Now, sirs, what do you think of this? are you able to bear it? Alas! 'who among us shall dwell with devouring fire? who among us shall dwell with everlasting burnings?' Isa. xxxiii. 14. This made the sinners in Zion afraid, and filled hypocrites with fearfulness; and will it not, sooner or later, have the same effect upon you who are out of Christ? If this condemnation or eternal death was total abolition or annihilation, as some Socinians make it to be,[1] it would not be so bad; this would be a great allay to it; for surely, whatever some learned men may say to the contrary, no being would be more desirable than such a being; but it is not so.

3. The condemnatory sentence being once passed, it will be irreversible and irresistible. When it is once out of the judge's mouth there is no reversing of it; as the penalty is intolerable, so the sentence is irreversible. The poor condemned sinner will presently fall upon his knees and most earnestly beg mercy, but all in vain; all his entreaties, beseechings, tears, wringing of hands, will avail nothing; time was when he would not hear Christ, and now Christ will not hear him. Now, to be sure, the season of grace is over—once condemned and ever condemned; there is neither appealing from the judge nor repealing of the sentence. And then too, I say, it is irresistible; as soon as it is passed, Christ will have his officers by him, who shall see it put into execution : his guard and retinue of angels shall be ready for this service, these reapers shall 'gather the tares and bind them in bundles to burn them,' Mat. xiii. 30, and who shall be able to resist? The judge amongst the Jews was to see the offender punished before his face, Deut. xxv. 2. Christ will not only pass sentence, but he himself will see execution done : Luke xix. 27, 'Those mine enemies, which would not that I should reign over them, bring them hither and slay them *before me.*' And as there will be no turning of

---

[1] Omnia Gehennæ supplicia superabit, Deum non videre, et bonis carere.—*Bernard.* See Bolton of the four last things, p. 95, &c.

[2] *Vide* Chrys. ad pop. Antioch., Hom. 49, very full upon this.

[1] See Calov. Socin. proflig. de morte æterna, Contr. tertia, p. 1113. Cloppenb. Compend. Socinian, cap. 8, p. 134, &c., with many others.

him, so neither will there be either flying from him or making resistance to him. When man condemns God can save, but who can save when God condemns? If the three children be thrown into the fire God can take them out, but when the unbeliever is thrown into hell-fire, or to be thrown into hell-fire, who then can either hinder or deliver? Oh come to Christ and get into Christ betimes! If you defer till the sentence be passed, you must suffer it, and there is no remedy. As God says, 'I will work, and who shall let?' Isa. xliii. 13. So when he condemns, and will have his sentence executed, who shall let? what can man do to defend himself, or to hinder God? Job xxxi. 14, 'What shall I then do when God riseth up? and when he visiteth, what shall I answer him?'

4. The unbeliever and Christless person will not only be condemned by God, but he will also be condemned by himself: self-condemnation will accompany God's condemnation, and that is very miserable. Next to being condemned by God, nothing so sad as to be αὐτοκατάκριτος, condemned by one's-self. When the poor sinner shall be upon his trial, conscience will accuse as well as the law, and condemn as well as the judge. And as soon as ever the judge shall have passed sentence, conscience will fall upon the guilty condemned person and say, Is not this just and righteous? 'hath not thou procured this to thyself?' Jer. ii. 17; must not such a course have such an end? is not this the fruit of thy sin? This will highly justify God, (for the more the sinner condemns himself, the more he acquits God,) but greatly heighten his own misery. You read how at the great day there shall be the opening of the books,[1] Rev. xx. 21; these books are mainly two, the book of Scripture, and the book of conscience. As to the latter, men keep it shut here, but God will open it to some purpose then; and sinners shall be forced to look into it, and read over the sins of their lives written there in very legible characters. And what a sad time will it then be, when as God condemns without and above, so conscience shall condemn below and within! Such as are out of Christ will feel also this to be true, to their inexpressible

---

[1] Per apertionem librorum significatur, unicuique conscientia sua (nec enim opus erit testibus externis) suggestura sit omnem suam vitam.—*Voss de Extr. Judicio.*

grief and torment, if it be not prevented by timely repentance.

5. I might add, (which indeed will be but a more particular explication of the former head,) this condemnation will be the sadder, especially to such who live under the gospel, because they will lie under the sense and conviction of this, that they have foolishly and wilfully brought all this misery upon themselves. For—and their hearts will tell them of it—Christ offered himself to them from time to time, but they refused to close with him; he tendered pardon to them, but they slighted it; and who will pity the traitor that dies for his treason, when his prince offered him a pardon and he scorned to accept of it? They might have been saved as well as others, would they but have hearkened to the free, gracious, hearty, often repeated invitations which in the gospel were made to them; how often would Christ have 'gathered them as the hen gathers her chickens, but they would not,' Mat. xxiii. 37; and therefore now their souls are lost for ever. O sinner! 'thy destruction is of thyself,' Hosea xiii. 9; and the consideration of this will sadly gnaw upon thy conscience for ever; this is the worm that never dies. The Jews, when they had adjudged a malefactor to die, the judge and the witnesses used to lay their hands upon him, and to say 'Thy blood be upon thy own head;' in imitation of which the murderers of our Saviour said, 'His blood be on us and our children,' Mat. xxvii. 25. Thus Christ, when he shall have passed the dreadful sentence of eternal death upon the impenitent and unbelieving, he will say, Your blood be upon your own heads.

Now is not here enough, if the Lord would please to set it home upon the conscience, to awaken and terrify secure Christless sinners? You who are out of Christ pray believe me, as sure as God is, and is a just and righteous God, as sure as his word is true, so sure are you, if you go out of the world before you have got into Christ, to be condemned for ever. And will ye not lay this to heart before it be too late? is it not high time for you to think of these things? will nothing awaken you but only the feeling of everlasting flames? will you not mind the damned state till you be in it? I tremble to think of that distress that you will be in at the great day, though now you are quiet and unconcerned; when your sins shall fly in your faces and accuse you, when the tremendous justice of God shall affright you, when, if you look downwards, there is a hell ready to receive you, if upwards there is an angry judge, if inwards there is the worm of conscience, if about you there is a world all in flames. Oh what a time will this be! what would you then give to be in Christ? take heed, I beseech you, of an after-wisdom.

Use 2. Secondly, I would exhort you to make sure of this exemption from condemnation, to labour to be in the number of those to whom there is no condemnation. It is infinite mercy that such a thing is attainable; surely he must be strangely besotted and utterly void of all sense of eternity, who doth not with the greatest care and diligence put in for a share in this happiness. No condemnation! Justification here and salvation hereafter! What can be so worthy of our utmost pains and endeavours as these? what pitiful trifles and very nothings are all other things in comparison of these! It is no great matter how things go at present, if the future everlasting state may be secured. Oh that all your thoughts, desires, pursuits, might be swallowed up in this! You dread such and such evils here; alas! what are these to the eternal evils which have been set before you? You are set upon the world's good, and what is that to an endless blessedness in the vision and fruition of God in heaven? Think of hell, and nothing here will be very evil, and of heaven, and nothing here will be very good. Should you come to a condemned man, and talk to him of the riches, honours, crowns, and sceptres of this world; Ah! saith he, what is this to me? I am a poor condemned man; can you tell me how I may get out of the condemnation that I lie under? Then you will say something which will suit my condition. Why, sirs, you trouble yourselves about the getting of wealth, the greatening of yourselves in the world, but you do not consider you are condemned men: such you were as you came into the world. 'By the offence of one, judgment came upon all to condemnation,' Rom. v. 13; and there is a worser condemnation for you when you shall go out of the world. Oh

¹ Indique erunt tibi angustiæ hinc erunt accusantia peccata, tremeda justitia, subter patens horridum chaos, desuper iratus judex, intus vermis conscientiæ, foris ardens mundus.—*Beres de Consc.*

what have you to do but to get out of this condemnation? It is to be feared that the greatest part of men (not out of any want of mercy in God, or from anything to be charged upon God, but merely through their own sin and folly) will perish therein. You read of the condemning of the world, Cor. xi. 32; now therefore what are you, or what do you do, that you may be exempted from the general misery? Certainly if you lie in the common state, and live in the common course, you must perish in the common condemnation; think of it, and make some timely provision against it. Your judge deals very graciously with you; he warns you beforehand, tells you how his terrible sentence may be prevented, nay, he offers life and pardon to you if you will but accept of it. And after all this, will you force him to condemn you? Then it will be condemnation with a witness. I would upon this consideration be the more earnest with you in the present advice, because though this condemnation will be sad enough to all, yet to you it will be superlatively sad. You living under the gospel, where the way of salvation is set before you, where tenders of grace are made to you, if you be not wise and serious in securing the main, this will not only make your condemnation more unavoidable,—'How shall we escape if we neglect so great salvation?' Heb. ii. 3,—but also more intolerable: it will be condemnation with an accent or emphasis to you. 'This is the condemnation, that light is come into the world,' &c., John iii. 19. The Scripture speaks of 'greater damnation,' Mat. xxiii. 14. It will be great damnation to pagans and infidels, but greater damnation to Christians. According to the different measures of that gospel light and gospel grace which men live under, so will the different measures of their future misery be. If they live and die in impenitency and unbelief. Oh how will these aggravate your condemnation! If there be one place in hell hotter than another, that very place shall be yours, whilst others shall *mitius ardere.* 'Thou Capernaum, which art exalted into heaven, &c. But I say unto you, That it shall be more tolerable for the land of Sodom in the day of judgment, than for you,' Mat. xi. 23, 24.

You will ask me, What are we to do that it may be to us no condemnation? For answer to this, several directions might be given and much enlarged upon; but I will give you only five or six, and be but short upon them.

Direc. 1. First, Let sin be condemned in you and by you. For thus the case stands: sin must either be condemned by you, or you for it; a condemnatory sentence must pass either upon the sin or the sinner. And is it not better it should pass upon the sin rather than upon the sinner? that it should die rather than you should die? Oh let not sin live in you, nor do you live in it, for if it be so it will be condemnation! This sin is the condemning thing. Had there been no sin there had been no condemnation; it is that, and that only, which makes the creature liable to eternal death: 'The wages of sin is death,' Rom. vi. 23. Did not the malefactor break the law, by stealing, murdering, &c., he would not be obnoxious to the law's penalties; and so it is here. We violate God's law, upon that violation there is guilt, upon that guilt there is obnoxiousness to punishment and to a sentence of death. Oh take heed of sin! Here lies the evil of it, it exposes to and ends in eternal condemnation. It pleases the sinner for a season, Heb. xi. 25, and then entails everlasting wrath upon him. Was it not for this a life in sin would be a fine life. I must recall myself. A life in sin a fine life? No. Was there no hell hereafter, yet such a life would be, and is, a base, sordid, cursed life. But hell, and wrath, and condemnation, and all follow upon it, and this spoils the pleasures and delights of a sinful life. Who would not fear and shun sin? A child of God dreads it for the hell that is *in it*. Methinks all should dread it for the hell that is procured *by it*. Now therefore what is your course? Every man's sentence shall be according to his course. Where it is a holy course, it shall be the sentence of life; where it is the opposite course, it shall be the sentence of death. Bring it down to yourselves; do not you live in sin? Maybe you are not drunkards, swearers, &c.; but is there not some other, some secret way of wickedness in which you walk—some bosom lust hid and cherished? Do you endeavour after universal holiness? These things must be inquired into, for the no-condemnation depends upon them. Mistake me not. I do not say, if no sin, then no condemnation, as if to be sinless was the condition of

or way to the future blessedness. God forbid I should go so high! for then I should condemn every man in the world; but this I say, no allowed sin, no reigning sin, no presumptuous sin, no course in sin, and then it is no condemnation. That God who is just to punish for known and presumptuous sins, is gracious also to pardon sins of infirmity. So that upon the whole, as ever you desire to see the face of God with comfort, to lift up your heads before your judge at the great day with joy, to be freed from the sentence of condemnation—I say, as ever you desire these blessed things, be holy, live a godly life, keep sin at a great distance, do not allow yourselves in it, but rather condemn it, that it may not condemn you. If any think that the present good of sin preponderates the future evil of condemnation, or that they may live in sin and yet rely upon God's mercy, as if he would not condemn them for it, I heartily beg of God that he will convince them of these soul-destroying mistakes, that they may not persist in them till condemnation itself will be a sad confutation to them.

Direc. 2. Secondly, Condemn yourselves, and God will not condemn you. Self-condemnation prevents God's condemnation. There is a self-condemnation which is judicial and penal, which pains and torments, but yet doth no good; such was that of Cain and Judas. Oh there is in some that condemnation from their own consciences, which is but a *prolepsis* to the condemnation of God at the great day. But then there is gracious and penitential self-condemnation, such as that of David upon his numbering of the people, and also upon his commission of other sins. Now this is that which I would urge upon you. Where the sinner, upon the sense of the heinousness of sin, condemns himself, God will not condemn him too: 'If we would judge ourselves, we should not be judged of the Lord,' 1 Cor. xi. 31; and so here as to condemnation. The penitent self-judger is safe; the self-condemning publican went away justified, Luke xviii. 14. When the sinner justifies, God condemns; but when he condemns, then God justifies. This signifies but little in the courts of men. Let the criminal person repent and judge himself never so much, that is nothing; for all this the law must be executed upon him; but this always carries it in the court of God. Oh, saith

God, there is a sinner, but he is a penitent sinner; he hath sinned, but he is angry with himself for it; he arraigns and condemns himself for it; well, upon this I will acquit him; he condemns below, and therefore I will absolve above.

Direc. 3. Thirdly, As you desire no condemnation, speedily get your peace made with God through Christ Jesus. A pacified God is never a condemning God. First, our apostle saith, 'Being justified by faith we have peace with God,' Rom. v. 1; and then he infers, 'There is now no condemnation,' &c. Your first work is to look after the atoning of God through the blood of Christ; if it be not reconciliation it will be condemnation. Are God and you reconciled? Is your peace made with him? You have a reprieve for some time, but have you sued out your pardon? Is the breach which sin hath made healed and made up betwixt God and you? Oh, as Christ speaks, 'Agree with thine adversary quickly whilst thou art in the way with him, lest at any time thy adversary deliver thee to the judge,' &c., Mat. v. 25, 26; this is a thing which admits of no procrastination.

Direc. 4. Fourthly, Pray that it may be to you exemption from condemnation. You would have others, yourselves, delivered from it, but are you often with God, and earnest with God about this matter? Of all evils, deprecate this as the greatest evil; tell God you are willing he should do anything with you, burn, cut, lance, *modo in æternum parcat*, if he will but save you from eternal misery. This is the thing you should every day, with the greatest ardency, be begging of God: Ah, Lord, do with us what thou pleasest, but for thy mercy sake do not condemn us. You are to pray daily that you may not 'enter into temptation,' Luke xxii. 40; surely much more that you may not enter into condemnation. Oh be often upon your knees pleading with God, and saying, Lord, 'what profit will there be in our blood?' Ps. xxx. 9. Why should such souls be lost for ever? What will follow upon our condemnation, but cursing and blaspheming of thy sacred name? Whereas if thou wilt pardon and save, we shall bless, adore, and magnify thy name for ever. If God give you a heart thus to pray for this mercy, the mercy of mercies, it is to be hoped he will not withhold it from you. It is good to

pray now whilst prayer will do you good; when the sentence is once passed, it will then do you no good at all. Is it not much to be lamented that there are so few who go to God to plead with him about the everlasting concerns of their immortal souls? Many go from day to day, from week to week, nay, from year to year, without prayer; let it be salvation or damnation, it is all one to them. Oh this is dreadful! How seldom are the most of men at the throne of grace beseeching the Lord, for Christ Jesus' sake, to deliver them from wrath to come! What can be expected upon this, but that their final state will be very sad? The end of the prayerless cannot be good. Nay, I have too just occasion to go higher; there is a sort of persons amongst us, who, instead of humble, serious calling upon God to free them from condemnation, in their hellish imprecations they dare to call God to damn them. Oh prodigious, amazing, astonishing profaneness! I tremble to speak of it; but oh that it was not too common in our ears! What! do men defy God, and even bid him do his worst? Is damnation a thing to be desired or wished for? Do they know what they say? What if God should take them at their word, and do that in his greatest wrath which they seem to wish for with the greatest wickedness? Oh let such take heed lest God hear them in a dreadful manner! I hope I speak to none of these; you, I trust, have a dread of God, and of the things of eternity upon your spirits. Let exemption from condemnation be the matter of your prayer; and do but join the right manner with the right matter, and this will secure your souls for ever. God never yet condemned a praying man: he that fears and prays, shall never feel what he fears and prays against.

Direc. 5. Fifthly, Make sure of faith, I mean true, saving, justifying faith; where that is, yea, but the least drachm of it, there shall be no condemnation. It secures from this, both as it is the grace which unites to Christ, and also as it is the great condition of the gospel upon which it promises life and salvation. Unbelief is the damning sin, and faith is the saving grace. If thou beest a sincere believer, it is not only thou shalt not be condemned, but thou shalt most certainly be saved; both are sure from the frequent, often-repeated declarations, attestations, promises of the word; the whole gospel revelation centres in this. God is as gracious to acquit, justify, save the believer, as he is righteous to charge, punish, condemn the unbeliever. He may set down what condition or conditions he pleases, in order to the giving out of his grace; which, when they are performed, he is engaged to make good what he promises upon them.[1] Oh, therefore, get faith, for this is the grand gospel condition: if you believe not, the gospel itself cannot save you; if you believe, the law itself cannot condemn you.

Direc. 6. I do not enlarge upon these things, because that direction which is proper to the text is this, As you desire no condemnation, get into Christ, so as to be in Christ Jesus; for they, and they only, are the persons who are out of the danger of condemnation. The privilege and the subject are of the same extent and latitude; just so many as are in Christ are safe, and no more. If thou beest one of these, do not fear; if otherwise, do not flatter thyself with false, presumptuous, and ungrounded hopes. All that were not in the ark perished in the common deluge; all out of Christ are lost. When it is a Christ, it is no condemnation; when it is no Christ, it is nothing but condemnation. When the guilty-pursued malefactor had got into the city of refuge, then he was secure. Oh thou poor awakened sinner, fly to Christ, it is for the life of thy precious soul, and get into Christ, the alone city of refuge for the poor guilty creature, then guilt may pursue thee, but it shall never hurt thee. And here I would admonish all to take up with nothing short of union with Christ. You are members of the church, but are you members of Christ? You are joined to the church upon baptism, but are you joined to Christ by a true and lively faith? Here lies your security from condemnation. The first Adam hath brought guilt upon us, and consequently death—how? we being united to him; so the second Adam frees us from this, and makes over righteousness to us—how? in the same way and upon the same ground, viz., we being united to him; without this all that Christ

---

[1] Gratia Dei speranda est et acceptanda ad normam et propositum miserentis Dei, (neque enim convenit, ut qui condemnationis reus est, formulas gratiæ præscribat ei a quo juste potest condemnari,) sed requiritur, ut præscriptum gratiæ ab illo accipiat et grato animo amplectatur—.*Muscul. in præfat. ad Ep. ad Rom.*

is, hath done, or suffered, will avail us nothing. But I shall more fully insist upon this in that which will follow.

Use 3. Thirdly, I would speak to those who are in Christ, to excite them to be very thankful, and highly to admire the grace of God. What? No condemnation? not one condemnation? Oh, the riches, the heights, breadths, depths, lengths of the love of God! How should such be even astonished because of this inexpressible mercy! They who deserve millions of condemnations, that yet there is not one condemnation belonging to them; they that have in them matter enough to condemn them over and over, that yet they shall never be condemned; how should God be admired by those to whom this blessedness belongs! Such as are not in this state, how should they be filled with self-awakening thoughts! Such as are in this state, how should they be filled with God-admiring thoughts! Oh you that are in Christ, what will you think of this happiness when you shall see it accomplished? The truth is, as sinners will never know, nor ever be suitably affected with, their misery till they feel it in hell; so the saints will never know, or be suitably affected with, their happiness till that day shall come wherein they shall be put into the possession of it in heaven. When God shall pick and single you out of the common crowd, and shall say, I here acquit you before all the world from all your guilt, I here pronounce you to be righteous persons, and I will by no means pass a condemnatory sentence upon you, though I know what I might have done to you, and what I will do to others; I say, when it shall come to this, how will your souls be drawn out (and if you had a thousand more souls, how would they all be drawn out) in the adoring and magnifying of the grace of God! But something should be done now whilst you are here, though but in the hopes and expectation of this felicity. Where there is no condemnation there should be much thankfulness. How doth the traitor admire the grace and clemency of his prince who sends him a pardon when he expected his trial and sentence to die!

And as you must be thankful to God the Father, so in special to Jesus Christ. It is he who hath 'saved you from wrath to come,' 1 Thes. i. 10. It is he who was willing to be condemned himself, that he might free you from condemnation. Judgment passed upon him—'He was taken from prison and from judgment,' Isa. liii. 8—that it might not pass upon you. He was made a curse that he might deliver you from the curse, Gal. iii. 13. When Adam had entailed guilt and wrath upon you, Christ came and cut off this sad entail, and procured justification for you: 'As by the offence of one judgment came upon all to condemnation: even so by the righteousness of one the free gift came upon all to justification of life,' Rom. v. 18. It is upon union with him that there is no condemnation to you. Oh let your whole soul go out in thankfulness to Christ! He, as your surety, paid your debt, else you had been arrested and thrown into prison for ever. In him there was nothing to deserve condemnation, and yet he was willing to be condemned; in you there is very much to deserve condemnation, and yet you shall never be condemned. Here is the admirable, boundless, infinite love of Christ!

Use 4. Lastly, The main tendency and drift of this truth is comfort to believers; and what a full breast of consolation is here for such as are in Christ! No condemnation to them! This *no condemnation* is the ground of all consolation. What a word is here for faith and hope! *O magnæ spei verbum!* as he cries out. What a mighty support is here for poor doubting and dejected souls![1] The great thing that such are afraid of is condemnation; but here is that which secures them from it. The assertion is very express and full, and it is grounded, too, upon a sure foundation—'There is now no condemnation to them who are in Christ Jesus.' Oh, you that are in Christ, as your thankfulness should be high, so your joy should be high also! And what will raise your joy if this will not? Pray, improve it upon all occasions, and be cheerful. Set this against all the present evils you meet with. God afflicts you, but he will not condemn you. Why should you be troubled? Affliction becomes very tolerable upon no-condemnation. What though it be sickness, pain, loss of relations, a low estate, so

long as the soul is safe and the main state secured? There may be 'fiery trials' here, 1 Peter iv. 12, but there is no 'unquenchable fire' to burn in hereafter, Mark ix. 43. Oh, there is comfort! What are the comforts of this world if we shall be kept out of heaven, and what are the crosses of this world if we shall be kept out of hell? Take the wicked, there is condemnation at the bottom of all their good; take the saints, there is salvation at the bottom of all their evil. Again, men condemn you; ah, but God will not condemn you. This is but man's day, 1 Cor. iv. 3, where you may have the worst of it; but God's day is coming, and then all will go on your side. Oh, let it be a very little thing to you to be judged of man, so long as God doth and will acquit. You have sin in you, (too much, God knows,) yet it is no condemnation; and if sin itself—it being pardoned and washed away by the blood of Christ, Rev. i. 5—if this, I say, shall not condemn you, what then shall? After Paul's sad complaints of sin, yet he here says there is no condemnation. Condemn yourselves for sin you do; and so you should do, provided this self-condemnation flow from repentance, not from unbelief; but the great God, by whose judicial sentence your everlasting state shall be ordered, will not condemn you for it. It will be so far from this, that, as some divines hold, the sins of believers shall not be so much as mentioned at the great day.[1] The law is a condemning thing: it is so indeed in itself, but it is not so to you who are in Christ. You must die and be judged; but welcome death, welcome judgment, so long as there is no condemnation. Why should you be afraid of these, which will only let you see the accomplishment of what is here affirmed? This is the happiness of you who are in Christ; will you act faith upon it, and take the comfort of it? I would have you live and die with this cordial always by you, 'There is therefore now no condemnation,' &c. And let me add, it is not only your privilege, but your duty to rejoice because of this; it is not only

---

[1] Ut frustra sibi blanditur homo carnalis, si de emendanda vita nihil sollicitus, hujus gratiæ prætextu impunitatem sibi promittat; ita habent trepidæ piorum conscientiæ invictum propugnaculum, quod dum in Christo manent, sciunt se esse extra omne damnationis periculum.—*Calv. in loc.*

[1] Hinc fidelium peccata non prodibunt in judicium. Quum enim in istac vita per sententiam justificationis tecta sunt et ablata, et ultimum illud judicium confirmatio erit et manifestatio ejusdem sententiæ, non esset consentaneum ut in lucem denuo tum temporis proferantur.—*Ames. Med.*, lib. i. cap. 41.

you *may*, but you *ought* to be cheerful: you cannot be otherwise, unless you either distrust or disparage what is here spoken of. The sinner hath no reason to be jocund and merry, for he is liable every moment to condemnation; the saint hath no reason to be dejected and pensive, for he is out of all danger of condemnation. The sinner is secure as though there was no hell; and the saint is sad and cast down as though there was no heaven. The good Lord convince the one, and comfort the other!

I will close all with two words of advice. 1. Get assurance in your own souls that there is to you no condemnation. It is a sad thing to live under *peradventures* about this; maybe God will save, and maybe too God will damn. To hang in doubtfulness 'twixt heaven and hell is a very uncomfortable state. Were you but clear in your evidences about this privilege, you could not but rejoice. Now, in order to this, do but make sure of your union with Christ, and that will assure you of no condemnation.

2. Let this happiness be a great incentive to holiness. It is good to infer duty from mercy. Are you secured from condemnation? What manner of persons should you be? How should you differ from others here, who shall so differ from others hereafter? Though sin shall not condemn you, yet do you condemn it. I will end with an allusion to that of our Saviour to the woman taken in adultery, 'Woman,' saith Christ, 'where are those thine accusers? Hath none condemned thee? She said, No man, Lord. And Jesus said unto her, Neither do I condemn thee; go, and sin no more,' John viii. 10, 11.

CHAPTER II.

OF THE SAINTS' UNION WITH CHRIST.

There is therefore now no condemnation to them which are in Christ Jesus, &c.—ROM. viii. 1.

The subject of the proposition next opened—What it is to be in Christ Jesus—The difference betwixt Christ's being in believers, and their being in Christ—Union with Christ a great mystery—A threefold union: The union of three persons in one nature; the union of two natures in one person; the union of persons where persons and natures are distinct—This is mystical, legal, or moral—Scripture resemblances, by which the mystical union is shadowed out—Its properties—It is a sublime, real, spiritual, intimous, total, immediate, indissoluble union—Use 1. For trial whether we be in Christ—A double distinction concerning this—Union with Christ is either material and natural, or spiritual and supernatural: either external and visible, or internal and invisible—How it may be known whether we be really and savingly in Christ—Some scriptures insisted upon for the evidence of this—Use 2. To excite all to get into Christ—Use 3. Some directions in order to it—Use 4. Several duties pressed upon those who are in Christ—Use 5. Comfort to such in eleven particulars.

Two things have been observed in these words, the privilege, and the subjects of that privilege. I have done with the first, and go on now to the second. Here is no condemnation, a very high and glorious privilege; who are the persons to whom it belongs? Such as are in Christ Jesus. This I have hitherto but touched upon in the general, but am now to fall upon the more particular opening of it.

To them which are in Christ Jesus. Here are the two great names or titles of our blessed Lord; *Christ* with respect to God, *Jesus* with respect to us. He is God's Christ and our Jesus; God's anointed and our Saviour. But I do not intend in the least to stay upon these titles; I will only speak to that one thing which here lies before me, viz., being in Christ Jesus.

To them (which are) in Christ Jesus.—So we fill it up; but in the original it is only τοις ἰν Χριστῷ Ἰησοῦ, 'to them in Christ Jesus.' The words are descriptive; the apostle doth not design in them to set down the meritorious cause of non-condemnation—no, not with respect to Christ himself—but only to describe the persons who have an interest therein; for he doth not say there is no condemnation because of Christ, or through Christ, though that be very true, but there is no condemnation to them who are in Christ. I grant that something argumentative may be fetched out of them, but in their first and main scope they are descriptive.

Quest. What is it to be in Christ Jesus?

Answ. It is generally opened by that mystical union which is betwixt Christ and believers through the Spirit and faith.[1] To be in Christ, it is to be ingrafted, incorporated, mystically united unto Christ. This union in Scripture is set forth, sometimes by the saints' being in Christ, sometimes by Christ's being in them. Sometimes, I say, by their being in Christ; so here in the text, and so in several other places. 1 John v. 20, 'We are in him that is true, even in his Son Jesus Christ.' 2 Cor. v. 17, 'If any man be in Christ he is a new creature.' 1 Cor. i. 30, 'But of him are ye in Christ Jesus,' &c. Then it is also set forth by Christ's being in them : 2 Cor. xiii. 5, 'Know you not that Christ is in you, except you be reprobates?' Col. i. 27, 'Christ in you the hope of glory.' Rom. viii. 10, 'And if Christ be in you, the body is dead because of sin,' &c.

Now I conceive these two expressions do both point to one and the same thing, viz., to the spiritual and mystical union betwixt Christ and believers. Yet possibly, as to some modes and circumstances, there may be some difference betwixt them ; which a reverend person in a late treatise thus sets forth :[2] Christ is in the believer, by his Spirit, 1 John iv. 13; 1 Cor. xii. 13 ; the believer is in Christ by faith, John i. 12. Christ is in the believer by inhabitation, Eph. iii. 17 ; the believer is in Christ by implantation, John xv. 2 ; Rom. vi. 3. Christ is in the believer, as the head is in the body, Col. i. 18, as the root is in the branches, John xv. 5 ; believers are in Christ, as the members are in the head, Eph. i. 23, as the branches are in the root, John xv. 7. Christ in the believer implieth life and influence from Christ, Col. iii. 4 ; 1 Peter ii. 5 ; the believer in Christ implieth communion and fellowship with Christ, 1 Cor. i. 30. When Christ is said to be in the believer we are to understand it in reference to sanctification ; when the believer is said to be in Christ, it is in order to justification.

Further, this union in Scripture is set forth, sometimes by the saints abiding in Christ, and Christ's abiding in them : John xv. 4, 'Abide in me and I in you,' 1 John iii. 24, 'Hereby we know that he abideth in us,' &c. Sometimes by their dwelling in Christ, and Christ's dwelling in them : 1 John iv. 13, 'Hereby know we that we dwell in him, and he in us, because he hath given us of his Spirit.' John vi. 56, 'He that eateth my flesh and drinketh my blood dwelleth in me, and I in him.' Eph. iii. 17, 'That Christ may dwell in your hearts by faith.' Sometimes by Christ's living in them, Gal. ii. 20, &c. —'Yet not I, but Christ liveth in me.' Sometimes by that oneness that is betwixt Christ and them, John xvii. 21, 22. And some make that ἀνακεφαλαί-ωσις, that gathering together in one all things in Christ, Eph. i. 10, to point to this union. I dispute not about that, but certainly this is that which is here held forth, when the apostle saith there is 'no condemnation to them which are in Christ Jesus.'

It being so, my business then will be, as God shall assist, to discourse of that admirable and glorious union which is betwixt Christ and believers. It is a very high, and noble, and excellent argument. Oh that I may, in some measure, reach the greatness, spiritualness, and glory of it ! I will not at all insist upon the proving of the thing, viz., that some persons are in Christ, or that there is this blessed union betwixt Christ and saints ; for the Scriptures beforementioned sufficiently prove it, and I do not meet with any who deny it. Though there are some different notions about it, and some different explications of it, yet all grant there is such a thing. So that my only work will be first to open, and then to apply it.

And indeed there is great need of the former, because this union is a very profound and abstruse point ; it is a mystery, a very great mystery ; a truth which lies very deep, and is not easily to be understood. All believe it, but few understand it; all grant the *quod sit*, but for the *quid sit* how much are the most knowing persons in the dark about it ! The apostle, speaking of it, calls it 'a great mystery,' Eph. v. 32 ; and, Col. i. 27, he sets it forth ' by the riches of the glory of this mystery' (what's that? why) 'Christ in you the hope of glory.' Indeed, it is such a mystery as that we shall never fully understand it till we come to heaven, where all mysteries shall be unfolded, and particularly this of the mystical

[1] Qui sunt in Christo, *i.e.*, qui credunt in Christum, et per fidem ei sunt insiti.—*Piscat. in Schol* ; so Beza. Esse in Christo Jesu, est fide Christo adhærere, Spiritu insitus esse ut membrum Capiti.—*Pare.* Conjunctis fide cum Christo Jesu. —*Vatabl.* Qui sunt incorporati per fidem et dilectionem et fidei sacramentum.—*Aquin.*

[2] Mount Pisgah, p. 22.

union : John xiv. 20, 'At that day ye shall know that I am in my Father, and you in me, and I in you.' *That day* refers either to the time when the Spirit should be given, which is promised ver. 16, 17, or to the glorified state, spoken of ver. 19. Upon the effusion of the Spirit men may come to know something of this union, but it will never be fully understood by them till they be in glory. In the opening of it, so far as the present state and the height of the mystery will admit of, I must look into the word, and keep to that, and fetch all from that; for it is revelation and not reason which here must give us light. The word having revealed it, reason may be useful, as a handmaid, to shadow it out by such and such resemblances, thereby to help us the better to conceive of it ; but that which must be our first and main guide about it is Scripture revelation.

Now the Scripture speaks of a threefold union :

1. There is the union of three persons in one nature.

2. There is the union of two natures in one person.

3. There is the union of persons, where yet persons and natures are distinct.

1. There is the union of three persons in one nature. This is in the Trin-unity, where you have three persons united in the Godhead, the Trinity in unity, and the unity in Trinity ; one in three, in respect of nature and essence, and three in one, in respect of personality. This is that ineffable, incomprehensible union, which is between the Father, Son, and Holy Ghost, in the same common nature of the Godhead. Of which the apostle speaks, 1 John v. 7, 'There are three that bear record in heaven, the Father, the Word, and the Holy Ghost, and these three are one.' Here are three, and yet one ; three as to their distinct personal subsistences, and yet one as to their common nature. This a mystery to be adored, not to be fathomed ; a mystery much too deep for the plummet of reason to reach ;[1] he that

[1] The union betwixt the Three Persons, &c. The knowledge of this is not, nay, cannot be attained unto by the light of nature. No example can illustrate, no reason, angelical or human, can comprehend the hidden excellency of this glorious mystery. But it is discovered to us by a divine revelation in the written word, and our faith must receive, and our piety admire what our reason cannot comprehend.—*Cheynel of the Divine Trin-Unity*, chap. iv., p. 19. *Vide* Aquin., p. 1, qu. 39, art. 1, 2 ; Lombard lib. 1, dist. 2, 3.

by reason would go about to grasp it is as foolish as he that would attempt to put the ocean into a bucket, or to grasp the universe in the hollow of his hand.

2. There is the union of two natures in one person. This is that which we commonly call the hypostatical union, or the union of the two natures in Christ, his Godhead and his manhood, both making up but one person. You may thus conceive of it : It is the substantial, supernatural conjunction of the two natures in Christ, the divine assuming the human, and giving it a subsistence in itself, so that both make but one person ; and yet so as that the being and properties of both natures are preserved entire. As to this twofold union, I am not at present concerned to speak to them ; when I shall come to the third verse, I shall have occasion there to speak to the latter.

3. There is the union of persons, where yet persons and natures are distinct ; and this is the mystical union, that which is betwixt Christ and believers ; this I am only now to speak to. Concerning which, that you may not mistake the nature of it, you must know here is union, but no transmutation, confusion, or commixtion ; here is the union of persons, but not personal union.

1. Here is union, but no transmutation, confusion, or commixtion ; I will put them together for brevity sake. Believers are united to Christ, but yet not so as that they are changed or transformed into the very essence or being of Christ, so as to be Christed with Christ, as some too boldly speak ; or that he is changed or transformed into the essence and being of believers : no, you must not entertain a thought of any such thing. Christ is Christ still, and believers are but creatures still, notwithstanding this union ; though they be really and nearly united, yet both keep their natures distinct, and are the same after the union that they were before it. As it is in the persons in the sacred trinity, there is union but no confusion ; they are essentially one, yet they have their personal properties and distinct subsistences.[1] And as it is in the two natures of Christ, they are under a near union, they make but

[1] Ἑνοῦνται, οὐχ ὥστε συγχρεῖσθαι, ἀλλ' ὥστε ἔχεσθαι ἀλλήλων καὶ τὴν ἐν ἀλλήλαις περιχώρησιν ἔχουσι, δίχα πάσης συναλοιφῆς καὶ συμφύσεως.—*Damasc. De Orthod. Fide*, lib. i. cap. 11, p. 42.

one person, yet for all this they are distinct ;[1] the Godhead is not turned into the manhood, nor the manhood into the Godhead ; they are united but not confounded or converted, for both of them, even after this union, do still retain their essential properties without confusion or conversion.[2] So it is in the union of believers with Christ; for thus far we may make use of the two former unions to open the mystical union by—they all agree in this, though in other things they differ. You may take a lower resemblance of it if you please. In man there is a near union between soul and body, and these two united make up the man ; yet upon the union the soul is not turned into the nature of the body, nor the body into the nature of the soul ;[3] they are not confounded though united, they yet retain their essence and properties distinct ; the soul is the soul still, and the body is the body still. So it is in the union between Christ and believers.

2. Here is the union of persons, but not personal union. And here lies the difference between the mystical union and the hypostatical union. The hypostatical union is personal, but not of persons ; the reason is, because in Christ there are two natures, but there is but one person. There is this nature and that nature in Christ, but not this person and that person in Christ, as Nestorius held ; there is in Christ ἄλλο καὶ ἄλλο, but not ἄλλος καὶ ἄλλος, *aliud et aliud* but not *alius et alius*, as the learned express it. Christ did not assume the person of man but the nature of man into his person, *Non assumpsit hominem personam sed hominem in personam.*[4] But now in the mystical union it is otherwise ; there it is the union of persons, but not personal union. This I will endeavour to clear as well as I can.

In the mystical union there is the union of persons ; the person of Christ is united to the person of the believer, and the person of the believer is united to the person of Christ. For faith being the uniting grace, and this faith receiving the person of Christ, 'to as many as received him,'[1] &c., it must also unite to the person of Christ. In the marriage union it is person joined to person, and so it is in the mystical union also. How is a believer said to be in Christ ? it cannot so properly be said that he is in the graces, or in the comforts, or in the gifts of Christ ; but the meaning is, he is in the person of Christ ; so that this is a union of persons. For, further, this union doth not lie only in some moral or spiritual acts, qualities, or gracious endowments, as oneness of will, or oneness of disposition, &c., but it lies in the oneness of person. And therefore Cyprian's explication of this union with Christ is not full enough. Our union, saith he, with Christ does not mingle persons nor confound substances, (so far very true,) but it unites affections and wills ;[2] (if he meant that this was all, then it is conceived he came short :) there is more in it than so, for there is besides this uniting of the affections and will, the uniting, though not the mingling, of persons. The Father, Son, and Spirit, are one, not only in respect of consent, as some most falsely tell us ; but also in respect of nature and essence. Now, far be it from me to say that Christ and the saints are one in this sense ; yet withal I say, even between them there is a higher union than barely that of oneness of affection and will. I say no more than what others who write upon this argument generally say.[3]

But that you may not go too high, I add, this

---

[1] John i. 12. Faith is a receiving of Christ himself ; we cannot receive the benefits that come by him without receiving of himself : as in marriage the consent is, I take thee, not I take thine, &c.—*Vines on the Sacram.*, p. 120.

[2] Nostra et ipsius conjunctio non miscet personas, nec confundit substantias ; sed affectus consociat, et confœderat voluntates.—*Cypr.*

[3] *Vide* Zanch. in cap. v. ad Eph., p. 245.; Polan., Synt. Theol., lib. vi. cap. 35. p. 454. Hujus unionis interventu fit, ut tum beneficiorum Christi tum substantiæ ipsius fiamus participes, quia beneficia omnia et vis illa vivifica quæ animas nostras sustentat in vitam æternam, non possunt a corpore et sanguine Christi cui inhærent, adeoque ab ipso Christo, divelli. —*Treltat Inst. Theol.*, lib. ii. p. 189. *Bucan* L. C. 48. pp. 818, 819. It is not a union of Christ with a believer in accidents only, as in opinion, affection, in consent of mind and heart, or in likeness of disposition and conversation ; but it is a union of substances, essences, persons. As Mr Perkins saith, the person of him that believeth is united to the person of Christ. —*Reyn. Præc.*, p. 49.

---

[1] Οὐδαμοῦ τῆς τῶν φύσεων διαφορᾶς ἀνῃρμένης διὰ τὴν ἕνωσιν, σωζομένης δὲ μᾶλλον τῆς ἰδιότητος ἡκατέρας φύσεως, καὶ εἰς ἕν πρόσωπον, καὶ μίαν ὑπόστασιν συντρεχούσης.—*Synod. Calced.*

[2] Τὰ φύσικα ἰδιώματα ἀσύγχυτα καὶ ἄτρεπτα.—*Damasc. Dial.*, cap. 66.

[3] *Vide* Nemes. de Nat. Hom., p. 97. Ὅτε δὲ ἀσύγκυτον μένει, &c.

[4] *Vide* Lombard, lib. iii. dist. 5.

union is not personal; it is but mystical, not personal. For then Christ and the believer would properly and physically make but one person; and then it would be so many believers, so many Christs; and then the believer would have no subsistence but in Christ, as the human nature of Christ hath no subsistence but what it hath in the Godhead; and then he would merit in what he did, as Christ *qua* man did by virtue of the personal union. Therefore we must conclude, that though here is a union of persons, the person of Christ in a mystical way being united to the person of believers, yet here is not any personal union, they both, notwithstanding this, remaining several and distinct persons. These things may seem, as indeed they are, abstruse and dark to you; I will come to that which will be somewhat more plain and easy.

For the further explication of this great mystery, there are three things which I will speak to:

1. I will endeavour to open the several kinds or branches of that union which is betwixt Christ and believers.

2. I will give you those scriptural resemblances by which it is shadowed and set forth.

3. I will give you the several properties of it.

1. First, Let me open the several kinds or branches of this union; it is threefold, mystical, legal, and moral. A believer is united to Christ three ways, mystically, legally, morally. Take any of these singly, and they will not be enough comprehensive; but take them jointly, so there is all in them.

(1.) First there is the mystical union, so we usually call it, which may be thus described: It is that supernatural, spiritual, intimous oneness and conjunction which is betwixt the person of Christ and the persons of believers, through the bond of the Spirit and faith, upon which there follows mutual and reciprocal communion each with the other.[1] If this description be taken in pieces, it contains in it the most considerable things to be known about the mystical union. For,

[1.] Here is the proper general nature of it, viz., oneness and conjunction. Christ and saints are united; how? why, in respect of that oneness and conjunction that is betwixt them. This the Scrip-

ture expressions do mainly refer to, and clearly hold forth. They are said to be in Christ, and Christ in them; they are said to dwell in Christ, and Christ in them; to abide in Christ, and Christ in them; to be one with Christ, as he is one with the Father; (the several scriptures which speak to these things have been already cited.) They are further said to be joined to the Lord, and to be one Spirit, 1 Cor. vi. 17; to be one flesh, Eph. v. 31, 32; Christ lives in them, Gal. ii. 20; he is the head, they the members, Eph. i. 22; he the root, they the branches, John xv. 5; he the foundation, they the building, 1 Cor. iii. 9–11; he the husband, they the wife, Eph. v. 28, &c. All these expressions, I say, point to that oneness and conjunction which is betwixt Christ and believers, in which the general nature of the mystical union doth consist.

[2.] Here is the qualities or properties of this union. It is a supernatural, spiritual, intimous union; to which I shall speak by and by.

[3.] Here is the subjects of this union, Christ and believers. And that too is set down with this modification, the oneness and conjunction is betwixt the person of Christ, and the persons of believers, (of which before.)

[4.] Here is the *media* or *vincula unionis*, the means or bonds of this union, the Spirit and faith.

[5.] Here is also the effect or consequent upon this union—namely, mutual and reciprocal communion each with the other. This will be opened in what will follow.

Only at present let me open the fourth head, the means and bonds of the mystical union. In all unions there is something which binds and knits thing and thing, person and person, together; what is it then which binds, knits, conjoins Christ to believers, and believers to Christ? I answer, it is the Spirit and faith. The Spirit unites Christ to us, and faith unites us to Christ. First, the Spirit is the bond of this union on Christ's part; for by this he takes possession of believers,[1] dwells in them, lays hold of them, apprehends them, as the word is Phil. iii. 12; in Tertullian's dialect,[2] *Spiritus nos*

---

[1] *Vide* Bodium in Eph. v. 28, p. 786, more fully describing of it.

[1] Christ lives in us, not by local presence, but by the special supernatural operation of his Spirit.—*Perkins upon Gal.* ii. 20 p. 216.

[2] De Trinit. et de Pœnit.

Christo confibulat, the Spirit doth join and button believers to Christ. And then faith is the bond or ligament on our part: Eph. iii. 17, 'That Christ may dwell in your hearts,' how? 'by faith.' Christ lays hold on us by the Spirit, and we lay hold on him by faith; he comes to us by the Spirit, and we go to him by faith. The Spirit of God does not only discover and make out the union of the soul with Christ,—'Hereby we know, that he abides in us, by the Spirit which he hath given us,' 1 John iii. 24—but he works, promotes, and brings it about. As it is in that union which is amongst the saints themselves, 'by one Spirit they are all baptized into one body,' 1 Cor. xii. 13, so it is in the union which is betwixt Christ and them; by this one Spirit they are all made one with Christ. Therefore, saith the apostle, 'If any man have not the Spirit of Christ, he is none of his,' Rom. viii. 9; he means he hath neither interest in him, nor union with him. And then there is faith, which unites on our part; for that is the uniting grace, the sinew or ligament which knits and binds the soul to Christ; that by which the soul clasps and clings about Christ. By faith we apply ourselves to Christ, and Christ to ourselves; and that application is the ground of union. So also by faith we receive Christ, John i. 12, upon which receiving of him we are united to him and made one with him. The spiritual ingrafting too is by this, as you may see, Rom. xi. 19, 20; and this is our eating Christ's flesh and drinking Christ's blood, upon which he dwells in us, John vi. 56. Thus the union is brought about both on Christ's part and on the believer's part; and this is the mystical union.

Secondly, There is the legal or law-union betwixt Christ and believers. The ground of this union is Christ's suretyship, Heb. vii. 22. He, as the saints' ἔγγυος, surety, struck hands with God, as the word imports, put himself into their stead, took their debt upon himself, and bound himself, upon their account, to make satisfaction to God. Now from this act of Christ there results that law-union which I am upon. Saints, as it is said by some, are united to Christ three ways, *Spiritu, carne, et vadimonio;* as they are partakers of his Spirit, as he hath assumed their nature, and as he hath engaged for them as their sponsor or surety. You know in law the debtor and the surety are but one person; the law looks upon them as one, and makes no difference betwixt them, and therefore both are equally liable to the debt; and if the one pay it, it is in the eye of the law as much as if the other had paid it. So it is with Christ and us; he is our surety, for he took our debt upon himself, engaged to pay whatever we owed, (as Paul once did to Philemon for his Onesimus, Phil. 18, 19,) entered into bond, though not *with us*, yet *for us*. Upon this, Christ and we are but one person before God, and accordingly he deals with us; for he makes over our sins to Christ, and also Christ's righteousness and satisfaction to us, he now, in a legal notion, looking upon both but as one person. And this consideration is of great use (and so accordingly it is improved by the orthodox against Socinians) to clear up and confirm those great truths which concern Christ's sufferings, and the believer's benefit thereby. For if it be asked, How could Christ—he being a person perfectly innocent—suffer in a penal manner as he did? He being altogether guiltless in himself, how could the Father, with justice, fall upon him as though he had been guilty? Or grant that he did sin suffer, yet how can any good by his suffering redound to others? I say, if any shall raise such questions, the answer is ready: That Christ and believers in law are but one person, he having submitted to be their surety, in a voluntary substitution of himself in their stead, and susception of their guilt. Whereupon it came to pass that their guilt was imputed to him, upon which the Father might, without the least impeachment of his justice, severely fall upon him; and his righteousness, merit, satisfaction, was imputed to them, (for that being performed by their surety, it is theirs to all intents and purposes, as if they had performed it in their own persons.) Briefly, upon this law-union resulting from Christ's suretyship, our sins were very well imputable to him, and his merits to us. This doth so exactly fall in with the common notion and case of suretyship amongst men, that I need not any further insist upon the illustration of it. The adversaries, therefore, who deny that Christ either did or could suffer in the sinner's stead, or that there is any imputation of his merit to believers, are so pinched with this—his being a surety—that they oppose it to their utmost, wholly deny that too, and are fain to make good one denial with another.   But here I digress.

Two things I shall add upon this head, and then dismiss it :

1. That the oneness of person betwixt Christ and the saints (which hath been affirmed of them more than once or twice in the opening of the matter in hand) is not to be carried further than that particular sense and respect in which it is affirmed. I mean this : they are not one person in respect of nature, essence, or any personal union ; only they are so in respect of that mystical and legal oneness of person that is betwixt them. And this latter oneness is very well consistent with the different natures of the subjects united, though the former is not so.

2. That this law-union is only proper to Christ the second person. The mystical and the moral union, in some sense, doth reach to the other persons ; for though the saints proximately and immediately are united to Christ, yet the union is not so terminated in him, but that through him they are united to the Father too. Therefore it is said, John xvii. 21, 'That they also may be one *in us* ;' it is not one in *me* singly, but one in *us* conjunctly. And the apostle saith, 1 Thes. i. 1, 2, 'To the church which is *in God the Father*, and in the Lord Jesus Christ ;' the same you have, 2 Thes. i. 1. So that believers, in some respects, are in both, and united both to Father and Son.[1] But as to the law-union arising from suretyship and vadimony, that is only proper to Christ—he of all the persons being the alone surety for believers.

Thirdly, There is a moral union between Christ and believers. It is called moral from the bond or ground of it, which is love ; and the word *moral* is used, not as it stands in contradistinction to *spiritual*, but to *natural* and *physical*. I say, the bond of this union is love, for faith unites mystically, and love unites morally. Love is a uniting grace as well as faith, though it doth not unite in the same way. Therefore it is said, 'He that dwelleth in love, dwelleth in God, and God in him,' 1 John iv. 16. It is all for union, and it produces union. Take two persons who love each other, their mutual affection

makes them to be one ; there is a real oneness between friend and friend. The philosopher very well defined friendship by one soul in two bodies, μία ψυχὴ ἐν δύοις σώμασι. A friend is but ἕτερος αὐτὸς, *alter idem*, another self.[1] Thus it is in that which is before us. There is a mutual, reciprocal, hearty love between Christ and believers ; he loves them, and they love him, and by virtue of this mutual love there is a real and close union betwixt them. The husband and wife are one, not merely upon the marriage covenant and external relation, but also, and chiefly, upon that love and affection that is betwixt them. So it is betwixt Christ and saints. Some, therefore, open this being in Christ Jesus (or oneness with him) by love ;[2] in respect of this love believers are in Christ. And so I have opened that threefold union which is between Christ and believers. I have a little insisted upon the two latter branches of it, but it is the first (the mystical union) that I shall further mainly speak to ; for the truth is, this is the union which the gospel principally sets before us.

The second thing propounded was to instance in those several Scripture resemblances by which the mystical union is set forth. These are very many ; for this being a very high and mysterious thing, it hath pleased God to make use of various resemblances for the better describing of it, that he might thereby make it to us more credible and more intelligible. And it is observable how the Spirit of God summons in all unions, natural, relative, artificial, that he might by all of them more clearly and distinctly shadow out the grand union betwixt Christ and saints. Yet I must tell you, though those are very useful as to the end designed, and are very high —the highest—in *genere unionis*, yet they all come short of the mystical union which they refer to. They may illustrate it, but they cannot reach or equalise it. I will but briefly go over them, both because they are fully handled by others, and also because that which is proper from them to the business in hand may be despatched in few words.

[1] Of the saints' union with the Father as well as with the Son, see Burg. upon John xvii. p. 586 ; Newton upon John, p. 450.

[1] Aristot. Ethic. lib. ix. cap. 3, 9.

[2] Qui scilicet dilecti a Christo vicissim Christum amant. Hoc enim est in Christo esse, non tantum a Christo amari, sed et Christum amare.—*Corn. Mussus.* Qui Christo incorporati sunt puro et perfecto amore.—*Idem.*

The first is that of husband and wife. A very fit and full resemblance (a [1] type say some) of the mystical union. Upon the conjugal relation there is a very near and close conjunction. If you please to look to its first institution, you will find a deep foundation of oneness laid therein: Gen. ii. 23, 24, 'This is now bone of my bone, and flesh of my flesh; therefore shall a man leave his father and his mother, and shall cleave unto his wife, and they shall be one flesh.' Now Christ and believers stand in this conjugal relation each to the other. He is their husband, they his spouse; they are 'espoused to Christ their husband,' 2 Cor. xi. 2; 'married to Christ,' Rom. vii. 4; 'betrothed' to God and Christ, Hosea ii. 19; their name is *Hephzibah* and *Beulah*, Isa. lxii. 4. The marriage-union, in the very height of it, the apostle brings down to Christ and believers: Eph. v. 28, 29, &c., 'So ought men to love their wives as their own bodies: he that loveth his wife loveth himself. For no man ever yet hated his own flesh; but nourisheth it, and cherisheth it even as the Lord the church; for we are members of his body, of his flesh, and of his bones. For this cause shall a man leave his father and his mother, and shall be joined to his wife, and they two shall be one flesh.' Well, what of all this? He adds, 'This is a great mystery: but I speak concerning Christ and the church.' As if the apostle had said, Do not misapprehend me; though I speak so much of the union that is betwixt husband and wife, according to the primitive institution, yet that is not the main thing which I drive at; I aim at a higher union than that, namely, at that spiritual union which is between Christ and the church. The husband and the wife are one; Christ and believers are so much more.

Another resemblance is that of the head and members. In the body natural there is a near and close union between these two; being fastened and joined each to the other, they make up one and the same body. Thus it is with Christ and believers in the body mystical; he is the head, they are the several members belonging to that head: Col. i. 18, 'He is the head of the body, the church.' Eph. i. 22, 'God gave him to be the head over all things to the church, which is his body.' 1 Cor. xii. 27, 'Now ye are the body of Christ, and members in particular.' So Rom. xii. 5. As truly and as nearly as the head and the members, so truly and so nearly are Christ and believers united also.

A third resemblance is that of the root and branches. There is also union betwixt these; otherwise, how should the one convey juice, sap, nourishment, life, growth, to the other? So it is with Christ and believers; he is the root, they the branches: John xv. 5, 'I am the vine, ye are the branches.' You read of being 'planted and ingrafted into Christ;' it is a metaphor which the Spirit of God much delights in, in the setting forth of that which I am upon. See Rom. vi. 5, and xi. 17, &c. Also you read of being 'rooted in Christ,' Col. ii. 7. There is a blessed analogy or resemblance between Christ and believers, and the root and the branches, in point of union, in point of influence. The root is united to the branches, and they to it; so is Christ to believers, and they to him. The root conveys life, and nourishment, and growth to the branches; so does Christ to believers.

Another resemblance is the foundation and the building. Here is union too; for in a building, all the stones and timber being joined and fastened together upon the foundation, make but one entire structure. So it is here. Believers are 'God's building,' and Christ is the foundation in that building: 'Ye are God's building,' 1 Cor. iii. 9. 'Other foundation can no man lay than that which is laid, which is Christ Jesus,' 1 Cor. iii. 11. Therefore they are said to be 'built upon the foundation of the prophets and apostles, Jesus Christ himself being the chief corner stone,' Eph. ii. 20. As a man builds upon the foundation, and lays the stress of the whole building upon that; so take the true Christian, he builds upon Christ; all his faith, hope, confidence, is built upon this sure foundation, (as Christ is styled, Isa. xxviii. 16, 'Behold I lay in Zion a sure foundation.') Hence also they are said, 'as lively stones to be built up a spiritual house,' &c., 1 Pet. ii. 5. Here is the mystical union under this resemblance also.

Take but one more, that of meat or food. That which a man feeds upon and digests, it is incorporated and united with himself; it is turned into his own substance and made a part of himself. The believing soul

[1] See Dr Cudworth's Union of Christ and the Church Shadowed.

F

by faith feeds upon Christ, digests him, and turns him, as it were, into his own substance ; so that Christ becomes one with him, and he one with Christ : John vi. 55, 56, 'My flesh is meat indeed, and my blood is drink indeed ; he that eateth my flesh, and drinketh my blood, dwelleth in me, and I in him.' All this must be taken, not in the literal, but in the spiritual notion ; the eating and drinking is believing, (so it is to be understood all along in that chapter.) Upon which believing the union follows, 'He dwells in me, and I in Him.'

Thus I have, with great brevity, given you those Scripture resemblances by which the mystical union is shadowed out. The handling of them in their utmost extent is a subject that would have admitted of great enlargement ; but my business was but to speak to that one thing from them which suits with the work in hand. In some of the preceding heads I was in the great deeps, but in this I have been in the shallows ; there the elephant might swim, here the lamb may wade ; there things were not so dark, but here they are as clear ; therefore I shall not need to make any further stay upon them.

I come to the third head, The properties of this union. I will name these seven :

First, It is a sublime union. And that,

1. In respect of its nature, as considered in itself. Christ and a poor creature made one, and *so* made one ? Oh, what a union is this ! We have many unions in nature, and some very considerable ; but, alas ! they all come short, and are but poor, mean, low things in comparison of this. Next to the union of the three persons in the sacred Trinity, and the hypostatical union of the two natures in Christ, the mystical union is the highest. Except but those which I have named, and all other unions must veil to it.

2. It is sublime in respect of its rise, original, and production. The more supernatural a thing is, the more sublime it is ; now, this union is purely supernatural. What can nature be imagined to do for the bringing about of such a thing as this ? Oh, surely it is all of the mere grace of God ! As it is not natural for the matter of it, so neither is it so for the production and application of it. It is supernatural as to the thing, and also as to the person to whom it belongs.

3. It is sublime in respect of the high and glorious privileges, effects, and consequents of it.

4. In respect of its mysteriousness and difficulty to be known. (Something I spoke to this at my first entrance upon this subject.) The mystical union is a mysterious union—so mysterious that we had known nothing at all of it if God had not revealed it to us in the word. And even now he hath revealed it, yet it is but very little that we do understand of it. *That* there is this union, that is as clear as the light of the sun ; but *what* this union is, oh, that is a hidden thing, and locked up from us. The union of the body and soul in man is a great mystery ; there is even in that union that which puzzles the greatest philosophers ; but the union of Christ and the believer is a far greater mystery. That persons every way so distant, so divided, should yet be made mystically one, here is a mystery indeed ! a mystery which no finite understanding, angelical or human, can comprehend.

Secondly, It is a real union. Not a notional, fantastic, or opinionative thing, something that is merely matter of fancy and imagination, or something that dull and melancholy persons please themselves with the thoughts of. Oh, it is not so ! but it is a real thing, and as great a reality as any, whatsoever it be. You have very many scriptures which speak to it, under great variety of expressions, all of which, with the greatest evidence and clearness, do point to it, and cannot be otherwise understood ; and yet will you doubt of it, and look upon it as a mere fancy ? As really as the members are united to the head, and the head to them ; the wife to the husband, and the husband to the wife ; the branches to the root, and the root to the branches ; so really are the saints united to Christ, and Christ to them, for these several unions do confirm, as well as represent and open, the mystical union. Nothing in religion is real if this be not ; take away this mystical oneness between Christ and the soul, and take away all. Is not the union betwixt God the Father and God the Son a real union ? surely that will not be denied ; if so, then this is real also ; for, John xvii. 22, 'The glory which thou gavest me I have given them, that they may be one, *even as we are one.*' Observe it, it is *one, even as we are one ;* but how ? not as to any equality, but only as to verity ; not as to the *modus* or *qualitas unionis*, but only as to the *veritas unionis*. This *as* is often but a note of likeness, not of sameness, (so Mat. v. 48, ' Be ye perfect, even *as* your Father which is in heaven is perfect.' So 1 Pet. i. 15, 16 ;) it is so to be interpreted here. Believers are not one with Christ, as he is one with the Father, in respect of the *manner* of the union ; but as to the *truth* and *reality* of it, so it is as verily, as truly one with Christ as Christ is one with the Father. It is a *higher* union betwixt the Father and the Son, but it is as *real* a union betwixt Christ and believers.

Thirdly, It is a spiritual union. Not a gross fleshly, corporal union—you must not so conceive of it—but a divine, inward, spiritual union. It is the uniting of hearts and souls together in an imperceptible way ; and the bonds of this union are spiritual, namely, the Spirit in Christ, and faith in us ; and the union is to be judged by that which is the bond of it. The husband and the wife are ' one flesh,' Eph. v. 31 ; but ' he that is joined to the Lord is one spirit,' 1 Cor. vi. 16, 17. I have set before you several external and material resemblances of it ; but the union itself is internal, immaterial, and spiritual. When Christ had been speaking so much of it under the resemblance of eating and drinking, he adds, to prevent mistakes, ' It is the spirit that quickeneth ; the flesh profiteth nothing ; the words that I speak unto you, they are spirit, and they are life,' John vi. 63 ; *q.d.*, You must take me in a right sense ; in all that I have said I do not intend any fleshly or corporal eating, as some grossly imagine ; I only mean spiritual eating and drinking by faith. Neither, saith he, would I be thought to speak of any union that is carnal and earthly ; it is the heavenly and the spiritual union only which I design in all that I have spoken.

Fourthly, It is a near, intimous union. The persons here concerned are not only truly and really, but nearly, closely, intimately united each to the other. The union betwixt them is so near, that there is no union, excepting what hath been excepted, to be compared with it ; so near, that we know not how to conceive of it, much less how to express it ; we may borrow some light here and there from the scattered unions of nature, but they all, in point of nearness, are vastly short of it. In the text cited but now, 1 Cor. vi. 17, the apostle tells us, ' He that is joined to the Lord is one spirit ;' where he opposes joining to Christ to joining to a harlot, (ver. 16.) Of which he saith, ' He that is joined to an harlot is one body ;' and though this be out of the due course, yet he carries it up to the marriage union —for two,' saith he, ' shall be one flesh.' But he heightens the mystical union with Christ : ' He that is joined to the Lord is one spirit.' This is the highest scripture which I know for the describing of the intimousness of the spiritual union. First the apostle says, *He that is joined to the Lord.* In the Greek it is κολλώμενος, he that is *glued* to the Lord ; it is the same word which is used, Eph. v. 31, ' He shall be joined (or glued, προσκολληθήσεται) to his wife.' It speaks the firmness and the nearness of the union. And then he says, ' He that is thus joined to the Lord *is one spirit*.' What an expression is this ! What could be spoken higher ? To be one spirit is much more than to be one flesh, inasmuch as the union of spirits is the nearest union that is imaginable. The apostle opposes the spiritual conjunction betwixt Christ and believers, to that carnal conjunction that is betwixt person and person. He that is joined to a harlot is one body and one flesh ; but he that is joined to the Lord is one spirit. Saints are not only flesh of Christ's flesh, and bone of his bone, (by which phrase the height of the conjugal union is set forth, and by which the Jews used to express the greatest nearness in consanguinity,[1]) but, which is much higher, they are one spirit with him. It is not said they have one spirit, or that believers are spirited as Christ was,[2] or that they are led, acted, animated by the same spirit that he was, (though I conceive that is the very thing intended in the expression ;) but the apostle says, the better to set off the intimousness of the union, Christ and they are one spirit, which is as high as anything that could be spoken. Again, believers are so near to Christ, that, in a sober sense, they may be said to be a part of him ; yea, such a part of him that he, as head and mediator, would not be complete without them ; for as he is so considered, they are his fulness :

[1] Quæ loquendi formula ex literis Veteris Testamenti videtur esse desumpta. Ita enim fratres et cognati de se mutuo loqui solent, os meum et caro mea.—*Pet. Mart.*

[2] *Vide* Grotium *in loc.*

Eph. i. 23, 'The fulness of him that filleth all in all.'
It is spoken of the church, the body of believers.
Once more, the union is so near, that they both have
one and the same name ; Christ's own name and title
is given to them : 1 Cor. xii. 12, 'So also is Christ.'
The apostle means Christ mystical, not Christ personal. Compare Jer. xxiii. 6, 'This is the name
wherewith *he* shall be called, the Lord our righteousness,' with Jer. xxxiii. 16, 'This is the name
wherewith *she* shall be called, the Lord our righteousness,' (which is spoken, too, of the church.) The
wife upon the marriage union loses her own, and is
called by her husband's name. And so it is here :
he—that is, Christ—shall be called the Lord our
righteousness ; and she—that is, the church—shall
be called, too, the Lord our righteousness. Here is
communication of names which speaks the nearness
of the union. Nay, Christ and the believer are but
one,[1] (mystically though not substantially ;) and this
is the highest of all. Oh this is a close and intimate
union indeed !

Fifthly, It is a total union. I mean this, the
whole person of Christ is united to the whole person
of believers, and the whole person of believers is
united to the whole person of Christ. Christ is not
in this or that single nature, but in both his natures ;
not in this or that office, but in all his offices, made
one with them ; and they too, reciprocally, are made
one with him as to the whole man ; not as to the soul
only, but as to the body also. The soul indeed is the
principal subject of this union, but the body too
hath its share in it ; therefore the apostle saith,
1 Cor. vi. 15, 'Know ye not that your bodies are
the members of Christ ?' As Christ in the assuming
of the nature of man took not the body only, or the
soul only, but both, and so united them to the Godhead ; so it is in the mystical union, the whole man
is knit to whole Christ. And, which puts marvellous sweetness into it, the totality of this union, on
Christ's part, reaches to every individual believer in
the world ; as the whole soul is united to every part
of the body, so it is whole Christ to every believer.

Sixthly, It is an immediate union. Christ and the
believing soul, they touch each the other,[1] if I may
so express it, and the word encourages me so to do ;
there is nothing that doth intervene or interpose
between Christ and it. In other unions it is not
so ; there is union between the head and the members, yet all the members do not touch the head.
The foot is at a great distance from the head, though
it be united to it. All the parts of the building are
united to the foundation, yet they are not all contig-
uous to it ; there is apposition, but no contiguity.
But now the union which I am upon is so immediate, that every believer touches Christ, as it were,
and lies close and near to him. Which yet is not to
be taken of any physical or local contact,[2] but only
of that which is moral and spiritual ; not of any *immedietas suppositi*, but only of that *immedietas virtutis*,
or *unionis*, which is through the Spirit and faith.

Lastly, It is an indissoluble union. The knot
therein is tied so fast that it shall never be again
untied or loosened. Christ and believers are so
firmly joined together that none shall ever be able
to part them ; all the powers of hell, with all their
united strength, shall never be able to disjoin or
separate one soul from Christ. As no distance of
place doth hinder the union,[3] so no force or violence
from devils or men shall ever be able to dissolve the
union. And herein lies the peculiar, transcendent
blessedness of this union above all other unions.
They all may cease, be broken, and come to nothing ;
the members may be separated from the head, and
the head from the members ; the tender husband
may, and shall, be parted from the affectionate wife ;
the building may be broken off from the foundation ;
the soul may be divided from the body ; but the
mystical union stands fast for ever. Christ and a
gracious soul can never be separated ; God hath

---

[1] Ex quo fit, ut ipsemet quoque Christus usque adeo arcte
noster evadat, et nos vicissim illius, ut apud Patris tribunal,
Christus, et Ecclesia (non quidem hypostatica substantiarum
unitione, sed quod ad istam communionem attinet mysticam)
velut unum et idem ὑφιστάμενον, et unus Christus efficacissme
censeamur.—*Bucan. L. Com.* 48, p. 821.

[1] See *Davenant* upon the Ἀφαὶ, Col. ii. 19. Per has com-
missuras Christus tangit nos, et nos tangimus Christum.

[2] Omnis physicus contactus excludendus est.—*Zanch. in
cap.* 5, *ad Eph.*, p. 242.

[3] Non obstat unioni huic intercapedo locorum, sive distantia
cœli et terræ, qua Christus (qua homo) et fideles peregre ab
ipso versantes disterminantur : quia unio non est existentia
corporis Christi intra corpora nostra, nec locali contactu, aut
inclusione constat.—*Alting. Explic. Catech.* part ii. qu. 76,
p. 266.

joined them, and ' what he hath joined together no man shall ever put asunder,' Mat. xix. 6. There are two abiding things in the saints, their unction and their union. Their unction abides : ' But the anointing which ye have received of him, abideth in you,' 1 John ii. 27 ; and their union abides, for it follows, ' and ye shall abide in him.' Our apostle makes his challenge in the close of this chapter : ' Who shall separate us from the love of Christ ?' He tells you none should ever be able to do it, vers. 38, 39. So, who shall separate us as to our union with Christ ? None shall—none can. Possibly the influences of it for some time may be suspended ; but yet the union itself is not, nay, cannot be, dissolved. As it was in the hypostatical union, for a time there was a suspending of the comforting influences of the divine nature to the human, insomuch that our Saviour cried out, ' My God, my God, why hast thou forsaken me ?' Mat. xxvii. 46 ; yet for all this, the union between the two natures was not in the least abolished. So here, in the mystical union, the sensible effects, comforts, benefits of which may sometimes be kept in and not appear, but yet the thing itself abides, and so shall abide firm and inviolable for ever. It is an inseparable, an insuperable, union. Yea, death itself, though that be the bane of all other unions, shall never reach this so as to put an end or period to it.

And thus I have finished the heads necessary to be spoken to for the opening of this admirable and blessed union ; in the clearing of which I have given you the explication of the subject of the proposition, ' There is no condemnation to them *who are in Christ Jesus*.' I must not dismiss so excellent, so useful a point, without some practical improvement of it.

Use 1. And first, Are they, and they only, the persons to whom there is no condemnation, such as are in Christ Jesus ? I would then put all of you upon the most serious examination whether you be thus in Christ Jesus. Pray bring it down to yourselves, and ask yourselves, one by one, this question, Am I in Christ ? Some are so in him, am I one of them ? What is this mystical union to me ? It concerns you to be very inquisitive about this, because the grand privilege in the text depends upon it. You cannot safely apply *no condemnation* if it be *no union*. If you desire a solid foundation to build upon for exemption

from condemnation, you must make sure of this union ; the happiness and safety of your future state wholly depends upon your present being in Christ. Oh that you would be persuaded, with the greatest diligence, faithfulness, impartiality, to search and examine yourselves about this. The apostle is very smart upon it : 2 Cor. xiii. 5, ' Examine yourselves whether you be in the faith ; prove your own selves. Know you not your own selves, how that Jesus Christ is in you (and you in him), except you be reprobates ?' (and say I, except you be liable to eternal condemnation.)

Now, that I may help you in this great inquiry, viz., whether you have that very union with Christ which will effectually secure you from this most dreadful condemnation ? I must first distinguish about it.

1. Union with Christ is either material and natural, or spiritual and supernatural. There is a material or natural union with Christ, consisting in oneness with him in respect of one of his natures : for he having assumed the nature of man, and hypostatically united it to the Godhead, upon this, wherever the nature of man is, there is union or conjunction with him, so far as the participation of one and the same nature with him will go. The spiritual and supernatural union is that which hath been opened, viz., that which is brought about by the Spirit, and by faith ; upon which the creature is not one with Christ merely in respect of his manhood, but he is one with him in a higher manner, as being also, according to his measure, made a ' partaker of his divine nature ;' that is to say, as the image of God is imprinted upon him, as the several graces of the Spirit are wrought in him, as Christ and he are not only one flesh, but also one spirit, both having the same Spirit dwelling in them, and both being animated and acted by one and the same spirit.

Now to apply this distinction. The first of these unions is not sufficient to secure from condemnation, or to entitle to salvation ; for then, that being common and general, all men living should be saved, and none should be condemned ;[1] even the graceless

[1] Nullus est hominum cujus natura non erat suscepta in Christo.—*Prosp. resp. ad cap. Gall.* cap. 9. Of this see Cyril, lib. x. cap. 13. In Joh. Dei Filius quia suscepit humanam naturam

and unregenerate are men, and have that very nature which Christ assumed; but is this enough for an everlasting state of happiness? Surely no! It is true, even this natural union is very precious, and the foundation of great joy and comfort to believers. Oh for such to remember that Christ hath matched into their family, sits in heaven in their nature, and is of the same flesh and blood with themselves; this, I say, must needs be very sweet. The apostle speaks of it as a very great thing: Heb. ii. 11, ‘He that sanctifieth and they that are sanctified are all of one.’ This ἐξ ἑνος admits of various interpretations; I conceive this is the best: Christ and the saints are all of one, that is, all of one nature, of one and the same flesh and blood; for it follows, ver. 14, ‘Forasmuch as the children are partakers of flesh and blood, he also himself took part of the same,’ &c., and, ver. 16, ‘For verily he took not on him the nature of angels, but he took on him the seed of Abraham.’ I say this union is matter of great comfort to believers; but for others who have nothing more than that Christ is man, and hath assumed their flesh, and is as they are, and they as he, what will this avail them? What is Christ's taking our flesh if he doth not give us his Spirit? What is it for him to be made like to us in our nature, if we be not made like to him in his nature? Christ with the human nature is in heaven, and yet thousands with the human nature are in hell. Oh rest not in mere manhood, though Christ be man! but get a higher, a closer, a more special union with him, or else it will be condemnation for all that.

2. I distinguish, secondly, union with Christ is either external and visible, or internal and invisible. The first is common and general, yet not so common as the material and natural union spoken of before; for all are men, but all are not Christians. This lies in church membership, the participation of church privileges, living under the word and sacraments, passing under the baptismal seal, making of some external profession of religion, &c. The second includes and supposes all this, but hath a great deal more in it; it notes real insition and implantation into Christ. This distinction is evidently grounded

cum omnibus hominibus conjunctus est, &c., sed ista conjunctio generalis est, et tantum (ut ita dicam) juxta materiam.—*Pet. Martyr.*

upon that of our Saviour, John xv. 2, where he saith, ‘Every branch *in me* that beareth not fruit he taketh away.’ Here is the external union, for here is a branch which bears no fruit, and yet it is in Christ. How? It must be understood in respect of church membership, external profession, &c. ‘And every branch that beareth fruit, he purgeth it, that it may bring forth more fruit.’ Here is the internal and special union, that which is, as was said, by real insition and implantation into Christ. Now the inquiry lies here, whether you be so in Christ as to be ingrafted and implanted into him? The former without this will signify but very little. It is indeed a great mercy to be a member of the visible church; but this, without a close and special membership with Christ, will not secure a man's everlasting state; if it be only external conjunction with Christ here, it may for all that be eternal separation from him hereafter. What is it for the branch to be tied or fastened to the stock, if it doth not coalesce and incorporate with the stock? What is it for a man to be in Christ's mystical body only as the wooden leg or eye of glass is in the natural body? (where there is apposition, but no coalition or union.) Certainly when Paul here tells us, ‘There is no condemnation to them who are in Christ Jesus,’ he means such a being in him, as is more than what is external and common, or founded upon any such bottom.[1] As particularly, such as is by mere baptism, I mean when it is the participation of the external sign only, and there is nothing more. They, therefore, who open the words by this, are too large and general.[2] Alas! baptism alone will not do it;[3] there must be some-

[1] Illi in Christo esse dicuntur hoc loco, non qui mediate tantum et secundum quid in Christo sunt, nempe, ratione ecclesiæ ipsius quæ corpus Christi mysticum, &c., sed κατ’ ἐξοχὴν intelliguntur veri Christiani, qui immediate in Christo sunt per unionem mysticam cum ipsius persona, fide et virtute Spiritus Sancti, &c.—*Gomar.*

[2] Τοῖς τοῦ βαπτισματος ἀξιωθεῖσιν.—*Theophyl.*

[3] Non loquitur Paulus de iis qui sacramentum tantummodo baptismi perceperunt, quos extrinsecus duntaxat unda alluit, non autem intus in animo gratia expiavit; sed eos intelligit qui sunt in Christo Jesu, *h.e.*, rem etiam sacramenti adepti sunt.—*Justinian in loc.* Qui sunt in Christo Jesu, *i.e.*, qui per baptismum Christum induerunt, eique per fidem et dilectionem incorporati sunt, factique tanquam vita ejus membra, et tanquam palmites Christo ut viti insiti.—*Perer. Disp.* 1,

thing more than the external badge and livery of Christianity, or else that will come short both of union here and non-condemnation hereafter. Oh how many are there who are baptized, live in the church, are visible members thereof, who yet are far from being inwardly knit to Christ, and therefore shall perish eternally! This is to be but on the outside of the ark, which will not save from drowning. It is the internal, special union which you must look after; whether you be in Christ so as to receive life, growth, spiritual influences from him, as the branch doth from the root. Other unions might be alluded to. It is very true, that baptism is an ingrafting ordinance into Christ, therefore it is set forth by being ' baptized into Jesus Christ,' Rom. vi. 3; and Gal. iii. 27, you read ' As many of you as have been baptized have put on Christ;' and again, 1 Cor. xii. 13, ' By one Spirit we are all baptized into one body.' But then it must be limited to such and such subjects, and as the Spirit accompanies it, working therein faith and regeneration; so that the matter comes to this, upon baptism alone in the external reception of it you cannot be confident; but if you can find that you are also true believers and regenerate persons, then you are right as to your union, and safe as to non-condemnation.

This twofold distinction being premised and opened in the general, the main question now lies thus before us: How may a person know whether the union in which he stands to Christ be internal, special, and saving, or whether it be only external, material, and common? It is a question of very high import; for answer to it I shall desire you,

1. To fix your thoughts upon the double bond of it.

2. To look into some trying scriptures which lay down marks and characters about it.

First make your search after and by the bonds of the mystical union—the Spirit and faith. As,

1. Inquire whether you have the Spirit; for it being the bond of the union, it is evident that none can be a partaker thereof who is not first a partaker of the Spirit. The apostle lays it down very expressly: ' If any man hath not the Spirit of Christ, he is none of his,' Rom. viii. 9; that is, he is none of

in cap. 8 *ad Rom.* Qui sunt insiti per baptismum, et in eo regenerati.—*Estius.*

those who are savingly united to him. Whoever is in Christ, the Spirit of Christ is first in him, that being the agent by which this blessed in-being is brought about. I told you the Spirit is the bond of the union on Christ's part; which yet you are to understand, not of the Spirit merely as it resides in Christ himself, but as it is given and communicated to us; he by his own Spirit, as poured out upon believers, and dwelling in them, takes hold of them and joins them to himself. Not that there is any priority of time betwixt the gift of the Spirit and the union, for they go together; at the very same instant wherein the Spirit is received the soul is united to Christ; but in order of nature, the reception of the one is antecedent to the union with the other. 1 John iii. 24, ' Hereby we know that he abideth in us, by the Spirit which he hath given us;' and chap. iv. 13, ' Hereby know we that we dwell in him, and he in us, by the Spirit which he hath given us.' Observe it, still the apostle grounds the evidence of the union upon the Spirit as given to the saints, not as it resides in Christ himself. Oh, therefore, let the serious, inquisitive Christian put such interrogatories as these to himself: Have I the Spirit? is he given to me? doth he dwell in me? for accordingly as he can answer these queries, so will he be able to conclude whether he be in Christ or not.

And he that would know whether he hath the Spirit, he must examine what he feels of its great acts in himself. To have the Spirit, it is for a man to be brought under the great and special effects and operations thereof. At present I say no more of it; I hope hereafter I shall. These are various: there is illumination; whence he is called ' the Spirit of wisdom and revelation,' Eph. i. 17. Quickening; whence he is called ' the Spirit of life,' Rom. viii. 2. Conviction; the promise is, ' He shall convince the world of sin,' John xvi. 8. He is ' the Spirit of grace and supplication,' Zech. xii. 10; the sanctifying Spirit, 1 Pet. i. 2; the Spirit enabling to mortify sin, Rom. viii. 13; working a person up to all holy obedience, Ezek. xxxvi. 27. Now then, what do you find in yourselves of these high and precious operations of the Spirit? Here lies your participation or having of it, and consequently the evidence of your union with Christ. This great

Spirit is never idle where he is; he is always an active, operative, working Spirit; is he so in you? doth he teach, enlighten, convince, humble, draw to Christ, raise up the heart to heavenly things, excite to duty, assist in duty? &c.; if so, then he is in you, and you are in Christ: if it be not so, then you have not the Spirit, and thereupon are none of Christ's.

2. Inquire about the other bond, viz., faith.[1] Ask yourselves in secret how the case stands as to faith. Say, Oh is this precious grace wrought in us? are we sincere and sound believers? have we heartily closed with Christ according to the gospel offer? have we received Christ, and whole Christ? is our trust, reliance, confidence, for pardon, life, salvation, grounded upon him, and upon him only? do we cast ourselves upon his alone merits, renouncing everything in ourselves? have we that faith which is wrought by the almighty power of God? Eph. i. 19; which purifies the heart? Acts xv. 9; overcomes the world? 1 John v. 4; works by love? Gal. v. 6; is attended with good works? James ii. 20. Is it more than a mere dogmatical or historical faith? than such an easy, common, presumptuous, false faith, as that which is in the generality of men? Oh that you would herein deal faithfully with your own souls! Let the search be deep and thorough; go to the very bottom of your deceitful hearts; bring things to an issue; be sure that you be not mistaken. If the faith be right the union is sure, yea, everything else is sure; but if that be unsound, do not flatter yourselves; you are not in Christ Jesus, but in the woeful state of disunion and distance from him.

Thus the examination must be made from the bonds of the union. To clear up the thing yet further, in order to your passing true judgment upon yourselves, I would direct you to a few trying scriptures.

1. Let the first be that, 2 Cor. v. 17, 'If any man be in Christ, he is a new creature.' What a glass is this for every one of us to see our faces in! The thing to be known is our being in Christ. And how may that be known? Thus, by our being new creatures. The apostle sets it down indefinitely, that he may reach every person, 'if any man be in Christ,' &c. This new creature is one of the greatest riddles of Christianity to men that have it not. It is that new creation which the soul passes under in the work of conversion; or that great and universal change which follows upon conversion. A converted man is a changed man; a quite other person than what he was before. He may say, with Augustine, I am not I; 'all old things are passed away, and all things are become new,' as it follows in the place alleged. Upon conversion, understanding, judgment, thoughts, will, affections, conscience, heart, tongue, life, all is new. When the sinner is turned from sin to God, he hath new principles from which he acts, new ends for which he acts, new guides and rules by which he acts. Is not here a wonderful change? Now are you acquainted with this new creature? What do you find of it in yourselves? It concerns you to make sure of it; for all is nothing without it. 'In Christ Jesus'—and so in reference to the proof of being in Christ Jesus—'neither circumcision availeth anything, nor uncircumcision, but a new creature,' Gal. vi. 15. Oh this is all in all! This must be the sure and infallible witness of your union with Christ.

Therefore examine yourselves about it. I beseech you look back; compare yourselves with yourselves. Hath any thorough change been wrought in you? Are you not the same you ever were—just such as you came into the world? Can any that hears me say, Oh, blessed be God, it is not with me as it hath been! Time was when I was blind, as ignorant a creature as any; but I hope now, in some measure, I am enlightened; God hath shined into me, and set up such a light in me that I see what I never saw before,—and I see it in another manner than I did before. Time was when I could swear, curse, be drunk, take God's name in vain, profane sabbaths, &c.; but I dare not now give way to such impieties. Time was when sin and I agreed very well; but now my heart rises at it: 'I hate every false way,' Ps. cxix. 104. Time was when I had no love for duty; I lived in the total omission of it; but

[1] Soli vere fideles sunt membra Christi, idque non quatenus homines, sed quatenus Christiani; nec secundum primam generationem, sed secundum regenerationem: ac proinde non secundum ipsam humanæ naturæ substantiam per se, sed quatenus illa in Christo ut altero Adamo renovatur, singulis ejus partibus nova ac spirituali qualitate sanctificatis, ut smus novi homines.—*Polan. Synt. Theol.*, p. 454.

now I love prayer, I love the word, and all the ordinances of Christ are precious to me. Time was when I was all for the world, my whole heart was taken up in it; but now, ' I count all but loss that I may gain Christ,' Phil. iii. 8. Now, none but Christ, none but Christ. Can any of you thus speak? Here is a change indeed!—upon that the new creature indeed! and upon that being in Christ indeed!

There is a double change which evermore accompanies the mystical union.

1. The state of the person is changed. He who, before he was in Christ, was a child of wrath, is now, upon his being in Christ, an heir of grace. He that before the union was in a state of condemnation, is now after the union in a state of salvation.

2. The nature is changed. There is a new nature, a new soul (not physically, yet morally) infused into the regenerate person; the divine nature itself is now communicated to him, 2 Pet. i. 4; whereupon he doth not think, speak, or act, as he did before; he doth not love or live as before; he ' walks in newness of life,' as it is, Rom. vi. 4. This is the change which we are to make sure of; for assuredly the Lord Jesus will put none into his bosom, or make them a part of himself, but first the new creature shall pass upon them, to prepare and make them fit for so near and so close a union. It is not consistent with his honour to take a sinner just as he finds him, and without any more ado to own him as a member of himself. There cannot be a passage from one head to another, but there must be some notable alteration. Christ will not break off a branch from the first root and ingraft it into himself, but he will first alter the very nature and property of it. It is not in the power of creatures to change those whom they take into union with them. The husband may take the wife into his bosom, but he cannot change her nature, temper, disposition. As Bernard saith of Moses: *Ethiopissam duxit, sed non potuit Ethiopissæ mutare colorem.* He married an Ethiopian, but he could not alter her Ethiopian complexion; much less could he alter her inward temper. But Christ can and doth thus work upon those whom he takes into near union and relation. If he joins the black, swarthy soul to himself, he puts a new complexion upon it: he makes it ' comely with his own comeliness,' as God speaks, Ezek. xvi. 14. So, then, by

this you may know whether you be truly, really, savingly, in Christ,—viz., if you be new creatures; without the new creation there is no mystical union.

2. Another trying scripture is that, Gal. v. 24, ' They that are Christ's '—who are in him—' have crucified the flesh with the affections and lusts.' This also is a very close word, and it speaks this: No crucifixion, no union. The crucified head will have crucified members. He that is planted in Christ's person, shall be ' planted in the likeness of Christ's death,' Rom. vi. 4. Oh, is sin crucified in you? Did you ever set that upon the cross which brought the Son of God to the cross? Is there in you that death to sin which carries some analogy to Christ's death for sin? Is the flesh, with all its cursed retinue, the affections and lusts thereof, mortified in you? Is the corrupt nature dead as to its former power and sovereignty in the soul? for that is the crucifixion here spoken of. Assure yourselves, Christ will not have a member in him to be under a foreign power; the flesh shall not be the ruler where he is the head; where he brings about the union he will have the dominion.

My text, too, speaks of this flesh; and it tells you that ' they who are in Christ Jesus do not walk after the flesh, but after the Spirit.' Paul here seems to rise and to go on step by step; would you know who are exempted from condemnation? he tells you, such who are in Christ; would you further know who are in Christ? he tells you, such who walk not, &c. Here, then, is the characteristical note of all who are in Christ, they live not the fleshly, carnal, sensual life, but the spiritual, heavenly, holy life. Sirs, what is your walking? It is the conversation that must discover the union. Do but reflect upon your course of life, and that will plainly tell you to what head you belong. ' He that saith he abideth in him, ought himself also so to walk even as he walked,' 1 John ii. 6. Many will be saying they are in Christ, pretending to union with him. Ay! but do they walk as he walked? Do they live the life of Jesus? Do they conform to his example? He that doth not thus do, he may say he abides in Christ, but he doth but say so,—it is not so in truth and reality.

3. Take but one place more: John xv. 2, ' Every branch in me that beareth not fruit, he taketh away:

G

and every branch that beareth fruit, he purgeth it, that it may bring forth more fruit.' As this text holds forth a twofold union betwixt Christ and men, so it was spoke to but even now, I am only now to consider it as it may be improved for trial. Some are in Christ, but it is not by real insition, but only by external profession and church membership, which will avail them but little ; for, notwithstanding this, they are cast forth as dead branches, and gathered, and cast into the fire, and burnt, (as you see ver. 6 ;) and all this befalls them because they bear no fruit. Others are in Christ in a saving and special way, which is the thing to be inquired after. For the finding out of which, let me ask you, What fruit doth grow upon you ? Are you so in Christ as to be fruitful ? then you are in Christ indeed. He will have no dead, barren branches in him, for that would reflect dishonour upon the root. All who are united to him shall bring forth fruit, John xv. 5, 8 ; much fruit, good fruit; fruits 'meet for repentance,' Mat. iii. 8 ; 'fruits of righteousness,' Phil. i. 11 ; fruitfulness 'in every good work,' Col. i. 10. And if so, oh how many empty, barren professors are declared to be out of Christ by this evidence ! Thus I have shewn, both from the double bond of the union, and also from some notable trying scriptures, how you may know whether you be really, internally, specially in Christ Jesus, so as that you may, with well-grounded confidence, lay hold upon the non-condemnation here pronounced to such. So much for the first use.

Use 2. The second shall be to exhort you all to endeavour to get into Christ. Oh that you would with the greatest diligence make out after this blessed union ! What can be so desirable as it ? What so worthy of your endeavours as to be one with Christ ? To have a soul so nearly, so inseparably knit to him, what a great thing is this ! It was exceeding high in Paul's eye, who counted all things but loss for Christ, &c., Phil. iii. 8, 9. Wherein ? why, that he 'might be found in Christ,' *i.e.*, be in him as his head, root, surety, city of refuge, &c., for the expression admits of these several illustrations, though I think the last is most proper. Now, did he thus highly esteem and value this being in Christ, and shall we slight and make little of it ? Surely, my brethren, it is better not to be at all,

than to be, and yet not to be in Christ. Better no union betwixt soul and body, than to have that, and yet no union of the soul with Christ. Here is no condemnation ; but for whom ? Only for them who are in Christ ; to such there is no condemnation ; to others there is nothing but condemnation, as hath been often said. Doth it not highly concern all, therefore, to endeavour to be one of them who are in Christ ?

To enforce the exhortation, I will give you but one motive, but that will be a very comprehensive and considerable one : it is this, Union with Christ is the foundation of all good by and from Christ. It is the fundamental blessing, I mean with respect to application. There can be no application of what Christ hath purchased without antecedent union with his person ; it is the very basis upon which all is built—the leading blessing—the inlet to all the grace of the gospel—the ground of all communion and communication. Ah, sinner ! thou canst hope for nothing from Christ unless thou beest in Christ ; *without Christ* and *without hope* go together, Eph. ii. 12.

I say union is the foundation of all communion. So it is in nature, so it is in grace too : 'But of him are ye in Christ Jesus, who of God is made unto us wisdom, and righteousness, and sanctification, and redemption,' 1 Cor. i. 30 ; mark it, it is first *in Christ Jesus*, and then he is wisdom, righteousness, &c. As it was with Christ in his manhood, first that did participate of the *Gratia unionis*, in its being united to the Godhead ; and then, after this, all other grace was poured out upon it. So it is with the believing soul ; it is first taken into union with Christ, and then upon that, all blessings, privileges, benefits are conveyed to it. You know the member receives nothing from the head unless it be united to it ; so it is with the branches in reference to the root : and so here, without union with Christ there is no justification, no pardon, no reconciliation, no adoption, no salvation by him ; for it is a most certain truth, *Omnis communio fundatur in unione.* If you be one with Christ and in him, all is yours : 1 Cor. iii. 21–23. 'All things are yours, whether Paul or Apollos, or Cephas, or the world, or life, or death, or things present, or things to come ; all are yours ; and ye are Christ's ; and Christ is God's.' Here is a vast propriety and possession, but it is all founded upon union ; we being Christ's, so God is ours ; the promises are ours, heaven is ours, life, death, &c., all is ours. As the wife upon the conjugal union hath a right and title to all that her husband hath, so as that she may say, *Ubi tu Caius, ibi ego Caia*, a proverbial speech used among the Romans at their marriages ; so the believer being joined and married to Christ, all that Christ is or hath becomes his ; but without this union there is nothing to be expected by him or from him. It pleases God to deal altogether with men according to their union, and according to the head which bears them : now there are two public heads, to one of which every man and woman in the world doth belong ; these are the two Adams, of whom you read, 1 Cor. xv. 45. There is the first Adam, and all the unregenerate seed are united to him as their head ; and upon their union with this head, they derive nothing but guilt and wrath and condemnation. Then there is the second Adam, Christ Jesus, and all the regenerate seed are united to him as their head ; and he, by virtue of union also, communicates pardon of sin, peace with God, justification, eternal life, &c. Both of these Adams and public heads proceed by the law, and upon the terms of union ; for the first Adam could do us no hurt,[1] were we not descended out of his loins, and in him as our common head ; and so the second Adam can do us no good, unless we be made one with him and in him as our head also. If we so be, then there shall be gracious communications, most blessed derivations from him ; but if not, none of these can be looked for. And who would not now desire to be in Christ ? who would not purchase this privilege with a world ? nay, who would not give ten thousand worlds for it ? Oh that you would all make sure of it ! Do not trouble your heads with curious inquiries into some difficulties about this union ; but let this be your business, to make sure of the thing. The poor low-gifted Christian may get it, though the highest-gifted man cannot grasp it.

Use 3. But I must direct as well as persuade. Methinks I hear some saying, How may this blessed

union be attained ? what shall we do that we may be in the number of those who are in Christ Jesus ? For answer to this, I must again refer you to its double bond and ligament, the Spirit and faith, and advise you to get both of them. Would you have Christ to be one with you ? then get the Spirit ; would you be one with Christ ? then get faith.

1. First get the Spirit, which may be done by attendance upon the word, and by prayer : Gal. iii. 2, 'Received ye the Spirit by the works of the law, or by the hearing of faith ?' The apostle means the hearing of the gospel, or the evangelical doctrine. The gospel doth highly conduce to the obtaining of the Spirit, for it is 'the ministration of the Spirit,' 2 Cor. iii. 8. Do any therefore want this Spirit ? let them wait upon the gospel dispensation and publication, and, through the grace of God attending that dispensation, they shall have it. Let me also recommend prayer as an excellent means for the procuring of the Spirit. Oh sirs ! what will bring you into Christ but the Spirit ? and what will bring the Spirit into you but prayer ? You should be praying *for* the Spirit, though you cannot as yet pray *with* the Spirit. Oh that you would often go to God and plead with him for the giving of it to you ! Say, Lord, we read, 'If any man have not the Spirit of Christ, he is none of his ;' now, Lord, we dread the thoughts of being none of Christ's. Oh to be out of Christ is a woeful state ! and we perceive that is our state till we have thy Spirit. We hear it is the Spirit that knits the soul to Christ ; till therefore we are partakers of it we cannot be knit to him : wherefore we beseech thee to give it to us. Oh whatever thou deniest to us, do not deny us this good Spirit ! Thou hast promised to 'give thy Spirit to them that ask him,' Luke xi. 13. Lord, upon our bended knees we ask him of thee ; oh now make good thy promise to us. I say, do you but thus pray, and the thing shall be done ; a good God never denies his good Spirit to the good seeker of it.

2. Get faith also. This is a grace highly precious and excellent. The apostle Peter speaks of several precious things, and faith is one of them : it is 'precious blood,' 1 Peter i. 19 ; it is 'precious Christ,' 1 Peter ii. 7 ; it is 'precious promises,' 2 Peter i. 4 ; and it is also 'precious faith,' 2 Peter i. 1. Now

---

[1] Sicut per peccatum Adami non potuissemus peccatores fieri, nisi fuissemus in ejus lumbis, ita per justitiam Christi non possumus justificari, nisi ei inseramur, uniamur, et unus spiritus cum eo fiamus.— *Streso.*

amongst many other things which make it so precious, this is one; it is the grace which unites to Christ.[1] The woman consenting to take the man for her husband, upon that the matrimonial union follows; so the sinner consenting to the receiving and obeying of Christ, which is one great act of faith, upon this he is united to him: this, I say, makes faith so precious. Oh this is one of faith's royal excellencies! nothing puts a greater worth and glory upon it than this great effect. Well then, see that you make sure of it. Are you yet without it? in the sad state of unbelief? You have no share in, and can make no claim to, this mystical union, so long as it is thus with you; you must be put into another state, and become true believers, then it will be well. These are the only persons who are in Christ: 'We who believe are in him that is true,' 1 John v. 20. For whom did Christ ask of his Father 'that they may be one even as we are one'? it was for them 'that should believe' on him, John xvii. 20, &c. Therefore let it be your great endeavour to be believers; for let me tell you, in the very first moment of believing you will actually be the members of Christ: the soul is in Christ as soon as ever faith is in it. I will say no more, but only add this, As you desire to get faith, first get the Spirit; for if you once come to have that Spirit, he will most infallibly work faith in you. Of all the several graces, he will not let that be wanting wherever he is.

Use 4. The uses hitherto have been general, I shall now more particularly direct myself to those who are in Christ Jesus.

And first, is it thus with any of you, that you are indeed taken into this near union with Christ? how should you admire the love of God! I here consider God personally, and so I would excite you to admire the love of the Father, of the Son, and of the Holy Ghost; for indeed all the persons have a great hand in this union, and the love of each of them in it is very admirable. The Father first lays the foundation of it, and then he orders the accomplishment of it; therefore it is said, 1 Cor. i. 30, 'Of him,' *i.e.*, of God the Father, 'are ye in Christ Jesus,' &c.; and

[1] Fidei gratia incomparabilis hæc est, quod animam copulat cum Christo, sicut sponsam cum sponso, &c.—*Luther*, tom. i. 466.

he also is said 'to call unto the fellowship of his Son Jesus Christ,' 1 Cor. i. 9. The Son is willing to be one with you; what a condescension is that! and he is the person in whom the union is primarily terminated. Then the Holy Ghost brings it about as one great agent therein. So that all the three persons are concerned in the mystical union; it is to the Son, by the will of the Father, through the agency and operation of the Spirit. Oh let Father, Son, and Spirit all be adored by you!

Which that I may the more effectually persuade you to, let the thing itself be considered, and how you stand in reference to it. To be in Christ Jesus, so nearly, so indissolubly united to him, what mercy is this! There are in the union many things of a very mysterious nature, but the greatest mystery of all is that there should be such a mystery; I mean, that there should be such a thing for such poor creatures. Oh consider, you 'who sometimes were afar off, even you are made nigh,' Eph. ii. 13, not only by Christ, but to Christ; you who were so far from being in Christ, that you were even 'in the wicked one,' and in him you did lie, even as the carnal world doth, 1 John v. 19; yet you are now under a blessed conjunction with Christ. You who by nature were grafted into the wild olive, are now grafted into and made partakers of the root and fatness of the olive tree, Rom. xi. 17. Oh incomparable, transcendent mercy! that so great a person as Christ, the 'only begotten Son of God,' John iii. 16; 'God blessed for ever,' Rom. ix. 5; 'the brightness of his Father's glory,' Heb. i. 3; should stoop so low as to be made one with dust and ashes: that you who are no better than worms which crawl on the earth, should be joined to so glorious a head; that he who did at first assume your nature into so near a union with himself, should afterwards take your persons also, and mystically unite them to his own person; that it should not only be God with you, Mat. i. 23, but God in you, and you in God. Oh how will you be able, in some suitable manner, to bless God and Christ for such unconceivable, astonishing love as this is! This being in Christ, as a limb and part of him here on earth, will certainly bear a great share in your highest thanksgivings and hallelujahs, when you shall be with him in heaven.

2. Endeavour after a further clearness in this union. This I would urge,

1. With respect to the nature of the thing.

2. With respect to your personal interest in it.

First, Get the thing itself more and more cleared up, that your knowledge of it may be more full and more distinct. Some further head knowledge about it would not be amiss. It is a mystery, that very 'mystery which hath been hid from ages and from generations; but it is now made manifest to the saints, to whom God hath made known the riches of the glory of this mystery, which is Christ in you the hope of glory,' as the apostle sets it forth, Col. i. 27. Now it is a mystery which hath been hid so long, but is now revealed in the gospel, and shall we not labour after a clearer light about it? It being a privilege that is common to all believers, there being also such a revelation of it, it is to be lamented that it is no better understood by us. It is true, in this life we cannot hope fully to comprehend it, yet we might know much more of it than generally we do. Paul speaks of the love of Christ as 'passing knowledge,' Eph. iii. 19; and yet he prayed for the Ephesians that they might know it; *i.e.*, that they might know as much of it as was possible, though all could not be known. The same I say concerning the mystical union. But chiefly,

In the second place, Labour to be more clear as to your personal interest in it. Are not many of God's people very much in the dark about this—often questioning with themselves whether they be in Christ or not? Is it better with you? have you assurance of your spiritual conjunction with Christ? As you value your comfort, your inward settledness and establishment, take pains after this assurance; so as that, with the apostle's evidence and confidence, you may be able to say, 'We are in him that is true,' 1 John v. 20. Could you but once arrive at this, how great would your rejoicing be! I have told you, it is a sad thing for a man to get no higher than a *peradventure* with respect to non-condemnation. Now the assurance of that depends upon the assurance of union. The apostle would have Christians know distinctly how the case stands with them in reference to their being in Christ, and Christ's being in them. 'Prove your own selves.

Know ye not your own selves, how that Christ is in you, except ye be reprobates?' 2 Cor. xiii. 5.

In order to this assurance, you must pray much for the Spirit's witness; for that Spirit which promotes it doth also discover and give the evidence of it. The objective evidence you may have in yourselves, viz., grace in the heart, the new creature, faith, &c.; but the subjective evidence you will not have till the Spirit, by a divine irradiation, doth make out the thing to you.

3. Are you in Christ? Oh maintain and keep up your union with him! This is the abiding in him which he himself speaks so much of: John xv. 4, 'Abide in me, and I in you;' so ver. 5–7. It is not enough to be in Christ unless you abide in him. You will say, Is not the union indissoluble—that which shall never cease? I answer, Yes, it is so; yet you may do that which may tend to the dissolving of it, though, through grace, it shall not actually dissolve it; and you may do that which may utterly deprive you of the sense and evidence and comfort of it, though the thing itself shall remain firm and sure: it concerns you therefore, upon these accounts, to be very careful. Wherein? why, do not sin willingly and knowingly against God, and do not abate in your constant and fervent performance of duty; for these things strike at the union, at the untying of that knot which God hath tied so fast. And if it should once come to that, what would become of you? No sooner is the branch broken off from the root but it immediately withers and dies. Could you imagine a believer to be broken off from Christ but for one moment, what a withering, dying person would he be! O sirs! your life, strength, fruitfulness, comfort, your all is in Christ, and secured by your union with him; if that should fail, all would fail: do nothing, therefore, to endanger it. John xv. 4, 'As the branch cannot bear fruit of itself, except it abide in the vine; no more can ye, except ye abide in me;' ver. 5, 'He that abideth in me, and I in him, the same bringeth forth much fruit; for without me ($\chi\omega\varrho\grave{\iota}\varsigma$ $\dot{\epsilon}\mu o\tilde{\upsilon}$, *seorsim a me*, separated from me, so Beza renders the word) ye can do nothing.' So long as you preserve your union you will be strong—strong to do, and strong to suffer; but if you once make a breach upon that, you will be no better than Samson

when his strength was departed from him, Judges xvi. 19. What is the cutting off the hair to divulsion and separation from the head?

4. Improve your union with Christ. Are you in him? You should always be drawing and deriving from him. So the member doth from the head; and Christ being your head, why do you not live under more constant, more free and full derivations from him? Why is not this union improved, as a standing cordial in and against those faintings and despondencies of spirit which sometimes you lie under? Why is not this more pleaded with God in the midst of sad thoughts and misgivings of heart. Many other things might be instanced in. It is too much a truth, all other unions are better improved than this great mystical union with Christ; the branch makes the best of the root, and draws from it as though it would exhaust all its life and virtue. Oh that we could carry it so to Jesus Christ! even to draw from him as though we would draw him dry, if such a thing were possible. We say in philosophy, the nearer anything comes to the first cause, the more abundantly it doth receive from it;[1] as the nearer a thing is to the sun, the more it doth participate of its light and heat. Now you, believers, are very nigh to Christ, in whom 'all fulness dwells,' Col. i. 19; you are even in him. Oh what full supplies of grace should you be fetching from him upon all occasions! why should they want, or what should they want, who are not only at the fountain, but in it!

5. Such as are in Christ must be very humble. Christians, your union is very high, but your spirits should be very low. High alliances are apt to puff men up; you are highly allied, indeed. Christ is your head, your husband, your brother; he and you are 'all of one,' Heb. ii. 11; yet be not proud. When the apostle was speaking of the ingrafting of the Gentile believers into Christ, he adds, 'Others by unbelief are broken off; you stand by faith; be not high-minded, but fear,' Rom. xi. 20: the same I say to you. Oh, ascribe nothing to yourselves; do not entertain or give way to any self-exalting thoughts; never think you can subsist by yourselves; live under a constant sense of your dependence upon

Christ; let there not be a thought in you that Christ is in the least beholden to you; it is 'the root which bears you; you do not bear the root,' Rom. xi. 18. You are one with Christ, yet you come infinitely short of him; he is in you, yet above you; it would be pride of the first magnitude to equalise yourselves with him. Especially, never think that, because of this union, you can merit anything of God. The papists would fain prove the saints meriting in what they do, from their union with Christ; but it is a weak proving of it; and our divines give a good reason against it,— because the union betwixt Christ and believers is only mystical, and not personal. Now it is the personal union only that is the ground of merit. Oh, 'when you have done all, say you are unprofitable,' Luke xvii. 10. How unprofitable, then, are you when you do so little! nay, when you do nothing at all as you ought to do!

6. Be very holy. They who are joined to such a head, how should they live! what holiness can be high enough for such a union! Will you pretend to be in Christ, and yet live in sin? will you dishonour Christ your head by a loose, vain, unholy, unsuitable conversation? How should they 'shew forth the virtues of Christ,' 1 Pet. ii. 9, who are the members of Christ! Methinks this union with him should greatly sharpen the soul against sin, and cause it to repel all temptations and solicitations thereunto with a holy detestation, as he once did: Gen. xxxix. 9, 'How shall I do this great wickedness, and sin against God?' What! I, a member of Christ, one with Christ, shall I do so and so? As for others, who belong to a degenerate root, they will bring forth degenerate fruit; but I, who am ingrafted into so noble, so excellent a stock, shall I bring forth no better fruit? This precious soul, which was so immediately created by God, and is so immediately united to Christ, shall that be prostituted to sin and Satan? This body, too, hath its share in this union; and 'shall I take the members of Christ, and make them the members of a harlot?' 1 Cor. vi. 15. Surely such who are one with Christ should in all things be like to Christ; where there is union and communion there should be conformity. Christians, if you live as others do, you will make the world to question whether there

[1] Unumquodque quo propius accedit causæ primæ, eo abundantius recipit.

be such a thing as union with Christ, or at least to think but meanly of it. Oh, therefore, 'as you have received Christ, so walk ye in him,' Col. ii. 6. It is obedience and holy walking which must evidence your union to others, to yourselves: 1 John iii. 4, 'He that keepeth his commandments dwelleth in him, and he in him; and hereby we know that he abideth in us, by the Spirit which he hath given us.' And the union itself calleth for it: 1 John ii. 6, 'He that saith he abideth in him ought himself also so to walk, even as he walked.' Oh, how should they live who live in Christ, and he in them! Gal. ii. 20.

7. Are you in Christ? then be heavenly-minded. Such as are in him should be much with him in the heavenliness of their thoughts and affections. Our union is with our Lord in heaven, and our conversation should be with him in heaven also, Phil. iii. 20; our head is there, Col. iii. 1; and our treasure is there, Mat. vi. 21. Should not our hearts be there also? What a contradiction is an earthly conversation to the heavenly union? How sad a thing is it, that a believer, who is so near to Christ, should yet live at so great a distance from him, and carry it as though he was rather in the world than in Christ Jesus? If thou beest glued to Christ, do not live as one who is glued to the world.

8. Be fruitful, and very fruitful. 'He that abideth in me bringeth forth much fruit,' John xv. 4. Christ saith it is so; sure I am it should be so. If you be branches ingrafted into Christ, there is a special obligation lying upon you to be very fruitful; for else you will disparage your root, and also frustrate the expectations of him who lays out much cost upon you in order to your fruitfulness. The husbandman, God the Father, looks for much fruit from such as you; and if you do not answer his expectations, he will purge you, that is, he will lay some sharp afflictions upon you, and thereby make you to bring forth more fruit; he will not take you away, as he doth those who are only externally in Christ, or cast you out for the fire, but he will afflict you to some purpose. This is our Saviour's own awakening doctrine, John xv. 2. The promise is, Ps. xcii. 13, 14, 'Those that be planted in the house of the Lord shall flourish, &c.; they shall bring forth fruit,' &c. Oh, how fruitful should they be who are planted in the Lord himself!

9. Such as are one with Christ should be one amongst themselves. Saints are under a double union; one with Christ, and one amongst themselves; and the latter is as real as the former, and purchased by Christ as well as the former—for the proof of which read and weigh Eph. ii. 14, &c. The members in the body natural, as they are united to the head, so they are also united each to the other; and so it is here. Oh that this union among saints was more conspicuous and evident! But, with grief of heart be it spoken, little is to be seen of that, whilst much of that which is opposite to it is everywhere too apparent. What schisms, rents, divisions, are there to be found even amongst them! Is not this spoken of in Gath? Are not the great enemies of Christianity too well acquainted with it? Now, what a sad thing is this, that when they are 'all one in Christ Jesus,' as it is in Gal. iii. 28, that there should be such divisions, fractions, and distances amongst themselves! Some divines make this to be the matter of Christ's prayer, John xvii., where he prayed that all believers might be one, as the Father and he were one; i.e., that they might be one in unity and concord amongst themselves. Which interpretation, though the higher union must by no means be excluded, is very probable, from the argument with which Christ twice backs his prayer: 'That the world may believe that thou hast sent me.' It must, therefore, be some external and visible union, of which the world, in order to this conviction, might take notice; which the saints' mystical union with Christ is not, but their union or unity amongst themselves is. And it appears that upon this very prayer of Christ there was a little after great unity and concord amongst the primitive Christians: Acts ii. 46, 'And they continuing daily with one accord,' &c.; Acts iv. 32, 'The multitude of them that believed were of one heart, and of one soul,' &c.—just as Christ had prayed. And oh that the virtue of this prayer might reach us also at this time! for surely our divisions are so many and so great, our breaches so wide, that I think nothing can or will unite us but the alone efficacy of Christ's intercession. A stronger motive to unity cannot be set before the people of God than that which I am upon. They who are so joined to Christ should not be disjoined amongst themselves: as they have but

one head, and are all members of the same body, so they should have but 'one heart and one way,' Jer. xxxii. 39.

10. Are you in Christ? You should then be well acquainted with him, so as to attain to a considerable degree of the knowledge of him. Others, who are afar off from him, may be ignorant of him, but you, who are so nigh to him, should know him well. He told his disciples that he would 'Pray the Father, and he would give them the Comforter,' &c. 'Even the Spirit of truth; whom the world cannot receive, because it seeth him not, neither knoweth him: but ye know him; for he dwelleth with you, and shall be in you,' John xiv. 16, 17. This was spoken of the saints' knowledge of the Spirit; but it holds true as to the knowledge of Christ himself. The world knows him not, but believers know him. How doth that come to pass? Why, from this, for he dwells in them, and is in them, and they in him. Oh, how should the consideration of this union excite you to labour after a clearer knowledge of the Lord Jesus! Persons we live with we know them fully. Christ lives in you, and you in him. What a shame will it be if you do not, so far as your capacity will admit of, know him distinctly! 'Surely,' saith Jacob, 'the Lord was in this place, and I knew it not,' Gen. xxviii. 16. Whoever thou art, if thou beest a gracious person, surely the Lord is in thee and thou in him; and yet thou neither knowest thy union, nor the person to whom thou art united. Pray, let this put you upon the daily diligent studying of Christ, that you may arrive at a higher knowledge of him. 'Acquaint yourselves with him,' Job xxii. 21, and do it thoroughly. Upon the intimateness of the union there should be intimateness of acquaintance.

Use 5. Hitherto I have been speaking to such who are in Christ by way of exhortation. I shall now further speak to them by way of consolation; and you that are such, oh rejoice and be exceeding glad, let your hearts be even filled with joy! What abundance of comfort is there wrapt up for you in this your union with Christ! It is a flower out of which all sincere Christians may suck a great deal of evangelical sweetness. For the setting forth of which let me go further than that special privilege which the text holds forth.

1. Are you in Christ Jesus? This speaks the excellency and dignity of your persons. How great and honourable must they needs be, who are thus nearly united to so glorious a person as Christ, the Mediator, the eternal Son of God! 'This honour have all the saints,' Ps. cxlix. 9. It is no great matter what the world says or thinks of you; men vilify you, and look upon you as the very 'scum and filth of the earth,' so they did long ago to far your betters, 1 Cor. iv. 13. 'The precious sons of Zion, comparable to fine gold, how are they esteemed as earthen pitchers!' Lam. iv. 2. And it is no great matter what your outward condition is in the world —that may be mean and inglorious enough. I say these are things not much to be regarded, so long as you are the members of Christ. You being so, what a glory and greatness must this needs reflect upon you! Mark that expression, John xvii. 22, 'The glory which thou hast given me I have given them.' What glory doth Christ speak of? it follows: 'That they may be one, even as we are one.' This is glory indeed. It is a great honour to be a member of the church; so the good emperor Theodosius judged of it, who preferred his being a member of the church before his being emperor of the world. But it is a far greater honour to be a member of Christ. It is a high expression concerning Israel, that they were 'a people near to God,' Ps. cxlviii. 14. You believers are near to God indeed, for you have not only communion with him who is God, but union also; you are one with the Father, and one with the Son. You must needs upon this be excellent and glorious. The excellency of persons and things is to be measured by their appropinquation or approximation to that which is most excellent. Then the saints are 'the excellent in the earth,' Ps. xvi. 3, because they are so near to Christ, the centre of all excellencies. How was the human nature advanced and dignified, even above the angelical nature, when it was so nearly united to the Godhead, as the woman of mean descent is when she is matched into some great family! And hath not Christ highly advanced your persons too, by taking them into so close, so intimate a union with himself? It was accounted honour for Esther to be taken into Ahasuerus's royal bed; it was a far greater honour to her to become his wife. But this is nothing to the

honour which Christ hath put upon you in his joining and marrying of you to himself. Oh let him first be adored who hath thus exalted poor worms! and then you should know how to judge of yourselves according to the advancement and dignity conferred upon you by your being in Christ. As to your being and order, the angels are above you: 'Thou hast made him a little lower than the angels,' Ps. viii. 5. But as Christ hath assumed your nature, and not theirs, and hath thus nearly united your persons to himself, so they are a little, nay, a great deal, lower than you. Let there be no pride or sinful self-exaltation in you; yet know how to put a right estimate upon yourselves according to your advancement by grace. The saint in his rags is greater than the sinner in his robes; for the one is in Christ, and the other is not, and that puts a superlative glory and excellency upon him.

2. Are you in Christ Jesus? Then, as your dignity is great, so your safety is great too. You need not fear the greatest dangers which threaten you; upon your being in Christ, even in the 'valley of the shadow of death,' you are safe, Ps. xxiii. 4. The evils you dread are either temporal and external, or spiritual, internal, and eternal. You are secure against all. That special providence which is over you secures against the first; and that special grace which is in you and towards you secures against the last: 'Upon all the glory shall be a defence,' Isa. iv. 5. You upon your union are a part of this glory, for it points to persons as well as things; therefore there is a defence upon you to keep off whatever might hurt you. You are not merely a part of Christ through your conjunction with him, but you are, in regard of his special and tender affection, as ' the apple of his eye,' Zech. ii. 8; and will he not guard the apple of his eye? He that is in this ark must needs be safe in the greatest deluge. The evil of evils is eternal condemnation. But what saith the text? 'There is no condemnation to them who are in Christ Jesus.' How can they perish who are one with Christ? Will he suffer persons so united to him to be miserable? So long as it is well with the head, shall it not be well with the members also? In the body natural the head may be safe, and yet some of the members may perish; but in the body mystical it is otherwise, where all

the members are safe in the head, and as safe as the head itself. O believers! you may with courage look the greatest dangers, evils, in the face, as knowing that none of them shall ever reach you, much less to hurt you, because you are so strongly engarrisoned in Christ. But more of this in the last branch of comfort.

3. Are you in Christ Jesus? Here is comfort for you; upon your union with him he sympathises with you in all your afflictions, and looks upon all done to you as done to himself. I say, Christ sympathises with you in all your afflictions, for he is a sympathising, compassionate, tender-hearted Saviour, as you read, Heb. iv. 15, and v. 2. As there is, by virtue of the union, a mutual sympathy betwixt the head and the members, the husband and the wife, so it is here betwixt Christ and you: 'In all your afflictions he is afflicted,' Isa. lxiii. 9. He that bore your griefs when he was on earth, really and properly, Isa. liii. 4, he bears them still, now he is in heaven, in a way of sympathy. Further, I add, he hath a tender sense of what is done to you, and looks upon it as done to himself; and no wonder, since he and you are but one: ' He that touches you, touches the apple of his eye,' Zech. ii. 8; 'Saul, Saul, why persecutest thou me,'[1] Acts ix. 4. When the saint is persecuted, Christ himself in him is persecuted. As if any kindness or love be shewn to believers, Christ looks upon it as done to himself: Mat. xxv. 40, 'Inasmuch as ye have done it unto one of the least of these my brethren, ye have done it to me;' so if any unkindness be shewn to them, Christ looks upon it as done to himself. Oh that enemies would be quiet, and let God's people alone, and fear to wrong or injure them! for they are so united to Christ, so incorporated with him, that they who strike at them do through them strike at Christ himself.

4. Are you in Christ? He will then most certainly supply you in all your wants. In temporal wants fear not, Christ will provide; will he suffer that body to starve which he hath united to himself? You are full of anxious thoughts 'what ye shall eat and drink; what ye shall put on.' Christ would have you 'take no thought' about these things, Mat. vi.

---

[1] Sic vocem pedis suscipit lingua; clamat, *calcas me.* In membris Christi Christus est.—*August. in Ps.* xxx.

26. Your bodies being in union with him, he will look after them, so that they shall not want what is necessary. O believer! hath Christ thus admirably joined thee to himself, and will he deny thee a little meat, and drink, and clothing? And then as to spiritual wants, in those Christ will supply too. Every member in the body from this head shall receive that grace, life, strength, that is proper for it. The root supplies every branch with what it needs. Christ will do the same to every believing soul; and this is part of that ἐπιχορηγία τοῦ πνεύματος, that 'supply of the Spirit' which you read of, Phil. i. 19. This union is operative and communicative. If thou beest in Christ, thou shalt most surely have from him that measure of grace and comfort which he sees best for thee, Rom. xii. 3. Every lamp in the golden candlestick was supplied from the two olives, Zech. iv. 12; and so every particular member of Christ is and shall, as need requires, be supplied from him. The apostle tells us, 1 Tim. v. 8, 'If any provide not for his own, and especially for those of his own house, he hath denied the faith.' You are Christ's own, John xiii. 1, of his house and kindred, nearly related to him, nay, members of himself, and therefore certainly he will provide for you. And that he will do in all your concerns, whether outward or inward. That, look, as you must 'glorify God in your body, and in your spirit, for both are God's,' 1 Cor. vi. 20; so Christ will supply you in your bodies, in your spirits, for both are his.

5. Are you in Christ? Then you have no reason to be afraid of death. Though it be 'the king of terrors,' Job. xviii. 4, of all terribles the most terrible, yet as to you there is no cause of fear. Why? Because it can never dissolve the union that is betwixt Christ and you; and so long as that abides, death can never do you much hurt. Hear me, thou sincere Christian! Dost thou live? thou art in Christ; dost thou die? thou art in Christ; neither life nor death, therefore, shall be hurtful to thee. Nay, it is so far from that, that death itself shall be thy advantage: 'To me to live is Christ, and to die is gain,' Phil. i. 21. You read of 'dying in the Lord,' Rev. xiv. 13, of 'sleeping in Jesus,' 1 Thes. iv. 14. The saints die, their bodies are thrown into the grave, (that vast repository,) yet there they are united to Christ; yea, their

very dust is so. This death cuts asunder all other knots, but it cannot do so to the mystical knot; it dissolves the union betwixt soul and body, betwixt husband and wife, &c., but it shall never dissolve the union betwixt Christ and the believing soul. When the body of a child of God shall be no better than a rotten carcase, Christ will say, Oh yet this very carcase is precious to me, for it is in union with me! David speaks of the saints favouring the dust of Zion, Ps. cii. 14. The very dust of dead believers is valued by Christ, insomuch that he will not lose the least atom of it.

6. Are you in Christ? Here is matter of comfort as to the certainty of a happy resurrection. Your bodies may be locked up in the grave for a time, but Christ, who hath the key of the grave—they being united to him—will certainly open it and take them out. He will raise them up again, and that with advantage too, for they shall then be fashioned like to his own glorious body, Phil. iii. 21. The head is risen, and the members shall rise also, by virtue of the union that is betwixt them. *Quod præcessit in capite, sequetur in corpore*, as Augustine speaks: 1 Cor. xv. 20, 'Now is Christ risen from the dead, and become the first-fruits of them that sleep.' Rom. viii. 11, 'If the Spirit of him that raised up Jesus from the dead dwell in you, he that raised up Christ from the dead shall also quicken your mortal bodies by his Spirit that dwelleth in you.' So John vi. 54, 'Whoso eateth my flesh, and drinketh my blood, hath eternal life; and I will raise him up at the last day.' And this is not to be limited to a bare resurrection; there is more in it than so, for all shall arise; the resurrection shall be general and universal, Dan. xii. 2; 1 Cor. xv. 22. But yet there will be a vast difference in it; it will be a happy resurrection to them who are in Christ, but a dreadful resurrection to others. The wicked shall be raised by Christ as a judge, in order to their trial, and the passing of the sentence of death upon them; but the saints shall be raised by Christ as a head, *virtute unionis*, in order to the receiving of the blessed sentence of life. John v. 28, 29, 'Marvel not at this: for the hour is coming, in the which all that are in the graves shall hear his voice, and shall come forth; they that have done good, unto the resurrection of life; and they that have done evil,

unto the resurrection of damnation.' How should believers rejoice in this !

7. Are you in Christ? Then great is the Father's love to you. Take believers as they are in themselves—the Father greatly loves them; but now as they are in Christ, and made one with him, there is an additional love, a higher love belonging to them from the Father, because they are so near to his own Son. Therefore, upon this union, God loves them with the same love wherewith he loves Jesus Christ himself: John xvii. 23, 'I in them, and thou in me, &c.; that the world may know that thou hast sent me, *and hast loved them, as thou hast loved me.*' O believers, what a love hath the Father for you upon this! And Christ's own love, too, is very great to you; for you are his flesh, and 'no man ever hated his own flesh,' Eph. v. 29, 30. Yea, he told his disciples, 'As my Father hath loved me, so have I loved you,' John xv. 9. So near a union must needs be accompanied with a very dear affection. It is not always so with us; but as to Christ, the strength of the affection from him shall always be answerable to the nearness of the union with him.

8. Are you in Christ Jesus? Here is comfort as to your perseverance, stability, and fixedness in the state of grace. This, upon which all depends, a child of God may be fully assured of; for will Christ lose a member, a part of himself? shall one united to him finally and totally fall away from him? No, that shall not be. So long as the union is firm and indissoluble, do not fear. I speak not against the *duty* of fear, but the *sin* of fear. It is not here in and out—in to-day and out to-morrow; but it is once in Christ, and ever in Christ; there is your safety. Indeed the saints stand firm upon several great foundations, as the Father's election, the immutability of his counsel, Heb. vi. 17, the tenor of the covenant, &c., but this also must be taken in, their inseparable union with Christ. You are not only in Christ's hands, (out of which none shall pluck you, John x. 28,) but you are in Christ as your head; and who shall be able to sever the members from this head? If Christ should lose a member, he would be imperfect as a head. You are his fulness, as hath been said, Eph. i. 23, now he will be *Christus plenus*, a full Christ, as he speaks,[1] which he

[1] Aug. in Ps. xxxvi.

would not be if any of his members should be taken away from him. If he might lose one, he might then lose another and another, and so he would be sure of none. Oh! 'your life is hid with Christ in God,' Col. iii. 3; therefore it is sure and safe. Take the saints apart from Christ, the strongest could not stand; take them as joined and united to him, the weakest shall not fall. When the first Adam was our head, our condition was mutable, in him we stood upon very slippery ground; but now, when Christ is our head, we stand fast and firm, 'even as mount Zion, never to be removed,' Ps. cxxv. 1. It is but the same grace now, which we should have had upon our first creation—I speak of the kind, not of the degree—yet it is not amissible as that was, because of our union with another head.

9. Are you in Christ? This assures you of the audience of your prayers. 'If ye abide in me,' saith Christ, 'ye shall ask what ye will, and it shall be done unto you.' What an encouraging word is this! God will grant your requests for the love he bears you upon other accounts; but to be sure he will do this for you, you being under such a near conjunction to the Son of his love.

10. Are you in Christ? Know then that union and communion go together, and is not this full of comfort? As all communion is founded upon union, so all union terminates in communion; and the closer is the union, the fuller is the communion. Union with Christ is a very enriching thing; it interests a person in all that Christ is or hath; this is that fellowship of the Son to which the saints are called, 1 Cor. i. 9. You being in Christ, his person is yours; you are his, and he is yours: 'My beloved is mine, and I am his,' Cant. ii. 16. Upon the covenant-relation God is yours; upon the mystical union Christ is yours. You being in Christ, all his attributes are yours: his wisdom yours to guide you; his power yours to protect you; his mercy yours to pity you; his all-sufficiency yours to supply you; and so in the rest. As the father in the Gospel once said to his son, 'Son, thou art ever with me, and all that I have is thine,' Luke xv. 31; so saith Christ to the believing soul, Thou art ever in me; all that I am or have is thine. Being in Christ, you share with him in all his offices, hence you are kings and priests as he is, in a spiritual and mystical

notion.[1] Rev. i. 6, 'And hath made us kings and priests unto God,' &c. 1 Peter ii. 5, saints are styled 'an holy priesthood,' and, ver. 9, 'a royal priesthood.' Being in Christ, you bear his name, as hath been shewn, and you partake with him in his high relations and dignities; he is a son of God, so are you: John xx. 17, 'I ascend to my Father, and your Father;' he is 'heir of all things,' Heb. i. 2; you 'joint heirs with him,' Rom. viii. 17. Being in Christ, all his merit is yours; his sufferings, satisfaction, are as much to your advantage, as if you had suffered and satisfied in your own persons.[2] You being in Christ, all the blessings, privileges, which he hath purchased are yours[3]—as justification, atonement, adoption, access to God, &c. You being in Christ, that very glory which he hath is yours. See Rev. iii. 21; John xvii. 24; Luke xxii. 29. You being in Christ, all 'the promises in him are yea and amen' to you, 2 Cor. i. 20; Gal. iii. 29. You being in Christ, all his victories and triumphs over enemies are yours, Rev. ii. 26, 27. Upon union with Christ, you have union, too, with the Father and the Holy Ghost.[4] In a word, you being Christ's, all is yours, 1 Cor. iii. 21, and what can be said further? Is not all this enough for your comfort? Here is blessed communion flowing from a blessed union; here is partaking indeed of the fatness of the olive, upon your being ingrafted into it, as it is Rom. xi. 17.

[1] Omnes Christiani sunt sacerdotes, quia membra unius sacerdotis.—*August. de Civ. Dei*, lib. xx. cap. 10.

[2] Caput et membra sunt quasi una persona mystica, et ideo satisfactio Christi ad omnes fideles pertinet, sicut ad sua membra.—*Aquin.*, 3 P. qu. 49, art 1.

[3] Unio hæc est spiritualis illa relatio hominum ad personam Christi, qua jus acquirunt ad omnes illas benedictiones quæ ab ipso præparantur.—*Ames. Medul.*, lib. i. cap. 26, sec. 2. Fides pure docenda est, quod per eam sic conglutineris, ut ex te et Christo fiat quasi una persona, quæ non possit segregari; ut cum fiducia dicere possis, Ego sum Christus, *h.e.*, Christi justitia, victoria, vita, est mea; et vicissim Christus dicat, Ego sum ille peccator, *h.e.*, ejus peccata et mors mea sunt, quia adhæret mihi et ego illi, conjuncti enim sumus per fidem in unam carnem et os.—*Luther.* Homo cum fiducia possit gloriari in Christo, et dicere, meum est quod Christus vixit, egit, dixit, passus est, mortuus est, non secus quam si ego illa vixissem, egissem, dixissem, passus essem, mortuus essem; sicut sponsus habet omnia quæ sunt sponsæ, et sponsa habet omnia quæ sunt sponsi, &c.—*Idem.*

[4] See Sedgw. on the covenant, p. 208.

11. Are you in Christ? Then it is no condemnation: so the text expressly tells you. Oh what a ground of rejoicing is exemption from condemnation! What can be sweet to him who is obnoxious to it? what can be bitter to him who is secured against it? this is the happiness of all in Christ. Poor Christless souls are condemned over and over; law, and gospel, and conscience, and, which is worst of all, the great God condemns them; but it is not so with you who are in Christ; to you it is no condemnation. You are justified here, and shall be solemnly, publicly, declared to be so at the great day. You are in Christ, not only as the members in the head, which is your mystical union, but as the debtor in the surety, which is your legal union. Christ's payment and satisfaction is yours, and God will not fall upon him and you too for payment. The wife under covert is not liable to an arrest or action at law, but all must fall upon her husband. You being married to Christ, this supersedes the process of the law against you; if it be not fully satisfied, it must seek its reparation at the hands of your spiritual husband, Christ himself: as to any condemnatory charge, it cannot fall upon you. Amongst all the damned in hell there is not one in Christ to be found; that is no place for such as are limbs of him. And, to shut up all, upon this union it is not only no condemnation, but it is also certain salvation: 1 John v. 12, 'He that hath the Son, hath life;' John xiv. 19, 'Because I live, ye shall live also.' Christ the head is in heaven, and where he is, there he will have his members also; this is his great request to his Father, John xvii. 24. Where it is union it shall be vision; *in Christ* here, and *with Christ* hereafter, are inseparable; a Christ in you is a sufficient ground for the hope of glory: Col. i. 27, 'Christ in you, the hope of glory.' You therefore who are in Christ should highly comfort yourselves with these things.

I would desire such not to put from them these cordials, as if they were not proper for them, because of the weakness of their graces, the imperfections of their duties, the meanness of their persons, or upon any other discouragement of this nature. Art thou a believer? be thou never so weak, yet thou art in Christ; thou art low in grace, in gifts, in thy outward condition, yet thou art in Christ. The meanest member in the body is united to the head, as well as that which is the highest; and so it is here. Though the eye was weak which looked upon the brazen serpent, yet it looking thereupon there was healing for all that. The weakest faith is healing faith; and it is so, not only because it takes a view of Christ, but also because it knits to Christ. O Christian! faith's uniting virtue doth not depend upon its strength, but upon its sincerity; the very *minimum quod sic* is enough to put thee into Christ; therefore be not discouraged because thy faith is so weak and low. And for thy outward condition, that is nothing at all to the state or privilege; the poor are in Christ as well as the rich, the ignoble as well as the noble. He doth not choose his members by any external considerations. If grace be in thy heart, though thou art very mean in thy outward state, hast scarce bread to put into thy belly, or rags upon thy body, Christ is not ashamed to own thee as one of his members and brethren, Heb. ii. 11.

Let this suffice for the opening of the subjects of the privilege, so far forth as they are described by their union: 'There is no condemnation *to them which are in Christ Jesus.*'

CHAPTER III.

OF THE HOLY AND SPIRITUAL LIFE, IN OPPOSITION TO THE SINFUL AND CARNAL LIFE.

There is therefore now no condemnation to them which are in Christ Jesus, who walk not after the flesh, but after the Spirit.—ROM. viii. 1.

The subjects of the privilege are further characterised by their course—The words repeated ver. 4, with some little variation—They are descriptive both with respect to the non-condemnation, and also to the being in Christ Jesus—Why the apostle singles out this character—What walking imports. The observation raised—Eight things taken notice of from the words: 1. The apostle doth not say, There is no condemnation to them in whom there is no flesh, but to them who walk not after the flesh; 2. He doth not lay his evidence upon particular acts, but upon the general course; 3. Here is not redditio causæ, *but only* descriptio personæ; *4. The description is not laid down in the negative only, but also in the affirmative; 5. The two walkings are supposed to be contrary; 6. First it is being in Christ Jesus, and then it is walking not after the flesh, &c.; 7. There always was and always will be different walkers; 8. The apostle lays it down in the general, and the reason given why he so doth—The parts of the description opened.—What is meant by flesh, and by walking or not walking after the flesh—Flesh considered, 1. More generally: what it is to walk after it in that respect; why the corrupt nature is set forth by flesh; a fivefold account given of that. 2. More particularly; what it is to walk after it in that respect—Of lust, or lusting, the most natural act of the flesh—What is here meant by the Spirit.—What it is to walk after the Spirit—That opened in five particulars—The doctrine confirmed—Applied, 1. By way of information, in three things; 1. That Scripture marks or signs, grounded upon sanctification and holiness, are not under the gospel to be rejected by believers; 2. That the popish calumnies against protestants and the protestant doctrine are causeless and groundless. 3. That there are but few who are in Christ Jesus— Use 2. To examine the walking, whether it be after the flesh, or after the Spirit—Use 3. 1. To dehort from walking after the flesh; several motives to enforce that dehortation; what is to be done for the avoiding of it; 2. To exhort to walking after the Spirit: three motives to that—Use 4. Such as do walk after the Spirit are exhorted, 1. To be very thankful; 2. To walk yet less and less after the flesh, and yet more and more after the Spirit; 3. To take the comfort of this walking; the great discouragement of troubled Christians about it removed.*

THERE is in the whole verse, as you have heard, the privilege, and the description of the persons who have a share in that privilege, they are described,

1. By their union with Christ: 'There is no condemnation *to them which are in Christ Jesus;* this hath been spoken to.

2. By their holy course: they are such who *walk not after the flesh, but after the Spirit;* this I proceed now to speak to.

In the Greek the words run thus: "Οὐδὲν ἄρα νῦν κατάκριμα τοῖς ἐν Χριστῷ Ἰησοῦ, μὴ κατὰ σάρκα περιπατοῦσιν, ἀλλὰ κατὰ πνεῦμα. There is no condemnation to them in Christ Jesus, not walking after the flesh, but after the Spirit. Our translators put in, 'to them *which are* in Christ Jesus, who walk not after,' &c. And they part the *being in Christ*, and the *not walking*, &c., and read them as distinct; but others put them together and make all but one sentence. Thus the Syriac version, cited before. Thus Grotius:[1] 'There is,' saith he, 'no condemnation to them, who by Jesus Christ, or by the gospel, are brought to this, not to go whither carnal affections do carry them, but having obtained the Spirit they constantly obey his motions.' Some difference there is in this double reading, but I will not inquire whether material or not.[2]

The apostle recites these words, ver. 4, with a double variation: 1. There he brings in the relative and joins it with the participle, which here he doth not; for there it is τοις περιπατουσιν, whereas the relative here is joined with ἐν Χριστῷ. 2. Here it is expressed in the third person, there in the first person; 'that the righteousness of the law might be fulfilled *in us*, who walk not after the flesh, but after the Spirit.'

This clause is descriptive of the persons who have an interest or share in that which goes before; and so it is an evidence or description either with respect to the no-condemnation, or to the being in Christ. There is therefore now no condemnation; to whom? why, to them 'who walk not after the flesh, but after the Spirit.' Wherever there is a holy conversation in this life, there shall be no condemnation in the life to come; and so *vice versa*. Or it refers to the other branch immediately foregoing; to them that are in Christ Jesus—who are they? or how may they be known? The apostle thus characteriseth them; they are 'such who walk not after the flesh, but after the Spirit.' A holy, spiritual course is an infallible evidence and inseparable concomitant of union with Christ. These two may reciprocally be predicated each of the other; thus, they who are in Christ walk not after the

flesh, but after the Spirit, and they who thus walk are in Christ. You may take the words in which of these two references you please, but their immediate conjunction seems to carry it for the latter, they being linked and coupled with the τοις ἐν Χριστῷ Ἰησοῦ, them that are in Christ Jesus; but both may very well be taken in. Which way soever we take it, certainly there is, as to both, a restriction and limitation in the words; the non-condemnation and the union belong only to those who walk not after the flesh, &c. Yea, they are conditional, as to the privilege, even to them who are in Christ Jesus. There is no condemnation to such, provided or upon this condition that they walk not after the flesh, but after the Spirit; and so the Arabic version paraphraseth upon them.[1]

The apostle designing to describe such who are freed from condemnation, or such who are in Christ, he pitches upon that evidence and character which is plain and obvious, and not upon that which might have been more dark, obscure, and hard to be understood. He grounds it upon the course of a man's life and conversation; and what may better be known than that? He does not lay it upon election or the secret decree of God, and say, there is no condemnation to them whom God hath chosen before the foundation of the world, Eph. i. 4, to them whom God hath ordained to eternal life, Acts xiii. 48, whose names are written in the book of life, Rev. xiii. 8, though that be a very great truth; but because persons possibly herein might not be so well able to judge of themselves, therefore he saith there is no condemnation to them 'who walk not after the flesh, but after the Spirit.' This walking is a thing that is manifest, and easy to be known. I cannot so easily find out my election, for that lies deep and hid, as I can my conversation, which, in a great measure, is exposed to the view of others, much more to my own. And whereas the apostle had been speaking of union with Christ, that being a great mystery, and men might not so well know how to judge of themselves concerning it; therefore he comes to that which would fully and plainly open it to them. He saith, whoever they be who are in

---

[1] Nulla condemnatio iis qui per Jesum Christum, sive per evangelium, eousque perducti sunt, ut non eant quo carnis affectus rapiunt sine discrimine, sed Spiritum sanctum adepti ejus motibus constanter obsequuntur.—*Grot.*

[2] Unica est in textu Pauli oratio, sed interpres distinxit in duas, &c., quamvis ad sensum non intersit.—*Cajet.*

[1] Non est igitur ulla damnatio eis qui sunt in fide Jesu Christi, dummodo se exerceant, non in his quæ propria sunt carnis, sed in his quæ propria sunt Spiritus.—*Vers. Arab.*

Christ, this is the course they take, 'they walk not after the flesh, but after the Spirit.' They that can find—which upon faithful searching may easily be found—that they do not live the carnal and sensual life, but the holy and spiritual life, though this being in Christ be a great mystery in itself, yet this walking will clear it up to them, so far as their interest in it is concerned, that they are indeed in Christ.

Who walk not after the flesh, but after the Spirit. It is a very usual metaphor in Scripture, to set forth the course of life by walking: 'Enoch walked with God,' &c., Gen. v. 24, *i.e.*—the course of his life was holy. 'I am God all-sufficient; walk before me, and be perfect,' Gen. xvii. 1. Zachariah and Elisabeth were righteous, 'walking in all the commandments and ordinances of God blameless,' Luke i. 6; with very many such places. That which in this verse is called walking after the flesh, in the 12th and 13th verses it is called living after the flesh. I might in several particulars shew you the aptness of this metaphor, how proper it is to set forth the course of life; but I will not stay upon that.

Obs. 2. This branch of the text leads me to that second observation, which I raised from the whole verse at my entrance upon it, namely, That such who are in Christ, and thereby freed from condemnation, this is their property or course, they walk not after the flesh, but after the Spirit.

In the discussing of which, my main work will be to open the twofold walking here mentioned; yet before I fall upon that, let me take notice of seven or eight things which lie very plainly before us in the words.

1. The apostle does not say, There is therefore now no condemnation to them in whom there is no flesh, or to them who have no flesh in them; but he saith, To them who walk not after the flesh. Alas! if the former should be the description and character of justified persons, and of such who are in Christ, then none would be justified or in Christ. There would not be so much as any one person in the world exempted from condemnation, or united to Christ; for there is not a man upon the earth, I except not one, in whom there is not more or less of this flesh, Rom. iii. 10. The very best of saints in their lower state are not wholly freed from it; the most spiritual whilst here below are but mixed, imperfect creatures,

made up partly of flesh, and partly of spirit; so it is in the natural, and so it is in the moral notion also. Paul himself lay under a sad sense of this, as you see Rom. vii. 24, 25. It is most truly said by one upon the words,[1] Perfect sanctification is the rule that is to be laid to the saints in heaven, not to those that are upon the face of the earth. And it is a saying of Bernard, *Velis, nolis, intra fines tuos habitabit Jebusœus;* the poor burdened Christian, whether he will or no, shall have the Jebusite, the flesh, dwelling in him. Men before conversion are entirely flesh, but they are not after conversion entirely spirit. The apostle here saith, 'There is now no condemnation;' but he doth not say, There is now no corruption, no flesh, no concupiscence in the children of God.[2] It shall be so hereafter, but it is not so at present; no, that perfect freedom from all mixtures of flesh is reserved for heaven. And therefore Origen's gloss upon the words is much too high:[3] There is no condemnation to them who walk not after the flesh, but after the Spirit; that is, saith he, to them who are so reformed and rectified, that there is nothing of sin, of any vicious act, or of flesh to be found in them. But who, Christ only excepted, did ever arrive at this pitch and measure of holiness and spiritualness here on earth? There is not only flesh in the best, but that is very stirring, active, and powerful even in them. It hath not only a bare being or existence in them, but a great activity and strength: 'The flesh lusteth against the Spirit,' Gal. v. 17. These two opposite principles, like Rebecca's twins in the womb, are daily contending in the gracious soul each against the other; and this combat will continue till the saint be in heaven. It is well, therefore, that the apostle grounds his description, not upon the not having of flesh, but upon the not walking after the flesh, which are two very different things.[4]

[1] Elton upon the text.

[2] Et ne putares hoc postea futurum, ideo additum est *nunc;* postea expecta illud ut nec concupiscentia sit in te contra quam contendas, quia nec ipsa erit.—*Anselm.*

[3] Nihil absurdius, neque magis falsum dici potest, Origenis in hunc locum expositione, qui hæc de iis dici vult, qui sunt (inquit) ita emendati, ut in seipsis nihil vitiosi operis inveniatur; *i.e.,* de iis, qui, uno excepto Christo, nusquam unquam fuerunt, neque sunt futuri.—*Beza.*

[4] Secundum spiritum ambulare dicit, non qui penitus exue-

2. He doth not lay his evidence upon particular acts, but upon the general course; not upon particular steps, but upon walking, which notes the continued, uniform course of life. In the trial of ourselves, about our union with Christ, or freedom from condemnation, or the truth of grace, we are not to judge so much by single acts, as by the general course. The reason is, because the state, whether present or future, may infallibly be known by the latter, but it cannot be so by the former; for as to some single acts, the bad may be very good, and the good may be very bad. The best sometimes tread awry, and take some steps—too many, God knows—in the way of the flesh; of which Noah's drunkenness, Lot's incest, David's adultery, &c., are too sad proofs; but yet they do not walk after the flesh, because this is not their general course. And on the other hand, the worst may seem to take a step or two now and then in the way of duty, to come up to some particular good acts; Cain sacrificed, Ahab humbled himself, Judas preached Christ, &c., but yet they do not walk after the Spirit; both because they are not thorough and sincere in the good they do, and also because it is not their course to do good. The coarsest web here and there may have some finer threads in it, but they are nothing to the whole piece. Even the blackest Moors have their white teeth; yet the whole body being black, from that they receive their denomination. The application is obvious. That which constitutes this walking after the flesh, or after the Spirit, is a constant, continued, uniform course of life; and therefore this is that which we must judge by. A godly man indeed is, and ought to be, careful as to his particular steps: David prayed, 'Order my steps in thy

rint omnes carnis sensus, ut tota eorum vita præter cœlestem perfectionem nihil redoleat, sed qui in domanda et mortificanda carne sedulo laborant.—*Calvin.* Omnes carnem habent, et violentiam peccati in se sentiunt, tamen modo ei non obediant, sed Spiritu actiones carnis mortificent, nulla est eis condemnatio.—*Pareus.* Attendendum est, non dicere apostolum sublatum in nobis esse peccatum, utpote regeneratis; sed nullam condemnationem in nobis superesse, quia summa et perfectissima naturæ nostræ in Filio Dei integritas, nostra facta per nostram cum ipso per fidem spiritualiter apprehenso unitionem, nos jam nunc licet vix ab illa nativa corruptione liberari cœptos, sistit in sese apud Patris tribunal prorsus integros et securos.—*Beza.* Non dicit, qui non peccant, &c. —Vide *Muscul. in loc.*, p. 120.

word, and let not any iniquity have dominion over me,' Ps. cxix. 133; but that which doth denominate him to be godly, it is that course of godliness which he drives on in his whole life; and this is that which must evidence his being in Christ. Every fleshly act doth not constitute fleshly walking,[1] though even they must be avoided as much as may be, and greatly repented of when they do prevail; but when the conversation is filled up with them, and the heart too delights in them, oh that is to walk after the flesh. And so it is *e contra*, as to walking after the Spirit.

3. This spiritual walking is not *redditio causæ*, but only *descriptio personæ*: or the words are not the assignation of the cause of the privilege, but only the description of the person to whom it belongs. Here is walking not after the flesh, but after the Spirit; how doth this come in? I answer, the apostle doth not assign this as the cause of the non-condemnation, as the popish doctors teach,[2] or of the union with Christ; only he brings it in as a description of the person who is freed from condemnation, and who is in Christ Jesus. He doth not say, 'There is no condemnation to them which are in Christ Jesus, *because* they walk not after the flesh,'[3] &c., but to them who walk not after the flesh, &c, so that this is merely descriptive of the person. The heavenly and spiritual life is

[1] Aliud est peccare etiam actu, aliud in peccato ambulare; *h.e.*, eo delectari, et illi operam dare, eique maxime servire.—*Gomar.* Qui Spiritum sequitur ducem, quamvis interdum a carne quasi pertractus extra viam vestigium ponat, secundum tamen carnem vivere non dicitur.—*Beza.* Non protenus secundum carnem ambulat, qui imprudens aut affectu aliquo abreptus delinquit. Lapsus hic est vel cespitatio quædam, non ambulatio, &c.—*Slichting.* Fidelis seipsum et omnes suas naturales facultates subdidit magisterio Spiritus, et secundum illum ambulat. Sed dum ambulat in obedientia Spiritus, violentis motibus inhabitantis carnis per externa objecta et externas occasiones excitatis, ita obruitur, ut labatur et vincatur, atque ita dictamen carnis aliquando sequatur. Sic fuit cum Noah, &c.—*Streso.*

[2] Causa hæc est cur non sit eis damnationis, &c.—*Tolet.* Ut hæc posteriora causam contineant, cur nihil condemnationis, &c.—*Justin.* Vide *Stapl. Antidot.*, p. 624, 625; *Contzen.* in ver. 2, chap. viii. ad Rom. Quæst. 2.

[3] Non dicit *quia non secundum carnem ambulamus*, sed *qui non secundum*, &c., ne faciat in hac justificationis causa primum esse, quod secundarium est, &c.—*Muscul. in Rom.*, chap. viii. ver. 4, p. 124.

not the cause of justification,[1] only it is the note or evidence of justified persons. And as to the union with Christ, the fruits of the Spirit and the effects of grace and sanctification begun in us, these do not unite us unto Christ, only they declare us to be so united:[2] they are evidences, not causes. Wherever there is justification and the mystical union, there is sanctification and holiness; yet the latter is not the ground of the former: as wherever life is there is sense and motion; yet these are not the cause, but only the sign, evidence, and consequent of life. There is a vast difference betwixt *who* is justified, and *why* or *upon what grounds* he is justified:[3] the holy walker is the justified person, but he is not justified because of the holiness of his walking. No, this causal influence upon justification is wholly founded upon the merits of Christ applied by faith. This is the Protestant doctrine, to which I shall have occasion from these two first verses to speak more than once.

4. The description is laid down, not in the negative only, but in the affirmative also: it is not only *who walk not after the flesh*, but it is also *who walk after the Spirit*. In order to the participation and evidence of the grace of the gospel, it is not enough not to be evil or not to do evil, but there must be being good and doing good.[4] Mere negatives will never justify or save; for a man may go so far upon bare restraining grace; and besides, God requires a great deal more. As when the repentance is right, there is not only a ceasing to do evil, but there is

also a learning to do well, Isa. i. 16; Ps. xxxiv. 14, 'Depart from evil, and do good;' so when the walking is right and evidential of gospel mercy, there is in it both the absence of sin and also the presence of virtue and grace. A religion made up of *nots* is but a half-religion. To be *magis extra vitia quam cum virtutibus*, as the historian describes Galba,[1] rather free from vice than virtuous, in the positive fruits and effects of virtue, this is not sufficient; it is to be as a cake that is baked but on one side, as the metaphor is, Hosea vii. 8. The first is well, but the last is better, as the philosopher tells us.[2] The gospel doth not only teach us to 'deny ungodliness and worldly lusts,' but also to 'live soberly, righteously, godly in this present world,' Tit. ii. 12. And it threatens not only those who bring forth evil fruit, but also those who do not bring forth good fruit, Mat. iii. 10. It is an expression of Theophylact upon the words, Mere abstinence from vice doth not crown, but there must be also the participation of virtue, and of that which is spiritual;'[3] and Chrysostom upon the fourth verse speaks to the same purpose.[4] You have in the description of the text therefore the negative and the positive part of holiness; and these two must go together, for holiness is made up of both: 1 Pet. i. 14, 15, 'As obedient children, not fashioning yourselves according to the former lusts, in your ignorance;' there is the negative part: 'But as he which hath called you is holy, so be ye holy in all manner of conversation;' there is the positive part. As some read the words, this head cannot be grounded upon them; for they only put in the negative, *not walking after the flesh*, leaving out the affirmative, *but after the Spirit*. So the Syriac, so the Vulgate, and the expositors who follow it. But generally the Greek copies have it; and the Syriac too brings it in ver. 4; and why not here as well as there? It is not put in only as a true interpretation, but it is a part of the text itself.[5]

---

[1] Non propter novam aliquam qualitatem quam in nobis operata est gratia Spiritus Sancti, extra condemnationem sumus; sed propter solam gratiam Dei, quam fide Christi apprehendimus.—*Muscul.* Non causa justificationis, sed conditio et nota justificatorum.—*Pareus.* See more Dub., ii. p. 773.

[2] Fructus spiritus sive sanctificationis in nobis inchoatæ effecta, nos non inserunt Christo, sed nos ei insitos esse declarant.—*Beza.*

[3] Sunt cohærentes quidem, sed diversæ questiones, *quare* eximamur omni condemnationi, &c., et *quinam* in Christo eximuntur condemnationi: ii videlicet qui se in Christo esse ex regenerationis fructibus ostendunt.—*Beza.*

[4] Non sat est non ambulare secundum carnem, abstinere a malis, non peccare; sed oportet secundum spiritum ambulare, bene agere: qui enim non bene agit, hoc saltem malum committit quod bonum omittit.—*Corn. Muffus.* Ut intelligamus non sufficere ad evitandam omnem damnationem abstinere a carnalibus, sed oportere proficere in spiritualibus.—*Cajet.*

[1] Tacit. Hist., lib. i. p. 313, ex edit. Lips.

[2] Τῆς ἀρετῆς τὰ καλὰ πράττειν μᾶλλον ἢ τὰ αἰσχρὰ μὴ πράττειν.—*Arist. Eth.*, lib. iv. chap. 1.

[3] Οὐ γὰρ ἡ ἀποχὴ τῆς κακίας στεφανοῖ; ἀλλ' ἡ τῆς ἀρετῆς καὶ τῶν πνευματικῶν μετοχή.—*Theop.*

[4] Δεικνὺς ὅτι οὐ κακῶν ἀπέχεσθαι δεῖ μόνον ἀλλὰ καὶ ἐν ἀγαθῷ κομᾶν.—*Chrysost. in ver. 4, hujus capitis.*

[5] Non est dubium, rectissime tanquam interpretationem

I

5. The apostle here brings in two walkings, and he supposes them to be contrary, for he sets them in opposition one to the other : 'who walk not after the flesh, *but* after the spirit,' implying a contrariety betwixt these two walkings. And so indeed there is : the flesh and spirit are two contrary principles, and therefore the walkings which proceed from these contrary principles must needs be contrary too. They are so contrary that they are incompatible and inconsistent in the same subject; there may be flesh and spirit in the same person, but there cannot be walking after both in the same person. Therefore saith the apostle, Gal. v. 16, 'Walk in the Spirit, and ye shall not fulfil the lusts of the flesh ;' as if he had said, He that doth the one cannot do the other too. He goes on, ver. 17, 'The flesh lusteth against the Spirit, and the Spirit against the flesh, and these two are contrary ;' contrary as to their natures, their originals, and, which suits best with the scope of the apostle in these words, contrary as to their propensions, tendencies, workings, lustings in the subject. Oh they put men upon different courses ! so different, as that, in their proper acceptation, they cannot consist; insomuch that he who walks after the flesh cannot walk after the Spirit; neither can he who walks after the Spirit walk after the flesh. A man cannot move to two contrary points, as east and west, north and south, at the same time ; no more can a man walk heavenward and hell-ward at the same time : now the flesh draws hell-ward and the Spirit draws heaven-ward, so that it is impossible *in sensu composito* to follow both. These are the two opposite masters, which none can serve together, Mat. vi. 24. Friendship with the flesh is enmity to the Spirit ; whoever therefore will be a friend of the flesh he must be an enemy to the Spirit. I allude to James iv. 4.

6. The order of the things here spoken of is to be observed. First it is being in Christ Jesus, and then it is walking not after the flesh but after the Spirit ; this I may briefly take notice of, though it be not the thing here directly intended. There must be union with Christ before there can be spiritual walking ;

addi *secundum spiritum :* qui enim non ambulat secundum carnem, necesse est ut ambulet secundum Spiritum ; medium enim in vita-humana nullum est.—*Contz. in chap.* viii. *ad Rom.,* Qu. 1.

for walking is an act or operation of life. Dead things do not move ; there can be no motion where there is no life. Especially spiritual and holy walking depends upon life ; but now there is no such life in the soul, till, being united to Christ, it be quickened by him. He who is out of Christ cannot live the holy life, for it is union with him that lays the foundation of all holiness in us. The branch must first be ingrafted into the stock, and then it bears fruit ; so here. Therefore saith Christ, John xv. 4, 5, 'Abide in me, and I in you. As the branch cannot bear fruit of itself, except it abide in the vine ; no more can ye, except ye abide in me. I am the vine, ye are the branches : he that abideth in me, and I in him, the same bringeth forth much fruit : for without me ye can do nothing.' Holiness is the evidence of union, so it comes in in the text ; and union is the ground of holiness, so it comes in in this head. Holy walking is an infallible consequent upon being in Christ, and that is a necessary antecedent to holy walking.

7. It is implied that there were in the apostles' time, and so will be to the end of the world, different walkers ; some will walk after the Spirit, and some after the flesh. As it was said with respect to persecution, Gal. iv. 27, 'As then he that was born after the flesh persecuted him that was born after the Spirit, even so it is now :' so it may be said with respect to the different conversations of men ; as then in Paul's days some walked after the Spirit and some after the flesh, even so it is now. So long as the world stands, some will be carnal as well as some spiritual ; the distinction of saints and sinners, of godly and ungodly, of good and bad, will abide whilst this world shall abide. There is the broad way of the flesh, there is the strait way of the Spirit, in both of which some or other will always be walking ; and the misery is, many walk in the broad way of the flesh, when but few walk in the strait way of the Spirit, Mat. vii. 13, 14 ; this may have its thousands, but that hath its ten thousands.

8. The apostle expresses it in the general only, by *not walking after the flesh, but after the Spirit.* He doth not instance in those particulars which are proper either to the one or to the other, (as he doth Gal. v. 17, &c.,) only he speaks in the gross. But all the several particulars are included in the general,

and run into that, as all waters do into the sea. Be it pride, covetousness, uncleanness, &c., all centre in the flesh; so, be it humility, heavenly-mindedness, holy love, &c., all centre in the Spirit, and derive their being, operation, efficacy from the Spirit. Therefore the apostle sets it down thus generally—under the *flesh* comprehending all evil, and under the *Spirit* all good; he sums up all the several sins under the former, and all the several graces under the latter.

These things being premised, I come now to the main point—such as are in Christ Jesus; this is their property or course, they walk not after the flesh but after the Spirit.

This I will, 1. Explain; 2. Prove; 3. Apply.

For explication, I must speak to the parts of the description severally, and shew,

1. What is meant by *flesh*, and by walking or not walking after it.

2. What is meant by *Spirit*, and by walking after it. And as I go along I will take in the doctrine, and particularly bring down to it the several explications of the description, negative and affirmative.

I begin with the first. Which that I may the better clear up, observe that there is a *being* in the flesh, and a *walking* in or after the flesh; which two, though they be never parted, yet they are distinct: the first refers to a man's state, the second to his course. There is a being in the flesh, of which you read Rom. vii. 5, 'For when we *were in the flesh*, the motions of sin, which were by the law, did work in our members to bring forth fruit unto death.' Rom. viii. 8, 9, 'So then they that *are in the flesh* cannot please God. But ye are not *in the flesh*, but in the Spirit,' &c. Then there is a *walking* after the flesh; this inevitably follows upon and suits with the former. They who are in the flesh will certainly walk after the flesh, for the conversation always agrees with the state.

Now it is this walking which the text speaks of. You have the same expression 2 Peter ii. 10, 'But chiefly them that walk after the flesh,' &c. It is also set forth by *living* after the flesh, ver. 12, 13 of this chapter.

If you turn to one scripture you will find the phrase there used in a quite other sense than that in which it is here used; it is 2 Cor. x. 3, 'Though we walk in the flesh, we do not war after the flesh.'

What may be the meaning of *walking in the flesh* in this place? I conceive it notes the apostle's living the same natural life with other men, and also the meanness of his external appearance in the eye of the world.[1] We walk in the flesh; it is as if he had said, we are poor, frail, mortal men as well as others; made with them of the same flesh, living in the same flesh, and encompassed with the same infirmities of flesh; and there is nothing from our outward condition and appearance to gain us any honour, esteem, or success amongst men. Thus, saith the apostle, we 'walk in the flesh.' But then, he adds, 'we do not war after the flesh,' *h.e.*, we do not carry on our work and business, as we are the apostles and ministers of Christ, by the flesh; it is not human power or any fleshly advantage which we go upon; it is only a divine power that helps, assists, and prospers us, by virtue of which God's work in our hands doth and shall go on in spite of all opposition from men and devils. This clearly seems to be the apostle's meaning, for it immediately follows, ver. 4, 'The weapons of our warfare are not fleshly and carnal, but spiritual and mighty through God.' Well! but now walking in the flesh, or after the flesh, here in the text carries a quite other sense along with it.

For the finding out of which we must first inquire what is meant by flesh?

Now as to this inquiry, to give you the several acceptations of the word *flesh* would be both tedious and unnecessary. Expositors generally agree about its sense in this place, only I find some few a little varying in their explications of it. They by flesh here understanding,—at leastwise taking in that sense as well as that which is usual and common,—the Jewish ceremonial law, with the several rites, ceremonies, appurtenances thereof;[2] and so they make the words to run thus: Such are exempted from condemnation who serve the Lord Jesus Christ, not

---

[1] Porro hoc loco Paulus aliter dicit 'ambulare secundum carnem,' quam alibi cum dixit 'in carne ambulantes non secundum carnem militamus;' ibi enim in carne ambulare, est mortalem adhuc vitam ducere; hic autem secundum carnem ambulare, idem est quod militare secundum carnem, *h.e.*, genio ac voluptatibus indulgere, et pravis cupiditatibus morem gerere.—*Justin.*

[2] Fortasse per carnem ceremonias legis intelligit; vultque dicere, Christianos illos a condemnatione exemptos et liberos esse, qui Christo Jesu serviunt, non carnali illa ceremoniarum observatione, sed spirituali.—*Mussus.*

according to the fleshly observation of the ceremonies of the law, but in a spiritual and evangelical manner. Now it is true those may come under this title of flesh, for they are called 'carnal ordinances,' Heb. ix. 10, and Paul, in part speaking of them, calls them flesh over and over, Phil. iii. 3, 4. Yet I conceive they do not fall within the great intendment of our apostle in these words. Our learned annotator,[1] in his paraphrase upon the text, and also upon the following verses, though for the main he opens it as others do, yet he makes it more specially to refer to the Jews as under the law, and to Christians as under the gospel. What there may be of that notion in the words I shall not meddle with, but rather come to the general and unquestionable interpretation of the word *flesh* as it is here used.

Where I will consider it,—1. More generally ; 2. More particularly.

1. More generally. So *flesh* in Scripture commonly notes that corrupt, sinful, depraved, vitiated nature that is in man as he comes into the world. This nature is variously set forth. Sometimes by 'the old man :' so Eph. iv. 22, 'That ye put off concerning the former conversation the old man,' &c. Sometimes by the 'law in the members warring against the law of the mind ;' so Rom. vii. 23. Sometimes by 'sin' in the general : so Rom. vii. 8, 'Sin,' *i.e.*, the corrupt nature, 'taking occasion by the commandment, wrought in me all manner of concupiscence.' Sometimes by 'indwelling sin ;' so Rom. vii. 17. Sometimes by 'the sin which doth so easily beset us ;' so Heb. xii. 1. And sometimes by 'flesh ;' so here, and so in several other places ; John iii. 6, 'That which is begotten of the flesh is flesh ;' John i. 13, 'Born again, not of the will of the flesh, nor of the will of man, but of God ;' Rom. vii. 18, 'I know that in me, that is, in my flesh, dwelleth no good thing ;' and ver. 25, 'So then, with the mind' (he means the renewed and

[1] There is therefore now no obligation lying on a Christian to observe these ceremonies of Moses's law, circumcision, &c., nor consequently danger of damnation to him for that neglect; supposing that he forsake those carnal sins that the circumcised Jews yet indulged themselves in, and perform the evangelical obedience in doing what the mind illuminated by Christ directs us to, that inward true purity, which that circumcision of the flesh was set to signify, that is now required by Christ under the gospel.—*Dr Hammond.*

sanctified nature) 'I serve the law of God ; but with the flesh' (he means the corrupt nature) 'the law of sin.' Gal. v. 17, 'The flesh lusteth against the Spirit,' &c. Once, indeed, in Scripture this corrupt nature is set forth by 'spirit :' James iv. 5, 'The spirit that is in us lusteth to envy ;' but usually it is set forth by 'flesh.' And several reasons might be given of that appellation. I will name some few ; but will not in the least enlarge upon them. The sinful nature in man is styled flesh,

1. Because it is conveyed and propagated as the flesh is.

2. Because it is propagated by the flesh, or by fleshly generation.

3. Because it is very much acted in the flesh, or fleshly part.

4. Because it is nourished, strengthened, and drawn forth by the flesh, or by fleshly objects.

5. Because of its baseness, sordidness, and degeneracy.

And by the most of these things the corrupt nature in man is distinguished from the corrupt nature of the apostate angels. Theirs is set forth by 'spiritual wickedness,' Eph. vi. 12, because it vents itself in spiritual, not in carnal acts, such as are envy, hatred, pride, blasphemy, fretting at God himself, and at his dispensations, &c. But ours is set forth by the flesh, because it is conveyed through the flesh, and acted in the flesh, and drawn forth by the flesh.

Now if you take flesh in this general notion, then to walk after it, it is this : to have the corrupt, sinful nature to be a man's principle and guide ; and not to walk after the flesh, it is not to have that nature to be one's principle and guide. For the text brings in these two, flesh and Spirit, as different and opposite principles and guides ; and therefore they who make flesh their principle and guide, they walk after the flesh ; as they who make the Spirit their principle and guide, they walk after the Spirit. Take men out of Christ, and such as are unregenerate, they 'walk after the flesh.' How ? Why, flesh is their principle and flesh is their guide ; the flesh is that which they act from, there is their principle ; and it is that which they act by, there is their guide. That which is the spring of action, that is the principle ; that which puts upon and orders in action, that is the guide. Now take

Christless men, the persons of whom I am speaking; flesh is the spring and flesh is the guide of their actings. If they think, it is from the corrupt nature; if they speak, it is from the corrupt nature; if they love, it is from the corrupt nature, &c.; and so all along, this is that spring in them which makes all the wheels to move; and this is that guide, too, by which they steer, order, direct their whole course. And it being so, their conversation must needs be a fleshly conversation, or a walking after the flesh, for that is always denominated from, and answerable to, its principle and guide; if it be a fleshly principle and a fleshly guide, it must needs be a fleshly walking. And thus it is with persons out of Christ, they act from the flesh and by the flesh, and so they are said to walk after the flesh. But such who are in Christ, they do not thus walk; corrupt nature is neither their principle nor their guide; there is another nature in them by which they are acted and guided—viz., the Spirit, as I shall shew you by and by when I come to the affirmative part. Expositors, whom to cite would be endless, do variously open and illustrate this walking or not walking after the flesh; but the most do pitch upon that illustration of it which I have given. This concerning flesh in the general consideration of it. But then,

2. Secondly, It may be considered, more particularly, with respect to its proper, radical, most natural and vital act, and that is lust or lusting. This lust is the great act, the most genuine issue of the flesh, —the stream which does most immediately and directly flow from that fountain. The most proper notion of the flesh is to conceive of it as a lusting thing. The apostle therefore, when he was speaking of it, presently he puts down this as its most proper and essential act: ' The flesh *lusteth* against the Spirit,' Gal. v. 17; and Rom. vi. 12, ' Let not sin reign in your mortal bodies, that ye should obey it in the *lusts* thereof.' Sin here is the flesh, and you see how it works. You read of ' the lust of the flesh,' Gal. v. 16; and of ' the lusts of the flesh,' Eph. ii. 3; Rom. xiii. 14; Gal. v. 24. These lusts, I say, are the most proper issue and the most genuine effects of the corrupt nature in man: Rom. vii. 8, ' Sin, taking occasion by the commandment, wrought in me all manner of concupiscence.' (or lust.) Eph. iv. 22, ' That ye put off concerning your former

conversation the old man, which is corrupt according to the deceitful lusts.' Observe how the flesh, the old man, the corrupt nature, and lust or lusts, are usually linked and coupled together.

To apply this now to the walking which I am upon. To walk after the flesh, it is to live and act as under the full power and strength of unmortified lust; it is to indulge, gratify, obey, and comply with the flesh as a lusting thing, or as it puts forth itself in sinful lustings. The apostle, 2 Pet. ii. 10, having spoken of walking after the flesh, immediately he instances in the gratifying of a particular lust, thereby shewing what that walking after the flesh is: ' But chiefly them that walk after the flesh in the lust of uncleanness,' &c. On the other hand, not to walk after the flesh, it is to keep lust under, to beat it down, to resist it, not to give way to it, in whatever form or shape it may assault the soul; to live in the daily mortification of it, not to suffer such hellish fire to smother and burn in the soul; to let it have no harbour or entertainment in the heart, but to thrust it out with abhorrency and detestation, &c. This is not to walk after the flesh.

But this lust being so near to the flesh, so connatural with it, that which issues from it, even as heat and burning doth from the fire, and the walking or not walking after the flesh being so much to be measured by it, I will, therefore, give you some further explication of it.

Lust in Scripture, as it is taken in a bad sense,— for the Spirit hath its lustings as well as the flesh,— sometimes notes the habit, the root itself—viz., the depraved nature; sometimes the act, that cursed fruit which grows upon the forenamed cursed root. The apostle James speaks of it as the mother-sin, if I may so express it: James i. 14, 15, ' Every man is tempted, when he is drawn away of his own lust, and enticed. Then when lust hath conceived, it bringeth forth sin,' &c. Paul speaks of it as the daughter-sin: Rom. vii. 8, ' Sin, taking occasion by the commandment, wrought in me all manner of concupiscence,' or lust. The one considers it as the fountain, the other as the stream. In this latter notion I am to open it; and so it is the bent and propension, the eager, fierce, vehement desire of the soul after fleshly objects or sensual things; for lust, in its strict and primary sense, mainly lies in the δύναμις ἐπιθυμητικὴ, the desiring or concupiscible faculty; therefore ἐπιθυμία is the word by which it is set forth. The soul of man is a desiring, craving, thirsting thing; it is a very mass of desires; and there is no faculty more natural to it, or wherein it puts forth itself more vigorously, than the desiring faculty. Now here is the principal seat of lust, and that which gives it its very being: when the soul is earnestly, vehemently, impetuously carried out after some sensual good, something that will please the fleshly part, if it will but do that, let it be what it will, this is lust. I say it refers principally to the desires, as inordinately set upon and drawn out after fleshly things. Therefore the apostle couples them together, 'the lusts of the flesh' and 'the desires of the flesh,' Eph. ii. 3. And the other apostle, speaking of the inordinate desire of worldly pleasure and profit, he expresseth it by ' the lust of the flesh, and the lust of the eyes,' 1 John ii. 16. I know, if you consider lust habitually and radically, there is more in it than this; for so it is the bent and propension of the soul to whatever is evil, and its aversation from whatever is good. But if you consider it actually and particularly, so fleshly and sensual desires are the main and most proper acts of it.

Here, further, you must distinguish of lust or lusts. Some are more rank and gross, such as lie in the sensitive and fleshly part; others are more refined and secret, such as lie in the upper part of the soul, the reason, mind, and will. You read, 2 Cor. vii. 1, of the 'filthiness of the flesh and spirit,' where the apostle describes the lusts of the lower faculties under the filthiness of the flesh; and the lusts of the higher faculties under the filthiness of the spirit: so Eph. ii. 3, 'Among whom also we all had our conversation in times past, in the lusts of our flesh.' How? Why, in 'fulfilling the desires of the flesh, and of the mind;'[1] so that all lusts do not lie in the desires of the flesh; but there are some which lie in the mind, and in the highest faculties of the soul.

Therefore the apostle in this chapter, ver. 6, speaks of 'the wisdom of the flesh:' where, God willing, we shall shew, against the papists, that the flesh and the lusts thereof are not to be confined to the lower and sensitive part in man, but that they do also extend to the nobler and higher part in him. And, to instance but in one place more, you read, Col. ii. 18, of 'a fleshly mind.' These are the lusts that are situated in the upper region of the soul; but then there are others which reside in that region which is lower; they are called 'fleshly lusts:' 1 Pet. ii. 11, 'I beseech you as strangers and pilgrims, abstain from fleshly lusts,' &c. They are also called 'worldly lusts:' Tit. ii. 12, 'The grace of God, which hath brought salvation, teacheth us to deny ungodliness and worldly lusts.' They are styled fleshly lusts, because they are altogether for the satisfaction of the fleshly and sensual part, or because they reach no further than the fleshly part; and they are styled worldly lusts, because they are drawn forth by worldly objects, or because they draw out a man in eager propensions after worldly things.

Now to bring this down to the business in hand. The flesh being thus particularly considered, so to walk after it, it is this: for a person to be under the regency and dominion of lust, in whatever part or faculty it may reside or exert itself, so that he acts in a ready, willing, full subjection to it and compliance with it. It is to be under the unbroken strength of sensual propensions, and to follow them in the course of life. More closely, it is to be carried out with vehemency of desire after some fleshly good, so as wholly to be swallowed up in pursuits after it and delights in it, even to the slighting, undervaluing, total neglect of what is truly and spiritually good; this is lust, by which whoever is thus acted he is a walker after the flesh; for wherever lust commands and is obeyed, in one respect or another, there it is walking after the flesh. Oh, doth it bear sway in any of you, that you obey and act by it in heart and life? The dark side of the character is towards you—you walk after the flesh, and not after the Spirit.

Saints in Christ Jesus do not thus walk; the flesh may sometimes be stirring and lusting in them, but they dare not hearken or give way to it; they repel its evil motions and propensions; do not follow or steer their course by the commands and counsels thereof; and they are not inordinately desirous of sensual things. In general, they do not, they dare not,

---

[1] Non corporis tantum, h.e., partis ratione carentis, sed etiam διανοίας opera esse vult omnes ejusmodi cupiditates, quas ex sola animæ parte, quæ censetur rationis expers, produci Platonici prohibent.—*Salmas. in Epictet.*, p. 117.

' obey sin in the lusts thereof,' Rom. vi. 12, or fall in with the cursed suggestions and solicitations of the flesh to that which is evil : ' They that are Christ's have crucified the flesh with the affections and lusts thereof,' Gal. v. 24. But let this suffice for the opening of the negative, *who walk not after the flesh ;* much more might be added, but that which follows will give more light about it.

Before I enter upon the applying of this, let me proceed to the opening of the positive or affirmative part, Such as are in Christ Jesus do not walk after the flesh. What then do they walk after ? Why, after the Spirit.

Quest. The question here to be answered is, What is it to walk after the Spirit ? or when and how may persons be said to walk after the Spirit ?

Ans. For the better answering of which question, we must first inquire what we are to understand by the *Spirit ;* for that being cleared, the walking after it will be the more evident.

Here also, not to insist upon the several significations and senses of the word *spirit*, in this place it must be taken either personally for the Spirit of God, the third person in the sacred Trinity ; or habitually for grace in us—the divine nature implanted in the soul in the work of regeneration ; or it must be understood of both. You find grace in Scripture set forth by spirit : John iii. 6, ' What is born of the flesh is flesh ; and what is born of the Spirit is spirit ;' where the latter spirit must be understood of the heavenly and renewed nature. Jude 19, the apostle speaks of some who were ' sensual, having not the Spirit,' which though it be chiefly to be understood of the spirit of grace, of which these persons were destitute, yet it takes in the grace of the Spirit too : so Gal. v. 17, ' The flesh lusteth against the Spirit, and the Spirit against the flesh ;' *i.e.*, the corrupt nature and the renewed and sanctified nature do reciprocally oppose and contend each against the other. So some interpret that of our Saviour, Mat. xxvi. 41, ' The spirit is willing, but the flesh is weak ;' but I cannot lay so great a stress upon this place for this import of the word. And as the sinful nature may very well be set forth by flesh, so grace or the sanctified nature may as well be set forth by this appellation of spirit. And that for these reasons :—

1. Because it is of the Spirit of God, it being immediately infused and created by him.

2. Because it is principally seated in the spirit— the soul of man.

3. Because it is a spiritual thing, and vents itself most in spiritual acts.

4. Because of the nobleness and excellency of it.

Now you will ask, In which of these senses is spirit here to be taken ? I answer, It is best to take in both ; namely, both the spirit of grace, and also the grace of the Spirit, or the renewed spirit in the creature. The thing here spoken of is applicable to both, and therefore why should we limit it to one ?

The word *spirit* throughout in this chapter is generally taken in the personal notion, for the Holy Ghost himself ; and no sooner had the apostle mentioned *spirit* in this verse, but presently in the second verse he speaks of the Spirit as considered personally : ' The law of the Spirit of life,' &c. ; he means the living and quickening Spirit of God : therefore to be sure this sense must be taken in. And grace habitually considered, or the renewed nature in the soul, that too may have its place here very properly ; for spirit being set in opposition to the flesh, which is the depraved nature, it must have some reference to that other nature which is opposite to this ; and interpreters generally so open it.[1] It is best therefore, I say, to take in both these notions of the word *spirit*.

The natural and philosophical notion of *flesh* and *spirit*, is *body* and *soul ;* though yet some philosophers sometimes speak of them in a somewhat different and more restrained sense. For *spirit* they make to be, as the whole soul in general, so sometimes only the highest part of the soul, viz., the intellectual and discursive faculty ; in compliance with whom, or rather with the Jewish writers[2] in their *Nephesh, Ruach,* and *Nesama ;* Paul seems so to use the word, ' I pray God your whole spirit and soul and body be preserved blameless,' &c., 1 Thes. v. 23.

---

[1] *Spiritus* sumitur pro animo regenerato per Spiritum.— *Pareus.* Per *Spiritum* intelligit novitatem naturæ, effectam per regenerationem Spiritus, vitiositate naturali emendata.— *Piscat.* Vocat *carnem* universam hominis naturam, ut quæ corrupta exciderit a pristina dignitate, cui opponitur *Spiritus,* eadem, viz., instaurata per Spiritum Dei.—*Beza.*

[2] *Vide* Drusium in 1 Thes. v. 23.

And as to flesh, that they make to be not only the body itself, but also the sensitive soul; that part which is void of, and sets itself against, reason, and refuses to be subject to the laws and dictates of the rational faculty. Thus the Platonists and Stoics do frequently make use of the word σάρξ, *flesh;*[1] only they differ about the diversity of the faculty, where it is seated, from the reasonable faculty. Now though flesh and spirit in the text contain in them something higher than what this philosophical notion of them reaches, yet it is not altogether to be rejected; and therefore in this discourse it will accordingly be made use of.

Now I come to answer the question, What is it to walk after the Spirit?

In general, it is to walk in the way of the Spirit. The flesh hath its way, and the Spirit hath its way: the way of the flesh is sin, wickedness, rebellion against God, &c.; the way of the Spirit is holiness, obedience, righteousness, &c. He then that walks in the way of sin, he walks after the flesh; and he that walks in the way of holiness, he walks after the Spirit; for the walking is according to the way that men go in.

So again, to walk after the Spirit, it is to bring forth the fruits of the Spirit. The Spirit hath its fruits, such as love, joy, &c., Gal. v. 22; and the flesh hath its fruits, several of which are recited Gal. v. 19; where the fruits of the Spirit fill up the life, there it is walking after the Spirit, and so, *e contra*, as to the flesh. In short, as to the general opening of it, to walk after the Spirit it is to live the holy and the spiritual life; it is to have God's Spirit, and to act in compliance with and obedience to it; and it is, too, to have the divine nature in the soul, to follow the motions and dictates of that nature, and to live in the exercise of the several graces which grow upon that root. I could very much enlarge upon this general description, but I shall choose rather to explain the thing particularly under these five heads:

To walk after the Spirit, it is,

1. To have the Spirit to be the principle of acting.

2. To have the Spirit to be the guide of life, and to follow its guidance.

[1] For this see Salmas. in Epict. and Simplic., p. 116, &c.

3. To have those affections which are proper to, and suit with, the Spirit.

4. To live under, and to close with, holy inclinations and propensions to what is good.

5. To act for spiritual ends.

Here I instance in more particulars than I did in the opening of the walking after the flesh, but they are as applicable to that as to this; and they being contraries, the one will illustrate the other.

1. To walk after the Spirit, it is for a person to be acted by the Spirit, or to act from the Spirit, as his principle.

That is the principle, as hath been said, which acts a man, or from which he acts; when the Spirit is this to a person, so that he lives and acts by its vital, quickening agency and working in him, then he may be said to walk after, or according to, the Spirit. You heard before, a man walks after the flesh when the flesh is his principle, and so he walks after the Spirit when the Spirit is his principle.

This is applicable to the Spirit in both of the respects which have been mentioned. As, 1. Take it personally; the Holy Spirit is in believers as the spring and principle of their obedience and holy actings. In a sober sense—all others I dread and detest—that which acts and animates the saints in their course, it is God's own Spirit; he is not barely in them, but he is in them as a lively and active principle, to actuate their graces, to quicken and excite them to all holy and spiritual acts. This is a part of that walking in the Spirit which you read of Gal. v. 25, 'If we live in the Spirit, let us also walk in the Spirit;' as if the apostle had said, If the Spirit hath been a quickening Spirit to us, and hath wrought a supernatural life in us, then let us walk in the Spirit; that is, let us all along live and act by this Spirit as our great principle. Such as are in Christ they pray, mortify sin, are heavenly-minded, love God, deny themselves, &c.; now in all these *acti agunt,* they act as they are acted from above; the Spirit, on his part, stirs them up to what is good, and gives out his influences to them in what is good; and they, on their part, fall in with his exciting and assisting grace, in opposition to all the interposures of the flesh; and so they walk after the Spirit.

Then, 2. Take the Spirit habitually, for grace or

the sanctified nature in the heart; this is a secondary or subordinate principle—the *principium quod*, as the former is *principium quo*—from which spiritual acts do proceed. You have the apostle speaking to this double principle: Gal. ii. 20, 'I am crucified with Christ, nevertheless I live: yet not I, but Christ liveth in me,' there is the supreme and first principle; 'and the life which I now live in the flesh, I live by the faith of the Son of God,' there is the subordinate and secondary principle. Faith and love, those two great branches of that general root which I am upon, make all the several wheels in a gracious heart to move; that which is done in the life comes from these in the heart: the spiritual walker doth all from these two graces, as his abiding principles; he 'lives by the faith of the Son of God,' and 'the love of Christ constrains him,' 2 Cor. v. 14.

Now he who is acted by this twofold principle, he is the walker after the Spirit. Pray observe, as there are two public heads to which all men in the world do belong, the first and the second Adam; and as there are two common states under which all are and shall be comprehended—at present it is the state of nature or the state of grace, and hereafter it is the state of blessedness or the state of misery; so there are also two common principles by which all men in the world are acted, viz., the flesh and the Spirit. They that have flesh for their principle, they walk after the flesh; they that have the Spirit for their principle, they walk after the Spirit. So far forth as our principle is divine and spiritual, so far forth is our walking divine and spiritual; for that is always answerable to its principle. Oh, are you acted in your course by an inward principle? is that the Spirit of God and grace in the heart? is all done by and from this Spirit? this is to walk after the Spirit.

2. To walk after the Spirit, it is to have the Spirit for the guide of life, and to follow its guidance. Where there is a fleshly guide, there it is fleshly walking; where there is a spiritual guide, there it is spiritual walking; for the course is denominated, as from the principle, so from the guide or rule. And indeed the latter is, in part, included in the former; for whatever is the principle, that carries in it too the nature and use of a guide, inasmuch as the action is always steered and ordered by

and according to the principle; but yet I consider them here as distinct. I say, when the Spirit is the guide, and followed as the guide, this is to walk after the Spirit. As I may be said to walk after one when he goes before me, shews me my way, and I follow him step by step—where he goes I go, as he bids me move so I move; so it is in reference to this walking after the Spirit. Thus it is very commonly opened: *Ambulare secundum spiritum, quid? est sequi in omnibus nostris actionibus ductum Spiritus sancti;* What is it to walk after the Spirit? it is for a man in all his actions and motions to follow the Spirit's conduct and guidance.

And here too, 1. God's Spirit is a guiding spirit; he leads, directs the soul to and in the way of holiness. I say in the way of holiness, for this pure and holy Spirit always leads to that which is pure and holy, never to that which is sinful, his excitations and guidance being evermore agreeable to his nature: Ps. cxliii. 10, 'Teach me to do thy will, for thou art my God.' How doth God teach or guide a man to this? it follows, 'thy Spirit is good,' good in itself, and good as a guide to us, 'lead me unto the land of uprightness.' Now when this Spirit is the *dux viæ*, a person's leader and guide, and he follows its guidance in his conversation, then his walking is right and good. It is set forth, ver. 14 of this chapter, by being 'led by the Spirit:' 'As many as are led by the Spirit of God, are the sons of God.' You read, Ezek. i. 20, of the living creatures, 'Whithersoever the Spirit was to go, they went; thither was their spirit to go.' And you read of the people of Israel, Num. ix. 16, 'As the cloud moved, they moved; as that stood, they stood,' &c. Thus it is with the spiritual walker; he is one who fetches his guidance from the unerring Spirit, and who regulates all his motions according to the Spirit's direction: what the Spirit bids him do, that he doth, what the Spirit forbids him to do, that he doth not; he moves or stands still as this great guide directs him. Let not any mistake me, as though I did in this assert or advance any enthusiasms, immediate inspirations or directions from the Spirit, without or besides, much less against, the written word. No, God willing, I shall shew the danger and vanity of such pretences when I come to the 14th verse. I am for the Spirit and the word conjunctly;[1] he guides, but it is by and in the word, and the guidance of the word is the guidance of the Spirit. He that squares his life by the counsels, commands, prohibitions of the word, he truly walks after the Spirit.

Again, 2. There is the sanctified nature, which is a guide also, though inferior to the former : Gal. vi. 15, 16, 'In Christ Jesus neither circumcision availeth anything, nor uncircumcision, but a new creature. And as many as walk according to this rule, peace be on them, and mercy, and upon the Israel of God.' The new creature, or grace, is a rule ; it is not only *regula regulata*, but, in some sense, also *regula regulans*. For, in subordination to the word, it shews a man what is good, and directs him to and in the doing of it ; what is evil, and how he is to shun it ; it leads him to those things which are suitable to itself, as to love God, to hate sin, &c. He that lives in compliance with this guide, he walks not after the flesh, but after the Spirit.

3. To walk after the Spirit, it is to have spiritual and heavenly affections, such as are proper to, and suit with, the divine Spirit. The Spirit himself, wherever he dwells, and the spiritual life, wherever it is wrought in the soul, are always attended with spiritual affections ; and indeed much of the influence and efficacy of both is exerted in the spiritualising of the affections. These are always suited to the nature ; the fleshly nature hath fleshly affections, and the divine nature hath divine and spiritual affections ; so that the walking after the Spirit, or after the flesh, is very much to be judged of and measured by them. Doth the poor creature love God ? is his delight and joy in spiritual things ? have they his most strong and vehement desires? this is to walk after the Spirit. Our apostle himself here opens the twofold walking by this : ver. 5, 'They that are after the flesh (or who walk after the flesh) mind the things of the flesh ; but they that are after the Spirit (or who walk after the Spirit) mind the things of the Spirit.' This *minding* the things of the flesh or of the Spirit is not to be limited either to the inward acts of the mind, in the thoughts only,

or to the outward endeavours, but it includes and takes in the affections also. Here, then, is the difference. Such as are after the flesh, they mind, *i.e.*, they savour and relish, the things of the flesh ; their affections are wholly set upon and drawn out after fleshly objects ; their love, delight, desires, run out altogether upon these things. But they that are after the Spirit, they mind the things of the Spirit ; their affections are fixed upon spiritual objects ; they run in the right channel, are placed upon God and Christ ; they are, in a word, pure and heavenly. The flesh hath carnal affections, and indeed it puts forth itself very much, if not most, in them ; therefore you have it coupled with them : Gal. v. 24, 'They that are Christ's have crucified the flesh with the *affections* and lusts.' On the other hand, the Spirit hath its affections too, but they are as contrary to the former as heaven is to hell. Pray observe what the apostle subjoins : ver. 25, 'If we live in the Spirit, let us walk in the Spirit.' This walking in the Spirit (for it will bear this sense as well as that which I mentioned before) is brought in by way of opposition to the affections and lusts of the flesh ; it is as if he had said, If we live in the Spirit, then let us not give way to those sordid affections which are of the flesh, and suit with it ; but let our affections be such as may suit with the Holy Spirit, and with that divine life which he hath wrought in us. Where any thus walk in the Spirit, they walk after the Spirit.

4. To walk after the Spirit, it is to live under and to close with secret inclinations and propensions in the soul to what is holy and good ; so that the bent, bias, tendency, and workings of the heart are for what is good, and against what is evil. These two contrary principles have always contrary propensions, they incline and draw contrary ways ; the good spirit and the sanctified nature are all for obedience, close walking with God, the exercise of the several graces, &c. ; there is their tendency. The evil spirit without, and the evil nature within, (I put them together, for they agree too well in that which I am upon,) they are altogether for sin ; they perpetually incline and urge to pride, passion, envy, covetousness, uncleanness, &c. ; there is their tendency. And these different propensions are so far in the saints themselves, that they are the ground of that civil war and conflict which they in this life feel so much of. They are

---

[1] Ambulare secundum spiritum est omnes actiones, qualescunque sunt, dirigere et instituere secundum dictamen Spiritus sancti in verbo, et in conscientia nostra secundum verbum loquentis.—*Streso.*

set forth by the lustings of the flesh against the Spirit, and of the Spirit against the flesh, Gal. v. 17. Now, according to the strength and prevalency of these two principles, and the closure of the heart with them in their different propensions and inclinations, so is the walking either after the flesh or after the Spirit. Let me not be misunderstood. I do not speak of the mere inexistence or inbeing of these contrary propensions, no, nor of the prevalency of them in some particular acts; for both of these may be in a child of God, and in one who walks after the Spirit, as you see in Paul himself, Rom. vii. 23, 25. I only speak of evil propensions in their full strength; when they are entire, unmixed, unbroken, do prevail as to the general course; when persons upon all occasions side with, and wholly give up themselves to them; where it is so, doubtless there it is walking after the flesh. But now, when these are resisted, and the soul doth rather fall in with the good inclinations of the good Spirit, so as to cherish, obey, comply with, and act according to them, then it is walking after the Spirit.

5. This walking after the Spirit consists in the spiritualness and supernaturalness of the aims and ends; for the Spirit of God, wherever he is, always raises and elevates a man in his ends; and the spiritual life too, wherever it is, always is attended with spiritual ends, namely, the glorifying of God as the supreme and ultimate end, and the saving of the soul as the subordinate end. Wherever there is a supernatural principle, there will also be a supernatural end, for the end is always adequate and answerable to the principle; as it cannot be higher, so it will not be lower. Men that are nothing but corrupt nature and flesh, their aims are answerable to their state; all that they drive at is the flesh, or self under some fleshly consideration; as they act altogether *from* self, (some base fleshly principle,) so they act altogether *for* self, (some base fleshly end;) the great end, the glory of God, is nothing to them; but flesh is all in all. Here is no halting in the case, this is downright walking after the flesh. But they that are spirit, and have the Spirit, oh they look higher; the mark which they aim at, with the greatest steadiness they can, it is God's glory. You see it in Paul: Phil. i. 21, 'To me to live is Christ, and to die is gain.' Christ was the matter of his life and the

end of his life, for these two things make the living Christ. Paul was all for this, as he there speaks, ver. 20, that Christ might be greatened or magnified by him. And he, speaking elsewhere of the saints in general, he thus sets them forth, 'None of us liveth to himself, and no man dieth to himself; for whether we live, we live to the Lord; and whether we die, we die to the Lord: whether we live or die, we are the Lord's,' Rom. xiv. 7, 8. Now, so far forth as any in their course come up to these high and spiritual ends, so far, and no farther, may they be said to walk after the Spirit. Flesh always centres in flesh; but grace causes a man to aspire and aim at the glory of God. The spiritual walker makes this his chief end, and looks upon all other things but as means to this; and herein lies the very essence of holiness, or of holy walking. Would any of you fully understand yourselves, so as to be able to pass decisive judgment about this? Let your inquiry run out here, What are our ends? what is it that we mainly design and intend in our course? As every man's end hereafter, happy or miserable, shall be according to his walking here; so every man's walking here is either spiritual or carnal, according to his end. Our Lord tells us, John vii. 18, 'He that speaketh of himself, seeketh his own glory; but he that seeketh his glory that sent him, the same is true, and no unrighteousness is in him.' So here, he that liveth to himself and of himself, he seeketh himself; but he that seeketh the glory of God, the same is a true walker after the Spirit.

Thus have I shewn in these five particulars what it is to walk after the Spirit; concerning which, it is not necessary that I should vouch an exact difference betwixt them; I give them but as so many illustrations of the thing, and so you must take them. From all that hath been spoken, it appears that this twofold walking is not to be limited to mere external and visible acts in the life, but it lies very much in the inward, secret acts of the heart. There is the principle, the affections, the propensions, the ends, and these are the things which do constitute the walking either fleshly or spiritual; but more of this in the use. I have done with the opening of the description in both its parts, not 'walking after the flesh, but after the Spirit,' which was my business in the explicatory part.

I go on to the second thing, the confirmation of the point, where it will be a very easy thing to prove that this is the property, and deservedly the character of such who are in Christ Jesus, they 'walk not after the flesh, but after the Spirit.' All Christ's mystical members are spiritual walkers; this is that very life which such do live, that very course which such do follow: 1 John iii. 6, 'Whosoever abideth in him, sinneth not;' that is, he doth not live in a course of sin, which is all one with not walking after the flesh: Gal. v. 24, 'They that are Christ's have crucified the flesh with the affections and lusts.' No sooner is a person brought into Christ, but sin and the flesh are crucified and dead in that person; so that there is no more walking after it: 1 Cor. i. 30, 'But of him are ye in Christ Jesus, who of God is made unto us wisdom, righteousness, sanctification, and redemption.' Here the apostle sets down what Christ is to believers, but first he sets down the ground of all, namely, the mystical union; and then he adds, to such who are in him he is not only righteousness, to free them from a guilty state, but he is also sanctification, to free them from a carnal, and to bring them over to a holy course. Wherever, then, there is this union, there is and must be also this spiritual, heavenly, and holy conversation, as the inseparable fruit and consequent of sanctification.

I shall not need to spend much time in the proof of it; two arguments, I conceive, may suffice for that.

1. The being in Christ Jesus, or the union with him, is brought about, as hath been opened, by the Spirit, and by faith; now both of these necessarily infer this walking after the Spirit. The Holy Spirit being in a person as the bond of his union with Christ, wherever he is he will be a spring and principle of holiness; he will not lie hid in the soul, but it shall be seen in the heavenliness and spiritualness of the conversation that he is there; wherever he comes, he comes as a commanding, overpowering guide and principle, working with great efficacy upon the sinner as to his walking: Ezek. xxxvi. 37, 'I will put my Spirit within you;' what then? 'and cause you to walk in my statutes, and ye shall keep my judgments and do them;' mark it, saith God, 'I will cause you,' &c. The way of God in his working upon the sinner is not merely by moral suasion, which leaves the will undetermined and pendulous, but it is by effectual inclination and overpowering; so that here is a complication of several things in the argument, which make it very strong. As, 1. It is the Spirit which unites to Christ; 2. This uniting Spirit is always an active, working Spirit; 3. The matter of his working is sanctification and universal holiness; 4. The manner of his working is effectual and irresistible. Now put all these considerations together, and it will most undeniably follow, that such who are in Christ, they shall walk not after the flesh, but after the Spirit.

Moreover, it is the very Spirit of Christ himself by which believers are united to him; so that the same spirit which was in him is in them also, though in a different measure. Now hereupon, where there is the same spirit, there will be the same course or walking; and therefore, as Christ was holy, so will they be holy too; and as Christ walked not after the flesh, but after the spirit, so will they walk also. If he indeed should take a person and immediately make him one with himself, possibly the certainty of this spiritual walking would not be so evident; but the union being carried on mediately by the Holy Spirit, that Spirit will have an infallible and powerful influence upon the way and walk of him who is united to Christ.

Besides this, there is the other bond, viz., faith; and that too, doth naturally operate and tend to the furtherance of that conversation which I am proving. For it is of a purifying nature; it first 'purifies the heart,' Acts xv. 9, and then consequently the several acts which issue and flow from the heart. Faith is the justifying grace, but it is a sanctifying grace too, Acts xxvi. 18; it justifies before God, but it also sanctifies before men. It is not only a bare instrument or condition of justification, but it is likewise an operative and influential grace upon sanctification. It is the lively faith which knits to Christ; and being so, it will shew its liveliness by its vigorous promoting of the holiness and spiritualness of the believer's course; insomuch that 'as the body without the spirit is dead, so faith' without this spiritual walking 'is dead also,' James ii. 26. It would be a very easy thing to descend to particulars, therein to shew the special methods in which the Spirit of God, and faith under it, do work for the keeping down of the walking after the flesh, and the promoting of the walking after the Spirit, in the distinct and several considerations proper to each of them; but I fear I am already too prolix.

2. The second argument is taken from Christ's tenderness of his honour. He will advance the creature, but he will do it in such a way as that he may secure and advance his own glory. Now, would this be for the honour of Christ, to take persons into so near a conjunction with himself, and yet let them live the carnal and sensual life? to walk just as others do who are afar off from him? Eph. ii. 13. To be in Christ, and yet to live in sin, immersed in flesh and sensuality, oh what dishonour would this reflect upon the head, if his members should thus walk! Christ will have his followers to differ from others, yea, and from themselves too; therefore all that are in him shall be 'new creatures,' 2 Cor. v. 17; and from the change in the heart there shall be a change in the life and walking also. He can join the greatest sinners to himself, but he will first prepare and adapt them for such a union, by making them other persons, and so causing them to live at another rate than they did before. Where there is nearness, nay, oneness, there, as you have heard, shall be likeness in a holy course. He that will not have us 'take the members of Christ and make them the members of an harlot,' 1 Cor. vi. 15, will not himself take the members of harlots—I mean great and gross sinners—they so continuing, and make them the members of himself. It shall be known by the goodness of men's walking that they belong to a good head; for Christ's honour is highly concerned therein. And hence it is that such who are in Christ shall walk not after the flesh, but after the Spirit. Thus you have the doctrine explained and confirmed, and I am now to fall upon the application of it.

Use 1. By way of information first, three things it informs us of.

1. That believers, even in the times and under the dispensation of the gospel, are not to lay aside or cast off Scripture marks, signs, or evidences grounded upon sanctification and holiness, in order to the finding out of their spiritual state and condition. For wherefore doth the Spirit of God here thus characterise persons 'in Christ' *which walk not after the flesh, but after the Spirit*, but for this end, that by this character or mark men may know whether they be indeed in Christ or not; the like you find in very many other places. The Antinomians do not approve of this doctrine; they will not hear of any evidences or signs of this or that privilege, fetched from sanctification or holiness, or anything inherent in ourselves; an opinion weak and false, yea, directly contrary to the tenor of the word. How great a part of the Bible might be blotted out, as altogether useless, if what they affirm herein was true. Read but the first Epistle of John, you will find it throughout to be characteristical or evidential of men's state from the fruits and effects of sanctification; the places therein are so many and so common, that I neither well can, nor do I in the least need to make any particular rehearsal of them. It is strange that men cannot distinguish betwixt grounds as to the thing, and evidences as to the person. Far be it from us to make sanctification or holy walking the grounds of our union with Christ, or of our justification; yet they are the evidences by which we come to know that we are in Christ and justified by him. And the question is not what the Spirit of God can do, or possibly sometimes may do, viz., whether he doth not in an immediate manner, without the making use of these signs, reveal to a believer his union with Christ, and interest in gospel-blessings; but the question is, What is the ordinary method of the Spirit in the witnessing and clearing up of these things to a soul? And surely that is first by the witnessing of faith, sincerity, holiness of life, and then by witnessing to them and upon them. And a Christian cannot ordinarily expect assurance of his union with Christ, or of any other thing, but in this mediate way. Very much might be spoken about this, but I think it is not now so necessary as sometimes it hath been, and divers have largely wrote upon it;[1] therefore I will pass it over.

2. Secondly, It shews us how groundless and injurious those high calumnies and sharp invectives are which some Romanists, in their writings upon this text, are pleased to cast upon and let fly against

---

[1] See Rutherf. Survey of Antinom., par. 2, cap. 55, p. 81, &c. Binning, who hath some sermons upon Rom. viii. lately published, speaks something to it, p. 23, &c.

protestants and their doctrine. Because the apostle here saith, that such who are freed from condemnation, and in Jesus Christ, do not walk after the flesh, but after the Spirit, how do some popish expositors from hence take occasion to oppose, traduce, revile, censure, and strangely misrepresent the protestant doctrine, and the worthy assertors of it! Amongst others, with what acrimony and virulency doth Stapleton and Contzen,[1] two who had τὰ στόματα πρὸς λοιδορίαν ἔυλυτα, as Libanius speaks of some, here fall upon Calvin, Beza, Pareus, &c., as if they did oppose, nay, quite nullify, the strict, holy, and spiritual life; and instead thereof, by their opinions did encourage and promote the carnal and fleshly life. I instance in these only, because they are the persons who in their expositions upon the text in hand, are pleased so freely to spit their venom upon this account; but it is that reproach and scandal which occurs very frequently in the body of their polemic writers. Amongst whom, what more common than to tell the world that protestants make holiness, good works, &c., to be unnecessary? that they are only for faith and imputed righteousness, that their principles tend to looseness and profaneness, and what not? Now did we not too well know the spirit which acts these adversaries, it would make us to stand and wonder that opinions so sound, so agreeable to the word of truth, as those are which in these matters the protestants hold in opposition to Rome, should yet be so maliciously reflected upon; that scandals so undeserved, so often answered, should yet be continued; that men's passions and censures should be so high and sharp, where their grounds and reasons are so low. How much hath been spoken and written, over and over again, for the vindicating of opinions and persons

from these imputations, for the due and right stating of things, and yet it is all one! Dissenters calumniated before, and so they will do still; protestantism was blackened and branded before, and so it shall be still.

I will not insist upon the making any apology or defence for this or that person, in what they have said by way of exposition upon the text; for they need no such thing, and, as to that for which they are censured, they say nothing but what the body of protestants hold. And for the forenamed authors, Calvin, &c., do they not upon this very place say that which might be enough to all ingenuous men to obviate these calumnies?[1] But let this pass. Give me leave only in the general to vindicate our faith in this matter, and to shew that what we believe herein is not at all repugnant to this, or any other scripture.

For do we hold that believers are exempted from condemnation, and shall most certainly be saved—upon their being in Christ—though they live a sinful, carnal, wicked life? How often have our opposers been told that we detest and abhor such an opinion? We say, indeed, that sanctification, holiness, or walking after the Spirit are not the meritorious causes of non-condemnation—that honour we give to the alone merits of our Saviour—yet withal we say, that whoever hath an interest in such blessedness he is a sanctified person, and he must and shall live a holy life. Is not this enough? as much as what the word will bear us out in? Can we not be for walking after the Spirit unless we make it to be a cause of our justification? Or can we not hold

---

[1] Ubi ergo umbraculum Calvinianum cum sola fide, et aliquo pietatis studio pene inefficaci? Stapl. Antidot., p. 624. *Vide plura*, pp. 625, 626. Contzen in quæst. 3, p. 308. An sectarii bona opera per suam expositionem condemnanda doceant? Et in v. 2, quæst. 2, p. 310. Si Phineez aliquis adulterum Calvinianum in ipsa libidine configat, cœlo eum continuo inserit, justus est enim, et nulla est ei condemnatio, quamvis secundum carnem cum occideretur ambularet. Justin. Magnopere falli necesse est hæreticos, qui *manere in Christo* nihil aliud esse putant, quam aliquem sibi certo polliceri, Christi merita sibi fuisse communicata, atque adeo peccatis omnibus expiatis se esse justum.

[1] Tria simul conjungit apostolus, imperfectionem qua semper laborant fideles, Dei indulgentiam in ea condonanda, regenerationem Spiritus: atque hoc quidem postremum, ne quis vana opinione se lactet, ac si liberatus esset a maledictione, carni suæ interim secure indulgens. Ut ergo frustra blanditur, &c.—*Calvin*. Non satis est Christum ore profiteri, oportet fide per opera efficaci Christo adhærere, quod fit non carnis sed Spiritus ductum sequendo in vita. Observa secundo quod connexam esse docet justificationis et sanctificationis gratiam, adeo ut divelli nequeant, ut frustra de priore glorietur, qui posteriorem non habeat. Qui igitur habenas laxant carni, testantur se in Christo non esse, &c. Hinc refutatur trita papistarum calumnia, &c. Atqui docemus cum apostolo, non esse in Christo nisi qui secundum Spiritum ambulant: qui carni indulgent eos inanem fidem profiteri, &c.—*Pareus*. Sunt cohærentes quidem, &c.—*Beza*.

imputed righteousness, but we must deny inherent righteousness? Are these two inconsistent? Our adversaries asperse us as if we denied the latter, which we do not; but what may we say of them who do most certainly deny the former? To go on. Do not we set inherent righteousness as high as they,—bate but perfection and merit—the first of which would make it impossible in this life, as the other would derogate from the freeness of God's grace, and the fulness of Christ's merit. And we appeal to the world, Do our censurers with their principles live more holily than protestants with theirs? We wish we could see it. Nay, take the whole model and platform of their doctrine and of ours, and let the world judge which doth most tend to the promoting of a strict and holy conversation.[1] Indeed, if we give way to the flesh, and walk after the flesh, we are to be blamed for our practices; but the principles of our religion are strict, holy, and good. In short, we are for the same things which they contend for, and that, too, in the highest measures and degrees, so far as the infirmities of the present state will admit of, but not upon the same grounds. We are for the spiritual life as the fruit and evidence of the union, and as always attending the person who is in Christ and shall not be condemned; but we dare not make it to be the meritorious ground, or to have any causal influence upon the one or the other. If this will not satisfy, let our revilers revile on!

3. If this be the way and course of such who are in Christ, that they walk not after the flesh, but after the Spirit, it informs us then that there are but few who are in Christ, or who have any interest in the mystical union. I would not straiten or narrow the grace of God or the happiness of the creature, further than the word itself doth; but, on the other hand, I must not make them wider than that doth. The most, it is to be feared, are out of Christ, because the most do walk after the flesh; it is but here and there some few who walk after the Spirit. Instead of walking not after the flesh, but after the Spirit, the generality of men walk after the flesh, and not after the Spirit. They are 'in the flesh,' (there is their state,) and they 'walk after the flesh,'

[1] See Dr Stillingfleet of the Idolatry of the Church of Rome, chap. iii. p. 178.

(there is their course.) Oh that this was not as evident as the light of the noonday! This flesh, as you have heard, is either the corrupt nature in the general, or more particularly it is the corrupt nature venting itself in and about fleshly and sensual things. Now, in both respects, how do fleshly walkers abound! As to the first, what an unholy, sinful life do the most live! How doth the depraved nature break forth and shew itself in their whole course? this is that which acts them all along, by which they steer and order their conversation. And as to the second, look upon the greatest number of men, how sensual are they? They lie tumbling and wallowing in the mire of lust; are even immersed and swallowed up in fleshly things, minding nothing so much as the pleasing of the flesh. Go to them at their tables, there is gluttony, excess in eating and drinking; they pamper the body, whilst they starve the soul. Mind them in their pursuits; it is some fleshly good they mainly drive at—some fleshly interest by which they steer their course. What do they most consult but the flesh's ease and interest? Oh, that is the thing which they 'make provision for,' that they may 'fulfil the lust thereof,' which the apostle so expressly forbids! Rom. xiii. 14. Their forecasts, projects, contrivances are for the flesh; yea, all their thoughts are employed as so many caterers or purveyors for their sensual lusts. Is not this walking after the flesh? And is not this, more or less, the walk of the most? Alas! as to that walking after the Spirit which hath been opened, how few are there that know anything of it! The generality are wholly strangers to it, understanding the angelical life in heaven, as well as the spiritual holy life of saints here upon earth. You can scarce make them believe that there is such a life, so far are they from the living of it. Thus it is with the multitude; and is not this, then, too clear an evidence, too full a demonstration, of the paucity of such as are in Christ? Oh that we could bewail and lament it! What more plain than that such who are in Christ do walk, not after the flesh, but after the Spirit? And what more plain too, than that the body of men do walk after the flesh, and not after the Spirit? Sirs, let us not flatter and think too well of ourselves. We talk of faith, make our boast of the gospel, glory in our baptism, lay a great stress upon our church privileges, when yet, notwithstanding all this, we are mere flesh-pleasers; our conversations are carnal and fleshly.[1] Doth not this proclaim us to be yet out of Christ?

Use 2. Secondly, Let me desire you to examine what your walking is, whether it be after the flesh or after the Spirit. Is spiritual walking the property of all who are in Christ? Must this evidence your union with him? How then doth it concern you all to judge aright about it! Here are two sorts of walkers, and every man in the world comes under the one or the other, for these two divide the world betwixt them. Now, where are you? what is your course? which of these walkings do you come under? what do you follow, flesh or spirit? I told you at the first this is a thing which may be known. The apostle doth not lay the evidence upon something that is abstruse and hard to be understood, but upon that which is easy to be found out. Surely with a little diligence every person may know what his walking is. I entreat you, therefore, to urge this home upon yourselves. Oh let every one say, How do I walk? what kind of life do I live— holy or sinful, spiritual or carnal? Brethren! your freedom from condemnation depends upon your union with Christ; will you not find out that? Then your union must be known by the holiness of your walking, and will you not understand yourselves about this also? Oh what a blessed thing is it when a man is clear in this! so that he can frame a syllogism upon it thus: He that walks not after the flesh, but after the Spirit, he is in Christ; but I, through grace, am one who walk not after the flesh, but after the Spirit, therefore I am in Christ. This is a good bottom to build assurance upon; these premises will bear the weight of such a conclusion. Be sure you take up with nothing short of this. It is only the spiritual life which must assure of the mystical union: 1 John i. 6, 'If we say that we have fellowship with him,

---

[1] *Ut eos omnes intelligamus esse exclusos, qui fidem et evangelium jactitant, cum interim volutentur in crassissimis vitiis, &c.—P. Mart. Addo quod fortasse Paulus non tam spectasse videtur vim baptismi, qua omnis macula penitus abstergitur, sed ad mores ac vitam eorum, qui, Christi gratia percepta, omnes vitæ suæ rationes ad Christi legem exigunt, atque ita pravæ cupiditati non obsequuntur.—Justinian.*

and walk in darkness, we lie, and do not the truth.' 1 John ii. 4-6 'He that saith, I know him, and keepeth not his commandments, is a liar, and the truth is not in him. But whoso keepeth his word, in him verily is the love of God perfected; hereby know we that we are in him. He that saith he abideth in him ought himself also to walk, even as he walked.' Faith, indeed, is the bond of the union, but holiness of heart and life is the mark or evidence of it. And it is the walking which makes the Christian; it is not external profession, the being of such or such a party, some good religious talking, but it is the course of life which is the distinguishing character betwixt person and person. Oh that God would direct every one of you to pass righteous judgment upon himself concerning this!

I need not add anything to what hath been laid down in order to the helping of you in this trial. The walking after the flesh and after the Spirit have been opened, and by the particulars which make up each of them you may be able to judge of yourselves. Pray go over them in your own thoughts again and again, and say, Is the flesh or the Spirit our principle, our guide? what are our affections? do we savour the things of the flesh or of the Spirit? what are our secret and strongest propensions? are our ends fleshly or spiritual? I say, go over these things again and again, and there is no question of it, but that serious and frequent examination in a little time will fully clear up the thing to you.

Only, to prevent mistakes, let me tell you there is a twofold walking after the flesh—one more gross and manifest, the other more close and more indiscernible. The first is when the flesh breaks forth and openly vents itself in external and bodily lusts, such as adultery, uncleanness, drunkenness, gluttony, &c.; this is 'the filthiness of the flesh,' 2 Cor. vii. 1. The second is when the flesh more secretly vents itself in internal heart-lusts, such as are kept in and lie smothering in the soul, as pride, self-love, envy, covetousness, &c.; this is 'the filthiness of the Spirit.' The apostle gives a catalogue of the actings of the flesh in both of these respects, Gal. v. 19, 20, &c. Now here is the mistake of men; they confine walking after the flesh to the first of these—the latter being little regarded by them—so that if they do not live in whoredom, gross intemperance, open profaneness, brutish sensuality, they think all is well; whereas they may be free from these gross practices, and yet be walkers after the flesh. The corrupt nature hath other outlets besides these, and there may be sins (ulcers) within, when they do not externally shew themselves. Oh be not deceived! You are not possibly so and so vicious in the outward conversation, but if there be within in the heart malice, hatred, envy, uncharitableness, self-exalting, inordinate affections to the world, covetousness, these are enough to bring you within the compass of walking after the flesh. Devils you will grant are bad enough; [1] it is because of their envy, pride, &c., for the grosser sins of the flesh they are not liable to them. Augustine proves [2] that the stoics (that strict sect of philosophers), were as guilty of this upon their inward unmortified corruptions, as the Epicureans themselves, a more debauched and sensual sort of men, if they be not wronged; for as to Epicurus himself, Laertius, Gassendus, &c., give a quite other character of him. [3] Do I see one living a brutish life, wallowing in his filthy lusts, laying the reins upon the neck of his corruptions? He is drunk, defiles his body, lives in open wickedness, &c. I am sure this man walks after the flesh; these are 'the works of the flesh which are manifest,' Gal. v. 19. Every eye sees and every tongue cries shame upon these courses. Ah! but there is another who is free from these scandalous courses; yet he is worldly, revengeful, envious, proud, haughty, under the power of earthly affections, full of evil desires: this man now is a walker after the flesh as well as the former, though not in so gross a manner. Therefore do not please yourselves upon your being kept from the notorious and external eruptions of the corrupt nature, if yet inward and more refined corruptions have their full power and strength over you. Oh, how many persons of a civil, unblameable, conversation, nay, how many fair professing hypocrites (though no adulterers, no drunkards, &c.) will yet be judged at the great day to be walkers after

the flesh! Pray look inward; any one allowed, cherished, unmortified lust in the heart will spoil your walking before God, though before men it may seem to be blameless, yea, very spiritual.

Use 3. Thirdly, The main use will be for counsel.

1. To dehort from walking after the flesh.

2. To exhort to walk after the Spirit.

1. First, Do not walk after the flesh. Particularly, let not flesh be your principle to act you in your course; for what can be expected but evil practices from so evil a principle? 'Do men gather grapes of thorns, or figs of thistles?' Mat. vii. 16. How impure must those streams be which flow from so impure a fountain? How bitter must that fruit be which grows upon so bitter a root? So also let not flesh be your guide, that you should choose to be ordered and directed by it. Will you choose or follow a blind guide? 'If the blind lead the blind, both fall into the ditch,' Mat. xv. 14; or will you follow a guide that will lead you to hell? God forbid! When you have the good Spirit of God, and the good word of God, to lead you, will you rather live under the leading and conduct of the flesh? Oh, have as little to do with its guidance as ever you can! It is not a thing that you must walk after, but rather fly from; for if you follow it, it will certainly carry you to those rocks and precipices which will endanger the dashing of you in pieces for ever.

I know the best will not be wholly freed from this flesh whilst they are here; but let not any tamely give up themselves to it, so as to be subject and obedient to it, or to walk after it: 'Let not sin reign in your mortal body, that you should obey it in the lusts thereof.' Avoid it, I beseech you, in all the parts and limbs of it, for it is all naught. There are 'the wills of the flesh,' τὰ θελήματα τῆς σάρκος, Eph. ii. 3; the 'affections or passions of the flesh,' τὰ παθήματα τῆς σάρκος, Gal. v. 24; Rom. vii. 5; 'the works of the flesh,' τὰ ἔργα τῆς σάρκος, Gal. v. 19; all these flow from one and the same spring, only they are several channels in which it runs. Now, I say, avoid it in all; as it works in the soul by its wills and affections, as it works in the body by its grosser lusts, do not in anything comply with it or walk after it; we must be always mortifying, never allowedly gratifying, this cursed flesh.

[1] Invidientia vitium diabolicum, quo solus diabolus reus est, &c. Non enim dicitur diabolo ut damnetur, adulterium commisisti, furtum fecisti &c., sed homini stanti lapsus invidisti. —*Aug. de. Disc. Chri.*, cap. 1.

[2] De Civitate Dei. lib. xiv. cap. 2.

[3] Against whom, see Dr Meric Casaubon of Incredulity, par. 1, p. 202, &c.

L

To enforce the dehortation one would think the motive in the text should be strong enough. If you do not walk after the flesh, then you are in Christ; and if you be in Christ you will not walk after the flesh, for such do never so walk. But besides this, there are some other motives which have a great force and efficacy in them.

(1.) Let it be considered that this walking after the flesh is directly contrary to your baptismal dedication and obligation. When you passed under that blessed ordinance, did you not then dedicate yourselves to the Lord? Have you not since owned and acknowledged that dedication? And shall persons so dedicated to the Lord walk after the flesh? That would be like Belshazzar's making of himself drunk, even out of the golden vessels which were dedicated to the service of God in the temple, Dan. v. 2-4. There is upon your baptismal dedication a sacredness upon your souls and bodies; and yet shall they be made common, and prostituted to the service of sin and lust? This is not only to rescind, retract, null your dedication, but even to profane that which was consecrated to holy uses and ends. When you were baptized, did you not then stipulate and covenant to renounce the flesh, as well as the world and the devil? And notwithstanding this, will you yet walk after it? What a high breach of covenant would that be! And shall any break covenant with God and prosper? Ezek. xvii. 15. If after baptism you will be flesh-pleasers and flesh-followers, where will that 'answer of a good conscience' be, which the apostle speaks of? 1 Pet. iii. 21. How will you be said to be 'baptized into Christ's death,' Rom. vi. 3, if the flesh yet live in you, and you in it? And what a poor insignificative thing is the outward washing, if heart and life continue under flesh pollutions! What will the sprinkling of baptismal water profit him who lies wallowing in fleshly lusts?[1] Oh think much of your solemn engagement in baptism, and surely you will not be so obsequious and pliable to the motions of the flesh as hitherto you

[1] Δείκνυσι σοι, ὅτι οὐκ ἀρκεῖ τὸ λουτρὸν ἡμῖν εἰς σωτηρίαν ἐὰν μὴ κάτα τὸ λουτρὸν ἄξιον ἐπιδειξώμεθα βίον της δωρεᾶς.—Chrysost. in v. 4 hujus capitis. Restringitur generalis propositio, contra eos qui in baptismo omnia collocabant, satis esse Christo per baptismum insitum esse, recte credere, in ecclesia versari, sacramenta participare: vitam Christanam dignam etiam requiri docet, vitam spiritualem non carnalem.—Contz.

have been! How ill doth the Christian mark and title agree with a pagan life!

(2.) Secondly, I would desire you to consider what the flesh is. He that knows it, and hath right apprehensions of it, certainly will not walk after it. In general, let it promise or pretend what it will, it is an enemy; and shall we cherish an enemy in our bosom, nay, let him have the command and guidance of us?

First, It is God's enemy; yea, his inveterate, implacable, irreconcilable enemy; the sinner may be reconciled to God, but sin itself, the flesh, the corrupt nature, never can. It is observable, ver. 7, 'The wisdom of the flesh'—the carnal mind we read it—' is enmity against God.' The apostle sets it forth in the abstract to note the greatness of the enmity; it is more than if he had said it is an enemy against God, for enemies may, but enmities cannot, be reconciled. And he speaks of the best of the flesh too, the very wisdom of the flesh is enmity against God; and see what a full proof he gives of it, for, saith he, 'it is not subject to the law of God, neither indeed can be.' Oh how evil a thing is this flesh! Now, shall that be your principle and guide which is God's enemy? Will you agree with that which is at such variance with God? and be subject to that which neither is nor can be subject to the law of God?

Then, secondly, It is your enemy too; ay, and the very worst enemy you have in all the world. For was it not for this, all your other enemies could never hurt you;[1] the devil and the world without do all their mischief to the souls by the flesh within. Christ not having any of it was impenetrable against all the fiery darts of Satan: John xiv. 30, 'The prince of this world cometh and hath nothing in me.' We cannot say so, he hath a corrupt nature in us, and that he works upon and endangers us by. This flesh is the womb where all is conceived and formed, the anvil upon which all is wrought; it is the false Judas that betrays us, the close enemy within that is ready upon all occasions to open the gates to the besieger. Was it not for this morbus mentis, the morsus dentis could never hurt us.

And besides this relative consideration of the

[1] Vide Najanz., tom. ii. in Carm., p. 93, describing the mischievous effects of the flesh.

flesh, as it gives advantage to our other grand adversaries, it is in itself a very dangerous enemy. Partly in respect of its malice; it carries on desperate aims and designs against the sinner; it is full of mischievous intentions, and those of a high nature too; it aims at nothing below the ruin of the precious soul. The apostle, speaking of one part of its working, viz., by 'fleshly lusts,' tells you that those 'war against the soul,' 1 Pet. ii. 11—how? why, not only as they would take away the soul's order, beauty, strength, peace, comfort, &c., but as they strike at the very life and happiness of the soul. And the same is designed by this malicious flesh in all its workings, for they all tend to the everlasting destruction of the soul. Oh what a pernicious enemy is the flesh! Partly also in respect of its subtlety; for, which makes it the more formidable, as it is a malicious and desperate, so it is a cunning and subtle enemy. How craftily doth it insinuate itself into us in order to the carrying on of its mischievous designs! how cunningly, by its blandishments and allurements, doth it entice us unto evil! James i. 14, 'Every man is tempted, when he is drawn away of his own lust,' there is the force and power of it, 'and enticed,' there is the fraud and cunning of it. How finely doth it represent some taking good to men in order to the alluring of them, whilst it slily conceals the evil which should deter them! It shews the bait, but hides the hooks; holds forth the milk, but keeps close the hammer and the nail; presents the apple, but conceals the death. Here is the flesh's subtlety, and oh how many poor souls are undone by it! Their eye is upon the good which the flesh promises, they not at all regarding the evil which indeed it designs, as you read of Amasa, 2 Sam. xx. 8, 9. Joab took Amasa by the beard with the right hand to kiss him, 'but Amasa took no heed to the sword that was in Joab's hand.' Oh what a cunning, deceiving enemy is the flesh! Rom. vii. 11, 'Sin taking occasion by the commandment deceived me.' Eph. iv. 22, 'That ye put off concerning the former conversation the old man, which is corrupt according to the deceitful lusts;' in the Greek it is τὰς ἐπιθυμίας τῆς ἀπάτης, lusts of deceit, they are made up of deceit, there is nothing but mere deceit in them. The apostle, Tit. iii. 3, says they were 'deceived;' how?

'serving divers lusts and pleasures;' whoever serves sin shall find at last he was sadly deceived by it. Upon the whole, then, is flesh a thing to be walked after? Will you trust yourselves, your souls, your everlasting concerns in the hands of an enemy, of such an enemy?

3. Thirdly, Consider what this walking after the flesh is.

(1.) It is sordid walking. It carries in it a great abasement of the human nature; man is degraded by it, and divested of that glory and excellency which God and nature hath put upon him. To be under the power of the flesh and the lusts thereof, especially such as are gross and lie in the sensual part, how doth this turn the man into a very brute! What is the difference, I pray you, between a brute and a man who lives a brutish life? Only this, that of the two the man is the worst, for he hath reason and religion to direct him to a better course, which the brute hath not. Is it the shape only which makes the man, without suitable actings to the nature?[1] To walk after the flesh? how base and unworthy is this for such a creature as man! who was once made after God's own image, and who yet hath a noble, spiritual, and immortal soul. Oh how is this soul depressed in its native excellencies by a carnal course! by this it is made an underling to the body, and, to make use of that proverbial allusion, the prince is forced to go on foot while the beggar rides on horseback. Oh that flesh-followers would often think of this! This walking is not only below the Christian, but the man too; he that was made by God like Nebuchadnezzar when upon the throne, he, by living after the flesh, makes himself like Nebuchadnezzar when grazing among the beasts, Dan. iv. 32, 33. Pray, sirs, know yourselves, consider your original, whose workmanship you are,[2] that you are soul as well as body,[3] how highly your maker hath advanced you, and scorn to

---

[1] Τί οὖν ἔλεγες ὅτι ἄνθρωπός ἐστι; μὴ γὰρ ἐκ ψιλῆς μορφῆς κρίνεταιτῶν ὄντων ἕκαστον.—Arrian. Epict., lib. iv. cap. 5, p. 391.

[2] Εἰ μὲν τὸ ἄγαλμα ἦς τοῦ Φειδίου, ἢ Ἀθηνᾶ, &c.—Arrian. Epict., lib. ii. cap. 8, p. 188.

[3] Ἀλλ' ἐπειδὴ δύο ταῦτα ἐν τῇ γενέσει ἡμῶν ἐγκαταμέμικται, τὸ σῶμα μὲν κοινὸν πρὸς τὰ ζῶα, ὁ λόγος δὲ καὶ ἡ γνώμη κοινὸν πρὸς τοὺς θεούς· ἄλλοι μὲν ἐπὶ τάυτην ἀποκλίνουσι τὴν συγγίνειαν τὴν ἀτυχῆ καὶ νεκράν, ὀλίγοι σέ τινες ἐπὶ τὴν θείαν καὶ μακαρίαν.—Idem., lib. i. cap. 3, p. 91.

live below yourselves. It is happy pride which makes men to disdain a sordid life.

(2.) It is foolish walking; that which is the fruit of ignorance, and only suits with the state of ignorance: 1 Pet. i. 14, 'Not fashioning yourselves according to the former lusts, in your ignorance.' It is both the effect and the evidence of ignorance; if men were not strangely blinded and besotted they would never carry it towards the flesh as they do. But here is the misery of it; first the flesh blinds and besots sinners, puts out their eyes, as the Philistines did Samson's, Judges xvi. 21, and then they are at its beck and dispose. Ah sirs! have ye no knowledge, no wisdom? are you under total darkness and gross infatuation? are ye so foolish that you do not know what the flesh is, and whither it leads? and yet will you walk after it? when there is a spiritual, heavenly, holy course revealed to you, will you yet choose that which is opposite thereunto? will you prefer the conduct of the flesh before the conduct of the Spirit? Oh, stupendous folly, most woeful infatuation! The apostle, describing the natural state, saith, 'For we ourselves also were sometimes foolish,' (ἀνόητοι, without any understanding or intellective faculty, wherein,) 'serving divers lusts and pleasures;' oh that is to be foolish indeed! And he elsewhere, speaking of lusts themselves, calls them too ἀνοήτους καὶ βλαβερὰς 'foolish and hurtful,' 1 Tim. vi. 9. Flesh-followers are apt to admire their own wisdom, but they fall under that sad character, Rom. i. 20, 'Professing themselves to be wise, they became fools.'

(3.) It is groundless and unreasonable walking. Bate but the sinner's pleasing himself, which is a pitiful reason, and what reason hath he to serve or gratify the flesh? what can it plead for any subjection or obedience to it? This our apostle here takes notice of: ver. 12, 'We are debtors not to the flesh, to live after the flesh.' We are debtors indeed to God every way; to him we owe our love, obedience, &c., our all; but what do we owe the flesh? what hath it done or suffered for us? hath it redeemed us? was it crucified for us? surely no! Justice and gratitude call upon us to live to God and Christ, but for the flesh we are under no obligation at all to live to it, rather the quite contrary. Why should we pay where we owe nothing, and not pay where we owe our all? Were we but so just and honest as to pay our debts, sure I am we should walk after the Spirit and not after the flesh.

(4.) It is uncomfortable walking: Isa. lvii. 20, 21, 'The wicked are like the troubled sea, when it cannot rest, whose waters cast up mire and dirt. There is no peace, saith my God, to the wicked.' Isa. lix. 8, 'They have made them crooked paths: whosoever goeth therein shall not have peace.' Sin and comfort cannot go together; he loses the one who closes with the other. A wicked life, saith Plato,[1] is not only a sordid, but a more unpleasant life than that which is virtuous; the bare light of nature led divers of the ancient moralists to assert this over and over.[2] And sinners may put the best face upon it, but they find this to be true by their own sad experience; they feel it, their consciences plainly tell them of it every day, that there is little true joy in a sinful, sensual course. Oh, the sad gripes of conscience which they meet with in the way of sin! which though they endeavour to smother, yet they pursue and vex them from time to time. But suppose the way of the flesh at present be not uncomfortable, to be sure in the final issue it will be so: when the sensualist and ungodly wretch shall see death making its near approaches to him, when conscience shall force him to take a review of his ill-spent life, when he shall be called to stand before the tribunal of his judge; I say, how will it be then? will it be joy and comfort? no, but instead thereof inexpressible anguish and horror of spirit. Oh let not the flesh deceive you! 'its pleasures are but for a season,' Heb. xi. 25; its delights are soon over and gone;[3] and then that which was honey in the mouth turns into gall and wormwood in the belly. Poor deluded creatures think to take their fill of it, but in a little time God finds them out, sets home their sin and folly, gives them the prospect of a dreadful eternity; and what follows? first, hell is in their souls, and then in a little time their souls are in hell.

[1] Ἀναγκαῖον τον ἄδικον βίον, οὐ μόνον αἴχιω καὶ μοχθηρότερον ἀλλὰ καὶ ἀηδέστερον τῇ ἀληθείᾳ τοῦ δικαίου τε εἶναι καὶ ὁσίου βίου.—Plato de Leg., lib. ii. p. 663.

[2] Ποῦ τὸ ἡδὺ της κακίας ἐστιν, &c.—Plutarch. Περὶ ἀρετῆς καὶ κακίας, p. 101. Τὸ ἡδέως ζῆν ἄνευ τοῦ καλῶς ἀνυπάρκτον ἐστίν.—Idem in Tract., &c., p. 1087.

[3] Delectatio occidit et praeteriit, vulneravit te transivit, miserum fecit et abiit, infelicem reddidit et reliquit.—August. de Temp., Serm. 3.

And therefore, as you desire to be kept from this misery, and to have peace and comfort in life and death, see that you abandon the flesh so as not to walk after it.

(5.) It is walking which ends in eternal perdition. Oh that this might be believed before it be felt! Sirs, whom will you believe? sin and the flesh, which are made up of lies, and do their business by lies, or the God of truth and the word of truth? He tells you therein, 'to be carnally minded is death,' Rom. viii. 6. 'If ye live after the flesh, ye shall die,' Rom. viii. 13. 'He that soweth to the flesh, shall of the flesh reap corruption,' Gal. vi. 8. 'There is no condemnation to them which walk not after the flesh but after the Spirit;' then there is condemnation to them who walk after the flesh, &c. 'Sin, when it is finished, it brings forth death,' James i. 15; with many such scriptures. Now shall not this deter you from a fleshly conversation? if this will not, what will? Solomon, speaking of the strange woman, tells us, 'her house inclineth unto death, and her paths to the dead,' Prov. ii. 18; just so it is with fleshly walking. Nothing more certain than that every man's end shall be according to his course: as he sows, so shall he reap, Gal. vi. 7. Now there are two very different ends, and two very different courses; there is heaven and hell, two very different ends; and there is walking after the flesh and after the Spirit, two very different courses. If you fall in with the former, that will most certainly lead you to hell; if with the latter, that will as certainly lead you to heaven. Which of these courses now will you choose? Condemnation is as sure to them who walk after the flesh, as no-condemnation is to them who walk after the Spirit. So much for the third motive.

4. Fourthly, Let me add but one dissuasive more, and that is the death of Christ. What a consideration is this to take men off from a carnal life! Oh when this flesh begins to stir and pirk up itself, you will do well, in order to the suppressing of it, to fix your thoughts upon your dying Redeemer. Say, When my Saviour hath died for sin, shall I live in sin? when he was 'manifested on purpose to destroy the works of the flesh and of the devil,' 1 John iii. 8, shall I yet walk after them? was the sinless flesh in Christ crucified, and shall the sinful flesh in me be cherished? You read of the crucifixion of the flesh, Gal. v. 24; we should be for nothing short of that, for no better usage doth it deserve from us. When Pilate asked the enraged Jews against our blessed Lord, 'What shall I then do with Jesus which is called Christ?' they all said unto him, 'Let him be crucified;' and when he a little hung off from this cruelty, 'What evil hath he done?' they cried out the more, saying, 'Let him be crucified,' Mat. xxvii. 22, 23. This was not so much their sin in being so cruel to the Lord of glory, but it is as much your duty to deal thus revengefully with the flesh. Oh let all cry out in the height of their hatred against it, Let it be crucified! Why, but what evil hath it done? nay, rather ask what evil hath it not done? therefore cry out the more, Let it be crucified. And indeed the crucifixion of our natural flesh in Christ, without the crucifixion of moral and sinful flesh in ourselves, will not profit us. Paul saith he was 'crucified with Christ,' Gal. ii. 20. How? why, in a spiritual and mystical sense, so as to be dead to the flesh, and so as to live the spiritual life. And the apostle lays it upon this, 1 Pet. iv. 1, 2, 'Forasmuch then as Christ hath suffered for us in the flesh, arm yourselves likewise with the same mind: for he that hath suffered in the flesh hath ceased from sin; that he no longer should live the rest of his time in the flesh to the lusts of men, but to the will of God.' It is a scripture somewhat dark; but the strength of it lies thus, 'Christ hath suffered for us,' and we, in an analogical sense, must be ready to suffer too,—this is the same mind here spoken of,—and Christ having suffered 'hath ceased from sin,' *h.e.*, so as to die for sin no more; so, saith the apostle, you too in your own persons must so die to sin as no longer to live in it. This is the being 'planted into the likeness of Christ's death,' Rom. vi. 5, and you find the apostle there in that chapter, from this very topic, the death of Christ, earnestly dissuading persons from walking after the flesh. I have done with the motives to enforce the dehortation.

Before I go off from this head, something must be hinted by way of direction. What is to be done, some may say, that we may no longer walk after the flesh? I answer:

1. Get out of the flesh. For being in the flesh is always attended with walking after the flesh; as the state is always according to the course, so the course is always according to the state. If you be in the fleshly state, your conversation will be a fleshly conversation. Such as the man is, such are the principles; and such as the principles are, such will the practices be also. Therefore get out of the state of nature—in which the flesh rules and carries a man whither it pleases—and get into Christ: persons out of Christ are all flesh, and thereupon will be wholly followers of the flesh. Spiritual walking discovers the union; but first the union is the ground of spiritual walking .That will certainly follow upon being in Christ, but being in Christ must necessarily antecede it. Till thou beest ingrafted into Christ, no good fruit can grow upon thee. He that is flesh must needs live and act flesh.

2. Get the Spirit, and walk after the Spirit. It is the divine Spirit, and the divine nature from that Spirit, which must dethrone and break the power of sinning and sinful nature. Till the Holy Spirit and grace come into the heart, the flesh lords an d domineers in the life (as you will hear more fully when I come to the second verse.) The apostle joins together *sensual* and *not having the Spirit*, Jude 19, where the latter clause is not only a further description of the persons spoken of, but it is also the assignation of the cause or reason of their being sensual, viz., because they had not the Spirit. Till the mighty Spirit of God comes into the soul, by saving illumination and overpowering influences, to say efficaciously to a man, 'This is the way, walk therein,' Isa. xxx. 21, there may be convictions, purposes, resolutions to the contrary; yet still there will be, one way or other, walking after the flesh. And so for grace; no sooner doth this take possession but the walking is altered, which it never is before to any purpose: Prov. ii. 10, 'When wisdom entereth into the heart, &c., discretion shall preserve thee, &c., to deliver thee from the way of the evil man, &c., who leave the paths of uprightness to walk in the ways of darkness, who rejoice to do evil,' &c. Your way to be rid of the flesh is to get the Spirit; set a thousand arguments, the most effectual considerations imaginable, before the sinner, to draw him off from this fleshly walking, till

the regenerating, sanctifying Spirit take hold of him, they are all weak and ineffective,

I add, Walk after the Spirit. Every man will be walking; there is no standing still. All will be in motion so long as they are *in via;* and every man's walking will be in one of these two ways, either after the flesh or after the Spirit, for *non datur tertium;* and these being contrary, do mutually exclude each the other. He that walks after the flesh cannot, *in sensu composito*, walk after the Spirit; and he that walks after the Spirit cannot walk after the flesh. Therefore, Gal. v. 16, 'Walk in the Spirit, and ye shall not fulfil the lusts of the flesh:' the reason, then, upon which this direction is grounded is strong and evident. And let me tell you, principles you will and must have, some or other, which, if they be not good, they will be bad. And so as to guides, affections, propensions, ends, these will be in every reasonable soul from one cause or another: so that if you be not spiritual, you will be carnal; for one of these two you must be, as both you cannot be. Oh, let it be the former, that it may not be the latter!

3. Take heed of particular, allowed fleshly acts, for they make way for that general course which you are to shun. Acts produce habits, as well as habits do produce acts. Particular acts of sin, especially if allowed and repeated, end in a course of sin. If you gratify the flesh in some things, it will grow upon you, as sad experience proves. The gangrene or leprosy at the first begins with some particular member, but if it be let alone, in a little time it diffuses itself over the wholy body; and so it is here as to sin, 'A little leaven leavens the whole lump.' It is true, as hath been observed, the apostle here fixes his character upon the course, and not upon single acts; but he that allows himself in them will not stay there—in time he will fall into a wicked and fleshly course.

4. Timely suppress the first risings of the flesh; it gains by delays. Oh as soon as the corrupt nature begins to stir and shew itself, see that you fall upon it presently, make speedy and vigorous resistance to it. If you give the enemy time, he will grow stronger, and the conquest will be the more difficult.[1] You read, James i. 15, of the conceiving of lust, 'When

[1] *Ῥᾷον ἀπὸ ἀρχῆς μὴ ἐνδοῦναι κακίαν*, &c.—Vide *Stobœum in Eclog.*, Serm. iii. p. 9.

lust hath conceived it bringeth forth sin.' Now sin must be taken at the first conception; as soon as the temptation offers itself, and begins to allure and tickle by something that it presents, so that the heart inclines to a closure with it, now fall on presently and parley no longer. This brat of Babylon must be dashed in pieces in its very infancy; it is good to kill the cockatrice in the very egg, to quench the fire at the first smotherings of it within, or else it will quickly flame forth in the life, even to the making the conversation carnal. Be very watchful over the initial suggestions of the flesh, and fall upon the timely exercise of mortification; upon the first motions of sin say, Satan, flesh, 'get thee behind me, thou art an offence to me,' Mat. xvi. 23. But I must not further expatiate upon these things. So much for the dissuasive part of this use, against walking after the flesh.

I go on to the persuasive part, wherein I would most earnestly exhort you to walk after the Spirit. I will be but short upon this, because that which I have already spoken hath a great tendency to the promoting of it; for the truth is, whilst I have been dissuading you from walking after the flesh, I have in effect been persuading you to walk after the Spirit; in beating you off from that, I have been drawing you on to this. You have heard what it is so to walk. What now remains but that you would all endeavour to put it in practice; and oh that this might be your way and course! Let others live as they please, let it be your fixed resolution that you will live the holy, spiritual, heavenly life. True, there are but few who do thus walk. The world is but a great Exchange, wherein the Spirit's walk is very thin, whilst the flesh's walk is full and crowded; but it is better to be with the few in the way of the Spirit, than with the many in the way of the flesh. And I desire you to lay it to heart, Have not you yourselves too long walked after the flesh? is it not high time for you to think of another course? 1 Pet. iv. 3, 'The time past of our life may suffice us to have wrought the will of the Gentiles, when we walked in lasciviousness, lusts, excess of wine,' &c. When will ye 'walk in newness of life?' as the expression is, Rom. vi. 4. When shall the renewing and the renewed Spirit command, govern, act, guide you in your whole conversation? When will you

so walk that you yourselves, and others too, may know, by the spiritualness of your deportment, that you are indeed in Christ Jesus?

Here consider, in opposition to what was said of the former walking, but three things:

1. This is excellent walking. The spiritual life is the excellent life. This speaks somewhat more than what is of man; there is something divine and supernatural in it.[1] To be acted by, to live under the conduct and guidance of, the blessed Spirit, to have affections, propensions, ends, all holy: this is truly great; this is the life which is most agreeable to the human nature, not only as considered in its primitive unstained glory and excellency, but as it is now under its sad ruins and decays. Oh how unbecoming, how ill doth a vicious conversation comport even with that reason, natural light, and those broken excellencies which are yet left in man! Man is not so low, but that by complying with sensual lusts, he yet acts below himself; nay, so far as he puts on the sinner, he puts off the man; where he unsaints himself, he unmans himself. Sensuality and wickedness carry in them a contradiction to his very being; nothing so well suits with that as a pious, religious, heavenly course. Further, the fleshly life is a base, sordid life; but the spiritual life is a raised, noble life. So much as the Spirit is above the flesh, the soul above the body, so much is the spiritual life above the sensual or carnal life.[2] The life which I am urging upon you is the very life of God himself; for the apostle speaks, Eph. iv. 18, of some men 'being alienated from the *life of God* through the ignorance that is in them;' by which life of God he means, in part, the holiness of God, or that holy life which God lives. The holy liver, then, he not being alienated from God's holiness, lives the life of God; he acts in conformity, though under a vast disproportion, to the great God.[3] Must there not, then, needs be unspeakable glory and excellency in spiritual walking? The more one lives

[1] Ὁ τοιοῦτος ἂν εἴη κρείττων βίος ἢ κάτ' ἄνθρωπον· οὐ γὰρ ᾗ ἄνθρωπός ἐστιν οὕτω βιώσεται, ἀλλ' ᾗ Θεῖόν τι ἐν αὐτῷ ὑπάρχει.—*Arist. Eth.*, lib. x., cap. 7.

[2] Τὸ οἰκεῖον ἑκάστῳ τῇ φύσει κράτιστον, &c., καὶ τῷ ἀνθρώπῳ δ ἡ ὁ κατὰ τὴν νοῦν βίος, εἴπερ μάλιστα τοῦτο ἄνθρωπος.—*Arist. ibid.*, p. 138.

[3] Ὁμοίωσις τῷ θεῷ δίκαιον καὶ ὅσιον μετὰ φρονήσεως γένεσθαι.—*Plato in Thœt.*

the fleshly life, the more he resembles the beast; the more one lives the spiritual life, the more he resembles God. The creature is not so much debased and depressed by the one, but he is as much advanced and dignified by the other. Saints may be censured and misjudged by the world, but in truth they come the nearest, and are most like to God: 'That they might be judged according to men in the flesh, but live according to God in the Spirit,' 1 Pet. iv. 6. I do but allude to these words, for I know in their first and proper sense they point to another thing than that which I cite them for. God's people are judged as if they lived according to men, walking in or after the flesh, as others do; but it is not so, they walk in or after the Spirit, and so live according to God. What a great thing is this for poor creatures, to live according to God! Who would not so live?

And this, too, is the life of the blessed ones in heaven. Take the glorified saints, how do they walk? Not after the flesh I assure you, for they have no such flesh to walk after. They are wholly freed from the sinning and sinful nature, are perfectly renewed and sanctified, and accordingly they act. All in them, or from them, is divine and spiritual; there is nothing that they do but what flows from a gracious principle; all their thoughts and affections are swallowed up in God; their love, joy, delight are unmixedly spiritual; the pleasures of the flesh are nothing to them; they have not the least inclination to the least evil; the great thing they mind and rejoice in is the glory of God. Oh what a holy, spiritual life do the saints live in heaven! Must not the same life then needs be excellent in the saints here, so far forth as they can reach it in their imperfect state? Surely none can undervalue or think low of it, but only they who are altogether ignorant of, and strangers to it. A child of God would not for a thousand worlds live any other life; nay, should God leave him to his liberty to make his own choice, and fully assure him of his future blessedness, let his choice be what it would, yet he would choose to live the spiritual rather than the carnal life. Was there no heaven nor no hell, yet the sincere Christian would be for holy walking, because of that excellency and intrinsic goodness which he sees in it.

2. Walking after the Spirit is pleasant, delightful, comfortable walking; that which begets true peace, solid joy, unspeakable comfort in the soul. The more spiritual a man is in his walking, the greater is his rejoicing; oh what peace have they who thus walk! Ps. cxix. 165. The flesh must not vie with the Spirit about true comfort; men exceedingly mistake themselves when they look for pleasure, delight, and satisfaction in a fleshly course; alas! it is not there to be had. Its very sweet is bitter; there is gall and wormwood even in its honey: 'Even in laughter the heart is sorrowful; and the end of that mirth is heaviness,' Prov. xiv. 13. It promises indeed great things, but it falls exceedingly short in its performances; eminently it doth so in its promises of joy and comfort. True peace is only to be found in a holy course: Rom. viii. 6, 'To be spiritually-minded is life and peace;' life hereafter, peace here: 2 Cor. vi. 10, 'As sorrowful, yet always rejoicing:' 2 Cor. i. 12, 'Our rejoicing is this, the testimony of our conscience that in simplicity and godly sincerity, not with fleshly wisdom, but by the grace of God, we have had our conversation in the world.' There is no comfort like to that which attends holy walking;[1] the true Christian would not for a world exchange that joy which he hath in his soul, in and from meditation, prayer, the word, sacraments, promises, mortification of sin, holiness, communion with God, the hope of glory, for all that joy which the sinner hath in the way of sin and in his sensual delights. Would you have the 'joy which is unspeakable,' 1 Pet. i. 8, the 'peace which passeth all understanding,' Phil. iv. 7, the 'consolations of God which are not small,' Job xv. 11, oh, walk after the Spirit! Men have false notions of religion, which experience must confute. The devil belies and misreports the ways of God, as if a godly life was a sad, pensive, melancholy life; pray try and then judge, be persuaded to fall upon this heavenly course, and then tell me whether wisdom's ways be not ways of pleasantness, and all her paths peace, Prov. iii. 17; Ps. cxix. 14, 'I have rejoiced in the way of thy testimonies as much as in all riches.' The flesh

---

[1] Τοῖς φιλοκάλοις ἐστὶν ἡδέα τὰ φύσει ἡδέα. Τοιαῦτα δὲ αἱ κατ' ἀρετὴν πράξεις· ὥστε καὶ, &c. Οὐδὲν δὴ προσδεῖται της ἡδονῆς ὁ βίος αὐτῶν, ὥσπερ περιάπτου τινὸς, ἀλλ' ἔξει τὴν ἡδονην ἐν ἑαυτῷ—Arist. Eth., lib. i. cap. 9.

is outdone by the Spirit; if it gives some outward, flashy joy, the Spirit, with advantage, gives inward, solid, abiding joy; should not this allure you to walk after it? We always love to walk where our walking may be most pleasant and delightful. Surely to walk with God, to live in communion with Father, Son, and Spirit, to be taken up in the contemplation and fruition of heavenly things, to be always sucking at the breasts of the promises, to act in the daily exercise of grace; I say, surely this must needs be pleasant and delightful walking indeed. And the spiritual walker hath not only this peace and satisfaction whilst he lives, but in a dying hour too he is full of comfort. Oh the soul-cheering reflections which he then can make upon a holy life! Oh that heart-exhilarating prospect which he hath of the world to come! Whether he looks backward or forward, all administers ground of rejoicing to him. Is it thus with the sinner, the sensualist? alas! it is quite otherwise. When death comes and lays his cold hands upon him, what bitter pangs of conscience doth he feel! what dreadful terrors do fill his soul! how doth the sense of judgment and eternity strike him with astonishment! All his sensual comforts do now fail him; and he did not live so full of joy, but he dies as full of sorrow. 'This shall ye have of mine hand, ye shall lie down in sorrow,' Isa. l. 11; but 'mark the perfect man, and behold the upright, for the end of that man is peace,' Ps. xxxvii. 37.

3. This is blessed walking, for it evermore ends in salvation. It doth not only at present evidence non-condemnation and union with Christ, but it assures of heaven, and certainly brings to heaven at last. Holiness and happiness never were, never shall be, parted. Every motion hath its *terminus* or end; the end of this motion or walking is eternal rest: Rom. viii. 13, 'If ye through the Spirit do mortify the deeds of the body, ye shall live:' Gal. vi. 8, 'He that soweth to the Spirit shall of the Spirit reap life everlasting:' Prov. xii. 28, 'In the way of righteousness is life; and in the pathway thereof there is no death;' so that if you will be persuaded to enter into and to hold on in the way of the Spirit, it will infallibly lead you to eternal life; and what can be spoken higher? The sum of all is this, I here set life and death before you, Jer.

xxi. 8; if the one will not allure you to a holy, heavenly conversation, nor the other deter you from a sinful, carnal conversation, I have then no more to say; but surely such as have any sense of God, of the worth of the soul, and of the things of the world to come, they will resolve for the spiritual life. Athenagoras, in his apology for the primitive Christians, states their practice thus:[1] If, saith he, we did believe that we should only live the present life, there might then be some room for suspicion that we might be as wicked as others, indulging flesh and blood, and drawn aside by covetousness and concupiscence; but we know that God is privy not only to all our actions, but to all our thoughts and words; that he is all light, and sees what is most hid in us; and we are fully persuaded, that after this life we shall live a much better life with God in heaven; and therefore we do not live as others do, whose life will end in hell fire. Oh that we could as easily draw men to the heavenly life, as we can apologise for those who leave it, or set down the grounds and reasons why they leave it!

And now you who are flesh-followers, will nothing prevail with you? Shall all these considerations be ineffectual? Will you yet persist in your fleshly course? Though an angel with a drawn sword stands before you to stop you in your evil way, yet, Balaam-like, will you go on? Num. xxii. 22. Will you 'set yourselves in a way that is not good,' as the wicked are described? Ps. xxxvi. 4. Are you at that language, 'We will every one walk after our own devices, and we will every one do the imagination of his evil heart'? Jer. xviii. 12. Or, as it is, Jer. vi. 16, 'Stand ye in the ways and see, and ask for the old paths, where is the good way, (the way of the Spirit,) and walk therein, and ye shall find rest for your souls. But they said, We will not walk therein'? Do you walk after the flesh, and resolve to do so still? Then it is sad indeed, but I would fain hope better of you. Pray be entreated to read the motives again which have been set before you, and in your most calm thoughts to pause and dwell upon the things which have been spoken. Shall I need to add anything further, in telling you that all your walkings, yea, every step you take, is known to

[1] Εἰ μὲν γὰρ ἕνα τὴν ἐνταῦθα βίον, &c.—*Athenag. Leg. pro Christian.*, p. 35.

M

God? Job xxi. 4, and xxxiv. 21; Ps. cxxxix. 3, and cxix. 168. That God judges of every man here, and hereafter will judge every man at the great day, according to his walking? Eccles. xi. 9; 2 Cor. v. 10; Eccles. xii. 14. That death will come with a dreadful aspect where the life hath been carnal and sinful; that in the way of the flesh you are in danger of treading upon serpents, vipers, adders, scorpions, every step you take; that by this course you 'forsake the path of life,' Ps. xvi. 11, and, for a little flesh-pleasing, put yourselves into the broad way to everlasting damnation? How much might I yet say upon this account, but enough and enough hath been already said, if God will but set it home upon the conscience. The Lord hedge up your ways with thorns, and make a wall that you may not find the paths of the flesh, and thereupon may resolve to get into the paths of the Spirit; for surely it will be better then than now it is;—I allude to Hosea ii. 6, 7.

Use 4. There is one use more, and that shall be directed to them who do walk after the Spirit. Three things to such.

1. First, I would, with the greatest earnestness, stir up such to be highly thankful to God. Are any of you through grace made spiritual, and do you live the spiritual life? Have you received the Spirit, and do you also walk after the Spirit? What cause have you to bless God! yea, what thankfulness can be high enough to him who hath brought you to this! Why do you not walk just as others do? Why is not the flesh as powerful, as predominant in you as it is in others? Why does not the very worst of the flesh prevail over you? Why are not you atheists, scoffers at religion, drunkards, adulterers, open and notorious sinners? Surely all must be resolved into the discriminating grace of God; that, and that only, hath made the difference. Time was when your walking was bad enough, when you were as carnal as any, and very tamely lackeyed it after every base lust; is not God to be admired upon that blessed change which he hath wrought in you? Eph. ii. 1-3, 'You hath ye quickened, who were dead in trespasses and sins; wherein in time past ye walked according to the course of this world,' &c. 'Among whom also we all had our conversation in times past in the lusts of our flesh, fulfilling the desires of the flesh and of the mind;

and were by nature the children of wrath, even as others. But God, who is rich in mercy, for his great love wherewith he loved us, when we were dead in sins, hath quickened us together with Christ:' Tit. iii. 3, 'For we ourselves were sometimes foolish, disobedient, deceived, serving divers lusts and pleasures.' See also Col. iii. 7; 1 Pet. iv. 3. Oh what a sad course do the best follow before conversion! and, as to yourselves, if God by his distinguishing and almighty grace had not seized upon you, as you began with that course, so you had continued in it to this very day. Oh let the Lord be for ever magnified, who hath delivered you from fleshly walking, and brought you over to that which is spiritual and heavenly. And this must the rather be done, because you now have so clear, so convincing an evidence of your being in Christ; is not that a great thing? The blessedness of this union with Christ hath been fully set before you; it is all yours, you not 'walking after the flesh, but after the Spirit.' Surely, though you cannot in your praises reach so great mercy, yet you should go as far as ever you can.

2. Secondly, Such are to be exhorted to walk yet less and less after the flesh, and yet more and more after the Spirit. For this walking admits of degrees; there are none, in the present state, so freed from the flesh and the fleshly conversation, but that yet they may be more freed from it; and so too there are none who have so much of the Spirit, and walk so much after the Spirit, but that yet they may be more spiritual in their walking. It is mercy that it is so well, as to the main, but surely it may yet be better. Saints! are you so universally acted by the Spirit of God and the sanctified nature as you might be? Oh do you so constantly live under the guidance and conduct of the Spirit as you might and should? is he your guide no sooner to shew you the right way, but presently and readily you engage therein?[1] are all your affections so pure and heavenly as God requires? are there not many strong inclinations to evil yet remaining in you? are your ends in all things so sublime and spiritual as the gospel commands?

---

[1] Ὡς ὁ ὁδοιπόρος πυνθάνεται παρὰ τοῦ ἀπαντήσαντος, ποτέρα τῶν ὁδῶν φέρει, οὐκ ἔχων ὄρεξιν πρὸς τὴν δεξιὰν μᾶλλον φέρειν ἢ τὴν ἀριστερὰν, οὐ γὰρ τούτων τινὰ ἀπελθεῖν θέλει, ἀλλὰ τὴν φέρουσαν· οὕτως ἔδει καὶ ἐπὶ τὸν θεὸν ἔρχεσθαι, ὡς ὁδηγόν.—*Arrian. Epict.*, lib. ii. cap. 7, p. 186.

Ah, something is yet wanting! there is yet room for growth; you have not yet arrived at perfection, as the apostle speaks of himself, 'Not as though I had already attained,' &c., Phil. iii. 12. Oh that every day you might rise higher and higher in heavenly walking! that the flesh might decrease and the Spirit increase; the carnal part, like the house of Saul, might still be going down, and the spiritual part, like the house of David, might still be getting up; that heart and life might be refined and spiritualised yet more and more! I beseech you, do not stay where you are, but still be 'pressing forward,' Phil. iii. 14. Walking, it is *motus progressivus;* so it should be in your walking after the Spirit: as there is a going 'from strength to strength,' Ps. lxxxiv. 7, 'from faith to faith,' Rom. i. 17, so there should be also from spiritualness to spiritualness. And walking it is *motus uniformis;* are you so steady, so even and uniform in your walkings as you ought? In a statue or piece of art all the several parts are uniform and proportionable, or else it loses in its exactness and curiosity;[1] and should it not be so too in the spiritual life? But I will only keep to the metaphor of the evenness of the Christian's walking. Oh the many crooked, wandering, extravagant steps which you take! Sometimes you are in the way of the Spirit, then presently in the way of the flesh; you do not make 'straight paths,' as the apostle advises, Heb. xii. 13: how do your partial closures and compliances with the carnal part too often intercept the light of God's countenance, interrupt your communion with him, and cause a damp in all your inward peace, as you know by reason of this it sometimes was with David himself! When will you walk in the path of holiness, so as not to turn to the right hand or to the left, as the word enjoins? see Prov. iv. 27; Deut. v. 32. Again, is your spiritual walking so visible as it should be—so as to convince the world that there is such a life, such a course as hath been described? Truly, men question whether there be such a thing, because you who pretend to it come so short of it; when you speak, act just as others, are as worldly, vain, passionate, selfish, revengeful as others, who will believe that there is in reality any

[1] Τοῦ βίου καθάπερ ἀγάλματος πάντα τὰ μερὴ καλὰ εἶναι δεῖ.— Socrat.

such walking after the Spirit? or that there is more in it than mere fancy and pretence? How did Paul's Spirit rise in him, upon the surmises and censures of some who thought of him as though he walked according to the flesh! 2 Cor. x. 2; and can you, as to yourselves, not only bear such censures, but, which is much worse, give too just occasion for them? Further, let me ask you, doth this holy walking intermingle itself with your whole conversation? even in your natural and civil actions do you walk after the Spirit? when you eat and drink is your eye upon the glory of God? 1 Cor. x. 31; in common actions have you special and peculiar aims and principles? the very animal life which you 'live in the flesh,' do you 'live by the faith of the Son of God,' as Paul did? Gal. ii. 20. It is a great mistake to limit this walking after the Spirit to actions materially spiritual, or to the positive duties of religion; no, at all times, in all actions you are so to walk, doing all from a spiritual principle, by a spiritual rule, to a spiritual end. It is one thing to be employed in some acts that are spiritual, and another thing to be spiritual in all acts; the fleshly walker may do the first, but saints must endeavour after the last. At your tables, in your shops, in your civil converses, you may, and ought, to live the heavenly life, as well as in hearing the word, prayer, and such religious duties. A carnal man sometimes engages in spiritual things, and yet even then he doth not walk after the Spirit; and a child of God sometimes is engaged in common things, civil and natural, and yet even then he walks after the Spirit— viz., as he intermingles grace with all he doth. Now is it thus with you? are you holy, spiritual 'in all manner of conversation,' in every winding and turn of the life, as the apostle exhorts? 1 Pet. i. 15. And once more let me ask you—and pray call your own souls to account about it—is there not some one or other secret by-path of the flesh which you walk in? This holy David prayed against, Ps. cxxxix. 24, 'See if there be *any wicked way* in me, and lead me in the way everlasting.' Upon the whole, I fear there is need to press this upon you, to walk yet more and more after the Spirit: and we 'beseech and exhort you by the Lord Jesus, that as ye have received of us how you ought to walk and to please God, so ye would abound more and more,' 1 Thes. iv. 1.

3. Thirdly, Are you such who walk not after the flesh but after the Spirit? Oh rejoice in this and take the comfort of it! Here is sufficient ground of assurance that there is no condemnation to you, that you are in Christ Jesus; and is not that matter of rejoicing? You are within the character here given of such who are in Christ, therefore you are in him, and being in him, must it not needs be well with you? And if you look into the following verses there is yet more comfort for you: they tell you that God sent his Son to condemn sin, to fulfil the law, and all for such spiritual walkers as you are, for upon them the character is repeated again.

Ah, you will say, if it was thus with us we would desire no higher comfort in the world, but we fear it is otherwise; we cannot find that we come up to this description, and therefore cannot apply the happiness annexed to it. And why so? why, because there is so much of flesh in us; oh there is a very sinful, carnal, and sensual part in us! yea, this often prevails and breaks forth in our conversation; upon which we cannot but judge that we walk after the flesh rather than after the Spirit.

Now to this I answer: Nothing more certain than that flesh is in you, and will be so whilst you are in the flesh; you must carry it with you to your very grave, the body of sin and the other body must both be buried together; you will never be wholly rid of a sinning nature and a carnal part till you be in heaven. And it is true too, this flesh doth and will sometimes prevail over you, though the seldomer the better: yet this doth not amount to walking after the flesh, or to the nullifying of the walking after the Spirit. Paul himself complained of the flesh, yea, of the strength and power of it, yet for all that he says here, ver. 4, 'We walk not after the flesh, but after the Spirit;' though it was so with him, yet his state was good, and his course good too. We must thus speak for the comfort of burdened souls, though enemies without take occasion from hence to revile, and sinners, amongst ourselves, to presume. It would be happy if you might wholly be freed from a corrupt nature;[1] but that is rather to

be desired than hoped for in this life. Yet here is this to support you; though that may carry the day as to some particular acts, yet the bent of the heart is for God, and as to the general course the renewed part is uppermost. The flesh sometimes is too hard for you, but you do not consent to it;[1] it hath not the full allowance and approbation of the will; you do not give up yourselves in a willing subjection to it; what it doth it is from mere force and strength; you cry out to God daily for help against it: well! God will not lay particular failings, thus circumstantiated, to your charge. The damsel under the law that was ravished, if she cried out for help and did not consent to the fact, was to be acquitted, Deut. xxii. 25; so you do to God under the assaults of the flesh, and so God will do to you. True, sin is sin though it hath not full and deliberate consent; but God is so gracious that where that is not, he will not impute it. I have also told you, that you must distinguish betwixt lapses into sin and walking in sin;[2] thou sometimes fallest by the flesh, but yet thou dost not walk after the flesh. Where the fleshly act, especially if it be gross, is not repeated, where the soul resists it, where there is a rising again by repentance, deep humiliation for what is past, and all diligent circumspection and steadfast resolution, in God's strength, for the time to come, there it is but a lapse, and not a walking. This I hope is your case; and if so, then what you allege against yourselves will not amount to make you walkers after the flesh.

And as to the positive part, the walking after the Spirit, though you come short as to degrees, and are not so raised in the spiritual life as you ought, yet in such a measure, which God accepts, you do live it. The Spirit is your principle, your guide; spiritual objects have your affections; the heart inclines and bends chiefly to that which is good; your great end is to enjoy and glorify God; oh be of good comfort, this is walking after the Spirit! You are imperfect in it, yet sincere; you aim at more than what you

---

[1] Desiderium tuum tale debet esse ad Deum ut omnino non sit ipsa concupiscentia cui resistere oporteat; resistis enim, et non consentiendo vincis, sed melius est hostem non habere quam vincere.—*Aug. Serm. de Tem.*, 45.

[1] Nulla condemnatio iis qui sunt in Christo Jesu, non enim damnatur nisi qui concupiscentiæ carnis consentit ad malum. —*Aug. contra duas Ep. Pelag.*, lib. i. cap. 10. *Vide plura in Aug. in Ps.* cxviii. conc. 3.

[2] Non dicitur vivere secundum carnem, qui Spiritum ducem sequitur, etiamsi aliquando extra viam vestigium ponat.—*Justin.*

can as yet arrive at; God accepts of you, and will deal with you as persons really ingrafted into Christ: your holy walking discovers your union, and your union secures your non-condemnation. What have you to do, but to beg of God that he will yet guide you, and more and more fix and stablish you in this your spiritual walking. He that knows the goodness of your way, knows also the weakness of your graces. Oh pray much for strengthening grace, that you may steadfastly continue in your holy course to the end! Ps. xvii. 5, 'Hold up my goings in thy paths, that my footsteps slip not:' Ps. cxix. 117, 'Hold thou me up, and I shall be safe: and I will have respect unto thy statutes continually.' So much for the application of this point. Two things should therein have been further spoken to, but now must be omitted, namely,

1. To vindicate the true notion of the spiritual life, against all the false monastic glosses and interpretations which some do put upon it.

2. To answer those usual and common objections which too many do raise against it. But the due handling of these two heads would take me up some considerable time, and they will in the following verses again offer themselves; and I fear I have already been too long upon this verse, therefore at present I shall not meddle with them. I have done with the first verse: 'There is therefore now no condemnation to them which are in Christ Jesus, who walk not after the flesh, but after the Spirit.'

CHAPTER IV.

OF THE SINNER'S BEING MADE FREE BY THE POWER OF THE SPIRIT FROM THE POWER OF SIN AND DEATH.

For the law of the Spirit of life in Christ Jesus hath made me free from the law of sin and death.— Rom. viii. 2.

Of the connexion of this verse with the former—Some bring in the words by way of prolepsis—The proper import of the particle for *cleared, and made good against the papists—In the words something implied, something expressed—All reduced to three heads: a gracious deliverance; the subject; the author of that deliverance—What sin is here mainly intended—How far the being made free from it doth reach—Whether it points to the guilt or power of sin—What is meant by the law of sin—Of deliverance from the law of sin and death—Paul instances in himself as the subject of it—How that is to be taken—Why he speaks in the singular number—The law of the Spirit, &c., opened—A fourfold exposition of the words—What that is which is in Christ Jesus—Is it the life, or the Spirit, or the law of the Spirit?—In the close, one truth briefly handled, that the Holy Spirit is the Spirit of life—How or in what respects he is so—Some short application made thereof.*

THE apostle having in the former verse more succinctly laid down that great truth upon which he designed to build his following discourse, he here in this verse falls upon the amplifying and enlarging of himself about it; and all that he says from this verse to the seventeenth is but by way of amplification upon what he had more concisely said in the first.

It is obvious, at the first view, that this verse doth not only immediately follow, but that in its matter it is linked and embodied with the former; the particle *for* plainly shews that it is brought in to prove or to explain something there asserted: 'For the law of the Spirit,' &c. Now the apostle having there, 1. Propounded the happy state of persons in Christ; and 2. Having described and characterised those persons, a question here doth arise, Which of these two doth he in this verse design to prove or open? I say to prove or open, for the words may come in by way of illustration as well as by way of proof or argumentation.

For answer to which, I see nothing of reason why both may not be taken in; the words will bear a fair reference both to the one and to the other too. [1]

1. First, as to the privilege. He had said, 'There is no condemnation to them who are in Christ Jesus.' Now this being the great prop or pillar of the be-

[1] Hinc utrumque dependet, quod versu præcedenti statuit. Prius, &c.—*Lud. de Dieu.*

liever's faith and hope, he will therefore fasten it sure; he is not satisfied barely to affirm it, but he will confirm and make it good, and also shew how it is brought about.

For the proof of it, he brings this argument: They who are freed from the law of sin and death, to them there is no condemnation; but such who are in Christ are thus freed from the law of sin and death, *ergo*, &c. All the difficulty lying in the minor proposition, he shews how this freedom from the law of sin and death is effected; and as to that he saith, it is 'by the law of the Spirit of life.' Which being done, in this method, in and for believers, they are in no danger of condemnation.

For the explication of it—if you take the words in that notion—the apostle sets down the way and manner how this non-condemnation is carried on. That is done two ways: partly by the Spirit of Christ; partly by the merit of Christ. In order to the sinner's justification and salvation two things are necessary: 1. He must be freed from the tyranny, usurpation, and dominion of sin; 2. He must be freed too from the guilt of sin, and the justice of God must be satisfied. Now, saith the apostle, both of these are accordingly done: the former by the Spirit of Christ, which is spoken to in this second verse; the latter by the merit or satisfactory obedience of Christ in his own person, which is spoken to in the third and fourth verses. Thus the apostle clears up the way and method of God in the bringing about of the non-condemnation of believers; and this is the double reference which the words will bear with respect to the privilege.

2. Then, secondly, they may refer, too, to the character or description, 'who walk not after,' &c. It might be asked, How doth the truth of this appear, viz., that persons in Christ do thus walk? or rather, How comes it about that such do arrive at this spiritual course? The apostle answers, 'The law of the Spirit of life hath freed such from the law of sin;' *q.d.*, I have spoken of the holy and heavenly course of believers, and do not wonder at it; you may believe me in what I have asserted, for the mighty power of the Spirit of God having subdued sin and broke its strength and dominion in these persons, upon this they are brought to holy walking, or therefore they do so walk. In this reference

several expositors carry the words; but this for their connexion. [1]

Some divines make them to be, in part, proleptical, as if the apostle, foreseeing some objections which might be made against what he had laid down, did here design to prevent and anticipate those objections. For as to both the forementioned things, doubts and discouragements might arise in some who were in Christ. They might object thus: Blessed Paul! thou sayest there is no condemnation to them who are in Christ; but how can this be? What! so much sin and guilt, and yet no condemnation? Can we who are nothing but a very mass of sin be thus safe and secure as to our eternal state? Oh, this we scarce know how to believe! And, again, thou speakest of 'walking not after the flesh, but after the Spirit.' Alas! who do thus walk? When we have so much of flesh in us, and that doth so often draw us to carnal acts, &c., how is this qualification practicable?

To obviate this double objection or discouragement, the apostle brings in these words, in which he renders both the privilege and the property of persons interested in it real and credible—viz., by their being freed from the law of sin and death through the law of the Spirit. It is as if he had said, It is too true that even such who are in Christ will have sin in them, and sin will too often be committed by them; yet for all this, I say that such shall not be condemned; why? because they are freed from the law of sin, and so, consequently, from the law of death. Sin, I grant, is in them; but it is not a law in them, or to them; it still keeps its residence in them, but its reign, its commanding power, is gone. Now, where it is not commanding it shall not be condemning. So then, this notwithstanding, the foundation of a believer's safety and comfort stands firm and unshaken.

---

[1] Lex spiritus vitæ quæ pertinet ad gratiam, et liberat a lege peccati et mortis, facit ut non concupiscamus, et impleamus jussa legis, &c.—*August. Octogint. Quæst.*, p. 575, t. iv. Verius et certius est, quod hoc versiculo rationem reddere apostolus voluerit, non illorum verborum *nihil nunc damnationis*, sed cur hanc quasi conditionem illis verbis adjecerit, *iis qui non secundum carnem ambulant.*—*Stapl. Antidot.*, p. 625. The apostle proves the spiritual walking, *à causa procreante*, quæ est Spiritus Sanctus.—*Piscat.* He gives a reason why the true members of Christ do walk according to the Spirit.—*Deod.*

And for the other discouragement here is a kind of tacit and implicit concession that the people of God are flesh as well as spirit, and that as to some particular acts, through infirmity, they may follow the guidance and motions of the flesh; but yet they are not under the law and command of the flesh. Why? because they are freed from the law of sin; there is another law which hath thrust out that law of sin, viz., the law of the Spirit. Indeed, time was when they were at the beck and command of the flesh, when they walked after it; but the law of the Spirit having taken hold of them, now, for the main, they do not, they cannot walk after the flesh.

I come more strictly and narrowly to look into the words, 'For the law of the Spirit of life,' &c. It is a scripture that either is dark in itself, or else it is made so by the various and different interpretations put upon it; which, before I can well speak to, the first word, *for*, must be a little considered; and the rather because it is made use of and insisted upon in some matters of controversy. That which unites verse and verse divides party and party; this little word is made to bear its part in some sharp contests; and though to us at the first view it may seem but inconsiderable, yet it is not so to the Romanists, who, in their arguings against protestants, make no small use of it. They tell us that it is here to be taken causally, as containing in it the ground of justification;[1] that it points to inherent righteousness as the cause of the non-condemnation before spoken of; and by this they attempt to prove that the believer is not justified by the imputed righteousness of Christ, but by his own personal inherent righteousness. For, say they, the apostle having said that there is no condemnation to them who are in Christ, he proves it from inherent righteousness as the proper and formal cause of it: there is no condemnation, '*for* the law of the Spirit,' &c. And, that the argument may be the more pressing and concluding to us protestants, they urge that Calvin and Beza themselves do make this law of the Spirit of life to point to grace, regeneration, inherent righteousness.

To whom I reply, 1. That it is not safe, either for them or us, in matters of great moment, to lay too great a stress upon little words, which only join verse and verse together, unless that which we build upon them or infer from them do agree with other scriptures where the thing is fully and professedly handled. I dare not undervalue the least, the meanest particle in God's word; yet I would be loath to bottom a fundamental article of faith upon such a particle, especially when it admits of various senses, as this here doth, if it hath not the current of the word to back it. For our opinion of justification by the alone righteousness of Christ imputed to the sinner, and laid hold on by faith, we ground it upon several full and entire discourses, where our apostle doth professedly handle that argument, proving justification to be according to what we hold; but our adversaries, to prove their justification by inherent righteousness, very often (I do not say always) catch at some little single word, and that they make the foundation which they build this opinion upon. In short, against this *for* in the text —I mean, too, only as they pervert it, for in truth they have not so much as even this little word to favour them—we set the whole third, fourth, fifth chapter of this Epistle to the Romans, where the apostle, in a full discourse upon it, doth plainly lay justification upon imputed, not upon inherent righteousness; and which of us now do build upon the surest and safest bottom?

2. What if this particle, supposing it to be causal, doth point to the description of the persons, and not to the privilege—some of their own authors do carry it so[1]—where, then, is the strength of their argument from it to prove the formal cause of no condemnation? All that then can be deduced from the words is this, that grace in the heart is the cause of a holy life; that men upon regeneration are delivered from the law of sin, and therefore they walk not after the flesh, but after the Spirit. What is this against us? And, with respect to their glosses, who questions or denies inherent righteousness, or that that doth free from sin, provided you take it with a double limitation?—(1.) That the freeing from sin upon regeneration be understood of the

<hr>

[1] Subscribit causam prædictæ liberationis.—*Soto.* Apostolus hanc libertatem a lege peccati per Spiritum Dei, ponit ut causam ejus quod prius dixerat.—*Stapl. Antid.,* p. 625; with many others.

[1] *Stapl.* ut prius. *Tolet:* causam exponit cur qui sunt in Christo non secundum carnem ambulant.

taking away its power; (2.) That it be not carried so far as quite to jostle out imputed righteousness, or set so high as to have that attributed to it which is only proper to Christ's righteousness. Our adversaries misrepresent our opinions, and trouble themselves, in a great measure, to prove that which we never deny, and then asperse us as though we did deny it.[1]

3. It is one thing to be the proof of a thing, another thing to be the cause of that thing. Regeneration, indeed, *proves* justification — for every regenerate person is a justified person; but it is not the *cause* of justification; for the person is not therefore justified because he is regenerated, but because Christ's righteousness by faith is made over to him. It is one thing to say, therefore a man lives because he hath sense and moves, and another thing to say, therefore a man lives because he hath a living soul in him; the sense and motion prove the life, but it is the living soul which is the cause of life. So here, the believer shall not be condemned because the law of the Spirit of life, &c.; this evinces the certainty of the thing; but it is not the proper cause of it. So that the *for* in the text is only *nota probationis*, but not *causalitatis*, and so it is used up and down in the Gospel in very many places.

4. It is very true that Calvin, in part, doth interpret the words of regeneration and inherent righteousness;[2] but then, foreseeing the objection that would be made upon it, he explains himself about it, and saith, If any shall reply that then pardon or justification doth depend upon regeneration, the answer, says he, is obvious; Paul doth not set down the cause wherefore we are absolved from guilt, only the manner wherein this is done.[3] He adds,

further, It is as much as if the apostle had said that regeneration is never separated or parted from the imputation of Christ's righteousness.[1] So that he doth not argue for non-condemnation or justification from inherent righteousness as the proper cause of it, but only as these two always go together, and as this is the order and method of God wherein he justifies. And it is true too that Beza doth take in here, under 'the law of the Spirit,' regeneration and sanctification;[2] but then it is very well known what he makes to be the law of the Spirit of life principally, viz., the sanctity and holiness of Christ's human nature, which, he saith, being imputed to the believer, he is thereupon justified. And now Calvin and Beza have lost all their credit.[3] So long as they expounded the words of inherent righteousness they were very sound and orthodox, but now they thus explain themselves, no censures are severe enough for them. Now, if Stapleton may be believed, they are not *adulteratores sed carnifices verbi Dei*. I know Pareus, to avoid the popish objection, closes with another interpretation of the words; but there is no necessity for that, as I conceive. In short, as was said in the handling of the foregoing verse, we are for inherent righteousness as well as our opposers, though they are pleased very freely to calumniate us, as if we denied the thing, because we deny it to be the cause or ground of justification.[4] We are for *infallibilis nexus*, an inseparable connexion betwixt justification and sanctification; where there is the blood there is the water also; for Christ came by both, 1 John v. 6. We further hold that regeneration,

---

[1] Si Spiritus vitæ vivificans, sanctificans, &c. Ergo liberati sumus a lege peccati et mortis, regeneratione, sanctificatione, non sola justitiæ imputatione; gratia ergo inhærens est quæ liberat a peccato.—*Contz. Quæst.* 1, *in ver.* 2, *cap.* viii. *ad Rom.* Torsit hic locus tam Calvinum quam Bezam, quia inhærentem justitiam per veram peccati victoriam luculenter probat, et imputativam subvertit.—*Stapl. Antidot.*, p. 625.

[2] Legem Spiritus improprie vocat Dei Spiritum, qui animas nostras Christi sanguine aspergit, non tantum ut a peccati labe emundet quoad reatum, sed ut in verum pietatem sanctificet. —*Calvin.*

[3] Siquis excipiat veniam ergo qua sepeliuntur nostra delicta pendere a regeneratione, facilis est solutio. Non assignari causam a Paulo, sed modum tradi duntaxat, quo solvimur a reatu.—*Calvin.*

[1] Perinde valet hæc sententia, ac si dixisset Paulus regenerationis gratiam ab imputatione justitiæ nunquam disjungi.

[2] Legem Spiritus vitæ, nec pro lege fidei, &c., sed pro ejus efficacia, per quam peccatum, *i.e.*, corruptio, ipsaque adeo mors, sensim aboletur, ut docet infra, v. 10 et 11, denique pro regenerationis gratia accipio, cui opponitur carnis, *i.e.*, naturæ nostræ, corruptio.—*Beza.*

[3] In his verbis Calvinum orthodoxæ et Augustinianæ expositioni conformiter dicere, quis dubitaverit? sed audiantur reliqua, et impostoris technæ ac fraudes apparebunt.—*Stapl. ubi supra.* Quam legem Spiritus cum probe intellexissent recentiores hæretici, perperam transferunt, non ad gratiam justis inhærentem, sed ad externam Christi justitiam, quam nobis quodammodo affingi volunt et imputari.—*Justin.*

[4] *Becanus Opusc de Justif. Calvinist.* cap. ii.; *Costeri Enchir*, cap. vi., p. 220; *Campian*, Rat. 8. Against which calumny vide *Chamier*, tom. iii. lib. i. cap. 2.

habitual and actual righteousness, are the indispensable conditions of eternal life, and absolutely necessary thereunto. Nay, some worthy divines[1] go so far as to make them *causa sine qua non*, even with respect to justification. But all this is nothing unless we make them the proper, formal cause of justification; which we cannot do, that being a thing so diametrically opposite to gospel revelation. This block being removed out of my way, now I proceed.

The law of the Spirit of life, &c. In the former verse you had contrary principles—flesh and Spirit; in this you have contrary laws. Here is law in opposition to law,—the law of the Spirit set against the law of sin, the law of the Spirit of life against the law of death; the law of sin enslaving us, against the law of the Spirit freeing us from that slavery.

In the words something is implied, and something is expressed.

That which is implied is this, that all men—the very best of them—for a time, viz., till they be converted, are under the law of sin and death.

That which is expressed is this, that believers by the law of the Spirit of life are made free from the law of sin and death. The opening of these things will be my present business, for I cannot well pitch upon the doctrinal observations till I have cleared up the sense of the words, and the apostle's main scope and design in them.

In order to which, I will reduce the whole matter contained in them to these three heads: A gracious deliverance, the subject, the author or efficient of deliverance.

1. Here is a gracious deliverance.—*Hath made me free from the law of sin and death.* As to the first of these, if you consider them as distinct—the being made free from the law of sin—for the better understanding thereof I desire you to take notice of the following particulars:—

(1.) That by sin the apostle chiefly aims at the root sin, the sin of nature, or the sinful depraved nature which is in fallen man. It is the same with the flesh spoken of before, as also with the indwelling sin, the law in the members, &c., in the foregoing chapter. This is that sin which hath the greatest

[1] Pareus in Respons. ad Dub. ii., p. 773; with some eminent divines of our own.

power in and over the soul. Particular and actual sins do but derive their power from this; all that dominion and strength which they have is but delegated; the supreme, sovereign, original dominion of sin is seated in the corrupt nature: there chiefly is that law of sin which believers are freed from; yet, in subordination to this, the power of particular sins, and deliverance from that, is here also to be taken in.

(2.) The apostle doth not say, that believers are simply and absolutely made free from sin, only that they are made free from the *law of sin*. There is a great difference betwixt sin and the law of sin:[1] a total freedom from the former none have in this life, no, not they who are most under the law of the Spirit. The dearest of God's children must wait for that till they come to heaven, the only place and state of perfection; there they shall be perfectly, completely freed from sin, yea, from the very being of it, but here the utmost they can arrive at is to be freed from its power in regeneration, and from its guilt in justification. The text therefore doth not speak of absolute freedom from sin, for that being unattainable here below is yet to come, and so it falls under the glorious liberty of the sons of God mentioned ver. 21: but the being made free in the text is spoken of as a thing that is past; ('*hath made me free,*' &c.;) and therefore it must be limited to freedom from the law of sin only.

(3.) There is in this life a twofold freedom from sin: the one respects its guilt, the other its power. It is a law in both respects: in reference to guilt, as it binds the creature over to answer at God's bar for what he hath done, and makes him obnoxious to punishment: in reference to power, as it rules, commands, and exercises a strange kind of tyranny and dominion over the sinner. Now believers are freed from sin in both of these respects, namely, as was said but just now, in justification from the guilt, in regeneration from the power of it.

[1] Non sunt idem *Peccatum* et *Lex peccati*; peccatum est vitium inhabitans in carne, Lex peccati dominium peccati, quod in carne non regenitorum plene exercet. Ab hoc peccati inhabitantis dominio, efficacia Spiritus regenerantis liberat fideles, frænando illud, non vero penitus tollendo.—*Pareus.* Attendendum, quod non dicit, &c : Non enim gratia hominem impeccabilem reddit, sed fomitis vim minuit, &c.—*Corn. Muss.* Nos ita a morte et peccato liberati sumus, ut tamen horum malorum non parum adhuc supersit.—*Pet. Mart.*

N

But here a question must be resolved, viz., Which doth the apostle here speak of? which of these two parts of the saints' freedom from sin is here primarily and principally intended?

For answer to which, divines do somewhat differ about it. Austine took in both, and therefore he sometimes opens it by the one, sometimes by the other.[1] Amongst modern expositors, some interpret the words of freedom from the guilt of sin, they making them chiefly to point to that grace which is given out in justification.[2] Others interpret them of freedom from the power of sin, they referring them to that grace which is proper to regeneration.[3] The opinion of the latter I prefer, and shall follow in the ensuing discourse. I conceive the law of sin mainly refers to the power of sin, and therefore the freedom from the law of sin must also mainly refer to the being freed from the power of sin. As to the taking away of its guilt, that the apostle speaks to in the following verse, for that is the condemning of it there mentioned; in this verse the taking away of its dominion was chiefly in his eye. You have him, chap. vii., sadly complaining of the law in his members, of the law of sin; now nothing more evident than that he hereby designs to set forth, not sin's guilt, but that great, though not full, power and strength which sin had in him; and if that be the proper notion of the law of sin there, then why not here? And besides, the word here used, ἠλευθέρωσε, 'hath made free,' both in Scripture and also in common authors usually notes the freeing of one who is un-

der bondage and slavery: it doth not so properly note the freeing of a malefactor from his guilt, and from that condemnatory sentence which he deserves; as the freeing of a slave or captive who is under the tyranny and dominion of another; and so it falls in exactly with that notion of freedom which I am upon. Therefore the Arabic translator well renders it by *emancipavit me à lege peccati, et mortis;* and Tertullian by *manumisit me,*[1] in allusion to the manumission of the Romans when they set their servants or slaves at liberty. Oh when a man is once regenerated he hath a blessed manumission, he being made free from that cursed servitude wherein he lived before under this cruel master, sin. I say, this is the strict and proper notion of the word; which though, it is true, it be here applied to death as well as to sin, yet that is either in a more large and improper sense,—for the apostle having first spoken of freedom from sin, and set it forth by that term which was proper to it, he was not solicitous to be so accurate as to vary his expression for the other, but would make the same to serve for both;—or else because there is a bondage in death as well as in sin, and therefore ἠλευθέρωσε will agree with it as well as with sin. And I desire that this may be considered, which I lay a great stress upon, the apostle in this verse speaks of the Spirit personally considered, as in the next verse of the Son personally considered also: it being so, we must then interpret their several making free from sin according to that which is proper to them in their personal consideration. Now it is the Spirit's personal act to free, by regeneration, from sin's power, as it is the Son's personal act, by satisfaction, to free from sin's guilt; therefore the first is meant in this verse, where the Spirit is mentioned; as the second is meant in the next verse, where the Son is mentioned.

(4.) *The law of sin.* It is a metaphor which our apostle often uses, and in which he seems much to delight; you have it often; Rom. vii. 21, 'I find a law, that when I would do good, evil is present with me': ver. 23, 'But I see another law warring against the law of my mind, and bringing me into

---

[1] Non damnatur nisi qui concupiscentiæ carnis consentit ad malum; lex enim Spiritus vitæ in Christo Jesu liberavit te a lege peccati et mortis, ne scil. consensionem tuam concupiscentia carnis sibi vindicet.—*August. contra duas Pelag. Ep.* lib. i. cap. 10. Liberavit, quomodo? nisi quia ejus reatum peccatorum omnium remissione dissolvit, (lex Spiritus vitæ in Christo,) ut quamvis adhuc maneret—in peccatum tamen non imputetur.—*Idem de Nup. et Concup.,* lib. i. cap. 32.

[2] A jure peccati, *i.e.,* a reatu, &c.—*Pet. Martyr.* Liberatio hæc non est regeneratio, qua liberamur ex parte a peccato inhærente, sed est peccatorum remissio, qua liberamur non ex parte, sed plene, perfecteque a peccatorum quorumcunque remissione.—*Rolloc.* Paulo post satis patebit de absolutione gratuita loqui, &c.—*Calvin.*

[3] Liberavit regenerando ad novam vitam.—*Beza.* Ut intelligamus legem Spiritus non solum hoc in nobis agere, quod non condemnemur propter imputationem justitiæ, sed et vim peccati in nobis extinguere, ut jam non regnet in nobis peccatum, sed gratia et virtus Christi.—*Muscul.*

[1] Tertull. de Resur. Carn., cap. 46 legit, *manumisit me.* Fuimus enim quasi mancipia peccati et mortis, sed a Christo manumissi et libertate donati sumus.—*A. Lapide.*

captivity to the law of sin, which is in my members: ver. 25, 'With my mind I myself serve the law of God, but with the flesh the law of sin.' What this law of sin is, and in what respects it passes under this appellation, hereafter shall be opened: at present only in general observe, that this metaphorical expression notes the power, dominion, tyranny of sin.[1] Some make the law of sin to be no more than barely sin itself; but, I think, it carries a special reference to and superadds the adjunct of sin, the power of it. And some would have us read it the *right of sin* rather than the *law of sin;* the matter comes much to one.[2]

So much for the being made free from the law of sin: in the opening of which, as yet I have not taken any notice of the opinion of some, who make the law of sin to be the old Mosaical law; but by and by I will. It follows, *and death.* Now this is either one and the same with sin, as being only an epithet for it; so several expound it *sin and death,*[3] that is deadly sin, or sin which is of a deadly nature. As the Spirit of life is the living spirit, so sin and death is no more than deadly sin; it is an expression like that of the poet,

> ' Pateris libavit, et auro ;'

(*i.e., aureis pateris.*) Or else you may take it as distinct from sin: and so there is a double deliverance held forth in the words, One from the law of sin, another from the law of death: thus the most of interpreters open it.[4] The law of sin is always at-

tended with the law of death, and freedom from the law of sin is always attended with freedom from the law of death: the power and dominion of death stands or falls by the power and dominion of sin.

But what is this law of death?

Austine answers[1]: The law of sin is, 'Whoever sins shall die;' the law of death is, 'Dust thou art, and to dust shalt thou return.' Cajetan[2] makes it to be *permanentia in morte,* the abiding or continuance in the state of death. So believers are freed from it; for though they may for a time be subjected under it, yet it shall not always have power over them so as to hold them for ever, (as the word is used concerning Christ, Acts ii. 24); they shall arise and live again; they are not under the law, *i.e.,* the everlasting, ever-continuing, full power and strength of death. You have, ver. 10, 11, the matter of this explication: 'If Christ be in you, the body is dead because of sin, but the Spirit is life because of righteousness. But if the Spirit of him that raised up Jesus from the dead dwell in you, he that raised up Christ from the dead shall also quicken your mortal bodies by his Spirit that dwelleth in you.' But to pass these by; as the law of sin is the power of sin, so the law of death is that power and right which it hath over men by reason of sin; for it hath its empire and dominion as well as sin. Therefore as you read of the reigning of sin, so also you read of the reigning of death. Rom. v. 14, 'But death reigned from Adam to Moses;' ἐβασίλευσεν, it reigned as a king, as the word imports. Death is either temporal or eternal, both of which carry that in them which may give them the title or denomination of a law; but regenerate persons, upon the law of the Spirit of life, are freed from both. From the first, not simply and absolutely, but only in a restrained sense, viz. as it is strictly a curse, or the fruit and product of that primitive curse, Gen. ii. 17. From the second, as it notes eternal condemnation, for these two are all one,[3] they are absolutely freed. This

---

[1] Ex adverso, legem peccati et mortis appellat carnis imperium, et (quæ inde consequitur) mortis tyrannidem.—*Calv.* A peccato inhabitante, quod instar legis mihi imperabat malas actiones, et ad eas me impellebat.—*Piscat.* Est lex peccati, quia ad peccatum movet incitatque velut lex quædam.—*Estius.* A lege peccati, *i.e.,* a lege fomitis, quæ inclinat ad peccandum, vel a lege peccati, *i.e.,* a consensu et operatione peccati, quod hominem tenet ligatum per modum legis.—*Aquin.* Dum absolvuntur a dominio peccati super ipsos, ab obligatione conformandi voluntarias suas operationes legi peccati, a quo vinculo non absolvebat lex.—*Cajetan.* A lege peccati, *h.e.* a dictamine, jure, dominatu, reatu concupiscentiæ.—*A. Lap.*

[2] Elegantius vertisset *a jure peccati.*—*Erasm.*

[3] Ἤγουν τῆς θανατοποιοῦ ἁμαρτίας.—*Œcum.* Apostolus conjunctionem interposuit, eodem tamen sensu, ac si peccatum mortiferum, ἁμαρτίαν θανατοφόρον dixisset.—*Piscat.*

[4] Ἡ τοῦ πνεύματος χάρις διὰ τὴν εἰς τὸν Χριστὸν πίστιν, δυὸ σοι ἐλευθερίας δεδώρηται, οὐ μόνον γὰρ τῆς ἁμαρτίας τὴν δυναστειαν κατέλυσεν, ἀλλὰ κάι τοῦ θανατοῦ τὴν τυραννίδα κατέπαυσεν.—

Theodoret. Confer supra cap. vii. 23 et 24 ubi utriusque legis, nempe legis peccati et mortis, mentio facta est. Quare non videtur hic esse figura ἓν διὰ δύο.—*Vorstius in Schol.*

[1] August. contra Fortunat., Disput. 2.

[2] Lex mortis est mortuum perseverare mortuum; est de morte non esse reditum ad vitam.—*Cajet.*

[3] Ut sibi respondeant mors et damnatio.—*Estius.*

death, they being in Christ, and by the sanctifying Spirit delivered from the law of sin, hath no power or authority over them; I say no authority, for it is ἐξουσία, Rev. xx. 6—'On such the second death hath no power.' This is the first general in the words, that gracious deliverance from the law of sin and death which they hold forth.

The second is the subject of this deliverance. This the apostle puts down in his own person: 'The law of the Spirit, &c., hath made me free from the law of sin and death.' Here is *enallage personæ*, the change of the person; it was *them* in the foregoing verse, it is *me* in this. I have already observed, and I would now more fully open it, that our apostle throughout this whole chapter, wherein he mainly treats of the saints' privileges, speaks altogether in the plural number, excepting only this one verse. It is true, where he is speaking of some high act of grace, as performed by himself, there he puts it in the singular number, as, ver. 18, 'I reckon that the sufferings of this present time are not worthy to be compared with the glory which shall be revealed in us.' And so too, where he is speaking of some high assurance, a thing not so common, there also he expresses it in the singular number, as, ver. 38, 'For I am persuaded that neither,' &c. But wherever the great and fundamental principles of believers are before him, there he always expresses himself in the plural number; then it is *us* all together. And it is observable that, even where he speaks of himself, as to some special act or enjoyment, yet even there, as to the main privilege, he takes in all the people of God. You may see this made good in the two forementioned places; it is *I reckon*, but it is the glory that shall be revealed *in us;* and it is *I am persuaded*, but it is 'shall separate *us* from the love of God.' Well, here he puts in himself as the subject of the privilege, but it is not to exclude or shut out others, only he propounds himself as one great instance of freedom from the law of sin by the law of the Spirit; here is application and appropriation as to himself, but no impropriation or exclusion with respect to others. He that had so much of faith and experience as to be able to apply this to himself, had withal so much of knowledge and wisdom as to know that it was with others, yea, with all regenerate persons, just as it was with himself. And therefore it is in

the persons [1] of all these that he here thus speaks, and this *me* is inclusive, not exclusive; every child of God in the world may say as here Paul doth, 'The law of the Spirit of life in Christ Jesus hath made me free from the law of sin and death;' and indeed every believer should be so well acquainted with the workings of the Spirit of God upon his own heart as to be able to apply this to himself.

But why doth Paul here particularise himself, and speak thus in the singular number in this place rather than in others? I answer—

1. Because he looked upon himself as a pattern. And, indeed, God all along dealt with him as so; in reference to pardoning grace he was a pattern. 1 Tim. i. 16, 'That in me first Jesus Christ might shew forth all long-suffering, for a pattern,' &c. So in reference to renewing grace he shall be a pattern too. God would and did so effectually work upon him in the miraculous changing of him, in the mighty rescuing of him from the power of ignorance, carnal confidence, prejudices against Christ, enmity to the gospel and the professors thereof, that he should be πρὸς ὑποτύπωσιν for a pattern, to all that should be converted, of the freeness and efficacy of converting grace. And therefore if he was thus freed from the law of sin, it should then be so with others also, for what was done to him was not done to him as a mere single or private person, but as to one that was to be an instance or pattern of the grace of God towards many.

2. Because he was the complainer, therefore he shall be the triumpher; because he was the combater, therefore he shall be the conqueror. And as

---

[1] Observandum est, in causâ gratiæ nullum esse inter apostolum, et quemvis Christianum (duntaxat verum) discrimen. Non est quod dicamus Paulus fuit apostolus, nos non item; ex eo quod sibi contigit per gratiam Christi, probat hoc quod tribuit omnibus Christianis.—*Muscul.* Continet argumentum á testimonio, viz. experientiâ apostoli, et ita simul argumentum à pari, quod enim apostolus in se expertus fuerat, id pari ratione omnes credentes in se experiuntur, nempe operationem illam Spiritus sancti regenerantis.—*Piscat.* Non ego solus, sed omnes quotquot in Jesu Christo sunt, &c.—*Zuingl.* Me, et fidelem quemvis.—*Gomar;* i.e., quemvis verè Christianum.—*Grot.* Pronomen *me* demonstrat ipsum in Christo ambulantem, &c., personam siquidem talium induit.—*Cajet.* In eorum personâ de se apostolus loquitur hæc verba.—*Estius.* Soto will be sure to extend it far enough, for he glosses upon it, *me,—i.e.,* genus humanum.

you have him in the foregoing chapter,[1] in the person of believers, complaining of the law of sin ; so here you shall have him, in the person of believers too, triumphing over the law of sin, he being made free from it by another and a higher law. But to close this head ; be thou who thou wilt, if thou beest a gracious person, and one upon whom the Spirit hath put forth his efficacious power, thou as well as Paul art made free from the law of sin. Therefore, to make this the more indefinite and universal, the Syriac, not without an emphasis saith Beza,[2] reads it not *me* but *thee :* ' The law of the Spirit of life hath made *thee* free from the law,' &c.

The third general in the words is the author or efficient of this freedom from the law of sin and death, and the way or manner how it is effected. It is by ' the Spirit of life,' and it is by ' the law of the Spirit,' &c. Now here lies the greatest difficulty, and that wherein expositors do most differ : I find no less than four several interpretations put upon these words.

1. First, Some would have them to refer to the sanctity and perfect holiness of Christ's human nature. This, say they, is the Spirit of life in Christ Jesus ; and the law of the Spirit of life is the power and virtue of Christ's unspotted holiness and purity, to acquit and make free the believer from the law of sin and death, *h.e.,* from the guilt of sin and condemnation. So that they bring the matter to this ; the habitual righteousness of Christ, as man, being imputed and made over to the believer, upon this he is discharged from all guilt, and looked upon by God in Christ as perfectly righteous. This interpretation is that which several expositors, some of whom are of great eminency, do pitch upon ;[3] yet, with

submission, I shall crave leave to prefer another before it.

For it is very well known, though I shall not in the least concern myself therein, that some very worthy persons do question the truth of the thing, viz., the formal imputation of Christ's habitual and original righteousness, they making the sanctity of his human nature to belong to his *justitia personæ,* rather than to his *justitia meriti* or *justitia fidejussoria,* and they looking upon it only as the necessary qualification of his person to fit him to be a mediator, and also as that which was necessary in order to the meritoriousness of his obedience, but denying that it is directly and formally made over by imputation to the believer. But as to this, (which is the *veritas rei,*) as I said before, I will not at all concern myself about that. I am only to inquire whether this interpretation be proper to the text, and rightly grounded upon it, (which is the *veritas loci.*) And truly that I question very much, and must say with the learned De Dieu, *Nescio an id spectaverit apostolus,* &c. I know not whether that was the thing which the apostle here had in his eye. I humbly conceive the words, without great straining, cannot be brought to this sense, their main scope and intendment looking to a quite other thing. And that branch of them, *in Christ Jesus,* upon which they who close with the exposition before us lay so great a stress, will bear another explication much more easy and genuine, as you will hear by and by.

2. Secondly, Others understand by *the law of the Spirit of life* and *the law of sin and death,* the law of faith and the law of works, or the evangelical and the Mosaical law. You read, Rom. iii. 27, of the law of faith and of works, two very opposite and

---

[1] Ponit se pro exemplo, ut prius infirmitatum et luctæ, ita nunc fiduciæ. Imo verbis quasi præit, quibus singuli hanc consolationem nobis applicemus.—*Pareus.*

[2] Et quidem non sine emphasi, quasi admonente Paulo, ut singuli credentes hoc sibi beneficium applicent.—*Beza.*

[3] Cum adeo imbecilla sit via Spiritus in nobis, quomodo inde possumus colligere, nullam esse condemnationem, &c. quoniam, inquit, vis ista Spiritus vivificantis, quæ tam imbecilla est in nobis, perfectissima et potentissima est in Christo, et nobis credentibus imputata, facit ut perinde censeamur, ac si nullæ prorsus reliquiæ corruptionis et mortis in nobis inhæererent. Nunc autem de perfecta sanctitatis humanæ naturæ Christi imputatione disserit, &c.—*Beza in Paraphr.* Distinguit legem Spiritus vitæ quæ est in ipso Christo Jesu, ab ea

quæ in nobis est ab eo effecta, *i.e.,* perfectam naturæ nostræ in Christo sanctificationem, ab ea quæ in nobis est duntaxat inchoata. Nam illa quidem nobis imputata, cum perfecta sit, nos liberavit, &c. Explicandum est igitur istud, de tertia justificationis nostræ gratuitæ parte, quæ consistit in sanctificatione ipsa Jesu Christi nobis communicata.—*Idem in Notis.* Et porro, vis illa Spiritus vivifici, cujus fons est in Christi carne, facit ut peccatum, seu vitiositas illa, cujus reliquiæ adhuc in me supersunt, et quæ me alioqui condemnationi adjudicarent, efficere nequeat ut condemner, quoniam quod est in me duntaxat inchoatum, in Christo perfectissimum est, cui sum insitus. This way goes Hemingius, Elton, Parr, Streso, &c. Thus Downham interprets it, Of Justific., book i. chap. 3.

contrary laws. Now by that twofold law some open the law of the Spirit and the law of sin and death. Thus Ambrose expounds it:[1] 'The law, saith he, of the Spirit of life, it is the very law of faith. The law of Moses was a spiritual law,[2] because it forbade sin; but it was not the law of the Spirit of life, because it could not remit sin, and so quicken the dead. But this law of faith is the law of the Spirit of life, because it doth not only restrain sin, but it also restores from death, &c. This law in Christ Jesus, that is by faith, doth free the believer from the law of sin and death. The law of sin is that which dwells in the members, which persuades to that which is contrary to the will of God. The law of death is the law of Moses, because it kills sinners. And no wonder that this law should be the law of death, when the gospel is to some the savour of death unto death; and so he goes on in the further explication of it. Amongst modern interpreters, Pareus follows this exposition, making the law of the Spirit of life to be the doctrine of the gospel, and the law of sin and death to be the law of Moses. The gospel, saith he, is the law of the Spirit, because it is attended with the conveyance of the Spirit; the law of Moses was spiritual, but not the law of the Spirit, because it did not convey the Spirit. And that was the law of sin, because it discovered sin, irritated sin, made sin to be sin; and of death too, because it had a killing virtue in it. 2 Cor. iii. 6, 'The letter killeth, but the Spirit giveth life.' Thus Pareus, who, after he had laid down and opened his opinion, thus concludes, With submission to other men's judgments, I judge this to be the most plain and genuine meaning of this place. This way very many others go, either as to the whole, or as to the most considerable part of it.[3]

But neither shall I close with this interpretation, and that for two reasons: 1. Because, though the gospel may very well be styled the law of the Spirit of life, yet it sounds somewhat harsh to call the Mosaical law—God's own law—the law of sin and death. There is, I grant, something of truth in it, and it may admit of a very fair and sound explication; but then there must be a great deal of stating and limitation and cautioning before you can come at it. And therefore many expositors do not approve of the application of this title to the Mosaical law.[1] Nay, our apostle himself warns us against it; whose way and custom it was, whenever he had touched upon anything which might seem to reflect any disparagement upon the law, presently to subjoin something for the vindication of its honour: Rom. vii. 7, 'What shall we say then? Is the law sin? God forbid. When the commandment came, sin revived and I died; and the commandment which was ordained to life, I found to be unto death,' &c. Yet, saith he, 'the law is holy, and the commandment holy, and just, and good; was then that which was good made death to me? God forbid. But sin that it might appear sin, working death in me by that which is good; that sin by the commandment might become exceeding sinful.' No man did ever depress the law more than Paul did, in the matter of justification; yet in other respects none did ever more vindicate and exalt it. Well, this is one reason why I shall not fall in with this sense.

A second is this, because the apostle here is not treating of the law state, or gospel state, or of the

---

[1] Lex ergo Spiritus vitæ est lex fidei. Nam et Mosis lex est Spiritualis, quia prohibet peccare, non tamen vitæ, &c. (It is too large to be written out.)

[2] Chrysostom distinguishes much to the same purpose. Καί τοι καὶ τὴν Μωυσεως οὕτῶς ἐκάλει, λεγων, οἴδαμεν ὅτι ὁ νόμος πνευματικὸς ἐστι, τί οὖν τὸ μεσον; πολὺ καὶ ἄπειρον; ἐκεῖνος μεν γαρ πνευματικός, οὗτος δε νόμος πνευματος, καιτι τοῦτο διεστηκεν; ὅτι ὁ μεν ὑπὸ τοῦ πνευματος ἐδόθη μόνον, οὗτος δε τὸ πνεῦμα ἐχορήγει τοῖς δεχομενοις ἀυτὸν δαψιλές.—Chrysost. in loc.

[3] Lex Spiritus, &c., est doctrina evangelii fide apprehensa. —Osiand. Fortasse et legem Mosis intelligit per legem peccati et mortis, a qua etiam lege liberati sumus, in vulgato Jesu

Christi evangelio.—Mussus. Utraque est Spiritus sancti ut actoris, utraque est spiritus nostri directiva, sed hæc est Spiritus sancti, quatenus est vivificator noster in Jesu Christo, &c.—Cajetan. Legem peccati vocat literam legis, quæ peccatum excitare solet, et damnationem revelare.—Vatabl. Opponitur hæc lex Spiritus legi Mosaicæ.—Crell. Posset etiam per legem peccati et mortis intelligi lex Mosis, &c.— Perer. Vide Lud. de Dieu in loc.—Baldwin. Dr Hammond in Paraphr.

[1] Ού τοῦ Μωῦσαικου, ὅταν γαρ λέγει ἠλευθέρωσέ με ἀπὸ τοῦ νόμου τῆς ἁμαρτίας, καὶ τοῦ θανάτου, οὗ τον Μωύσεως νόμον λέγει ἐνταῦθα, οὐδαμοῦ γαρ ἀυτὸν νόμον ἁμαρτίας καλει, &c.—Chrysost. Legem peccati et mortis non ausim cum quibusdam accipere pro lege Dei, &c. Quamvis enim peccatum augendo mortem generet, Paulus tamen ab hac invidia consulto supra deflexit. —Calvin. His verbis non significatur lex Mosaica, &c.- Pet. Mart.

covenant administration proper to either; but he is, more closely, treating of the state of nature and of grace, of freedom from condemnation by the taking away of sin's power and guilt; in pursuance of which, he pitches upon sanctification by the Spirit and satisfaction by the Son. And therefore, though the former notion may be taken in, yet certainly that which directly falls in with the latter, as that sense will which I shall presently give, must be most agreeable to the apostle's scope in this place.

3. Thirdly, By *the law of the Spirit of life in Christ Jesus*, some understand nothing but the very Spirit of Christ Jesus. They make the law of the Spirit to be the very Spirit itself, and nothing more; thus Chrysostom and his followers.[1] This is a very good foundation to build upon, but yet without some further addition, it will not so fully reach that special matter in the words, which hath a great weight and emphasis in it.

4. Fourthly, Therefore others do interpret them not only as pointing to God's Spirit, but, to make it the more express, they consider the Spirit of God as renewing, as regenerating, as working the new and heavenly life in the soul with great power and efficacy. The Spirit is styled the Spirit of life, both as he is a living Spirit himself, and also as he is a quickening Spirit to the creature; as he makes sinners who, Eph. ii. 1, were 'dead in trespasses and sins,' to live, by working grace and regeneration in them, and so life thereby. But what is the law of the Spirit of life? Why, it is the mighty power of the regenerating Spirit put forth upon men in order to the freeing of them from the power and dominion of sin. There are, I know, sundry other explications given of it; Origen makes it to be the law of God in general, which, saith he, is also the law of the Spirit;[2] Erasmus opens it by the spiritual law;[3] Pererius and Estius, by that grace of Christ

or of the Spirit by which he 'writes the law in the heart;[1] Zuinglius by the grace of faith;[2] several such glosses are put upon it, which I shall not further make recital of. That explication which I have laid down is most usual and common;[3] and so, to be brief, all comes to this; *the Spirit of life* is the Holy Spirit of God, which is a living Spirit in himself, and which also as a regenerating Spirit works the divine and spiritual life in the soul; and *the law of the Spirit of life* is the power and commanding efficacy of the sanctifying Spirit in his gracious operations upon the hearts of such and such persons, by which they are made free from the law of sin and death; that is, from the absolute domination, tyranny, and full power of sin and death. Before I go off from this, one thing must be added, viz., that though *law* be here joined with the *Spirit of life*, yet it is to be taken not as ultimately referring to the life, but rather to that which follows, 'hath made me free from the law of sin,' &c. I mean this; great is that power which the Spirit puts forth in renewing, and thereby quickening the soul, yet his power, as terminating in that effect, is not here mainly intended; but it is the power of the Spirit terminating in the deliverance of the sinner from sin's dominion which is here intended; that, I say, is the proper *terminus* of the Spirit's power in this place, and whatever power the Spirit puts forth in the life or regeneration, that is here mentioned but as the way or medium of the Spirit in his making free from the law of sin and death.

This interpretation of the words I judge most agreeable to the apostle's scope in them, and therefore I shall handle them according to it; and then the connexion will lie thus, 'There is no condemnation to them who are in Christ Jesus, &c., because by the mighty power of the regenerating and enlivening

---

[1] Νόμον πνεύματος τὸ πνεῦμα καλῶν, ὥσπερ γὰρ νόμον ἁμαρτίας τὴν ἁμαρτιαν, οὕτω νόμον πνεύματος τὸ πνεῦμα φησί.—*Chrysost.* Theophyl., Œcumen., Theodor., say the same. Lex Spiritus, *i.e.*, lex quæ est Spiritus.—*Aquin.*

[2] Lex Spiritus vitæ una eademque est quæ et lex Dei, sicut una eademque est lex peccati et mortis; nihil damnationis erit his, qui a lege peccati, quæ est lex mortis, liberantur, et legi Dei, quæ est lex Spiritus, serviunt.—*Orig.*

[3] Lex Spiritus perinde sonat, *q.d.*, legem Spiritualem, juxta proprietatem sermonis Hebraici.—*Erasm.*

[1] Est periphrasis legis gratiæ, quam Spiritus sanctus renovator et vivificator mentis humanæ scribit in cordibus quæ inhabitat.—*Perer.* Legem Spiritus vocat gratiam Christi, qua lex Dei per Spiritum sanctum scribitur in cordibus nostris.—*Estius.*

[2] Lex Spiritus vitæ, *i.e.*, certa et indubitata in Christum fides, &c. Per antithesin legi peccati, fidem in Deum per Christum legem appellat, abutens vocabulo legis.—*Zuinglius.*

[3] Cum Paulus utitur voce legis, loquitur metaphorice, nam per legem intelligit vim et efficaciam.—*Pet. Martyr.* Lex Spiritus metaphorice, vis quasi imperans et dominans.—*Gomar.*

Spirit such are freed from the command and rule of sin, so that it doth not reign over them as formerly it did; and they being thus freed from the power of sin, consequently they are also freed from the power of death, especially of eternal death; so that most certainly there is no condemnation to them.'

But now against the truth of what is here asserted a question or objection may be raised: How doth Paul here say that he was made free from the law of sin, when in the preceding chapter he had so much complained of it? You have him there bewailing it over and over, therefore how is that consistent with what he here lays down? I will not at present stay to answer this objection, but in the handling of one of the observations it shall be answered.

Upon the review of the words I find one thing in them which as yet hath scarce been touched upon, that therefore must be a little opened; and then I shall have done with the explication of them. It is here said 'the law of the Spirit of life *in Christ Jesus.*' Now it may be asked, what doth this *in Christ Jesus* refer to? or what is that in special which is in Christ Jesus? Is it the life, or the Spirit, or the law of the Spirit? for all of these go before. I answer, each and all of them in different respects may be said to be in Christ Jesus, but I conceive it is spoken chiefly with respect to the Spirit itself.

1. The life, wrought in the soul at and by regeneration, that is in Christ Jesus; partly as he by the Spirit doth work that life, and partly as he preserves and keeps up that life when it is wrought. The spiritual life here, as well as the eternal life hereafter, is in Christ; that of the apostle, though it be spoken of the latter, yet is applicable to both: 1 John v. 11, 'And this life is in his Son.' Beza, with others,[1] some of whom do a little differ in their notion of the life itself, carries it in this reference, according to his explication of the *Spirit of life;* and to make the thing more express he would have an article inserted and added to the words, thus, τοῦ πνεύματος τῆς ζωῆς τῆς ἐν Χριστῷ Ἰησοῦ.

2. The Spirit is in Christ Jesus. And it may be

said to be so upon a fourfold account: (1.) As it was at first poured out upon him in his human nature, and doth yet reside in him in a very high and eminent manner. For 'God gave not the Spirit by measure to him,' as he doth to us, John iii. 34; he was 'full of the Holy Ghost,' Luke iv. 1; 'anointed with the Holy Ghost,' Acts x. 38; it was prophesied of him that 'the Spirit of the Lord should rest upon him,' Isa. xi. 2. Christ as man hath the special residence of the Spirit in him, and the special communication of the Spirit to him; it is in all the saints, but eminently it is in Christ Jesus. (2.) It is the Spirit of life in Christ Jesus, not only in respect of the great acts and operations of this Spirit in and upon Christ himself, but also in respect of the order of the Spirit in its operations; for it first wrought in and upon Christ,[1] in the sanctifying of his human nature, in the fitting of him for his sufferings, in the supporting of him under his sufferings, &c., and then subsequently it works in and upon believers according to their capacity. (3.) The Spirit may be said to be in Christ Jesus, as he doth convey and give this Spirit where he pleases. Then the *in Christ Jesus* is as much as *by Christ Jesus:*[2] the Spirit is given and doth work as a regenerating Spirit, or the Spirit of life, according to the will and good pleasure of Christ. (4.) As this Spirit is given only to those who are in Christ.[3] Men out of Christ have nothing to do with it; his members are only its temples; without the Spirit there is no union, and without the union there is no Spirit. As the member doth not participate of the animal spirit but as it is united to the head, so a man doth not participate of the blessed quickening Spirit of God but as he is united to Christ; but these things will be more largely insisted upon when I come to the ninth and tenth verses. Now the words, which I am opening, mainly point to this; what is it which is in Christ

---

[1] Lex Spiritus vitæ, est vis Spiritus quæ vitam eam inspirat quæ est in Christo, quæque vivitur ejus Spiritu.—*Bucer.* Illius inquam Spiritus, qui ad vitam æternam ducit quam Christus daturus est.—*Grot.*

[1] See of this Dr Sibbs in The Spiritual Jubilee, p. 36, &c.

[2] Αὐτὸς ἡμῖν αἴτιος τῆς δωρεᾶς τοῦ πνεύματος, καὶ ἐπισπασάμενος καθὸ ἐστιν ἄνθρωπος τὸ πνεῦμα, καὶ ἡμῖν μεταδούς.—*Œcumenius.* Lex Spiritus vitæ, *i.e.,* gubernatio Spiritus vitalis, quem suppeditat Christus, non solum admonens nos exemplo mortis suæ ad charitatis opera perficienda, sed etiam operans illam in cordibus nostris.—*Œcolamp.*

[3] In Christo Jesu, quia non datur nisi his qui sunt in Christo Jesu.—*Aquin.*

Jesus? Why, it is the Spirit itself; therefore some also would have an article inserted here to make the reference to the Spirit more clear, thus, τοῦ πνεύματος τῆς ζωῆς τοῦ ἐν Χριστῷ 'Ιησοῦ.[1]

3. Then as to the third and last thing, *the law of the Spirit*: that too is in Christ Jesus. Thus, that mighty power which the Spirit at any time doth exert in the work of regeneration, it is conveyed to a person, and doth take hold of him in Christ Jesus, that is, in and through Christ; viz., as this effectual operation of the Spirit is grounded upon Christ's purchase, and is put forth in pursuance of Christ's redeeming love. This is a truth which might be largely opened, but I fear I have been too long already upon the clearing up of this branch of the text.

And yet I cannot omit to tell you that there is one reference more, which some do mention;[2] as this, *in Christ Jesus*, may refer to and be joined with the word, ἠλευθέρωσε, 'hath made free.' Then the sense would be this, it is by Christ that saints are made free from sin and death; whatever spiritual freedom believers have they owe it all to Christ, he hath the great hand in it as the efficient and meritorious cause thereof. But this I will pass by, because though it be a thing unquestionably true, yet the generally received pointing of the words will not admit it to be here intended.

I have now finished the explicatory part; the difficulty of the words, and the different expositions put upon them, all of which may be useful, though all are not so pertinent and proper, must be my excuse for my being so tedious and prolix upon it.

Having given you their proper sense and meaning, I should next draw out those doctrinal truths which are contained in them; but that I shall not do at present. Only there is one of them which I shall mention and briefly close with; it is this, the holy and blessed Spirit is the Spirit of life; so he is here expressly styled, 'the law of the *Spirit of life*.' Which words are applied to the witnesses, Rev. xi. 11, where it is said of them that 'the Spirit of life

from God entered upon them;' but yet know, though it is the same words, yet it is not the same sense. For by the Spirit of life, as applied to the witnesses, nothing is meant but their civil living again in their restoration to their former power, office, liberties of service, &c.; but when it is applied to the great Spirit of God it carries a quite other and much higher sense in it. What is that? Why, it notes his living in himself, and also his being the cause of life to the creature. He is the Spirit of life;—

1. Formally. 2. Effectively or causally. A few words to each.

1. First, as to the formal notion. The Spirit of God is the Spirit of life as he is a living Spirit, as he lives in himself, or hath life in himself. For 'as the Father hath life in himself,' and 'hath given to the Son to have life in himself,' John v. 26, so the Spirit hath life in himself also. And it is not an ordinary or common life which the Spirit lives, but it is the selfsame life which the Father and the Son do live; he being truly God, lives the same uncreated, infinite, independent, blessed life which the two other persons do. Expositors[1] generally observe that *life*, when it is here joined with the *Spirit*, is not to be taken *substantivè* but *adjectivè*: it is according to the Hebrew idiom, where when two substantives are put together, the latter of which is in the genitive case, that is to be rendered as an adjective or as an epithet of the former; as the *bread of life* is *living bread*, the *water of life* is *living water*, the *glory of grace* is *glorious grace*, &c.; so here the *Spirit of life* is the *living Spirit*. Theophylact, joining this life with the law going before, saith this is spoken πρὸς ἀντίαςολὴν, as if the law of life was set in opposition to the law of sin and death; but *life* is not to be joined with the *law*, but with the *Spirit* himself.

2. Secondly, the Holy Spirit is the Spirit of life effectively or causally. He is a quickening, a life-bestowing or life-working Spirit in the creature; he makes sinners to live, and is the spring of that heavenly and supernatural life which is in the gracious soul. As he hath life in himself, so he communicates it to others; he is not only a 'living Spirit,' but he is also πνεῦμα ζωοποιοῦν, a 'quickening Spirit.' And

---

[1] Placet supplementum *qui* ut referatur ad Spiritum, et in Græco subaudiatur τοῦ, quasi scriptum sit τοῦ πνεύματος τῆς ζωῆς τοῦ ἐν Χριστῷ 'Ιησοῦ.—*Piscat.* So *Erasm.*

[2] Quamquam nihil vetat, quin illa verba, ἐν Χριστῷ 'Ιησοῦ, construantur cum verbo sequente ἠλευθέρωσε, &c.—*Piscat. in Schol.*

[1] Genitivus Hebraico more pro epitheto ponitur.—*Calvin.* —Est genitivus epitheti loco.—*Estius.*

O

this is one of his great acts, namely, to quicken; he is the Spirit of liberty, 2 Cor. iii. 17, and he is also the Spirit of life; he is a teaching, enlightening, convincing, strengthening, comforting, purifying Spirit, and he is also an enlivening and quickening Spirit. And as the father and the Son live in themselves, and quicken whom they will, John v. 21; so the Holy Ghost too hath life in himself and quickens whom he will, as he is said to 'divide gifts to every one severally even as he will,' 1 Cor. xii. 11. The Spirit is χόρηγος καὶ δότικος,[1] the guide and the giver of the spiritual life. As the soul gives life to the body, so the Spirit of God gives life to the soul; in which respect he is called the Spirit of life.[2]

And this life or quickening by the Spirit is either that which is at the first conversion, or that which is subsequent and follows after conversion.

1. First, there is that life which is proper to the first conversion. When the sinner is converted he is quickened or made alive; for, indeed, till that great work was done in him, in a spiritual sense he was no better than a dead man: before renewing grace there is no life. It is the regenerating Spirit which inspires this into the soul. I say into the soul, for that is the receptive subject of this life. There is another life or quickening, to be wrought also by the Spirit, which is proper to the body, of which the apostle speaks here, ver. 11, 'Shall also quicken your mortal bodies by his Spirit that dwelleth in you,' in reference to which Christ too is called a quickening Spirit, 1 Cor. xv. 45; but the proper subject of the present and spiritual enlivening by the Spirit is the soul. Now, take a man before conversion. He hath a soul spiritually dead, he lives the life of nature, the common animal life, and that is all; but when the Spirit comes and renews him, it breathes a divine and excellent life into him. Eph. ii. 1, 'You hath he quickened, who were dead in trespasses and sins.' Luke xv. 32, 'For this thy brother was dead, and is alive again.' The Spirit of life is the Spirit of regeneration, and he, working as a regenerating Spirit, is the Spirit of life.

2. There is the Spirit's quickening after conversion.

[1] Œcumen.
[2] Dicitur Spiritus vitæ, quod animam vegetet et vivificet divina gratia.—*Contzen.* Sicut spiritus naturalis facit vitam naturæ, sic Spiritus divinus facit vitam gratiæ.—*Aquin.*

For this, in such a sense, is a continued, abiding, repeated act; we are but once regenerated, and therefore but once habitually quickened, but the actual and subsequent quickening is renewed and reiterated from time to time. This lies in the exciting and actuating of the several graces, the taking off the deadness of the heart in holy duties, the drawing out of vigorous and lively desires after God and Christ, the raising and stirring up of the affections, &c. And all this is done by the Spirit of life also; the life and liveliness too of a Christian is from the vital, quickening influences of the Spirit, without which there can be no spiritual vivacity in him. Therefore the spouse prayed, Cant. iv. 16, 'Awake O north wind, and come thou south, blow upon my garden, that the spices thereof may flow out.' She directed her prayer to the Spirit, and what did she pray for? For that which I am upon, viz., the enlivening and exciting of her graces; she expresses it metaphorically, but this was the thing which her soul breathed after. To apply this in a word, for it is not a point which I intend to stay upon.

Use.—Sirs! you see whither you are to go for life. Here is the Spirit of life, to him therefore you must apply yourselves for life; it is the living Spirit which must make you live. Are you not spiritually dead? Is not this the sad condition of all who lie in the natural state? What are such but as so many walking ghosts? they are no better than dead even whilst they live, as the apostle speaks of the widow that lives in pleasure, 1 Tim. v. 6. Is not grace the life of the soul? What is life itself but a kind of death without Christ and grace? θανατός ἐστιν ἄνευ Χριστοῦ ζωὴ saith Ignatius. Alas! you may move, walk, breathe, eat, drink, sleep, put forth all the several acts of the animal life, and yet for all this, in reference to any spiritual life, be but dead persons. And is it so with any of you? Oh why do you not fly to the Spirit of life that you may be quickened? God convince you of the misery of spiritual death, that you may endeavour to get out of it! and God convince you of the glory, excellency, necessity of the spiritual life, that you may with the most earnest desires pursue after it! What is it to have the life of nature, and to want the life of grace? to have living bodies without and dead souls within? to be able to do whatever is proper to nature, and not to be able to put forth one vital act of grace ? Is not the spiritual death a certain forerunner of the eternal death ? Can he that is dead here, being without God, hope to live with God hereafter? O that you would be persuaded to make out after the spiritual life ! I would in hearty desires say that for every dead soul which they once wrote upon the tomb of dead Brutus, *utinam viveres*, would to God that thou mightest live ! But how shall that be accomplished ? Why, thus, here is the Spirit of life, whose office it is to quicken the dead ; whoever thou art, therefore, if thou wilt but betake thyself to this Spirit, he can and will give thee life. Life thou *must* have, for it is better to have no life than not to have this life. Life thou *mayest* have, nay, life thou *shalt* have, if thou wilt but implore, improve, wait, depend upon this Spirit of life.

Further, you that are saints, in whom the quickening Spirit hath effectually wrought, yet do not you find yourselves too often under great deadness ? Certainly you are great strangers to yourselves if you do not find it to be so ; you are not dead, yet often under deadness. Oh now, whenever it is so with you, and you groan under it as your burden, do you also apply yourselves to this Spirit of life. You go to duty, attend upon ordinances, pray, hear the word, receive the sacrament, and you would fain be lively in all ; would you be so indeed? look upwards then, as knowing it is the Spirit of life that must make you so. Quickening grace is very precious to the soul that is sincere, a child of God cannot be without it ; he cannot be satisfied in the bare having of grace, unless it be lively; nor with the bare performance of duty, unless he be lively in it. How earnest was David in his prayers to God for it ! Ps. cxix. 25, 37, 40, 88, 'Quicken thou me, according to thy word :' 'Quicken thou me in thy way :' 'Quicken me in thy righteousness :' 'Quicken me after thy loving kindness.' The earnestness of his desires after it made him go over it again and again. And no wonder it is so, for how sweet are ordinances to a gracious person when he hath life in them ! when therein he can get his graces up, his affections up and lively, when he prays and hath life in prayer, hears and hath life in hearing, receives and hath life in receiving, oh then great is his joy ! Deadness very much hinders comfort in duty ; as the soul is quickened, so proportionably it is comforted. In order therefore to this, how doth it concern you to improve the Spirit of God as the Spirit of life ! Who can thus animate and enliven you but he ? He who freed you from the law of sin and death must also free you from all that dulness and deadness of spirit which sometimes possesses you : therefore when David was desiring this mercy he puts the Spirit before it, 'Thy Spirit is good, &c. : Quicken me, O Lord, for thy name's sake,' Ps. cxliii. 10, 11. Indeed, as none can cleanse the filthy heart but the purifying Spirit, nor soften the hard heart but the mollifying Spirit, so none can enliven the dead heart but the quickening Spirit. When the child was dead the prophet sent his staff, but that would not do the work ; the child did not revive till the prophet came himself ; so you may have quickening means, and quickening ordinances, and quickening providences ; but if this quickening Spirit doth not come himself, you will be dead still. Oh therefore, whenever you find the heart under inward deadness, presently carry it to this quickening Spirit for quickening grace ! I would not have any here mistake me, to put a wrong interpretation or make bad inferences from what hath been spoken, so as to slight, neglect, cast off external means, ordinances, duties, because they are but dead things of themselves, and it is the Spirit only which gives life ; some infer such a practice from the premises, but they do it very unwarrantably. For it is true that the Spirit of life only quickens, but then he doth this for men when they are in the use of and in attendance upon the means ; he first quickens *to* duty and then *in* duty and *by* duty : his way and method is to give out his enlivening influences when the soul is waiting in holy ordinances. And therefore these must be highly valued and duly attended upon, though it be the Spirit only which works in them effectually upon the heart. It was the angel moving the waters that did the cure, yet the poor cripples were to lie by the pool side ; so it is here. It is a good *caveat*, therefore, that of Musculus upon the words, *Ista Spiritus Dei efficacia*, &c., that efficacy of the Spirit, saith he, is always to be prayed for, yet we must take heed that we have a due respect for those outward means which the Spirit will have us to make use of. But no more of this.

CHAPTER V.

OF THE LAW OR POWER OF SIN UNDER WHICH ALL MEN ARE BY NATURE.

For the law of the spirit of life, in Christ Jesus, hath made me free from the law of sin and death.—ROM. viii. 2.

The whole matter in the words drawn into several observations—The main observation broken into three—The first of which is spoken to, viz., That every unregenerate person is under the law of sin—That law of sin is opened in the twofold notion of it—Two questions stated : (1.) How doth sin act as a law in the unregenerate ?—(2.) How it may be known when it is the law of sin ; or wherein doth the difference lie betwixt the power of sin in the regenerate and in the unregenerate ? The point applied by way of information : to inform us (1.) of the bondage of the natural state—The evil and misery of that set forth in some particulars—(2.) To inform us of the necessity, power, and efficacy of restraining and renewing grace—Both spoken to.

HAVING opened the words, and fixed upon that interpretation of them which I judge most proper and genuine, which was my work the last time; I come now to fall upon those observations which are grounded upon and do best comply therewith.

It hath been already observed, first, That the Holy Spirit of God is the spirit of life : this I have given some short account of, and will add nothing further upon it.

I might secondly observe, That this spirit of life is in Christ Jesus : the regenerating Spirit is in Christ, though not as the regenerating Spirit, according to our common notion of regeneration. This was also cleared up in some particulars when I was upon the explication of the words; and in the following verses I shall have occasion to handle it fully ; therefore here I will pass it over.

There is a third observation, which takes in the principal matter in the text, that therefore I shall only insist upon ; namely, That all regenerate persons by the law of the spirit of life are made free from the law of sin and death. For this is that

which Paul here affirms concerning himself ; and he speaking here not as an apostle but as one regenerate *quatenus* regenerate, that which he saith of himself is applicable to all such, they are all made free from, &c.

This being more generally laid down just as it lies in the words of the text, and it being very comprehensive, I will therefore more particularly branch it out into three observations :

Obs. 1. That every man in the world, as he is in the natural and unconverted state, before the Spirit of life, or the regenerating Spirit, takes hold of him, is under the law of sin and death.

Obs. 2. That such who are truly regenerate are made free from the law of sin and death.

Obs. 3. That it is by the law of the Spirit of life that these are made free from the law of sin and death. Each of these points are of great weight and importance, therefore I shall distinctly and largely speak to them.

Obs. 1. I begin with the first, which you may shorten thus : Every unregenerate man is under the law of sin and death. In the handling both of this and also of the two other, I shall mainly direct my discourse to the law of sin ; as to the law of death, that I shall only speak to in the close of all.

This first doctrinal proposition is not so express in the letter of the words as the two following, but it is strongly implied, and very naturally deducible from them. Paul himself, that chosen vessel, Acts ix. 15, who was so eminent in the love of God, the graces of the Spirit, the work and privileges of the gospel, till it pleased the Lord savingly to work upon him, was under the law of sin ; for he says here he was made free from it, implying there was a time when he was enslaved under it. As to the civil freedom of a Roman, he tells us he was born to that, Acts xxii. 28 ; but as to evangelical freedom from the command and bondage of sin, he doth not say he was born free, but made free; this was not the result of nature, birth, or any such thing, but the mere effect of divine grace. Further, he saith, ' the law of the Spirit of life in Christ Jesus hath made me free ;' whence it follows that till this law of the Spirit had taken hold of him he was under the law of sin ; before the mighty power of the regenerating Spirit did effectually work in him to convert and sanctify him, sin had its full power and dominion over him. He gives a sad account of this, Eph. ii. 3, ' Among whom also we all had our conversation in times past in the lusts of our flesh, fulfilling the desires of the flesh,' &c. And Tit. iii. 3, ' For we ourselves also were sometimes foolish, disobedient,' &c. It is true, even after conversion, you have him complaining of the law of sin : Rom. vii. 21, ' I find a law, that when I would do good, evil is present with me,' &c. ; but there was a great difference between that law of sin which he was under before conversion, and that which he was under after conversion, as you shall hereafter understand.

And thus it is with all men in the world before regenerating grace ; in the natural and unconverted state, all are under the law of sin. Every man is born a subject and vassal to sin, and is, as he comes into the world, under the power, tyranny, and domination of a cursed nature. Sin is that truly universal monarch which hath all men, before they be converted, under its empire and sovereignty ; let them be high or low, bond or free, in other respects, till they be renewed and rescued by the law of the Spirit of life, they are all under sin's command and regency. For the proof of this, in the general, I shall only refer you to Rom. vi., from the 12th verse to the end ; where you have the law of sin, and the sinner's bondage under its dominion, set forth in great variety of expressions ; I will not recite any of them, it is best to take them together as they lie in the whole discourse of the apostle.

For the better handling of the truth before us, I will, 1st, Open this law of sin, and shew what is included in it, and why that is set forth by this metaphor ; then, 2d, Prove that men whilst unregenerate are under this law of sin.

Yet since, without any prejudice or disadvantage to the matter contained in each of these heads, they may be spoken to conjunctly as well as apart ; and because, too, the putting of them together will somewhat shorten the work ; therefore that shall be my method.

The word *law*, as a worthy person[1] hath observed to my hand, is taken either properly or improperly. Properly, so it is the edict or sanction of a person or persons in authority, wherein he or they do order

[1] Dr Owen ' On the Power, &c., of Indwelling Sin,' ch. i. and ii.

and enjoin something to be done, backing his or their commands with promises of rewards, as also their prohibitions with threatenings of punishment ; this is the nature of a law in the strict and proper notion of it. Now, if you insist upon this its exact consideration, and take in all in this description, so sin cannot be said to be a law, or to impose a law upon the creature,—the reason is obvious, because it hath no right of dominion or rightful authority, which is essentially requisite to the law-maker, and to the validity and obligation of the law. The power of sin is but usurped, it hath dominion *de facto*, but not *de jure*. God never gave the corrupt nature in man any authority to be or to make a law which should bind his creatures. He himself hath made excellent laws, which are unquestionably and universally obligatory ; and he hath set up magistrates, his vicegerents, to whom he hath delegated a power of making laws, which shall, in a lower degree, be obligatory also. But now for sin, what hath that to do with this law-making or law-obliging authority ? so that this consideration of a law doth not all suit with it ; yet there is something in the description that will suit with it well enough, insomuch that it may be truly called the law of sin.

For, first, a law is a commanding thing : it lays its imperative injunctions upon men, and expects their obedience ; it doth not barely notify or represent to men what they are to do or not to do, nor only advise and persuade them to do so and so, but it commands authoritatively ; it carries dominion in it, Rom. vii. 1, ' Know ye not the law hath dominion over a man as long as he liveth ?' This is wrapped up in the very nature of it, and is inseparable from it. Now in this respect sin is a law, it commands the sinner to act so and so, lays its precepts upon him in a very imperious manner, assumes a strange kind of authority over him, though justly it hath none ; therefore you read of the reigning of sin, of obeying sin, of the dominion of sin, Rom. vi. 12, 14. This is the nature of a law in general, in reference to which sin hath this appellation of a law. In this respect such as are in the natural state may too justly be said to be under the law of sin, for it hath the command over them, and doth from time to time lay its commands upon them. The subject is not more under the law of his sovereign, nor the servant of his master, than the sinner is under the law of sin; it commands very proudly, and he as tamely obeys. Oh, there is the law of sin!

There are indeed two things in a law; it is a commanding, and it is a condemning thing. It first commands men to order their actings according to what it prescribes; and if they do not so do, in case of disobedience, then they are by it tried and condemned. Unregenerate persons are in both of these respects under the law of sin: (1.) Sin hath a commanding power in them. Oh, that is upon the throne in their hearts! It rules them, and with a strange kind of sovereignty, orders them to do what it pleases; it kings[1] and lords[2] it over them, as the words are, Rom. vi. 12, 14. And as there is this domination on sin's part, so there is subjection on the sinner's part. No sooner doth it command, but it is presently obeyed; it doth but speak the word and it is done. If it will have such a lust gratified, the sinner readily yields to it. As the centurion speaks of his soldiers, Mat. viii. 9, 'I am a man under authority, having soldiers under me; and I say to this man, Go, and he goeth; Come, and he cometh; Do this, and he doeth it.' Just such a power or sovereignty hath sin in and over graceless persons. They are at its beck; according to its commanding propensions, they order and steer their course. May they not therefore be said to be under the law of sin? Then (2.) for the other property of a law; as it is a condemning thing, that belongs to sin too. Oh, it is not only of a commanding, but also of a condemning nature. And, which is not usual, where it commands and is obeyed, there it condemns; which shows the difference betwixt the law of sin and all other laws. They do not condemn where they are obeyed; it is only the breach or non-performance of them which makes a person liable to condemnation. But herein lies the cursedness of the law of sin; upon the obeying of it, it becomes a condemning law, and it only condemns where it is obeyed. But observe how this comes about, for there is a difference in this double act of the law of sin. To command, that is sin's proper and natural act; to condemn, that is sin's act only eventually or meritoriously. It rules of itself directly and properly, but it condemns only as it lays the

foundation of condemnation by another; for there is another law which formally is the condemning law, viz., the law of God upon the violation of it. And this speaks the inexpressible misery of the unregenerate; they are under that law which tyrannically commands them here, and which, upon their obeying of it, will most certainly condemn them hereafter.

2. Secondly, That I may further clear up this expression of the law of sin, let me compare it with other laws—divine and human. Take the laws of God or men; they are usually backed with rewards and punishments,[1] and it is convenient it should be so, if not for the strengthening of the laws in themselves, yet, however, for the furtherance of men's obedience to them: for men, generally, do not obey them upon the authority of the legislators, or the intrinsic goodness of the matter of the law, but as they are thereunto either allured by rewards or deterred by punishments. These are the things that do most prevail with them to yield their obedience to the laws both of God and men. Answerably now to this, sin (indwelling sin, the corrupt nature,) will be backing its commands with promises and threatnings; it will be pretending to rewards and punishments, which though in themselves they are but sorry things, yet they have a great power and efficacy upon besotted sinners. For instance, Sinner! saith sin, I enjoin thee to fall in with me and my ways; to do as I bid thee do. I will that thou dost go and swear, and steal, and be filthy, and profane Sabbaths, and please the flesh, &c. Here is the laws or commands of sin. Well! how doth it strengthen and back them? Why thus, Sinner! Do but obey me, and here are such profits, pleasures, delights, honours, preferments, all of which, upon thy compliance with me, shall be thine. If thou wilt but be my loyal subject, and do what I would have thee, thou shalt live at ease, flourish in the world, pass thy days in mirth, be respected by all, with a great many more promises of this nature. Therefore, why dost thou demur? why dost not thou presently submit and obey? Particularly you

_____
[1] Μὴ βασιλευέτω.   [2] Οὐ κυριεύσει.

[1] Some, therefore, define a law, Ordo rectam gubernandi rationem includens, ex prudentia prodiens, transgredientibus pœnam, obtemperantibus præmium decernens. See *Wendel. Polit.*, lib. ii., cap. 11.

read of 'the pleasures of sin,' Heb. xi. 25 ; now it represents and heightens these to sinners, and by them urges and almost enforces obedience to its commands. Oh, saith sin, do but hearken to me and do thus and thus, then what a delightful, pleasant life will you live ; how will all comforts then flow in upon you ! Then your good days will begin, when you once resolve to comply with my laws, but it will never be well till then. And are all these promises and solicitations of sin in vain ? No ! the poor deluded sinner believes, hearkens, yields, closes with them, and knows not how to resist its commands backed with such promises and rewards.

But if these soft and mild insinuations, these enticing and alluring arguments will not do, sin then appears in the lion's shape, and begins to menace and threaten : it alters its language, and saith, Sinner ! wilt thou cast off my laws, and choose to be subject to some other ? Then look to thyself, and take what follows. Wilt thou engage in a course of duty, and fall in with a strict and godly life ? Then know what will be the fruit of this. (Much better than thine, O thou cursed liar !) Thou must expect the loss of all that is good, the undergoing of all that is evil ; thou must look for nothing but prisons, reproaches, derision, contempt, poverty, persecution, and what not ; thou must bid adieu to all thy comforts, prepare for the carrying of a heavy cross, live a pensive, afflicted life ; this will cost thee dear, expose thee to the loss of liberty, estate, relations, credit, nay, of life itself. Oh how doth sin, to draw and hold the sinner in vassalage to itself, and to keep him off from the way of holiness, bestir itself and summon in all its threats and menaces. And may not unrenewed souls too truly be said to be under the law of sin in these respects ? With what efficacy doth it entice them to what is evil by what it promises, and deter them from what is good by what it threatens ? Do not these promises and threatenings of sin carry it with men in their natural state (the former for sins of commission, the latter for sins of omission,) that they know not how to withstand them ? Oh that what we do see every day was not too full a demonstration of their being under the power of sin, as promising and as threatening !

By this you understand what there is in a law, in the strict notion of it, that is applicable to sin, upon which the apostle might ground his metaphor of the law of sin ; it is a commanding thing, and it urges and seconds its commands with promises and threatenings, both of which are proper to a law.

One thing further I desire you to take notice of, and it is this ; that sin, considered as simply commanding, so it is not a law ; but it then becomes formally and completely a law when it commands and the sinner obeys ; so that he owns the power of it, and willingly subjects himself to its dominion. O now it is a law indeed ! As it is in the laws of usurpers, they, merely as imposed by them, are no laws, because not made by persons in lawful authority ; but if a people freely own these usurpers, and willingly put themselves under subjection to them, then to them their laws become valid and obligatory ; so here as to sin, it hath not the least right to any dominion over the soul, it hath no power but what is by usurpation, and therefore its laws are mere nullities ; but yet if men, which is the case of the unconverted, will voluntarily put themselves under its government and consent that it shall rule them, to them *de facto* it becomes a law, and hath the force and authority of a law, though *de jure* it can challenge no such thing. This for a law in its proper sense.

2. Secondly, the word *law* is taken improperly, for anything that hath an impelling or impulsive virtue in it, which though it be not strictly and properly a law, yet it may pass under that appellation, because it hath the virtue and force of a law, and doth that which a true and proper law uses to do. And so an inward, operative, lively principle, that which efficaciously moves and acts a man, or impels and urges him so and so to act, may be styled a law, because of its powerful and authoritative influence in and upon the man in his acting. A principle is a virtual law, or that which is equivalent to a law, inasmuch as it inclines, urges, impels with power and efficacy to such and such operations which are suitable to it. And therefore when sin is the principle which acts a person in his general course, and which doth efficaciously excite and impel him to those things which are suitable to its own nature ; I say when it is thus, there sin may be called a law, and there it is the law of sin. So that when Paul here supposes himself before his

conversion to be under the law of sin, he means that then sin was his principle, the sole and active principle in him,—that which with a strange kind of power and efficacy did urge, excite, impel him to wicked and sinful acts all along in that state. The law of sin notes the power of sin, as hath been shown. Now that is twofold, moral or physical. I will not upon several accounts undertake to justify this distinction in the rigid acceptation of things; I only make use of it to help your conceptions in that which I am upon. Sin's moral power lies in its being a law, for that is the power of a law; its physical power lies in its being a principle, for that is the power of a principle. As to its moral power, it directs and regulates, prescribing to the sinner what it would have him to do, and, in a sense, commanding him to do accordingly: as to its physical power, it doth so and so excite and act by its inward, effectual, powerful inclinations and impulsions. I distinguish here between a law and a principle, because I now consider the latter strictly in itself, and not according to the improper application of the word *law* to it: and I make use of this distinction of sin's twofold power, not as designing to assert any special difference betwixt them; possibly something might be objected against that; I only design thereby to set forth the several ways and modes wherein sin doth exert its power; for though it is very true that moral and physical power, as considered in themselves and when applied to such and such things, are distinct kinds of power; yet when they are applied to sin, they are but different modes, the nature of the thing admitting nothing more.

Now to bring this to the point in hand. Unregenerate persons are under the law of sin, inasmuch as in that state sin, the depraved nature, is the principle which acts them, and which strongly, effectually, nay impetuously, inclines and excites them to what is sinful. Every agent hath its principle, which acts it strongly and irresistibly; as natural agents in natural acts have their principle working with great efficacy in them. The fire burns, and cannot do otherwise, because it is determined and influenced by that natural principle which is in it: so moral agents in moral acts have their efficacious principles too, which work as strongly and powerfully in them, the difference being always preserved betwixt natural and free agents. But now these principles are very different according to men's different state; where it is the law of the Spirit of life in Christ Jesus, there the Spirit is the principle, and the new nature too in the soul as the principle doth with a great deal of power and efficacy excite and quicken to what is good, 2 Cor. v. 14, 'The love of Christ constraineth us.' But where it is the law of sin, there sin is the principle which doth also strongly excite to what is evil. The natural man hath no other principle than this, and it is very active in him, ever working with great power and strength to draw out his corruption; and so he is under the law of sin.

I conceive this law of sin, as to its most proper import, notes the activeness and efficacy of a principle, rather than the authority or sovereignty of a law, though that be the word here used. But however it is best to take in both notions, and in both the doctrine holds true; so long as any man is unrenewed, sin is both a law to him to command, rule, and govern him, and also a principle powerfully and efficaciously to act him in his whole course; in both respects before regeneration it is nothing but the law of sin. By which expression the apostle seems to superadd something to what he had said, ver. 1. He had there spoke of walking after the flesh, thereby intimating the flesh to be the principle by which men out of Christ do act; but now here in calling it the law of sin, or of the flesh, he intimates the power and strength of that principle in those persons; it is a commanding principle in them, which takes in the sum of both the significations which I have been enlarging upon; it rules and acts them as it pleases; it hath over them the authority of a law, and in them the energy or efficacy of a principle, both of which do centre and are comprehended in one word, the power of sin. So much for the first thing, to show what the apostle means by the law of sin, and in what respects it is so styled.

Two questions here arise, the answering of which will give further light unto the doctrine; the first is this, How or wherein doth sin, as a law, exert and put forth its power and dominion in and over unregenerate persons?

In the answering of this, should I fall upon particulars, to set forth the various workings of sin in the matter or kind of them, or the various arts and methods of sin in the manner of its working, it would occasion a discourse too large for my present design. I will therefore limit myself to two general heads, under which the several particulars will fall.

The law of sin shews itself, partly with respect to what is evil, and partly with respect to what is good. You may understand its workings in the unregenerate by its workings in the regenerate, for it is the same in both, only in different degrees. Now how doth it work in these? that you shall see in our great instance in the text. Paul complaining of this law, as in himself, shews how it did put forth its power and strength in him, namely thus: (1.) It did strongly excite, impel, and draw him to what was evil; so Rom. vii. 15, 'That which I do, I allow not; what I hate, that do I.' Ver. 17, 'It is no more I that do it, but sin that dwelleth in me.' Ver. 19, 'The evil which I would not, that I do.' Ver. 23, 'I see another law in my members,' &c. 2. It did strongly oppose, resist, hinder him as to what was good: ver. 15, 'What I would, that do I not.' Ver. 18, 'To will is present with me; but how to perform that which is good I find not. For the good that I would I do not.' Ver. 21, 'I find then a law, that, when I would do good, evil is present with me.' Thus sin acted in Paul, in whom its power and strength was much broken, and thus it doth, in a much higher degree, act in the unregenerate, in whom it is in its full strength and vigour.

1. Sin in such exerts its power in its vehement urging and impelling of them to what is evil. I say *to what is evil;* for indeed all its impulsions are to that; sin is for nothing but sin; sin in the habit is altogether for sin in the act, indwelling sin is wholly for dwelling in sin; it bends and works entirely that way, *urget ad peccata peccatum.* And no wonder that it so doth, since the principle always moves and excites to those acts which are consentaneous to itself; therefore sin agreeing with sin, the sinful nature solely stirs up a person to that which is sinful. And how entire, restless, unwearied, impetuous is it in this! The truth is, though there was no devil to tempt the graceless sinner, yet that law of sin which is in himself would be enough to make him sin, in a great measure, as he doth: as to many men, and

many sins of those men, it is but the devil's over-eagerness which puts him upon tempting of them, for without that the thing would be done to his hand, as dry wood would burn without blowing. Corrupt nature is continually egging, soliciting, exciting the unsanctified man to what is evil; it will not let him alone day or night unless he gratify it; and its motions are so urgent and violent that he, poor creature, either cannot or will not make any considerable resistance. What an instance was Amnon of this! He was under the law of sin; it had such a power and sovereignty over him, and was so impetuous in its workings in him, that he walked sadly, pined away, fell downright sick, and all because he knew not how to satisfy that lust which wrought so strongly in him towards his own sister; read 2 Sam. xiii. 2, &c. So Ahab; sin put him upon the coveting of Naboth's vineyard, and this it did with such violence that he would eat no bread, because he could not have his will, 1 Kings xxi. 5. Solomon tells us of some who 'sleep not except they have done mischief; and their sleep is taken away unless they cause some to fall,' Prov. iv. 16. O the law of sin! it solicits to this and that evil, and its solicitations thereunto are so pressing and earnest that it will receive no repulse; yea, the sinner is so overpowered that he is even carried away with it, like an empty vessel in a fierce and rapid stream. In whatever point the wind stands, it blows so fiercely, so strongly, that there is no standing against it; I mean, whatever the lust be in which the sin of nature vents itself, whether uncleanness, or ambition, or covetousness, or what you will, that comes with such a force and violence upon the natural man that he falls before it and yields to it. We speak much, in another sense, of the law of nature; truly the grand law of nature as depraved is to command and incline men to sin against God; and this it must needs do with a mighty power and efficacy in those in whom it is wholly depraved.

2. Secondly, This law of sin shews itself in its opposing and hindering of what is good. It is a law which always runs counter to God's law; it will be sure to further what that forbids, and to hinder what that commands, for it always sets itself in a direct opposition thereunto. Doth that call for such and such duties? are there some convictions upon

the sinner's conscience about them? doth he begin a little to incline to what is good? how doth sin now bestir itself to make head in the soul against these convictions and good inclinations! how doth it endeavour to nip the blossoms, to stifle and smother the initial propensions to what is good, to kill the infant in the cradle, as Herod would have done with Christ, to make all conceptions, in order to obedience and holiness, to prove abortive! There is in sin a fixed, rooted aversation to whatever is holy and spiritual, which it puts forth to its utmost wherever it is upon the throne; it doth not only work a loathness to duty, but a loathing of duty; it countermands, where it is in its full power, all the motions and excitations of the blessed Spirit there-unto. Oh sometimes the Spirit comes to a man and says, Thou hast neglected prayer hitherto; it is high time now to set upon it; thus long thou hast lived, and all this time thou hast not minded the reading of the Scriptures, the hearing of the word preached, &c.; come now, let them be minded; all thy days thou hast been a stranger to holiness, now be holy; thou hast been a despiser of Christ hitherto, now love, fear, receive, honour him: thus the good Spirit would draw on the sinner to what is good. Well, is indwelling sin quiet now? Oh no! it puts forth itself with its greatest vigour and strength in opposition to the breathings of the good Spirit. It saith, Sinner, let word and Spirit say what they will, do thou hold on thy course; keep on thy way, God is merciful, fear it not; duty is burdensome, meddle not with it; what need is there of all this praying, hearing, believing, repenting, holy walking? &c. These are the bold oppositions and subtle insinuations of sin against what is good, set forth by the lustings of the flesh against the Spirit, Gal. v. 17; these are its cursed renitencies and reluctancies against duty. Now, till the regenerating Spirit comes with his victorious grace to conquer them, the sinner is wholly under their power, so that they do most effectually and prevailingly keep him off from what is good. You have it exemplified in the young man, Mat. xix. 22; in Felix, Acts xxiv. 25, and in several others. This is the very case of men before conversion: whether you consider the law of sin as it puts forth itself with respect to evil or with respect to good, the unconverted are under it; it

hurries them on to what is wicked, and as powerfully holds them off from what is holy; in both respects they are entirely under the command of it as a law, and entirely acted by it as a principle; it is no better than thus—and worser it cannot be—with unregenerate persons. Let this general answer to the first question be sufficient.

Quest. A second is this, How may it be known when persons are under the law of sin? or how may we distinguish betwixt the law of sin as it is in the unregenerate, and as it is in the regenerate? For even the latter find too much of this law in them. Paul here saith he was freed from it, and yet in the foregoing chapter he sadly laments it, as you have often heard. Renewed and sanctified souls do by sad experience feel the corrupt nature strongly urging and pressing them to what is evil, and as strongly opposing and hindering them in what is good; yea, in both often prevailing. May not they, therefore, as well as others, be said to be under the law of sin? If not, where lies the difference? or what is it that doth indeed denominate a man to be under that law?

Ans. This being a question of great importance, I shall be larger in the answering of it than I was of the former, yet not so large as the nature of the subject would admit of, nor as some of our own divines are who write upon it: I shall reduce all to three heads.

1. First, Where the whole bent and tendency of the heart is towards sin—that the propensions of the soul thereto are entire and unmixed—there it is the law of sin, and that law of sin which is proper to the unregenerate. This speaks sin to be upon the throne indeed, that its power and dominion is habitual, plenary, and absolute. A child of God may have very strong corruptions in him, and they sometimes, too, may break forth into external acts; the sinful nature may vehemently incline him to what is evil, and sometimes prevail too, yet the bent of his heart is for God against sin, and the stream doth not run wholly one way: he hath propensions unto good as well as unto evil, whereupon he is not under the law of sin. But take an unsanctified person, it is otherwise with him; his heart is in sin and set for sin, that is the thing to which it altogether bends, inclines, and works. There is

not a stronger bent in heavy bodies to descend, or in light things to ascend, than there is in such a one to sin against God. And further, he is not divided in what is evil, he is all of a piece; the sinful nature in him is entire, and doth all. Now where it is thus, certainly there it is the law of sin. Paul, in his saddest complaints of this law, as in himself, yet says, 'It is no more I that do it, but sin that dwelleth in me.' It was not he that did it, because the bent of his heart was against it. And he says, 'With the mind I myself serve the law of God.' The habitual tendency and inclination of his soul was towards good, and as he was himself it was thus with him, for he puts *I myself* only to the serving of the law of God, not to that of the law of sin: so that though the law of sin was in him, yet he was not under it, strictly, as the law of sin. Sin had too great a strength in him, but it had not the sole and full command of him.

2. Secondly, When all the several faculties of the soul are altogether on sin's side, and wholly take its part, then it is the law of sin, and that which is proper to the unregenerate. If this head be not distinct from the former, yet it may be useful as a more particular explication of it. In such persons, understanding, will, affections, all are engaged on sin's side, and therein lies its power and dominion over them. The understanding assents, the will consents, the affections answerably are drawn out. Oh here is the law of sin, or sin regnant. The understanding gives in its final and positive dictate that sin is good, represents it as eligible to the will. The will, upon this, closes with it, embraces it, cleaves to it; the affections, desire, joy, delight, &c., run out upon it. Where it is thus, the case is determined. But this must be taken with a threefold proviso: (1.) That the assent of the understanding be deliberate, for even a child of God upon a sudden surprisal, *pro hic et nunc*, may judge better of sin than it deserves. (2.) That the consent of the will be plenary and full, for there may be in gracious persons sometimes a broken half-consent to what is evil. (3.) That both assent and consent be understood of a course in sin; for as to particular acts, no question but one who is regenerate, under the power of a temptation, may do both of these. This threefold proviso being taken in, the thing is clear; whoso-

ever shall be so far besotted, as upon deliberation to judge a sinful course to be the best course, and thereupon shall choose, embrace, fall in with and continue in it, yea, shall delight and please himself in it, unquestionably in this man it is the law of sin. Sin never gets thus high where grace is, for the proof of which we must recur to our great instance. Paul, after his conversion, found sin to be too powerful in him, which was his great burden; yet notwithstanding, the fixed acts of the several faculties of his soul were for God against sin. As, for example, in his understanding he assented to the goodness of the law of God, but not to the goodness of the law of sin: Rom. vii. 12, 'Wherefore the law is holy,' &c. In his will he also consented to this: ver. 16, 'If then I do that which I would not, I consent unto the law that it is good;' and for his affections, he saith, 'I delight in the law of God after the inward man.' Now these being, as I said, the fixed acts of the several faculties in Paul, in him it was not the law of sin. And thus for the main it is with every gracious soul, but for others in whom sin hath all, all the faculties—understanding, will, affections—in their proper acts being entirely for it, it is evident that they are under the law of sin.

Of all the faculties the will doth most discover the power of sin, for there its dominion and sovereignty is chiefly seated and acted. Oh, when it once gains that, then it ascends the throne indeed! That is the time, as it were, of its inauguration, when it is invested in all its regalities. It comes to the sinner and says, Art thou willing that I should rule thee? Yes, saith he, with all my heart; I like thy commands and government, I am thine, I submit to thee to be at thy dispose, I here swear fealty and allegiance to thee, &c. Dreadful language! Oh that ever it should be uttered by the heart of man! Sinner! dost thou know what thou sayest? Pray thee, make a little pause, be persuaded to consider what thou dost. Is this spoken in good, or rather in bad, earnest? Dost thou resolve upon it? Wilt thou stick to it? Oh then thou art a mere vassal, thou puttest thyself under the reign of the worst tyrant in all the world; from this day forward thou must carry chains and fetters about thee, from this act of thine sin's reign commences. Therefore, if it be not yet done, let it never be done ; if it be done, let it be rescinded speedily. But I forget myself.

The lowest act of the will, in order to the constituting of this law of sin, is election or choice. There is good and evil, holiness and sin, set before the soul, and it chooses the evil before the good; this is a sad evidence of sin's power : Isa. lxv. 12, 'But did evil before mine eyes, and did choose that wherein I delighted not :' Isa. lxvi. 3, 4, &c., 'They have chosen their own ways, and their soul delighteth in their abominations,' &c. But though I say that this is the lowest act of the will in sin's being a law, yet even this is enough to put a person under that law. The godly man chooses the way of holiness : Ps. cxix. 30, 'I have chosen the way of truth.' The sinner chooses the way of sin ; this he prefers before the other. Now, should there be nothing more than this choice, (supposing it to be deliberate, full, and peremptory,) that would be enough to evince sin's dominion ; for wherever it hath the preference, it hath the power. But there are higher acts of the will than this, which do more highly constitute and more fully demonstrate the law of sin, and which are to be found only in the unregenerate. As, namely, when the will doth not merely choose, embrace, prefer sin before holiness, but it is pertinaciously set for sin, its full purpose and resolution is for sin against holiness. The sinner says he hath sinned, and so he will do still ; he is fixed and obstinate in his wickedness. Instead of cleaving to the Lord with full purpose of heart, as Barnabas exhorted the Christians at Antioch to do, Acts xi. 23, he cleaves to sin with full purpose of heart : Jer. ii. 25, 'I have loved strangers, and after them I will go :' Jer. viii. 5, 'They hold fast deceit ; they refuse to return :' Jer. xxix. 16, 'As for the word that thou hast spoken to us in the name of the Lord, we will not hearken to thee, but we will certainly do whatsoever goeth out of our own mouth,' &c. Now, wherever it comes to this, that sin is thus enthroned in the will, there most certainly it is the law of sin. But I must yet go one step further ; there is one act of the will higher than this too, viz., when the heart is wholly set for sin, and is not only resolvedly, but impetuously carried out after it. Eccles. viii. 11, 'Because sentence against an evil work is not executed speedily, therefore the heart of the sons of

men is fully set in them to do evil :' Jer. l. 38, 'They are mad upon their idols :' Eph. iv. 19, 'Who being past feeling have given themselves over unto lasciviousness, to work all uncleanness with greediness :' Jer. viii. 6, 'Every one turned to his course, as the horse rusheth into the battle.' Here the power of sin rises high indeed, when the will doth not barely consent to it, but it is eager and fierce for it. Oh this speaks not only its own great wickedness and most woeful depravation, but also the sinner's full subjection to sin. This is the law of sin with a witness ; where it is thus, it may easily be known who bears rule in the soul. Sin never arrives at this height of power in the regenerate ; this is altogether inconsistent with grace. Upon conversion the will is sanctified, and the sanctified will can never carry it thus towards sin.

You see what that is in the interior faculties of the soul, which doth constitute and evidence the law of sin in unregenerate persons. I might instance also in the exterior parts of the body, for though sin's power doth mainly reside and put forth itself in the former, yet it reaches to these also ; therefore the apostle brings them in upon this account, Rom. vi. 12, 'Let not sin reign in your mortal bodies,' &c. ; ver. 13, 'Neither yield you your members instruments of unrighteousness unto sin,' &c. ; ver. 19, 'As ye have yielded your members servants to uncleanness,' &c. When the body is prostituted to sin's drudgery, the several parts thereof employed in its service—as the eyes, to let in external objects for the exciting and feeding of lust within ; the feet, to run on sin's errands ; the tongue, to utter vanity and frothiness, &c. ; this is a great demonstration of a man's being under the law of sin. It is true, it chiefly reigns in the heart ; there is its imperial seat, or the palace where it hath its imperial residence, that is the inward citadel where its main strength doth lie ; but yet from thence it issues out its laws and edicts to the body also, and that is its outward fort or territory, where it hath a great strength and command also. Indeed the law of sin is best discerned, as to others, by its venting of itself in and through the body ; for so long as sin keeps in its power within the interior faculties of the soul, it is known only to the sinner himself ; but when that once breaks out in sins committed in and by the body, as intemperance, drunkenness, uncleanness, &c., then it becomes discernible to all to whom such sins shall be known. And though it is certain that sin may have its full dominion in the heart without the external eruptions of it in the life, in gross and corporeal acts, yet where they are added, they infallibly discover that sin lords and domineers. Oh therefore how evident is it that all who abuse and defile their bodies, who use them as instruments for sin, and wear them out in its service, are most particularly under the law of sin! But it is not thus with any who are truly sanctified; sin hath not the command of their bodies; they 'yield up their members servants to righteousness unto holiness,' Rom vi. 19; they look upon their bodies as the 'temples of the Holy Ghost,' 1 Cor. vi. 19, and accordingly they keep them holy; they know they are themselves bought with a price, and that their souls and bodies are both God's, 1 Cor. vi. 20, and therefore both to be employed in the glorifying of God; they scorn to let their bodies be drudges to sin and Satan, and in this respect they are not under the law of sin.

3. Thirdly, The law of sin, and its different workings in the people of God and others, may be opened by the modification of the act of sin. As,

(1.) Where sin is committed industriously and designedly, there it is the law of sin, and that which is peculiar to the graceless. Some there are who set themselves to sin; it is the thing they aim at, which they deliberate, contrive, muse how to bring about, their serious thoughts from time to time are at work in order to it; like to that person whom David describes, Ps. xxxvi. 4, 'He deviseth mischief on his bed, he setteth himself in a way that is not good:' like to the wickedness of men before the deluge, Gen. vi. 5, &c., 'Every imagination of the thoughts of his heart was only evil continually:' it is meant not only of imaginations which had sin in them materially and subjectively, but also of those which were for sin and in order to sin intentionally and finally. The apostle sets it forth by 'making provision for the flesh,' Rom. xiii. 14, when the sinner hath his forecasts and projects for sin. Now where it is thus,[1] unquestionably it is the law of sin, this

doth most certainly discover the absolute, unbroken, full power and dominion of sin: John viii. 34, 'Whoever commits sin'—ὁ ποιῶν, who makes it or frames it, as an artist doth a thing which is proper to his trade or art, who sins *de industria data, opera*; what of him? why, he is the servant of sin, that is, he is fully under its command, and is a perfect slave and vassal to it. It is never thus with regenerate persons; this 'spot is not the spot of God's children,' Deut. xxxii. 5. 1 John iii. 9, 'Whosoever is born of God doth not commit sin;' he doth not frame sin, or contrive how to sin, in the sense named but now. It cannot be denied but that even a child of God may sin after deliberation, nay, as to some particular sinful act he may deliberate in order to the doing of it; there was a great deal of deliberation in David's killing Uriah—it was a plotted, contrived sin, that which was brought about by many deliberate thoughts: oh but in such a one this is very rare and seldom, it is but in this or that particular act, it is not a thing that he holds on in, God forbid it should be so! And therefore though this be a great aggravation of sin, when it is committed deliberately, and a sad evidence that it hath too much power and strength in the heart, yet every deliberate sin is not enough to prove a man to be under the law of sin; when the designing and contriving is customary, and that too as to a course in sin, oh then it is the law of sin.

(2.) When the temptation easily prevails, and there is little or no resistance and opposition made to sin, then it is the law of sin, and that which is proper to the unregenerate. If the town be surrendered, and yields upon the first summons, it is a sign that the assailers are very strong, and the defendants very weak; if the tinder takes fire upon the first little spark that falls into it, surely it is very dry; so here, when Satan doth no sooner lay the temptation before the sinner but he immediately closes with it, and falls before it, and yields to it, this argues that sin and Satan have a full power in and over him. But I lay the main stress of this head upon little or no resistance to the motions, suggestions, commands of sin. Possibly it no sooner commands but the sinner readily obeys; if he chance to

[1] When the flesh hath the (πρόνοιαν) providential, projecting, and forecasting ability at command and at her service, it is certain her supremacy is in the full.—*Mr Rich. Bifield* 'The Gospel's Glory,' &c., 255.

make some opposition, it is as bad as none at all; it is not lively, vigorous, resolute, but cold, dull, faint, and languid. Oh, this is a sad demonstration of sin's height and regency in the soul! The bare commands of sin, as hath been said, do not make it to be a law; but when there is a ready, willing subjection to those commands, then it is a law. Rom. vi. 16, 'Know ye not, that to whom ye yield yourselves to obey, his servants ye are to whom ye obey, whether of sin unto death, or of obedience unto righteousness?' It is a brand upon Ephraim that he willingly 'walked after the commandment,' Hosea v. 11; may not this be charged upon men before renovation with respect to the commands of sin? We read of Satan that he takes some captive at his will, 2 Tim. vi. 26; and truly so it is with the sinful nature too; it doth with the unregenerate what it will; it commands, governs, orders them even as it will; it meets with little or no resistance; upon all occasions it doth but speak the word, and the thing is done. The true convert stands upon his guard, fights it out to the last; he will die rather than yield. Sin doth not so easily do his work in him; he may sometimes be a captive to it, as being overborne with its strength; but he will not be a subject to it, so as to give willing obedience to it; which shews that he is not under the law of sin. When it is willingness in the way of duty, then it is the day of God's power, Ps. cx. 3; when it is willingness in the way of sin, then it is the day of sin's power. There may be some resistance made to sin, and yet its dominion may be high; but when it is no resistance, then its dominion is high indeed. A sinner sometimes, from the stirrings of conscience, may make a little opposition; but sin having his will in its entire consent, that opposition soon goes off, and so sin's sovereignty is as absolute as ever it was.

(3.) When sin carries it in spite of all opposition, then it is the law of sin, and that power of sin which only suits with the unregenerate state; when it is committed with little opposition *ab intra*, and in spite of all opposition *ab extra*, I assure you then it hath a great power. Many there are who are so much under the strength and dominion of the hellish nature, that nothing shall hinder them from what is evil. As the sincere Christian, set never so many

hindrances and discouragements before him, yet, being under the law of the Spirit, he will be and do good; so, *e contra*, the man that is destitute of grace, set what hindrances or discouragements you will before him, yet, being under the law of sin, he will be and do evil. Let the threatenings of the law of God stand in his way, like the angel with a drawn sword in his hand, yet he will sin; let the sceptre of the gospel be held out to him, yet he will sin; set the love, grace, mercy of God before him, yet he will sin; set the wrath, justice, severity of God before him, yet he will sin; set the death, sufferings, agonies, wounds, blood of the Lord Jesus before him, yet he will sin; let conscience smite him, let word, ministers, Christians, reprove him, yet he will sin; let him resolve, purpose, vow, promise, covenant, yet he will sin; tell him of heaven or hell, that he will waste his estate, impair his health, undo his family, ruin his body, nay, his precious soul, it is all one, yet he will sin; come plague, pestilence, war, fire, yet he will sin; set the law of Scripture before him, yet he will sin; nay, as to some acts, set the very law of nature before him, yet he will sin. Here is the law of sin to some purpose, the power and strength of sin in their ἀκμὴ, and yet all graceless and Christless souls are under this, though not all in the same way or in the same degree; but sin never rises thus high in God's people, they are more easily stopped and kept off from sinning against God. You know the stream in a flood runs very fiercely, and will not be stopped by any opposition; it tears and breaks the banks which would give a check to it; but let the flood be but over, and then it comes to itself again, and its motion is not so boisterous and impetuous; so it is with the true Christian; possibly in some single act, under some strong temptation, upon some fit of passion, he may break through all that lies in his way as a let or hindrance to him in sin; but when the sudden gush of corruption and the power of the temptation are a little over, he comes to himself again, and then the word and Spirit do easily stop him in what is evil.

(4.) When it is sinning and no sense of sin, no after repentance for it, then it is the law of sin, and that power of it which is only in the unconverted. Sin always rules most where it is least felt, but it never arrives at the highest pitch of dominion where the soul groans under it as its burden. As it was with Paul, the corrupt nature was too powerful in him, but he was very sensible of it: he cried out, 'Oh wretched man that I am, who shall deliver me from this body of death!' Thus, too, it is with all gracious souls; they may have much of sin in them, yea, it may be so strong in them as that in some particular acts they may be overcome by it, yet it is but *peccatum vincens, non regnans*—sin conquering, not commanding—because they are greatly humbled in the sense of this, and because they ever recover themselves again by true repentance. Oh how do they mourn and grieve over corruption, especially when it hath been too hard for them! If you read of David's sins, you shall also read of David's tears. Now when it is thus, it is never the law of sin—sin bewailed is never sin reigning; but when a man sins insensibly and impenitently, there is no after-shame or after-grief in him for sin, no rising again after falling; verily in this man it is the law of sin. But so much for the answering of this question, and also for the explication of the point in hand.

Use. In the applying of it, there is but one use which I shall insist upon, and that shall be for information. It is thus: that every person before regeneration is under the law of sin. It informs us of two things:

1. Of the bondage of the natural state.

2. Of the power, efficacy, necessity of restraining and renewing grace.

1. Here is a sad demonstration of that bondage which attends the natural state, and those who are in it. Such being under the law of sin, and that importing what you have heard it doth, hence it follows that they are under bondage—the very worst bondage and thraldom that is imaginable. This sinners will not believe nor lay it to heart, but so it is; they being sin's subjects, and governed by its laws, they are no better than slaves and vassals, for so all its subjects are. We pity those who live under tyrants, usurpers, hard masters, &c., and judge their bondage to be very great; but, alas! what is that if compared with this of graceless souls living under the tyranny, usurpation, dominion of sin? Oh poor creature! art thou out of Christ, unsanctified and unregenerate, and consequently acted, ruled, governed by sin? Know thyself; thou art, in a

spiritual sense, no better than a slave; yea, there is no servitude or vassalage in the world comparable to thine. The poor Christians who are captives and bondmen under the barbarous Turks, or such who are condemned to mines and galleys, are in a better condition than thou who art under the power of thy base lusts. The state of nature is a quite other thing than what men imagine it to be; they think there is nothing but freedom and liberty in it; such who are in it fancy none live so free and happy a life as themselves; but God knows it is quite otherwise. 'While they promise themselves liberty, they are the servants of corruption; for of whom a man is overcome, of the same is he brought into bondage,' as the apostle speaks, 2 Pet. ii. 19. There are very many sad attendants upon unregeneracy, as blindness, darkness, death, enmity, distance, and alienation from God, &c., but none worse than the spiritual bondage which accompanies it. I add, too, there is none of all these which sinners are with more difficulty convinced of, and more hardly brought to believe, than that which I am upon. We see it in the Jews: John viii. 33, 'We be Abraham's seed, and never were in bondage to any man; how sayest thou we shall be made free?' Never in bondage to any man! that was false; were they not once in bondage in Egypt, which, therefore, was called the house of bondage, Exod. xx. 2, where they were under hard bondage? Exod. i. 14. Were they not again in bondage in Babylon? yea, were they not now in bondage under the Romans? But this not being the bondage which Christ aimed at, he passed by this—their vaunting of their exemption from it—and fell upon their spiritual bondage, with respect to which he told them, 'Whosoever commits sin is the servant of sin.' So go to many now and tell them they are under servitude, they will not believe it. What! they in such a condition? No, they are so and so descended; such and such is their birth and parentage; they have such noble blood running in their veins; they live in the enjoyment of such privileges; have so many under them at their beck, whilst they themselves are commanded by none; they can go and come and do as they list,[1] being free from that στέρησις αὐτοπραγίας

[1] Μόνοι ἃ δεῖ βούλεσθαι μαθόντες, ὡς βούλονται ζῶσι.—*Plutarch Mor.*, p. 35.

wherein the stoics placed bondage, and yet are they slaves? Yes, notwithstanding all this, they may be so, and are so, if sin hath the rule and regency over them; they have all liberty but that which is the best, and are exempted from all bondage but that which is the worst. The moralists, by the light of nature, had true notions about this, for they could say that virtue and goodness only did entitle to liberty—that vice and wickedness were always attended with servitude.[1] The satirist falls severely upon some high pretenders to liberty,[2] because they were their own masters, at their own dispose, did what they pleased, were not they free? He answers them sharply, shewing there might be external and civil liberty, and yet they might be under bondage, if vice had the mastery and command of them; nay, if any one vice or lust did prevail over them, whether covetousness or intemperance, &c., that would be enough to prove them no better than vassals and slaves, let their outward condition be never so high and good. Now surely we may be more clear and positive in this than they, who by Scripture light know more of the law of sin than they could do by the bare light of nature. Every regenerate, good man is free, but every unregenerate, wicked man is a very slave, and under most dreadful thraldom.[3]

Now it being thus, that I may the better convince you of the evil and misery of this bondage, and also excite you to the most vigorous endeavours to get out of it, let me lay a few particulars before you. As,

1. Consider that bondage to sin is always accompanied with bondage to Satan. Whoever is under the law of sin, he is thereupon also under the law of Satan, for sin's and Satan's power always go together.

[1] Δουλοπρεπὴς ἡ κακία, ἐλευθεροπρεπὴς δε ἡ ἀρετή—*Plato Alcib.*, i.

[2] 'An quisquam est alius liber nisi ducere vitam
   Cui licet ut voluit? licet ut volo vivere, non sum
   Liberior Bruto?
   Liber ego? unde datum hoc sumis tot subdite rebus?
   An Dominum ignoras nisi quem vindicta relaxat?
                                        Servitium acre;
   Te nihil impellit, nec quicquam extrinsecus intrat
   Quod nervos agitet; sed si intus et in jecore ægro
   Nascantur domini, qui tu impunitior exis?'
                                        —*Persius,* Sat. 5.

[3] *Vide* Philon. Jud. in Tract. cui titulus, *Quod omnis probus liber,* p. 670.

The truth is, these two are, as it were, allies and confederates; nay, they are copartners in dominion, they ever share in the government of the soul, and rule jointly, so that he who is under the power of the one is under the power of the other also. There is a oneness of interest and dominion betwixt them; as Satan gets up sin gets up, and as sin gets up Satan gets up too. The devil's reign depends upon the reign of sin. Where it is not the law of sin his power is very low; it is said of him that 'he rules,' Eph. ii. 2; where, or in whom? Why, 'in the children of disobedience.' Where it is disobedience to the laws of God, and obedience to the laws of sin, there Satan's kingdom is very high; there he rules and doth what he will, as he is said to take some men captive at his will, 2 Tim. ii. 11. Now is not this a dreadful thing—the most deplorable bondage that a creature can lie under? what? to be the devil's subject? a slave to him who is in chains himself? ruled by him who is the grand rebel, and the head of all the lower rebels against God? What more woeful! Sinner, when wilt thou consider it; shall a damned creature be thy lord and sovereign? shall he be thy ruler here, who will be thy tormentor hereafter? wilt thou live in subjection under him who is but a jailer and executioner of God's displeasure? What bondage can be so great, so much to be detested as this!

2. Secondly, Let it be considered what sin is, both as it is in itself, and also as it manages its power, command, and regency in and over the sinner.

1. Look upon sin in itself. It is the basest, the vilest thing that is; the whole world hath nothing in it of so vile a nature as it. It is that only thing which God never made. Other things may seem to be vile, and comparatively they may really be so, yet they being God's creatures there is something of excellency in them; but as for sin, God hath nothing to do with it, only as he doth dispose and overrule it to his own glory. It is the only thing that God cannot do. There are many things which he will not do, but sin is the only thing which he cannot do. God can make a world, uphold a world, destroy a world; he can do all, only he cannot sin. Now, whoever thou art, let this be thought of: Shall a thing so vile and base, so contrary to God's nature, shall that have the rule and command of thee? How can the spirit of a man bear a thing so inde-

cent, so unworthy of him? But if he will stoop to what is so much below him, what slavery and bondage must needs result from it! It is sometimes matter of affliction to us to see vile and base men exalted to places of high power and dignity: Ps. xii. 8, 'The wicked walk on every side, when the vilest men are exalted.' Yet this must be submitted to, because the all-disposing God, in the methods of his wise providence, hath a hand in it, as we read, Dan. iv. 17, 'That the most high ruleth in the kingdom of men, and giveth it to whomsoever he will, and setteth up over it the basest of men.' But that a man, by his own act and choice, should set so base a thing as sin upon the throne, and put himself under the dominion of it, this is most strange, and indeed would be incredible did we not see it done every day. To be subject to a prince of high extraction, that hath greatness and majesty in him, who refuses that? But to be subject to a fellow taken off from the dunghill, that was born for the kitchen, not the throne, to hold the plough rather than the sceptre, who can bear that? The application is obvious as to that which I am upon. Sin is of so vile a nature that every heart should rise against its power. All subjection doth not infer bondage, but when it is to a person or thing that is below one's-self, then it is bondage: now that is the case as to sin. It is sad that that which is so much below us in worth and excellency should be above us in power and dominion. It was Noah's curse upon Ham to be 'a servant of servants,' Gen. ix. 25. What a servant or slave is he who is a servant to sin and the several lusts thereof!

2. Look upon sin in the management of its power, and by that you will the better see into the evil and misery of that bondage which arises from subjection to it. What are the laws of sin? always evil. Usurpers amongst men often make good laws; our own histories, as to matter of fact, tell us that some of our kings who had the worst titles made the best laws; and indeed they had need use their power well who get it ill. But now sin doth not only usurp that power which of right belongs not to it, but it also manages its power very wickedly, particularly with respect to the laws which it makes and imposes upon its subjects. Oh it is sad living under its government! The philosopher tells us that the intention of the legislator is to make his subjects good

—certainly it is either so, or it should be so—but when sin gets upon the throne, and assumes a legislative authority to itself, its intention is only to make its subjects bad, for the worse they are the better they suit with it. It is a blessed thing to live under the rule of Christ, because of the holiness, purity, goodness of his laws; but it is a woeful thing to live under the rule of sin, because its laws are quite contrary, hellish, and wicked; for here it holds true, Like lord, like law. Nay, the laws of men, I do not say all, have real goodness in them, so far as they are founded upon reason and designed for good ends, viz., to excite persons to what is good, and to restrain them from what is evil;[1] and so far it is the happiness of any to live under them, and their duty readily and cheerfully to comply with them. But it is not thus with the laws of sin, inasmuch as they are always contrary to right and sound reason, and always tend to what is evil, which therefore, so far as any man is subject to, he must needs be miserable.

It is commonly said, *Ex malis moribus bonæ leges*, bad manners sometimes produce good laws; but bad laws, especially when they are written in the heart and are the principle of action, as the laws of sin are, can never produce good manners. If sin make the law, I know what will be the life.

Further, this sin is not only out of measure sinful in the exercise of its power where it is uppermost, but it is also out of measure tyrannical. There have been too many tyrants in the world, but never was there such a one as sin. All the Neros, Caligulas, Domitians, &c., that ever lived, were nothing to it; this first acted the part of a tyrant in them before they acted the part of tyrants over others. The tyranny of sin appears in many things. I will instance in a few: 1. Its commands are innumerable; there is no end of its laws; and multiplicity of laws always speaks either a bad people or a bad prince.[2] 2. Its commands are contrary; one law thwarts another. The poor sinner, under its dominion, is haled contrary ways, that he scarce knows whither

---

[1] Lex est nihil aliud nisi recta et a numine Deorum ratio, imperans honesta, prohibens contraria. ——profecto ita se res habet, ut quoniam vitiorum emendatricem legem esse oportet commendatricemque virtutum, ab ea vivendi doctrina petatur. —*De Legib.* lib. i.

[2] In corruptissima republica plurimæ leges.—*Tacit.*

Q

to go or what to do. Lust clashes with lust; one draws one way, and another another, so that the poor enslaved soul is at a loss, and knows not how to please all: Tit. iii. 3, 'Serving divers lusts,' ποικίλαις ἐπιθυμίαις, divers for their number, and diverse for their nature and kind also. *O quam multos habet dominos qui unum non habet!* How many lords and masters hath he who hath not Christ only for his Lord! 3. It is very rigorous in its demands; it must have full obedience or none at all: Eph. ii. 3, 'fulfilling the lusts of the flesh.' Partial and half obedience will neither satisfy a holy God nor an unholy nature; and as God, for whom the all is too little, so sin too, for which the least is too much, is for the doing of all it requires. 4. Its commands are never at an end. Let the poor bondman sin to-day, he must sin again to-morrow, and so on *in infinitum;* yea, the more he doth in obedience to it, the more it grows upon him in its commands, just as tyrants and hard masters use to do. 5. When sin once gets upon the throne, it is so imperious and cruel that its vassals must stick at nothing. Be the thing never so base, the costs and hazards never so great, yet if sin calls for the doing of it, it must be done. Sinners! you must waste your estates, blast your credit, impair your health, destroy your bodies, damn your souls; you must part with God, peace of conscience, heaven itself; you must quit all that is good, and venture all that is bad in its service, and in compliance with its edicts. Oh what an imperious, insolent, insatiable thing is sin! Here is the tyrant indeed, both *in titulo*, and also *in exercitio*. And now is not the poor, unregenerate sinner very miserable who lives under such a tyrant? is not his bondage exceeding great? Who that is not highly besotted would be willing to continue under sin's power, that may be brought under the holy, gracious, excellent government of the Lord Jesus?

3. Thirdly, The evil of this bondage, arising from the law of sin, appears from its principal subject; it is a soul-bondage. Of all evils soul-evils are the worst; soul-famine is the worst famine, soul-death the worst death, soul-plagues the worst plagues; and so here soul-bondage is the worst bondage. The bondage of Israel in Egypt was very evil, yet not comparable to this which I am upon; because that was but corporal and external, but this is spiritual and internal. When the best part is enslaved, that must needs be the worst slavery. There may be a servile condition without, and yet a free and generous soul within, as Seneca observes of servants;[1] but if the soul itself be under servitude, then the whole man, the very top of man, all is in servitude. Sin is of so proud and aspiring a nature that no place will serve it for its palace, or principal seat, but the very soul. Oh there it delights to have its residence, and to exercise its dominion! And this is its subtlety as well as its pride, for it knows if it can but rule the soul, that then the soul will easily rule the body; as the main fort within the town being gained, that will with ease command all the outward forts. And it is the whole soul too that sin must have. God, who made it, will have the whole heart, and sin, which designs to enslave it, will have the whole heart too. It is not satisfied with this or that faculty, but all must be subject to it. It must reign in the understanding, by darkness, ignorance, false conceits of God, prejudices against the good ways of God, &c.; it must reign in the will, by perverseness, obstinacy, and rebellion against God; it must reign in the affections, by disorder, earthiness, and sensuality; it must reign in the conscience, by insensibleness and searedness. Oh how great is sin's ambition! Nothing will serve it but a universal empire, so as that all men, and all in men, may be under its dominion. Now what a dreadful thing is this, that the soul, the whole soul, should be thus under the law of sin? Who can express the greatness, the sadness of this bondage, that the best in man should serve the worst in man? for the soul is the best, and sin is the worst in him; that that which was immediately created by God and for God, which did at first participate of the image of God, and was designed for the fruition of God here and hereafter, that so glorious, so excellent a being should be subjugated, enslaved, to such a cursed thing as sin. Oh the misery and evil of this is inexpressible, and yet thus it is with all who are unregenerate!

4. Fourthly, Of all bondage this is the most unprofitable. As to other bondage there may be some

---

[1] Errat siquis existimat servitutem in totum hominem descendere; pars melior ejus excepta est; corpora obnoxia sunt, et adscripta dominis, mens sui juris est, &c.—*Sen. de Benef.*, lib. iii. cap. 20.

profit in that, but there is none in this. The master may be cruel enough to his poor servant, and hold him to very hard and slavish work, but then he makes him some amends by giving him good wages; but here is the sinner's unhappiness, he serves that master which pays him no wages at all, death excepted. What doth he get by all his service? drudging and toiling for sin; even nothing but what he may put into his eye—I mean, to mourn and weep over. 'What fruit had you then in those things whereof ye are now ashamed?' Rom. vi. 21. Oh, this sin is the basest master that any can serve! God is the best: there is enough to be gained under him; but sin the worst, for there is nothing to be got in its service but broken bones, terrors of conscience, the loss of God's favour, and hell at last. You must drudge for it from morning to night, be at its call and beck upon all occasions, grind in its mill, run upon its errands, carry its burdens, &c.; and what recompense shall you have for all this? I will tell you: the loss of all that is truly good, and the bearing of all that is truly evil; you shall have shame before men, trouble in your own souls, and the eternal wrath of the great God; these are the rewards and recompenses of sin. Now, are not they miserable who serve such a master? and yet so it is with all men before conversion.

5. Fifthly, Sin's bondage is the worse, because they who lie under it are altogether insensible of it. Where it is external and civil bondage, men are sensible enough of that. Oh, they groan under it, would fain be rid of it, all their thoughts are employed to contrive how they may get out of it! The people of Israel 'sighed, and groaned, and cried to God because of their bondage,' Exod. ii. 23; and you read in this chapter how the poor irrational creatures, being under the bondage of corruption, do groan after deliverance, ver. 21, 22. The poor Christians in slavery under infidels, what a sense have they of their thraldom! how would they rejoice might they be but set free! But here is the evil of spiritual bondage; men do not feel it, nay, they will not believe it; they have other thoughts of themselves than that they are under any such thing. Who thinks himself so free as he that is a vassal to sin? The poor deluded sinner, like some distracted persons, plays with his chains, sports himself with

his fetters, and looks upon them as if they were his crown. Oh how doth sin, where it is in its full command and power, besot its subjects, and make them carry it as though they were in a plain frenzy! Have you not sometimes been in bedlam — it is a mercy you have been there only as spectators of the misery of others—where you saw poor creatures in a very dismal and deplorable condition, chained, beaten, almost starved, lodged in straw, sadly used; and yet how do these carry it? why, they laugh, sing, are merry, behave themselves as if they were the happiest persons in the world; who so jovial as they? Is not this a dreadful sight? Ah, my brethren, the world in a spiritual sense is little better than a large bedlam, where sin hath men in its chains and fetters, doth with them what it pleases, keeps them under cruel bondage; and yet they eat, drink, feast, game, live a merry life, and feel nothing. Oh how insensible, how stupid are sinners in the natural state! Nay, they are so far from lamenting and groaning under this bondage, as their infelicity, that they affect it and make it the matter of their choice; they love to have it so, and refuse to have it otherwise; they refuse the olive, the vine, and choose rather the bramble to reign over them—I allude to that parable, Judges ix. 7, &c.; they had rather swear allegiance and fealty to sin than to God; Christ's government and dominion is rejected, and sin's is preferred; they rather hold their bondage than their bondage them, according to that of the moralist, *Paucos servitus, plures servitutem tenent.*[1] In a word, they are slaves, and it pleases them exceedingly to be so. Now here is a twofold aggravation of the evil of this bondage, partly that it is voluntary—for of all servitude that is the worst which is voluntary, *Nulla servitus turpior quam voluntaria*[2]— and partly that it is not laid to heart. I know God hath a judicial hand in this, as also in the power itself which sin hath over the sinner; but yet the sinner's own will is as free, full, and entire in his closing with it, and submitting to it, as though God was not at all concerned in it.

6. Lastly, This bondage is the most hurtful and most dangerous bondage; for it is deadly, yea, it makes way for, and most certainly ends in, eternal death. Death puts an end to other bondage; the

---

[1] Senec., Ep. 22.   [2] *Ibid.*, Ep. 47.

slave when he is dead is a slave no more : 'There the prisoners rest together; they hear not the voice of the oppressor. The small and great are there, and the servant is free from his master,' Job iii. 18, 19; but the worst of spiritual bondage follows after death; this ends *in* death, but it doth not end *with* death. And other bondage doth not make any liable to eternal death; for that, simply considered, is nothing either to heaven or to hell. God may love and save the true penitent though in chains, and condemn the impenitent though never so free and flourishing in the world; the everlasting concerns of the soul do not at all depend upon civil liberty or civil servitude; but where this spiritual servitude is, there God hath no love, there the sinner must die eternally. You have in the text the 'law of sin' and the 'law of death' coupled together. Oh what a dangerous thing is the law of sin! Where sin hath its full power over the creature to make him wicked, death upon this will have its full power also to make him miserable. So Rom. vi. 16, 'Know you not, that to whom ye yield yourselves servants to obey, his servants you are to whom you obey, whether of sin *unto death*, or of obedience unto righteousness?' Ver. 21, 'For the end of these things is death.' Ver 23, 'The wages of sin is death.' And is it so? Who then would be sin's servant? who would serve that master who pays no better wages than death? You that are servants, would you enter into the service of one that would pay you such wages? Such a master sin is, and such wages it doth pay. Oh, therefore, quit its service! be wise for your souls, be sensible of the danger of continuing under the law of sin, otherwise this law of sin will soon be turned into the law of death. And indeed it is this which ends in death; it is not barely sin which condemns, but it is the law of sin which condemns. When it hath the supreme and sovereign commanding power in the soul, and reigns there as lord paramount, then it is killing and damning.

And now, sirs, may not that which hath been spoken be sufficient to convince you of the evil of that bondage—that miserable hereditary bondage—which you all lie under so long as you are in the natural and unregenerate state. And will you not be prevailed with to endeavour speedily to get out

of it? by the law of the Spirit to be made free from the law of sin? You may be freed from this bondage if you will; Christ is come, as for other ends, so for this, to 'give liberty to the captives, and to open the prison to them who are bound,' Isa. lxi. 1; to knock off sinners' bolts and chains, and to make them free indeed, John viii. 36. In his name I do this day tender freedom to you, and deliverance from sin's vassalage; will you not accept of it? And here is the law of the Spirit too, to make you free from the law of sin; why, then, shall not this be done? Will you still like sin's yoke? I assure you Christ's is not so easy, but sin's is as uneasy. Will you have its dominion yet kept up in you? are you loath to part with your old master? then your ears must be bored for sin and Satan, as the servant under the law was to be served, Exod. xxi. 5, 6, who might have been set at liberty from his master, but he had no mind to it. If it be thus, I can say nothing more; only pray that the Lord will convince you what the reign and power of sin is, what a miserable bondage attends it, that you may with the greatest earnestness press after conversion and the law of the Spirit of life, in order to freedom from it. So much for the first branch of this use of information.

Secondly, It informs us further of the necessity, power, and efficacy of restraining and renewing grace. I will speak to them apart.

1. For restraining grace. By which I mean that grace whereby God keeps in men's corruptions, and sets bounds and limits to them in sin, so as not to suffer them to be as vile and wicked as otherwise they would be. That such a thing is done by God, all grant; he that bounds the sea, that it doth not break forth and overflow all—it is most elegantly set out, Job xxxviii. 8, 10, 11, 'Who shut up the sea with doors, when it brake forth, as if it had issued out of the womb? And brake up for it my decreed place, and set bars, and doors, and said, Hitherto shalt thou come, but no further: and here shall thy proud waves be stayed?' As also Jer. v. 22, 'Which have placed the sand for the bound of the sea by a perpetual decree, that it cannot pass it: and though the waves thereof toss themselves, yet can they not prevail; though they roar, yet can they not pass over it:'—I say, he that thus bounds the

sea, that unruly body, doth also bound the wickedness of man's heart, a far more unruly thing than the sea itself; this God keeps in or lets out as seems good unto him. You see it in the case of Abimelech, whose lust did strongly work in him towards Sarah, but, saith God, Gen. xx. 6, 'I withheld thee from sinning against me, therefore I suffered thee not to touch her;' the like you have in several other instances. Now this law of sin proves both the necessity and also the mighty power and efficacy of this restraining grace; for the making out of which be pleased to take notice of the following particulars:

(1.) That the most of men are under the law of sin. All are born under it, and the most continue under it, for the most are in the state of nature, and in that state the law of sin carries it. Here and there you have a soul brought in to God, converted, savingly wrought upon, 'one of a city, and two of a family,' Jer. iii. 14; but the generality of men are strangers to this work, and therefore they are under the full power and dominion of a cursed nature. It being so, how necessary is restraining grace! for the less there is of regenerating grace, the more need there is of restraining grace.

(2.) Men naturally being under this law, it doth vehemently and impetuously put them upon sin; for herein lies its being a law and a principle, as you have heard. The depraved nature doth not barely dispose men to sin, or faintly persuade them to sin; but it doth powerfully and efficaciously incline, urge, impel, nay, necessitate them to sin; they 'cannot cease from sin,' 2 Pet. ii. 14.

(3.) It is not this or that sin which this law urges men to; but, if it be left to itself, it urges to every sin, yea, to the very worst of sins. This indwelling sin contains all sin in it; the corrupt nature is the πανσπερμάτιον, the seminary or seed-plot of all wickedness; in that one sinful habit all sinful acts do lie, seminally and radically; and sin, where it is a law, is for all sin; it will excite, instigate, provoke not only to lesser evils, such as the world puts a fairer interpretation upon, but also to those which are most enormous, hideous, and horrid, as atheism, blasphemy, murder, theft, adultery, &c.

(4.) This law of sin hath great advantages in and over men; for it is a law that is in them, an innate, ingenit, inbred law; it is written and engraven in their very nature. Sin is now connatural to them, yea, it is as natural, in some respects, for apostatised man to sin, as it is for the fire to burn or the stone to descend. I have told you, and there is too much of truth in it, that the great law of nature, it being considered as depraved, is to sin against God. This law of sin is written in the heart, and that gives a mighty power and efficacy to it, and must needs strongly incline a person to comply with it; as God, when he would have men readily and effectually to close with his will, he writes his law in their heart, Jer. xxxi. 33, and that being done, they cannot but do what that law enjoins; just so it is with sinners in reference to the law of sin upon the writing of it in their hearts.

These things being considered and put together, what is the reason that there is no more sin in the world? God knows there is too much of it; the law of sin is too prevalent in the hearts and lives of the most; but yet, I say, what is the reason that there is no more of it? for certainly this law of sin leads the unregenerate to do more evil than what many, yea, any of them do. Doubtless there are divers who are fully under sin's power, who yet are kept from many external gross acts of it, and are not altogether so bad as it and Satan would have them to be. Sometimes it breaks forth in this or that unconverted person, but why doth it not do the same in every such person? And sometimes, too, it breaks forth in this or that act; but why doth it not so do in every act, yea, in the grossest acts? Whence is it that every unconverted man is not a Cain, a Judas, a Nero, &c., the law of sin inclining him to all this wickedness? I answer, the reason why it is not so, is wholly grounded upon the restraining grace of God. It pleases God, for the good of the world, of human society, especially for the good of his own people, to keep in and bound that wicked nature which is in wicked men, that it shall not in all such, at all times, in all acts proper to it, vent itself as it pleases. And was it not for this mighty restraint which God in his providence lays upon sin and sinners, there would be no living in the world, there would be nothing but killing, and slaying, and stealing, &c., and, in a word, the perpetration of all villanies imaginable. Was it not for this, whither would not the law of sin carry men? They being under the full dominion of it, what would they stick at? Oh but God restrains them; he lets out so much of their corruptions as may be to his own glory, and the *residuum* or overplus he keeps in, according to that of the psalmist, Ps. lxxvi. 10, 'Surely the wrath of man shall praise thee, the remainder of wrath shalt thou restrain.' How necessary, therefore, is restraining grace! it is necessary in respect of the good, much more in respect of the bad; even they do need it for themselves, but these much more for others. Ravenous and fierce creatures must be kept in chains, or else they would worry and tear all that should come within their reach; if God had not devils and men in chains, they would be so exorbitant that the world could not long subsist; blessed be God for restraining mercy! And how doth this also hold forth the mighty power of this mercy, when sin lords it at such a rate in the hearts of men, hath such an absolute power over them, doth so impetuously urge them to all kinds and degrees of evil, that yet they should be so bounded and limited that some order and decorum should be kept up in the world? Oh the power of restraining providence! It is like the fire's not burning into which the three children were cast, or like the lions' not tearing of Daniel when he was in the very midst of them; which certainly proceeded from the mighty restraint which God laid upon the one and upon the other, in the suspending and hindering of them in their natural operations. It is no less power that which God puts forth in the restraining of men's sinful natures, that they do not so fiercely break forth in all wicked acts as otherwise they would. And if this be so admirable in the restraining of men, how much more admirable is it in the restraining of devils! Their power, rage, malice, wickedness, is greater by much than that in men; oh therefore, why do not they do all the mischief they could and would? Why do not they destroy and worry all before them? Especially as to the saints, whom they most hate, why do they not tear them in pieces every day? Why? No thank to themselves; they cannot do it because God restrains them, binds and bounds them as he pleases; here is the great demonstration of the power of restraining grace.

2. Secondly, It shews us also the necessity, power,

and efficacy of renewing grace. There is more in this grace than in the former: in restraining grace sin is a little curbed and kept in, but yet it retains its inward strength and power, as it was with Samson when he was only bound, or as it is with fierce creatures when they are in cages or chains; but in renewing grace sin is subdued, conquered, much weakened in its strength, divested of its former absolute power, not only kept in but brought under, and the soul brought over to the will and command of God. Now this being effected in and by renewing grace, it is evident that there is a mighty power and efficacy in that grace; for that which frees from so great a power as that of sin before conversion, must needs have a great power in it. If renewing grace was a weak thing, or did act in a weak manner, it could never do what it doth; was there not the law of the Spirit in it, the law of sin would be too hard for it. It is not to be imagined that sin will ever be persuaded to resign or tamely to quit its power and dominion, which it so dearly loves and so fiercely contends for; no, it must be forced to this and plainly overpowered, or else it will keep what it hath; therefore in regeneration God comes with that effectual, almighty grace which shall infallibly pull sin off from the throne, let it do its worst, with that power which all the power of sin cannot withstand; and so the work is done. As you see in the case of Peter—that I may open it by an allusion—you read Acts xii. 5, &c., how he was kept in prison, bound with two chains, the keepers before the door kept the prison, besides he had soldiers by him, and he sleeping betwixt them: one would think that now Herod had him fast enough, and yet Peter is brought out; how? Why, the angel of the Lord comes, in the strength of God, awakens him, bids him arise, makes his chains fall off from him, breaks open the prison doors, and so sets him free. The like you read of Paul and Silas, Acts xvi. 23: they were thrown into prison, the jailer charged to keep them safely; he throws them into the inner prison, made their feet fast in the stocks, yet for all this they were delivered; how? 'Suddenly there was a great earthquake, so that the foundations of the prison were shaken, and immediately all the doors were opened, and every one's bonds were loosed:' what could have brought these persons, under these circumstances, out of prison, but the miraculous interposures of the mighty power of God? and that did it effectually. Thus it is with men in their natural state; sin and Satan have them fast bound, secured in chains and fetters, they cannot stir hand or foot to help themselves, are fully under the power of their enemies; how are these now released? why, God comes, and the Spirit comes, by renewing grace, and therein he opens the doors of their hearts, though shut up very fast, knocks off their fetters, conquers the guard that is set upon them, breaks all the power and force of sin, and so rescues them from that thraldom and bondage which they were under. Oh the power of renewing grace! Well might Paul say, Eph. iii. 20, 'According to the power that worketh in us.' The truth is, in the freeing of a soul from the law of sin, no less power is put forth than that very power of God put forth in the raising up of the Lord Jesus from the dead; so the apostle makes the parallel, Eph. i. 19, 20; and that was much above that power which was exerted in the rescuing of the forementioned persons out of their confinement. It had been morally impossible that ever the children of Israel should have been freed from the power of Pharaoh, and that woeful bondage they were under, if God himself had not made bare his arm and brought them out with a strong and mighty hand, as it is Deut. vi. 21; Ps. cxxxvi. 12; but it is a much harder thing to free the sinner from his spiritual bondage, he being under a sadder captivity, and held therein by a far greater strength than what Pharaoh had. Oh surely no deliverance could be expected from sin's dominion, unless infinite power was engaged in the bringing of it about: therefore how necessary as well as efficacious is renewing grace! But more of this when I come to the third observation.

One use I have finished; several others should have been made of the point in hand, as to shew you yet further how you may find out your particular cases, whether you be under the law of sin or not; how you may be freed from this law, if as yet you be not so; why you should labour after this freedom, &c. But these things will as well fall in under the next observation, and therefore I will there insist upon them.

CHAPTER VI.

OF REGENERATE PERSONS BEING MADE FREE FROM THE LAW OF SIN.

For the law of the Spirit of life in Christ Jesus hath made me free from the law of sin and death.—Rom. viii. 2.

The second observation spoken to, viz., That persons truly regenerate are made free from the law of sin—This is, 1. cleared and stated: where it is shewn, that the freedom is not to be carried further than the law of sin—How sin is in the best, yea, and hath a great power in them, and yet they are not under the law of sin—when persons may be said to be so; or what that is which constitutes the law of sin—That not to be found in those who belong to God—The observation 2. confirmed by scriptures and reasons—It is, 3. applied: First, By way of examination—Mistakes about things which look like freedom from the law of sin, and yet are not so: five particulars instanced in —Secondly, All are exhorted to make out after this freedom—One direction in order to it—Thirdly, Such as are made free, &c., are exhorted, 1. to be humble; 2. To stand fast in their liberty, and also to walk suitably thereunto; 3. To bless God—Fourthly, Gracious persons are comforted from hence.

The sum of these words, after the giving their proper sense and meaning, hath been drawn into three observations: the first of which hath been spoken to; the second now follows, and it is this, That persons truly regenerate are made free from the law of sin; this is the privilege of all such, and that which always accompanies the state of grace or regeneration, viz., freedom from the law of sin. Paul being such a person, here saith he was made free from the law of sin.

For the better opening and stating of this truth, the first thing to be done, I must necessarily remind you of some things, which, in the explication of the words, and elsewhere too, I have had occasion to insist upon. As,

1. Though the apostle here speaks in his own person, 'the law of the Spirit of life hath made *me*

free,' &c., yet the thing spoken of is not to be limited to him, individually considered, but to be extended to all who are regenerated and sanctified; his knowledge of it might be somewhat special, but the thing itself is common and general in all saints.

2. That the freedom mentioned in the text refers to the being made free from the commanding, reigning power of sin, rather than to the being made free from the condemning power of sin.

3. The apostle speaks of it as an act that is past —'*hath* made me free,' &c.; therefore that freedom from sin which the saints shall have hereafter in their glorified estate is not here primarily intended, but rather that which they have already upon their sanctification.

4. This especially must be observed, which I must more enlarge upon, that the thing which the saints are freed from is but the law of sin. So the apostle here states it, and therefore the words are to be carried no further than to deliverance from that in sin which doth properly denominate it to be a law, or which doth belong to it in the notion and appellation of a law; so far the saints in this life are made free from it, but no further.

For the preventing of mistakes, and the due bounding of the point, two things must be laid down and made good:

As, 1. That this freedom is not to be taken simply and absolutely for perfect deliverance from the very being and inhesion of sin, but only for deliverance from sin in the notion of a law. The highest saints — God knows, and they themselves know too well — in their present state are far from being wholly, completely, perfectly made free from sin in this respect; yet the very lowest saints are truly and really made free from the law of sin. There is a great difference betwixt the inbeing and the law of sin, betwixt the residence and the reign of sin, betwixt sin's mansion and sin's dominion. Sin will have a being in God's people though it be not a law to them, a residence in them though it doth not reign over them, a mansion though it be cast out of dominion. There are none on this side of heaven so pure but that there is some mixture in them; they have corruption as well as grace, as the best grain has its chaff, and the brightest marble its spots and flaws: the regenerate themselves, whilst here on earth, are but like gold in the ore, which hath much of baser matter mingled with it. Oh this sin cleaves fast to us! it will live as long as we live, and will not die till we die; it will be in the soul so long as the soul is in the body; upon conversion it is cast down, but not wholly cast out; and therefore all that we can safely ground upon from the text, or that is designed in the present truth, is deliverance only from the law of sin. It is here according to what you read of Daniel's beasts: Dan. vii. 12, 'They had their dominion taken away; yet their lives were prolonged for a season and time.' Sin's dominion at the first moment of the sinner's conversion is taken away, yet for some time it lives and hath a being in the soul. Or as you read of the Canaanites, they were to be divested of all their power, yet God, for some reasons, would have them to continue in the Holy Land, and not cut them off all at once, Exod. xxiii. 28, &c.; just so he orders it with his people in reference to sin. You have in the words, according to some, a double freedom—one from sin, and another from death; now we are not absolutely freed from death, but only from the law of it, that is, from the tyranny and curse of it; so neither are we absolutely freed from sin, but only from the law of it, that is, the power and tyranny of it.

Nay, 2. Even the deliverance of regenerate persons from the power of sin must be taken but in a limited and qualified sense; not as if they were wholly freed even from that, so as that sin should have no power in them, for as to that too in this life they come short. Alas! it is the affliction of true converts not only to have sin, habitual and actual, but, which is much worse, that sin hath a great power and strength in them and over them. True indeed, it hath not such a power in them as it hath in the unregenerate, for its power is very much broken, and is not so entire and absolute in them as it is in the other; yet it hath too much of power even in them also. By which I do not mean only sin's molesting power,[1] as it can and doth here greatly molest, disturb, disquiet, trouble, vex the dearest of God's children; nor only sin's assaulting power, as it can and doth often invade and set upon the saints, wherever they are or whatever they are

[1] Of these things, and of sin's dominion, as to the whole, read Sedgwick's Anatomy of Sin, chap. iv.

about, in order to the overcoming of them ; nor only sin's tempting and provoking power, as it doth strongly excite, urge, provoke, solicit them to what is evil ; we may go higher than so, it hath a worser power than all these, namely, a prevailing power : now at some times and in some cases God's own people may be brought even under that. Oh sin may carry the day and be victorious over them ! it may with great efficacy and success prevail even in them, both in the keeping of them from what is good, and also in the drawing of them to what is evil. Is this a thing to be questioned, though the truth of it is much to be lamented ? Do we not see it by sad experience made good in ourselves and others ? Did not Paul himself, who here saith he was made free from the law of sin, yet, which hath often come in my way, a little before, when he was in the same state in which here he was, make sad complaints about it ? 'I find,' saith he, 'a law, that when I would do good, evil is present with me ;' as if he had said, others may dream of perfection, and please themselves with the thoughts of their high attainments, but, as to myself, I cannot pretend to any such thing ; for my part, 'I find a law,' &c. ; there is such a law, such a corrupt, cursed nature in me, which hath too much strength and power over me ; and, saith he, this law I find, I plainly perceive it and cannot but take notice of it ; I do not only hear of it, but I find and feel it in myself, in the sad fruits and effects of it ; yea, saith he, this is no weak or languid thing, but that which hath a great power in me ; for it wars against the law of my mind, and leads me captive, &c. : thus this great saint did groan under sin's power. And if a Paul thus complains, how may others complain ? If sin had such a power in him, what hath it in poor Christians of a far lower size and stature? We have too many instances, not only of the having and bare inbeing of sin, but of the prevailing power of sin even in truly, yea, eminently gracious persons. David commits adultery, plots the death of Uriah, numbers the people, &c. Noah is drunk, Lot incestuous, Hezekiah proud, Job impatient, Peter denies Christ, &c. Oh the strength and efficacy of sin even in the regenerate themselves ! It may and it doth sometimes prevail in the strongest, though it never rules in the weakest ; yet you must know that

these partial successes of sin do not amount to the law of sin : it may conquer and yet not command, its prevalency doth not evince its regency ; the invader may win the field in some battles, and yet for all that not be upon the throne. But, I say, sin *pro hic et nunc* may have a prevailing power even over the best, notwithstanding their being made free from the law of sin.

All then that we can warrantably and truly fix upon in this matter is this, that such who are in the state of grace, in whom the Spirit hath wrought as the Spirit of life, they are made free from the law of sin ; that law being taken in its strict and proper notion, according to the explication which hath been given of it, and as noting something more than the bare power of sin with respect to some particular acts. In some sense sin may be said to be a law *in* the regenerate, namely, in regard of that power and strength which it hath in them ; but yet it is not a law *to* the regenerate, because they do not own it or submit to it, as to that which hath the authority or dominion over them. You have heard there are two things which make sin to be a law : one is authoritative commanding on its part, the other is full and free resignation on the sinner's part to its commands and impulsions. Now the unsanctified in both of these ways are under the law of sin, but with the sanctified it is not so, especially in the latter respect. Indeed, sin, on its part, will often be laying its commands upon them, magisterially and imperiously enough, but they do not, on their part, yield obedience or subjection to those commands ; possibly now and then through infirmity they may hearken to something that sin enjoins, but as to their general course, and to the bent and purpose of their hearts, they say, sin shall not reign over us. Sin is only then a law when it hath habitual, universal, entire, absolute dominion, and when the sinner gives up himself in willing, ready, total subjection to it. Now it is never thus bad with the regenerate, sin's power never rises so high where grace is ; in this respect every child of God is made free from the law of sin, and in this notion the apostle here takes the law of sin. In the former chapter he speaks to it as it notes the power and strength of the relics of sin, and as its power is but somewhat broken, and so he felt too much of it ; but here in the text he speaks to

R

it as it is in its full power and strength, and so he was freed from it.[1]

Several of these things have occurred in what goes before, but they being most necessary and proper in this place, I could not but again mention them. Having thus stated the doctrine, and given you the explication of it, I am now, secondly, to make out the truth of it, and to prove that persons truly regenerate are made free from the law of sin. And surely so it is; as certain as the unrenewed are under this law, so certain are the renewed freed from it. Paul here attests it as to himself: 'The law of the Spirit,' &c.; and elsewhere he asserts the same in a more general manner. That text is not impertinent to my present purpose, in 2 Cor. iii. 17, 'Where the Spirit of the Lord is' (as the Spirit of life, as renewing and regenerating,) 'there is liberty,' (or freedom from the law of sin;) for I conceive the apostle doth not only speak of liberty of spirit, in opposition to bondage of spirit, or the spirit of bondage, but also of the liberty of the state, in opposition to the state of bondage; and that, too, is not to be limited only to the liberty of the gospel state, in opposition to the bondage of the law, though I grant the words are brought in more immediately upon that account; but it is applicable to persons with respect to their inward and spiritual state, as by the sanctifying Spirit they are freed from the power of sin, and from that bondage which they were under to it in their natural condition: so that the liberty here spoken of is, in a great measure, one and the same with the being made free from the law of sin in my text; and if so, then you see how positively it is asserted, 'where the Spirit of the Lord is, there is liberty.' So, again, the apostle, Rom. vi., speaks much of the law or reign and dominion of

sin; which he having dehorted from, ver. 12, 'Let not sin reign in you,' &c., he then backs his dehortation with a promise, ver. 14, 'For sin shall not have dominion over you, because you are not under the law, but under grace.'[1] The grace here mainly intended is that assisting, helping, strengthening grace which always accompanies the gospel or new covenant state; the law commanded much, but gave no strength for the doing what it commanded; but the gospel, where it requires duty, it always enables a person to perform it. Now upon this grace Paul assures believers that, they endeavouring on their part and making vigorous resistance to sin, it should not have dominion over them, because they should certainly have such strength and assistance given them from God, as that their endeavours should be successful against all sin's assaults,—this, I say, is the grace primarily intended in this place; yet you may take in, too, converting and renewing grace, and then the words will run thus: Sin neither hath nor ever shall 'have dominion over you,' who are believers, 'because you are not under the law,' i.e., that law which only discovers sin, but doth not help to conquer it, which leaves the person as it finds him, without any changing of his heart or state, 'but you are under grace,' i.e., regenerating grace, which always delivers from, and secures against, the dominion of sin.

And besides these Scripture proofs, in point of reason it must needs be so, because upon regeneration there is another active, operative, commanding principle infused into the soul, viz., grace; now grace and the law of sin are inconsistent. It may consist with sin, for otherwise there would be no grace in this lower world; but it cannot consist with the law of sin, or with sin in its full and absolute dominion and power. Two contrary principles cannot be together in the same subject in their full vigour and strength; the like, *cæteris paribus*, may be said of contrary powers; if sin be the principle in its full efficacy so as to make it a law, then there is no grace, because if this was in the soul it would

[1] At inquies, quomodo Paulus se liberatum jactat a lege peccati, qui capite præcedente questus sit se adhuc mancipari legi peccati, et adhuc servire legi peccati? Dixit se carne ei servire, at mente legi Dei. Si carne tantum, non mente, ergo vere liberatus; a mente enim, non a carne, fidelis æstimandus est, &c. Adde quod lex peccati non eodem prorsus modo hic sumitur atque præcedente capite. Hic significat plenum illud peccati dominium, cui totus homo naturalis extra Christum constitutus, subjectus est, &c. Illic autem per legem peccati intelligebantur reliquiæ quædam istius dominii, quod peccatum non in totum hominem fidelem, sed in membra, sive in carnem ejus tantum, *i.e.*, in corruptam naturam, adhuc exercet, &c.—*Lud. de Dieu.*

[1] Homo consideratur ante legem, sub lege, sub gratia, in pace. Ante legem non pugnamus, sub lege pugnamus, sed vincimur, sub gratia pugnamus et vincimus, in pace non pugnamus quidem.—*Aug. Lib. Octog.*, Quæst. 56; et in *Expos. quarund. Propos. Ep. ad Rom.*

certainly break the full strength of the opposite principle. True grace is a commanding thing as well as sin; there is such a holy pride in it that it disdains and scorns to be subject to corruption, or to let sin be above it; it can, though not without reluctancy, bear the inbeing of sin, but it cannot bear sin as a co-rival or competitor with it in point of rule and dominion. Here the elder must serve the younger, (to allude to that of Jacob and Esau, Gen. xxv. 23;) I mean, the corrupt nature must be an underling to that which is sanctified. If Hagar will be content to live in the house in a state of inferiority, well and good, that for a time must be submitted to; but if she will be presuming to vie with her mistress for authority and rule, and nothing will serve her below that, she must then be made to know herself. The application is obvious.

To make the thing unquestionable, pray consider what that in special is which is done by God at the converting of a soul; it is this very thing, the dethroning of sin and Satan, and the enthroning of Christ and grace. Where God converts, he doth in effect say: Sin, thou must now come down, and Christ and grace shall now ascend the throne. Whenever the sinner is regenerated, in the first moment of that state sin is divested of its usurped power and regency, and the kingdom of Christ, in and by grace, is set up in him. Now Christ's kingdom and sin's kingdom are incompatible; where he reigns it shall not, for he is *impatiens consortis;* but especially he will not have such a base thing as sin to share with him in the government of the soul. Where Christ comes and takes possession, he always abolishes the law of sin, and instead of that sets up another law; for new lords will have new laws, and different lords different laws. Therefore, in the work of conversion, God promises to write his law in the heart: Jer. xxxi. 33, ' But this shall be the covenant that I will make with the house of Israel, I will put my law in their inward parts, and write it in their hearts.' Now upon the doing of that the law of sin is defaced, antiquated, and cancelled, for since contrary laws cannot be together in their full force, the former must be abolished upon the introduction of the latter.

Once more. In the text you have ' the law of the Spirit of life' brought in in opposition to, and in order to the abolition of, ' the law of sin;' which being considered, it affords a very weighty argument for the proof of the truth in hand. The law of the Spirit is the mighty power of the Spirit put forth in the regenerate soul, for the rescuing of it from the power of sin, and the bringing of it under the rule and sceptre of the Lord Christ. Now shall this Spirit put forth such a mighty power for this very end, and yet sin continue as high in its sovereignty as before? What advantage, then, would the believer have by the law of the Spirit, if the law of sin should yet be kept up in him? Certainly when this great Spirit shall vouchsafe to exert his great power, there must be some great effect produced by it. And what can that be but the delivering of the poor captive sinner from sin's bondage, the destroying of Satan's kingdom, and the setting up of Christ's sweet and gracious government in the soul. But I spend time in the proving of that which indeed needs not much proof.

In the application of the doctrine, which I judge will be more useful and necessary, I might here take occasion to confute those who, misunderstanding this passage, ' Being made free from the law of sin,' do from thence infer and argue for the saints' perfection in this life. But having given you all that this freedom contains in it, which comes exceeding short of perfection, I think I need not—I am sure I will not—speak anything further for the obviating and refuting of that proud opinion. He that here saith he was made free from the law of sin, elsewhere saith also he had not already attained nor was already perfect, &c., Phil. iii. 12, and surely he went as far, nay, much further, than any of our modern perfectionists. God make us sensible of imperfection in this state, and ever to be pressing after and waiting for that perfection which only belongs to the future state!

I might also from hence infer the happiness of such who are truly regenerate, and the preciousness, excellency, advantage of regenerating grace: oh how happy are they who are delivered from sin's yoke! and how precious is that grace which instates the soul in such liberty!

Use 1. But passing by these things, I will in the first place desire you to make diligent search whether you be thus freed from the law of sin. O sirs!

how is it with you? what can you say of yourselves about this? You heard in the former point that all in the natural state are under this law. Adam hath entailed this bondage upon all his posterity; had he not fallen we had come into the world with the law of God written in our hearts, but now we are born with the law of sin written in them; are we therefore brought out of the state of nature? In this point you have heard that they who are regenerate are made free from it; so that if you be not such, you are concluded to be yet under the law of sin; these two do mutually prove each the other: if it be the state of unregeneracy, it is the law of sin, and if it be the law of sin it is the state of unregeneracy. Well, it highly concerns you to be most seriously inquisitive about this; I pray, therefore, bring it down to yourselves one by one, and ask, How is it with me? Am I under the law of sin? or am I made free from it? Some law or other I must be under, for every man in the world is so, therefore what is the law which hath the authority over me? is it the law of Christ, the law of grace, or is it the law of sin? hath not the sinful nature in me the dominion of a law, and the efficacy of a principle? is not all that which makes up the law of sin to be found in me?

To help you in this inquiry I need not say much more than what I have already said: do but look back to the explication of sin's being a law, as also to the answer of that question how this may be known, and there is enough to direct you in examination and passing judgment upon yourselves. Yet, however, a little further to help you herein, and also to quicken you to the more serious searching into it, let me tell you there are very great and dangerous mistakes in this matter; oh how far may sinners go, and how well may they think of themselves, and yet for all that be under the law of sin! men catch at false evidences, and lay that stress upon them which they will not bear. Let me instance in a few particulars, to shew how far persons may go and yet not be made free from the law of sin, or to set forth the weakness of some grounds which men build upon for this.

1. They make some resistance to sin, and therefore they conclude they are not under its power. But, alas! this will not prove it, for (1.) This resistance may be but a faint, weak, half-resistance; (2.) It may be but to this or that sin, not to every sin:

(3.) It may be to sin, but not as sin—that is, sin may be resisted because of the effects and consequences of it, as it kindles God's wrath, brings punishment, ends in hell, exposes to shame before men, &c., and yet as considered in its own nature, as it is an offence to God, a breach of the holy commandment, an aberration from the straight rule, so no resistance may be made to it, but the sinner readily closes with it, and likes it well enough: now such a resistance as this will not amount to a proof or evidence of not being under the law of sin. There is a resistance, indeed, which will undeniably prove it, as when it is hearty, thorough, vigorous, universal; when it is such that the utmost strength of the soul goes out in it against sin, when it is made to every sin, and to sin as sin; where it is thus, it is no law of sin; he that thus opposes and resists it, it is most certain he is none of sin's slaves and subjects: if therefore it be thus with any of you it is well, but you must not bottom too much upon mere resistance, if it be not thus qualified and stated. Indeed no-resistance is a good affirmative argument to prove sin's dominion, but every kind of resistance is not a good negative argument to prove no dominion thereof. Sincere Christians may fetch much comfort from their resistings of sin; but as to those which are common and ordinary in others, little comfort can be fetched from them.

2. Persons may be free from very many sins, may not have such violent inclinations to some particular sins, and yet for all this be under the law of sin. The reason is this, because there may be some other sins in which, though not in these, it may exercise full authority over them. Possibly they are not proud, but they are covetous; they are not openly vicious, but they are worldly; they are not unclean, but they are spiteful and malicious. Now reigning sin never limits itself to any one sin, though it be not obeyed in this or that; if its commands be observed in any other sin, it is enough; willing and full subjection to it in any one sin—I speak not of particular acts, but of the kinds of sin—evinces its dominion. Thou pleasest thyself because such corruptions and lusts do not prevail over thee; ay, but if any other single lust rules thee, so that it hath thy heart, and thou yieldest free and entire obedience to it, this sufficiently determines thy case; thou art under the law of sin. As 'whoever keeps

the whole law of God, and yet offends in one point, is guilty of all,' James ii. 10; so whoever opposes the whole law of sin, and yet in some one point resigns up himself to it, he is as truly under the power of it as if he obeyed it in all its commands. There needs not thirty tyrants at once to enslave a people; one is enough.

3. Sin may seem to lie still and quiet in the heart, to let sinners alone, that they shall not feel its urgings and impulsions to what is evil—especially in such a violent and impetuous manner—and yet they may be under its full strength and empire; for this stillness and quietness of sin may proceed merely from the entireness of its reign, or because it meets with no opposition—the soul doth whatever it will have it do; no wonder, then, that it is still. Pharaoh himself was so till the people of Israel would cast off his yoke; but then he bestirred himself, and marched in all his rage and fury against them. Oh, when the sinner begins to think of changing his master, when Christ and grace are competitors with sin, who shall rule? how doth it then, though it was quiet before, shew itself, and put forth all its strength for the securing of its dominion! We say, *Natura vexata seipsam prodit;* when sin is vexed and crossed a little, then you shall see and feel what it is; but so long as it is pleased, all is still and calm. And do any say they feel not the impetuous risings, stirrings, motions of sin? doth not this proceed from their insensibleness? If so, then sin's power is very high; for the less is the sinner's sense, the greater always is sin's power; if all be in peace, it is a sign the strong man keeps the house, Luke xi. 21. Sin evermore hath the fullest dominion where it gives the least disturbance; where it troubles least it rules most. If there be little or no sense, no conflict, no trouble, it is a very bad sign that sin is entire upon the throne.

4. There may be some trouble upon the conscience after the commission of sin, and yet it be the law of sin. It was so in Cain, in Ahab, in Judas, &c. Where there is no after-grief, sin indeed reigns; there may be some after-grief, and yet for all that sin may reign too. Upon the commission of some known sin, natural and enlightened conscience may fall upon a man and vex him sorely. Sin usually hath not that power in the conscience which it hath in the other

faculties; it may entirely have the will and affections, whilst yet conscience stands off, and is not so fully on its side. No, that—unless it be a cauterised conscience—will give in its dictates against sin, and, if it be not hearkened to, it will smite and vex and gall the sinner to some purpose. And because sometimes it is fast asleep and neglects to do its office, therefore God himself interposes to awaken and set it on the sinner. Conscience, saith God, go and do thine office; make such a man know what he hath done, tell him of his sin and spare him not, pursue him from place to place with the sense of his guilt, &c. Well! now all this may be but in order to his smarting, and not in order to his healing; this trouble may be only penal, and not medicinal or penitential, and therefore doth not amount to any proof of freedom from the law of sin. I would not discourage any true penitent. Know, therefore, sin never reigns where the soul grieves for it, provided, (1.) That the ground of this belief be right, viz., because God is offended, the good Spirit grieved, the holy law violated, &c.; (2.) That the effect of this grief be reformation, and the leaving that sin which the soul seems to mourn over.[1] If there be not these two things accompanying the trouble upon the conscience, it speaks nothing against the dominion of sin.

5. Men may do that which materially is very good, and may hold on in so doing for some time, and yet be under the law of sin. Oh, there are many who pray, hear the word, attend upon ordinances, give alms, &c., and yet sin is still regent in them; because, (1.) Though they do all this, yet the heart is not at all changed in them. Now sin's power never goes off till the heart be made new. (2.) Because, which is more demonstrative, the heart is rotten in all this. Christ hath the external duty, but sin hath the heart. Some outward respect is shewn to God, but yet the heart is set for some lust against God; as you read of those, Ezek. xxxiii. 31, 'And they come unto thee as the people cometh, and they sit before thee as my people, and they hear thy words, but they will not do them; for with their mouth they shew much love, but their heart goeth

---

[1] *Pœnitentia est mala præterita plangere, et plangenda iterum non committere.—Ambr. de Pœn.* Inanis est pœnitentia quam sequens inquinat culpa, et nihil prosunt lamenta si iterantur peccata.—*Aug.*

after their covetousness.' It is a thing too common for men, even in their external serving of God, to serve sin more than God; and God's work is done by them for the matter of it; but sin so far interposes its authority and strength as that it carries it in the sinner as to his ends in what he doth, and if it can but sway and order him in them, God may have the external act, but still it hath the sovereignty and power within. The same holds true, too, as to a plausible, outwardly good conversation; external piety is too well consistent with the internal reign of sin; it rules in the fair professing hypocrite, as well as in the gross and scandalous sinner.

By this, you see, you may run yourselves upon great mistakes in taking up with such evidences as will not prove your being made free from the law of sin. Oh that the consideration thereof might make you the more careful lest you, as many thousands are to their eternal undoing, should herein be deceived; as also quicken you to the trial of yourselves by those things which will infallibly prove the thing in hand! What are they? Why, no allowed subjection to sin; no tame, quiet submission to its commands; inward renouncing, nay, abjuring of its authority; a rooted, vigorous opposition to it in all its cursed suggestions; an utter dislike and hatred of it; the bent and *impetus* of the heart set against it; universal resignation of a man's self to the law and will of God; a hearty willingness, nay, desire, to come under the rule and government of the Lord Jesus, &c.; these are the things you are to inquire after and to judge by, for these are sure evidences which you may rely upon. Happy is that man who finds these in himself! he may with confidence build upon them that he is indeed made free from the law of sin; but he that is confident upon anything short of these, will, sooner or later, find he was too credulous. So much for this use.

Use 2. The next shall be to exhort you and others, yea, all men in the whole world, if I could reach them, to labour after and make sure of a share and interest in this blessed freedom from sin's power and dominion. Regenerate persons, you hear, have it; shall the unregenerate sit still, and be quiet and contented under the want of it? God forbid! To be made free from the law of sin, what a mercy or privilege is this! Oh how much is there in it to ex-

cite, draw, allure sinners to desire, love, and value it, and to be industrious after it! He that can upon good grounds say over the words of the text, needs no higher happiness. It was more for Paul to say 'the law of the Spirit of life,' &c., than if he could have said that God had given him all the kingdoms, crowns, diadems, riches, honours, pleasures of this world. You see he applies it to himself, and surely he had comfort enough in that application. Now, sinners, when will you be able to say the same of yourselves, that you also by the power of the Spirit are made free from the law of sin? Oh, as Eliphaz once said to Job, 'hear it, and know it for thyself,' Job v. 27; so I would say to you, Hear this and know it for yourselves, so as to get it for, and to be able to appropriate it unto, your own selves; so as to take the *me* here as coming out of Paul's mouth concerning himself, into your mouths one by one concerning yourselves. Sirs, this is a thing of such importance that we ministers cannot speak too much, or be too earnest about it. It is the great end of our Lord and master, in his employing us in the work of the ministry, 'to open your eyes, to turn you from darkness to light, and from the *power of Satan unto God*,' Acts xxvi. 18; and therefore, though I have said so much already to press the thing upon you, yet I must further plead with you in order to the more effectual pressing of it.

Therefore consider, hath not this sin tyrannised long enough over you? Are you willing still to continue under its thraldom and vassalage? Must this cursed usurper for ever sit upon the throne? Shall it yet command and give law to you? What woeful and miserable bondage attends its empire and government hath been described largely, shall all that be nothing to you? to be slaves, the very worst of slaves, shall that be but a little thing in your eye? Other bondage, not half so bad, you cannot bear, you detest and dread it; shall the worst bondage only be tolerable, nay, eligible? Pray look back to the description of sin's bondage, p. 120, &c., and methinks your heart should rise at it. It is an astonishing thing to consider that so excellent a creature as man, who hath such an excellent being in him as a reasonable and immortal soul, should so tamely submit to so base a thing as sin, and make no more of servitude to it. Doth God, in the gospel, so graciously tender liberty, privative and positive, to you, and will you not accept of it? May you be made free, and will you not? Oh stupendous folly! Is this after the manner of men with respect to external liberty or bondage? When God sent Moses to deliver Israel out of their bondage, what madness would it have been in them not to have accepted it! Let there be a ransom sent to the poor captives under Turkish cruelty, would they not readily embrace it? Ah, sinner! the Lord Jesus came from heaven on purpose to redeem thy poor captive soul out of the hands of sin and Satan; he hath, on his part, effected what he came about; he now offers his merit and Spirit to make thee free; nay, he invites, entreats, solicits, beseeches thee that thou wilt accept of the liberty purchased for thee; and yet wilt thou hug thy chains, play with thy fetters, love thy dungeon, be fond of thy bondage, and prefer it before liberty? What is this but madness not to be paralleled! What ingratitude is this to thy Saviour! what cruelty to thyself! As to thee I may well alter Tiberius's *O gentem*, &c., into *O animam ad servitutem natam!* Further, I pray you, think of this: if sin rule you, will Christ save you? You cannot but know the contrary. You know that he rules wherever he saves; that he will be the governor where he is the Saviour; that sin's yoke must be taken off, and his yoke taken up, or no salvation, Mat. xi. 29; and yet shall sin be obeyed, and be thy lord and sovereign, rather than Christ? The business comes to a narrow issue. Let Christ rule thee and he will save thee, but let sin command thee and it will condemn thee. The law of Christ and of the Spirit is the law of life, but the law of sin is the law of death. But these things have been insisted upon. Oh that this Spirit, which frees from the law of sin, would shew you what there is in the law of sin! Men do not endeavour to get out of it, because they are not convinced of the evil that is in it; did they but know what it is, they would choose to die rather than to live under it. And as for you, let me ask you how you carry it in other respects. You hate the tyrant without, will you love the tyrant within? You groan under the laws of men when they are a little heavy, shall there be no groaning under the far heavier laws of sin? You will not be called slaves to any, will you be content to be indeed slaves to

sin? Is a barbarous Turk cried out of, when a devil and a cursed nature are never regarded?

But one consideration more. As God made you at the first, you had nothing to do with this law of sin. No, he made you for his own government, to be subject to himself; his law was written within you, to command and act you in your whole course; how, then, came sin by this power? how did it get up thus into the throne? Why, only by the first apostasy from God. Adam's fall was sin's rise. Its reign commenced from man's rebellion. It is a mere upstart and intruder. God never designed this power to it. Will you now, by your liking of it and continuance under it, give an after-ratification or approbation of its power? It hath deprived you of your primitive liberty, and will you not endeavour to regain it? When Sardis was taken by the Grecians, Xerxes commanded that every day when he was at dinner one should cry aloud, Sardis is lost, Sardis is lost, that hereby he might be reminded of what he had lost, and stirred up to endeavour the regaining of it. O sirs, your original liberty is lost! Sin hath got it out of your hands. This we proclaim in your ears from time to time, that you may never be quiet till you have recovered it, and yet will you do nothing in order thereunto? Will you even sit still under this inexpressible loss? Oh that is sad!

All this hath been spoken to set you against sin's dominion, to excite you to the most earnest endeavours to be rid of its sovereignty, to cause you to fly to the Spirit of life that you may be made free from the law of sin, to work holy purposes in you that sin shall no longer reign over you, that you may say with the church, Isa. xxvi. 12, 'O Lord our God, other lords besides thee have had dominion over us, but by thee only will we make mention of thy name.' Oh that I might prevail with some soul to say with respect to sin, Ah, Lord, other lords have had dominion over me; lust, pride, passion, covetousness, sensuality, have ruled me just as they pleased, but I desire it may be so no longer; I am resolved now only to be subject to thyself; oh do thou dethrone sin and enthrone thyself in me, let me be brought under universal, hearty, ready subjection to thy laws, and let not the law of sin carry it in me any longer, &c.

In what ways and by what means a poor enslaved sinner may be made free from the law of sin, is a very weighty inquiry; and I would hope that some sinners, being convinced by what hath been spoken, have it in their thoughts. For answer to it there is one direction only which I shall at present give: it is this: Get into the regenerate state. Regenerate persons are the adequate subjects of this freedom; they, and none but they, are freed from sin as a law. Paul, so long as he was unconverted, was as much under this law as any person whatsoever, but as soon as it pleased God to convert him he was made free from it. This deliverance depends upon the state; it must be the state of regeneracy, till which, sin will keep up its regency and sovereignty in the soul. Oh, as you have heard, when grace once comes into the heart the kingdom of sin goes down, and the kingdom of Christ goes up therein; but never before. All your strivings, endeavours, convictions, purposes, promises, will never make sin's throne to shake and fall, till you be renewed and sanctified. Therefore pray much for the regenerating Spirit, and attend much upon the regenerating, word in order to this great work: John iii. 5, 'Except a man be born of water and of *the Spirit,* he cannot enter into the kingdom of God.' James i. 18, 'Of his own will begat he us by the *word of truth,*' &c. 1 Cor. iv. 15, 'In Christ Jesus I have begotten you *through the gospel;*' it is this Spirit and this word which must renew and bring about the new birth in you, and so 'deliver you from the power of darkness, and translate you into the kingdom of God's dear Son,' as the apostle speaks, Col. i. 13. But this will be more properly enlarged upon when I shall come to the third observation, therefore here I will say no more about it.

Use 3. I will direct myself to those who by the Spirit of life are made free from the law of sin. Something to them, 1. By way of counsel; 2. By way of comfort.

By way of counsel I will urge three duties upon them:

1. The first is hearty and deep humiliation; and this is incumbent upon such, partly upon what is past, and partly upon what is present.

First, Hath the Lord been so gracious to any of you as to bring you out of the natural bondage, to dethrone and bring down this sin which did at such a rate domineer over you? Oh you must be deeply humbled upon your taking a view of what is past. You are now—God be blessed for it!—made free, but how long was it before this was done? How many years did you pass over in the unregenerate state, in which you were as much under the command and at the beck of sin as any? How great a part of your life hath been spent in its drudgery and vassalage? For how long a time did you tamely submit to its yoke, when you would by no means be brought to submit to the yoke of Christ? Do you not remember how it was with you a few days or years ago, when the sceptre was in sin's hands, and it ruled and acted you even as it pleased? Should not this now be thought of with the greatest grief and sorrow? Oh the bondage, rebellion, enmity of the natural state should, even by converted ones, often be remembered and bitterly bewailed! That is a soul-humbling, heart-melting word, Eph. ii. 3, 'Among whom also we all had our conversation in times past, in the lusts,' &c.; who can read that sad description of a sinner before conversion, Ezek. xvi. 3–5, &c., and not be affected?

Secondly, You must be humbled upon the consideration of what is present. It is better than it hath been, yet not so well as it might and should be; sin hath lost its absolute, full, entire power, but yet it lives, nay, yet it hath a great strength and power in and over you, ay, and against you too, so as that it is still able to do you much hurt, notwithstanding its being weakened; as Samson, though he was much debilitated when his locks were cut, yet he had strength enough left to do mischief to the Philistines. Do not you to this very day find the corrupt nature very strong and powerful? sin rising and stirring in you with great vigour? many very evil inclinations assaulting you with such vehemency that you scarce know how to resist? Doth not corruption, this and that lust, too often foil you, and triumph over you as its captives? Now, though these things are not enough to evince sin's dominion, yet surely they call for deep humiliation. It doth not rule you here, it shall not damn you hereafter; but it defiles you, often separates betwixt you and your God, draws you off from him, prevailingly hinders you from what is good, and prevailingly also excites you to what is evil. Is not this sad? Is there nothing to afflict a gracious heart but only the unbroken power of sin? Oh why are you not more in crying out, 'O wretched man that I am, who shall deliver me from this body of death!' He that gloried here in his deliverance from the law of sin, in one sense, was as much abased before because of the law of sin, of which he felt so much in another sense. The wise God orders it thus, that sin shall not only have a being in his people, but also a considerable power over them in this life; amongst other ends for this, that he may keep them humble, and draw out and heighten their godly sorrow; and indeed there is more in the relics of sin to humble the true Christian, than in all the outward evils that either do or can befall him. Oh never think how it hath been, how yet it is, without great self-abasement and humiliation! When you begin to be 'exalted above measure,' 2 Cor. xii. 7, remember what you were, consider what you are.

2. Are you made free from the law of sin? let me say to you what Paul once said to the Galatians, in reference to their being made free from the ceremonial law, 'Stand fast in the liberty wherewith Christ hath made you free, and be not entangled again with the yoke of bondage,' Gal. v. 1. Is sin brought down? be sure you keep it down; it is pity it should get up again, or ever recover its pristine power. When a people have once got the usurper off from the throne, it concerns them to look to it that he doth not regain it; for should he so do, their condition then would be much worse than before. Saints! just so should you carry it towards sin. That is brought under at present; ay, but it watches all opportunities for the regaining of that power which it hath lost, for it is of a proud nature, and cannot bear the loss of superiority; you must therefore always be upon your guard, with your weapons in your hands, ready to make resistance against it in all its attempts, or else it will soon rally its forces and make head again upon you, and endanger all. I know all its attempts are in vain as to the recovery of its former dominion; God will not suffer it again to lord it over you as before it did; yet if you be careless, especially if you in the least side with it, it will strangely get ground and grow upon you.

Therefore, as Christ once charged the healed man, John v. 14, 'Thou art made whole, sin no more;' so would I charge you, You are made free, oh sin no more, that you may never come under its bondage again. Though God had so miraculously brought Israel out of Egypt, and out of that miserable servitude that there they were in, yet upon all occasions how desirous were they to be in Egypt again. Shall it be thus with you? shall your gracious deliverance be so undervalued? have you such low thoughts of sin's servitude as that you can be willing to come under it again? Pray learn how to put a due value upon your liberty; prize it at a high rate, and so prize it as to continue in it and to maintain it to your utmost. Amongst other conditions which were anciently imposed upon those who were set at liberty this was one, that they should not *servitutis jugum iterum sponte suscipere*, willingly submit to the yoke of bondage again; and is not this obligation laid upon souls in their being made free by Christ and the Spirit? The historian tells us a good man will lose his life as soon as his liberty;[1] oh, how should you defend that spiritual liberty which you have by Christ and by grace! I beseech you take heed lest by your carelessness and little compliances with sin, you provoke God to permit its former power and tyranny in a great measure to return upon you, that he may thereby let you see the difference betwixt his and sin's government; read and apply Deut. xxviii. 47, 48. It would be sad if God should deal with any of you as once that master in Athens did with his servant, whom he had formerly made free, but upon some unworthy carriage he reversed and retracted that freedom, saying to him, The city shall never have one as a free denizen of it, who doth so little know how to value such a privilege. Go thy way, therefore, and be a slave again, since thou knowest not how to carry it as becomes one that is free.[2] Now I say, if God should deal thus with any of you, would it not be sad? True, he will never wholly reverse what he hath done in you and for you, but thus far he may go, he may let corruption at some

[1] Libertatem nemo bonus nisi cum anima simul amittit.— *Salust. in Conjur. Cat.*

[2] Supersedeo te, habere civem tanti muneris impium æstimatorem, &c. Abi igitur et esto servus, quoniam liber esse nescisti.— *Val. Max.*, lib. ii. cap. 6.

times and in some acts prevail over you, and he may wholly deprive you of the sense and comfort of your spiritual liberty; and would not these be bad enough?

Let me under this head press another thing upon you, viz., to walk suitably to this your freedom. Wherein doth that consist? why, in this, in being holy, and very holy. If you so be, this will suit with the deliverance from the law of sin which you have upon regeneration, and which you must therefore be, because it is one great end of God in doing that for you: Luke i. 74, 75, 'That we being delivered out of the hands of our enemies, might serve him without fear, in holiness and righteousness before him all the days of our life.' It is observable how God ushers in the ten commandments with his delivering the people of Israel out of the Egyptian bondage, thereby to lay the greater obligation upon them to obey and keep those commandments: Exod. xx. 2, 'I am the Lord thy God, which have brought thee out of the land of Egypt, out of the house of bondage;' then the several commandments follow. And as to that particular command of keeping the Sabbath, you find God enforcing of it with this argument only: Deut. v. 15, 'Remember that thou wast a servant in the land of Egypt,' &c. Oh how holy, how obedient should they be whom God hath brought out of the state of spiritual bondage, the obligation rising higher from this deliverance than from the former. Christians, you should be very holy, partly from a principle of gratitude, partly because now the life of holiness is made more easy and facile; if you be not so now, the power of sin is broken in you, it must be from your sloth, or something worse. Some observe[1] upon the latter clause of the preceding verse, 'who walk not after the flesh,' &c., that now under the gospel it is much more easy to live the heavenly life than it was formerly under the law; so that, say they, if men do not live that life it must be charged merely upon their own negligence: so here, I say, persons being delivered from the reign of sin, to them now it is much more possible, nay, easy to be holy in their walkings than sometimes it was; and

therefore if they do not so walk, it is merely from their idleness and sinful neglects. Sirs, now the holy life is made practicable to you, what an engagement doth this lay upon you to live it! The apostle here, according to that connexion of the words which some pitch upon, brings in freedom from the law of sin as the ground of not walking, &c.; therefore they who are in Christ do not follow the sinful and carnal, but the holy and spiritual course, because they are freed from sin's power. I am sure, as to the thing, it is the duty of such so to walk upon this account.

Let me add a third consideration: regenerate persons upon this must be very holy, that there may be some proportion betwixt nature as renewed in the way of holiness, and nature as depraved in the way of sin; pray observe it, so long as depraved nature was upon the throne you were very sinful, therefore now, when renewed nature is upon the throne, you should be very holy. I do not from hence plead for an equality,—that I very well know is not possible, and the reason is, because corrupt nature before conversion was entire, not broken or weakened by any contrary habit or principle; but it is not so with the renewed nature after conversion, for that hath sin mingled with it, striving against it, making opposition to it; therefore men cannot be so entirely good after grace as they were entirely evil before grace;—yet I may, and I do, plead from hence for some proportion. Whilst sin ruled you, you were very sinful, therefore, now Christ and grace rule you, you should be very holy; so the apostle argues: Rom. vi. 19, 20, '*As* you have yielded your members servants to uncleanness and to iniquity unto iniquity; *even so* now yield your members servants to righteousness unto holiness. For when ye were servants to sin, ye were free from righteousness;' therefore (which though it be not expressed, yet it is implied) proportionably, now when you are the servants of righteousness, you should be free from sin. Upon this threefold consideration such as are made free from the law of sin should be holy.

Now, that I may be somewhat more particular about this, sin being that which is opposite to holiness, and much of the nature of holiness lying in refraining from sin, and also the dominion of any particular sin very ill agreeing with deliverance

---

[1] Δεικνὺς ὅτι ἐκ ῥαθυμίας τὸ πᾶν λοῖπον της ἡμετέρας, δύνατον γὰρ νῦν μὴ κατὰ σαρκὰ περιπατεῖν, τότε δε δύσκολον ἦν.—*Chrysost.* Ἐπὶ του νομοῦ οὐδέ ὁ βουλόμενος ζῆν ὀρθῶς ἰσχυε, μηδενος βοηθοῦντος, μηδὲ συνεπισχύοντος.—*Œc.*

from the law thereof, therefore in both of these respects I would caution all regenerate persons against it; but it is the latter only that I shall speak a few words unto. Where I would be very earnest with you who have passed under the regenerating work of the Spirit, to take heed even of the actual and partial dominion of sin; and there is great need of this admonition, for though upon regeneration you are secured from its habitual and universal dominion, yet as to some particular sin and some particular evil acts it may have that which looks too much like dominion, though strictly and properly it be not so. Here therefore I desire you to be very careful that you do not suffer any one sin to reign in you, for how would this consist with your being made free from the law of sin? since, as hath been said, the power of any one sin and subjection thereunto, if it be full and free, plenary and voluntary, doth as certainly prove its dominion as the power of many, nay, of all. Oh take heed that this and that sin do not rule or be too high in you! It was David's prayer, Ps. xix. 13, 'Keep back thy servant also from presumptuous sins; let them not have dominion over me: then shall I be upright, and I shall be innocent from the great transgression.' He goes further, and takes in all, Ps. cxix. 133, 'Order my steps in thy word, and let not *any iniquity* have dominion over me.' Saints are not so freed from the law of sin by the Spirit, but that there is need of daily prayer, and that there be all endeavours and care on their part against it; and their care must reach even to this, that not any single iniquity may have dominion over them.

And here especially you must be careful and vigilant about that particular sin to which you are most strongly inclined, or which hath the greatest strength in you; about the Diotrephes sin, the Herodias or darling sin, that which is as the right eye or the right hand; I say your eye must be chiefly upon this, that it do not prevail and domineer over you. Every man in the world hath some one sin which is uppermost in him, which carries it before all the rest, to which all do veil and stoop; it is pride in one, fleshly lust in another, greediness after the world in a third, and so on; nay, a child of God too usually hath some particular sin which is predominant in him, which though it doth not ab-

solutely reign in him, for then he would be under the law of sin, yet comparatively it doth, *i.e.*, it hath a greater power over him than any other sin hath. David calls it his iniquity, Ps. xviii. 23. Look, as the saints, though they have every grace in them, all being planted together in the new nature, yet there is some particular grace which shews itself more eminently in one than in another, as faith in Abraham, meekness in Moses, patience in Job, zeal in Hezekiah, &c. So *e contra*, though they and others have every sin in them radically and seminally in the corrupt nature, yet there is some particular sin which ordinarily vents itself with more strength than the rest, which having the advantage of the constitution, education, calling, condition, &c., is stronger than others; how that may be known divines shew in several things,[1] but I must not stay upon it. Now you that are regenerate, look to yourselves here, act your greatest vigilancy, and make your strongest opposition, with respect to your particular sin; here is your weakest part, and therefore here you must set your strongest guard, as keepers of garrisons use to do; as he said, 1 Kings xxii. 31, 'Fight neither with small nor great, save only with the king of Israel,' so I would say to you, Fight against neither small nor great, but only against the king sin or master sin in you. This is to kill Goliath himself, which being done all the Philistines fly; to stab sin at the very heart, upon which wound it must needs die; and here is the great evidence of sincerity, 'I was also upright before him, and I kept myself from my iniquity,' Ps. xviii. 23; and herein deliverance from the law of sin mainly shews itself.

3. Thirdly, You that are upon regeneration thus freed from sin's power, I am to bespeak your thankfulness, your highest and most hearty thankfulness, for so great a mercy. In the doing of this, what hath God done for you! oh whilst you pity others who are under sin's bondage, bless God for yourselves who are delivered out of it! The remainders of sin call for your deepest humiliation, but withal the not reigning of sin calls for your highest thankfulness. Are you made partakers of such liberty, and will you not be thankful? Is there any deliverance from any servitude whatsoever like to this?

[1] See Burg. Refin., part ii. p. 232. With many others.

Sin is the worst of evils, the power of sin the worst of sin; are you delivered from that? oh admirable mercy! Israel's deliverance out of Egypt and Babylon, the rescuing of subjects from the dominion of tyrants, the fetching poor captives out of chains and bonds, are good things, yet all but very nothings in comparison of the freeing a soul from the power and vassalage of sin; and this is done for you; shall not the Lord be greatly blessed for it? Here is a great part of that benefit which you have by Christ as a Redeemer; for what doth redemption point to but to the sinner's release from his spiritual captivity and bondage by sin? what did Christ come for but to 'proclaim liberty to the captives,' &c.? Isa. lxi. 1. Now as you were captives in God's hands by reason of guilt, so Christ redeemed you by paying down a price or ransom for you; as you are captives in sin's and Satan's hands, so he redeems you by power; for they are no other way to be dealt withal, by rescuing you out of their dominion and slavery in spite of all the resistance they can make; and Christ redeeming both these ways, so he becomes a full and complete Redeemer. So that your being made free from the law of sin is a part of Christ's redeeming love; and what the Spirit of life doth therein, it is but in conjunction with Christ in the carrying on of that love; and if so, have not you great reason to be very thankful? I pray look into that precious promise, the matter of which is that God will not only pardon your iniquities, but also subdue them, he being every way as gracious in the latter as in the former: Micah vii. 18, 19, 'Who is a God like unto thee, that pardoneth iniquity, and passeth by the transgression of the remnant of his heritage? &c. He will turn again, he will have compassion upon us; he will subdue our iniquities.' It is as great a mercy to have sin subdued in its power as pardoned in its guilt; you magnify God for the one, oh do the same for the other also! If God himself had not brought about this freedom, you had been without it for ever. Alas! you yourselves in the time of the natural thraldom never thought of or desired it, you were altogether unable to accomplish it, nay, you were set against it, and opposed it to your utmost; the law of sin was in the heart and had the heart, you liked and loved its government above any other, all your strength was

engaged for it; insomuch that God was fain to conquer, not only Satan and it, but your own selves too, and by a mighty power to make you willing to accept of deliverance out of its servitude; what ground of thankfulness is here! Once more, why should you be made free when others are let alone? what was there in you to move God to vouchsafe this distinguishing mercy? You had indeed been eternally undone without it; but was he under any necessity or motive, but what was from his own grace, to do it for you? O you that are renewed, shall not the Lord be admired by you? I pray be much in blessing of him for all mercies, but amongst the rest be sure you never forget to bless him for sin-subduing, sin-dethroning mercy. See how Paul upon this account blesses God for others: Rom. vi. 17, 'But God be thanked, that ye were the servants of sin, but ye have obeyed from the heart the form of doctrine, which was delivered you.' He that was so thankful for others surely would be so much more for himself; and so he was: Rom. vii. 24, 25, 'O wretched man that I am! who shall deliver me from the body of this death? I thank God through Jesus Christ our Lord.' Titus iii. 3-5, 'For we ourselves also were sometimes foolish, &c.; but after that the kindness and love of God our Saviour toward man appeared, not by works of righteousness which we have done, but according to his mercy he saved us, by the washing of regeneration and renewing of the Holy Ghost.' He lays it upon the kindness and love of God, which indeed are admirable in the freeing of a soul from the law of sin by the regenerating Spirit; this kindness of God should draw out the thankfulness of every gracious heart. So much for this use of counsel.

Use 4. A word, in the fourth place, for comfort. I would have every truly gracious person upon this truth to be even filled with joy. What glad tidings doth it bring to thee, whoever thou art, upon whom regenerating grace hath taken hold! it tells thee thou art made free from the law of sin. Sin may, and doth, trouble thee, but it doth not rule thee; it lorded it over thee too long, but now its dominion is gone; from the very first moment of thy conversion thou hast been made free; believe it, and take the comfort of it. What think you? had not Paul great joy in himself when he uttered these words,

'The law of the Spirit,' &c.; thou mayest say the same concerning thyself, the new birth having passed upon thee, why therefore shouldst not thou be brimful of joy also? This is so great a thing that the sense and comfort of it should revive and cheer thy spirit under all outward evils; the laws of men possibly may be somewhat heavy upon thee, thou mayest groan under such and such external pressures, there may be much of bondage in thy outward condition, but the law of sin is abolished, thy soul is made free, the spiritual bondage is taken off; is not this well—very well? Under the law, how were the poor servants overjoyed when the year of jubilee came, which gave them a release from all their servitude? O Christian, thou hast lived to see a glorious jubilee! wilt not thou rejoice? So also when oppressed subjects are freed from cruel usurpers, it is a time of great rejoicing; men's joy then runs over, and will be kept in no bounds or limits; what a full tide of joy should be in their souls whom God hath graciously delivered from sin's tyranny and usurpation! True, sin never had any right to rule, yet *de facto* rule it did, therefore triumph over it as though its authority had been just, as the people of Rome once did with a mean person.[1] That sin which once had you under is now brought under itself, and it is subdued, therefore cannot much hurt you. Adoni-bezek himself when in chains, Bajazet when in an iron cage, the fiercest enemies when broken in their power, cannot do much mischief; God be blessed so it is with sin; and therefore, as to the main state, fear it not. I know you lie under many discouragements; you feel such cursed inclinations to evil, sin doth so often prevail over you, repeated backslidings afflict you greatly, your corruptions daily pursue you, &c. Well, I would have you to be very sensible of these things, and mourn over them; but yet know the reigning, commanding power of sin is gone, notwithstanding all these, yet it is not the law of sin. How much good may an unregenerate person do and yet sin reign in him, and how much evil may a regenerate person do and yet sin not reign in him! Under the law every scab did not make one a leper, neither

[1] Hoc illi in malis suis indulgente fortuna, ut de eo populus Romanus quasi de vero rege triumpharet.—*Florus*, lib. ii. cap. 14.

doth every prevalency of sin make one a slave to it. The Spirit of life hath freed you from its dominion, that being duly stated, and that too in such a manner as that you shall never again be brought under it: 'Sin shall not have dominion over you,' &c., Rom. vi. 14. Is all this nothing or but little in your thoughts? is not here sufficient matter of great joy? oh know what God hath done for you, and make the best of it! Being freed from the law of sin you are freed from guilt, wrath, hell, eternal condemnation; for the apostle having said 'There is no condemnation,' &c., he proves his assertion by this, 'For the law of the Spirit of life,' &c. And where it is not the law of sin, there it is not the law of death; these two laws are linked and fastened each to the other, therefore he that is delivered from the one is delivered from the other also. Believers, there is but one thing remaining to be done for you —which in due time shall most certainly be done too—and that is to free you from the very being of sin, and from all those remainders of power which yet it hath in you; do but wait, and a little time will put an end to these also; be of good comfort, sin is dying and weakening and wearing out every day, shortly it will die indeed, so as never to molest you more. As you are justified its guilt is gone, as you are sanctified its power is gone; it will not be long before you will be glorified, and then its very being shall be gone too. Here in grace Pharaoh's yoke is broken, but above in glory sin shall be like Pharaoh drowned in the bottom of the sea. Oh let every regenerate soul greatly rejoice in these things! So much for the second observation.

CHAPTER VII.

OF THE POWER OF THE HOLY SPIRIT IN THE MAKING OF PERSONS FREE FROM THE LAW OF SIN.

For the law of the Spirit of life in Christ Jesus hath made me free from the law of sin and death.—ROM. viii. 2.

The third observation, viz., That it is the law of the Spirit of life which frees the regenerate from the law of sin

—How this is brought about by the Spirit, by the Spirit of life, by the law of the Spirit, &c.—What this imports—Of the necessity, sufficiency, efficacy of the Spirit's power for and in the production of this effect—The particular ways and methods of the Spirit in it opened—Of its workings at the first conversion—Of its subsequent regency in the renewed soul—Use 1. Of the greatness and glory of the Spirit; his Godhead inferred from hence—Use 2. To shew the true and proper cause of freedom from the law of sin; where men are exhorted, 1. To apply themselves to the Spirit for this freedom: 2. In case it be wrought in them, to ascribe and attribute the glory of it only to the Spirit—Saints exhorted, 1. To love and honour the Spirit; 2. To live continually under the law of it; 3. To set law against law.

Two observations I have gone through; I come now to the third and last. It is the law of the Spirit of life which frees the regenerate from the law of sin; or thus, It is by the mighty power of the living and regenerating Spirit that any are delivered from the power and dominion of sin. This is the great effect here spoken of, and the apostle shews who is the author and efficient of it, or how it is brought about: 'The law of the Spirit of life hath made me free from the law of sin.' I shall, as much as conveniently I may, contract in what I have to say upon this point, that I may draw towards the close of this verse, which I fear I have stayed too long upon.

Now here observe, 1. The Spirit frees from the law of sin; he is the true and proper agent in the production of this effect. In reference to which you may consider him either essentially as he is God, or personally as he is the third person, distinct from the Father and the Son, in both of which considerations he makes free from the law of sin. As to the first, so there can be no question made of the thing, because the Spirit, so considered, acts in common with the two other persons, and they with him;[1] what the Father doth and the Son, as God, that the Spirit doth also, and so *vice versa*. I speak of *actiones*

 ad extra, which only are *indivisæ*.[1] As to the second, so the thing is also clear, because it is the Spirit's personal and proper act to weaken and dethrone sin in the heart; for as it is the Son's proper act to free from the guilt, so it is the Spirit's proper act to free from the power of sin; that being a thing done within the creature, this person is the proper author of it—it belonging to the Son to do all without, and to the Spirit to do all within. The Father and the Son are by no means to be excluded, yet it is the Spirit which doth immediately bring about in the soul that blessed freedom which I am upon. If you cast your eye a little upon what lies very near the text, you will find all the persons mentioned, as all concurring to the advancement and promoting of the good of believers. It is Chrysostom's observation upon the words:[2] That, saith he, which the apostle always doth, going from the Son to the Spirit, from the Spirit to the Son and Father, ascribing all to the Trinity, that here he doth also. For when he said, 'Who shall deliver me from the body of this death? I thank God through Jesus Christ our Lord,' he shews that the Father doth this by the Son; then he shews that the Spirit also doth this by the Son, when he says that 'the law of the Spirit of life which is in Christ Jesus,' &c. Then he brings in again the Father and the Son, ver. 3, 4. But, I say, this freedom from the law of sin, it is the proper and immediate effect of the Spirit; therefore it is said, 'Where the Spirit of the Lord is, there is liberty,' 2 Cor. iii. 17, the meaning of which scripture I had occasion to touch upon before. That which God once said to Zerubbabel, in reference to the building of the temple, 'Not by might, nor by power, but by my Spirit,' Zech. iv. 6, is applicable to deliverance from sin's dominion, which is not brought about by any external and visible force and strength, but only by the internal, effectual operations of the Holy Spirit.

2. Secondly, Observe this is done by the Spirit of

---

[1] Factum Spiritus S. factum filii Dei est, et propter naturæ et voluntatis unitatem. Sive enim Pater faciat, sive Filius, sive Spiritus sanct. Trinitas est quæ operatur, et quicquid tres fecerint Dei unius est operatio.—*Aug. in Qu. N. T.*, quæst. 51.

[1] August. in Enchirid., cap. 38.

[2] Ὅπερ ἀεὶ ποιεῖ ἀπὸ τοῦ υἱοῦ εἰς τὸ πνεῦμα μεταβαίνων, ἀπὸ τοῦ πνεύματος εἰς τὸν υἱὸν καὶ τὸν πατέρα, καὶ τῇ τριάδι πάντα τὰ παρ' ἡμῶν λογιζόμενος, τοῦτο καὶ ἐνταῦθα ἐργάζεται· καὶ γὰρ εἰπών, τίς με ῥύσεται ἐκ τοῦ σώματος τοῦ θανάτου τούτου; ἔδειξε πατέρα διὰ υἱοῦ τοῦτο ποιοῦντα· εἶτα πάλιν τὸ πνεῦμα τὸ ἅγιον μέτα τοῦ υἱοῦ, ὁ γὰρ νόμος, &c. Εἶτα πάλιν τὸν πατέρα καὶ τὸν υἱόν, τὸ γὰρ ἀδύνατον, &c.—*Chrysost.* Κοινῇ εὐδοκίᾳ τῆς ἁγίας τριάδος σεσώσμεθα.—*Œcumen.*

life. He doth not say only the Spirit had made him free from the law of sin, but he joins this with it, the Spirit *of life*. What is contained in this, as it is considered abstractly and in itself, I shewed at my first entrance upon this verse, but I conceive it here hath some special reference to the effect spoken of; it being either a description of the Spirit who frees from the law of sin—he is a living Spirit; or it pointing to the special time when the Spirit doth this, viz., when he quickens and regenerates a man; or it noting the way and method of the Spirit wherein or whereby he frees from the law of sin, that is, by working the spiritual life or regeneration. The Spirit *who renews, when he renews, by renewing*, brings sin under. These are distinct things, and yet are all couched in this *Spirit of life*. I might enlarge upon each, but I will not; because that which I have in my eye doth not much depend upon them.

3. Then observe, thirdly, It is the law of the Spirit by which this is done. It is a metaphorical expression, as was shewn in the opening of the words. The law of the Spirit is the power of the Spirit, as the law of sin is the power of sin. Here is law against law, power against power; the power and efficacy of the Spirit against the power and efficacy of sin. The apostle elsewhere speaks of δύναμις ἐνεργουμένη, an inworking power: Eph. iii. 20, 'According to the power that worketh in us.' That is the same with the law of the Spirit in the text; so that when he saith the law of the Spirit, &c., he means this, that through the mighty power of the Holy Ghost, authoritatively and effectually working in him, sin's power was abolished, its dominion brought down, its kingdom in him destroyed; and not only so, but likewise Christ's kingdom was erected in him; for this law of the Spirit doth both conjunctly—wherever it dethrones sin, it also at the same time enthrones Christ and grace in the heart. When I was upon the law of sin I told you it hath a two-fold power—a moral and a physical power—in reference to both of which it is called a law; so it is with the Spirit; he hath his moral power, as he doth persuade, command, &c.; and he hath his physical power, as he doth strongly, efficaciously incline, urge, impel the sinner to such and such gracious acts; yea, which is highest of all, as he doth effectually, nay, irresistibly, change his heart, make him

a new creature, dispossess sin of its regency, and bring him under the sceptre and government of Christ. And herein the law of the Spirit is above the law of sin; for though that puts forth a great efficacy in the manner of its working, yet it doth not rise to such a pitch or degree of efficacy in what is evil as the Spirit of God doth in what is good. Set corrupt nature never so high, yet it is but a finite thing, and so hath but a finite power; but the Spirit is an infinite being, and in his saving and special workings he puts forth an infinite power, and therefore he must work more efficaciously than sin can do. The law of the Spirit must carry it against and notwithstanding the law of sin; for though both pass under the same appellation of *laws*, yet they are laws of a different kind and nature with respect to their power and efficacy.

This law or power of the Spirit is that which I will speak to; and for the better opening of the truth in hand, which mainly points thereunto, I will do two things:

1. I will speak to the necessity, sufficiency, efficacy of the power of the Spirit, in order to the freeing of men from the power of sin.

2. I will shew in what way or method the Spirit doth work and exert his power in his rescuing of souls from sin's power.

In the first of these heads three things are put together, which must be spoken unto apart.

1. First, Of the necessity of the power of the Spirit. Concerning which, I may confidently affirm that it is indispensably, absolutely necessary for the divesting sin of its long-possessed sovereignty. No less a power than the mighty power of this Spirit can bring down sin's power. Oh, it is no easy thing to rescue the poor enslaved captive soul out of its bonds. Omnipotency itself is requisite thereunto: that is the strong man which keeps the palace, Luke xi. 21, 22, till Christ through the Spirit, which is stronger than it, comes upon it and overcomes it. Israel had never got out of their bondage under Pharaoh if God himself had not brought them out of it 'through a mighty hand and by an outstretched arm,' as you read, Deut. v. 15; and so it is here. Let us bring it to a particular case. Take a sinner who is under the law of unbelief—as there are too many such, God knows—nothing shall ever free this

sinner from the power of his unbelief unless a divine and an almighty power from above be put forth upon him; until this be done, all the calls, commands, invitations, promises of the gospel are all weak and ineffectual; therefore it is said to be 'the faith of the operation of God,' Col. ii. 12; and the apostle prayed that God would 'fulfil the work of faith with power,' 2 Thes. i. 11; and, says the prophet, 'Who hath believed our report? and to whom is the arm of the Lord revealed?' Isa. liii. 1. Without the revealing of God's mighty arm there is no believing; and you read that God in sanctification and the working of faith doth put forth 'the exceeding greatness of his power, according to the working of his mighty power, which he wrought in Christ when he raised him from the dead,' Eph. i. 19, 20. What can be spoken higher than this? You see the law of the Spirit is necessary to the freeing of a person from the law of unbelief; and is it not so in all other things wherein sin's power shews itself? The power of nature, which some do so much magnify, can never conquer the power of sin. Alas! it is *impar congressus*, there is no even match betwixt them; and, besides, nature's greatest strength is on sin's side; its relics only, where it is good, are for God against sin; but its full and entire strength, as it is bad, are for sin against God; God hath but its shattered forces, as it were, but sin hath its full body. What can enfeebled nature, what will depraved nature, do against sin? Let it be considered, if the power of grace in the regenerate be so small that by that alone, without the concurrence of divine and special assistance from above, they can do nothing, which Christ affirms, John xv. 5, no, not so much as think a good thought, as the apostle affirms, 2 Cor. iii. 5; what, then, can be expected from mere nature in the unregenerate, in whom sin is in its full strength, as to the weakening or subduing of it? In things of a spiritual nature the Scripture doth not only deny the act, but the power too: John vi. 44, 'No man *can* come to me except the Father draw him;' 1 Cor. ii. 14, 'The natural man receiveth not the things of the Spirit of God, neither *can* he know them, because they are spiritually discerned;' Jer. xiii. 23, '*Can* the Ethiopian change his skin, or the leopard his spots? then may ye also do good that are accustomed to do evil.' So in that which I am

upon; it is not only the sinner *doth not* free himself from the law of sin; but of himself, without the mighty power of the divine Spirit, he *cannot* so do. He that is not strong enough to subdue some one particular lust, how shall he be able to subdue the whole body of sin in all its united and combined force?—as he that cannot conquer one single soldier can much less conquer the whole army. If God leave a man to grapple with sin merely by his own strength, woe be to him!

That the power of the Spirit is absolutely necessary to free from the power of sin will be very evident, if you consider those several advantages which it hath for the securing and holding up of its power in the sinner. As (1.) It is in possession. (2.) It hath been so a long time; maybe twenty, forty, threescore years, to be sure from the time of the sinner's coming into the world, for its power and his birth are of the same date; now usurpers in possession, and who have long been so, are not so easily conquered. (3.) Its dominion is entire, it hath all on its side; the whole soul is for sin, insomuch that when the Spirit of God comes to grapple with it, he finds nothing there to side with him or to take his part, which argues the necessity of his infinite power. When there is a party within a kingdom ready to fall in with the foreign force that comes to depose the tyrant, he may with more facility be vanquished; but if all the people unanimously stick to him, then the conquest is the more difficult. As Christ once said, 'The prince of this world cometh, and hath nothing in me,' John xiv. 30; so the poor sinner may say, The sin-subduing Spirit comes, but he finds nothing in me to close with him. (4.) The natural man likes the power of sin; it hath his heart, which is worst of all for the securing of its empire; he is fond of his vassalage, and loves sin's government better than Christ's. Oh the commands of it suit better with him than the commands of a holy God! so that upon the whole matter he is peremptorily resolved to adhere to it against whatever shall oppose it. (5.) Sin's strength is not only very great in itself, but it hath also those additional advantages which render it, as to any finite power, invincible; therefore it is set forth by the strong man, and by the strong man armed too, Luke xi. 21; it is engarrisoned in the heart, which of all places is the most inaccessible; it hath its τὰ ὀχυρώματα, strongholds, in which it is fortified, 2 Cor. x. 4. (6.) Sin is very resolute for and in the maintaining of what it hath; it hath a power, and it will keep it; it will fight it out to the last, and die rather than yield; all the persuasives in the world signify nothing to it; if the Spirit of God will gain the soul he must gain it as soldiers do strong towns which refuse to surrender, *unciatim*, to borrow the comedian's word, inch by inch. (7.) Sin and the sinner are under a covenant, Isa. xxviii. 15; they have engaged, as it were, to live and die together; now to dissolve and break this engagement is no easy matter. (8.) Satan sets in with it, and upon all occasions gives it all the help he can, as allies and confederates use to do; he says to sin what Joab once did to Abishai, 2 Sam. x. 11, 'If the Syrians be too strong for me, then thou shalt help me: but if the children of Ammon be too strong for thee, then I will come and help thee.' If he can hinder it, sin's kingdom shall never be demolished, no, not in any one soul. Now put all these things together, and it will appear that the power of the Spirit is highly necessary to deliver from the power of sin; yea, that nothing below the almighty strength of this almighty Spirit can free a soul from its dominion. Who but he who is God could subdue and conquer such an enemy as this is?

2. Secondly, There is the sufficiency of the Spirit's power, as he is every way able to produce the effect we are speaking of. It is indeed a great thing to break the yoke of sin, to pull the crown off from its head, to conquer it notwithstanding all the things which have been alleged; yet as great a thing as it is, this great Spirit is able to do it. If he once engage in the work it is enough; the power of an almighty God must needs be above the power of what is but finite and limited, as was said but now. As Christ is able to save to the utmost from sin's guilt, Heb. vii. 25, so the Spirit also is able to save to the utmost from sin's power; let it be never so high and lofty, if this Spirit take it in hand I will warrant you it shall be brought down. God once said to Paul, 'My grace is sufficient for thee,' 2 Cor. xii. 9; it is meant chiefly of strengthening and supporting grace; now as that grace is sufficient to bear up under the heaviest afflictions, so this sanctifying,

sin-subduing, sin-mortifying grace is sufficient to bring down the strongest corruptions. All things considered, we may stand and wonder at the rescuing of a soul out of sin's thraldom. Oh the bringing of sin under, that but just now was so high, is a strange and wonderful thing! But if we consider the strength of that person who is employed about it, the wonder is at an end; as it was said upon another account, Zech. viii. 6, 'If it be marvellous in the eyes of the remnant of this people in these days, should it also be marvellous in mine eyes? saith the Lord of hosts.' Jer. xxxii. 27, 'Behold, I am the Lord, the God of all flesh: is there any thing too hard for me?'—this is applicable to the Spirit in the personal consideration of God. We, alas! must cry out, as David once of the sons of Zeruiah, Sin is too hard for us, we cannot get it down; but it is not too hard for God and his Spirit. Though it hath its strongholds, he takes them or batters them all down with ease; it captivates the sinner, but the Spirit captivates it: 2 Cor. x. 4, 5, 'The weapons of our warfare are not carnal, but mighty through God to the pulling down of strongholds; casting down imaginations, and every high thing that exalteth itself against the knowledge of God, and bringing into captivity every thought to the obedience of Christ.' Oh the boundless, infinite power of the Spirit! nothing, no not sin itself, even when it is at the highest, can stand before him; that which all the creatures in heaven and in earth cannot do, that he can do *omnipotentissima facilitate*, as Augustine phrases it.[1] 'Who is sufficient for these things?' why, he, and none but he, who hath illimited and infinite power.

3. Thirdly, There is the efficacy of the Spirit's power, or the effectual working of the Spirit, in the freeing of a person from the law of sin. When this great agent comes to bring about this freedom, how doth he act? *Ans.* Efficaciously and irresistibly; I mean, he puts forth such a power as that the work is certainly done. He doth not only in a moral way advise, counsel,[2] persuade the sinner to cast off sin's bondage, but he in order thereunto puts forth an insuperable and irresistible strength upon him, and

[1] Epist. 107, ad Vitalem.
[2] *Vide* Twiss. Vind. Grat., lib. i. par. 2, sec. 16, p. 160, &c; and Digress. vi. p. 163, &c. With many others who everywhere write upon this argument.

T

so goes through with the work; he conquers all opposition both from without and from within, so that it shall not be victorious, and in spite of all makes the soul free; he works herein *omnipotenter, indeclinabiliter, insuperabiliter*, as that great champion of effectual grace expresses it. Further, when he comes about this or any other saving act, he doth not leave the sinner's will in suspense, pendulous, *in equilibrio*, hanging like a pair of scales, even, and not going down on either side; but, in a way congruous to its liberty, he overcomes and determines it for God against sin, so as that it shall neither hesitate nor make any successful resistance to his grace.[1] I am, before I was well aware of it, fallen upon a nice and much controverted point, viz., the efficacy of divine grace in its special operations, a thing strongly defended of old by Augustine against the Pelagians, and of late by the Dominicans and Jansenists against the Jesuits; and I could wish the controversy had lodged there, but there are other persons and parties concerned in it. Well, I am thus fallen upon it, but I will presently get off from it; for it being a point only incidental in my passage, I am not bound to stay upon it. In short, therefore, this I assert, that *gratia liberatrix est gratia efficax*, soul-freeing grace is effectual grace; wherever and whenever the Spirit undertakes to deliver any man out of sin's power he doth it effectually; he then puts forth such a mighty power as that he infallibly doth effect what he designed, which is all that divines mean by that so much disliked word *irresistibly*.[2] As the power of nature, take it at its best, cannot much further this freedom, so the power

of nature, take it at its worst, as to the final issue, shall not be able to hinder it. The Scriptures, which hold forth the efficacy of saving grace in general, are applicable to that particular branch of it which I am upon: Cant. i. 4, 'Draw thou me, we will run after thee.' John vi. 45, 'Every man that hath heard and learned of the Father comes to me.' Jer. xxxi. 18, 'Turn thou me, and I shall be turned.' Ezek. xxxvi. 27, 'I will put my Spirit within you, and cause you to walk in my statutes, and ye shall keep my judgments, and do them.' There is much in each of these texts to prove what is before me, might I but stay upon them. It is in the acts of grace as it is in the acts of providence, in which sometimes the stream runs with such a mighty force that there is no resisting of it: Isa. xliii. 13, 'I will work, and who shall let it?' And so, I say, it is in the acts of grace; it works with such a power that none can let it. Our apostle himself here before conversion was as much under the law of sin as ordinarily any are, and yet as soon as the renewing acts of this Spirit took hold of him, he yielded presently and made no prevailing opposition; indeed at first he was at his 'Who art thou, Lord?' but it was not long before he threw himself down at the feet of Christ, saying, 'Lord, what wilt thou have me to do?' Acts ix. 5, 6. So much for the three-fold consideration of the power of the Spirit with respect to the effect here mentioned, making free from the law of sin.

The second thing propounded was to shew in what ways or methods the Holy Spirit doth exert his power in the making a person free from the law of sin.

For the explaining of which we must distinguish of his workings: they are either those which are at the first conversion, by which sin's habitual dominion is destroyed; or those which follow after conversion and continue the whole life, by which sin's actual dominion is prevented and kept down; by the first he *makes* free, by the second he *keeps* free from the law of sin. With respect to each of these workings the Spirit hath his different ways and methods, which therefore must be distinctly spoken unto.

1. As to the first in the general; he puts forth his power in and by the doing of the main work, viz.,

---

[1] Deo volenti salvum facere, nullum humanum resistit arbitrium.—*Aug. de Corrept. et Grat.*, cap. 14. Vide *Jansen. August.*, t. iii. lib. ii. cap. 24. *Habertus* de Grat., lib. ii. cap. 16. Vide etiam celeberrimum *Doct. Ward* de Grat. discr., p. 24, &c.

[2] Non aliam irresistibilitatem propugnant nostri, quam realem et efficacem operationem, cujus vi effectum certo vel infallibiliter existit.—*Ames Coron.*, art. 4, cap. 3. Dicimus gratiam efficacem, quæ operatur velle et perficere, adeo potenter in opere conversionis et quovis opere salutari voluntatem movere, ut certo causaliter tollat non resistibilitatem aut connatam aut adnatam, aut etiam omnem actualem resistentiam, sed actualem resistentiam vincentem; adeo ut gratia semper eliciat consensum et acceptationem: ac proinde eo momento impossibile sit quod voluntas non annuat, aut de facto resistat.—*D. Ward*, Conc. de Grat. discrim., pp. 31, 32.

the converting of the soul. He comes and turns it from sin to God, Acts xxvi. 18; brings about the new creature in it, 2 Cor. v. 17; forms Christ therein, Gal. iv. 19; translates it out of one state into another, Col. i. 13; and herein you have the law or mighty power of the Spirit exerted. I say the mighty power of the Spirit, for this is a work which calls for such power, without which it would never be done. Oh it is no easy thing to convert a sinner! indeed there is nothing more difficult than that is. Though all things are alike easy to an almighty agent, as God and his Spirit are, yet as things are considered in themselves, and as we conceive of them, so some are more easy or hard than others are. As here, it is easier to create a world than to convert a soul; the new creation is more difficult than the old; for in the latter there was nothing to oppose or make resistance, but in the former there is sin, Satan, a wicked heart within, a cursed world without, all uniting and combining in all their strength to oppose to their utmost the work of conversion. There the matter was indisposed and unfit to be cast into such a form, and that was all; but here it is not only unfitness, but renitency, reluctancy, the highest opposition that is imaginable; it being so, it follows that that must be a mighty power by which the work is done notwithstanding all this resistance. The Spirit therefore puts forth such a power, whereby he makes mountains to become plains, Zech. iv. 9, cuts his way through the very rock, conquers all that vast host which is mustered up against him, in spite of all opposition converts the sinner; here is the law of the Spirit. Now upon and by this he frees from the law of sin, for upon conversion sin is as much deposed and pulled off from the throne as Athaliah once was, 2 Kings xi.; then its reign expires, from that time forward it must not any more lord it as before it did;—but this hath been already spoken to. Observe it, it is the law of the Spirit of life which frees from the law of sin; it is not absolute or mere power that doth it, but it is power as regenerating, as changing the heart, as implanting the divine nature, by which sin is brought under.

But more particularly; in freeing from the law of sin this is the way of the Spirit: (1.) He effectually works upon the understanding; that being the lead-ing faculty, and there being in it several things by which in special sin's dominion is kept up, and he working upon reasonable creatures in that way which best agrees with them as such, therefore there the Spirit of God begins and first exerts his power upon that faculty. And whereas he finds it under darkness, blindness, woeful ignorance, he is pleased to act as a Spirit of illumination, irradiating the mind with beams of divine light, dispelling the opposite darkness, filling the soul with heavenly and saving knowledge. This is the Spirit's proper act, and that which carries a marvellous power in it. It is no easy thing to open a blind eye; this is just such a thing as that. When the world lay in the abyss of darkness it required omnipotency to say, 'Let there be light,' Gen. i. 3; no less a power is requisite to the saving enlightening of the sinner, who is not in darkness, but 'darkness' itself, Eph. v. 8. But this being done, sin is exceedingly broken in its power by it; for ignorance is one of the great supporters of its throne, one of its royal forts wherein its main strength lies; where that is in the head, sin domineers in the heart and life. You read, Eph. iv. 19, of some 'who being past feeling, have given themselves over unto lasciviousness, to work all uncleanness with greediness;' here was the law of sin to purpose, sin at the very height and top of its dominion; how did things come to this pass? why, ver. 18, their 'understanding was darkened,' and they were 'alienated from the life of God through the ignorance that was in them, because of the blindness of their heart.' What a friend to sin is ignorance; how by this is the sinner at its beck, even to do whatever it would have him. No wonder, then, that the Spirit, when he comes to take sin down, first removes this ignorance: Acts xxvi. 18, 'To open their eyes, and to turn them from darkness to light, and from the power of Satan unto God,' &c. Here is the order or method in which the Spirit acts; he first opens men's eyes, and turns them from darkness to light, and so he frees them from the power of sin and Satan. Again, whereas the understanding lies under sad mistakes, misapprehensions, misjudgings, having false notions of things, and accordingly passing false judgment upon them, by which sin's power is highly strengthened and kept up; therefore the Spirit doth rectify it, delivers it from these mistakes, &c., makes it to judge aright of things as things, brings it to pass true dictates, that sin is evil, Christ good, holiness excellent, &c., gives that ' sound mind ' which the apostle speaks of, 2 Tim. i. 7. This too being done, sin as commanding exceedingly falls and sinks; upon this there is a great abatement and diminution of its power, for that never continues absolute and entire in a rectified judgment; the convincing Spirit, working as such, always destroys commanding sin. Its kingdom stands by lies and falsehoods; let but the soul be enabled to see into them and through them, so as no longer to be deluded by them, and down goes that kingdom. To be made free from a deceived and deceiving judgment, Isa. xliv. 20, is the way to the being made free from the law of sin; therefore the Spirit will be sure to have that done. Once more, the understanding is full of high and proud thoughts, of strange imaginations and reasonings, which lift up themselves against God and subjection to his will. Oh, saith the Spirit, these I must take a course with, these must be thrown out of the heart, or else Christ's kingdom will never go up in it; till something be done to bring these down, sin's regency will continue as high as ever; wherefore I will do it effectually. 2 Cor. x. 5, ' Casting down imaginations, and every high thing that exalteth itself against the knowledge of God, and bringing into captivity every thought to the obedience of Christ.' I assure you this is an act of great power, but the Spirit goes through with it when he comes as a sin-dethroning Spirit; thus he exerts his power in the understanding.

(2.) He then proceeds to the will, where you have heard sin chiefly exercises its dominion, and which of all the faculties is most enslaved to it and by it. The liberty of the will is very much cried up by many, and in such a sense none can deny it; but, out of that sense, there is nothing in man more under bondage than his will; it is not now *liberum*, but *servum arbitrium*, as Luther used to phrase it;[1] and Augustine long before him.[2] In natural and purely moral acts there is no question but it yet retains its freedom; but in things of a spiritual and

supernatural nature, that upon Adam's fall it hath wholly lost, since which it is only *libera quatenus liberata*, free no further than as it is made free. Well, the Spirit undertakes this faculty, lays forth his power upon it, that he may rescue it out of the hands of sin, and bring it over to God; and surely it is most necessary he should so do, for till the will be effectually wrought upon and subdued, how can it be imagined that ever the law of sin should be abolished? Of all the faculties, sin contends most for the will, which when it hath once gained it will not easily part with; whatever it loses, that it will not lose; it puts forth its utmost strength to defend and make good its conquests over that. And so, too, of all the faculties, the blessed Spirit contends most for the will; that being the determining faculty with respect to sin's reign, he puts forth the greatest efficacy of his grace for the setting of that right and straight for God, that it may choose, close with, cleave to his good and holy commands, in opposition to what it was wont to do to the laws and commands of sin.

But it will be asked, How far or wherein doth he exert his power upon the sinner's will in order to the freeing of him from sin as a law? I have already answered this in what I said but now, when I affirmed that the Spirit doth not work upon it only in a persuasive way, barely presenting some alluring considerations or motives for the inclining of it to this or that, but still leaving it under a perfect indifferency, so as that the sinner may after all yet choose whether he will believe or not, repent or not, cast off sin's yoke or not; but he doth efficaciously incline, bow, overpower, determine it, so as that it shall most certainly, yet most freely, consent to what is good, and close with it. And if God by his Spirit did not thus determine the will, either the sinner would never be converted, or if he should be converted, the completing of his conversion would be brought about by the determination of his will as his own act, God doing no more than only leaving it to its own indifferency; and so he would have whereof to glory, he himself having done that which was the highest and the hardest thing in conversion.[1] And herein lies the mysterious operation of

---

[1] *See him*, De Servo Arbitr.

[2] Vide *Jansen. Aug.*, lib. i. p. 3, cap. 3 and 5.

[1] Domine, gratias ago tibi, quod supernaturale auxilium mihi contuleris misericorditer, nempe posse, velle, convertere.

the Spirit, in that though he acts thus efficaciously and victoriously upon the will, yet he doth not at all violate, infringe, or intrench upon its natural liberty;[1] which is yet secured, because the Spirit exerts all this power in such a way as doth very well agree with that liberty, for he carries on the work *suaviter*, as well as *fortiter*, with efficacy, but without any co-action or violence; all being done by him in an accommodation and congruous attemperature of things to the will's native and ingenite liberty, and he working *per certam scientiam et victricem delectationem*, as Augustine speaks.[2] Therefore it is said, Ps. cx. 3, 'Thy people shall be willing in the day of thy power.' Mark what a sweet harmony and consistency there is betwixt the efficacy of grace and the will's liberty: Cant. i. 4, 'Draw me, we will run after thee.' *Draw me*, there is efficacious grace; *we will run*, there is free and voluntary obedience. And see how well they agree: 'Draw me, *and* we will run;' what more forcible than the former, what more free than the latter? Let us but fix upon the right notion of liberty, viz., spontaneity, not indifferency, and that which I have said will be clear enough. But to come to what is easy, the converting Spirit so puts forth his power upon the will that he makes it willing to close with what is good; he removes that averseness, obstinateness, reluctancy, that is in it against what is holy and spiritual, whereupon it most readily complies therewith. And in reference to the casting off the yoke of sin, and the

At vero simile æqualeque auxilium condiscipulo Judæ contulisti, sed ego superaddidi quod tu mihi supernaturaliter non dedisti, viz., velle convertere; cumque non amplius receperim quam ille, tamen ego amplius feci quam ille, cum jam justificatus evadam, et ille in peccato permaneat; itaque non amplius tibi tuæque gratiæ debeo, quam iste Judas, qui non est conversus. Hoc autem Christianæ aures audire exhorrescunt. —*Bannez* in *D. Ward*, De Grat. Discrim., p. 40.

[1] Ne arbitreris istam asperam molestamque violentiam; dulcis est, suavis est, ipsa suavitas te trahit.—*Aug.* Gratia Dei humanum arbitrium non aufertur, sed sanatur, &c.—*Fulgent.*, lib. ii. De Verit. Præd. Divina hæc actio non lædit voluntatis libertatem, sed roborat; neque tamen extirpat radicitus vitiosam resistendi possibilitatem, sed efficaciter et suaviter dat homini firmam obediendi voluntatem.—*Theol. Mag. Brit.* in Acta Syn., part i. p. 679. Deus ita utitur volunate, ut ipsa voluntas sese elective, vitaliter, et ex practico rationis judicio agat.—*Rhætorf.* De Grat. Exerc., iii. cap. 3. Vide *Norton's* Orthod. Evangel., p. 114.

[2] De Peccat. Mer. et Rem., lib. ii. cap. 19, tom. vii.

taking up of the yoke of Christ, he never gives the will off till he hath brought the sinner to say, "Sin! from this day forward I break off all my allegiance to thee; I will be ruled by thee no longer; I resolve now to change my master. Lord Jesus, I am thine! I have been a traitor and rebel against thee too long, but now I fully surrender up myself to thy government; thy laws only I will be subject unto; do thou rule, command, order, dispose me as thou pleasest; put thy yoke upon me, I willingly stoop to it." Thus his will is subdued, and now he is made free from the law of sin. So much of the power of the Spirit, and of its way of working upon the will in order to this effect.

(3.) I might go on to shew the way of the Spirit's agency upon the affections, as he doth disengage and disentangle them from sin, nay, set them directly against it, and so freeing the sinner from the law of sin; but this being necessarily consequential upon the two former, I will not at all stay upon it. So much for the Spirit's workings at the first conversion.

2. Secondly, I am to consider the exertings of his power in his subsequent workings after conversion, during the whole life, by which he keeps free from the law of sin, and secures from its actual dominion. This being not so proper to the text, I will despatch it very briefly. The good Spirit doth not put forth his power only in his first regenerating, sin-subduing acts; but he continues so to do to the end of the believer's life. Having brought sin under, he will keep it so; it will be endeavouring to regain what it hath lost, but this gracious Spirit will not suffer it. Having made the conquest, he will *parta tueri*, make good the conquest. Having gained the throne in the heart for God and Christ, he will order it so that that shall be secured for them, that sin shall never ascend it any more. And truly there is much power in this, as well as in that which went before. Oh this corrupt nature will be stirring, making head upon all occasions to get up again! It must be a mighty strength which must suppress and break it in all its attempts; therefore, here too it is the law of the Spirit.

But how is this done by him? *Ans.* By his constant and continued agency in, and regency over, the renewed soul. The law of the Spirit may have reference to these also ; that look, as sin is a standing law in the unregenerate, it having in their whole course the command of them, and it being the constant, active principle in them, efficaciously urging and exciting them to what is evil; so the Spirit is a standing law in the regenerate, it, too, in their whole course having the command of them, and it being the constant, abiding, lively principle in them, efficaciously urging and exciting them to what is good, by which continued actings he keeps sin under for ever. For if it shall offer at any time, by its solicitations, promises, threatenings, to recover its former dominion, the Spirit is ready at hand to set in with other commands, promises, threatenings, thereby to obviate and countermine sin in its interposures. He watches sin in all its motions and assaults, and accordingly applies himself in his guiding, governing, strengthening grace, so that sin can make but little of it in all its endeavours. You read here in this chapter, ver. 14, of the leading of this Spirit, ' As many as are led by the Spirit of God, they are the sons of God ;' and it was David's prayer, Ps. li. 12, that God would ' uphold him with his free Spirit ;' so we read it ; but Chrysostom renders it by πνεῦμα ἡγεμονικὸν, the leading, governing, commanding Spirit; which, he saith, is so called, because it doth ἡγεμονεύεσθαι τῶν παθῶν, &c., bridle and command the affections, and put forth its power over sensual pleasures.[1] This is certain, the Spirit of God doth authoritatively lead and govern the children of God in their course ; and by virtue of that constant regency which it keeps up in and over them, sin's power is kept down. Here also is the law of the Spirit freeing from the law of sin.

Use 1. I have done with the doctrinal part, let me make some short application. Where, first, we see what a great and glorious person the Spirit of God is. He is the Spirit of life ; by a mighty power he delivers from the law of sin ; the corrupt nature, with all its strength and advantages, cannot stand before him ; that which to the creature is invincible he overcomes with ease. Oh, he that doth such great things must needs be a great Spirit ! the excellency of the effect proves the excellency of the agent. Some from this very passage fetch an argument to prove the Godhead of the Holy Ghost ;

[1] De Spir. Sanct., lib. vi. p. 213.

Cyril, from his being the Spirit of life ;[1] Chrysostom, from his making free from the law of sin.[2] Hast thou not, saith he, heard Paul saying, The law of the Spirit, &c. ; doth the Spirit make slaves free, it not having liberty in its own nature ? if it be created and in subjection itself, it cannot make others free. The argument may be thus drawn up : He that in the way of primary efficiency is the Spirit of life to quicken the dead soul, and the spirit of liberty to free the enslaved soul, he is God ; but the Holy Spirit of God in this way is and doth all this, *ergo*. I put in these words, *in the way of primary efficiency*, because other things as means or instruments, by a derived and subordinate power, may have some influence upon these things, and yet not be God ; but whoever doth produce them by an immediate, primary, underived power, as the Spirit doth, certainly he is more than a bare creature, he is truly God. To make free from the law of sin is work for a God, and for a God only : for to this, infinite knowledge is requisite, in order to the finding out of all the secret recesses and close workings of sin ; and also infinite power, for none below that is fit to grapple with so great a power as that of sin. So long as it is finite against finite the match is but equal, and so there would be no victory ; if therefore the Spirit carries through such a work as this, it speaks him to be infinite in his knowledge and in his power, and consequently to be God. But this I do but touch upon here ; hereafter, if the Lord give leave, I shall have occasion to speak more fully to it.

Use 2. Secondly, We have here the assignation of the true and only cause of freedom from sin's bondage. Mistakes about this are very dangerous ; and yet nothing more common than for men to run themselves upon such mistakes. The apostle here speaking of his being made free from the law of sin, what doth he fix upon as the proper cause thereof ? doth he resolve it into the power of nature ? alas ! that is a thing so feeble and weak that corrupt nature despises it, not fearing that that will ever do

[1] γυμνότερον δὲ διὰ τῶν ἐφεξῆς, ὅτι θεὸς εἴη τὸ πνεῦμα, δεικνύει βοῶν, ὁ νόμος τοῦ πνεύματος της ζωῆς, &c.—*Cyril Alexandr. in Thesaur.* Assert. 34. p. 235, t. v.

[2] Οὐκ ἤκουσας Παύλου λέγοντος, ὁ γὰρ νόμος, &c. ; ἐλευθεροῖ τὸ πνεῦμα τοὺς δούλους, τὸ μὴ ἔχον ἐν τῇ φύσει τὴν ἐλευθερίαν ; εἰ γὰρ ἔκτισται καὶ δεδούλωται, οὐκ ἐλευθεροῖ.—*Chrys. de Spir. Sanct.*, p. 206.

any great thing against it. Doth he resolve it into his own free-will?[1] no, that he understood little of. I challenge the whole world to give me one instance of a sinner that was ever, by the power, election, and determination of his own will, made free from the reign of sin. The will, as now constituted, is so corrupted that it is rather for the continuance than for the shaking off of sin's dominion. Oh it is loath to be delivered even by a foreign power, it likes its bondage so well! One of the greatest things that the converting Spirit, when it so works, hath to do, is to bow and incline the sinner's will so as to make it willing to accept of deliverance from sin's yoke; and he is never brought to this till the day of God's power dawn upon him: Ps. cx. 3, 'Thy people shall be willing in the day of thy power.' The evangelist, setting down the proper causes of regeneration, first removes the false ones, among which man's will is one, and then assigns the true one: John i. 13, 'Which were born, not of blood, nor of the will of the flesh, nor of the will of man, but of God:' the same holds true of that which is a consequent upon regeneration, viz., being made free from the law of sin. How can he that is a captive himself deliver others out of their captivity? how can that bring down sin's power which is itself most under that power? This was not the thing in Paul's eye when he was giving an account of his happy state; it was free grace and not free will that he magnified.[2] Again, doth he resolve it into anything out of himself, as the word, ordinance, the means of grace? &c. No; it is very true that these, God having set his divine stamp upon them, he also being pleased to accompany them with his own presence and blessing, may be productive of high and great things; yet, as considered in themselves, they are but means or instruments, and therefore do not operate from any natural or inherent virtue, but only as they are used by the first cause, and as the Spirit of life puts energy and power into them.

[1] Neque liberum arbitrium quicquam nisi ad peccandum valet, si careat veritatis via.—*August. de Sp. et Lit.*, cap. 3. Liberum arbitrium captivatum non nisi ad peccatum valet.—*Aug. adversus duas Pelag. Ep.*, lib. iii. cap. 3.

[2] De corpore mortis hujus non liberum hominis arbitrium, neque legis sanctum justumque mandatum, sed sola nos liberat gratia Dei per Jesum Christum. 'Lex enim Spiritus vitæ,' &c.—*Fulg. de Incarn. et Grat.*, cap. 16.

'Our weapons,' saith the apostle, 'are not carnal but spiritual, and mighty, *through God*, to the pulling down of strongholds,' &c., 2 Cor. x. 4; the same may be said of all gospel institutions. Oh how many live under the most effectual means, the ordinances of God in the most lively and powerful administration thereof, and yet sin stands its ground and keeps up its full power in and over them! It is not Goliath's sword that makes execution upon the enemy, unless it be wielded with Goliath's arm: the word is 'the sword of the Spirit,' Eph. vi. 17, which when he manages himself with his own arm, Isa. liii. 1, then sin falls and dies before it, but in any other hand it doth but little execution. I would fain convince you of the insufficiency, inability of all causes or things, within or without, and consequently of the absolute necessity of the Spirit's efficiency, in order to the divesting sin of its dominion; and thence it is that I stay so long upon this argument; but I will close it with this one consideration, viz., take the saints themselves, such as have true grace wrought in them, who consequently are made free from the law of sin, and put even these upon particular and gradual mortification, the mortifying of some one lust, be it what it will, or the mortifying of it in a higher degree than before; I say, take these very persons, and let things too be brought thus low, yet they of themselves, without the mighty assistance of God's Spirit, can do nothing about them: special grace from above is requisite to every act and degree of mortification by the saints themselves: Rom. viii. 13, 'If ye, *through the Spirit*, do mortify the deeds of the body, ye shall live.' It was spoken to renewed persons, therefore it must be understood of gradual and progressive mortification: now saith Paul, 'If ye *through the Spirit*,' &c., implying that even such persons, in such mortification, which of all is most easy, must be enabled thereunto by strength from the Holy Spirit conveyed to them. Whence I infer an utter inability in the unregenerate to free themselves from the law of sin; they having no principle in them to further such a thing, as the saints have for their mortification, sin having its full unbroken strength in them, which it hath not in the other, their work not being gradual mortification but habitual, and the first mortification of the whole body of sin, which therefore is much harder than the former. I say, upon this stating of things, how unable must these be to throw off sin's power! If the saint be so weak, how weak is the sinner? if the saint must have the Spirit's help or else sin will be too hard for him in its relics, how much more must the sinner have it, in whom sin is in its full strength? He being under the law of sin, what can he do, further than attend upon the means, to free himself from it? Blessed be God that this Spirit is engaged in this work, otherwise there would be no such thing in the world as freedom from the law of sin.

It being so, two things I would infer by way of advice:

1. Let such who desire this mercy betake themselves to the Spirit for it. Such who desire it, did I say? Methinks, upon what hath been said, all should passionately desire it. Will any be willing still to continue under sin's command? I will suppose all that hear me to be heartily desirous to cast off its yoke, no longer to live in subjection to it, &c.; the only thing that troubles them is the difficulty of the thing, and all their inquiry is how they may be rid of this tyrant who hath so long domineered over them. If so, then I would give them this direction: Fly to the Spirit of life; let them cast themselves down at the feet of the Spirit, expecting only deliverance by and from him. It is a great while before sinners will be brought to desire such a thing; when they are brought to that, then they mistake themselves about the way of obtaining it; fain they would be made free, but they do not betake themselves to that Spirit which alone can make them so. Sirs, your case is desperate if this Spirit of life do not undertake it; no power in heaven or in earth can relieve you but his. As that evil spirit once said to him that would undertake to cast it out, 'Jesus I know, and Paul I know; but who are ye?' Acts xix. 15; so here, sin despises and defies all that will meddle with it; it only knows and cannot stand before this omnipotent Spirit. Christ's infinite merit alone frees from its damnation, the Spirit's infinite power alone frees from its dominion; therefore to that you must fly for this freedom. You may possibly think this and that may do the work, but you will be deceived. Suppose you are brought under some convictions, sin will do well enough for

all them; suppose you resolve thus and thus for the future, sin's throne may stand fast enough for all that; suppose you sit under such a ministry, sin can let you hear the word powerfully preached, and yet rule you as much as ever. Oh do not deceive yourselves! I tell you, nothing will or can effectually pull the sceptre out of this usurper's hand, and disengage the heart from obedience and bondage under sin, but this one thing, the law of the Spirit of life. With the most humble, hearty, fervent prayer, therefore, go to him, and say, 'O blessed Spirit, pity and help me; deliver a poor captive that is held in sin's chains and fetters; break its yoke for me, rid me out of the thraldom I have so long lived in, put forth thy power in me to free me from sin's power over me; I am undone for ever if thou dost not help me; I know not what to do against sin's mighty host, only 'mine eyes are unto thee,' 2 Chron. xx. 12. I have heard that it is thy office to rescue and set free poor enslaved souls; such a one am I. Oh do this for me, thou blessed Spirit! I must not let thee alone until this be done; take thine own course and method; convince, humble, terrify, &c.; do anything with me, only let not lust, pride, ignorance, passion, covetousness, sensuality, any sin whatsoever, any longer reign over me.' Could I but bring you thus to pray, the thing was done; if it be the 'Spirit of supplication,' it will be the law of the Spirit, &c. Never did any sincerely desire to be freed from sin's dominion but it was done for them, at the Spirit's time, in the Spirit's method, and according to that measure which the Spirit sees best.

In your betaking of yourselves to him in prayer,

1. See that you pray in faith, believing the sufficiency of his power. Let sin be never so high, he is able to bring it down. Do you believe this? All other things are weak, and can contribute but little to your help; but the mighty Spirit can do it easily and effectually. Sin cannot stand before him, no more than you can before it; when he undertakes it, he will subdue it to purpose, notwithstanding all its strength. You cannot be too diffident as to yourselves, nor too confident as to the Spirit.

2. Let all other means be joined with prayer. They are but means, and therefore not to be relied upon; yet they are means, and therefore not to be

neglected. In things of this nature men are very prone to run themselves upon one of these two rocks: either they rest upon the means, not looking up to the Spirit; or they cast off the means, casting all upon the Spirit; either they are proud, and can do all without God, or dejected and slothful, so as that God must and shall do all without them;[1] both of which are most dangerous mistakes. You have heard that it is the Spirit's sole act to free from sin's power—that you yourselves, and all causes and means whatsoever, are utterly unable to produce this effect; what now will you draw from hence? What! that you have nothing to do? that it is a vain thing for you to use any endeavour on your part, or to attend upon any means, for it is God and his Spirit that must do all? Oh pray do not so argue! You will err most perniciously if you do. The Spirit's sole efficiency, as to the formal production of the act, is very well consistent with the creature's endeavours; he indeed doth the thing, yet he will have the creature do what he can in order to it; he doth all in us and for us, yet he will do nothing without us; therefore the confidence must be on him, but yet diligence is required of us. It is the warmth and influences of the sun which make the fruits of the earth to grow; yet the husbandman must plough the ground and sow his seed. It was the angel stirring the waters that wrought the cure; yet the poor cripples were to lie by the pool-side, which allusion was before made use of upon this account; and thus it is here. So then as to that which I am upon, unquestionably it is the power of the Spirit which alone frees from the power of sin; but yet you in your sphere are to be active, and to do what in you lies in order to this very thing; as, namely, you are to attend upon the word, the several ordinances in and by which the Spirit works; to read the Scriptures, to be much in consideration of the evil of sin, and the sad effects

[1] Quosdam nimia voluntatis suæ fiducia extulit in superbiam, et quosdam nimia voluntatis suæ diffidentia dejecit in negligentiam. Illi dicunt, quid rogamus Deum ne vincamur tentatione, quod in nostra est potestate? isti, quid conamur bene vivere, quod in Dei est potestate? O Domine, O Pater, qui es in cœlis, ne nos inferas in quamlibet istarum tentationum, sed libera nos a malo.—*August.* Agendæ gratiæ sunt, quia data est potestas, et orandum ne succumbat infirmitas.—*Bradw.*, lib. ii. cap. 4, p. 473.

of its dominion; not to do anything that may tend to the strengthening of its power, by abstinence, fasting, &c.; to keep it under where it vents itself in some bodily lusts, &c. And in the doing of these things, with all faithfulness and diligence, you may with the greater confidence expect that the Spirit will exert his power for the real and thorough delivering of you from the law of sin.

2. The second word of advice is this: Let such who are made free from the law of sin own the Spirit of life as the author of their freedom, and ascribe the glory of it to him. Is this done for any of you? You are infinitely engaged to God and to his Spirit. How high should you be in the admiring of him, how humble in the ascribing of all to him! how should you evermore be crying out, 'Not unto us,' O Lord and Spirit, 'not unto us,' nor unto anything in all the world besides, 'but unto thy name be all the glory.' Assuredly if this Spirit had not effected this liberty for you, you had been to this day as much under sin's bondage as you yourselves ever were, or as any others yet are; you may take the comfort, but God must have the sole glory of it. The apostle prayed for the Romans that God would 'fill them with all joy and peace in believing, that they might abound in hope, through the power of the Holy Ghost,' Rom. xv. 13. It is this power of the Holy Ghost that hath done your work; keep your eye there: Acts iii. 12, 'Why look ye so earnestly on us,' saith Peter, 'as though by our own power we had made this man to walk?' Possibly God was pleased to make use of such instruments in order to your spiritual rescue; but why is your eye so much upon them, as though they had done it by any power of their own? No, it was not so; all was done in the power of God. We poor ministers must say, 'We have this treasure in earthen vessels, that the excellency of the power may be of God, and not of us,' 2 Cor. iv. 7; and all other things whatsoever must say the same. But is nothing to be ascribed to a man's self; to the acting and determination of his own will; to the improvement of his natural abilities? is it not enough to ascribe part, yea, the better part, to the Spirit, but some part to the creature? Oh this we like dearly, to divide betwixt God and ourselves, to share with him in part of the glory due upon his special grace! Some seem

highly to cry up the grace of God, and very much to assert the impotency of nature;[1] and yet in after-positions and distinctions the creature must come in for a part; maybe God shall have the nine hundred ninety-ninth proportion, but the thousandth part man himself must have; which, if it be granted to him, in a little time he will put in for more, till at last it come to this, man did all, and God did nothing.[2] It is safest and best to ascribe all to God. It was a good speech of Prosper, 'It is not devotion to give almost all to God, but it is dishonesty to keep the very least part from him.[3] The *all* is not too much to be attributed to him; the *least* is too much to be attributed to the creature.

I cannot confine my advice to God's people to this only head; three things further I would say to them, and I have done.

1. You are greatly to love and honour the Spirit. This you do, or ought to do, to the Father, to the Son; pray do the same to the Spirit. He is the great agent in your regeneration, deliverance from sin's sovereignty, illumination, conviction, turning to God, believing, mortification, &c. From him your light, life, strength, liberty, joy, peace, do all proceed. Why do you not more love and honour the Spirit? Oh love the Son for what hath been done without, but love the Spirit also for what he hath done within! the whole management of soul-work within, in order to salvation, now lies upon the hands of the Spirit; let him be adored and honoured by all saints.

2. As you have found the law of the Spirit in your first conversion, so you should live under the law of the Spirit in your whole conversation. There is the power of the Spirit at the first saving work, that is here spoken of; and there is, in what sense you have heard, the continuation of it in the whole life. Now this you are to labour after. I mean two things: 1. You are to live under the constant influences; 2. Under the constant government and rule, of the Spirit. Blessed is the man that hath it

always working in him and ruling of him! What a life doth he live who ever lives under the Spirit's authoritative guidance! Col. iii. 15, 'Let the peace of God rule in your hearts,' &c. Ay, and let the Spirit of peace rule in your hearts. It is a great motive to men to come under the rule of Christ, to consider that where he rules, there he saves; and it is also a great motive to sanctified persons to live under the rule of the Spirit, to consider where he rules there he comforts; his governing and his comforting go together. He that is acted by the Spirit's command, and yields up himself to the Spirit's guidance, shall neither want peace here, nor come short of heaven hereafter.

3. Set law against law; the law of the Spirit against the law of sin. You yet find too much of this latter law, and it goes to the heart of you that sin should yet have so great a power over you. Well, what have you to do in this case? Why, set law against law, power against power, the power of the Spirit against the power of sin. This should humble you, that should support you. That power which could baffle sin when in its full strength, can it not subdue it in the remainders thereof? That power which could bring you in to God, in spite of all opposition, is it not sufficient to keep you now you are brought in to God? 1 Peter i. 5, 'We are kept by the power of God through faith unto salvation.' That very power is put forth for your establishment now, which was put forth for your conversion at the first. Oh fear not the law of sin against you, so long as the law of the Spirit is for you! When you are beset, and enemies press hard upon you, see that you improve, both for duty and comfort, this power of God's own Spirit. Thus I have finished the three observations which take in the sum of this verse.

CHAPTER VIII.[1]

From the law of sin and death.—ROM. viii. 2.

Of the law of death—The connexion betwixt sin and death—Where it is the law of sin, there it is the

[1] Aquin. 1, 2, Quæst. 109, A. 6 and 7; Syn. Trid., Sess. 6, cap. 2. cant. 3; Bellar. de Lib. Arb., lib. vi. cap. 15; Remonst. in Acta Syn., pp. 1, 64; Armin. Declar. Sent., p. 98, and in Ep. ad Hip. Addo illum doctorem mihi maxime placere, qui gratiæ quam plurimum tribuit, &c.

[2] J. G. Red. red. in Præf.

[3] Non est devotionis dedisse prope totum, sed fraudis retinuisse vel minimum.—*Contra Collat*, cap. *ult*.

[1] Reader, the contents of this chapter were insisted upon only in the close of a sermon; I having under the former

law of death—Regenerate persons are made free from this law: that opened with respect to death temporal and death eternal—Use 1. Men persuaded to believe that sin and death go together; dehorted from thence not to sin—Use 2. Of the happiness of God's people.

THE apostle here sets a twofold law before us—the law of sin, and the law of death. The former I have been large upon, the latter I must despatch in a few words.

And death. The word *law* is not repeated, but according to that interpretation which some put upon the words, it is to be repeated;[1] it is the law of sin, and it is the law of death too. As if the apostle had said, The law, &c., hath made me free both from the law of sin, and also from the law of death.

In the opening of them I told you there is a twofold sense given of them.[2] 1. Some tell us there is in them the figure ἐν διὰ δυο, wherein one thing is set forth by two words; therefore they render this *and death* as being only an adjective or epithet of sin; thus, the law, &c., from the law of sin and death, that is, from deadly sin, or from the law of sin, which is of a deadly nature. 2. Others take the word *substantivè*, making the law of death to be a law by itself as well as the law of sin; as if this death was not to be melted into sin, and the deliverance from it into the deliverance from sin, but that they are distinct things, and point to distinct deliverances.

Now both of these senses are very true and good, and indeed I know not which to prefer. From the first, one single point offers itself to us, viz., that sin is a deadly thing; from the second, these three, which, *mutatis mutandis*, perfecty answer to the three former under the law of sin:

1. That men by nature, and before regeneration, are under the law of death.

2. That upon regeneration, or such as are regenerate, are made free from the law of death.

3. That it is the law of the Spirit of life which frees from the law of death.

The due handling of these heads would take up a

great deal of time; but I having already stayed too long upon this verse, and upon some other considerations, I am necessitated to contract; and therefore, for the better shortening of the work, I must pitch upon another method, wherein I may draw all into a narrow compass.

Three things only shall be observed:

1. That sin and death go hand in hand together. There is an inseparable connexion or conjunction betwixt them; they come here in the text very near each to the other; there is but an *and* betwixt them, and that too is copulative, 'the law of sin *and* death.' And well might the apostle put them together, when God himself in the methods of his justice, and in the threatening of his law, hath so put them together; and surely what he hath so joined no man can put asunder. When sin came into the world death came along with it; the one trod upon the heels of the other; if man will sin, he shall die: Rom. v. 12, 'Wherefore, as by one man sin entered into the world, and *death by sin;* even so death passed upon all men, for that all have sinned.' Ver. 17, 'For if by one man's offence, death reigned by one,' &c. Here is death, and the law of death too; by sin it hath got a power over men so as to reign over them. Had there been no sin there had been no death; if man had continued in his sinless and innocent state, he might have been mortal, *i.e.,* under a *posse mori,* he being but a creature and made up of contrary principles;[1] but he had not actually died, much less had he been under a necessity of dying, if he had not sinned. Death did not come into the world upon God's mere dominion and sovereignty, or merely upon the frailty of the human nature, as Pelagians of old and Socinians of late assert,[2] but as the fruit and punishment of sin.[3] Immortality was a part of God's image at first imprinted upon man;[4] that

---

head, the law of sin, exceeded the bounds allowed by the press, cannot upon this head, the law of death, make any considerable enlargement.

[1] *Ut lex* ad utrumque ex æquo referatur.—*Erasm.*

[2] See p. 99.

[1] *Vide* Grot. de Sat., cap. 1, p. 18.

[2] Mors non erat pœna vel effectus transgressionis Adami, sed conditionis naturalis consequens.—*Socin. de Statu primi hominis.* Vide *Prælect.,* cap. 1, and *contra Puccium,* cap. 5.

[3] Calov. Soc. Prost., p. 250; Hoorn Soc. conf., vol. i. lib. iii. cap. 4, p. 583, &c.; Franz. Scho. Sacr., Disp. 1, p. 7.

[4] Molin. Enod. Grav. Qu. de Statu Innoc., Tract. 3, p. 62; Gerhard. Loc. Com. de Imag., &c., tom. i. cap. 4, p. 199; Zæem de Imag., &c., cap. 8, art. 2; Moreton's Threefold State of Man, p. i. cap. 2, p. 35.

image being defaced, mortality took place. You know, in God's dealing with our first parents, how he backed his command or prohibition with the threatening of death: Gen. ii. 17, 'Of the tree of knowledge of good and evil, thou shalt not eat of it ; for in the day thou eatest thereof, thou shalt surely die ;' they disobeyed this most equitable commandment, and thereby brought death both upon themselves, Gen. iii. 19, and also upon all their posterity. Besides the guilt of this sin, made over to all mankind by imputation, there is men's personal sin, habitual and actual, which renders them yet more obnoxious unto death; and that too not only to temporal, but also to eternal death: Rom. vi. 21, 'The end of those things is death ;' ver 23, 'The wages of sin is death.' The apostle, in James i. 14, 15, treats of the first and last of sin, shews where it begins and where it ends, sets down its rise, progress, and final issue : 'But every man is tempted, when he is drawn away of his own lust, and enticed ; then when lust hath conceived it bringeth forth sin ; and sin, when it is finished, it bringeth forth death ;' sin is the issue of lust, and death is the issue of sin. So that our apostle here in the text might upon very good grounds link and couple sin and death.

2. Observe that it is the law of sin and the law of death which is here coupled together ; so that where it is the law of sin, there, and there only, it is the law of death. When sin is reigning and commanding, then it is ruining and condemning ; it is the power of sin that exposes to the power of death : Rom. vi. 46, 'Know ye not, that to whom ye yield yourselves servants to obey, his servants ye are to whom ye obey, whether of sin unto death, or of obedience unto righteousness ?' It is true every sin in its own nature deserves death ; the Scripture knows no such thing as venial sin ; it being judge, all and every sin is mortal. Indeed, as to event, the apostle saith, 'There is a sin not unto death,' 1 John v. 17, but as to merit, every sin, be it what it will, deserves death ; yet God is so gracious as that sin shall not condemn and end in death where it doth not command. Pray mark it how in the words the *law of the Spirit* is joined with *life*, and the *law of sin* with *death ;* as where the power of the Spirit is there is life, so where the power of sin is there is

death. I know the death in the latter clause doth not carry a direct opposition to the life in the former ; for the life there referring to grace and regeneration, and not to glory hereafter, the death, which refers to eternal condemnation and the misery of the future state, cannot be looked upon as directly opposite to that life ; yet there is a truth in the parallel. As upon the law of the Spirit there is life, spiritual and eternal, so upon the law of sin there is death, spiritual and eternal too. Further, I know there is a great disparity betwixt the Spirit's working life, and sin's working death ; the law of the Spirit works life in the way of proper efficiency and causality, the law of sin works death only in a final, consequential, meritorious way ; yet here also we may speak by way of parallel ; as the power of the Spirit works life in its way, so the power of sin works death too in its way. That which I drive at is very plain, if I be so happy as to express myself clearly about it.

3. Observe that such who are brought under the power of the regenerating Spirit, they are made free from the law of death. This was Paul's happiness here laid down, and it is the same to all that are regenerate ; the proof of which I need not insist upon, for this deliverance undeniably follows from the former ; they who are made free from the law of sin, by that grace are also made free from the law of death, it being the law of sin which subjects the creature to the law of death. The power, or right, of death stands or falls by the power of sin ; so that if the person be freed from the latter, as you have heard every regenerate person is, it certainly follows, in the course and methods of God's grace, that every such person shall be freed from the former too ; for the law of death is penal, or the effect of the law of sin ; now take away the cause, and the effect ceases.

Quest. But a little explication will be necessary. How may regenerate persons be said to be made free from the law of death ?

For answer to this, you know death is either temporal or eternal ; (I do not instance in spiritual death, because though it is very true that the saints upon the law of the Spirit are made free from this death, yet I conceive that is not so much intended here :) the former lies in the separation of the soul from the body for a time, the latter in the everlasting separation of both soul and body from the love and favour and presence of God. This separation from God is the death of this death, or that wherein it mainly consists; hence though it doth not carry in it any annihilation, yea, though it be attended with a kind of life, both soul and body retaining their physical being, existence, and union, yet it is called death, because there is in it a separation from the fountain of true life and of all blessedness; upon which account it is not only death, but the worst death; and this too is the worst part of this worst death, for though there be more included in it than the loss of God's presence, viz., the punishment of sense, eternal torment in hell fire, yet it might easily be proved that herein lies its greatest evil; the departing from God is worse than the going into everlasting fire, Mat. xxv. 41. But to apply this distinction to the business in hand.

1. The law of the Spirit of life frees the regenerate from death temporal. Not simply and absolutely, from death considered abstractly and in itself, for so all must die. Believers themselves are within the compass of the general statute: Heb. ix. 27, 'It is appointed unto men once to die;' Ps. lxxxix. 48, 'What man is he that liveth, and shall not see death? shall he deliver his soul from the hand of the grave?' but it frees from death as so qualified and so circumstantiated; in the language of the text, it frees from the law of death. How is that? why, take a gracious man, death hath not a full right or an absolute power over him, so as to keep him under its dominion for ever, for so I shewed you some open this law of death. Such a one may die, but he shall live again; the grave shall not always hold him; he may be thrown into prison for a time, but Christ will fetch him out, and then death shall never again exercise its power over him; after he hath died once he shall die no more, as it is said of Christ, Rom. vi. 9. Again, grace frees from the law of this death, that is, from the hurtfulness, sting, and curse of it. Death carries much of a curse in it; it is the result and fruit of the primitive curse, Gen. ii. 17; now in this notion sanctified persons are freed from it. The nature and property of death is altered to a godly man; to him it is now but the paying of that debt or tribute which is due to nature; but a sleep,

1 Thes. iv. 14; but a change, Job xiv. 14; but a departure or going out of prison, Luke ii. 29; but a going to bed, Isa. lvii. 2; but an unclothing, 2 Cor. v. 4; but a passage into an endless and everlasting life, an inlet into the immediate fruition of God. Oh set but sense aside, what a harmless, innocent thing is this death to such a person! the lion being slain by Christ, there is honey now in the belly of it; I allude to that of Samson, Judges xiv. 8; 1 Cor. xv. 55, 'O death, where is thy sting? O grave, where is thy victory? The sting of death is sin, and the strength of sin is the law; but thanks be to God, which giveth us the victory through our Lord Jesus Christ.' Christ by death hath overcome death, unstung it and taken off its hurtful quality; by dying himself he hath expiated sin, vanquished Satan, atoned God, satisfied the law, secured from hell, purchased eternal life, and, these things being done, where is now the law of death? Heb. ii. 14, 15, 'Forasmuch then as the children are partakers of flesh and blood, he also himself likewise took part of the same; that through death he might destroy him that had the power of death, that is, the devil; and deliver them who through fear of death were all their lifetime subject to bondage.'

2. There is that death which is much worse than this, viz., eternal death; that which indeed is the death incomparably surpassing any other. As no life like to eternal life, so no death like to eternal death. To have the body separated for a while from the soul is a thing to nature very dreadful, but what is that to the separation both of body and soul from God for ever? This is sometimes set forth by *death* without the addition of any epithet, as John viii. 51, 'If a man keep my sayings he shall never see death;' Rom. vi. 23, and viii. 6, *et passim*. Sometimes by *the second death;* and it is so styled because it succeeds upon, and doth not commence till after the first death: Rev. ii. 11, 'He that overcometh shall not be hurt of the second death;' Rev. xx. 6, and xxi. 4. This is that death which the unconverted and impenitent are obnoxious unto,[1] but such as turn to God by true repentance, and live a holy life, they are freed from it. And this deliverance is absolute;

[1] Sicut is qui liberatur a lege Spiritus vitæ, permanet in Christo qui est vita; ita qui servit legi peccati permanet in morte, quæ venit ex damnatione peccati.—*Orig.*

the former was but in such [1] a qualified sense, but this, I say, is absolute. Even such may, and shall, die the first death, but they shall never die this second death: Rom. xx. 6, 'Blessed and holy is he that hath part in the first resurrection; on such the second death hath no power.' You read of the abolishing of this death by Christ, 2 Tim. i. 10; eternal death is quite abolished to all regenerate persons. But this very much falls in with the no-condemnation in the foregoing verse; of which having there said enough I will add nothing more.

Use 1. By way of use, 1. I would exhort you all to live in the steady belief of this, and often to revive it upon your thoughts, that it is sin and death. Especially when at any time Satan and your own hearts solicit and tempt you to sin, be sure then you think of this, so as to retort it upon the temptation speedily. What! shall I sin and die? shall I for the pleasures, delights, satisfaction of sin, which are but for a season, Heb. xi. 25, expose myself to death? yea, to eternal death? no, that I dare not, that I must not do. It is good to break the force of a temptation by such reasonings as these; for though it is true the great restraints from sin should be taken from the love of God, the fear of offending God, &c., yet it is good, and God allows it, to take in the advantage of self-love too, and the fear of self-destroying. Surely if men did indeed believe, or did not strangely smother and suppress all serious convictions about this, that it is sin and death, they durst not sin as they do. Where is the man, let him be never so thirsty, or let the draught be never so alluring, that would venture upon it should he be told there is poison in it, and that if he drinks it he is a dead man? Oh the stupendous folly, nay, madness of men! We tell them from God's own mouth there is death at the bottom of sinful practices; and yet, because these suit with and please their sensual part, they will venture upon them. The fear of temporal death to be inflicted by the magistrate keeps off many from those enormous acts which otherwise they would commit; they dare not thus and thus transgress the law, by stealing, killing, &c., though they have a good mind to it. Why? because they know if they so do, they must die. Ah, sinner! God backs his laws with the penalty of eternal death,

to which thou makest thyself liable by the violation of them, and yet wilt thou dare to do it? shall the fear of this not at all restrain thee from what is evil? Here is the devil's cunning in his temptations; he presents the bait, but hides the hook; he tempts from and by the pleasure, delight, contentment that is in sin, but conceals the death that will follow upon it; nay, he doth not only conceal the evil threatened, but, either *in thesi* or *in hypothesi*, he flatly denies it. This lying spirit will tell the sinner he may sin without danger; what! die for it? no, there is no such thing: 'Thou shalt not die.' Thus he began in his first assault upon our first parents: Gen. iii. 4, 'And the serpent said to the woman, Ye shall not surely die;' and thus he doth with sinners to this very day. He always sharpens his temptations by blunting the edge of the law's threatening, assuring the poor besotted creature that he may sin and yet not die. Now, I beseech you, do not hearken to him or believe him, for he is what he always was, a liar, and so a murderer, John viii. 44. Let the temptation be never so inviting and alluring, yet I pray, consider, death is in the pot, 2 Kings iv. 40, and therefore there is no meddling with it; let the enticements of sin be never so specious and plausible, yet know nothing less than eternal death will inevitably follow upon it; and doth not the evil of that infinitely weigh down all the good which sin promises? Sin is the falsest thing in all the world; its promises are very fair, but its performances are quite contrary; it pretends to this and that, which takes with the sinner exceedingly, but the very upshot and end of all is everlasting destruction. Suppose it be as good as its word, as to some temporal concerns, yet, alas! its good is soon over and gone, but its bad abides for ever; the pleasant taste of its honey in the mouth is but short, but its gall lies fretting in the bowels to all eternity; now what madness is it for a man for a few minutes' delight to run himself into everlasting and endless torments! It is one of the saddest things that is imaginable, that men do, and cannot but know that it is sin and death; and yet in a strange defiance of God, and in a bold contemning of all that he threatens, yea, even of eternal death itself, they will venture upon sin: Rom. i. 32, 'Who knowing the judgment of God, that they which commit such things are worthy of death, not only do the same, but have pleasure in them that do them.' But surely did they but know and consider what this death is, they would not carry it thus. I cannot now enter upon any particular description of it, only let me tell them what there is in it, the absence of all good, the presence of all evil; is not this enough? that, in short, it is the summary and abridgment of all that misery which the human nature is capable of; and should not such a thing make a poor creature tremble? As to this death, the sinner would fain die, but cannot; he must live, though he be dead even whilst he lives. At the first death the body and soul are loath to part, but in the second death they would fain part if they might;[1] but the just God will keep them together, that as they sinned together, so they shall suffer together. What a sad meeting will there be betwixt these two at the general resurrection, when they shall be reunited only in order to their being eternally miserable! Now do not sinners tremble at this? do they not dread that which will bring all this upon them? if not, what can we further say or do?

As to you, dearly beloved, I hope you are not given up to a reprobate mind, to this desperate hardness of heart to make nothing of dying eternally; pray therefore, 'stand in awe, and sin not,' Ps. iv. 4; do not dare to live in that for which you must die and perish for ever; let sin die that you may never die, for it must be either its death or yours. If you love sin, you love death; and is death a thing to be loved? Prov. viii. 36, 'He that sinneth against me wrongeth his own soul: all they that hate me love death.' Methinks that is a very sad description of the carriage of the poor amorous wanton under the enchantments of the whorish woman: Prov. vii. 21–23, 'With much fair speech she caused him to yield, with the flattering of her lips she forced him. He goeth after her straightway, as an ox goeth to the slaughter, or as a fool to the correction of the stocks; till a dart strike through his liver; as a bird hasteth to the snare, and knoweth not that it is for his life.' Sirs, will you carry it thus

under sin's enchantments, not considering that it aims at your life, and exposes you to eternal death? A fool sees but a little way, but a wise man looks to the issues and consequences of things; you know what I mean. Simply to die is not so much, but to die eternally, oh that is a formidable thing! as you would shun that, shun sin; for 'its house is the way to hell, going down to the chambers of death,' Prov. vii. 27.

Use 2. Let the people of God see their happiness, and take the comfort of it. You that by the power of the regenerating Spirit are made free from the law of sin, know that upon this you are also made free from the law of death; oh precious and admirable mercy! what a cordial is this to revive you under all your faintings! As to temporal death, you are not wholly exempted from it, that is common to you as well as to others; yet it is a quite other thing to you than what it is to others; oh whenever it shall come, bid it welcome and do not fear it![1] For to you it will come without a sting, and you know the serpent that hath lost its sting may hiss but cannot hurt. It is in itself an enemy, and the last enemy, 1 Cor. xv. 26; but to you it is a harmless, because a conquered enemy; it may seem to threaten the greatest evil, but, in truth, it shall do you the greatest good. But here lies your main happiness, you are wholly exempted from eternal death, the second death; you shall die but once, and then live with God for ever. It is this second death that makes the first to be so formidable; for a man to die that he may live, that is not at all dreadful; but to die here in order to a worser death hereafter, there is the thing which is only dreadful. When death is but an inlet to eternal life, a departure to be with Christ, Phil. i. 23, when there is no condemnation to follow after it, you may and you should meet it with joy and holy triumph. And know, that to you it shall not be bare freedom from eternal death, but it shall also be the possession of eternal life; there is very much in the privative part of the mercy, but when the positive part too is joined with it, how high doth it rise! oh admire and adore the grace of God! The least of your sins

---

[1] Mors prima pellit animam nolentem de corpore, mors secunda detinet animam nolentem in corpore.—*Aug. de Civit. Dei*, lib. xxi. cap. 3.

[1] Non est formidandum quod liberat nos ab omni formidando.—*Tertull.* Ejus est mortem timere, qui ad Christum nollet ire.—*Cypr.*

deserve death, the best of your duties doth not deserve life; and yet you are freed from that which you so much deserve, and shall be put into the possession of that which you so little deserve; here is the riches of the grace of God towards you. Sin and death are the two comprehensive evils;[1] all evil is summed up in and under them, but you are freed from both; what reason have you to rejoice and to admire the Lord's boundless goodness! Oh the damned in hell, who are under this death and feel it, what would they give to be freed from it! You, through the merit of Christ and the power of the Spirit, are made free from it, therefore you should first be very thankful and then very cheerful. What great things hath the gracious God done for you! he hath delivered you from the rule of sin whilst you live, from the hurt of death when you die; have not you abundant cause of blessing and rejoicing? It will not be long before this death will look you in the face and lay its cold hands upon you; it is every minute making its nearer approaches to you; by every breath you draw it gets ground upon you: well, be not troubled at this; you know the worst of it; it is death, but not damnation, it is the parting of the soul from the body, but no parting of the soul from God; it is but dying temporally that you may live eternally: how great is your happiness! proportionable to which, how great should your thankfulness and holy joy be! So much for this verse.

CHAPTER IX.

OF THE LAW'S INABILITY TO JUSTIFY AND SAVE.

For what the law could not do, in that it was weak through the flesh, God sending his own Son, in the likeness of sinful flesh, and for sin condemned sin in the flesh:

That the righteousness of the law might be fulfilled in us, who walk not after the flesh, but after the Spirit. —ROM. viii. 3, 4.

High and glorious matter contained in these two verses

---

[1] Peccatum et mors sunt duæ partes adæquatæ humanæ miseriæ; nam in culpa et pœna tota miseria hominis consistit. —*Streso.*

—Of their coherence with what went before—The difference amongst expositors about that—The general sense and meaning of the words—The various readings and explications of them—They are divided into five parts—There is a complication in them of the several causes of the sinner's justification and salvation—The first branch of the text insisted upon, 'What the law,' &c.—Four things observed in it—Of its literal exposition—What is here meant by law— *What that was which the law could not do—How it is said to be* weak—*What the* flesh *is by which it is weakened—The whole matter drawn into one observation—Of the special matter of the law's impotency, as it refers to justification and salvation—Three grounds or demonstrations of its impotency: 1. It requires more than what the fallen creature can perform; 2. It doth not give what the fallen creature needs; 3. It cannot make reparation for what the fallen creature hath done—Use 1. To humble us, because we have a nature in us by which God's own law is thus weakened: where something is said against the power of nature—Use 2. First, To vindicate the honour of the law, notwithstanding the weakness charged upon it; secondly, The law's obligation not to be cast off because of this; thirdly, Nor yet is it to be looked upon as altogether weak or useless—Use 3. To take men off from expecting righteousness and life from and by the law—Use 4. To stir up believers to adore the love and mercy of God in sending his Son, when the law was under an utter inability to justify and save.*

OUR apostle here, eagle-like, soars aloft, and rises up in his discourse to the most sublime truths of the gospel. These two verses set things before us so high and glorious as may fill heaven and earth, angels and men, with amazement and astonishment. Here is the whole gospel summed up in a few words, contracted and brought into a narrow compass. Here is in one view man undone and man recovered, the depths of the creature's misery and the heights of God's mercy, in a short abridgment. Here is God's sending his Son, which surely was the greatest thing that ever he did, it being the highest contrivance of his infinite wisdom, and the highest product of his infinite love. Here is this Son sent in our flesh, the first and the great mystery of the gospel; for it comes in the front of the gospel mysteries, 1 Tim. iii. 16. Here is sin condemned and the sinner acquitted; the law represented as impossible for us to keep, yet fulfilled for us in a most strange and wonderful manner; as Christ hath done, and suffered that for us which we were utterly unable to do and suffer ourselves. Oh the breadths, lengths, depths, heights of the wisdom, mercy, justice, holiness of God! Eph. iii. 18; for all these several attributes, in what is here set forth, do concur and shine forth in their greatest lustre. Who can hear or read these two verses with due consideration, and not be in a divine transport and ecstacy? For the truth is, whatever is short of the most raised workings in the soul is too low for the glorious things here spoken of.

We must first inquire into their coherence or connexion with what goes before. They are a further proof or confirmation of the main proposition laid down in the first verse, ' There is no condemnation to them that are, in Christ Jesus.' That which might endanger as to condemnation was sin, and there are two things in sin to endanger about it, its power and guilt; therefore the apostle shews how such who are in Christ are freed from both of these. As to the taking away its power, that is spoken to in the second verse: 'The law of the Spirit of life, in Christ Jesus, hath made me free from the law of sin,' &c. As to the taking away its guilt, that he speaks to in these two verses, ' What the law could not do,' &c. As if the apostle had said, If anything could condemn God's people it would be sin, but that cannot, for it is condemned itself. Christ, or God by him, hath condemned sin, and so the sinner himself shall not be condemned by it or for it. The guilt of sin being expiated, and the sinner made righteous upon the imputation of Christ's obedience and satisfaction, which are the two things here asserted, surely there is, there can be no condemnation to those who have an interest in this grace. And this I judge to be the chief scope and proper reference of the words, which I will endeavour to clear up a little further.

The believer's non-condemnation, as you have heard, is brought about, partly by sanctification, in which the strength and dominion of sin is broken; and partly by justification, in which the guilt of sin is done away and not imputed. The first of these is done by the Spirit in the heart within, in the put-

ting forth of his mighty power in the work of regeneration : ' The law of the Spirit of life,' &c. The second is done by the Son for the person without, in that propitiatory sacrifice which he offered up to God, upon which God is atoned, reconciled, satisfied, and so doth acquit the sinner. Now the apostle, having spoken to that act which is proper to the Spirit, ver. 2, he here expressly speaks to that which was proper to, and to be effected by, the Son : ' God sending his Son in the,' &c. And he speaks of condemning sin for sin, that is, for Christ's being a sacrifice for sin ; and therefore this must properly and strictly refer to justification rather than to sanctification. Yet I would not be too nice ; for as, in a large sense, the law of sin in the foregoing verse may point to the guilt as well as to the power of sin, so here, in a large sense too, the condemning of sin may point to the abolishing of the power, as well as to the expiating of the guilt of sin. Expositors take in both, and I would not straiten the words more than needs ; though yet I conceive, in their main and primary intendment, they refer to what is done in justification. The apostle's argument then stands thus : To them for whom God sent his Son, all other ways being impossible, for sin to condemn sin, and in their stead to fulfil the righteousness of the law, to them there is no condemnation. But for believers, and such who are in Christ, God upon these terms sent his Son ; therefore to them there is no condemnation. I shall follow those interpreters who make the main scope and drift of the words to lie in this.[1]

I know there are several who go another way ;[2]

[1] Nunc sequitur expositio vel illustratio probationis, quod scilicet Dominus gratuita sua misericordia nos in Christo justificavit, id quod legi erat impossibile.—*Calvin.* Duobus argumentis consolationem de indemnitate piis confirmavit; quorum prius fuit, quod *Lex Spiritus,* &c. Alterum, quod *Deus misso filio suo,* &c.—*Pareus.* Jam accedit ad probationem sententiæ prioris, quæ fuit de justificatione; nempe credentes in Christum esse justificatos, seu nullam esse eis condemnationem.—*Piscat. in Paraphr.* Observandum sententiam hanc non cohærere cum proxime præcedente, sed cum priore membro versiculi primi.—*Id. in Schol.; vide* Cajet. *in locum.* Quorum causa Deus Pater misit Filium suum coæternum in carne conspicuum fieri, iis nulla est condemnatio; at qui nostra causa, &c.—*Gryn.; see* Dutch Annot.

[2] Firmamentum est in hoc versu superioris conclusionis, &c. —*Beza.* Pertinent ista declarationis vice ad id quod dixit, se

X

they making the words to be rather the further explication or continuation of that matter which is laid down in the second verse. The saints are made free from the law of sin and death. How is that brought about? Why thus, God sent his Son into the world, by whom he is reconciled to them; being reconciled, upon this he hath taken away from sin that commanding power that it had before, abolished its strength, divested it of its former dominion and regency; and this they make to be the condemning of sin in the text. Well, I will not now object anything against this interpretation. Hereafter I shall speak more to it, when I come to the more particular opening of the clause, 'And for sin condemned sin,' only at present give me leave to prefer the former.

Let us now consider the words in themselves. As to their general sense and meaning, it is plainly this, though somewhat more darkly expressed: what the law, it standing in such circumstances, could not do for the guilty, undone sinner, that God through Christ hath fully done for him.[1] This is that plain truth which they resolve themselves into.

I find some considerable difference amongst expositors in the reading of them. Some would have a word inserted, as ἐποίησε, ἐτέλεσε, *fecit*, *præstitit*:[2] thus, 'What the law could not do, in that it was weak through the flesh, God *did*, he sending his own Son,' &c. They conceive, with the addition of this one word, the sense would be more clear, and the words

would run much more smooth; but others will not admit of this addition.[1]

Some again would have the conjunctive particle καὶ, *and*—' and for sin,' &c.—to be expunged, apprehending that it makes the words to be more obscure.[2] They would have us read them thus: ' What the law,' &c., ' God sending his own Son in the likeness of sinful flesh, for sin condemned sin in the flesh.' But this, too, is not approved of, for Calvin lays a great stress upon that particle, as heightening the matter spoken of,[3] ' and for sin;' it is as much as *yea* or *even* ' for sin condemned sin,' &c. It is not a pleonasm or superfluous word, but it is *particula intensiva*, to shew the greatness and strangeness of the thing spoken of. It is not omitted by any of the Greek scholiasts, and I see no reason why we should put it out.

Tolet would solve all, first, By adding some illative word, as *ideo*, *igitur*, &c. Secondly, By turning the participle *sending* into the verb *sent*. Of which hereafter.

Take the words in the gross, as I am now considering them, I think our translators render them very well; and there will be no necessity either to add to them, or to take from them. Only it is necessary that you make this variation or addition, whereas it is said, ' and for sin condemned sin,'—read, ' and by a sin-offering, or sacrifice for sin, condemned sin.' And so they will run thus, ' For what the law could not do, in that it was weak through the flesh, God sending (or sent) his own Son in the likeness of sin-

---

per legem Spiritus, &c., et transfert totius hujus negotii causam et meritum in gratiam Dei.—*Muscul.* He proves the foresaid making free, because that God being reconciled by Christ's death, he hath taken away from sin that power, which he had granted it over man for a punishment of his first transgression. —*Deod.* Hic affertur ratio, qua ostenditur istum Dei Spiritum liberatorem nobis donatum esse, &c.—*Pet. Mart.* Ratio superioris sententiæ, qua explicat apostolus quomodo lex Spiritus, &c.—*Justin.* Hic versus continet ætiologiam itemque exegesin eorum quæ versu secundo dicta fuerunt.—*Vorst.* So *Staplet.*, *Streso*, *Rolloc*, &c.

[1] Quod impossibile erat legi, Deus in Christo fecit.—*Anselm.* Mens apostoli hoc loco est etsi verbis obscurioribus expressa, id nobis præstitum per gratiam quod lex præstare non potuit.—*Estius.* ὁ ὁ νόμος ἐβούλετο, ἠσθένει δὲ, τοῦτο Χριστὸς ἐποίησε δι' ἡμᾶς—*Theophyl.*

[2] Mihi locum hunc pro virili mea perpendenti, videtur aliquid verborum deesse ad explendam sententiam, veluti si sic legamus; nam quod lex Mosaica non potuit juxta partem carnalem, secundum quam imbecillis erat et inefficax, hoc Deus *præstitit* misso Filio suo, qui Spiritualem legis partem absolvit.—*Erasm.*

Subaudiendum verbum *præstitit*, aut aliquid simile.—*Estius.* Omnino videtur ἐλλείπειν verbum ἐποίησε aut simile.—*Piscat.* Ut huic malo succurreretur tale quid enim necessario intelligendum est.—*Staplet. Antid.*, p. 626. Sane conjunctio et postulare videtur, ut aliquid subaudiatur, ut sensus sit, *perfecit* id Deus quod lex efficere non poterat.—*Justin.* Subaudiendum videtur *præstitit*, aut aliquid hujusmodi.—*Bucer.* To the same purpose, *Salmer*, tom. xiii. p. 531; *Catharin Vorst.*, *Muscul.*, *Heming.*, &c.

[1] Hoc supplementum non est necessarium.—*Tolet.*, &c. Sed non est opus, et Socinus hæreticus illud ad suam blasphemiam trahit.—*Pareus.* Mihi videtur aliter contextus optime fluere. —*Calv.*

[2] Una tantum conjunctione expuncta, nullo præterea opus est supplemento.—*Soto*, with divers others.

[3] Copula καὶ Erasmum decepit, ut insereret verbum *præstitit*, ego vero amplificandi causa positam fuisse sentio.— *Calv.*

ful flesh, and by a sacrifice for sin condemned sin in the flesh : that the righteousness,' &c.

There are great difficulties in their several branches and parts ; but they shall be opened as I go over them in their order.

If you take them in pieces, you have these five things in them :—

1. It is here implied that something was to be done in order to the recovery, justification, salvation of the lost sinner.

2. Here is an express assertion of the weakness, inability of the law to do what was to be done ; with the true cause of that inability of the law : ' What the law could not do, in that it was weak through the flesh.'

3. The way and method which the wise and gracious God took upon this, that he might effectually do that which the law could not do : he ' sent his own Son in the likeness of sinful flesh.'

4. The double effect produced by this, or the double end and design of God in this sending of his Son : ' For sin he condemned sin in the flesh ; that the righteousness of the law might be fulfilled.'

5. The description of the persons who have an interest in all this grace : ' Who walk not after the flesh, but after the Spirit.'

We have in the whole a complication of the several causes of the sinner's justification and redemption. Here is the deficient cause, the law ; here is the principal efficient cause, God the Father ; here is the subordinate agent, (I mean with respect to the Father,) or the meritorious cause, Christ the Son ; the formal and also the material cause, ' for sin condemning sin in the flesh ;' the final cause, the *finis cujus*, ' that the righteousness of the law might be fulfilled,' and the *finis cui*, ' in us, who walk not after the flesh, but,' &c. Here I bring in the words ' for sin condemned sin' under another head of causes than that laid down but now in the division of the words ; but that I may do well enough, because they will bear diverse causal respects.

I begin with the *causa deficiens*, which comes in also as the procataric or impulsive cause, as that which moved God to send his Son, viz,, the weakness and impotency of the law to help the lost sinner.

For what the law could not do, in that it was weak through the flesh. Here observe,

1. The thing spoken of, *the law.*

2. That which is asserted concerning this law, *it could not do.*

3. The ground or reason of this its inability to do, *in that it was weak.*

4. The assignation of the true cause of its weakness, viz., the flesh, *in that it was weak through the flesh.* It could not do because it was weak, and it was weak because of the flesh.

I will a little insist upon the literal explication of this branch, and then come to the matter contained in it.

For what the law could not do. In the Greek it is τὸ γὰρ ἀδύνατον τοῦ νόμου ; which, if you render word for word, runs thus : For the impossible of the law, or the invalid of the law ; so Tertullian renders it.[1] The sense and meaning of the expression is plain enough ; our translation gives us that very well, ' What the law could not do ;' but the form and manner of it in the original, especially when it is turned into our language, is somewhat harsh and unusual.

Interpreters, for the opening of the phrase and the clearing up of the connexion of the matter, do several ways comment upon the words. Some bring in this first paragraph under a parenthesis ; but that signifies but little one way or another. Some would read it absolutely, and change the nominative case into the genitive, the Greeks using that case as the Latins do the ablative in that form of expression ;[2] thus, for τὸ ἀδύνατον τοῦ νόμου, they turn it τοῦ νόμου ἀδυνάτου, or ἀδυναμένου, the law being unable, in that it was weak through the flesh, God sent, &c. Some take it in the accusative case, and put in the word ἐποίησε ; the impossible part of the law God performed or made good by the sending of Christ. Some change the τὸ into ὅ, putting in ἦν, (ὅ ἦν ἀδύνατον ;) what was the impossible of the law, or to the law, that God supplied by the sending of his Son ; this comes nearest to our transla-

---

[1] Quod invalidum erat legis.—*De Resur. carnis*, cap. 46.

[2] τοῦ ἀδυνάτου τοῦ νόμου, impotentia legis existente.—*Beza.* Mihi placet, ut ἀδύνατον nominativus positus sit absolute loco genitivi, ut sensus sit, cum enim esset impossibile, &c.—*Erasm.* Fateri necesse est Pauli orationem mutilam esse et imperfectam, nisi dicamus, τὸ ἀδύνατον positum esse absolute loco secundi casus, quo Græci eo firme modo utuntur quo Latini casu auferendi, &c.—*Justin.*

tion. Some make the *impossibile legis* to be taken
substantivè, for *impossibilitas implendæ legis ;*[1] which
impossibility of fulfilling the law proceeded from
hence, because the law was weak through the flesh.
Some tell us[2] the words are an atticism, and they
make a double atticism in them ; it is first τὸ ἀδύνατον
for διὰ τὸ ἀδύνατον, and then it is διὰ τὸ ἀδύνατον for
διὰ τὴν ἀδυναμίαν. Then the sense of them runs
thus : For the impotency and inability, or because
of the impotency and inability of the law, therefore
God sent his Son. The ancient versions bring it in
with a *since* or *because;*[3] since there was an utter
impossibility or inability in the law to justify or recover lost man, therefore God pitched upon another
way, viz., the incarnation, obedience, satisfaction of
his own Son. I thought it not amiss to put down
these several explications and readings of the words
for the satisfaction of more inquisitive persons concerning the expression itself, and the coherence of
the matter ; but as to the plain sense, that our translators, as I said before, give us very well : 'For what
the law could not do, or because of the law's inability to do, in that it was weak through the flesh,
therefore God sent his Son,' &c.

I pass from the letter of the words to the matter
contained in them ; and that may be summed up in
these two propositions :

Prop. 1. There was something to be done by and
for the sinner which the law could not do ; it was
under an impossibility of doing it.

Prop. 2. Therefore the law could not thus do, because it was weak through the flesh.

For the better understanding of which propositions, it will be necessary to resolve these four
questions :

1. Of what law doth the apostle here speak ?
2. What was the τὸ ἀδύνατον τοῦ νόμου, that which
the law could not do ?

3. How is the law said to be weak ?
4. What is meant by the *flesh*, from which the
law's weakness proceeds ?

Quest. 1. First, Of what law doth the apostle here
speak, when he saith, What the law could not do ?

Ans. I answer, Of God's own law, and that too
in its strict and proper acceptation. For the word
law is taken sometimes in an improper, allusive,
metaphorical notion ; as in the verse foregoing,
where you read of the 'law of the Spirit' and of
the 'law of sin,' which is nothing but the power
and commanding efficacy of the Spirit and of sin.
But here in this verse it is to be taken in the strict
and proper notion of a law, viz., as it notes that declaration or revelation which God, the great lawgiver, hath made of his will, therein binding and
obliging the reasonable creature to duty. I know
some understand the law here of that law of the
mind spoken of, chap. vii. 23,[1] which lies in strong
propensions, efficacious and commanding impulsions
to what is holy and good, springing from the sanctified nature in regenerate persons. But I conceive
this interpretation is not so genuine, nor so well
suiting with the apostle's scope in the words ; where
he is treating not of the law which is in some persons, but of the law which is imposed upon all ; of
that law the righteousness of which was to be fulfilled, as it follows, ver. 4 ; and therefore it must
be understood of God's own law, that being it which
Christ was to fulfil and satisfy, and not any other
law.

Since then the words point to the law of God,
we must bring the question into a narrower compass, and inquire, What law of God is here spoken
of ? For answer to which, that I may as much as I
can avoid unnecessary excursions, I shall only say
this, that it is either that primitive law which God
imposed upon Adam, and in him upon all mankind,
upon the keeping of which he promised life, upon
the breaking of which he threatened death, it being
the summary of the covenant of works ; or else it is
that law which God gave the people of Israel from

---

[1] Impossibile legis: *i.e.*, impossibilitas implendæ legis ex
eo procedebat, quoniam lex infirma erat per carnem.—*Tolet.*

[2] So Camerarius. τὸ ἀδύνατον τοῦ νόμου Attica constructione
usitata accipi commode potest, pro ἥτις ἦν ἀδυναμία τοῦ νόμου.
—*Beza.* Propter impotentiam legis, eo quod per carnem erat
infirmata.—*Pare.*

[3] Quum impotens esset lex propter infirmitatem carnis, &c.
—*V. Syr.* Ob defectum virium legis, quo laborabat in carne,
&c.—*V. Arab.* Et cum impotentes eramus ad præstandum
mandata legis, &c.—*V. Ethiop.*

---

[1] Lex mentis, quæ impleri non poterat propter carnem peccati.—*Tolet.* Crediderim ego, non hic legem Mosis, sed legem
illam mentis accipiendam esse.—*Justin.* Potest et de lege
mentis intelligi, quam supra dixit velle facere bonum, sed per
infirmitatem et fragilitatem carnis implere non posse.—*Orig.*

Mount Sinai, namely, the decalogue or moral law. Which law was but a new draft of the law first made with Adam; for that being by his fall much defaced, nay, almost quite obliterated, as it was written in his heart, it pleased the Lord to copy it out again, and to write it afresh, in tables of stone, in fair and legible characters. And this, too, was a scheme or transcript and summary of the covenant of works first made with Adam, though it was not given to the people of Israel purely and absolutely as the covenant of works, for in reference to its end and design there was much in it of the covenant of grace. For matter and substance they were both but one and the same law; the terms and conditions of both were the same, 'Do and live,' Rom. x. 5; but there were certain appendixes of grace to the moral law, which were not in that made with Adam in the state of innocency, as is fully made out by several writers upon the covenant;[1] so that it was a mixed thing, there being something in it of the covenant of works, and something also of the covenant of grace. Now the law considered as first given to Adam, and then as renewed to the people of Israel, so far as in both it was the covenant of works, is the law here spoken of as being concluded under an impossibility of doing what was requisite to be done. It was not the ceremonial law which the apostle here had in his eye, but the moral law itself,[2] which, if it was necessary, might be evinced by several considerations; but this one is enough, he speaks of that law, the righteousness of which was to be fulfilled in believers, for law in the 3d verse must be expounded by law in the 4th verse; now it is the righteousness of the moral law which is fulfilled in us; ergo, it is very true, Paul insisting upon the law's weakness, doth sometimes direct his discourse to the ceremonial, and sometimes to the moral law; and it would be of great use to us to understand his epistles, if we could exactly hit upon the true notion of that law of which he occasionally speaks; but undoubtedly here it was the moral law,

as the covenant of works, of which he affirmeth that 'it could not do,' &c. Let this suffice for answer to the first question.

Quest. 2. The second is, What doth this impossible of the law refer to? or what is the thing in special which the law could not do?

Ans. To this it is answered several ways. You read, ver. 1, of exemption from condemnation; now this the law could not do; the law, in separation from Christ, and especially in opposition to Christ, can condemn millions, but it cannot save one person from condemnation. Thus some do open it.[1] You read, ver. 2, of being made free from the law of sin and death. Herein, too, was the law impotent; it might lay some restraints upon sin, but it could never bring down the power of sin. Some apply it to this.[2] There is the blessed empire or regency of the Spirit over the flesh, as also the full and perfect obeying of the law's commands; neither of these could the law effect. So Cajetan opens it.[3] There is the amendment and reformation of the life and manners; this the law could not do. This explication some fix upon.[4] The text speaks of the condemning of sin; this the law could not do; it can condemn the sinner, but it cannot, in a way of expiation, condemn sin itself. So De Dieu paraphraseth upon it.[5] Musculus puts many things together.[6] What is it, saith he, that was impossible to the law? He answers, To abolish sin, to make righteous, to free from the law of sin and death, to give that the righteousness which it taught and exacted should be fulfilled in us.

All these several explications are very true; but,

---

[1] Camero de tripl. Fœdere; Cocceius de Fœdere; Bulkely on the Covenant, p. 57.

[2] Legem dicit, non præcepta sacrificiorum, et cætera quæ erant umbra usque ad tempus Christi data, sed illam quam, &c.—*Hieron.* Quare nihil est quod quisquam cavilletur, illud quod Paulus ait impossibile fuisse legi, non ad moralem sed ad ceremonias referri.—*P. Martyr.*

[1] Nempe condemnationem ab homine auferre.—*Piscat.*

[2] Aptissimus mihi sensus videtur, ut illa verba non modo sequentia, sed multo magis præcedentia respiciant, &c., ut in carnis contumaciam domandam vires non haberet.—*Contz.*

[3] Duo quantum ad propositum spectat subordinata sunt, quæ lex nequit efficere. Alterum est Dominium Spiritus super carnem, alterum hinc consequens est, perfecta præceptorum legis executio.—*Cajet.*

[4] Dr Hammond.

[5] Quæ erat impossibilitas legis? nempe id facere, quod Deus deinde fecit in carne Filii sui, condemnare peccatum.—*Lud. De Dieu.*

[6] Quid est illud, quod legi erat præstitu impossibile? Abolere peccatum, et reddere justos, liberare a jure peccati et mortis, dare ut justitia, quam docebat et exigebat, in nobis impleretur.—*Muscul.*

further, there is the reconciling of God and the sinner, the atoning and propitiating of an incensed God, the satisfying of infinite justice, the paying of vast debts contracted, the justifying of the guilty, the giving of a right and title to heaven, with many other such-like great things. Now the law was under an impossibility of doing or effecting any of these; insomuch that God must send his Son, or no justification, no reconciliation, no atonement, no satisfaction, no payment, no pardon, no righteousness, no salvation [1]—which will be by and by particularly made out in the two most eminent branches of the law's impotency.

I must mind you, that I am in all this speaking of the moral law. The inability of the ceremonial law—abstracted from Christ, who was the pith and marrow, and who put energy and efficacy into all the types, rites, shadows of that law—I say, its inability to do anything, further than to point or direct and lead to Christ, is easily granted. It is the very thing which the apostle largely insists upon the proof of in his excellent Epistle to the Hebrews, chap. vii. 18, 19, 'For there is verily a disannulling of the commandment going before, for *the weakness* and unprofitableness thereof; for the law made nothing perfect; but the bringing in of a better hope did, by the which we draw nigh unto God.' Heb. ix. 9, 'Which was a figure for the time then present, in which were offered both gifts and sacrifices, that *could not* make him that did the service perfect, as pertaining to the conscience.' So Heb. x. 1, 'For the law having a shadow of good things to come, and not the very image of the things, *can never*, with those sacrifices which they offered year by year continually, make the comers thereunto perfect,' (οὐδέποτε δύναται; here is a total negation of the ceremonial law.) And that law had its ἀδύνατον also; for the apostle adds, ver. 4, 'It is not possible' (ἀδύνατον γὰρ) 'that the blood of bulls and goats should take away sins.' Thus it was with that law, of which it is very clear Paul speaks in these places. And it was but little better with the moral law itself, though that was a far higher and better law; even this was and is as weak as the former. This

very law, which is so much for doing, which requires and commands the creature to be so much in doing, itself can do little or nothing. The lost sinner hath great things to be done by him and for him; but in all these the moral law, though God's own law, and an excellent law, cannot, without Christ, give the least help or assistance to him.

Quest. 3. The third inquiry is, What is the weakness of the law here spoken of?

Ans. The word is ἠσθένει, which is used to set forth any debility or weakness, whether it be natural or preternatural, as being occasioned by some bodily disease or distemper, in which sense it is often used in the New Testament. It is applied here to the law; and it is brought in as the ground of its τὸ ἀδύνατον before mentioned. Elsewhere the apostle uses it, he speaks of the τὸ ἀσθενὲς τῆς ἐντολῆς, 'the weakness of the commandment,' Heb. vii. 18. And speaking of the ordinances, rites, injunctions of the ceremonial law, he calls them τα ἀσθενῆ καὶ πτωχὰ στοιχεῖα, 'weak and beggarly elements,' Gal. iv. 9. Here, in the text, a higher law was in his eye, and yet he attributes weakness to it also: it could not do because it was weak, and it was weak because it could not do; for these two do reciprocally open and prove each the other.

And let me add, that this weakness of the law is not gradual or partial, but total;[1] it is not the having of a lesser strength, but it is the negation of all strength; it is so weak that it hath no power at all to accomplish what is here intended. The apostle carries it up to an impossibility: he doth not say it was somewhat hard or difficult for the law to do thus and thus, or that it could do something, though but imperfectly; but he says this was impossible to it, as being utterly above its power and ability. A man that is weak may do something, though he

---

[1] ἠσθένει ὁ νόμος εἰς τὸ δικαιωθῆναι τὸν ἄνθρωπον.—*Athan.* Significat legem fuisse imbecillem et invalidam ad justificandum hominem.—*Perer. Disp.* 3, in cap. 8, ad Rom.

[1] Ἀσθένεια ex qua τὸ ἀδύνατον τοῦ νόμου nascitur, virium non imbecillitatem, sed omnem destitutionem declarat.—*Beza.* Non dicit, quod legi erat grave et difficile, sed quod, &c., quibus sane verbis adimit legi in universum justificandi vim, &c.—*Muscul.* Infirmitatem legis accipe, quomodo solet usurpare apostolus vocabulum ἀσθενείας, non tantum pro modica imbecillitate, verum pro impotentia; ut significet legem nihil prorsus momenti habere ad conferendam justitiam.—*Calv.* Quamquam per verbum *infirmari* ἀσθενεῖν ab interprete versum sit, vis tamen illius verbi Græce potius significat vires nullas quam imbecillas.—*Salmer.*, tom. xiii. p. 532.

cannot do it vigorously, exactly, and thoroughly; but now, as to justification and salvation, the law, considered in itself, is so weak that it can do nothing; it cannot have the least influence into these effects, further than as God is pleased to make use of it in a preparatory or directive manner. Its weakness as to the great things of the gospel is like the weakness of the body when it is dead. 1 Cor. xv. 43, 'It is sown in weakness,' (ἐν ἀσθενείᾳ, it is the same word with that in the text concerning the law,) 'it is raised in power.' A dead body is so weak that it cannot put forth one vital act; it may be weak in part whilst it lives, but when it is dead it lies under a total weakness. Such is the weakness or impotency of the law in reference to the taking away of guilt, and the making of a person righteous before God.

Quest. 4. Fourthly, It will be queried what the flesh is here by which the law is made thus weak?

Ans. The word *flesh* occurs thrice in this verse, &c.: 'In that it was weak through the *flesh*, God sent his Son in the likeness of sinful *flesh*, and for sin condemned sin in the *flesh*.' As it is used in the first place, it carries in it a very different sense from what it doth in the two following places; and it is not unusual in holy writ for one and the same word in one and the same verse to be taken in different senses; as you may see Mat. xxvi. 29, and viii. 22. When it is said the law was weak through the flesh; here flesh is taken morally for the corrupt nature in man: but when it is said, God sent his Son in the likeness of sinful flesh, and so on, there flesh is taken physically, for the human nature of Christ. But to come to the business in hand. The law was 'weak *through the flesh.*' By this flesh, the Manichees of old understood the very being and substance of flesh, that which constitutes the body in man; but this interpretation is rejected by all. Origen, with some others, expounds it of the ceremonial law,[1] with re-

spect to the gross and literal sense and meaning of that law. Now it is true, as hath been already observed, that that law may be styled *flesh*, because it lay very much in fleshly things; it is called 'the law of a carnal commandment,' Heb. vii. 16; 'it stood only in meats, and drinks, and divers washings, and carnal ordinances, imposed till the time of reformation,' Heb. ix. 10. And it is also most true, that they who looked no further than the fleshly part, the letter of that law, who did *hærere in cortice* and only *rodere literarum ossa*, as the Jews did, to them it must needs be weak, and unable to bring about any evangelical and saving good. But this is not the law, as you have heard, which the apostle here doth mainly intend. Beza is very sharp against Origen for this his exposition of the flesh.[1] Cajetaine interprets it of the carnal state of the Jews under the law; they being in that state, by means thereof to them the law was weak. But, as to this explication, our learned annotator well observes,[2] that *flesh* here is not so properly the state of men under the law, as that which is the means by which occasionally the law became weak and unable to restrain men, viz., the carnal or fleshly appetite which is so contrary to the proposals of the law; therefore he expounds it by that, and Grotius before him went the same way.[3] The fullest and best interpretation of this *flesh*, and that which is most generally followed, is this: it is the corrupt, sinful, depraved nature that is in fallen man.[4] Oh this is

---

carnalem legis intelligentiam, sive carnis infirmitatem, cui deerat evangelica gratia.—*Erasm.* Origenes per carnem intelligit crassam, literalem, et carnalem legis intelligentiam; atque etiam legis infirmitatem in eo collocat, quod impossibile fuerit legis ceremonias omnes secundum carnem, *i.e.*, secundum literam observare.—*A Lapide.*

[1] Distinguit hoc loco impurissimus ille scriptor legem in carnem et spiritum, &c.—*Beza in loc.*

[2] Dr Hammond in Annot. (a)

[3] Caro, *i.e.*, carnales judæorum affectus vires ejus retuderant. Acts xiii. 38; Heb. ix. 15.—*Grot.*

[4] Per carnem, *i.e.*, vitiatam hominis naturam, *Piscat*, &c., *i.e.*, per carnis desideria, et per fomitem vitiorum qui est in carne.—*Anselm.* Ideo lex infirma est, quia in vitiatam naturam incurrit.—*P. Mart.* Quum vel legem infirmatam fuisse, &c., nemo sibi finget damnari hic substantiam carnis aut naturam corporis, nam hæc a Deo creata sunt bona; sed per carnem intelligit pravitatem et corruptionem, quæ per lapsum Adami transivit in nostrum genus.—*Idem.*

---

[1] Puto quod legem Mosis in duas partes apostolus dividat, et aliud in ea carnem, aliud Spiritum nominat; et illam quidem observantiam quæ secundum literam geritur, sensum carnis appellat, illam vero quæ accipitur spiritualiter, Spiritum nominat—impossibile legis eo quod, &c. Intellectus qui secundum literam est accipi potest, ipse enim impossibilis erat, &c.—*Orig.* Vel per carnem infirmabatur lex, *i.e.*, per carnalem intellectum, et per carnalem observantiam erat imbecilla, non per seipsam.—*Anselm.* Per carnem, *h.e.*, Per

that which puts such a weakness and inability upon the law, to help and recover the undone sinner! it is by this that the law is so enfeebled and debilitated as to its production of any spiritual or saving effects. The apostle lays it upon this, 'the law could not do, *in that* it was weak through the flesh,' that is, because it was weak through the flesh. For the ἐν ᾧ, is causal;[1] therefore it is usually rendered here by *quia, quoniam, quandoquidem, eo quod,* &c. And so it is in other places, as Heb. ii. 18, 'For *in that* he himself hath suffered,' ἐν ᾧ γὰρ πέπονθεν, because he hath suffered, 'being tempted, he is able to succour them that are tempted:' it is as much as the ἐφ' ᾧ, Rom. v. 12. Sometimes indeed it is only expressive of such a time or state or condition: as Mark ii. 19, 'Can the children of the bride-chamber fast *while* the bridegroom is with them?' ἐν ᾧ ὁ νύμφιος. Sometimes again it is rendered by *whereas,* as 1 Peter ii. 12, and iii. 16; but here in the text it is taken causally.

Let it then be observed, that the weakness of the law is not properly inherent or from the law itself, only it is adventitious, accidental, and from the state and condition of the subject with whom it hath to do.[2] It is the wickedness of man's nature which is the sole cause of the law's weakness. If man was the same now that at first he was, the law would be the same too now that at first it was, and have the same power and ability that then it had; but he being fallen now the law is weakened. It is not, I say, from any intrinsic defect or weakness in the law, but only because it meets with a subject in which there is flesh, a depraved nature; and so it cannot do that which before it did, when the nature was holy and good. When man was in the state of innocency, the law, Samson-like, was in its full strength, and could do whatever was proper to it; yea, as to itself, it is able yet to do the same; but the case with us is altered: we cannot now fulfil this law, nor come up to what it requires of us, and therefore it is weak. True, the apostle lays it upon

the weakness of the law: he saith it was weak; but then he tells you what was the ground of that weakness, namely, our flesh. The law is only weak *to us* because we are weak *to it:* the strongest sword in a weak hand can do but little execution; the brightest sun cannot give light to a blind eye, not from any impotency in itself, but merely from the incapacity of the subject; and that is the case in the law's ἀδυναμία with respect to the sinner. Pray observe, the law strengthens sin, and sin weakens the law: 1 Cor. xv. 56, 'The strength of sin is the law;' viz., as the law gives it a killing and condemning power, and as, through man's corruption, it makes sin to be more active, impetuous, and boisterous, thus sin is strengthened by the law. But then the weakness of the law is sin, for because of that it cannot now do what formerly it could.

Thus I have answered the four questions propounded; under which I have cleared up the words, and also, in part, the matter contained in them. Which being done, I might from the whole raise this observation, that the law, yea, the moral law itself, though it was an excellent law, the law of God's own making, and designed by him for high and excellent ends, yet it having now to do with fallen man, with sinners that have flesh (a corrupt nature) in them, it is become weak and altogether unable to justify and save.

I must not enter upon any large prosecution of this point, yet let me speak something to it, both to fill up what I have hitherto but just touched upon, and also to supply what as yet I have said nothing to. There are but two things which I would further open:

1. The special matter of the law's weakness.

2. The grounds or demonstrations of the law's weakness.

For the first, the special matter of the law's weakness, that will be cleared up,

1. With respect to justification.

2. With respect to salvation and eternal life. 'What the law could not do in that it was weak.' What was the thing particularly which the law could not do? what did its weakness especially refer to? *Ans.* The Scripture mainly fixes it upon these two things; it could not justify, it could not eternally save. There are indeed many other things—some

---

[1] ἐν ᾧ valet hic *quia,* more Hebraico.—*Grot.*

[2] Impotentia legis, &c., non fuit ex ipsa lege, quasi justificare homines eam præstantes nequiret, sed ex carne, *h.e.,* ex corruptione naturæ humanæ, quæ hominem reddit impotentem ad præstandam legem.—*Pareus.* Non infirmitatem illi impingit quasi intrinsecus inhærentem, sed quasi extrinsecus ratione carnis ei adjacentem.—*Soto.*

of which have been already hinted—which the law could not do; but these two are most usually instanced in, in the word when it speaks of, or would set forth the law's weakness.

1. The law, upon its terms of doing and working, ever since man's fall, always was, and yet is, unable to justify; it may possibly attempt such a thing, or rather the sinner may look for such a thing from it, but it cannot carry it on to any good issue. This, I conceive, Paul's thoughts were in special upon, when he says 'what the law could not do;' for it is the sinner's justification which he in this place is discoursing of, and he first begins with the law, as being impotent and insufficient to accomplish this justification. God by Christ condemned sin, i.e., he abolished and cut off sin's guilt, and by him he brought about a righteousness for the sinner; but the doing of this by the law was a thing altogether impossible—that could not make the creature to cease to be guilty, or to become righteous. The proving of this truth was elsewhere his main business, as, namely, in the 3d, 4th, 5th chapters of this epistle, where he doth professedly and largely insist upon it. That one place is a sufficient proof of it, chap. iii. 20, 'Therefore by the deeds of the law there shall no flesh be justified in his sight: for by the law is the knowledge of sin.' He pursues the same argument in his Epistle to the Galatians, where he goes over it again and again: Gal. ii. 16–21, 'Knowing that a man is not justified by the works of the law, but by the faith of Jesus Christ, even we have believed in Jesus Christ, that we might be justified by the faith of Christ, and not by the works of the law; for by the works of the law shall no flesh be justified. I do not frustrate the grace of God; for if righteousness come by the law, then Christ is dead in vain,' Gal. iii. 11, 21, 22, 'But that no man is justified by the law in the sight of God, it is evident: for the just shall live by faith. Is the law then against the promises of God? God forbid: for if there had been a law given which could have given life, verily righteousness should have been by the law. But the Scripture hath concluded all under sin, that the promise by faith of Jesus Christ might be given to them that believe.' So also in his sermon at Antioch, Acts xiii. 39, 'By him all that believe are justified from all things,

from which ye could not be justified by the law of Moses.' How full and positive are the Scriptures in the denial of any power to the law to justify! It can discover sin, accuse and judge for sin, but it cannot expiate sin, or make a man righteous before God. There is indeed the righteousness of the law, and upon that, righteousness by the law; but that now is altogether unattainable, further than as it is brought about and accomplished in the hands of Christ. The law in Christ's hands can do great things, but in ours it can do nothing.

2. So also the law is weak in reference to eternal life. 'It could not do,' i.e., it could not save; it never yet, as separated from Christ, carried one sinner to heaven: it is above the ability of the law to save one soul. Consider it as the covenant of works; so its language is 'Do and live:' Rom. x. 5, 'For Moses describeth the righteousness of the law, that the man which doth these things shall live by them.' Now man in his lapsed state cannot do according to the law's demands, therefore by it there is no life for him. Had he continued in the state of innocency, he had been able to have done all which the law required, and so would have attained life by it in the way of doing; but now the case is altered. If salvation depended upon the creature's perfect and personal obedience, not a man would be saved. There must indeed be obedience to the law, or no salvation; but should it be that very obedience which the law calls for, and as the law calls for it, viz., as the condition of the first covenant, this would make salvation absolutely impossible. You know Moses brought Israel to the borders of the Holy Land, but Joshua must lead them into it; so the law, as God uses it in subserviency to the gospel, may do something towards the saving of a poor creature; but it is the alone merit and obedience of the Lord Jesus, applied by faith, which must put the sinner into the possession of the heavenly rest. That which now saves is Christ, not Moses; the gospel, not the law; believing, not doing: I mean only in the old covenant sense. So much for the matter of the law's impotency.

Secondly, Let me give you the grounds, or, if you will, the demonstrations of the law's impotency and weakness to justify and save. I will instance in three:

1. It requires that which the creature cannot per-
Y

form. Before the law do any great thing for a person, it must first be exactly fulfilled. For that is its way, the terms and condition which it stands upon, and it is as high in these terms now as ever it was : for though man hath lost his power, the law hath not lost its rigour ; it doth not sink or fall in its demands because of man's inability to answer them. Though the sinner be as the poor broken debtor, utterly undone, yet the law will not compound with him, or abate him anything, but it will have full payment of the whole debt. Now this, *in statu lapso*, as I shall shew when I come to the 4th verse, is impossible.[1] None but such a one as Christ could thus answer the law's demands. For nothing will serve it below perfection : inherent righteousness, actual obedience, all must be perfect, or else the law despises them. The gospel accepts of sincerity, but the law will bate nothing of perfection ; if there be but the least failure, all is spoiled : Gal. iii. 10, 'For as many as are of the works of the law, are under the curse ; for it is written, Cursed is every one that continueth not *in all things* which are written in the book of the law to do them :' James ii. 10, 'For whosoever shall keep the whole law, and yet offend *in one point*, he is guilty of all.' And is it thus ? Are these the terms and demands of the law ? What then can it do ? or rather what can we do ? It must needs be weak to us, because, in these rigours, we are so weak to it ; it cannot do much for us, because we can do but little to it ; it cannot do what we desire, because we cannot do what it demands. Oh how exceeding short do the best come of the high measures of the law ! 'Who can say, I have made my heart clean ; I am pure from my sin,' Prov. xx. 9. 'In many things we offend all,' James iii. 2. 'There is not a just man upon earth, that doeth good, and sinneth not,' Eccles. vii. 20. 'Our very righteousness is as a polluted rag,' Isa. lxiv. 6. 'How should man be just with God ? If he will contend with him, he cannot answer him one of a thousand. If I justify myself, mine own mouth shall condemn me ; if I say I am

perfect, it shall also prove me perverse,' Job ix. 2, 3. See Job xv. 14–16 ; Job xxv. 4–6. 'If thou, Lord, shouldst mark iniquities, O Lord, who shall stand ?' Ps. cxxx. 3. 'Enter not into judgment with thy servant, for in thy sight shall no man living be justified,' Ps. cxliii. 2.[1]

2. The law doth not give what the creature needs ;[2] it asks above his strength, and gives below his want. He must have grace, sanctification, holiness, &c., but will the law help him to these ? no ; it is high in the commanding of them, but that is all, it doth not work them in the soul ; it asks very high, but gives very low. It is holy itself, but it cannot make others holy ; it can discover sin, but it cannot mortify sin ; as the glass discovers the spots and blemishes in the face, but doth not remove them. The law is a killing thing, 2 Cor. iii. 6, but it is of the sinner, not of the sin : it hath by accident, by reason of the flesh here spoken of, a quite other effect ; for it doth rather enliven, increase, and irritate sin, as water meeting with opposition grows the more fierce and violent ; and the disease, the more it is checked by the medicine, the more it rages.[3] Paul found in himself this sad effect of the law : Rom. vii. 8, 'But sin taking occasion by the commandment, wrought in me all manner of concupiscence : for without the law sin was dead.' Moreover, the law calls for duty, but it gives no strength for the performance of it,[4] Pharaoh-like, who exacted

---

[1] Unde sequitur plus in lege præcipi, quam præstando simus, quia si pares essemus implendæ legi, frustra aliunde esset quæsitum remedium.—*Calvin.* Hic locus efficacissime convincit justificationem non esse ex operibus, &c.—*P. Martyr.* Non implet legem infirmitas mea, sed laudat legem voluntas mea. —*August.*

[1] Quis melior propheta de quo dixit Deus, inveni virum secundum cor meum, et tamen ipse necesse habuit dicere Deo, 'Ne intres in judicium cum servo tuo.'—*Bernard. in Annunt. Mariæ.* Sine peccato qui se vivere existimet, non id agit ut peccatum non habeat, sed ut veniam non accipiat.—*August. Enchirid.* In pessimis aliquid boni, et in optimis nonnihil pessimi, solus homo sine peccato Christus.—*Tertul.*

[2] Lex Moysi quamvis spiritualis esset, quia tamen non adjuvabat intus per gratiam, lex erat infirma et imbecillis ob statum carnalem hominum, in quo relinquebat illos.—*Cajet.* Non quod ipsa infirma sit, sed quod infirmos faciat, minando pœnam, nec adjuvando per gratiam.—*Anselm.* Lex præterquam quod peccati rationem aperiebat, nihil præterea auxilii præstabat Spiritui adversus carnem, et ideo neque sufficiebat ad justificandum, neque ad perficienda legis opera.—*Soto.*

[3] Non de legis præstatione hic agitur, sed de ipsius vi in nostris immutandis animis, et ad illud legis præscriptum efformandis, utpote quæ corruptionem illam in qua nascimur non modo non sanet, sed augeat potius.—*Beza.*

[4] Per legem non adjutorium sed nostri mali indicium et monitorium habemus.—*Luther.*

brick, but allowed no straw. The gospel helps where it commands, the law commands but helps not : *Lex jubet, evangelium juvat.* Remember I still speak of the law as it stands in opposition to the gospel, and as it is the matter and transcript of the first covenant. It neither pardons what it forbids, nor doth it enable to do what it enjoins ; and much of the ἀδυναμία, impotency of the law, lies in these two things.[1] Take a particular instance, great is the sinner's need of faith ; for without this, no justification, no peace with God, no heaven ; it is the gospel-condition on which all depends. Now the law knows nothing of this faith ; nay, it is diametrically opposite to it ; it is so far from working it that it hinders it to its utmost. It is all for working, for doing : Gal. iii. 12, 'And the law is not of faith : but the man that doth them shall live in them.' Believing belongs only to the gospel ; therefore that is styled the law of works, and this the law of faith, Rom. iii. 27. If faith come under the law, it is only that faith which is a general faith, or as it is a part of obedience, not as the condition of gospel grace. The law therefore not helping as to these things, so indispensably necessary for grace here and hereafter, what can it do for the lost sinner ?

3. The law could not do, because it could not heal that breach which sin had made betwixt God and the sinner. It still looks forwards, and is always calling for perfect obedience ; but what if sin hath been committed for the time past ? Oh there the law is weak ! It can make no reparation for what is past ; as to that, all it says to the guilty person is, as they to Judas, Mat. xxvii. 4, 'What is that to me ? see thou to that.' Suppose the sinner could for the future come up to a full conformity to the law, and in everything answer its highest commands. Suppose him now to arrive at such a pitch of perfection that he should do nothing which this law forbids, and do everything which this law commands : yet, supposing the fall from God, and

the guilt thereby contracted, or any one sin committed, the law would be weak, and the creature could not thereby be justified ; the reason is, because here is now reparation and satisfaction to be made for what is past, which to make is impossible to the law. This perfect obedience, present and future, might do the work, was it not for what is past ; but guilt hath been contracted, God hath been offended, his first covenant violated ; therefore there must be reparation made to him for this. Now this the law cannot do, nor the creature upon the terms of the law ; for all that he can arrive at is but perfect obedience, and that is his duty ; he is under an obligation to it, and therefore by it he can make no satisfaction for what is past : this is but the paying of the present debt, which can quit nothing of the former score. This is very well if we look forward, but what becomes of us when we look backward ? So that the apostle did very deservedly thus speak of the law, 'what the law could not do,' &c. So much for the opening of the matter held forth in these words ; let me close this head with some application.

Use 1. First, Here is matter of deep humiliation to us. How should we lament that sinful nature, that flesh which is in all of us ! we all come into the world under a sad and woeful depravation of nature. Well, suppose we do, what of this ? Oh this should bitterly be bewailed by us, because by reason of this the law is weak, that it cannot do that for us which otherwise it could and would have done. As we were created at the first, before our nature was corrupted, we were strong to the law and the law strong to us ; we could fulfil its highest demands, and it could fulfil our highest desires ; we were able to keep it and it was able to save us ; its perfect righteousness was not above us, and we had been righteous in that righteousness. But now it is far otherwise ; sin hath got into us, our natures are now depraved and vitiated, insomuch that even from this law itself we can look for nothing : it is upon our degeneracy weakened to us to all intents and purposes ; and is not this sad ? Oh that there should be such natures in us as even to debilitate and weaken God's own blessed law ! And would to God the sad effects of the flesh in us stayed here ! but it goes further : it doth not only bring a weakness upon the law, but upon the gospel too. The gospel

---

[1] Necessarius fuit adventus Christi, qui legi suppetias ferret, &c. Nam illa quidem recte docuerat, &c. Verum adhuc duo erant necessaria quæ lex conferre non potuit, 1. Ut condonentur ea quæ contra ejus precepta admissa fuerint : 2. Ut vires hominis corroborentur, quibus possit legis jussa perficere. —*P. Martyr.*

itself, the new and remedial law, though it be the power of God, Rom. i. 16, yet it would be altogether ineffectual to our justification and salvation, if God did not accompany it with a mighty power. It tenders and holds forth that in Christ which is every way sufficient for these great things; yet we should be never the better for it, this too 'could not do,' if God, in spite of all opposition from our cursed natures, did not overpower us to believe, to close with Christ, to accept of restoring grace in the way of the gospel. Truly if God should leave us to ourselves, and should not rescue us from the power of natural corruption, neither law nor gospel could do our work; notwithstanding both we should perish for ever. Should not this be greatly bewailed and lamented by us, that sin should be so rooted in our nature, and have such a strength in us, as that it should be too hard both for law and gospel, and bring both under an inability to do us good?

And is it so? I might then from hence infer, that certainly in the fallen creature the power of nature is very low; nay that, with respect to the keeping and fulfilling of the law, it is quite lost. Pelagius of old, with whom some in latter ages do almost concur, only they put a better varnish upon their opinions, held that though nature by the fall is somewhat weakened and impaired in its strength, yet still it can do great things; yea, especially with some ordinary assistance, it may enable a man to fulfil the law of God. Now against this the argument in the text is considerable :[1] is the law weak, and yet is the sinner strong? is that under an impossibility, and yet is this and that possible to the creature? The flesh is but extraneous to the law, and yet by reason of that it cannot do; but it is inherent in the sinner, and yet he can do; what more absurd! Especially it being considered, that the law's weakness is not attributed to it in respect of itself, but only in respect of us; so that if we now

could perfectly obey, perform, keep the law, its τὸ ἀδύνατον would then cease; and if so, why was Christ sent? But no more of this.

Use 2. Secondly, It is necessary that I should vindicate the honour of the law, and obviate those mistakes and bad inferences which some possibly may run upon from what hath been spoken. Three things therefore let me say to you.

1. Notwithstanding this weakness of the law, yet keep up high thoughts of it, and give it that honour and reverence which is due to it.

It is weak indeed, but yet remember whose law it is, as also what an excellent law it is in itself. It is a perfect draught or model and delineation of original righteousness; it is the measure, standard, test, of that purity and perfection which man would have had in the state of innocency; yea, it is the copy, transcript, exemplar of God's own holiness, for God framed and modelled this law according to his own purity and sanctity. And let us be what we will, still the law, in itself, is all this, and the same that ever it was, though we be not so. And therefore we should adore, and reverence, and magnify it, though now to us accidentally it be thus weak.

But doth not this weakness reflect disparagement and dishonour upon the law? *Ans.* No, not in the least. Two things will sufficiently vindicate it as to any such reflections : 1. The apostle only says of it that it was weak; he chargeth nothing upon it but only weakness. He doth not say that it was any way impure, or unholy, or unrighteous; he affirms the contrary: Rom. vii. 12, 'The law is holy, and just, and good,' only he saith it was weak. This the Greek expositors take notice of, and from it apologise for the law.[1]

2. It is weak, but how comes it to be so? Why, through our flesh.[2] It is not so in and from itself,

---

[1] Quid hic dicent naturalium virium prædicatores ac doctores? Reddant rationem quare per carnem infirma fuerit lex Dei; ita ut necessitas humanæ salutis opus habuerit missione Christi, &c. Si virtus et judicium rationis tam potens est, ut quæ bona præcipiuntur, agnoscat, approbet, et præstare valeat, quomodo in illis non potuit qui sub pædagogio legis fuerunt?—*Muscul.* Paulus ait legem sine Christo infirmam esse; isti aiunt, nos priusquam simus participes Christi posse bene operari, et obtemperare legi Dei.—*P. Martyr.*

[1] Δοκεῖ μὲν διαβάλλειν τὸν νομὸν, εἰ δὲ τις ἀκριβῶς προσέχοι, καὶ σφόδρα αὐτὸν ἐπαινεῖ, σύμφωνον τῳ Χριστῷ δεικνὺς, &c. οὐδὲ γὰρ εἶπε τὸ πονηρὸν τοῦ νόμου, ἀλλὰ τὸ ἀδύνατον. καὶ πάλιν ἐν ᾧ ἠσθένει, οὐκ ἐν ᾧ ἐκακούργει· καὶ οὐδὲ τὴν ἀσθένειαν αὐτῳ λογίζεται, ἀλλὰ τῇ σαρκὶ.—*Chrysost.* Ὁρᾶς ὅτι οὐ τοῦ νόμου καταψηφίζεται, &c.—*Oecum., Theophyl.* to the same purpose. Οὐ τοίνυν πονηρὸς ὁ νόμος, αλλ' ἀγαθὸς, ἀδύνατος δε.—*Theodor.*

[2] Ne legem incusare videatur, culpam rejicit in carnem, *i.e.*, concupiscentiam, quæ fomes est peccati—*Estius.* Vide quanta arte legem simul extollit, deprimit, et excusat. Deprimit, cum dicit quod non potuit peccatum damnare; excusat, cum dicit

but only through our depraved nature; it is merely by accident, *et aliunde*, that it lies under this impotency. The law is not to be blamed, but we; had not we sinned, the law would have been still as able and mighty in its operations as ever it was. Did it but meet with the same subject, it would soon appear that it hath the same power which it had before Adam fell. So that, I say, the law is not at all in the fault, but only we because of the flesh. Observe here the wisdom and care of our apostle; wherever he seems to tax the law, there he will be sure to vindicate it. As where he speaks of its irritating of corruption, he there lays the blame upon his own wicked nature, not at all upon the holy law: Rom. vii. 8–11, 'Sin taking occasion by the commandment, wrought in me all manner of concupiscence: for without the law sin was dead. For I was alive without the law once, but when the commandment came, sin revived, and I died. And the commandment which was ordained to life, I found to be unto death. For sin taking occasion by the commandment deceived me, and by it slew me.' Yet verses 12–14, 'The law is holy, and the commandment holy, and just, and good. Was then that which is good made death unto me? God forbid. But sin, that it might appear sin, working death in me by that which is good; that sin by the commandment might become exceeding sinful. For we know that the law is spiritual: but I am carnal, sold under sin.' And thus we should carry it with respect to the law's weakness. Oh in itself it is mighty and powerful, but there is sin in us by which only the law is made weak; there, therefore, the blame must lie. Could we but get rid of this sin, we should soon find what a mighty thing the law is, so mighty that nothing would be too high or too hard for it.

2. Secondly, Take heed that you do not cast off the law upon this pretence. It is indeed weak, as

hoc non accidisse ejus vitio, sed carnis potius; extollit quam maxime, cum concludit Christum advenisse ut legi contra carnem subsidium ferret.—*Mussus.* Transfert legis impotentiam alio, ut legem absolvat a culpa, quam dat carni, viz., nostræ, *i.e.*, corruptæ nostræ naturæ.—*Muscul.* Ne quis parum honorifice legem impotentiæ argui putaret, vel hoc restringeret ad ceremonias, expressit nominatim Paulus defectum illum non a legis esse vitio, sed carnis nostræ corruptela.—*Calvin.*

to such ends, but yet it is a law, and that which is obligatory to all, even to believers themselves under the gospel state and covenant. Shall we, because of this weakness (especially it being occasioned by ourselves) cast off the law, and pretend that we are not under the obligation of it? We must not so argue. Observe it in the apostle, even when he was proving the weakness of the law as to justification, and shewing that God had found out another way for that, viz., the way of faith; yet foreseeing that some might run themselves upon this rock, and infer from hence that they had nothing to do with the law, he therefore adds, 'Do we then make void the law through faith? God forbid. Yea, we establish the law,' in its proper place and sphere, Rom. iii. 31. The creature, as a creature, is under a natural, and therefore indispensable, obligation to this law, so as that nothing can exempt him from that obligation. It commands to love, fear, serve, honour, obey God; wherein it obliges so strongly that God himself—with reverence be it spoken—cannot free the creature from its obligation to these duties. True, indeed, believers are not under the curse, rigour, or bondage of this law, or under it as it is the condition of life; but they are (and it cannot be otherwise) under the obligation of its commands as to a holy life. There may be, and blessed be God there is, a great change as to circumstances, a great relaxation as to the law's rigours, severities, and penalties; but for the main duties of obedience and holiness it is eternally obligatory, and never to be abrogated. Oh therefore do not look upon yourselves as made free from this law, though it be weak and unable to justify and save you! It can damn upon the breaking of it, though it cannot save by the keeping of it.

3. Thirdly, Neither must you, upon this, look upon the law as altogether weak or useless. I say, not as altogether weak; for though as to some things it be under a total impotency, yet as to other things it still retains its pristine power. It cannot take away sin, or make righteous, or give life, which it promised at first, and for which it was appointed; for 'the commandment was ordained to life,' Rom. vii. 10. Here is the weak side of the law, as to these it is τὸ ἀδύνατον τοῦ νόμου. But as to the commanding of duty, the directing and regulating of

the life, the threatening of punishment upon the violation of it, here it can do whatever it did before. The law's preceptive and punitive part, where it is not taken off by Christ, are yet in their full strength; only as to the promissory part of it, viz., its promising life upon the condition of perfect obedience, there it is at a loss. In a word, its authority to oblige to duty or punishment is the same that ever it was, but its ability to give righteousness or life, in which respects only the apostle here speaks of it, is not the same. If God open this law to you, and set it home upon your consciences, you will find it hath yet a very great strength and efficacy in it. Let it not, therefore, be altogether weak in your eye.

Nor altogether useless. For some will be ready to say, If the law be thus weak, then what use is there of it? to what end doth it serve? what is to be looked for from that which can do so little for us? But do not you thus reason! For though the law be not of use to you as to justification, (I mean in a way of immediate influence upon the act or state: a remoter influence it may have,) yet in other respects it is of great and admirable use, viz., as a monitor to excite to duty, as a rule to direct and guide you in your course, as a glass to discover sin, as a bridle to restrain sin, as a hatchet to break the hard heart, as a schoolmaster to whip you to Christ, Gal. iii. 24. The Lord Jesus, indeed, hath taken sin-pardoning, God-atoning, justice-satisfying, soul-saving work into his own hands. He would not trust this in the hands of the law any longer, because he knew the weakness of it; but for other work, the awakening and convincing of a sinner, the terrifying of the secure, the humbling of the proud, the preparing of the soul to close with Christ,—though this last act be only eventual and accidental as to the law,—all this work, I say, yet lies upon the law. Be you who you will, believers or unbelievers, regenerate or unregenerate, the law is of marvellous use to you. It is a rule to all, whether they be good or bad, and as so none are exempted from it, as is by several divines sufficiently proved against the Antinomists; and it hath, too, very good and useful effects upon all, whether called or uncalled, saints or sinners. Our apostle, who here doth so much depress the law in respect of justification, doth else-

where in other respects speak much of its usefulness: Rom. iii. 19, 'Now we know that what things soever the law saith, it saith to them who are under the law, that every mouth may be stopped, and all the world may become guilty before God:' Rom. vii. 7, 'What shall we say then? Is the law sin? God forbid. Nay, I had not known sin but by the law; for I had not known lust, except the law had said, Thou shalt not covet:' Gal. iii. 19–24, 'Wherefore then serveth the law? It was added because of transgressions, till the seed should come to whom the promise was made; and it was ordained by angels in the hand of a mediator. Wherefore the law was our schoolmaster to bring us unto Christ, that we might be justified by faith.' I must not launch out into this vast ocean. You have variety of treatises upon this argument,[1] namely, to prove that the law is still a rule, and still very useful in those great effects which have been mentioned. I refer you to them for further satisfaction. This I only touch upon as it lies in my way, both that I may prevent dangerous mistakes, and also shew you how you are to carry it towards the law. Oh let it be highly esteemed, reverenced, honoured by you! Yea, bless God for it; for though, indeed, it is weak and unprofitable, as the covenant of works, yet as it is a rule, and as it produces such effects upon the conscience, so it is of great use and highly beneficial. So much for the second use.

Use 3. Thirdly, Was the law thus unable to do for the sinner what was necessary to be done? Then never look for righteousness and life from and by the law. For as to these, it cannot do your work unless you could do its work; it cannot justify or save you unless you could perfectly obey and fulfil it. Oh pray expect little from it, nay, nothing at all in this way! You cannot answer *its* expectations, and it cannot answer *yours*. It highly concerns every man in the world to make sure of righteousness and life; but where are these to be had? Only in Christ in the way of believing, not in the law in the way of doing. We would fain make the law stronger than indeed it is; and it is natural to us to look for a

---

[1] Taylor's Reg. Vitæ; Burg. Vinde. Legis; Bolton's Bounds, &c.; Baxter, in several treat., with divers others. Facessat longe ex animis nostris profana ista opinio, legem non esse regulam; est enim inflexibilis vivendi regula.—*Calvin*.

righteousness from it, because there was our righteousness at first, and that suits best with the pride of our hearts. Man is not so averse to the law in point of obedience, but he is as apt to rest upon the law for heaven and happiness, if he can but do something which the law requires. Oh this he looks upon as a sufficient righteousness, and as a good plea for heaven. Especially when conscience is a little awakened, then the poor creature betakes himself to his doing, to his obedience to the law; and this he thinks will do his work, till God lets him see his great mistake. As it is said, Hosea v. 13, 'When Ephraim saw his sickness, and Judah saw his wound, then went Ephraim to the Assyrian, and sent to King Jareb, yet could he not heal you, nor cure you of your wound;' just so it is with the convinced sinner in reference to the law, both as to his practice, and also as to his success.

I would not be mistaken in what I have said, or shall further say, as if I did design to take off any from obedience to the law. God forbid! All that I aim at is only to take men off from trusting in that obedience, and from leaning upon that as their righteousness. We should be doers of the law; for 'not the hearers of the law are just before God, but the doers of the law shall be justified,' Rom. ii. 15; yea, we should go as far as ever we can in our endeavours after a law-righteousness; for though that be not sufficient to justify us before God, yet that must make us righteous in his eye as to qualitative and inherent righteousness;[1] and so we are to understand that text, Deut. vi. 25, with many others of the same import: 'It shall be our righteousness if we observe to do all these commandments before the Lord our God, as he hath commanded us.' But yet, when we have gone the furthest, the righteousness which we are to rely upon is only the gospel righteousness, or the imputed righteousness of the Lord Jesus; if we take up with anything short of that we are miserable and lost for ever.[2] As to the law, is it thus weak, or rather, are you thus weak, and yet will you bottom your expectation and confidence there? can you fulfil or satisfy it in its demands of perfect, personal, universal, constant

obedience? If you cannot—than which nothing more certain—it can never then do your business; nay, upon the least failure it will be your enemy, to plead against you for the non-performance of its conditions; and so, though it cannot as a friend do you much good, yet as an enemy it can and will do you much hurt. What a sad case is the legalist in! The law condemns him because he doth no more obey, and the gospel condemns him because he doth no more believe. He is lost on every hand. Oh this is woeful! And yet how many precious souls split themselves upon this rock! Millions of men look no higher than the law; that is the foundation upon which they build their confidence for life and salvation. Could we but get into them, and be privy to the grounds of their hope, we should find that it is not Christ and faith in him, but the law and some imperfect obedience thereunto, upon which they bottom. They deal honestly, wrong nobody, live unblameably, make some external profession, perform such duties, are thus and thus charitable to the poor, &c., and hereupon they are confident of their salvation. Now I deny not but that these are very good things; I wish there was more of them; yet when any rest in them or upon them for righteousness and life, they set them much too high. As good as they are, in reference to these great concerns they are no better than so many fig-leaves, which will not cover a sinner's nakedness when God shall come to reckon with him. Whosoever bottoms his trust and confidence upon these, he builds upon the sand, and sooner or later there will be a sad downfall of all his hopes. These are things which glitter in our eye, but they are but coarse and mean things, without Christ, in God's eye.[1]

Sirs, I am upon a point of as great importance as any that can be spoken to; and therefore give me leave to stay upon it a little, and to deal plainly and faithfully with you about it. I would fain leave every one of you upon a good bottom, built upon the rock, that 'sure foundation,' Isa. xxviii. 16, which will stand firm and steady in all winds and weather, having that anchor-hold which will abide under all storms. And therefore let me prevail with you to cast off all legal confidence, and to rely, trust, rest

---

[1] *Vide* Burg. of Justif., p. ii. Serm. 22, p. 215.
[2] Oh nos miseros, si vel tantillum nostra salus basi tam infirma nitatur!—*Beza* in 1 John i. 8.

[1] Sordet in districtione judicis quod fulget in conspectu operantis.—*Gregor.*

upon nothing short of Christ and his righteousness. Duties, graces, holiness, obedience, good works—all, in their proper places, are excellent things; but it is the alone merit, righteousness, satisfaction of Christ that must justify and save you. Would you have that righteousness which will bear the test at the great day?—that righteousness in which you may be able to stand before the disquisition of the righteous God? Oh, then, fly to Christ, to his imputed righteousness, and there let all your trust and reliance be placed! What is that 'one thing' which the New Testament revelation mainly drives at? It is this: to carry sinners from Moses to Christ, from the way of the law to the way of the gospel, from doing, as the old covenant condition and ground of life, to believing. The not understanding, receiving, embracing of this grand truth, was the sin and ruin of the Jews; all that Christ and the apostles could say or do would not prevail with them to shake off their depending upon the law; but still they 'rested in the law,' Rom. ii. 17, 'followed after the law of righteousness,' and 'sought righteousness not by faith, but, as it were, by the works of the law,' Rom. ix. 31, 32; they, 'being ignorant of God's righteousness, and going about to establish their own righteousness, would not submit to the righteousness of God,' Rom. x. 3. Oh, therefore, how full, how earnest was Paul in his dealings with them, and with others too, to undeceive and convince them about this! He saith the whole matter of righteousness was now taken out of the law's hands and put into the hands of Christ. 'Christ is the end of the law for righteousness to every one that believeth,' Rom. x. 4. 'Therefore by the deeds of the law there shall no flesh be justified in his sight, &c. But now the righteousness of God without the law is manifested, being witnessed by the law and prophets: even the righteousness of God which is by faith of Jesus Christ unto all and upon all them that believe,' Rom. iii. 20–22. He sets down the miserable state of those who would be resting upon the law, such as were ἐκ τῶν ἔργων τοῦ νόμου, as he describes them: 'For as many as are of the works of the law are under the curse; for it is written, Cursed is every one that continueth not in all things written in the book of the law to do them,' Gal. iii. 10. He tells them, by this they made the

sending, dying of Christ to be to no purpose: 'I do not frustrate the grace of God; for if righteousness come by the law, then Christ is dead in vain,' Gal. ii. 21; see, too, Gal. v. 3, 4. He tells them, further, that God had such a respect for his own law, that if righteousness and life had been possible by it, he would have taken no other way: 'If there had been a law given which could have given life, verily, righteousness should have been by the law,' Gal. iii. 21. But why do I give you a few gleanings, when you yourselves may go into the full field?—Now was all this spoken only to the Jews and Gentiles who lived at that time? doth it not concern us also? have not these several considerations their strength to us as well as to them?

To come nearer home. The text tells us 'the law could not do.' Will you not be convinced of the law's inability to help you, so as to betake yourselves to that better and effectual way of justification and salvation which God hath so graciously provided for you? The law is weak, as weak now as ever; but Christ is strong, as strong now as ever. The law can do nothing, but Christ can do all. Till it pleases God to convince you of the law's impossibility to make you righteous and happy, you will never seek out after help in Christ, or close with him; for as Christ had never come to you, had it not been because it was impossible for the law to save you; so you will never come to him till you see that it is impossible for the law to save you. This is that which moved God to send Christ, and this is that which moves the sinner to embrace Christ and his way of salvation. If this work of conviction was but once passed upon you, oh you would soon quit the law, and all your confidence would be bottomed upon Christ. Well! shall I bring it to a head? Here are two ways set before you for righteousness and life,—the way of the law and the way of the gospel, the way of doing and the way of believing. Now which of these two will you choose? If the former, so as to venture your souls upon what you can do, your case is desperate. By this you plainly put yourselves under the covenant of works, and there is nothing but perishing, as things now stand with us, under that covenant. If the latter, there is hope, nay, certainty—supposing you close with the gospel way in a right gospel manner—that it shall be well with you. Who would not now say with David, ‘I will make mention of thy righteousness, even of thine only’? Ps. lxxi. 16; who would not, with Paul, ‘count all but dross and dung, that he may win Christ, and be found in him, not having his own righteousness, which is of the law, but that which is through the faith of Christ, the righteousness which is of God by faith’? Phil. iii. 8, 9.

Use 4. Fourthly, See here the admirable love of God, and be greatly affected with it. The law was weak, utterly unable to relieve us in our forlorn condition; as to that *conclamatum est*, the case is desperate; and now the merciful God finds out another way, pitches upon another course, he will see what that will do, the former failing; what is that? he ‘sent his own Son in the likeness,’ &c. Oh the infinite love, mercy, compassion of God! The weaker was God’s law, the stronger and higher was God’s love. Oh that he should not let us all perish under the law’s impotency! that he should employ one for our recovery who was every way able to do what the law could not! How should we adore his mercy in this! But this leads me to the following words in the text, ‘God sent,’ &c., where I shall have occasion more fully to press this duty upon you. So much therefore for this first branch of the words, ‘What the law could not do, in that it was weak through the flesh.’

CHAPTER X.

OF CHRIST’S MISSION, AND OF GOD’S SENDING HIM.

God sending his own Son in the likeness of sinful flesh,
&c.—ROM. viii. 3.

Man being utterly lost upon the terms of the law, it pleased God to find out and to pitch upon another way, which he knew would be effectual—That was the sending of his own Son, &c.—Four things observed in the words; all reduced to three observations—Of Christ’s mission: how he was sent: and sent by God—It notes his pre-existence, before his mission and incarnation; his personality; his being distinct from the Father—It is opened first negatively: 1. It was not Christ’s

ineffable and eternal generation; 2. It was not any local secession from his Father—Secondly, Affirmatively: It was, 1. God’s preordaining of him to the office and work of a mediator; 2. His qualifying and fitting of him for that office and work; 3. His authorising and commissionating of him to engage therein; 4. His authoritative willing of him to assume man’s nature, and therein so to do and so to suffer; 5. His trusting of him with his great designs—How was this sending of Christ consistent with his equality with the Father? this answered two ways—Why was Christ sent? answered first more generally, then more particularly in four things—Use 1. To stir up persons, 1. To admire God; 2. To admire, in special, the love of the Father; 3. To love Christ; 4. To imitate Christ, with respect to his sending; 5. Not to rest in the external sending of Christ; 6. To believe on him whom God hath sent—Use 2. This is improved for the comfort of believers.

THE law’s impotency and weakness, nay, utter inability to recover, justify, and save the lost sinner, hath been spoken to; I go on to that which thereupon the wise and gracious God was pleased to do. And what was that? Why, to the praise of his glorious grace, he ‘sent his own Son in the likeness of sinful flesh.’ The great God is never at a loss; if one means fails he hath another, if all means fail which fall within the view of the creature, yet God hath his secret reserves, and that under the deck, which shall do the work. Upon Adam’s sin all mankind was lost, plunged into a woeful abyss of misery, obnoxious to eternal wrath, and accordingly God might have dealt with them in the utmost severity of his justice. What is there now to prevent this, to give any relief to man in this deplorable state? Alas! the sinner cannot help himself; the law stands with a withered arm and can do nothing; there is no creature in heaven or earth to interpose; as to all of these the case was desperate. Therefore God himself engages to let the world see what he could do:[1] ‘He looked and there was none to help, therefore his own arm brought salvation,’ Isa. lxiii. 3. Here indeed was Θεὸς ἀπὸ μηχανῆς, a God helping at a dead lift, in the greatest straits,

---

[1] Deus solus in hac intricata causa poterat prospicere remedium.—*Streso.*

and in the most admirable manner. If ever—with reverence be it spoken—infinite wisdom was put to it, now was the time; yet, even in this intricate and perplexed state of things, that found out a way which would do the business, a way which none could have thought of but God alone; he 'sent his own Son,' &c. None could cry εὕρηκα to this but God himself; this was his alone invention and contrivance. The restoring of fallen man was impossible to the law, yet it shall be done; God will take another strange and wonderful course, which shall do it effectually.[1] What his own law cannot do his own Son can, therefore him he will send. A very high and costly way! yet rather than all mankind shall perish, God will make use of it. Here is the very mirror of the wisdom, love, grace, pity of the blessed God.

God sending his own Son, &c. To make the sense run more smoothly, some turn the participle πέμψας into the verb ἔπεμψε, reading the words thus: 'God sent his,' &c. If the following conjunctive particle *and* be kept in, this reading is not much amiss. Some render it in the passive form, *Deus misso Filio suo*, &c.[2] Some would put in the word *ideo*, *therefore:*[3] 'Since the law was weak through the flesh, *therefore* God sent his own Son, and for sin,' &c. But as to these things there is no great difficulty.

In the whole paragraph you have, 1. The act, or the thing done—namely, the sending of Christ; 2. The person whose act this was, or the person sending, viz., God the Father: '*God* sent,' &c. It is a known rule, when the name or title of God is set in contradistinction to the Son, it is then taken not essentially, but personally, for the first person, God the Father, instances of which are very common. It is here said God sent his own Son, therefore it must be understood of God the Father, Christ being

his Son, and upon that consideration he being styled the Father. And this person is called God, not because he partakes more of the Godhead than the other persons, Son and Holy Ghost, do, but because he is the first in the order of the three divine persons; and because he is the beginning of the Son and of the Holy Ghost, but hath no beginning of his own person; for he doth not receive the Godhead, in the personal consideration of it, by communication from any other; in which respect he is in Scripture more frequently styled God than either the Son or the Holy Ghost.[1]

3. You have the person sent, our Lord Jesus Christ; and he is set forth, 1. By his near relation to God: God sending *his Son*. In order to the sinner's redemption God did not employ an ordinary person, a mere servant, a creature that stood at a great distance from him; but, so great was his love, he employed a Son. 2. By the speciality and peculiarity of this relation, God sending *his own Son*. In the Greek it is τὸν ἑαυτοῦ υἱόν, the Son of himself. In ver. 32 it is τοῦ ἰδίου υἱοῦ, his proper Son, or his own Son. There is that in this expression which very much heightens Christ's sonship; he was not barely a Son, but God's own Son, a Son in a special, extraordinary, incommunicable manner.

4. Here is the further explication of this sending with respect to the way and manner of it; how did God send his Son? Why, *in the likeness of sinful flesh.* If you go further into the words than that branch of them which I have now read, there are two generals more to be observed in them; but they will be taken notice of in their proper place.

There are three great doctrinal truths here to be handled:

Obs. 1. That Christ was sent, and sent by God the Father.

Obs. 2. That Christ, thus sent, was God's own Son.

Obs. 3. That Christ, God's own Son, was sent in the likeness of sinful flesh.

I begin with the first, That Christ was sent, and sent by God the Father. Here are two things to be spoken to, Christ's being sent, and his being sent by the Father; but they may very well be put together.

---

[1] Noluit propterea quod lex imbecillis erat per pravitatem humanæ naturæ, opus salutis humanæ abjicere; quasi non posset per aliam, quod ista legis via non succedebat, efficere. —*Musc.*

[2] Dictio interpretata *mittens* participium est, &c., et propterea ad servandum et participium et tempus, aliqui interpretes verterunt, et recte, activum in passivum, legendo sic, *Deus Filio suo misso in carne.—Cajet.*

[3] Duplex est Hebraismus, unus est, oportet supplere Latine *ideo ;* alter, quia participium *mittens* ponitur loco verbi *misit.* —*Tolet.*

[1] Mr Perkins on Gal. iv. 4, p. 271.

Before I fall upon the close handling of this sending of Christ, there are three things which it presents to our consideration : his pre-existence, his personality, his personal distinction from the Father; let me therefore a little touch upon each of these.

1. This sending of Christ strongly implies his pre-existence before his incarnation. For if he had not had a being before, how could the Father send him? That which is not, cannot be sent. It is not said here that God now created him or made him, as if he did not exist before, but he sent him, which must, as I said, strongly imply that he did exist before this sending.[1] This the Socinians fiercely oppose; and therefore in this matter they are worse than the Arians.[2] For these, though they denied that Christ was from all eternity, and made him to be only first created by God, upon the misunderstanding and perverting of his being called 'the first born of every creature,' Col. i. 13; the 'beginning of the creation of God,' Rev. iii. 14; yet they asserted Christ's existence long before his incarnation. But the Socinians, following Photinus, deny that he had any being or existence before he was conceived and brought forth by the virgin Mary; so that their opinion about the person of Christ is somewhat worse than that of the old Arians, for which they are admonished and dealt with a little sharply by a late Arian writer himself.[3] The or-

thodox fully prove the eternity of Christ against the one, and consequently the pre-existence of Christ before his incarnation against the other.

And one would think the Scriptures are so clear in this, that there should not be the least controversy about it; for they tell us that Christ was in Jacob's time: Gen. xlviii. 16, 'The Angel which redeemed me from all evil,' &c. It might easily be proved that this angel was Christ.[1] That he was in Job's time, for he said, Job xix. 25, 'I know that my Redeemer liveth,' meaning Christ. That he was in the prophets' time under the Old Testament, for the 'Spirit of Christ was in them,' 1 Pet. i. 11. That he was in Abraham's time, yea, long before it : John viii. 56, &c., 'Your father Abraham rejoiced to see my day, and was glad. Then said the Jews unto him, Thou art not yet fifty years old, and hast thou seen Abraham? Jesus said unto them, Verily, verily, I say unto you, Before Abraham was, I am.' That he was in the Israelites' time, for, 1 Cor. x. 9, it is said, 'Neither let us tempt Christ, as some of them also tempted;' *him* is added in some translations, however the sense will so carry it. That he was in the prophet Isaiah's time, for John xii. 41, you read, 'These things said Esaias, when he saw his glory, and spake of him,' that is, of Christ. Now were not these periods of time before, long before, Christ's being born of the Virgin? therefore he had an existence before that. How fully and plainly is this asserted in the Gospel! John i. 1-3, 10 : 'In the beginning was the Word, and the Word was with God, and the Word was God. The same was in the beginning with God. All things were made by him; and without him was not any thing made that was made. He was in the world, and the world was made by him, and the world knew him not.' Eph. iii. 9, &c., 'Who created all things by Jesus Christ;' by him, not as an instrument, but as a social or co-ordinate cause. Col. i. 16, 17, 'By him were all things created, that are in heaven and that are in earth, visible and invisible,

---

[1] Non de novo creans vel faciens, sed quasi præexistentem misit.—*Aquin.* Misit, non creavit aut condidit, sed qui secum erat coæternus, eundem ad nos delegavit; non ut esset ubi non fuerat, &c. Sed ut appareret ubi invisibili modo erat.—*Soto.*

[2] The whole body of the Socinian authors agree in this, except Erasmus Johannes, who fell in with the Arians. See Socinus's Disp. with him, De Filii Dei existentia.

[3] Sandius in Nucleus Histor. Eccles., who, p. 229, lib. i., concerning the pre-existence of Christ thus expresses himself: Licet dogma de præexistentia Christi antesæculari, in symbolo dicto non contineatur, &c., nihilo minus præstat tutiorem viam sequi, Christi præexistentiam non denegando. Nam si Christus præextitit, quanti res plena periculi Christo id nolle concedere quod ei jure competit, et quam mitem judicem habituri sunt qui ita sentiunt? Et si Christus non fuit ante Mariam, periculo tamen vacat confessio præexistentiæ; nam Christus non succensebit illis qui ei nimium honoris attribuerint. Nec est quod timeant se eo ipso detrahere majestati Patris : Nam, ut taceam non esse contra rationem vel impossibile, filium fuisse primogenitum ante omnes creaturas; certe majestati patris magis convenit, quod talem filium ante sæcula genuerit. Deinde nec habent, quod vereantur se per præexistentiam

tollere veri Christ humanitatem, potest enim virtute Divina quilibet angelus incarnari et uniri cum carne in unitatem personæ, sic ut ille unitus simul dici possit et homo et angelus; et Plato non negavit animas præexistentes post incarnationem fieri homines.

[1] *Vide* Franzii Disput. Theolog., Disp. 14, The. 40, p. 436.

whether they be thrones, or dominions, or principalities, or powers; all things were created by him, and for him; and he is before all things, and by him all things consist.' Heb. i. 2, 'By whom also he made the worlds.' Now could Christ have thus cooperated with the Father in the creation, and yet not have a being before his incarnation, which was so long after the creation? John i. 15, 'John bare witness of him, and cried, saying, This was he of whom I spake, He that cometh after me is preferred before me; for he was before me.' How was Christ before John Baptist, if he did then only exist when he was born? for in reference to that John Baptist was before Christ, he being born before him. John xvii. 5, 'And now, O Father, glorify thou me with thine own self, with the glory which I had with thee before the world was:' mark the latter words, 'With the glory which I had with thee before the world was.' Phil. ii. 6, 'Who being (ὑπάρχων, subsisting, existing,) in the form of God,' &c. John xvi. 28, 'I came forth from the Father, and am come into the world: again, I leave the world, and go to the Father.' John vi. 62, 'What and if ye shall see the Son of man ascend up where he was before?' in respect of his divine nature, or as he was the Son of God. Do not these scriptures sufficiently evince that Christ had a being before he was incarnate? The drawing forth of their full strength, and the answering of the several cavils and evasions of the adversaries about them, would fill up a volume; the learned know where and by whom both of these are fully done.[1]

This sending of Christ therefore speaks his existence before he assumed flesh; he must have an antecedent being, otherwise he would not have been capable of being sent.[2] And he was first sent, and then incarnate, his mission being antecedent to his incarnation, though this be denied by the enemies

with whom we have to do.[1] For God sent him, that is, appointed that he should assume the human nature; and this is his being sent in the likeness of sinful flesh, as a judicious expositor descants upon the words.

2. Secondly, This sending of Christ speaks his personality. He did not only exist before he took flesh, but he existed as a person; he had his τρόπος τῆς ὑπάρξεως, wherein the notion of a divine person consists, his manner of subsistence distinct from the subsistence of the Father and of the Holy Ghost. But this explication of Christ being a person more properly belongs to the next head. Here I say Christ was a person, by which I mean he was not a thing, quality, dispensation, or manifestation, as some fondly and dangerously speak; but he was, and is, a person, having a proper, personal subsistence. And he must be so, or else he could not be the subject of this sending. It is very true, God may be said to send or give that which is but manifestative, as he sends his gospel, which yet is not a person, but only a manifestation of his will, grace, love, wisdom, &c. But now in Christ there is something more than bare sending, even that which will amount to the proving of him to be nothing less than a person; for he is sent to be incarnate, to take the likeness of sinful flesh upon him. Now a bare quality or manifestation are under an utter incapacity of being thus, or doing thus. Who will be so absurd as to assert such a thing? If Christ be sent by God the Father, and upon that doth assume flesh, then certainly he was a person, for none but a person could do this. Had the apostle only said that God sent Christ, the truth in hand had not been so evident, at leastwise from this text; but when he adds 'he sent him in the likeness of sinful flesh,' this undeniably proves his personality.

3. Thirdly, It notes the distinction that is betwixt the Father and Christ. Which appears not only as one is the Father and the other is the Son, though that evidently infers a distinction, for the same person in the same respects cannot be Father and Son

[1] See Arnold. Catech. Racov. Major de Persona Christi, p. 187, &c.; Hoorneb, Socin. Conf., tom. ii. de Christo, cap. 1. Calovius Socin. Proflig. de Filio Dei, controv. 1; but especially Placei Disput. de Argum. quibus efficitur Christum prius fuisse, quam in utero beatæ Virginis secundum carnem conciperetur. This is fully and learnedly discoursed of by Dr Pearson on the Creed, art. ii. p. 213 to 237.

[2] Necesse est ut qui mittitur existat priusquam mittatur, fatente Enjedino.—*Calov.*, Socin. Proflig., p. 183.

[2] Misit a se per virtutem Spiritus Sancti genitum, et ex matre sua natum, et ad virilem ætatem perductum, non adhuc generandum et oriturum, quod dictu ipso absonum est et Scripturæ plane dissonum.—*Slichting.*

too—cannot beget and be begotten too ; but also as the one sends and the other is sent.[1] The Father and the Son are one in nature and essence, with respect to which he saith, John x. 30, ' I and my Father are one ;' yet they are distinct persons.[2]   The number and distinction of the persons in the Trinity is usually taken notice of by divines from this scripture.   The apostle, saith Theophylact, had spoken of the Spirit in the former verse, in this he speaks of the Father and of the Son, τὴν τριάδα διδάσκων, teaching the Trinity. And saith Peter Martyr from these words, the number and distinction of the persons in the holy Trinity doth appear.[3]   Which great truth is also frequently held forth in other places : Isa. xlviii. 16, ' Come ye near unto me,' (Christ is the person here speaking,) ' hear ye this : I have not spoken in se- cret from the beginning ; from the time that it was, there am I : and now the Lord God, and his Spirit, hath sent me.'   A full Old Testament proof of the distinction of the persons.   But it is most plainly held forth in the New Testament.   At the baptism of Christ there was a manifestation of God in the Father, Son, and Spirit ; the Spirit descended in the form of a dove, the Father gave the testimony, ' This is my beloved Son,' &c. ;[4] Christ was the object of it.   Christ directed his apostles to baptize ' in the name of the Father, Son, and Holy Ghost,' which surely he would not have done had there not been a personal distinction betwixt them : John xiv. 16, ' I will pray the Father, and he shall give you an- other comforter,' &c.   Here is all the persons as dis-

tinct : John xiv. 1, ' Ye believe in God, believe also in me.'   John xii. 44, ' He that believeth on me, believeth not on me ' (i.e., on me only,) ' but on him that sent me.'   John v. 32, ' There is another that beareth witness of me, and I know that the witness which he witnesseth of me is true.'   Many such places might be cited, but these may suffice.   Here is enough in the text ; the same person, considered in the same respects, cannot both send and be sent too, therefore the Father and the Son are distinct persons.   True, as Augustine observes,[1] in some sense Christ might be said to send himself, that is, consider him essentially, so he did what the Father did, so he sent himself ; but if you consider him personally, so he did not send but was sent : upon which he and his Father are distinct.   So much for these three things, which are but implied in Christ's mission.

I come more closely to the thing itself, and to the point which lies before us, namely, That Christ was sent, and sent by God the Father.   The redemption of lost man was a blessed work, a most glorious un- dertaking ; never was there any like to it, or to be paralleled with it ; yet our Lord Jesus would not of his own head engage in it, or thrust himself upon it ; no, he must first be sent ; then, and not till then, did he undertake it.   And who sent him ?   Surely he who only had authority to employ and commis- sionate him about such a work, viz., God the Father : ' God sent his own Son,' &c. ; where, as hath been already hinted, God is to be taken in the personal notion, and as relating to the first person.[2]

This sending of Christ, and that by the Father, are two points of such unquestionable verity to all who pass under the denomination of Christians, that as to them—and with Jews and heathens I will not meddle—it is not necessary to spend the least time in the proving of them.   Yet, even as to them, it is needful that these truths should be a little opened and explained.

In order to which I will endeavour,

1. To clear up the nature of the act.

---

[1] Ἄλλος ὁ ἀποστέλλων, ἄλλος ὁ ἀποστελλόμενος.—Epiphan. adv. Hœres., p. 740.   See Gerhard. Loc. Com, tom. i. cap. 6, p. 263, De personali Filii a Patre et Spiritus Sancti dis- tinctione.

[2] Una est Patris, et Filii, et Spiritus Sancti essentia, in qua non est aliud Pater, aliud Filius, aliud Spiritus Sanctus ; quamvis personaliter sit alius Pater, alius Filius, alius Spiritus Sanctus. —Fulgent., lib. i. De Fid.   Ecce dico alium est Patrem, et alium Filium, et alium Spiritum Sanctum.   Male accepit idiotes quis- que aut perversus hoc dictum quasi diversitatem sonet, et ex diversitate separationem pretendat Patris et Filii et Spiritus. —Tertul. adv. Praxeam.   Of the distinction of the three di- vine persons, see Dr Cheynel on the Trin-unity, chap. vii. p. 181, &c., and p. 227 to 248.

[3] Ex his verbis apparet divinarum personarum in Sancta Triade numerus et distinctio.

[4] Pater auditur in voce, Filius manifestatur in homine, Spi- ritus dignoscitur in columba.—August.

[1] Lib. ii. De Trin. cap. 5.   Vide Lombard., lib. i. Dist. 15.

[2] Personaliter sumpto vocabulo, quia opponitur persona mittens personæ missæ.—Grynœus.   Ubi ait quod Deus misit Filium, nominatione Dei Patrem intelligit, ad quem Filius refertur.—Soto.

2. To remove a difficulty or answer an objection about it.

3. To give the grounds and reasons of it.

As to the first, the question is, What was the Father's sending of Christ? in what respects is he said to be sent, and sent by the Father? for I shall open both together.

To which I answer, 1. Negatively, in two things:

(1.) This sending of Christ was not his ineffable and eternal generation, or Sonship grounded upon that. He was sent who was the Son of God; but he was not the Son of God as he was sent, nor said to be sent as he was the Son of God.[1] His Sonship was the result of his generation, not of his mission. These two are very different things; for Christ was begotten of the Father from everlasting; but he was sent by the Father—the sending being taken in its strict and most proper notion—in time: 'When the fulness of time was come, God sent forth his Son,' &c., Gal. iv. 4. He was a Son long before he was sent; and he was not a Son because he was sent, but he was sent because he was a Son.

(2.) Christ's sending was not any local secession from his Father,[2] or any local motion from the place where he was to some other place where he was not. You must not so conceive of it, nor fetch your measures concerning it from your own sending of persons; for there when you send one upon your errand or business, he leaves the place where he was, and goes to the place where he was not; but so it was not with Christ. The Father sent him to this lower world, yet here he was before; the Father sent him from heaven, yet, as to his Godhead, he remained in heaven still. He saith, indeed, John xvi. 28, 'I came forth from the Father'—yet not so but that he was still with the Father—'and am come into the world' —yet not so but that he was there before; for 'he

was in the world, and the world was made by him, John i. 10; 'again I leave the world and go to the Father,' he speaks in respect of his bodily presence. Look, as when Christ ascended, he went from earth, and yet he was on earth still as to his spiritual presence; for he saith, 'Lo, I am with you unto the end of the world,' Mat. xxviii. 20. As man he went from us, but as God he is as much with us as ever.[1] So when Christ descended, he came from heaven, and yet he was in heaven still; for he tells us, 'No man hath ascended up into heaven, but he that came down from heaven, even the Son of man which is in heaven,' John iii. 13. So that in Christ's sending there was no mutation of place, only upon that he assumed the human nature, and so became visible; whereas before, as God, he was invisible.[2] He was but where he was, only he was more than what he was, for he was now God-man; and he was here in a different manner, for now he was visible. You see what the sending of Christ was not.

2. Secondly, To open it affirmatively, this sending of Christ lies in five things:

(1.) In God's choosing, appointing, ordaining of Christ from everlasting to the office and work of the mediator. This, I confess, is somewhat remote from that strict notion of his sending in which the Scripture usually speaks of it. However, I take it in, it being the foundation of his being sent in time. God the Father from all eternity did choose, decree, ordain that his Son should take flesh, and in that flesh redeem man; therefore he calls him his elect: Isa. xlii. 1, 'Mine elect, in whom my soul delighteth.' And Rom. iii. 25, it is said, 'Whom God hath *set forth* to be a propitiation through faith in his blood,' &c.;

---

[1] Non eo ipso quod Patre natus est, missus dicitur Filius, sed eo quod apparuit huic mundo, verbum caro factum est.—*Aug. de Trin.*, lib. iv. cap. 10. Duobus modis dicitur mitti Filius, præter illam æternam genituram quæ ineffabilis est; secundum quam etiam missus posset dici, (ut videtur quibusdam,) sed melius ac verius secundum eam dicitur genitus.—*Lomb.*, lib. i. dist. 15.

[2] Non missus est mutando locum, quia in mundo erat. Quapropter Pater invisibilis una cum Filio secum invisibili, eundem Filium visibilem faciendo, misisse eum dictus est, &c. —*August. de Trinit.*, lib. ii. cap. 5.

[1] A quibus homo abscedebat, Deus non recedebat.—*Aug. Tract.* 78, *in John.* Et abiit et hic est, et rediit et nos non deseruit.—*Idem. Tract.* 50, *in John.*

[2] Missio divinæ personæ convenire potest, secundum quod importat ex una parte, processionem originis a mittente; et secundum quod importat ex alia parte, novum modum existendi in alio. Sicut Filius dicitur esse missus a Patre in mundum, secundum quod incepit in mundo esse per carnem assumptam, et tamen ante in mundo erat, ut dicitur John i.— *Aquin.*, part i. qu. 43, art. i. in corp. art. ; et in Resp., ad 2. Illud quod sic mittitur ut incipiat esse ubi prius nullo modo erat, sua missione localiter movetur. Sed hoc non accidit in missione divinæ personæ, quia persona divina missa, sicut non incipit esse ubi prius non fuerat, ita nec desinit esse ubi fuerat.

προέθετο, it relates to God's πρόθεσις or purpose; and it notes not only God's setting forth and revealing of Christ in the gospel, which was done in time, but also, and chiefly, his decreeing, foreordaining of Christ in his secret purpose from all eternity to the work and office of a Redeemer. So the word is used, Eph. i. 9; and therefore the marginal rendering of it, *whom God foreordained*, is better than that in the text itself, *whom God hath set forth*. The apostle Peter speaks expressly of it: 'Who verily was foreordained before the foundation of the world, but was manifest in these last times for you,' 1 Pet. i. 20. You read of a decree concerning Christ, Ps. ii. 7, 'I will declare the decree,' &c.; but that which I am upon was not the matter of the decree there spoken of.

(2.) Christ's sending—I take it passively—lies in God's qualifying and fitting of him for his great work. This also is more remote from the close intendment of the sending; yet it also may be taken in. The wise God first fits and then sends; he never puts a person upon any special service but first he qualifies and fits him for that service. You have it exemplified in Moses and in several others. Now the restoration of man to God's image and favour, the redeeming and reconciling of the sinner to God, was the greatest work that ever was undertaken; and therefore if God will employ Christ about such a work, his wisdom engaged him first to fit him for it. Which accordingly he did; for in order thereunto, whereas Christ must have a body to fit him for dying and suffering, that God provided for him. 'Wherefore, when he cometh into the world, he saith, Sacrifice and offering thou wouldst not, but a body hast thou prepared' (or fitted) 'me,' Heb. x. 5. And whereas he must also have the Spirit, in a large proportion and plentiful effusion thereof, that too the Father doth furnish him with: Isa. xlii. 1, 'I have put my Spirit upon him;' John iii. 34, 'God giveth not the Spirit by measure unto him.' Our blessed Saviour could need nothing more than a body and the Spirit to qualify and fit him for his work, and both, you see, were given to him: John x. 36, 'Say ye of him whom the Father hath sanctified and sent into the world, Thou blasphemest, because I said I am the Son of God?' What was the Father's sanctifying of

Christ? I answer, It was partly his setting of Christ apart to, and partly his gifting and qualifying of Christ for, his office and undertaking; the latter of which the Father did for him as well as the former; and so he sanctified him. And observe, it was first sanctifying, and then sending. 'Whom the Father hath sanctified and sent,' &c.

(3.) Thirdly, It lies in God's authorising and commissionating of Christ to what he was to be and to do. The Father sent him, that is, gave him authority to engage as the Redeemer of the world. Christ had a commission from God under hand and seal, as it were, before he meddled in his great negotiation: John vi. 27, 'Him hath God the Father sealed,' or authorised by special commission; for though that be not all which is intended in the sealing, yet that is a great part of it. As princes, when they send abroad their ambassadors, or appoint their officers at home, they give them their commissions sealed to be their warrant for what they shall do; so God the Father did with Christ. He did not intrude or thrust himself upon what he undertook; no, but though he had in himself a strong inclination thereunto, yet first his Father must call him to it. He did not run before he was sent, as those prophets did, Jer. xxiii. 21. So the apostle tells us, Heb. v. 4, 5, 'No man taketh this honour to himself, but he that was called of God, as was Aaron. So also Christ glorified not himself to be made an high priest; but he that said unto him, Thou art my Son, this day have I begotten thee.' John viii. 42, 'I proceeded forth and came from God; neither came I of myself, but he sent me.' You see how his sending is opened by this; the due consideration of which doth administer matter of great support and encouragement to faith, as you will hear in the applying of the truth in hand.

(4.) Fourthly, This sending of Christ consists in the Father's authoritative willing of him to take man's nature upon him, and in that nature so to do, and so to suffer. This is higher than the former; God did not only authorise Christ to engage, so as that he might, if he so pleased, undertake to redeem sinners, without any intrusion or usurpation; but he made this known to him as his will, and so, to speak according to our conceptions, he laid his command upon him to act accordingly. So as that

Christ was under an obligation—which yet did not in the least destroy or lessen his liberty, or his merit, or his love—to come and to do as he did. Sending is an authoritative act amongst men; it was so in God towards Christ; the Father did not proceed with him in a way of mere offer or bare proposal or entreaty, but in a way of authority; he laid his injunction upon him to assume flesh, and in that flesh to make satisfaction. Therefore when Christ entered upon this work, speaking to his Father, he saith, ‘Lo, I come, (in the volume of the book it is written of me,) to do thy will, O God,’ Heb. x. 7. And when he was discoursing of laying down his life, he adds, ‘This commandment have I received of my Father,’ John x. 18; the apostle also tells us that ‘he became *obedient* unto death, even the death of the cross,’ Phil. ii. 8, which obedience necessarily supposes a command. And Christ was under a command in reference to his incarnation, as well as to his death and passion, for indeed without that there could have been none of this; therefore the text saith, ‘God sent him in the likeness,’ &c., that is, God ordered him to take our flesh. This sending then of Christ was the Father’s authoritative calling of him to the office and work of a Redeemer, which call was also backed with positive and peremptory commands as to the management of both; in respect of which God is said to send him, for *mittere Deus dicitur ubi mandata dat*, as Grotius glosses upon it. And the truth is, Christ in the management of the whole work of our redemption was under, acted by, and according to, his Father’s command; whereupon God calls him his servant, Isa. xlii. 1, and liii. 11; and Christ himself, speaking to his Father, says, John xvii. 4, ‘I have glorified thee on the earth, I have finished the work which thou gavest me to do;’ mark that, *which thou gavest me to do*, intimating that all his work was cut out for him by the will of his Father. So John iv. 34, ‘Jesus saith unto them, My meat is to do the will of him that sent me, and to finish his work.’ John vi. 38, ‘I came down from heaven, not to do mine own will, but the will of him that sent me;’ upon this account therefore Christ may well be said to be sent by the Father. In Scripture it is sometimes God *gave him*, and sometimes God *sent him;* Christ was *given*, in respect of the

freeness of the grace of God towards us, and he was *sent*, in respect of the Father’s authority over himself.

(5.) Fifthly, Take one thing more, God’s sending of Christ imports his trusting of him with his great designs; this comes in too, if not directly, yet at leastwise collaterally or concomitantly. In all sending there is trust; when we send a person about our affairs we repose a trust in him, that he will be faithful in the management of our concerns; God sent Christ, that is, he put a great trust into his hands. It is as if the Father had said, ‘My Son! here is a great work to be done, a work upon which my glory doth infinitely depend, all now lies at the stake, as this is managed it will be well or ill with souls. Well, I will send thee, I will put all into thy hands, venture all with thee; I know thou wilt be faithful to secure my glory and to promote the good of souls; I will trust thee, and none but thee, with such great things as these are.’ This, I say, is implied in God’s sending of Christ.

And now, by all put together, you see how or in what respects Christ was sent, and sent by God the Father. You may, both to strengthen what hath been said, and also further to clear it up, take his own parallel: John xx. 21, ‘As my Father hath sent me, even so I send you.’ So that look, what Christ’s sending of the apostles was in reference to their office, the same was God’s sending of Christ in reference to his office. How then did he send them? Why, 1. He designed, chose, selected them to and for the work of the ministry; 2. He qualified and fitted them for that work; 3. He authorised them by his special commission to undertake it; 4. He sent them out authoritatively to preach the gospel, and laid his commands upon them so to do; 5. He reposed a special trust in them that they would be faithful. Just thus—allowing for the pre-eminence of the person and of his office—did God send Christ, which fully agrees with the particulars that have been insisted upon. And as to the apostles, Christ had said the same before to his Father: John xvii. 18, ‘As thou hast sent me into the world, even so have I also sent them into the world;’ not that there was a parity or perfect equality betwixt the one and the other, only a harmony and great agreement.[1] So much for the first thing, the opening the nature of the act.

I proceed to the second, to answer an objection, or to remove a difficulty which here lies before us. That which hath been spoken seems to derogate from the greatness and glory of Christ's person; for did God thus send him? Surely then, as some argue, he is a person inferior to the Father; this sending seems to be inconsistent with his equality to his Father; if he was sent, and thus sent, doth not that speak his inferiority to that God who sent him, and by consequence that he is not God? Thus the Socinians argue from it; and this is one of those heads from which they fetch their arguments against Christ's deity.

For the explaining of the thing, and the answering of the adversary, divines commonly lay down two things about it:

1. That sending doth not always imply inferiority or inequality; for persons who are equal, upon mutual consent, may send each the other, and if the person sent doth freely concur and consent with the person sending, there is no impeachment or intrenchment then upon the equality betwixt them.[2] And thus it was between God the Father and Christ. Had he been sent merely from the will of the Father, whether he himself would or no, then indeed the case had differed, and the objection would have carried strength in it; but it was quite otherwise. For Christ readily consented to and perfectly concurred with the Father, and he was as willing to be sent as the Father was to send him: 'Lo, I come to do thy will, O God.' When the master sends the servant he goes because he must, but when the Father sends the Son he goes readily, because his will falls in with his Father's will; he obeys not upon necessity, but upon choice and consent. So it was with Christ in reference to his Father's sending of him; the will of the Son was as much for the work as the will of the Father himself. You must not look upon Christ as merely passive in the sending, for, in some respects, he sent himself; and his

coming upon that great errand of man's redemption was his own act as well as the Father's. As the Father is said to sanctify him, John x. 36, and yet he also is said to sanctify himself, John xvii. 19; and as the Father is said to give him, Rom. viii. 32, and yet he also is said to give himself, Gal. ii. 20; so here the Father is said to send him, yet he also, as he was one in nature and in will with the Father, may be said to send himself; thus Augustine opens it.[1] The expression in the text, 'God sent his Son,' doth not exclude the Son or the Spirit from the sending, or wholly appropriate it to the Father; it only notes the order of the persons in their working. The Father being the first in working, therefore the sending of Christ is ascribed to him; but there being nothing more in it than so, that will not prove any inequality in the persons, or any superiority that one hath over the other. The schoolmen give some nice and curious distinctions about Christ being sent by himself, and by the Holy Ghost, as well as by the first person; but it is not convenient to perplex the reader with them. This is one answer for the clearing up of the difficulty, and the weakening of the objection which we have to do with.

2. The learned further distinguish of a twofold inferiority; one in respect of nature, and one in respect of office, condition, or dispensation. As to the first, Christ neither was nor is in the least inferior to the Father, both having the same nature and essence, in respect of which he 'thought it not robbery to be equal with God,' Phil. ii. 6. As to the second, Christ being considered as Mediator, as having assumed flesh, put himself into the sinner's stead, and undertaken to make satisfaction to God; so, without any derogation, it may be said of him that he was inferior to the Father. In reference to which it follows in the forementioned place, ver. 7, 8, 'He made himself of no reputation, and took

---

[1] Vocula καθὼς non omnimodam paritatem, sed aliquam convenientiam indicat. Nam et ab alio, et alio modo, et alio fine Christus missus est quam apostoli.—*Bisterf. contra Crellium*, lib. i. sec. 2, cap. 31.

[2] See Mr Perkins on Gal. iv. 4, p. 271.

[1] Forte aliquis rogat, ut dicamus etiam a seipso missum esse Filium, quia et Mariæ conceptus et partus operatio Trinitatis est. Sed inquit aliquis, quomodo Pater eum misit, si ipse se misit? Cui respondeo quærens ut dicat, quomodo eum Pater sanctificavit, si ipse se sanctificavit? utrumque enim Dominus dicit, &c. Item quæro quomodo Pater eum tradidit, si ipse se tradidit? utrumque enim legitur. Credo respondebit, si probe sapit, quia una voluntas est Patris et Filii, et inseparabilis operatio.—*Aug. de Trin.*, lib. ii. cap. 5.

2 A

upon him the form of a servant, and was made in the likeness of men; and being found in fashion as a man, he humbled himself, and became obedient unto death, even the death of the cross.' And upon this he saith, John xiv. 28, 'My Father is greater than I.'[1] He was in nature every way as great as the Father, but he having submitted to be made man, to be a surety, having condescended to the office and work of a redeemer in our flesh, so in respect of economy and dispensation the Father was greater than he. And by virtue of his superiority over Christ, as considered in this his voluntary exaninition, so he sent him, and laid his commands upon him, and dealt with him as you have heard: but yet his natural and essential greatness or equality with the Father was not at all by this impaired or lessened,[2] which was the great truth to be secured against the adversary.

The third thing which I am to speak to is to inquire, so far as the word will warrant, into the grounds and reasons of Christ's mission; wherefore did God send him? He who is so wise that he doth nothing, be it never so little or mean, but he hath his reasons for it, surely in so great a thing as the sending of his own Son he had very high and weighty reasons upon which he acted. And though it is most certain that he neither had, nor could have, any motives *ab extra*, in a way of merit, to move

him to this; yet it is as certain that he had great and urgent grounds for it, even such as might become a God in doing such a thing. He that in other things is a 'God of judgment,' Isa. xxx. 18, undoubtedly in this, which was his masterpiece, he would shew himself to be a God of judgment. It will therefore be worthy of a modest inquiry, to find out the reasons which the wise and gracious God went upon in the sending of his Son.

In the general, some must be sent. When I say *must*, I do not mean any simple or absolute necessity, as though it was simply and absolutely necessary that God should take some course, or employ some person from heaven for the redeeming and saving of the world: God forbid that I should assert a thing so utterly false, and so highly derogatory from the freeness of the grace of God in what he did! I only mean therefore that which we call hypothetical or conditional necessity; and so the business stood thus. God designed to glorify and advance his mercy to sinners, he had gracious purposes in himself towards man; and whereas all mankind lay before him in an undone and ruined condition, he would not leave them to perish eternally in that condition. Then supposing this, which cannot be denied, God must send, something must be done, or else these gracious purposes of God will be lost, and all men must inevitably perish for ever. For as to all other ways the sinner's case was desperate, with respect to them there was no hope or help; some new and strange course must be taken, or else, as things stand, on the creature's part there is nothing to be looked for but hell and damnation. Now things being brought to this pass, therefore God will send, yea, he will send his own Son; for he will be sure to pitch upon a way which shall infallibly and effectually do the work. Observe it in the text, when, or because, it was impossible for the law to do, then, or therefore, God sent his Son; since neither the law, nor anything else, could operate to any purpose towards the advancing of God's honour, and the promoting of the sinner's good, it was necessary, in order to these great ends, that God himself should interpose in some extraordinary way, which thereupon he accordingly did in the sending of Christ.

But more particularly; let us take it for granted that there was a necessity of sending, yet why did

---

[1] See this text fully opened in Estwicke against Biddle, p. 121, &c., vid. etiam *Epiph. adver. Hæres.*, lib. ii. tom. ii. p. 775, &c. Loquatur Filius hominis, Pater major me est; loquatur Filius Dei, ego et Pater unum sumus.—*Aug. de Temp.*, Serm. vi.

[2] Non ideo arbitrandum est, minorem esse Filium quia missus est a Patre, nec ideo minorem Spiritum Sanctum quia et Pater eum misit, et Filius. Sive enim propter visibilem creaturam, sive potius propter principii authoritatem vel commendationem, non propter inequalitatem vel imparitatem et dissimilitudinem substantiæ, in Scripturis hæc posita intelliguntur. Non ergo ideo dicitur Pater misisse Filium, vel Spiritum Sanctum, quia ille esset major, et illi minores; sed maxime propter authoritatem principii commendandam, et quia in visibili creatura non sicut ille apparuit.—*Aug. de Trin.* lib. iv. cap. 21. Missio importat minorationem in eo qui mittitur, secundum quod importat processionem a principio mittente, aut secundum imperium aut secundum consilium, quia imperans est major, et consilians est sapientior. Sed in divinis non importat nisi processionem originis, quæ est secundum equalitatem.—*Aquin.* i. p. Quæst. 43, Art. 1, resp. ad primum. Δῆλον ὅτι τὸ μεῖζον ἐστι τῆς αἰτίας, τὸ δὲ ἴσον τῆς φύσεως.—*Naz. Orat.* 2 de Filio, p. 582.

God pitch upon his Son and send him? Might not some other person have been sent as well as he? or might not some other way have been found out as good as this?

I answer, no; Christ the Son must be the very person whom God will send. And him he pitched upon, so far as we poor shallow mortals are able to judge of his deep and unsearchable actings, or to assign the reasons of them, for these reasons:

1. First, Because he was the person with whom the Father had covenanted about this very thing. There was a covenant, commonly called the covenant of redemption, which had passed betwixt these two persons, in which the Father engaged so and so to Christ, and Christ reciprocally engaged so and so to the Father—a considerable part of the terms and matter of which covenant is set down, Isa. liii. 10, 'When thou shalt make his soul an offering for sin, he shall see his seed,' &c. The Father covenants to do thus and thus for fallen man; but first, in order thereunto, the Son must covenant to take man's nature, therein to satisfy offended justice, to repair and vindicate his Father's honour, &c. Well, he submits, assents to these demands, indents and covenants to make all good; and this was the covenant of redemption. Now upon this covenant God sends his Son, that being done in pursuance of, and agreeable to, that admirable compact or stipulation that had passed betwixt them both. So that this sending was not founded merely upon the Father's absolute will or sovereignty over Christ, but upon the federal agreement made betwixt them as to this very matter: of which I will say no more here, having formerly had an opportunity to publish some thoughts about it.

2. Secondly, God sent Christ because he saw that was the very best way which could be taken, and therefore in wisdom he pitched upon it. Oh there was no way like to that! The Father had great designs now to carry on; as, for example, to let the world see what an evil thing sin was, what a dreadful breach it had made betwixt himself and the creature, how terrible and impartial his justice was, what an ocean of love he had in his heart to promote the sinner's happiness, yet so as, in the first place, to secure and advance his own glory in the magnifying of all his attributes, to endear himself, his Son, and all his mercies to his people, to lay a sure foundation for the righteousness and salvation of believers. Were not these great and glorious designs? Now there was no way for the accomplishing and effecting of these comparable to this of God sending his Son. What God might have done some other way by his absolute power and will, abstracting from his decree, I dare not inquire into, much less determine anything about it; or whether this was the only way, I leave to others to discuss. But certainly this was the best, the fittest way, and therefore the wise God pitched upon it. Augustine went no higher than thus.[1]

3. Christ was sent, because as this was the best and the fittest way, so he was the best and the fittest person to be employed in such an embassy. God always sends the fittest messengers upon his errands. It was a great errand for Christ to come from heaven to earth about man's redemption, but God saw that he was the fittest messenger to be employed therein, and therefore he sent him. For as he employs none in his work, especially when it is high and of great importance, whom he doth not either find or make fit for it; so the more fit any are for his work, the rather he doth employ them; and therefore this was that which induced him to send Christ, none being so fit for the managing and transacting the work of redemption as he was, which I shall endeavour to make out in a few particulars.

Christ's superlative fitness for it appears from, and was grounded upon,

(1.) His two natures, the hypostatical union of both in his person. He was God, John i. 1; Phil. ii. 6; 1 John v. 20; Rom. ix. 5; Isa. ix. 6; Tit. ii. 13; he was also man, 1 Tim. ii. 5; then too he was God-man in one person, Col. ii. 19. Now who could be so fit to bring God and man together, as he who was himself both God and man? who so fit to negotiate with both, as he who was a middle person

[1] Eos itaque qui dicunt, itane defuit Deo modus alius quo liberaret homines a miseria mortalitatis hujus, ut unigenitum Filium, &c. Parum est sic refellere, ut istum modum, quo nos per Mediatorem Dei et hominum hominem Jesum Christum Deus liberare dignatur, asseramus bonum et divinæ congruum dignitati: verum etiam ut ostendamus non alium modum possibilem deo defuisse, cujus potestati æqualiter cuncta subjacent, sed sanandæ nostræ miseriæ convenientiorem alium non fuisse. *Aug. de Trin.*, lib. xiii. cap. 10.

betwixt both? who so fit to treat with an offended God, as he who was God? who so fit to suffer as he who was man, and to merit by suffering as he who was God-man? Had he been only God, he could not have suffered; had he been only man, he could not have merited; but being both he was eminently fit for both, viz., for suffering and meriting, for obeying and satisfying. Thus his not to be paralleled fitness was grounded upon his personal consideration.

(2.) It was grounded upon his glorious attributes, his power, wisdom, mercy, goodness, faithfulness, holiness, &c. He that will undertake to redeem sinners must have all these, for they all were indispensably requisite to such an undertaking. The Lord Jesus had them all, and that too in an eminent and extraordinary measure, as I might easily shew at large. Never did any mere creature arrive at that pitch of wisdom, power, holiness, &c., which he did, therefore none so fit to be sent as he.

(3.) It was grounded upon his Sonship and near relation to God. Who so fit to make others the adopted sons of God, as he who was himself the natural Son of God?

(4.) Upon the glory and dignity of his person. He was 'the image of the invisible God,' Col. i. 15; 'the express image of his Father's person,' Heb. i. 3. Now who so fit to restore man to God's image, as that man who was the essential image of God?

(5.) Christ's admirable and transcendent fitness was grounded upon his threefold office, as he was king, priest, and prophet. For hereupon he was, and is, fit to deal both with God and man; he is a priest to deal with God, a king and prophet to deal with man. Doth God stand upon satisfaction? Christ is a priest to die, and to offer up himself an expiatory sacrifice; or will God keep his distance from the creature, and be known in his greatness? Christ is a priest to mediate and intercede. Then is the sinner under ignorance and darkness? Christ is a prophet to enlighten and teach. Or is he under the tyranny of sin and a rebel against God? Christ is king to rescue, subdue, and conquer him to himself, to bring and keep him under his own dominion and government. To sum up all. There are but two things to be done for the sinner in order to his happiness, viz., impetation and application. Now

both of these are done by Christ's threefold office. By the first part of his priestly office, his oblation, there was the impetration, for by that he procured, purchased, merited all good; by the second part of his priestly office, his intercession, there is the application. And because both God and the creature are to be dealt withal in order to this application, therefore Christ doth accordingly deal with both of them. With God he deals in the way of prayer or intercession; for God, because of his majesty and sovereignty, will be treated in this manner; with the creature he deals in the way of power, partly by dispelling the darkness of the mind, which he doth as a prophet, and partly by taking off the rebellion of the will, and bringing the stubborn sinner under a ready subjection to God, which he doth as king. Which things being done, all that Christ hath purchased is now made over and actually applied to the creature. Upon the whole, then, it follows, that Christ being invested with these offices, which are every way so full, of so great virtue, so suited to the nature and demands of God, and the condition of the sinner, he must needs be by many degrees the fittest person to be sent by God.

Before I go off from this head, I desire one thing may be taken notice of. It must be granted, that the sending of Christ was previous and antecedent to several of the things which have been mentioned, as the demonstrations of his superlative fitness to be sent, and the grounds of his being sent. Yet nevertheless they may be alleged and made use of in that notion, because though in our apprehension, if not also in the nature of the thing, they were after the sending, yet in the eye and estimation of God they were before it. For instance, Christ, just at his sending, had not then assumed the human nature, (we suppose that to antecede his incarnation,) yet God judged him a person fit to be sent because of that nature. And so he might very well; for though the incarnation, as considered in itself, was future, yet as to the knowledge, consideration, estimation of God, it was present and done already. I thought it necessary to put in this, for the preventing of an objection which might arise in the thoughts of some upon the reading of what had been laid down.

4. Fourthly, God therefore sent Christ, not only because he was the fittest person to be sent, but be-

cause indeed he was the only person that could be sent; for none but he could effect or accomplish man's redemption. If God will be so gracious as to send, it was not only convenient but necessary that he should send this very person, his own Son, for there was none other in heaven or earth that could go through an undertaking of this nature. There were evils to be endured which were above the strength of any mere creature to endure; there were evils to be removed—the wrath of God, the guilt of sin, the curse of the law—which no mere creature was able to remove; there were also blessings to be procured—as reconciliation with God, justification, adoption, eternal salvation—which no such creature possibly could procure. Oh no! Therefore Christ himself must come, or nothing can be done. Why did not God send an angel rather than his Son? Why, because he knew redemption-work was no work for an angel; no, not for the whole body of angels. If the whole order of them had come from heaven and combined all their strength together, they could not have redeemed so much as one soul. I dispute not how far God, by his mighty power, might have enabled an angel to have borne up under the greatest sufferings. Suppose he might have had such a strength as to have been able to undergo all that Christ did, yet under the highest communications of the grace of God to him, he, being still a mere creature, could never satisfy for what was past, nor merit for what was to come; he could neither expiate sin nor procure eternal life. No; these are things which could only be accomplished by him who was more than a mere finite or created being, even by the Lord Jesus, who was man, but God too; wherefore he is the person whom the Father will send. And he very well understood himself in what he did; if the work had been possible to have been effected by any creature, God would have employed that creature and spared his own Son; nothing but absolute necessity made him to fix upon this course.

So much for the reasons why God sent his Son; which we poor dim-sighted creatures do but in a manner guess at, but he himself understands them fully. As 'all his works are known to him,' Acts xv. 18, so also the special reasons of all his works are known to him, and eminently those which he went upon in this his highest and greatest work.

When we come to heaven we shall more fully know why Christ was sent, but here our knowledge is very dark and imperfect about it.

I have done with the three things which I propounded to open, and so have despatched the doctrinal part. I am now to make some practical improvement of it.

Was Christ sent, and did God thus send him? What doth this great act of God call for from us? I will tell you in a few things.

Use 1. It calls upon us greatly to admire God. Oh how should all our souls be drawn forth and elevated in the adoring of God, for his sending of Christ! What rich mines of grace have we in these few words, *God sent his own Son!* Here is the greatest thing that ever God did, or ever will do. It was much that he should make a world, but what is the making of a world to the sending of a Son? The apostle, in the text, seems to ascend step by step, and to crowd together variety of great and glorious things, that he might the more heighten God's love, and draw up the hearts of believers to the admiration of it. For, 1. Here is sending; 2. God sending; 3. God sending a Son; 4. His own Son; 5. The sending of this Son in our flesh; yea, 6. In the likeness of sinful flesh; yea, 7. In that flesh to offer up himself as a sacrifice for sin; 8. Doing this for this end, that sin might be condemned, and that the righteousness of the law might be fulfilled in us; 9. Doing this too when the sinner's case was desperate as to the law. Is not here *magnum in parvo?* and doth not the apostle thrust things together, heaping one thing upon another, that he might the better set off and aggrandise the love of God? There is enough in any one of them to make you stand and wonder; but when you have them conjunct, and all set before you in their proper emphasis and import, how should you be affected and wrought upon to admire the grace of God! The truth is, take all together, and you have here a representation of that love, mercy, goodness, which was too great and big for any but a God. If you read no further than *the law could not do, in that it was weak through the flesh,* there man is utterly lost; but if you go on to *God's sending of his Son, &c.,* there the day of salvation begins to dawn; there is an effectual remedy for a desperate malady; now the case is altered.   Oh let the blessed God be therefore for ever magnified and adored !

2. More particularly, this calls upon you to admire the love of God the Father, and always to entertain good thoughts of him ; they are distinct heads, however let me put them together.   I would not too curiously divide or distinguish betwixt the sacred persons in their several acts ; much less would I set them in competition, or prefer one before another, as if we were more beholden to the one than to the other.   As they centre in the same common essence, it is the same love and the same gracious actings in all ; but yet they being personally distinct, and they having those acts which are proper to them as so distinguished, so they have their special and peculiar love.   And it is very good for us to understand what is immediately done by the Father, what by the Son, what by the Spirit ; which we must the rather endeavour after, because the Scripture usually, I do not say always, applies this effect to the first, that to the second, and another to the third person.   I am at present only to speak to the acts of the Father, wherein he hath displayed that love which is proper to him ; which if you please to look into, as the Scripture sets them forth, you will find yourselves under a strong obligation to admire him, as personally so considered. For I pray, observe, who did from all eternity predestinate, elect, choose you ? was it not God the Father ?   Predestinating love is the Father's love : Eph. i. 3–5, 'Blessed be the God and Father of our Lord Jesus Christ, who hath blessed us with all spiritual blessings in heavenly places in Christ ; according as he hath chosen us in him before the foundation of the world, &c. : having predestinated us unto the adoption of children by Jesus Christ to himself, according to the good pleasure of his will.' After this came redeeming love, and had the Father no hand in that love ? nay, had not he the first and the chief hand therein ?   For did not he find out the ransom ?   Job xxxiii. 24, 'I have found a ransom.' Did not he contrive and lay the whole model and platform of redemption in his eternal purpose and ordination ?   Therefore it is said, Isa. liii. 10, 'The pleasure of the Lord shall prosper in his hand ;' that great work resolves itself into the will and pleasure of the Father, as the first and principal cause of

it ; Christ, as mediator, is brought in but as subordinate to him, as being but the ministerial and executive agent in redemption, for it is but in his hands that the pleasure of the Lord should prosper. Who chose, sent, called Christ to that work, and fitted him for it, but the Father, as you have heard ?   So also who assisted and strengthened him in it, but the Father ?   Isa. xlii. 1, 'Behold my servant, whom I uphold ;' of which upholding and strengthening grace by the Father Christ assured himself beforehand, as you read, Isa. l. 7, 9 ; and it was accordingly made good to him, as you read, Mat. iv. 11 ; Luke xxii. 43.   Then again, who rewarded Christ when he had finished his work, but the Father ?   Therefore to him Christ prayed for this : John xvii. 4, 5, 'I have glorified thee on the earth : I have finished the work which thou gavest me to do.   And now, O Father, glorify thou me with thine own self with the glory which I had with thee before the world was.'   And now Christ hath made the purchase, who doth authoritatively collate upon persons the blessings purchased, but the Father ?   Rom. viii. 33, 'It is God that justifieth.' 2 Cor. v. 18, 'All things are of God, who hath reconciled us to himself by Jesus Christ,' &c.   Luke xii. 32, 'Fear not, little flock ; it is your Father's good pleasure to give you the kingdom.'   Who is it that works in sinners their meetness for heaven, but the Father ?   Col. i. 12, 'Giving thanks unto the Father, which hath made us meet to be partakers of the inheritance of the saints in light.'   Who is it that reveals the great mysteries of the gospel, but the Father ?   Mat. xi. 25, 'I thank thee, O Father, Lord of heaven and earth, because thou hast hid these things from the wise and prudent, and hast revealed them unto babes.'   Who bestows and gives the Spirit, but the Father ?   John xiv. 16, 'I will pray the Father, and he shall give you another Comforter, that he may abide with you for ever ; even the Spirit of truth.'   And, to shut up this, who secures and keeps in a state of grace, but the Father ? John x. 29, 'My Father, which gave them me, is greater than all ; and no man is able to pluck them out of my Father's hand.'   Now, Christians, may you not be fully convinced by all this, that the Father's love to you is very great ? and if so, will you not admire him for it ?   You must 'honour the

Son, even as you honour the Father,' John v. 23; and you must adore, bless, love the Father even as you do the Son. God forbid that I should go about to lessen your most thankful sense of what the Son and Spirit have done for you! but yet know, that these the Father, as the first cause doth work by, it is he who by them doth so great things for you: I pray, think high of their love, but then think high of his love too.

Further, I would persuade you to entertain good thoughts of the Father. It is a temptation, though not so usual, which some gracious persons lie under, they can with more comfort think of the Son than of the Father; they do not so much question the love of the Son as of the Father; they cannot deny but that the Son is indeed a very gracious person, for he came from heaven to seek and to save what was lost, Luke xix. 10; to save sinners, yea, the chiefest of them, 1 Tim. i. 15, &c. Hereupon they can, in some comfortable manner, encourage themselves to hope in him. But as to the Father they are not so confident; they are more jealous and suspicious, and have a greater dread of him than they have either of the Son or of the Spirit. Doth Satan assault any of you in this manner? Or do such thoughts as these prevail over you? Oh be convinced of your mistake! You have as great encouragement for faith and hope from the Father as you have from the Son; for you hear it was he who sent Christ, and whatever Christ was or did, all was but in pursuance of his good pleasure; therefore have you any reason to think otherwise than well of him? Surely ' God is love,' 1 John iv. 16. This very thing, his sending of his Son, represents him as full of mercy, goodness, and grace; the sinner hath not the least cause to be jealous or afraid of him. Oh when unbelief and hard thoughts of God the Father begin to rise, beat them down by arguing thus: Was not he the first spring from which redeeming grace did flow? the great contriver and willer of man's recovery? Who set Christ on work but he? Who sent him into the world to be a Saviour but he? Who employed his own Son for the good of sinners but he? Oh that you would labour to get your faith encouraged and strengthened as to the first person; and that it might rise up to the first cause of all, and there fix and terminate, ' that your faith and hope may be

in God,' as the apostle expresses it, 1 Pet. i. 21. Christ says, John xiv. 1, ' Let not your heart be troubled: ye believe in God, believe in me also;' and let me say, Ye believe in Christ, believe in God also, as the fountain and original of all your happiness.

3. It calls upon us to love Christ greatly. Oh how should the consideration of this endear Christ to every gracious heart! God sent him, but not against his will. How willing was he to be sent upon the errand of your salvation! He freely consented to whatever the Father was pleased to put him upon for your good. He very well knew beforehand what would follow upon this sending, what he was to undergo, how he was to be abased, if he do engage to redeem and save you; yet notwithstanding this, no sooner did the Father call him to it, but he most readily and cheerfully obeyed. Oh the infinite love of Christ! He came down from heaven that he might carry you up to heaven; he that was a Son, for your sake stooped to be a servant, that you of slaves might be made sons. What had become of you if Christ had refused to come when the Father sent him? Oh love the Lord Jesus! let his person be very dear and precious to you; admit him into your hearts, who was willing to take the whole business of your salvation into his hands. What love can be enough for a Father sending, and a Son coming! It is true God sent him; but his obedience to his Father was no diminution of his love to you; and it is true in this embassy he acted in a way of inferiority to his Father; but it was his pity to you which made him willing to put himself into such a state of subjection and inferiority: for that did not proceed from his nature, before he had assumed yours, but merely from his dignation and gracious condescension. And now, after all this, will you not love him? How can you do otherwise than love him? Suppose you had heard him, as soon as ever God had signified his pleasure to him, and said, Son! the fulness of time is come, I must send thee down to earth to redeem man! saying, Father, I am ready; here I am, send me whithersoever and about whatsoever thou pleasest. To promote thy glory, and the good of souls, I am willing to go wherever thou wilt have me; yea, I will stick at nothing which thou shalt judge necessary for the

preventing of the sinner's everlasting ruin. Send me to be made flesh, I submit; to lie in a manger, I submit; to die upon a cross, I submit; lay what commands upon me thou pleasest, to further the salvation of souls, they shall all be obeyed. Suppose, I say, you had heard Christ uttering such words to his Father, doubtless it would have wrought very much upon you; your hearts would have been all in flames of love to him. O wretched creatures! we know all this was spoken and done too by our Lord Jesus, and yet how cold, how weak, is our love to him!

4. It calls upon you to imitate Christ in his carriage with respect to his being sent. Thus never go till you be sent, then go readily; both of these were admirably done by our Lord Jesus. He went not till he was sent. Before he would move one step he would have his Father's mission and commission. A great mind he had to be at redeeming work, his heart was exceedingly set upon it; yet he would stay till he was sent, called, authorised thereunto by his Father. But as soon as he was so called, how readily and cheerfully did he engage! 'Lo, I come to do thy will, O God!' Heb. x. 7. Now, in this his deportment he hath set us an excellent copy to write after, teaching us always humbly to wait for a call from God, and when it comes, let it be what it will, faithfully to comply with it. Whatever rank or station God hath set you in, see that you therein abide, 1 Cor. vii. 17, 20, 24, and that you meddle with no work, employment, office, undertaking, further than as you are called thereunto. This is a duty in special incumbent upon public officers, magistrates, and ministers, as also upon Christians in a private capacity, with respect to public offices; none must presume to invade an office, or to intrude themselves into it, where they are not sent by God. Oh that is an act of high presumption, and usually attended with sad and fatal consequences, as several instances shew. Concerning the office and work of the ministry the apostle is very smart: Rom. x. 13, 'How shall they preach except they be sent?' The interrogation carries a vehement negation in it, viz., without a call and mission from God none ought, none can, (that is, lawfully, warrantably, you may put in too successfully,) preach the gospel.[1] But now, though

[1] Deus non fortunat labores eorum qui non sunt vocati, et quamvis salutaria quædam afferant, tamen non ædificant.— *Luther.*

in things of this nature a divine call be eminently requisite, yet it is not to be limited to them. Whoever you be, whatever work or service you engage in, you must look to your call and commission from God. For you can no further expect assistance, acceptance, success in anything you do, than as you are thereunto called. When it is so, you may rely upon it God will assist, accept, succeed, prosper; but when it is otherwise, nothing can be hoped for. Our Lord being sent, it was prophesied that the work should prosper in his hands, Isa. liii. 10, and we find that from the consideration of his sending all along he fetched encouragement, that his Father would be with him, and would not leave him alone, as you see John viii. 29, *et passim.* Hence, therefore, I would give you this advice: in every undertaking, especially when it is very weighty and momentous, make sure of a call and commission from above. To run upon anything without this you will find to be not only uncomfortable, but very dangerous. And in order to the finding out of this call, *pro hic et nunc*, there must first be the serious studying of the word, and then the prudent weighing and considering of providences, so far as they comply with the word; for providences, so bounded, may sometimes, in such and such particular cases, give much light concerning the will and call of God. But I must not engage in this point.

But then I add, which is the second branch of this exhortation, When once you are clear in your call, stick at nothing. If God bids you go, be sure you go, let the errand be what it will. Suppose the work be difficult, dangerous, contrary to the interest of the flesh, &c., it is no matter for that; if God commands, you must obey; if God sends, you must run. No dangers, difficulties, discouragements, sufferings, fleshly concerns, are then to be regarded. Paul's example herein was excellent, and most worthy of our imitation. Gal. i. 15, 'When it pleased God, who separated me from my mother's womb, and called me by his grace, to reveal his Son in me, that I might preach him among the heathen; immediately I conferred not with flesh and blood.' No question but flesh and blood were very apt to suggest many things, to make this blessed man to balk the call and work of God. Ay! but, says he, I would not confer with them, so as to hearken to their suggestions, so as to fetch my guidance and direction from them.

No; these he laid aside, that he might wholly steer his course by God's will. Oh let the service be what it will, be it the preaching of the gospel amongst heathens, there must be no consulting with carnal reason or carnal interest against a divine call and command. But I am upon a far higher example, the example of Christ himself. Never was any sent upon such work as his was. That was hard work indeed, abasing work indeed, painful work indeed, never was any to be compared with it; and yet, upon his Father's call, with what readiness did he set upon it! And this is that very thing wherein the apostle would have us to conform to Christ: Phil. ii. 5, 'Let this mind be in you which was also in Christ Jesus.' What mind doth he mean? Why, this; upon all occasions, in ready compliance with the will and call of God, to be willing to be emptied and abased, to be, to do, to suffer anything. It is a great evil for any, upon carnal and selfish grounds, to shift off and withstand a call from God. Therefore the Lord took it very ill from Moses that he was so backward to go upon his sending, and would so fain have put it off: Exod. iv. 13, 'Send I pray thee by the hand of him whom thou wilt send;' but it follows, ver. 14, 'The anger of the Lord was kindled against Moses.' Jonah's disobedience in this cost him dear. God sent him to Nineveh, but thither he would not go; wherefore God sent him to the bottom of the sea, and thither he shall go. Oh let all dread the like disobedience! Pray be always willing to observe and obey God's call; balk not any service which he puts upon you; stir not a step till he sends; be sure you run when he sends. It is the wisdom of a Christian not to stir a foot till he be sent; it is the zeal of a Christian to run when he is sent. It is a blessed thing when we can so carry it as neither to be over-forward in running before we are sent, (for which, though possibly in a sense somewhat different from that which I am upon, God so much complained of the false prophets, Jer. xiv. 14, and xxiii. 21,) nor over-backward in demurring and hanging off after we are sent. When God asked the prophet, Isa. vi. 8, 'Whom shall I send, and who will go for us?' see how presently he answered, 'Here am I, send me.' Oh that there was such a readiness in all of us to comply with God's call! Believe it, no errand is, or can be, bad, which he sends about.

5. A word of cautionary advice will here be very necessary; it is this, take heed that you do not rest or take up with the external sending of Christ. When the everlasting concerns of your souls are upon your thoughts, and you are casting with yourselves what may be necessary to bring you to heaven, take heed of looking no farther than merely a Christ sent. True, this is the great thing which faith builds upon, the proper and sole foundation of all its reliance and confidence; for that which it doth ultimately eye in the hope of pardon, justification, eternal life, is merely a Christ sent by God; but yet as to the qualification and actual entitling of the person to the things believed and hoped for, so there must be something more than the bare external sending of Christ. Every one knows there is a twofold sending of him, the one external and visible, the other internal and invisible:[1] the first was Christ's sending to be man—that is past and over, and was to be but once; the second is Christ's sending into man—that yet continues, and is reiterated from time to time. Now these two, though they are of a different nature, must not be parted; he that would regularly hope for salvation by Christ must have the latter as well as the former sending; for it is most certain that a Christ without, if it be not also a Christ within, will never save. A Christ in our flesh must be accompanied with a Christ in our hearts; there must be not only a Christ sent to us, but also a Christ sent into us, or else he will not profit us. The whole business of merit lies upon the Christ without, as he took our nature and therein fulfilled the law; but the fitting or qualifying of persons to have a share in the blessings merited, that lies in the Christ within, as he is received into the heart. In a word, the impetration is by Christ without, but the application is by Christ within. Now therefore, I say, you must not rest in the one, unless you find the other too; there are very dangerous mistakes abroad in the world about this.

[1] Ecce distincti sunt duo modi missionis Filii, et secundum alterum semel tantum missus est Dei Filius, secundum alterum sæpe missus est, et mittitur quotidie. Nam secundum alterum missus est ut sit homo, et semel tantum factum est; secundum alterum vero mittitur ut sit cum homine, quomodo quotidie mittitur ad sanctos, et missus est etiam ante incarnationem, et ad omnes sanctos qui ante fuerunt, et etiam ad angelos. Vide *Aug. de Filio*, &c.; *Lomb.*, lib. i. d. 13.

2 B

Some are all for a Christ within, making nothing of a Christ without; a most pernicious opinion, and destructive of all Christianity. Others again are all for a Christ without, contenting themselves with this, that he was sent into the world to save sinners, and this to them is enough for future happiness, they look no farther. But now, whoever would be wise to salvation, must take in both; so as to adore, believe in, rest upon a Christ as externally sent, and yet so as to make sure of a Christ in himself, Col. i. 27, through the gracious operations of the Spirit. Paul here in this verse speaks of the external sending, in the 10th verse he speaks of the internal sending, 'And if Christ be in you,' &c.; all that live under the gospel know the former, but few know the latter. Oh how is it with you? Christ was sent *to* you, but is he *in* you? He was formed in the Virgin's womb, but is he formed in your hearts? as the expression is, Gal. iv. 19. He came from heaven in a corporeal manner *for* you, but did he ever in a spiritual manner come *into* you? You have the external mission, but have you also the mystical union? Hath the Father, who sent his own Son in your flesh, sent also his own Spirit into your hearts? which is the great promise of the New Testament, as the former was the great promise of the Old; see John xiv. 26, xv. 26, and xvi. 7. Pray search diligently into these things, for be assured that a Christ as only sent in the likeness of sinful flesh, if he and his Spirit be not also received within, I say a Christ, so stated, will never make you happy.

6. Did God thus send Christ? It calls aloud to you all to believe in him. Hath the Father chosen him, set him apart, every way fitted him to be a redeemer, sent him into the world for that end, and after all this, will you not receive, embrace, fly to, and venture yourselves, your all upon him? Oh what an argument is this to draw sinners to a hearty closure with Christ! What will engage souls to believe on him if this will not? Christ, as sent, is the object, the ground, and also the great encouragement of faith. Sinners! you may very safely believe on him, for he is no imposter or deceiver, but that very person whom God sent to be the Saviour of the world. And it is not only so, that you may safely believe on him, but it is your great duty to believe

on him; for he who sent him, lays this as his great command upon you so to do: 1 John iii. 23, 'And this is his commandment, that we should believe on the name of his Son Jesus Christ.' John vi. 29, 'This is the work of God,' that great work which he enjoins, 'that ye believe on him whom he hath sent.' It is observable how high Christ speaks of the knowledge of himself under this notion, as he was sent of God: John xvii. 3, 'This is life eternal, that they might know thee the only true God, and Jesus Christ whom thou hast sent.' As also how desirous he was that the world might know and believe that he was thus sent of God: John xvii. 21, 23, 'That they all may be one, as thou, Father, art in me, and I in thee; that they all may be one in us, that the world may believe that thou hast sent me:' 'I in them, and thou in me, that they may be made perfect in one, and that the world may know that thou hast sent me.' Now what was it that Christ propounded to himself in all this? Certainly he had more in his eye than the bare notional knowledge of, or naked assent to, this great truth, that he was the person sent of God. Yes, his desire reached to a practical and fiducial knowledge of it, to such a knowledge as might be attended with true and saving faith. So that it is not enough for you to know and believe, in a common and general way, that Christ was indeed sent of God, which will only make you differ from Jews and heathens; but you must so know and so believe it as to receive, accept, close with, rest upon him in a saving manner, which will make you differ from all outside and formal Christians.

Further, let it be considered what was God's great design in the sending of Christ. It was this, that sinners believing in him might live; so the gospel tells you over and over: 'God so loved the world, that he gave, or sent, his only begotten Son, that whosoever believeth in him should not perish, but have everlasting life. For God sent not his Son into the world to condemn the world, but that the world through him might be saved,' John iii. 16, 17. Is not here a strong engagement as well as a high encouragement to believe? And it being God's act to send his Son, he looks upon himself as highly concerned according as men carry it towards him: therefore saith Christ, Mat. x. 40, 'He that receiveth me, receiveth him that sent me;' Luke x. 16, 'He that despiseth me, despiseth him that sent me.' And especially this holds true in the matter of believing or not believing. Oh do you close with Christ and receive him upon the gospel offer! not only he himself, but his Father also is highly pleased herewith, and takes it very kindly at your hands. Ay! says God, here are souls that do not throw away or tread upon that costly remedy which I provided for them; who give me the glory of my wisdom and mercy; who would not have my great designs, in the sending of my Son, to be frustrated; who duly entertain the messenger whom I sent to transact the great affairs of my glory and their good; who answer my expectations in my highest love, &c.; I say, this pleases God exceedingly. But, on the other hand, do you reject Christ, make little of him, stand it out against him, refuse to believe? how heinously doth God resent such carriage! This he looks upon as a high despising and undervaluing of his mercy, a desperate striking at his glory, which is very dear to him, a very unworthy requital of his love, a dangerous attempt to make all his grace to be to no purpose; and must not all this highly provoke him? Suppose some great person, hearing of the sad condition of some poor captives, should, out of mere compassion to them, send from a far country his own and only son to redeem them; and this son should in person come to them, and treat with them about their redemption, he offering to pay down their ransom, to free them from all their misery, provided they will but trust on him and be subject to him; if now these captives should slight all this, and choose still to continue in their chains, rather than upon these terms to accept of deliverance, would not this folly and obstinacy greatly incense both father and son? Or suppose, again, some offended prince, against whom the treason had been committed, should send his son to the traitor with a pardon in his hand, and he should take no notice of this son, or pardon brought by him, but reject and slight both, what could be expected to follow upon this but the greatest indignation? Now is not this the very case of unbelievers? nay, is not theirs much worse, in respect of the person sending, the person sent, the benefits offered, the conditions required? and therefore must not they incur a higher dis-

pleasure, and make themselves obnoxious to a worser severity? Sinners! shall not these things be thought of? will nothing prevail upon you to believe? Was Christ sent, and did he come to you, and will not you come to him? will you not yet understand that it is he only who must save you? To allude to that Acts vii. 25, 'He supposed his brethren would have understood, how that God by his hand would deliver them, but they understood not.' Do you look for another Son or another Saviour to be sent? indeed hath God such another Son to send? or was not the once sending of his Son enough? Hath not God in Christ given you his last way and method for salvation, so that there is no other to be expected after that? And was he only sent? Did he not do all for which he was sent, and so returned back again to his Father? Is there anything further to be done, but only that you will repent and believe? Methinks these considerations should work upon you; and yet I am sure they will not, unless the Lord persuade your hearts to believe, and he himself be pleased to work faith in you. We may speak much to convince you of your duty; but when we have said all, it is God who must both incline and enable you to believe, who must overpower against unwillingness, and strengthen against weakness. Faith is his gift, Eph. ii. 8: he who gives the Christ to be believed on, must give the grace to believe with; he who sent Christ to you, must draw you to Christ: John vi. 44, 'No man can (or will) come to me, except the Father which hath sent me, draw him.' So much for the duties proper to be urged upon God's sending of Christ, in which you have the first use.

Use 2. Secondly, It affords abundant matter of comfort to all sincere Christians. The truth which I have been upon, Christ sent by God, may be useful, not only as a powerful incentive to duty, but also as a firm foundation of inward comfort. O believers! set your faith, hope, joy, as high as ever you can, this sending of Christ will bear you out in it; you cannot, God having done this, over-believe or over-rejoice. I will shew you what there is wrapped up in a Christ sent; and for the better raising of your comfort I will instance in particulars; for it is with gospel-truths as it is with your perfumed things, which so long as they are wrapped up do but weakly affect the sense; but when they are taken out, opened and parted, then they do more strongly send forth their fragrant odours.

1. Did God send Christ? Surely then great was his good-will towards you; for had it not been so, would he ever have done such a great thing for you as this? Therefore that heavenly choir of angels singing in concert upon the birth of Christ made this a part of their spiritual song, Luke ii. 14, 'Glory to God in the highest, and on earth peace, good-will toward men;' I follow our reading of the latter clause, though I know it might be, and is, otherwise rendered; why did they say, *good-will toward men?* Oh because now in the sending and incarnation of Christ God had given out the highest demonstration that was possible of his good-will towards them. Had there been anything but that in his heart, and had there not been an abundance of that in his heart, he would never have sent, and so sent, his own Son.

2. Did God send Christ? Surely then he is in good earnest, real, hearty in the matters of salvation. After such a thing as this saints have not the least reason to be jealous of God, or to question the reality of his call, offers, invitations, intentions, promises, declarations concerning their happiness. What higher assurance could God give of his heartiness and reality in these than this? If he once send his Son there is no room left for suspicion or doubting. This assures us that God is real in his promises, and will be faithful to his promises, for by it they are all at once ratified and confirmed. If God make good the grand promise of sending his Son, what other promise will he not make good? A Christ sent is the seal of all the promises; see Isa. vii. 14.

3. Did God send Christ? Then you need not fear but that the work of redemption is completed. When such a person sends, and such a person is sent, the thing shall be done effectually and throughly; be it never so high, so hard, if Christ undertake it, he will accomplish it. Had a creature been sent, there might have been some ground of fear that he would not have been able to have gone through such a work; but when Christ is pitched upon, all ground of fear is removed; to be sure he can and will finish what he engages in. And it is evident that he perfected

what he came about, from the Father's re-admitting him into heaven; had there been anything left undone by him, would the Father have given him such a reception as he did? Believers, do not fear, all is finished, John xvii. 4; Christ gave not over till he brought it to that, John xix. 30. You do your work by halves, very weakly and imperfectly, but Christ did his completely; yea, though the law itself, through your flesh, was weak, yet Christ, in your flesh, was strong; he did that throughly which the law was altogether unable to do.

3. Did God send Christ? Know to your comfort he hath not yet done. As to his own satisfaction he hath no more to do, but as to your glory and happiness he will yet do more. He sent Christ once into the flesh, and he will send him again in the flesh, not to suffer and die again; no, Christ being dead dies no more, Rom. vi. 9, &c. There is now no further need of any suffering and dying, but to appear like himself in glory, and then to take you up into glory.[1] Once already he came down from heaven to earth, from thence he will come again; for what end? why, to carry you up from earth to heaven. Heb. ix. 28, 'Christ was once offered to bear the sins of many;' that is past: 'and unto them that look for him shall he appear the second time, without sin, unto salvation;' this is yet to come! Oh long for it, and rejoice in it! His first sending was to make the purchase, his second shall be to put you into possession; which shall be done as certainly as the former is done, and then there will be nothing further to be done.

5. Wherefore did God send Christ? For most gracious ends and purposes: 2 Tim. i. 15, 'Christ Jesus came into the world to save sinners,' &c. 1 John iv. 9, 10, 'In this was manifested the love of God toward us, because that God sent his only begotten Son into the world, that we might live through him. Herein is love, not that we loved God, but that he loved us, and sent his Son to be the propitiation for our sins.' John iii. 17, 'For God sent not his Son into the world to condemn the world, but that the world through him might be saved.' Now were these God's ends, and shall they

---

[1] Τὴν δευτέραν αὐτῷ πάλιν πρὸς ἡμᾶς ἔνδοξον καὶ θείαν ἀληθῶς ἐπιφανείαν, ὅτε οὐκ ἔτι μετ᾽ εὐτελείας, &c.—*Athan. de Incar. Verbi.*, p. 110.

not be accomplished? May not faith fetch strong encouragement from these? for in order to the strengthening of faith we are to look to God's works and their great ends, as well as to his word and promise.

6. Did God send Christ? Set this against all. Against the weakness of the law: that which the law could not do, Christ did; that which was too hard for it was not too hard for him. The text tells you he was sent on purpose to make up what was defective in the law. Set it also against the guilt of sin; upon Christ's sending, presently you read of the condemning of sin: 'God sent his own Son, &c., and for sin condemned sin in the flesh.' Sin was to be destroyed, and the wise God took a fit course, employed a fit messenger for that end, as the scape-goat with the sin of the people was to be sent away by the hand of a fit man into the wilderness, Lev. xvi. 21. Several other things might be instanced in; whatever it is which troubles the dejected Christian, let him therein study a God sending, a Son sent, and there he may find very proper and considerable satisfaction in every case.

7. God sent Christ, for whom? for you who see your lost and undone condition: Mat. xv. 24, 'I am not sent but unto the lost sheep of the house of Israel.' So his commission was straitened at first, but afterwards it was enlarged to the lost sheep of the Gentiles also: Luke xix. 10, 'The Son of man is come to seek and to save that which was lost;' Mat ix. 13, 'I am not come to call the righteous, but sinners to repentance;' 1 Tim. i. 15, 'This is a faithful saying, and worthy of all acceptation, that Christ Jesus came into the world to save sinners, of whom I am chief.'

8. He that sent Christ was also pleased to lay a special trust and charge upon him to secure all the elect, and to look to it that not one of those should perish. Here is a truth which is like the full honeycomb; you cannot touch it but honey and sweetness drops from it. And I the rather here take notice of it, because I find our Saviour himself, when he is speaking of his sending, to make mention of it; or when he mentions it, to take in also his sending; as John vi. 39, 40, 'This is the Father's will which hath sent me, that of all which he hath given me I should lose nothing, but should raise it up again at the last day. And this is the will of him that sent me, that every one which seeth the Son and believeth on him may have everlasting life, and I will raise him up at the last day.' Oh, when the Father sent Christ he made this known to him as his will and pleasure, that he should take special care of all his elect, and see that not one of them should be lost. And this Christ submitted to as a part of his suretyship, and ever since he hath with all faithfulness observed this his Father's will, and made good his trust in the securing of every sincere Christian. And, for your comfort, know that this trust doth as much lie upon Christ's hands now as ever it did; that even as to your individual persons, if you be true believers, it is the Father's will to Christ that he should not lose one of you, or let one of you perish. A child of God perish! Oh, by no means! that neither Father nor Son will permit. Rather than that should befall any of the elect, God would send his Son again to do and suffer all over again, if such a thing was to be imagined. Here then, believers, is matter of strong consolation for you, viz., as to your spiritual and eternal state you are safe. Christ is under a special obligation to secure you. For the Father did not only send him in order to the bringing of you into a good estate, but he did also then entrust him with the keeping of you in that estate when he should have brought you into it. And what can be spoken higher for your support and comfort? But I must leave these things with you. Oh that you would often think of them, especially in soul distresses, and be ever drawing from them till your hearts be even brimful of heavenly consolation!

Use 3. A third use offers itself, which might be as useful in order to information as the two former were in order to exhortation and consolation. Something hath been spoke for the opening of the nature and grounds of Christ's being sent; but as to the determination or close application of that to his person, wherein we have to do with Jews and infidels, little hath been spoken—I mean in that way and method which is proper to those opposers of Christ and Christianity. Here, therefore, I should lay down and make good these two propositions:

1. That that Jesus in whom we Christians believe, even he who was born of the Virgin Mary, suffered

under Pontius Pilate, was crucified, dead, and buried, and rose again, &c. I say this Jesus was the very person whom God sent, and consequently that he was the *Shiloh* or *Messias* prophesied of.

2. That this Jesus was so sent by God to be the true and only Messiah, as that besides and after him no other person is to be expected in that nature or quality to be sent by God.

Now though these be two as weighty and as fundamental truths to us Christians, as Christians, as any whatsoever; and though I could not hope to reach the great enemies of the gospel so as to fasten any conviction upon them, yet probably I might, in the pursuing of this argument, reach some weak Christians, so as to confirm and stablish them in the belief of these great truths; yet I shall not at present engage in the discussing of these two propositions. First, Because in so great points it is better to say nothing, than not to speak fully and thoroughly to them; which if I could, other discouragements being removed, hope to do, yet here in this place, without making the work in hand too vast and big, to be sure I could not. Secondly, Because however pertinent this undertaking might be to some other texts, to that which I am upon it would not be so pertinent; where the apostle's drift and design is not so much, in opposition to Jews and infidels, to assert that Christ was the very person sent of God, as to assign, for the comfort of believers, the way and course which God took to bring about their salvation, when upon the terms of the law it was impossible—namely, he sent his own Son, &c. The text, therefore, not tying me to it, I may waive it; I shall have work enough to go over what the proper and immediate sense of the contents of this chapter will lead me to, and therefore I may well cut off what is of a more remote and foreign consideration; so that this shall suffice for the first observation, Christ was sent, and sent by God the Father.

CHAPTER XI.

OF CHRIST BEING THE NATURAL AND ETERNAL SON OF GOD.

God sending his own Son in the likeness of sinful flesh.
—ROM. viii. 3.

The second observation spoken to, Of Christ being God's Son—How his Sonship is attested in Scripture—Of his being God's own Son—That opened as he is considered both relatively and absolutely—That he is the natural Son of God, co-equal, co-essential, co-eternal with the Father, is asserted and proved by sundry Scriptures—The true notion and ground of Christ's Sonship vindicated against the Socinians—Where it is made good against them, that he is not the Son of God, 1. In respect of his miraculous conception; nor 2. Of his extraordinary sanctification; nor 3. Of his resurrection; nor 4. Of the dignity and advancement of his person; nor 5. Of the Father's special love to him; nor 6. Of adoption; nor 7. Of his likeness to him—But he is the Son of God in respect of his participation of his Father's essence, and of his eternal generation—Some others, besides Socinians, somewhat concerned in this controversy—Of the different communication of the divine essence from the Father to the Son and to the Holy Ghost—Use 1. In which, by way of inference, it is shewn, 1. That Christ is God; 2. That he is a very great and glorious person; 3. That the work of redemption was a high and costly work—Use 2. Christians from thence are exhorted, 1. To study Christ in this relation, as God's own Son: some directions given about that; 2. To believe him and on him as such; 3. To honour and adore Christ; 4. To admire the greatness of God's love—Use 3. To draw forth the comfort wrapped up in this relation of Christ.

I PROCEED to the third general observed in the words—the description of the person sent. He is described by his near and special relation to God, as being God's own Son. From whence the second observation will be this, That the Lord Jesus, the person sent by God, as you have heard, was his Son, yea, his own Son: 1 John iv. 14, 'We have seen and do testify, that the Father sent the Son to be the Saviour of the world.'

Here two things are to be spoken to : 1. Christ was God's Son ; 2. He was God's own Son.

1. First, Christ was God's Son. He was truly the Son of man, but not only the Son of man, for he was also the Son of God ; and he was as truly the latter as the former. In reference to his human nature he is styled 'the seed of the woman,' Gen. iii. 15 ; 'the seed of Abraham,' Gal. iii. 16 ; 'the Son of David,' Mat. i. 1 ; the 'branch of the root of Jesse,' Isa. i. 1 ; Jer. xxiii. 5, 6 ; Zech. vi. 12 ; the Son of man. In reference to his divine nature he is styled the Son of God. This relative appellation or title is so frequently applied to Christ that if I should cite the several texts where it occurs, I must transcribe a great part of the New Testament.

Yet it will not be amiss to take notice of the several attestations there upon record to this great truth. As that of John Baptist : John i. 34, 'I saw, and bare record that this is the Son of God ;' that of Nathanael, John i. 49, 'Rabbi, thou art the Son of God ;' that of Peter, Mat. xvi. 16, 'Thou art Christ the Son of the living God ;' that of the centurion, Mat. xxvii. 54, 'Truly this was the Son of God ;' that of the eunuch, Acts viii. 37, 'I believe that Jesus Christ is the Son of God ;' that of Martha, John xi. 27, 'Yea, Lord, I believe that thou art the Christ, the Son of God, which should come into the world.' The devils themselves witnessed to it, Mat. viii. 29 ; they cried out, saying, 'What have we to do with thee, Jesus thou Son of God ?' Mark iii. 11, 'Unclean spirits, when they saw him, fell down before him and cried, saying, Thou art the Son of God.' Christ himself, even when he was speaking to God the Father, often asserted and pleaded his Sonship. And the Father himself, in a most solemn and open manner, attested it ; first at Christ's baptism, Mat. iii. 17, 'Lo, a voice from heaven, saying, This is my beloved Son, in whom I am well pleased ;' and then at his transfiguration, Mat. xvii. 5, 'Behold a voice out of the cloud which said, This is my beloved Son.' The apostle, 1 John v. 7, 8, speaks of the witness of heaven and of earth : 'There are three that bear record in heaven, the Father, the word, and the Holy Ghost ; and these three are one. And there

are three that bear witness in earth, the Spirit, and the water, and the blood ; and these three agree in one.' Now what is the thing which they bear witness to ? It is Christ's Sonship ; for that is instanced in as to the first and supreme witness : ver. 9, 'If we receive the witness of men, the witness of God is greater : for this is the witness of God, which he hath testified of his Son.' You see how fully this truth is attested, and how abundantly God was pleased to clear it up in the first promulgation of the gospel, it being the great thing necessary to be known and believed. Indeed the Jews, as to the body of them, had a veil before their eyes, so that they could not discern this near relation of Christ to God ; they saw the Son of man, but they did not see the Son of God. They went no higher than, 'Is not this the carpenter's son ; is not his mother called Mary ? and his brethren James, and Joses, and Simon, and Judas ? and his sisters, are they not all with us ?' Mat. xiii. 55, 56. 'Is not this Jesus the Son of Joseph, whose father and mother we know ; how is it then that he saith, I came down from heaven ?' John vi. 42. Nay, when Christ plainly and boldly told them that he was the Son of God, they could not bear it : John x. 33, 'For a good work we stone thee not, but for blasphemy, and because that thou, being a man, makest thyself God.' You may know what they meant by this by Christ's reply, ver. 36, 'Say ye of him whom the Father hath sanctified, and sent into the world, Thou blasphemest, because I said, I am the Son of God ?' Nay, they were so offended at it, that for this very thing they took away his life : John xix. 7, 'The Jews answered him, We have a law, and by our law he ought to die, because he made himself the Son of God.' You have a full account of it, Mark xiv. 61-65, 'Again the high priest asked him, and said unto him, Art thou the Christ, the Son of the blessed ? And Jesus said, I am, &c. Then the high priest rent his clothes, and said, What need we any further witnesses ? Ye have heard the blasphemy : what think ye ? and they all condemned him to be guilty of death.' Thus the eyes of that people were then—and oh that they were not so still !—so blinded, that they could not perceive Christ to be the Son of God ; but the Lord hath given sufficient evidence thereof to all who do not wilfully shut their eyes upon the light. It is a truth out of all question to us who are called Christians; yet about the nature and manner of Christ's Sonship there are some unhappy controversies raised amongst us.

2. Secondly, Christ was God's own Son: so it is here *signanter*, God sending *his own Son*. I have told you in the original it is τὸν ἑαυτοῦ υἱὸν, the Son of himself, or τὸν ἴδιον υἱὸν, his proper Son, as it is ver. 32. God is Christ's proper Father, ἴδιος πατὴρ, John v. 18; and Christ here is God's proper Son, ἴδιος υἱός. He is not barely a Son, but a Son in a special and peculiar manner, God's own Son. This being a truth of very high import, a most fundamental point, I will endeavour first to explain and prove it, and then to vindicate and make good its true and genuine notion against opposers.

Our Lord Jesus Christ is God's own Son, whether you consider him comparatively and relatively, I mean in reference to other sons, or absolutely as he is in himself, abstractly considered from all other sons.

1. Consider him comparatively. And so he is thus styled to difference or distinguish him from all other sons. For God hath three sorts of sons: (1.) Some are so by creation, or in respect of their immediate creation by God. So the angels are the sons of God; of whom divines commonly interpret these passages in Job, chap. i. 6, 'There was a day when the sons of God came to present themselves before the Lord;' chap. xxxviii. 7, 'When the morning stars sang together, and all the sons of God shouted for joy.' So Adam upon this account, he being immediately made by God, is called the 'son of God,' Luke iii. 38. (2.) Some are the sons of God by grace, viz., the grace of regeneration and adoption. Thus believers are the sons of God, as they are spiritually begotten of him, and adopted by him: John i. 12, 13, 'As many as received him, to them gave he power to become the sons of God, &c.; which were born not of blood, nor of the will of the flesh, nor of the will of man, but of God.' James i. 18, 'Of his own will begat he us with the word of truth,' &c. Gal. iv. 3, 'To redeem them that were under the law, that we might receive the adoption of sons.' Eph. i. 5, 'Having predestinated us unto the adoption of children by Jesus Christ to himself, according to the good pleasure of his will.' Rom. viii. 14, 'As many as are led by the Spirit of God,

they are the sons of God.' Gal. iii. 26, 'Ye are all the children of God by faith in Christ Jesus.' 1 John v. 1, 'Whosoever believeth that Jesus is the Christ, is born of God; and every one that loveth him that begat, loveth him also that is begotten of him.' Then (3.) in contradistinction to these there is God's own Son, or his Son by nature; one that is a Son of another rank and order than the former. In this respect God hath but one Son, namely, Christ. True believers are his sons, which speaks the exuberancy of divine love towards them: 1 John iii. 1, 'Behold what manner of love the Father hath bestowed upon us, that we should be called the sons of God!' Therefore Christ owns them for his brethren: Heb. ii. 11, 'Both he that sanctifieth, and they who are sanctified, are all of one: for which cause he is not ashamed to call them brethren;' and ver. 17, 'In all things it behoved him to be made like unto his brethren.' But yet they are not sons as Christ is; his Sonship and theirs are of a very different nature, differing no less than specifically. Upon which account he sometimes appropriates the paternal relation in God unto himself: Luke x. 22, 'All things are delivered to me of my Father,' &c. John xiv. 2, 'In my Father's house are many mansions.' And elsewhere he distinguishes betwixt God as being his Father, and as being the Father of believers: John xx. 17, 'Go to my brethren, and say unto them, I ascend to my Father and your Father, to my God and your God;' where he plainly makes a difference, for he doth not say, I ascend *to our Father*, as though he and they had one and the same common interest in this near relation to God, as he teaches us to say *our Father*, because we all stand upon the same foot and bottom of filiation: but he saith, 'I ascend to my Father and your Father,' thereby intimating that there was a difference betwixt God's being a Father to him, and a Father to them. And so indeed there is a vast one, for he is the Father of Christ by nature and by eternal generation;[1] but he is the Father of saints only by grace, by adoption and regeneration, which also are not eternal but accomplished in time. Thus in this comparative notion Christ may be called God's own Son.

[1] Ἄλλως ἐμοῦ κατὰ φύσιν, ἄλλως ὑμῶν κατὰ θέσιν.—*Cyrill. Hieros.*

2. Consider him absolutely and abstractly from all other sons, so he is God's own proper Son. It will be asked, how or wherein?

That I may a little insist upon the explication of this sublime mystery, I answer, Christ is God's own Son, not only as God hath a special interest or propriety in him, as believers are said to be οἱ ἴδιοι, Christ's own, John xiii. 1; nor only as Christ is the Son of no other father but of God, as the Socinians would turn off the word ἴδιος;[1] for so the saints themselves may be called God's own sons, they being sons as to their spiritual sonship by and from God the Father only: there must be therefore something higher than this intended in this glorious title of God's own Son. What may that be? *Ans.* That Christ was, and is, God's natural and essential Son; that he was in a peculiar manner begotten of him and from him in his eternal generation; that he did participate of the Father's own nature and essence; that he was a Son co-equal, co-essential, co-eternal with God the Father.

To draw all into as narrow a compass as may be. Our Lord Jesus is God's own Son, as God the Father did from all eternity, in an ineffable manner, beget him in his own divine essence; so that it points to two things—to his being eternally begotten, to his being begotten in the divine essence. As to the latter, I choose to express it so, because it is more safe, if not more true, to say that the Son was begotten *in* that essence rather than *out of* it. And some, who endeavour to open these profound mysteries, tell us that here we are not to consider Christ essentially as he is God, but personally as the divine essence subsists in him as the second person. In the first consideration, as he was God, he had the divine essence in and of himself, and so he could not be begotten to it, for he was αὐτοθεὸς, God from himself; though some, who yet were no Arians, do not agree to this.[2] In the second notion, as he was God personally considered, or as he was the second person and the Son, so he was of the Father and not of himself; for though he was αὐτοθεὸς, God of himself, yet he was not αὐτουιὸς, Son of himself. The usual

language of the ancients was 'God of God, very God of very God,' &c.; and this was very true; but then you must take it as spoken of God, personally considered with respect both to the person begetting and the person begotten;[1] for in the sacred persons essence doth not beget essence, but person begets person, as it is usually expressed.[2] I fear these things may be too high for our weak capacities, that they do but darken rather than illustrate the Sonship of Christ; yet divines know not how to speak more plainly concerning these mysteries. Well, I, for my part, will not venture too far into these great depths. That Christ is the Son of God, yea, thus the Son of God, as hath been laid down, is evident enough; but he that will engage in a curious inquisition into all particulars resulting from or referring to Christ's natural and eternal Son-ship, will find at last he attempted that which was infinitely too high for him.

Contenting ourselves, therefore, with this more general explication of it, and not launching out too far into particulars, that we may be the more firmly rooted in the belief of this great article of the Christian faith, viz., that Christ is the natural and eternally begotten Son of God, and therefore called his own Son, it will be necessary for us to look into the word of truth, to see what foundation we have there for

[1] Proprius Dei Filius jure optimo dicitur, propterea quod non sit alienus, nec cujuspiam alterius, &c.—*Slichting.*

[2] Amongst others see Armin. Declarat. Sent., p. 100, &c., et Resp. ad Artic., p. 131.

[1] Christus non est Filius essentiæ sed personæ; non Dei essentiæ sed Dei Patris. Genitus enim est non essentiatus, ergo non suæ essentiæ, vel sui Filius. Est Filius unius veri Dei, videlicet Patris, non divinæ in Patre essentiæ, &c.—*Hoorneb.*, Socin. conf., lib. i. cap. 1, p. 36. Cum dicitur quod Filius est a Patre, novimus ex ipsis fidei principiis hoc ita esse explicandum, ut Filius sit a Patre quoad personalitatem, nimirum secundum quod est Filius; non quoad Deitatem, et secundum quod est Deus. Siquidem cum Deitas Filii sit una illa simplex et ipsissima Patris Deitas, ab alio esse non possit; nam et Filius juste αὐτοθεὸς dicitur. Cum ideo in symbolo Nicæno de Christo occurrit, quod sit φῶς ἐκ φωτός, θεὸς ἀληθινὸς ἐκ θεοῦ ἀληθινοῦ, hoc sensu Catholico intelligendum est, ut sit Deus de Deo, non quoad Deitatem et essentiam, sed potius quoad personalitatem et subsistentiam, &c.—*Barlow*, Exercit. 5, p. 107, &c. The Son, in respect of his person, is of the Father, but in respect of his Godhead he is of none. The Son of God, considered as he is a son, is of the Father, God of very God; but considered as he is God, he is God of himself, because the Godhead of the Son is not begotten more than the Godhead of the Father.—*Perkins* on Gal., p. 271; see *Cheyn.*, Trin-unity p. 134.

[2] Alting. Theol. probl., loc. 30, probl. 32 and 34.

2 C

this our belief.   For it would be equally dangerous for us to believe it if the word doth not affirm it, as not to believe it if the word doth affirm it, because we cannot fathom several things in it by the plummet of reason.   I shall desire you, therefore, to weigh the following scriptures :

John vii. 29, 'I know him, for I am from him, and he hath sent me.'   They are the words of Christ uttered with reference to God the Father, concerning whom he saith that he was παρ' αὐτοῦ, from him.   How was Christ from the Father?   I answer, Not only in respect of his mission by and from the Father, that indeed follows immediately upon it, 'and hath sent me,' but not as the sole or main thing in respect of which Christ is said to be from his Father.   I conceive, his being sent is brought in as a quite other thing and distinct from that.   But Christ saith he was from the Father in respect of his eternal generation by the Father: that was the thing principally intended by him in this expression.   As the Holy Ghost is said to be from the Father, because of his procession from him, that is the reason I go upon : John xv. 26, παρὰ τοῦ Πατρὸς ἐκπορεύεται, 'He proceedeth from the Father;' so the Son, the second person, is said to be from the Father because of his generation by him, and I find the ancients thus opening the place.[1]

Another text for the proof of this eternal Sonship of Christ is Ps. ii. 7, 'The Lord hath said unto me, Thou art my Son; this day have I begotten thee.' To me this is a very considerable scripture for the confirming the truth in hand, though our adversaries, I know, make a contrary use of it, and some others who are friends speak somewhat diminutively about it.[2]   It is beyond all dispute that Christ was the person here spoken of; it was not said to David, further than as he was a type, but to Christ himself, 'Thou art my Son,' &c.   Thus some of the Jewish writers themselves do carry it,[3] and the matter of

the psalm, with the several expressions in it, are only applicable to Christ; see verses 8, 9, &c., to the end.   And as to that verse which I have to do with, you have it thrice cited in the New Testament, and it is always applied to Christ : so Acts xiii. 33 ; Heb. i. 5, and v. 5.   Well, then, what doth God here say concerning Christ?   Why, 'Thou art my Son.'   But how did Christ come to be his Son? Why, as he had 'begotten' him, for that comes in as the *fundamentum relationis*, 'Thou art my Son, I have begotten thee.'   But when did God thus beget him?   Why, from all eternity : '*to-day* have I begotten thee.'   Various are the apprehensions of men about the import and reference of this word, *to-day*, and what that matter or period of time is to which it refers.   Some make it to point to the time of the rage and opposition of enemies against Christ, spoken of ver. 1, &c. ; some to the time of the New Testament administration ; some to the time of Christ's resurrection and advancement, as we shall see hereafter.   But I must concur with those who do not understand it of this or that particular, determinate day or time, but make it to point to and be expressive of eternity.[1]   This eternity is but one day, or but one continued now, in which there being no succession, whatever God doth from eternity, he may be said to do it now, or to-day.   So here, 'this day have I begotten thee,' that is from everlasting. True, indeed, the word itself, in its first and strictest sense, doth not signify or import eternity ;[2] yet because in this place it must be interpreted according to the matter spoken of, therefore here it must have that signification, the nature of the thing so determining it.   For God's begetting of his Son being an immanent act, it must, as all acts of that nature

<hr>

[1] Ab ipso (inquit) sum, quia Filius de Patre, et quicquid est Filius de illo est cujus est Filius.   Ideo dominum Jesum dicimus Deum de Deo ; Patrem non dicimus Deum de Deo, sed tantum Deum.—*August.*

[2] As the learned Dr Jackson, who saith he dares not insist upon this text to prove Christ's eternal generation.—*On the Creed,* 7 B. sect. 3, chap. xxv. p. 257.

[3] One of which hath this notable passage about this 2d Psalm : Magistri nostri quicquid hoc psalmo canitur, de rege

Messia interpretati sunt ; sed secundum verborum sonum, et ob refutationem hæreticorum, (he means us Christians,) convenit, ut eum interpretemur de ipso Davide.—*Rabbi Solomon Jarchi.*

[1] *Hodie* non tempus certum, sed æternitatem designat.   Est descriptio naturæ æternitatis optime conveniens, omne præteritum a Deo removens, omne futurum a Deo præscindens, omnem successionem excludens, æternitatem his omnibus carentem optime explicans.—*Arnold. Catech. Racov. Major.*, p. 208.

[2] Non volunt nostri vocem hodie æternitatem significare, sed pro subjecta materia exponi debere ; et quando Deo tribuitur, non infringere ejus æternitatem, sed ei propter nos et ἀνθρώπινον duntaxat adjungi—*Hoorneb de Christo,* cap. 1, p. 17.

are, be from everlasting; and it being spoken after the manner of men, it must be so understood as may best suit with the nature of God, and with the nature of the thing which it speaks of. When, therefore, you read, 'Thou art my Son, this day have I begotten thee,' it is as if God had said, Oh my Son, I own thee to be so before the world, and I here attest that from all eternity I have begotten thee, and that thou art my Son by eternal generation. And thus the great lights of the ancient church, in their contest swith the Arians, did make use of and expound it.

That text in Prov. viii. is exceeding full and clear: ver. 22–24, &c., 'The Lord possessed me in the beginning of his way, before his works of old. I was set up from everlasting, from the beginning, or ever the earth was. When there were no depths I was brought forth; when there were no fountains abounding with water. Before the mountains were settled, before the hills, was I brought forth.' This is further, with great elegancy, set forth, ver. 26–28. He concludes, ver. 29, 30, 'When he gave to the sea his decree, that the waters should not pass his commandment; when he appointed the foundations of the earth; then I was by him, as one brought up with him, and I was daily his delight, rejoicing always before him.' Of whom can all this be understood but of Christ?[1] to whom is it applicable but to him who is the personal Wisdom of God the Father? and if so, doth it not then plainly hold forth his eternal existence, and also his eternal generation? So Micah v. 2, 'Thou, Bethlehem Ephratah, though thou be little among the thousands of Judah, yet out of thee shall he come forth unto me that is to be ruler in Israel, whose goings forth have been from of old, from everlasting.' In the Hebrew it is 'from the days of eternity.'

If we look into the New Testament this will yet be more clear. There Christ is styled 'the only begotten of the Father,' which title the evangelist John often repeats. The other evangelists speak much of Christ's manhood, and of his birth as man; but John is altogether taken up with the Godhead of Christ, and with his eternal generation as the Son of God;[2] whence Nyssene saith of him that he did

indeed θεολογεῖν; and some think he was from hence called 'John the divine;' in reference to which he calls him over and over God's only begotten Son, as you see John i. 14, 18, and iii. 16–18; 1 John iv. 9. Now how is Christ the only begotten Son of God? Surely it must be in respect of some extraordinary way and manner of his Sonship peculiar to himself; and what can that be but that which I am upon? Never was any person so begotten of the Father as he was.[1] God hath other sons begotten of him, as some pre-alleged scriptures testify, but yet Christ is styled his only begotten Son, because of his special and incommunicable generation, because he is the Son of God by nature, and hath that very nature and essence which God the Father hath. Take away this specialty of his Sonship, and how shall we interpret this exclusive title of Christ, the only begotten of God? He is not only called God's own Son, but also his only Son; and nothing can make him to be so, as will appear by and by, but his being the natural Son of God, and by eternal generation. It is observable, after the evangelist had been speaking of the sonship of believers, John i. 12, 13, immediately he speaks too of the Sonship of Christ, ver. 14; and he speaks of this as being of a different kind and order from the former, upon which he calls him 'the only begotten of the Father.' The old Arian heretics had a pretty evasion for this. Christ, says Eunomius, whom Basil and his brother Nyssene have so profoundly confuted, was the only begotten of the Father, inasmuch as he was begotten only of the Father; which evasion exactly falls in with that modern gloss which some Socinians give upon the text, Christ was God's own Son, i.e., he was the Son of no other but of God. But to this it is answered, there is a great difference betwixt being begotten only of the Father, and being the only begotten of the Father. The first makes God to be the only begetter, but not Christ to be the only begotten; without which this title of his would

---

[1] Vide *Synopsis Critic.*, vol. 2 in cap. viii. Prov. in initio.

[2] Τέταρτος ὁ Ἰωάννης τὴν κορωνίδα καὶ τὸ ἀκραιφνὲς τῆς ἄνω

τάξεως, καὶ ἀεὶ οὔσης θεότατος, τὸ ὕστερον ἐδήλωσεν.—*Epiphan. adv. Her.*, lib. ii. tom. ii. p. 747.

[1] Λέγεται μονογενὴς ὅτι μόνος ἐκ μόνου τοῦ Πατρὸς μόνως ἐγεννήθη, οὐδὲ γὰρ ὁμοιοῦται ἑτέρα γέννησις τῇ τοῦ υἱοῦ τοῦ Θεοῦ γεννήσει, οὐδὲ γὰρ ἐστιν ἄλλος υἱὸς τοῦ Θεοῦ.—*Damasc.*;—Nazianz. Orat. ii. de Filio et Sp. Sancto, page 590, puts in another word, μονοτρόπως.

signify nothing. For it is true as to the saints, they are begotten only of the Father; but yet it is not true that they are the only begotten of the Father. Indeed this belongs not to them at all, but only to Christ; their sonship by regeneration, and Christ's Sonship by eternal generation, are things of a quite different nature and species; and it must be so, or else he could not truly be styled 'the only begotten of the Father.'

The apostle in this chapter, ver. 32, calls Christ God's own Son, 'he that spared not his own Son,' &c. Now the word ἴδιος imports as much as God's proper or natural Son. That is the signification of it in other references: Luke vi. 44, 'Every tree is known by his own fruit;' it is ἴδιος καρπός, that fruit which is proper and natural to it; so that ἴδιον σῶμα is to be taken, 1 Cor. xv. 38, 'God giveth it a body as it hath pleased him, and to every seed his own body.' And so Christ is ἴδιος υἱός, God's own Son, that is, his Son who hath the same nature and essence with himself.

There are three properties, if the two first be not one and the same, belonging to Christ in his Sonship, which are incommunicable to any other. As,

(1.) He is a Son co-equal with his Father: John v. 18, 'The Jews sought the more to kill him, not only because he had broken the Sabbath, but said also that God was his Father, making himself equal with God.' The Jews were in the right as to the thing, only they erred as to the person, because they would not see that Christ was this Son of God, and therefore equal to the Father. Their argument was good, and their inference proper and genuine; if Christ do claim to be the proper Son of God, then he must be equal with God; nothing could be more true. And he had and must have such a sonship as will rise up to this; therefore his whole discourse, in which he is very large, John v. and x., tends to the proving of nothing lower than his natural Sonship, and consequently his equality with his Father. And if he had been only the Son of God in a lower way, why did he not so explain himself? why did he suffer the charge of blasphemy upon it? nay, why did he lose his life upon it? Had he been the Son of God only as others are, the very telling of that had quieted the people, acquitted him from blasphemy, and saved his life; but he lets them alone to go on in their malice against him, because that was the very truth which they pitched upon, and which he would have to be known, namely, that he was so the Son of God as to be equal with God. For a further proof of this, take that of the apostle where he speaks it out expressly, Phil. ii. 6, 'Who being in the form of God, thought it not robbery to be equal with God.' Surely there is more in this, being equal with God, than what some, particularly Grotius, are pleased to make it to be.[1] It notes equality of nature and essence, not only some external show, or appearance, or estimation by others. The latter clause must be expounded as it is joined with the former, and then its sense and emphasis will be clear enough. Christ being in the form of God, existing in the divine nature, and really participating of that nature, thought it no robbery, no bold encroachment upon the honour of God, to be equal with God, to assume and apply that nature to himself which he had in truth. And, which will much strengthen this exposition of the words, as that which follows, ver. 7, 8, speaks Christ's natural equality with us, as he was man, and must be so interpreted; so this here speaks Christ's natural equality with the Father as he was God, and must be so interpreted also.

(2.) Christ is a Son co-essential with the Father. He is not only like him, but of the same nature and essence with him; not only under some resemblance of God, ὁμοιούσιος, but under a perfect identity and oneness of essence with God, ὁμοούσιος: John x. 30, 'I and my Father are one.' Hence he is styled 'the image,' the essential and substantial image of God, Col. i. 15; Heb. i. 3. This was that great truth which the Nicene fathers asserted and maintained with such renowned courage and zeal. But I will but touch upon this head, because it is the same with the former; that is more comprehensive, but in its main import it perfectly agrees with this.

(3.) Christ is the co-eternal Son of God the Father. They were both of the same standing, if I may with reverence so express it, both from everlasting. Christ was eternally a Son; there never was any time when he was otherwise, or when he began so to be, οὐκ ἦν ὅταν οὐκ ἦν, as the ancients used to express it. If the

---

[1] Εἶναι ἴσα θεῷ est spectari tanquam Deum.—Grotius. As though there were no more in τὸ εἶναι ἴσα θεῷ, than in τὸ εἰσορᾶσθαι ἴσα θεῷ.—Dr Pearson on the Creed, p. 246.

Father was eternal and always a Father, then the Son was eternal and always a Son, for relatives must be simultaneous.[1] This was that which greatly troubled and vexed Arius, so often to hear the orthodox speaking of *semper Pater semper Filius, simul Pater simul Filius;* I say, this offended him very much, as appears by what he himself wrote in his letter to Eusebius; but the thing is never the less true because he was offended at it. The Scriptures are very plain concerning Christ's eternity and eternal generation, some of which have been already cited; take a few more: Rev. i. 8, 'I am Alpha and Omega, the beginning and the ending, saith the Lord, which is, and which was, and which is to come, the Almighty.' Rev. ii. 8, 'These things saith the first and the last, which was dead and is alive.' As soon as the apostle had spoken of Christ's Sonship, Heb. i. 5, presently he falls upon his eternity: ver. 8, 'Unto the Son he saith, Thy throne, O God, is for ever and ever.' Thus I have shewn in what respects Christ is styled God's own Son, and how far those are grounded upon the word of truth.[2]

But all this being vehemently denied and opposed by some, and it highly concerning us truly to apprehend and firmly to believe a thing of so high a nature, upon these considerations I judge that it will not be enough barely to assert the truth, but it will be necessary also to hear what opposers say against it, and how they endeavour to undermine it; give me leave therefore to spend some time about that.

I think I may confidently and warrantably affirm, that amongst all the articles of faith which make up the Christian religion, not any one of them ever met with so much opposition, and was the ground of so many and so fierce disputes, as this great article which refers to the Godhead of Christ, and to his being the natural and essential Son of God. They who know anything of what hath passed in former times in the matters of religion, know what contests there were about it in the first ages of the church. In the very infancy of the gospel Satan stirred up some, as Ebion, Cerinthus, &c., to oppose it, for it being the great fort and bulwark of Christianity, he would be sure first to make his batteries against it.[1] But things never came to their full height till about three hundred years after Christ, when Arius and his party with great zeal, such as it was, set themselves against it, boldly denying Christ to be God, or the eternal Son of God.[2] After a long flux of time, these controversies were pretty well composed, yea, the church had, in a great measure, after its sharp conflicts, gained the belief of this fundamental truth, and was in the quiet possession of it; till in these latter ages that unhappy Socinus came upon the stage, and he muddied the waters again, revived the old Arian heresies which seemed to be dead and rotten, and did, with no less boldness and more subtlety, *veterem serram reciprocare.* With him and his followers, all of which do unanimously agree in their denial of Christ's Sonship in that sense wherein it hath been opened, we now have to do;[3] and the difference betwixt them and us stands thus: they agree with us that Christ is the Son of God, but as to the nature, quality, manner, foundation, of his sonship, there they differ from us. We say he is the proper, natural Son of God; they make him, in effect, no better than an improper, allusive, metaphorical son of God; we say he is the eternal Son of God, they say he is only so in time; we say he is the Son of God by eternal generation, and thereupon called God's own Son, they say he is God's

---

[1] Ποτὲ ὁ πατήρ; οὐκ ἦν ὅτε οὐκ ἦν, τοῦτο οὐκ καὶ ὁ υἱός.— *Nazianz. Orat.* 35, tom. i., p. 563. Θεὸς ἀκατάληπτος ὢν θεὸν ἀκατάληπτον ἐγέννησε πρὸ πάντων τῶν αἰώνων, καὶ πρὸ χρόνων: καὶ οὐκ ἔστι διάστημα ἀναμέσον υἱοῦ καὶ πατρός, ἀλλ' ἅμα νοεῖς πατέρα, ἅμα νοεῖς υἱὸν, ἅμα ὀνομάζεις υἱὸν ἅμα δεικνύεις πατέρα, &c., πόθεν γὰρ υἱὸς εἰ μὴ πατέρα ἔχει; καὶ πόθεν Πατήρ, εἰ μὴ ἐγέννησε τὸν μονογενῆ, &c.—*Epiph. adv. Hæres.,* lib. ii. tom. ii. p. 796. ὥστε παρ' αὐτῷ τὸ γέννημα ἀεὶ γεγέννηται, καὶ μὴ ἐν χρόνῳ ἀρξάμενον, ἀλλ' ἀεὶ σὺν Πατρὶ γεγεννημένον ὑπάρχει, καὶ οὐδέποτε διαλείπει.—*Id.,* p. 794.

[2] He that would see the texts which have been cited, and divers others, opened and improved in reference to Christ's Sonship, as it hath been stated, let him read *Zanch. de Tribus Elohim,* lib. iv. cap. 6, &c., p. 125, &c.

[1] Of whom Ignatius is conceived to speak when he saith, ἀλλοτριοῦσι τοῦ πατρὸς, they made the Son to be of another and different essence from the Father, and so the Father from the Son; so the expression is usually opened.—*Ep. ad Trallian.,* p. 69. Edit. Usser.

[2] *Vide* Hist. Trip., lib. i. cap. 12 and 13.

[3] Socinus contra Wiekum. lib. Suasor. Animadv. in Assert. Posnan.; Smalcius de vera Divinit. Jesu Christi. Refut.; Franz. contra Smiglet; Crellius de uno Deo Patre; Slichting, contra Meisner; Ostorod. contra Tradel; Enjedinus. Catech. Racov. de Pers. Christi, cap. 1.

own Son upon other grounds and causes; which
what they are we are now to inquire after, and
whether they be true and consonant to the word.
This is a work which hath been done over and over
by many, by some in our own language, yet the
subject in hand necessarily leads me also to speak
something to it.

1. First, They affirm that Christ is God's own
Son in respect of his miraculous conception and production in the womb of the Virgin by the Holy
Ghost; for the proof of which they allege, Luke i.
35, 'The angel answered and said unto her, The
Holy Ghost shall come upon thee, and the power of
the highest shall overshadow thee: therefore also
that holy thing which shall be born of thee shall be
called the Son of God.'

Here the defenders of the truth take notice of the
adversaries' fallacious and fraudulent dealing, which indeed is very gross; for the greatest of them sometimes
seem to grant that Christ is the natural and essential
Son of God—it is the very title which they prefix
before some of their treatises—in which one would
think that they did concur with us, holding the same
thing which we do, and giving the same honour and
respect to Christ which we do, when in truth there
is no such thing; they do but speak fraudulently,
according to the custom of their old predecessors.[1]
For here is the fallacy; they mean by all this nothing
more than that Christ was the Son of God in regard
of his wonderful conception and nativity by the Virgin
Mary. But to pass by their frauds, let us come to the
thing. We say Christ's filiation or Sonship was
grounded upon something of a far higher nature
than this, that he was the Son of God antecedently
to it, even from all eternity. They ground his Sonship upon it only, making it but then to commence,

when he was begotten by the Holy Ghost, conceived
and born by the Virgin.

Against which dangerous opinion we argue thus:

(1.) If Christ's Sonship did result from this, as the
true and proper ground of it, then the Holy Ghost,
the third person, should rather be intituled the
Father of Christ than the first person;[1] because that
effect, which was the foundation of Christ's Sonship,
was more immediately produced by him than by the
first person. But this is notoriously false; for all
along, in the whole current of the word, Christ is
brought in as the Son of the Father, and as standing
in this relation to the Father and not to the Spirit.

(2.) Christ himself never resolves his Sonship into
his miraculous conception or birth. You find him
sometimes professedly treating upon it, and giving
the world an account about it, and what doth he then
ground it upon? Why, he carries it up to his doing
what the Father did, John v. 19; to his quickening
whom he will, even as the Father doth, John v. 21;
to his having life in himself, as the Father hath life
in himself, John v. 26; to his being one with the
Father, John x. 30; to his being in the Father, and
his Father in him, John x. 38. He doth not at all
mention his miraculous conception, which in all pro-
bability he would have done if that had been the
proper ground of his Sonship, but he insists altogether upon things tending to the proof of his participating of his Father's nature and essence, and by
them he designs to make out his Sonship; yea, and
that it was such a Sonship as did render him equal
with his Father; but this he could not have done,
either with truth or evidence, had he been only the
Son of God upon what is here pretended.

(3.) Though Christ's conception and temporal generation was very wonderful, yet that did but reach
to his flesh or human nature, and there terminate.
Now the Scripture doth not place his great Sonship
in his human, but in his divine nature; therefore as
to that it speaks him to be the Son and seed of David,
or the Son of man,[2] in contradistinction to his being

---

[1] Τὸ μὲν υἱὸς ὀνόματι ὁμολογοῦσι, τῇ δὲ δονάμει καὶ διανοίᾳ
ἀρνοῦνται, &c. See much of the fraud of the Arians in this,
in Epiphan. adv. Hæres., lib. ii. tom. ii. p. 738. Of them
Hilarius speaks to the same purpose:—Tribuunt Christo Dei
nomen, quia hoc et hominibus sit tributum. Fatentur Dei vere
Filium, quia sacramenti baptismi vere Dei filius unusquisque
perficitur. Ante tempora et sæcula confitentur, quod de angelis
et diabolis non est negandum. Ita Domino Christo sola illa
tribuuntur, quæ sunt vel angelorum propria vel nostra. Cæterum quod Deo Christo legitimum et verum est, Christus Deus
verus, i.e., eadem esse Filii quæ Patris divinitas, denegatur.—
Contra Auxent. Mediolan.

[1] Vide Stegm. Photin. Dip. 16, p. 180. Arnold. Catech.
Racov. major., p. 176.

[2] Qui factus est ex semine David secundum carnem, hic erit
homo et Filius hominis, qui declarandus est Filius Dei secundum
Spiritum sanctificationis, hic erit Deus, et sermo Dei Filius.—
Tertul. adv. Praxean. Torquetur frustra locus Luc. i. 35, &c.

the Son of God. And his Sonship to God cannot be grounded upon that which was the ground of his Sonship to man, for where the sonships are so different, they must needs have different grounds and foundations. Pray let these two texts be well weighed, and they will sufficiently prove what I say: Rom. i. 3, 4, 'Concerning his Son Jesus Christ our Lord, who was made of the seed of David according to the flesh; and declared to be the Son of God with power, according to the Spirit of holiness, by the resurrection from the dead.' Rom. ix. 5, 'Whose are the fathers, and of whom as concerning the flesh Christ came, who is over all, God blessed for ever.' The sum of all: Christ hath two natures, according to which two natures he hath two distinct sonships; he is the Son of God, and he is the Son of man; these different sonships must have different causes and grounds, therefore his conception, upon which he was the Son of man, cannot make him also to be the Son of God.

(4.) As to the text alleged by our adversaries to prove their opinion, there is a double answer commonly given to it.

[1.] The particle *therefore* in it is not causal but illative. It is not brought in as signifying the ground of Christ's Sonship, but as a note of inference, wherein something is inferred from what went before. The angel had told Mary that 'the Holy Ghost should come upon her, and the power of the highest should overshadow her,' and then adds: 'Therefore also the holy thing which shall be born of thee shall be called the Son of God.' *Therefore?* what may be the force of this word in this place? It is a mere deduction, drawn from the premises to this effect: since such a thing shall be done by the Holy Ghost, therefore, according to what was prophesied, Christ shall be called the Son of God. The words plainly refer to the prophecy, Isa. vii. 14, 'Therefore the Lord himself shall give you a sign: Behold, a virgin shall conceive, and bear a son, and shall call his name Immanuel.' The evangelist brings them in

A nuda enim conceptione et nativitate carnis ex Virgine, manavit non Filii Dei, sed Filii hominis appellatio. Quod vero angelus porro affirmat, illud est, hac filiatione non obstante, etiam vocandum Filium Dei; adhibita exacte particula καὶ, ad conciliandam utramque filii hominis et Filii Dei uni Christo tribuendam appellationem, per communicationem idiomatum, &c. *Cloppenb. Ant. Smalc.*, p. 71.

expressly in that reference, Mat. i. 21, and xxii. 23, 'And she shall bring forth a son, and thou shalt call his name Jesus, for he shall save his people from their sins. Now all this was done, that it might be fulfilled which was spoken of the Lord by the prophet, saying, Behold, a virgin shall be with child, and shall bring forth a son, and they shall call his name Emmanuel, which being interpreted is, God with us.' And their sense and tendency is the same here, 'therefore also that holy thing,' &c.; as if the angel had said, This being the thing which was foretold, which must be accomplished, and is now near to be accomplished, therefore it shall so be, 'that which shall be born of thee shall be called the Son of God.' So that this *therefore* is only a note of consequence, as to the event or the fulfilling of the prophecy, not a note of causality as to the thing itself, viz., Christ's Sonship to God.

[2.] It is, 'therefore he shall be called the Son of the Most High.' It is not, therefore he shall *be* the Son, &c., but therefore he shall be called, &c. And so it points not to that which was constitutive of Christ's filiation, but only to that which was manifestative and declarative of it.[1] Christ was God before he assumed flesh, but he was God manifested in the flesh, 1 Tim. iii. 16; so Christ was the Son of God before he was thus conceived, but this was a great manifestation or declaration that he was the Son of God. It is true, as to us, our being 'called the sons of God,' 1 John iii. 1, notes our being made the sons of God; but here, as to Christ, it only notes that he should be declared, evidenced, acknowledged to be the Son of God. He was not now made the Son of God—that was done by his eternal generation—only it was now made to appear that he was the Son of God. In short, the Lord Jesus, who was thus miraculously conceived, was the very Son of God; but as he was thus conceived, or because he was thus conceived, so he was not the Son of God; for of this

[1] Angelus non dixit quare sit Filius Dei, sed quod sit Filius Dei, et quare fideles ipsum pro Filio Dei sint agnituri. Christum autem ab æterno a Patre esse genitum, humanamque naturam in unitatem Filii esse assumendam, satis indicavit, dum dixit, *quod nascetur ex te sanctum, Filius Dei vocabitur*, &c. Nec tamen hoc vult, quod Mariæ Filius, qua Mariæ Filius est, etiam sit Filius Dei; sed quod inter alia signa ex quibus Christum Dei Filium esse agnoscatur etiam hoc sit.—*Bisterf. contra Crellium*, lib. i. sec. 2, cap. 31, p. 305.

there was an antecedent foundation, that which was
of a far more ancient date, namely, his being begotten of the Father from everlasting.

2. Secondly, It is said that Christ was the Son of
God in respect of his sanctification and mission :
John x. 36, ' Say ye of him, whom the Father hath
sanctified, and sent into the world, Thou blasphemest ; because I said, I am the Son of God ?' Christ
being sanctified by the Father, that is, the Spirit of
grace and holiness being in so eminent a degree
poured out upon him, and he being designed and set
apart and fitted by God to, and for, a most high and
eminent office ; as also he being sent upon a great
work, for an extraordinary end, to redeem and save
lost sinners ; therefore upon these grounds, and not
upon his being eternally begotten of the Father, he
was God's Son.

Ans. More is inferred from this text than what
it will bear ; we may thus far very well argue from
it, He who was sanctified and sent was undoubtedly
the Son of God ; but if we go further and infer, He
who was sanctified and sent was therefore the Son
of God, as if the sanctification and mission were the
ground of his being so, we stretch the words too far,
and endeavour to fetch that out of them which is not
at all in them.[1] There is a great difference betwixt
the applying of such a relation to such a person, and
the assigning of the proper cause and foundation of
that relation. Christ being sanctified and sent is
the Son of God ; upon these that relation may truly
be attributed to him ; but yet they do not amount
to the being the cause of that relation. *Christus qui
fuit sanctificatus et missus est Filius Dei* is a proposition very true ; but *Christus qua fuit sanctificatus et
missus est Filius Dei*, as pointing to the *fundamentum
Filiationis*, is a proposition very false ; and there lies
the controversy betwixt us and our opponents. The
words cited have reference to the preceding verses,
where Christ is vindicating himself from that blas-

phemy which the Jews charged him with, ' because
he made himself God,' ver. 33. Now this he doth
first in a lower way, by an argument drawn from
the title usually given to men in places of office and
authority ; they are called gods, and if so, then,
saith Christ, do I blaspheme because I call myself
God, and the Son of God, whom God hath sanctified
and sent, and invested with such high offices ? Do
not mistake here ; Christ is not God only in a titular
way, because of his office, he is so truly, properly, in
respect of his nature and essence ; this he speaks to,
vers. 30, 37, 38 ; but he instances only in his office
in this place, and from thence fetches that argument
which was very proper to his present design, viz.,
the vindicating of himself as to the charge of blasphemy : vers. 34–36, ' Jesus answered them, Is
it not written in your law, I said, Ye are gods ?
If he called them gods, unto whom the word of God
came, and the scripture cannot be broken ; say ye
of him, whom the Father hath sanctified, and sent
into the world, Thou blasphemest : because I said,
I am the Son of God ?' Now what is there in this
to undermine Christ's eternal Sonship, or to make
his sanctification and mission the ground of his filial
relation to God ?[1] One word further, as to the latter of these. If Christ was the Son of God before
he was sent, then his sending did not make him to
become the Son of God ; but so he was ; for it is said,
here in the text, ' God sent his Son, implying he was
a son before he was sent. Had it not been so, it
must have been said, God *sent him to be his Son*, and
not God *sent his Son*, which supposes him before the
sending to be actually a son.

3. Another cause assigned of Christ's Sonship, and
of the appellation here given him, God's own Son, is
his resurrection. That begetting which the psalmist
speaks of, Ps. ii. 7, is not, say they, to be interpreted
of Christ's being eternally begotten of the Father,
but only of what the Father did when he raised him
up from the dead. For so the apostle brings it in,
Acts xiii. 32, 33, ' We declare unto you glad tidings,
how that the promise which was made unto the
fathers, God hath fulfilled the same unto us their
children, in that he hath raised up Jesus again : as

---

[1] Ex loco Joh. x. 36, negamus hoc effici posse, Jesum Christum Deum, ac Filium Dei unigenitum dici aut esse, &c. Sanc-
tificatio et missio qua Pater Filium sanctificavit et missit in
mundum, nec Deitatem Filii nec filiationem fundat, sed fundatur in illa, atque illam demonstrat a posteriori. Quia ad
munus mediatorium sanctificari et mitti in mundum non poterat, qui non esset co-æternus et co-essentialis Patri mittenti
Filius.—*Cloppenb. Compend. Socin.*, p. 38.

[1] Hoc non dicit causam suæ filiationis, sed præstantiæ supra alios, unde potius queat nuncupari Dei Filius quam illi
dii.—*Hoornb. Socin. Confut. de Christo*, cap. 1, p. 39.

it is also written in the second psalm, Thou art my Son, this day have I begotten thee.'

For answer to this, (1.) How many causes and grounds shall we have of Christ's Sonship? We have had two already; here is a third; we shall have, by and by, a fourth and a fifth, and I know not how many more; where shall we stop? Christ's Sonship is but one, I mean as he is the Son of God, and therefore admits not of the multiplication of causes. In all relations there is some single act which is the foundation of them, upon which in their relative notion they are complete. And why should it not be so here in the relation betwixt God and Christ? Our opponents tell us that Christ upon his miraculous conception was the Son of God. I then ask, Was he so, truly, fully, perfectly, completely? if so, which they by their principles cannot deny, then what need is there of anything further? or how doth the nature of the thing admit of anything further? For he that is a son already, perfect and complete, cannot by any addition or new emergency be made more a son, because the essence of things, whether absolute or relative, cannot be intended or remitted. We are inquiring what is it which makes Christ the Son of God? We ground it, as we should and must, upon one thing, namely, upon the Father's begetting of Christ from all eternity, and communicating his own nature and essence to him; they who oppose lay it upon several things, as you have already heard in part, and will yet further hear in what follows. Now we say this cannot be, for there can be but one foundation of one and the same relation; therefore they must pitch upon some such one foundation and waive all the rest. I know what they say: Christ upon his conception, &c., was the Son of God in a way of inchoation, but upon his resurrection and exaltation he was the Son of God in a way of consummation. I reply, (1.) Then the texts urged before are out of doors, and signify little or nothing; for they only prove that Christ, upon his conception and sanctification and mission, began to be a Son of God; but he was not so, indeed, fully and properly; for there must be yet something more which must follow after to complete and consummate his Sonship. (2.) This is a very strange and most ungrounded distinction, it arguing a growth and progress in Christ's Sonship, for which there is not the least warrant from the

word of God. We read, Luke ii. 52, of Christ's 'increasing in wisdom and stature, and in favour with God and man;' but we never read of his increasing in his Sonship; that admitted of several manifestative evidences as to us, but not of several perfective degrees as to itself. Even the sonship of believers at the first moment of their conversion is entire and full; they may grow and be more perfect in their gifts, graces, comforts; but as to their covenant-state and relation to God, that is complete at the first, and admits of no further addition. And shall the Sonship of the blessed Son of God be a partial, imperfect, progressive thing? Neither the glory of the person, nor the nature of the relation itself, will bear such a thing.

(2.) Secondly, Nothing more evident than that Christ was the Son of God before his resurrection: Mat iii. 17, 'Lo a voice from heaven, saying, This is my beloved Son, in whom I am well pleased.' Was not this witness given of Christ before his resurrection? Rom. viii. 32, 'He that spared not his own Son, but gave him up for us all, how shall he not with him also freely give us all things?' Christ here is called God's own Son, which must be understood of him before his resurrection; for the Father's not sparing of him was antecedent to that, and yet then he was his own Son, otherwise how could it be said that God spared not his own Son? Mat. xvi. 16, 'Thou art Christ, the Son of the living God.' Was not this confession made by Peter before Christ's resurrection? I might go much higher in the dating of Christ's Sonship than merely before his resurrection; but that is high enough to shew the falsity of what is asserted by the adversary.

(3.) We say Christ was declared and manifested, but not made or constituted, the Son of God, by his resurrection.[1] So the apostle himself states it, Rom. i. 4, 'Declared to be the Son of God with power, according to the Spirit of holiness, by the resurrection from the dead'—that the word ὁρισθέντος is truly rendered by declared is sufficiently proved by many. It is one thing to be made God's Son, another thing to be declared God's Son. The first Christ had from his eternal generation; it was only the second that

[1] Non quod tum Filius Dei esse cœperit, qui ab æterno fuerat, sed quia tunc res aliqua fieri dicitur, quando talis cognoscitur; seu tum demum dicitur facta γένεσις cum fuit facta γνῶσις.—Portus contra Ostorod., cap. 9, p. 67.

he had from his resurrection. You read, ver. 19 of this chapter, of the 'manifestation of the sons of God.' Believers are not made the sons of God when they enter upon the glorified estate, but they are then manifested both to be the sons of God, as also what their glory is upon their being so: 1 John iii. 9, 'Now are we the sons of God, and it doth not yet appear what we shall be; but we know that when he shall appear we shall be like him.' Mark it, the relation itself is present, ' *now* are we the sons of God;' but the dignity and glory which is to follow upon this relation, that 'doth not yet appear,' but hereafter it shall. So here, Christ was the Son of God long before his resurrection, but the manifestation thereof was when God raised him from the dead. Till then his Sonship and glory had been very much veiled and hid, but then it broke forth like the sun after it hath been shut up under a dark and thick cloud; then God owned him as his own Son before all the world, and made it to appear who and what he was. And this is that which the apostle aimed at in the place cited; his only design there being to prove that God had given the world sufficient evidence that Christ was his very Son; and amongst other evidences of it he instances in the miraculous raising of him out of the grave. So that the begetting in Ps. ii. and in Acts xiii. are of a quite different nature, the one being proper, as relating to the thing itself, the other improper, as relating only to the declaration or manifestation of the thing. We argue from the proper and primary sense of the words, 'Thou art my Son,' &c., the adverse party from their improper and secondary sense, as the apostle makes use of them in that place. In the Scripture dialect several things are said to be done, when they are declared and manifested to be done; so Paul brings in Christ as begotten at the day of his resurrection, because it was then declared that he was the eternally begotten Son of God.

4. It is said Christ is God's Son, and so called, because of the pre-eminence and dignity of his person, or because of his great advancement and exaltation to the offices of king and priest:[1] Heb. i. 4, 5, 'Being made so much better than the angels, as he

[1] Deus misit suum Filium, *i.e.*, Christum illum suum, cui communis alioqui Filii Dei titulus, propter singularitatem et excellentiam, proprius est factus.—*Slichting in loc.*

hath by inheritance obtained a more excellent name than they. For unto which of the angels said he at any time, Thou art my Son, this day have I begotten thee? And again, I will be to him a Father, and he shall be to me a Son.' Heb. v. 5, 'Christ glorified not himself to be made an high priest; but he that said unto him, Thou art my Son, to-day have I begotten thee.' Here, you see, Christ's Sonship comes in upon his exaltation with respect to his person and office.

I answer, this proves as little as that which went before; for here also,

(1.) It is clear that Christ was the Son of God before he was thus exalted.

(2.) His exaltation was not the ground, but the result and consequent of his Sonship. He was not a Son because he was exalted, but he was exalted because he was a Son. First the apostle describes him in what relates to the formality and essence of his Sonship: Heb. i. 3, 'Who being the brightness of his glory, and the express image of his person;' and then he sets down the honour which the Father put upon him, not *to be* a Son—for that he was already—but because he *was* a Son; for that is the ground of the more excellent name given to him; and so the words in ver. 4, 5 come in.

(3.) It is strange that this day of Christ's begetting should be so multiplied. There is the day of his nativity, and then it was '*to-day* have I begotten thee;' there is the day of his resurrection: and then, too, it was '*to-day* have,' &c.; there is the day of his exaltation: and then again it was '*to-day* have,' &c. Had this text been cited forty times in forty several cases, we must have had so many several grounds and causes of Christ's Sonship.

But why then, some may say, is this place so often repeated in the New Testament?

I answer, not only because it is applied to the several declarations of Christ's Sonship, but also to shew that all which the Father did to and for Christ was all to be resolved into his eternal Sonship as the ground thereof. He was raised again because he was the Son of God, exalted to great honour and dignity because he was the Son of God, entrusted to be mediator because he was the Son of God; all was grounded upon this his relation. And therefore, whenever such great things are brought in concerning Christ, this text is mentioned as pointing to that Sonship which was the ground of them, but not to assert that they were the ground of it.

(4.) Though the glory which the Father hath conferred upon Christ as king, prophet, and priest, be very great, yet it will not reach that which is wrapped up in his being the proper and only begotten Son of God.[1] Sonship and office are different things, and the highest office can never come up to what is in Sonship by eternal generation.

5. Fifthly, It is said that Christ is the Son of God in respect of that special love and affection which the Father bears to him: Mat. iii. 17, 'Lo, a voice from heaven, saying, This is my beloved Son, in whom I am well pleased.' And whereas Christ is called 'the only begotten Son of God,' they with whom I have to do say there is no more in it than only this, that Christ is the most beloved of God. As Isaac is styled Abraham's only son, Gen. xxii. 2, his only begotten son, Heb. xi. 17, now how is this to be taken? Had not Abraham an Ishmael as well as an Isaac? how is Isaac, then, called his only begotten son? Why, only as he had a greater share in his father's love than Ishmael had. For the same reason Solomon calls himself an only son, Prov. iv. 3; therefore the Septuagint render the word there used, וְיָחִיד, by τὸν ἀγάπητον, the beloved; and so our translators fill it up, 'and only beloved in the sight of my mother.' So, say they, it is here as to Christ's being the only begotten Son of God; God hath a special love for him, and that is all.

Ans. But we must not suffer this great title of our Lord Jesus to be thus wrested out of our hands. Without all question God hath transcendent, superlative love for Christ; his 'dear Son' he is called, Col. i. 13; but yet we say,

(1.) As before, this love is not the cause of his Sonship, but his Sonship the cause of it. He is not a Son because beloved, but he is beloved because a Son; therefore it cannot be the cause which is but the effect,

(2.) If this was the proper foundation of Christ's Sonship, then there would be only a gradual difference betwixt his Sonship and the sonship of believers.[1] For they being beloved of the Father as well as he, and even as he is—for the nature and quality of the love, though not for the degree of it: John xvii. 23, &c., 'And hast loved them as thou hast loved me'—I say it being so, if the love of the Father to Christ was the proper ground of his Sonship, it would then follow that they are sons just as Christ is, only in a lower degree. But surely the Scripture holds forth more than a gradual difference betwixt his Sonship and theirs; that τὸ διαφορώτερον ὄνομα, 'more excellent name,' which the apostle speaks of, Heb. i. 4, carries more in it than barely a higher degree of sonship; it points even to a different kind and order thereof.

(3.) As to the instances alleged for that use and signification of the word which might undermine that which we put upon it, it is answered that Isaac is called the only son and the only begotten of Abraham, not only because of all the sons he had his greatest love, but there were other grounds and reasons of it; he was the only son by Sarah, the only son by promise, and the only heir of the promise, upon which accounts, as well as upon the highest proportion of his father's love to him, he is styled the only begotten son. The same, under different circumstances, may be said concerning Solomon. But suppose that this was the only thing held forth in the unigeniture of these persons, will it follow that therefore it is all in the unigeniture of Christ too? when there is so great a disparity betwixt person and person, sonship and sonship, as hath been already, and might yet further be demonstrated if it was needful?

(4.) There is in Scripture another title given to Christ, to which the Father's greater love towards him than towards others doth more properly belong; namely, his being the πρωτότοκος, 'the first-born,' or 'the first-begotten:' Heb. i. 6, 'When he bringeth in the first-begotten into the world,' &c. Col. i. 15, 'The image of the invisible God, the first-born of every creature.' And elsewhere, upon some special and particular considerations with respect to his resurrection, he is called 'the first-born from the dead,' Col. i. 18; 'the first-begotten from the dead,' Rev. i.

---

[1] Christ not the Son of God because of his kingly dominion. Vide *Jacob. ad Portum* contra Ostorod. Def. Fid. Orthod. cap. 37, p. 512 ad 518. Not because of his pre-eminence, &c., *Epiph. adv. Heres.* p. 740. Εἰ γὰρ ὀνόματι μόνον, &c.

[1] Εἰ μὲν οὖν υἱὸς μόνον ἐγκαλεῖται ὡς καὶ πάντες ἐκλήθησαν υἱοὶ θεοῦ, ἄρα οὐδέν διαλλάττει τῶν ἄλλων, καὶ πῶς ὡς θεὸς προσκυνεῖται.—*Epiph. adv. Hær.*, lib. i. cap. 2, p. 741.

5. But as the title in that reference is applied to Christ, I am not now to meddle with it.

What doth his being the first-born or first-begotten hold forth?

Ans. Some expound it of his eternal generation by the Father;[1] some of the pre-eminence and dignity of his person, as also of the immunities and privileges which belong to him above others. As the first-born under the law had an excellency put upon him from his primogeniture, to him the dominion and authority over the family did belong, Gen. xxvii. 29, and xlix. 8, as also the double portion in the inheritance, Deut. xxi. 15–17, and he was the most beloved; in reference to which the people of Israel are styled God's first-born: Exod. iv. 22, 'Israel is my son, even my first-born;' because of that great glory which God put upon that people, and that singular affection which he bore to them. In all these respects Christ is God's first-born; if you understand it of his eternal generation, so it is incommunicable to any other, so he is *primogenitus et unigenitus*, first-begotten and only begotten too; but if you understand it of the excellency of his person, and of the other particulars mentioned, so, in such a degree, it is communicable to others. For Israel you see in a subordinate and allusive sense was styled God's first-born; and all believers too may be so styled in respect of the dignity of their persons, and of God's special love towards them. As Christ is the only begotten of the Father, that is exclusive to all, as he is the first-begotten of the Father, that signifies prelation but not exclusion. Saints are excellent, though not so excellent as Christ; beloved, though not so beloved as Christ; heirs, though not such heirs as Christ. And therefore, had Christ been called only the first-born, and that too in its second import and significancy, something then might have been inferred from it for the nulling of that sonship which we plead for, as only belonging to him; but besides this he is also called the only begotten, wherefore he must be alone in this relation. And though the saints do in a lower degree share with him in the Father's love as he is the first-born, yet they do not at all share with him

in the glory of his eternal generation as he is the only begotten.

6. Sixthly, We are told that Christ is the Son of God in respect of adoption; that he is not the natural or essential, only the adopted Son of God.

This our opposers are not afraid or ashamed to assert. Oh how low will they bring the Sonship of our blessed Lord and Saviour! they will make him anything rather than grant what indeed he is; but for answer. This is no novel opinion, or that which was never broached in the church before; it was the old heresy of those two Spanish bishops, Felix and Elipandus,[1] condemned in a council held at Frankfort very near a thousand years ago;[2] both fathers and schoolmen, all but Durandus, argue much against it.[3]

Take, in brief, these four arguments against it.

(1.) In all the Scriptures Christ is never styled the adopted Son of God;[4] nay, there is nothing there to be found in the least to countenance the attributing of such a sonship to him; it is a mere forgery of man, to evade and put off what the word expressly asserts. We read much of God's adopting of saints, but nothing at all of his adopting of Christ.

(2.) Then Christ and believers would have the same sonship, they being sons by adoption as well as he, and he having no higher foundation for his Sonship than they.

(3.) Christ is the true and proper Son of God, but should he be his Son by adoption he would then cease to be his true and proper Son;[5] for he that is

---

[1] Quomodo primogenitus esse potuit, nisi quia secundum Divinitatem ante omnem creaturam ex Deo Patre Sermo processit.—*Tertull.*

[1] See Forbesii Instruct. Historico-Theolog., lib. vi. cap. 1.

[2] Concil. Tom. xx. p. 82, &c., secundum Edit. Reg. Paris.

[3] υἱος τοῦ θεοῦ ἐστὶ φύσει, καὶ οὐ θέσει γέννηθεις ἐκ πατρὸς.— *Cyrill. Hierosol.* Quod si etiam unigenitus Filius dicitur ex gratia, non vere genitus ex natura, proculdubio nomen et veritatem unigeniti perdidit, postquam fratres habere jam cæpit. Privatur enim hujus veritate nominis, si in unigenito non est de Patre veritas naturalis.—*Fulgent.* Si quæritur, an Christus sit adoptivus Filius secundum quod homo, sive alio modo: Respondemus, Christum non esse adoptivum Filium aliquo modo, sed tantum naturalem, quia natura Filius Dei est, non adoptionis gratia.—*Lombard.* Vide alios e Scholasticis in Hoorneb. Socin. Confut., tom. ii. cap. 1, de Christo, p. 30, et e Patribus in Zanch. de Tribus Elohim, p. 249.

[4] Legi, et relegi Scripturas, Jesum Filium Dei adoptione nusquam inveni.—*Ambros.*

[5] In materia et negotio filiationis, proprius et adoptivus opponuntur; ut proprius non sit adoptivus, et adoptivus non

adopted is only a son in an improper and allusive notion, and but in the esteem and repute of him who doth adopt. Socinus himself so describes such an one :[1] An adopted son is one who is accounted a son, but in truth and reality he is not so ; then according to his own explication of it, if Christ be an adopted son, he is no true and proper son, but only so as the Father doth so repute him. And is not Christ now greatly beholden to these persons? is he not highly advanced by them? do they not shew great respect and give great honour to him, according to what they pretend, in making of him only a putative Son? Adoption, indeed, is not so much too high for us, but it is as much too low for Christ.

(4.) If begotten, then not adopted, for these two are incompatible or inconsistent : the same son cannot be begotten and adopted too, therefore adoption comes in to supply the want of generation. Christ must be the one or the other; and if he be the one, he cannot be the other; if begotten, then not adopted, and if adopted, then not begotten. It is true, in the sonship of believers there is both ; they are sons by regeneration and adoption too ; but the reason of that is because they are sons but in an improper and metaphorical respect ; I mean in contradistinction to Christ, who is the very true and natural Son of God.

7. Once more, they say Christ is God's own Son because of his resemblance and likeness to him.

This comes exceeding short, for it is not likeness but oneness, not resemblance but equality, upon which Christ is called God's Son ; he himself draws it up to that, as you have already heard. No likeness here will suffice but essential likeness, answerable to that, Gen. v. 3, 'Adam lived an hundred and thirty years, and begat a son in his own likeness, after his image.' Amongst us you know likeness is not the foundation of sonship ; the son is a son, not because he is like his father, but because he is begotten by his father ; and so it is with respect to Christ. There may be resemblance where yet there is no filial relation : in the glorified state we shall be 'like the angels,' Luke xx. 36, yet I never

read of any paternal and filial relation betwixt them and us. In time I fear, according to the old heresy of some, it will come to Christ's being the Son of man too but in likeness. He is the Son of man as he hath the very nature and essence of man, and why is he not the Son of God also, as he hath the very nature and essence of God ?

Thus I have both laid down the truth, and also made it good against opposers. And now the false grounds and notions of Christ's Sonship being removed, the true ground and notion of it is more evident, viz., that he is God's own Son as he partakes of his essence, and was from everlasting begotten by him. He that would read full and large discourses upon this great subject, let him peruse the writings of those worthy instruments whom God hath raised up and enabled to assert and defend it.[1] If any think I have been too long, or have unnecessarily troubled myself and the reader about it, I must, for several reasons, crave leave to differ from them. We cannot say too much, or too often go over those things in which the honour of God's own Son, our Lord and master, and the good of souls, are so highly concerned. Give the Socinians their due—it is but a sad commendation—all along they make their thrusts at the very heart of religion, they fight against neither great or small, but only against the great King of all the world, the very Son of God ; whom they strike at in his deity, eternal Sonship, incarnation, satisfaction, in what not ? Surely we cannot too much endeavour to antidote men against their desperate soul-destroying venom and poison, especially in times wherein men seem more than ordinarily to incline to close with their pestilent opinions ; upon which considerations I would encourage myself to hope, that such who are friends to Christ and souls will put a candid interpretation upon what hath been done. Yet as to the learned, if any such shall cast their eye upon these papers, I beg their pardon for the

---

sit proprius ; sed adoptivus opponitur naturali, et proprio, et naturalis non est adoptivus ; adoptivis liberis opponuntur naturales ac veri, dicunt jurisconsulti.—*Hoorneb.*

[1] Adoptivus filius est, qui pro filio quidem habetur, sed tamen revera non est filius.

[1] Bisterf. contra Crell., lib. i. sec. 2, cap. 31. Smiglet. de Vero et naturali Dei Filio contra Smalcium. Jacob. ad Portum adv. Ostorod. Def. Fid. Orthod. cap. 9. Arnold. Catech. Racov. Maj. cap. 1, de Person. Christi. Idem against Biddle, cap. 7. Calov. Socin. Proflig. De Filio Dei Controv., iv. Hoorneb. Socin. confut., tom. ii. cap. 1, de Christo. Dr Owen against Biddle, chap. vii. Estwick against Biddle, p. 110, &c. ; et 375 Cheynal Trin-unity, p. 190, &c. Alting. Theol. Elenctica, p. 149 ad 187.

repeating of things so well known and common to them, and which they have elsewhere with great advantage. I have only this to say for myself, my eye hath been upon private Christians, to make things plain to them, and to set that before them here which, as written in other languages, they could not reach.

So much for these. But though I have been too prolix already, I have not yet done: there are some others, of a different party and denomination, who do, in part, concur and symbolise with the afore-named dissenters; for though they hold that Christ in a more special manner is the Son of God by eternal generation, yet they also hold that he is the Son of God too in respect of his conception, office, resurrection, and exaltation. Arminius himself pitches upon the first as the only ground of the Sonship of Christ;[1] but his successors take in the latter also: so the Remonstrants,[2] so Episcopius, a person of great eminence.[3] These tell us that God is the proper Father of Christ, and he the proper Son of God; but how? why, not only as he was eternally begotten by him, but also as he was miraculously conceived by the Virgin Mary, that agreeing to none but only to him. And therefore in this point, upon their blending of these things together, they are judged by some to Socinianise.[4]

Now though this opinion doth come incomparably short of that which absolutely denies Christ's eternal generation, provided that the abettors of it who seem to grant this generation do state it right, that is, that they hold Christ to be begotten in the very nature and essence of God and therein equal to him, ὁμοούσιος, of which there is just matter of doubting as to the person named but now, he making the Son in the deity itself not co-ordinate but subordinate to the first person.[5] I say, though this opinion, thus stated, be nothing near so bad as the former, yet divines of another persuasion cannot close with it, or let it pass without some confutation.[6]

The arguments against it do very much fall in with those which have been insisted upon already.

1. First, If Christ be the Son of God as eternally begotten with respect to his divine nature, and also the Son of God as conceived in time, &c., with respect to his human nature, then the Scripture doth groundlessly and needlessly distinguish betwixt his being the Son of God in reference to the one, and his being the Son of man in reference to the other nature. Why doth it make him to be God's Son ' according to the Spirit of holiness,' i.e., his divine nature, and the 'Son of David according to the flesh,' i.e., his human nature, Rom. i. 3, 4, if with respect to both he be the Son of God? This is to confound those things which the Scripture makes distinct, and places under several references. Christ's Sonships, as the Son of God and as the Son of man, are two very different things, and therefore they cannot have the same foundation. It is true, he who is the Son of man is also the Son of God; but as he is the Son of man, or in what is proper to him as the Son of man, so he is not the Son of God. And it is true these two in concreto may convertibly be predicated each of the other, thus, the Son of God is the Son of man, and the Son of man is the Son of God; but this is founded not upon the oneness of the foundation of the relation, nor upon the oneness of the two natures; but upon the communication of properties, and the union of the two natures in one person.[1] It comes to this, where the relations are distinct the grounds of these relations must be distinct; and therefore Christ's Sonship, as the Son of God and as the Son of man, being distinct, there cannot be one and the same ground of them.

2. If this was so, that Christ was the Son of God conjunctly upon his eternal generation, and also upon his conception and advancement in time, then he would strangely differ in the same relation. I do not contradict myself in what I said but now under the former head; for there I spake of both the Sonships of Christ, which differ very much, and must not

---

[1] *Vide* Disput. publ. Thes. v.

[2] Confess., cap. 3, sec. 2, p. 14 ; et Apolog. contra Censur., cap. 2, p. 48.

[3] Instit Theol., lib. iv. sec. 2, cap. 33.

[4] See Peltius Harm. Remonstr. et Socin., Art. 4.

[5] Instit. Theol., lib. iv. cap. 32.

[6] Censura Profess. Leid. in cap. 3, p. 51. Trigland. in Exam. Apolog., cap. 5. Alting. Theol. Elenc., p. 151, &c., et p. 181, &c.

[1] Inficiamur Christum esse ψιλὸν ἄνθρωπον ἀποθεοθεντα, &c., quamvis propter naturam humanam personæ divinæ hypostatice unitam, dicamus etiam in concreto, hunc hominem Jesum Deum ac Filium Dei unigenitum esse, per communicationem idiomatum, &c.—*Cloppenb. Comp. Socin.*, p. 38.

be confounded, but here I speak only of his single Sonship as he is the Son of God, which is but one, and must not be divided. Observe me, as the difference of the Sonships of Christ, as the Son of God and as the Son of Mary, depends upon the difference of their grounds; eternal generation being the ground of the one, and temporal generation being the ground of the other; so the oneness of the same single Sonship of Christ, as the Son of God, depends upon the oneness of the ground of it, viz., his generation by the Father: for if you add any other ground to this, then Christ ceases to be one Son, then he is the Son of God partly by nature and partly by grace; partly begotten and partly made; partly from eternity and partly in time: what a strange Son would Christ be upon these terms!

3. There can be but one true and proper cause of one and the same filiation; this hath been already proved. Divines are so tender of multiplying this relation of Christ, that several of them, though they grant the distinction of his natures, and hold his twofold generation, yet they argue but for one sonship to belong to him; for, say they, sonship belonging to the person, and being founded upon the person, Christ being but one person, therefore he can have but one sonship; so Aquinas argues.[1] I concur with others who attribute a twofold sonship to Christ;[2] but then I affirm that each of them have but that one single cause or foundation which is respectively proper to them; it is only eternal generation of the Father which makes Christ to be the Son of God, and it is only temporal generation of the Virgin which makes him to be the Son of man.

4. We say *oppositorum opposita ratio*, if Christ be the Son of man only because he was conceived of the substance of his mother, then he is the Son of God only upon the account of his being begotten of the substance of his Father, as a worthy author argues.[3]

5. Whatever is over and above eternal generation is but manifestative and not constitutive of Christ's sonship. This hath been made out in the several particulars alleged, therefore it will be needless to add anything further upon it.

I have shewn wherein and how Christ is the Son of God, his own proper Son. I will but propound one question, and very briefly answer it, and then I shall have finished the explicatory part; it is this, If Christ be God's Son because in his ineffable generation the divine essence was communicated to him, why may not the Holy Ghost, the third person, also be styled the Son of God, to whom the same essence was communicated as well as unto Christ?

I answer no, for two reasons:

(1.) Because it is the same essence in both, yet not the same person. When we speak of the communicating of the divine essence from the first to the second and third persons, we must be understood, as was before hinted, to speak this of them as persons, or as they are personally considered; for that essence, simply and absolutely considered, is not communicated to the Son and Spirit, but only as it subsists in them as such persons; the Godhead itself they have in and from themselves, but their distinct personalities, in which the Godhead subsists, are of the Father. It being thus, from hence it follows that, according to the distinction of the persons there must also be a distinct communication of the divine essence; not that there is one essence in the Son and another in the Spirit, for both are God; only that is distinguished according to their personal consideration and the personal properties belonging to them, which, notwithstanding their oneness in nature, do always remain. Well, then, Christ's Sonship being a personal thing, proceeding not simply from the divine essence, but as it subsists in the second person, therefore it must be proper and peculiar to him, and not common to the Holy Ghost, he being another person, and the divine nature subsisting in him accordingly, with respect to his personal properties.

(2.) Because though the same divine essence be communicated to both, yet not in the same way and manner. For though both come from the Father, yet it is in divers respects, the Son coming from him by generation, the Spirit by procession. And therefore, though both are God, and both come from God, yet both are not the sons of God, because it is com-

[1] 3 p. quest. 35, art. 5 in Corpore Art.

[2] See Durandus, Rada, &c., Junius, Martinius, Amesius in Hoorneb., Socin. Conf., tom. ii. de Christo, cap. 1, p. 30-32.

[3] Dr Owen ag. Biddle, p. 179.

ing from God in the way of generation only which
entitles to sonship. Thus Augustine answers it:
Thou askest of me, saith he, if the Son be of the
substance of the Father, and the Holy Ghost be of
the substance of the Father also, why is one the
Son and not the other? I answer, whether you
comprehend it or not, the Son is of the Father, the
Holy Ghost is of the Father, but the Son is begotten, the Spirit proceeds.[1] Thus this great divine
did solve this difficulty, stopping here and going no
further. If any will be so curious as to inquire
further wherein the difference lies betwixt eternal
generation and eternal procession, I am not
ashamed to give them this answer; I cannot tell, it
is a mystery far above my reach; God hath not revealed it, and there is nothing in nature which will
give us any light about it, therefore it becomes us
rather to adore than to be inquisitive. I know the
schoolmen, who are privy to all secrets, and have a
key to open every difficulty, though it be locked up
never so close, attempt the opening of it, but they
had better have let it alone; here humble ignorance
is better than saucy curiosity. I think they speak
best who say, we know and believe there is a difference betwixt generation and procession, but what
that is, and wherein it lies, that is to us incomprehensible.[2] It is time therefore for me to leave this point,
and to come to the application of the main truth.

Use. 1. Is Christ thus God's own Son? I infer then
That he is God. Not a mere titular or nuncu-
pative god; not a god by office only; not a made
god, a contradiction in the adject; but he is God
truly, properly, essentially—which great truth is
most strongly asserted and proved by various convincing arguments against Jews, Arians, Socinians,
all the opposers of it. I must not engage in so vast
a subject, I will only argue from this relation wherein Christ stands to God as he is his own Son, which
indeed by itself is sufficient, if there was nothing
more, to demonstrate his Godhead. He who is the

true Son of God, and such a Son of God, is truly
God; but Christ is the true Son of God, and such a
Son of God, (his own Son,) therefore he is truly God,
&c. The apostle joins the *true Son* and the *true God*
together, therefore the argument is good: 1 John v.
20, 'We know that the Son of God is come, and
hath given us an understanding that we may know
him that is true; and we are in him that is true,
even in his Son Jesus Christ: this is the true God,
and eternal life.' I do not say that every son of
God is God, for the saints are sons, and yet not God;
but I say he who is such a Son as God's own proper, natural, consubstantial, co-essential, only begotten Son, he is God: wherever this sonship is, there
is the deity or the divine essence. Now Christ is
thus God's Son, therefore he is God. What the
Father is as to his nature, that the Son must be
also; now the first person, the Father of Christ, is
God, whereupon he too, who is the Son, must be
God also. A son always participates of his father's
essence; there is betwixt them evermore an identity
and oneness of nature. If, therefore, Christ be God's
Son, as hath been fully proved, he must then needs
have that very nature and essence which God the
Father hath, insomuch that if the second person be
not really a god, the first person is but equivocally
a father.[1] Therefore he himself tells us, John x. 30,
'I and my Father are one:' where he is speaking
of a far higher oneness than that of consent or will
only. Christ being both the natural Son of God,
and also his Son by eternal generation, that makes
the one thing unquestionable; for what is that generation but the Father's communicating of his own
nature and essence to him? This is that which is
done in all generations, for generation is always the
production of another in the same nature.[2] Like

---

[1] Quæris a me si de substantia Patris est Filius, de substantia
Patris est etiam Spiritus Sanctus, cur unus Filius sit, et alius
non sit Filius? Ego respondeo, sive capias sive non capias, de
Patre est Filius, de Patre est Spiritus Sanctus, sed ille genitus
est, iste procedens.—*August contra Maxim.*, lib. iii. cap. 14.

[2] τὸ ὄντι hujus differentiæ sciri et credi ex divina revela-
tione. At τὸ διότι est nobis incomprehensibile et ineffabile.—
Alting. Theolog. Prolem., loc. 3, problem 38, p. 238.

[1] Nisi esset Jesus Christus φύσει θεὸς, natura Deus, non esset
φύσει υἱὸς θεοῦ natura seu naturalis Dei Filius.—*Cloppenb. Anti-
Smalc.*, cap. 3, p. 72. *Vide* Jacob ad Portum contra Ostorod,
cap. 9, p. 59. Estwick against Biddle, p. 442, &c.

[2] Πᾶν τὸ γεννῶν, ὅμοιον τὶ γεννήσει. Ἄνθρωπος ἄνθρωπον
γεννᾷ, καὶ θεὸς θεόν. οἷος ὁ γεννῶν ἄνθρωπος, τοιοῦτος καὶ ὁ
ὑπ' αὐτοῦ γεννώμενος, &c.—*Epiph. Hœres.*, 69, p. 750. Κοινὸν
ὑπάρχει πᾶσι καὶ αὐτοδίδακτον ὁμολόγημα, ὡς ἅπας υἱὸς τῆς
αὐτῆς ἐστι τῷ γεγεννηκότι οὐσίας καὶ φύσεως, ὥσπερ ὁ τὸν πατέρα
δημιουργικῆς οὐσίας καὶ ἀϊδίου φύσεως, εἰδὼς, τῆς αὐτῆς εἶναι καὶ
τὸν υἱὸν συναναμολογήσειεν.—*Phot.* Ep., p. 4. Αὕτη φύσις
γεννήτορὸς καὶ γεννήματος, &c.—*Nazianz.*, Orat. 35, tom. i. p. 568.

ever begets like, as it is said of Adam ; he begat a son in his own likeness, after his image, Gen. v. 3. And must it not be so here in the Father's begetting of Christ ? If man begets man, then God begets God ; this being taken in that sense which I laid down in my first entrance upon this subject. I know this will not hold as to all modes and circumstances, (with respect to which I grant there is a great disparity,) but as to the conveyance of the same nature and essence, so far it will hold. The Jews, therefore, John v. 18, argued very well ; if God was Christ's Father, and he God's Son, then he was equal with God, for such an equality must naturally and necessarily result from such a relation : John x. 36, ' Say ye of him, whom the Father hath sanctified, and sent into the world, Thou blasphemest ; because I said, I am the Son of God ?' Why doth he say *because I said I am the Son of God ?* He should have said *because I said I am God*, for that was the blasphemy charged upon him : ver. 33, ' Because that thou, being a man, makest thyself God.' But the answer is obvious, Christ knew that these were equipollent terms ; to be *God*, and to be the *Son of God*, are all one ; if Christ be the one, he must be the other too. You find Nathanael breaking forth into this witness concerning him : John i. 49, ' Thou art the Son of God,' &c. His meaning was ' thou art God ;' for that which drew this confession from him was that which was proper to him as God, namely, his omnisciency : see John i. 48. *God* and the *Son of God* are so much one, that he who speaks Christ to be the Son of God speaks him to be God also. As soon as the apostle had set down Christ's Sonship, Heb. i. 5, presently he falls upon those testimonies which relate to his Godhead : verses 6, 8, 10–12, ' When he bringeth in the first-begotten into the world, he saith, And let all the angels of God worship him. Unto the Son he saith, Thy throne, O God, is for ever and ever ; a sceptre of righteousness is the sceptre of thy kingdom. Thou, Lord, in the beginning hast laid the foundation of the earth, and the heavens are the works of thy hands. They shall perish, but thou remainest ; and they all shall wax old as doth a garment ; and as a vesture shalt thou fold them up, and they shall be changed ; but thou art the same, and thy years shall not fail.' You see how Christ's Sonship is linked with the Godhead, therefore the argument is good to prove the latter by the former. And indeed, as his being the Son of man doth most evidently evince him to be truly man, so his being the Son of God doth as evidently evince him to be truly God.

2. Is Christ God's own Son ? I infer, surely then he is a very great and glorious person : such a relation cannot but be the foundation of great glory. Though Christ's dignity and pre-eminence is not the ground of his Sonship, yet his Sonship is the ground of his dignity and pre-eminence. He is styled ' a great high priest,' Heb. iv. 14, not only because of the greatness of his sacerdotal office, but also because of the greatness of his person who doth manage that office, he being God's own Son ; therefore it follows, ' seeing we have a high priest, &c., Jesus the Son of God.' It is no small honour amongst us to be the son of some great man ; oh what an honour is it to Christ to be the own and only Son of the great God ! It puts a marvellous glory and greatness upon the saints, that they are the adopted sons of God, upon the angels that they are the created sons of God ; but what is this to Christ being the natural, only-begotten Son of God? Herein and hereby ' he hath obtained a more excellent name' than either angels or men, Heb. i. 4 ; for ' in all things (or amongst all persons) he must have the pre-eminence,' Col. i. 18. The higher and nearer the relation is to God, the higher and greater is the glory which accrues to a person standing in that relation. Now what relation to God can be higher and nearer than this of Christ, as he is his own Son? Therefore his glory must needs be exceeding great. Oh let not any entertain low thoughts of him who is thus the Son of God ! The Lord Jesus is the Father's best Son for gifts, grace, holiness, &c., and he is the Father's greatest Son for dignity, glory, and majesty. I say he is the Father's best Son : how short do all sons come of this Son ! We read of one who feared he might seem to adopt better sons than those whom he begat.[1] There is no such thing to be imagined with respect to God ; to be sure, his only-begotten Son shall infinitely exceed all his adopted sons, for ' God hath anointed

[1] Micipsa in Salust.—*Ne ego meliores liberos sumpsisse videar quam genuisse.*

2 E

him with the oil of gladness above his fellows,' Ps. xlv. 7. And he is the greatest Son too, for God 'hath set him at his own right hand in the heavenly places, far above all principality, and power, and might, and dominion, and every name that is named, not only in this world, but also in that which is to come,' Eph. i. 20, 21. True, indeed, this great Son for a time emptied himself of his glory, Phil. ii. 7, and for our sake submitted to great abasement; but yet even then in himself he was very high and glorious. He who clothed himself with our rags, put on our flesh, condescended to lie in the manger, to die upon the cross, he even under all this was the proper Son of God, and therefore full of glory. And it is very notable to consider how in Christ, even when he was under his lowest abasement, when this Sun was hid under the thickest cloud, I say how even then there were some beamings out and breakings forth of his glory suitable to this his relation.[1] He is laid in the manger, but there the wise men come and worship him; he is tempted by Satan, but then the angels minister unto him; he is crucified, but then the veil of the temple was rent, the earth quaked, the rocks were rent, the graves opened, the sun stepped in and hid itself, as being ashamed to be seen in its glory when the far brighter Sun was under such an eclipse; upon all which the centurion might well cry out, 'Truly this was the Son of God.' But what a person is Christ now, when the time of his humiliation is over, and when he appears in all things like himself, as the Son of God in his greatest glory!

3. Thirdly, Was Christ God's own Son? I infer, certainly then the work of redemption was a very great work; for God sent his own Son about it, and therefore surely it was no ordinary or common thing. Always the greater the person is who is employed in the work, the greater is that work; it is thus from the wisdom of a man, much more shall it be thus from the wisdom of a God. Kings do not use to

[1] Infantia parvuli ostenditur humilitate cunarum, magnitudo altissimi declaratur vocibus angelorum; similis est rudimentis hominum quem Herodes impius molitur occidere, sed Dominus est omnium quem magi gaudentes veniunt suppliciter adorare.—*Leo Magn.* Ep. ad Flavian, Ep. Const. Nazianzen. Orat. 35, tom. i. p. 375, instances in several particulars about this, and very elegantly enlarges upon them.

send their sons upon mean and petty services, but only upon such as are high and weighty; and can it be imagined that ever God would have sent his own Son into the world to redeem sinners, if this had not been a work very high and great in his eye? Indeed this makes redemption to be the greatest work that ever was done by God himself. The making of the world was a great thing, but God never sent his Son about that; that was despatched by a word; he did but speak the word and it was done. Works of providence are very great, but there is no sending of a Son about them; but when redemption work was to come upon the stage, in order to that Christ, God's own Son, must come from heaven, and be incarnate, and do, and die, and all was necessary for the accomplishing of that. Oh how great a work was this! So much for the first use by way of inference.

Use 2. Secondly, Was Christ God's own Son? Let me from hence urge a few things upon you.

1. Study Christ much in this relation, that you may know him as the proper, natural, essential Son of God. The knowledge of Christ, in whatever notion you consider him, is very precious; it was so to Paul, who determined not to know anything save Jesus Christ,' &c., 1 Cor. ii. 2, and who 'counted all things but loss for the excellency of the knowledge of Christ Jesus,' Phil. iii. 8; but to know him as he stands in this near relation to God, as God's own Son, oh this is precious knowledge indeed! Now, sirs, you have heard much of him, read much of him, but do you know him, and know him as the eternal, only-begotten Son of God? This is that truth upon which all religion depends; in which you have the very heart and spirit of the gospel; upon which the whole stress of your happiness is laid; it is one of the most fundamental articles of the Christian faith; and yet will you be ignorant of it? You all have some general knowledge of it, and you all profess to believe it, it is a part of your creed; but do you distinctly and clearly know, always allowing for the mysteriousness of the object and the dimness of your faculties, how Christ is the Son of God? how his Sonship was brought about, and wherein it lies? that he is God's natural Son, begotten by him from all eternity in a most mysterious and admirable manner; do you understand anything about this? Some tell

us that the knowledge and belief of Christ's Sonship, according to the particulars wherein it hath been opened, is not necessary to salvation.[1] I will not engage in this controversy, wherein some do as much affirm as others deny; but this I say, it being so momentous a truth in itself, and the Scriptures speaking so much of it, and giving so much light about it, it is of great concern to all who live under gospel-revelation to endeavour to know as much of it as the height of the thing and the lowness of their capacities will admit of.

And because I would hope that there are some here whose thoughts are taken up about it, and who desire to arrive at a fuller knowledge of it, therefore to such I would commend three things by way of direction.

(1.) In all your inquiries and searchings into Christ's Sonship, especially into the ground and mode of it, viz., eternal generation, be sure you keep within the bounds of sobriety. I mean this, take heed that in this deep mystery you ' be not wise above what is written,' 1 Cor. iv. 6; that you do not therein consult your own purblind and carnal reason, but Scripture revelation altogether. Pray study it, but in so doing do not pry too far into those secrets which God hath locked up from you;[2] content yourselves

with what he hath revealed in his word, and stay there.

It is both sinful and also dangerous for poor shallow creatures to venture too far into these depths, where, if they once lose their bottom, the written word, they drown themselves presently; there is no clue but that to guide us in this labyrinth. That Christ is the Son of God is very clear; that he is the Son of God by eternal generation is very clear; but will you be inquisitive further to know what this generation is? What can your reason, the Scripture being silent about it, say of that? Oh go not too far there! Human reason, considered as merely natural, is a very incompetent judge of this divine and sublime mystery; a mystery to be adored by faith, not to be comprehended by reason. Isa. liii. 8, ' Who shall declare his generation?' I may make use of this text, though possibly the generation mentioned in it be not that which I am treating of; for I much incline to think that it here notes that numerous issue and seed that Christ should have upon the preaching of the gospel, rather than his being eternally begotten by the Father. Yet it is very well known that several of the fathers take it in the latter sense, they making this to be the meaning of the words : Who can be able to understand in himself, or to declare to others, the hidden, ineffable, incomprehensible generation of the Son of God? Surely none can. Without controversy this, as well as Christ's incarnation, is a great mystery, 1 Tim. iii. 16. Nicodemus was a knowing man, yet strangely puzzled at the regeneration of believers : John iii. 4, ' How can a man be born when he is old? can he enter the second time into his mother's womb, and be born?' Certainly the eternal generation of God's own Son is a thing much more abstruse and unsearchable. And there are riddles in natural generation which we cannot resolve : Eccles. xi. 5, ' As thou knowest not the way of the spirit, nor how the bones do grow in her that is with child.' Now, are we so much at a loss and nonplus there, how much more shall we be at a loss when the far more unconceivable generation of Christ is before us![1] Oh, therefore, I advise you to be very humble and sober in all your disquisitions about that! There are two things in reason which you must always oppose and beat down,

---

[1] Cognoscere quando Filius Dei primum extiterit, et utrum ex ipsius Patris essentia necne genitus fuerit, non est necessarium creditu ad salutem.—*Socin. Solut. Scrupul.* resp. ad scrup., 1. So *Episcopius Inst. Theol.*, lib. iv. cap. 34, per totum.

[2] Quæro abs te quando vel quomodo Filium putas esse generatum? mihi enim impossibile est generationis scire secretum, mens deficit, vox silet, non mea tantum sed et angelorum; supra potestates, et supra angelos, et supra cherubim, et supra seraphin, et supra omnem sensum est, &c. Tu ergo ori manum admove, scrutari non licet superna mysteria. Licet scire quod natus sit, non licet discutere quomodo natus sit. Illud mihi negare, non hoc quærere metus est. Ineffabilis enim est illa generatio.—*Ambros. de Fide*, cap. 5. Si Christus dixit se nescire de die illa et hora, sed solum Patrem, quanto minus possumus nos scire quomodo genitus sit Filius ex Patre? Non debere igitur nos erubescere fateri, neminem hunc modum nosse, sed solum illum qui genuit, et eum qui genitus est.— *Iren.*, lib. ii. cap. 48. Quomodo Deus Pater genuerit Filium, nolo discutias, nec te curiosius inferas in profundi hujus arcanum.—*Cyprian. in Symbol.* Ἀφ' ἑαυτοῦ ἐγέννησε τὸν μονογενῆ ἀρρήτως καὶ ἀκαταλήπτως.—*Epiph. adv. Hæres.*, lib. ii. tom. ii. p. 739. The mystery of mysteries, which corrupt and wanton reason derides, but prudent faith admires and adores.—*Cheyn. Trin-unity*, p. 190.

[1] *Vide* Nazianz. Orat. 35, tom. i. pp. 566, 567.

viz., the curiosity of it—for it loves dearly to be prying into God's ark, into things which he sees good to lock up from the creature—and the pride of it— for it also loves to sit upon the bench as judge of the matters of faith, to be giving out its decrees and edicts as to believing or not believing—now do not you give way to it in either of these respects ; in your most earnest desires after knowledge still keep within the compass of what the word reveals, and let the word alone command and order your faith ; and especially in such profound mysteries as that which I am upon, see that these things be done by you. When I consider the several nice and curious questions which some have raised and discussed about the generation of the Son of God, I cannot but stand and wonder at the pride and sauciness of the wit of man; and so far I do concur with that learned person[1] in his severe censure upon these men. What is more than the thing itself, the Father's communi- cating of his own nature and essence to Christ, we must humbly submit to be ignorant of ; by soaring too high we shall but scorch and hurt ourselves.

(2.) In your eyeing of God the Father's active gen- eration of Christ, take heed of all gross conceptions about it, so as not in the least to measure it by, or to parallel it with, any physical or carnal generation. Our apprehensions must be rightly informed about this, otherwise what absurd and wretched notions shall we run ourselves upon ! So far as there is that in common generations which speaks goodness and perfection, so far you make use of them to help you in your conceiving of the divine generation of the Son of God ; but there being much in them which speaks defect and imperfection, all that you must prescind, and cut off, and lay aside, when you are thinking of that generation which is the ground of Christ's Sonship. As, for instance, for like to beget like, for one thing to convey its nature and substance to another, this is good in physical generations, and so far they may be improved to shadow out unto us the mystery of God's eternal generation. But now

there being sundry other respects which carry imper- fection in them, these you must be sure to keep out of your thoughts, and by no means to conceive by them of that which I am upon. As in our know- ledge and conceptions of God by the creatures we pick out of them what is good and perfect, and lay aside what is evil and imperfect, and so by them we ascend to know and conceive of God ; so we must do in natural and physical generations, with respect to God the Father's supernatural and hyperphysical generation of Christ.

To shew the difference betwixt these two, let me particularise, in a few things, without much enlarg- ing upon them.[1] Natural generation, upon the fail- ing of individuals, is necessary for the preservation of the species ; in God the Father's begetting of Christ it was quite otherwise. In natural generation there is multiplication ; there, though the thing be- getting and the thing begotten have the same nature and essence, yet numerically they are not the same; but in the Father's begetting of Christ these, as the learned prove, are perfectly one and the same ; they have not only the same specifical, but the same numerical essence. Here, as the divine essence was not divided, so neither was it multiplied ; for it is as incapable of multiplication as of division. Na- tural generation in the creature is a transient act, that in God was an immanent act. In natural gen- eration the thing begetting precedes the thing begot- ten, and begets that which is after it in time ; in God the Father's generation of Christ it was not so, both Father and Son being co-eternal. In natural gene- ration there must be such a time before things arrive at their prolific virtue ; far be it from us to entertain such a thought as to the Father's generation of Christ. So that you see there is a vast disparity betwixt these two, and therefore you must in your apprehensions reverently distinguish betwixt them, and not in com- mon judge of the one by the other. God forbid that you should so sadly mistake! Though the Father's communicating of the divine essence to the Son was a true and proper generation, so far agreeing with generations amongst us, yet in other respects it was quite of another nature ; and so you are to conceive

[1] Non dubito asserere, quando in Scholasticorum quæstiones de his rebus incido, quin in totidem salebras, labyrinthos, Syrtes, Charybdes, ipsaque adeo βάθη ματαιότητος incidere mihi videar. Quanto satius tutiusque est intra Scripturæ limites se arcte continere, et sapere nolle ὑπὲρ τὰ γεγραμμένα. —*Episcop. Inst. Theol.*, lib. iv. cap. 33, sect. 2.

[1] Of this see Zanch. de tribus Elohim, lib. v. cap. 8, p. 254; Alting. Theol. Elenct., pp. 170, 171 ; Estwick against Biddle, p. 443 ; Dr Pearson on the Creed, p. 275, &c.

of it, otherwise you will entertain very gross and unworthy thoughts of God.

(3.) Join study and prayer together. Would you know Christ as the eternal Son of God? especially, would you go beyond a literal, speculative, notional knowledge of him as such, so as to know both him and his Sonship practically and savingly? Oh then be much in prayer! Read and pray, hear and pray, meditate and pray, study and pray. He studies this mystery, and all others, best, who studies it most upon his knees. This special and supernatural Sonship of Christ is not savingly to be known without special and supernatural illumination from Christ through the Spirit. It is observable that in Mat. xvi. 17, when Peter had made that good confession, 'Thou art Christ, the Son of the living God,' see what Christ resolved it into: 'Blessed art thou, Simon Bar-jona; for flesh and blood hath not revealed it unto thee, but my Father which is in heaven.' You know that passage, Mat. xi. 27, 'All things are delivered unto me of my Father, and no man knoweth the Son,' or makes others to know him, 'but the Father; neither knoweth any man the Father save the Son, and he to whomsoever the Son will reveal him.' These two persons do make known each the other; the Father reveals the Son, and the Son reveals the Father. The Son is a fit person to reveal the Father, for he is his only-begotten Son, and lies in his bosom; therefore he saith, John i. 18, 'No man hath seen God at any time; the only-begotten Son, which is in the bosom of the Father, he hath declared him.' And the Father is also a fit person to reveal the Son; for he having begotten him, and having had him with himself from everlasting, he knows him exactly. Oh, therefore, go to him by prayer, and beseech him to reveal his Son to you! It is a great thing to know Christ in this relation—so great that there must be a heavenly light, a spiritual understanding given to a man before he can come up to it. Mark that of the apostle, 1 John v. 20, 'And hath given us understanding that we may know him that is true.' He speaks of the knowing of Christ as the true Son of God. It is as if the apostle had said, If God had not illuminated our understandings, and irradiated them with a divine light, we had never known Christ savingly in this notion. He who begat the Son of himself from all eternity, to him it appertains by his Spirit in time savingly to reveal this Son to the creature; and therefore your work lies with him in prayer to beg of him this revelation of his Son. So much for the first thing.

2. A second branch of the exhortation shall be this: Is Christ God's own Son? Then do you believe him to be such, and believe on him as such? The first we call dogmatical, the second justifying and saving faith; the first is assent to the proposition that Christ is God's own Son, the second is reliance upon the person who is, and as he is, God's own Son. The first is more general and common; for all who bear the name of Christians, in some sense or other, come up to it; yet notwithstanding there is much worth and excellency in it, though not so much as in the latter; and that is absolutely necessary in order to the second; for how can he believe on Christ as the Son of God, who doth not first dogmatically believe him to be the Son, and such a Son, of God? And this general faith too, as well as that which is more special, admits of degrees; for though all Christians believe it, yet some are more confirmed, rooted, stablished in the belief of it than others are. Now, therefore, this is that which I would press upon you, to labour after a more steady, unshaken, fixed believing of this great foundation truth. I hope you do believe it; but do you believe it in such a degree? doth not your faith sometimes waver about it? is not your assent weak and languid, attended with doubtings and questionings? are you rooted and stablished in the faith, Col. ii. 7, as of other things, so in special of this great article of the Christian religion? Are you come up 'unto all riches of the full assurance of understanding, to the acknowledgment of the mystery of God, and of the Father, and of Christ,' as the apostle speaks? Col. ii. 2. I could most heartily wish that it was thus with you, and with all who do profess that they believe Christ to be the Son of God; but I fear it is not so. Now, my brethren, that I may the better excite you to labour after a full and firm assent hereunto, consider that one special reason or end why a great part of the New Testament was written was this, that you might believe and be confirmed in your belief of this very thing: John xx. 31, 'But these are written that ye might believe that Jesus is the Christ, the Son of God, and that believ-

ing ye might have life through his name.' You may observe, concerning this evangelist St John, as of all the other evangelists he was most inspired in the revealing of Christ's divine Sonship, so he was also most inspired in the pressing of men to believe it, and in the setting out of the weightiness of the belief of it : 1 John ii. 23, 'Whosoever denieth the Son, the same hath not the Father : but he that acknowledgeth the Son, hath the Father also.' 1 John iv. 15, 'Whosoever shall confess that Jesus is the Son of God, God dwelleth in him, and he in God.' 1 John v. 5, 'Who is he that overcometh the world, but he that believeth that Jesus is the Son of God?' What a mighty stress did this great apostle lay upon it! Oh how doth it concern all, upon the considerations laid down by him, to live under a steady belief of Christ's being the Son of God! Indeed this is the foundation truth ; Christ himself is the personal foundation, and this truth, not exclusively, but eminently, is the doctrinal foundation, to both of which that famous and so much controverted text is applicable, Mat. xvi. 18, 'I say also unto thee, that thou art Peter, and upon this rock I will build my church ; and the gates of hell shall not prevail against it.' Upon this rock? What rock doth Christ mean? Was it Peter, personally considered? or was it Peter and his successors? as some would have it, they meaning by these successors the popes of Rome, whom I trust I shall never close with in this interpretation so long as it is this rock, and not this sand. Undoubtedly, let but persons be unbiassed, and not wedded to parties and opinions calculated for worldly designs and interests, nothing is more clear than that by this rock we are to understand either the person of Christ, or that doctrinal proposition which Peter had laid down concerning him, ver. 16, 'Thou art Christ the Son of the living God;' after which it immediately follows, 'upon this rock I will build my church;' or else we may put them together and take in both. Upon this person and this faith the church of God is built, and therefore it shall stand fast for ever ; so that, according to this exposition, which is with great strength defended by our protestant divines, this Sonship of Christ is the foundation truth. And therefore no wonder that in all ages the zeal of the church hath been so much engaged therein ; for it is very well known that in its drawing up of creeds and summaries of faith, this

one article, viz., Christ's being the co-essential, co-eternal, only-begotten Son of God, hath ever been put in — witness the Nicene, Constantinopolitan, Athanasian creeds—because this was judged a thing most necessary to be believed. And indeed there is not any one branch of the Christian faith which the church hath gained more out of the fire, after much trouble and opposition, than this one. Nay, this was that very truth for the owning and asserting of which above any other our blessed Lord lost his life, as you may plainly see by the evangelical history, John xix. 7 ; Mark xiv. 61, &c. And I desire that it may yet further be considered, that as God himself began and ended with the witness and declaration of Christ's Sonship ;—for as soon as he entered upon his public ministry the Father set him out with this witness, 'This is my beloved Son,' &c., Mat. iii. 17 ; and when he had well-nigh finished his work, and was going off the stage, then the Father renewed his witness again, 'This is my beloved Son,' &c., Mat. xvii. 5 ;—so the devil, too, he began and ended with the Sonship of Christ ; for presently after the Father's testimony thereof he took him aside to tempt him, and when he had him alone, and began the duel with him, how did he assault him! Why, 'If thou be the Son of God, command that these stones be made bread,' Mat. iv. 3. He comes over it again, 'If thou be the Son of God, cast thyself down,' &c., ver. 6. *If thou be the Son of God?* Why did Satan harp so much upon this? what might his design be in laying his temptation thus? I answer, it must be for one or for all of these reasons ; either that he might, by the observing of Christ's behaviour in the contest, more fully inform himself whether Christ was indeed the Son of God, which was the thing he was deadly afraid of, knowing that such a person would be the ruin of his kingdom ; or that he might see whether he could make Christ to doubt of his Sonship, after and notwithstanding the plain testimony of his Father ; or that he might go as far as ever he could to draw him to the doing of what was evil, and so, if such a thing had been possible, null this his near relation to God. Surely there was some special cause why Satan picked out this, and so much insisted upon it. Well! here he began ; these were the very first words which this cursed spirit uttered when he dared to assault our Saviour, wherein he plainly struck at his Sonship itself, though cunningly he made his temptations to point to some wicked inferences which he would have had drawn from Christ's relation, rather than directly to the truth of the relation itself. And as he began with this, so he ended with this; for it was he—which speaks a prodigious infatuation in him, that he should be so forward in the promoting of that which certainly would end in his ruin—who stirred up Pilate, the high priest, the body of the Jews, against Christ, and they through his instigation fell upon Christ and took away his life; for what? for this very cause, because 'he made himself to be,' as indeed he was, 'the Son of God.' By all this you see of what great moment and importance this truth concerning Christ's Sonship is. And, to add yet one thing further, pray look to that grand seducer and enemy of Christ and of the Christian faith—I mean Mohammed, of whom we read that he also set himself to his utmost to oppose and decry the Sonship of Christ. He was willing to grant Christ to be a great prophet, but by no means to be the very Son of God. This particularly and expressly he principled his followers against in his ridiculous Alcoran; and he gave them in special this command, "Ἑνα μόνον τροσχυνεῖν θεὸν καὶ τὸν χριστον τιμᾶν ὡς λόγον τοῦ θεοῦ μεν, οὐχὶ υἱὸν δὲ, to worship one only God, and to honour Christ as the word of God, but not as the Son of God.[1]

From all these premises I infer, is this such a foundation-truth, and shall not we firmly assent to it? Hath the church with such zeal contended for it, and shall we yet doubt of it? Do heathens, Jews, Turks, so much oppose it, and shall not we Christians, who have and own Scripture revelation, steadily believe it? Hath Christ sealed it with his blood, and yet shall we stagger about it? Have we such attestations from God and man, and yet shall there be questionings and reasonings in our souls against it? 1 John v. 9, 10, 'If we receive the witness of men, the witness of God is greater; for

this is the witness of God which he hath testified of his Son. He that believeth on the Son of God, hath the witness in himself: he that believeth not God, hath made him a liar, because he believeth not the record that God gave of his Son.'

But some will say, To what purpose is all this? who questions whether Christ be God's own Son?

I answer, Oh that there was not too much need of this advice! Many poor souls think they do fully and firmly believe it, and yet it is to be feared they do not; and the truth is, that weakness which is in our faith of adherence proceeds in part from that weakness that is in our faith of assent, much of that dejectedness which is upon our spirits under trouble, and of those inward sinkings under the sense of guilt, comes from one of these two causes, either we do not revive upon our thoughts, or else we do not fixedly believe in our hearts, that Christ is God's Son, and his own Son. And as to loose and common professors, if ever Arianism, old or new, should get upon the throne, which God forbid, I fear the belief of Christ's Godhead and eternal Sonship would soon be laid aside. Oh therefore, I would be very earnest with you to get your faith yet more and more strengthened and confirmed about it.

But though this be very good, yet it is not enough; besides the believing of Christ *to be* the Son of God, there must be believing *on* Christ *as* the Son of God. You find in Scripture that saving faith is described by its special reference to Christ as standing in this relation; so Gal. ii. 20, 'The life which I now live in the flesh, I live by the faith of the Son of God, who loved me, and gave himself for me.' Why doth the apostle thus express it by *the faith of the Son of God?* I answer, Partly because Christ the Son of God is the efficient and author of faith, Heb. xii. 2, partly because this Son is the great object of faith, and partly because faith in its essential act doth very much eye Christ as thus related to the Father, for it is a believing or relying upon him as the Son of God. It is very usual in the gospel, where it speaks of believing, to mention Christ with it as standing in this relation: 1 John iii. 23, 'This is his commandment, that we should believe on the name of his Son Jesus Christ.' 1 John v. 13, 'These things have I written unto you that believe on the name of the Son of God; that ye

[1] Constanter dic illis, Deum unum esse, necessarium omnibus, et incorporeum. Qui nec genuit, nec est generatus, nec habet quenquam sibi similem.—*Azoar.*, 122; Alcor. in Bibliandri. edit., p. 188. *Vide* Cribrat. Alcorani. per Nicol. de Cusa., lib. i. cap. 10, 11, 13, 14, &c. See Dr Pearson on the Creed, p. 272.

may know that ye have eternal life, and that ye may believe on the name of the Son of God.' John iii. 16, 'God so loved the world that he gave his only-begotten Son, that whosoever believeth in him,' as the only-begotten Son, 'should not perish, but have everlasting life.' Oh what a person is God's own Son for sinners to believe on! What an all-sufficient Saviour, how 'able to save to the utmost' must he needs be who is God and man, the Son of God and the Son of man! Heb. vii. 25. And indeed it is not enough barely to believe on Christ, but there must be such a believing on him as may in some measure be answerable to this his relation: is he God's own Son? At what a rate should we believe! What a faith should we act upon him! What great things should we expect for him and from him! Can anything be too high for our faith, when we have the proper, natural Son of God in our eye as its basis and foundation? Saints should have their faith raised not only upon the encouragement of the promises, but also upon the consideration of Christ's person, as he is so near and dear to God. I have formerly observed how our apostle in the text rises higher and higher in the setting forth of the love of God. He says God *sent*, there was love; he sent his *own Son*, there was more love; this own Son he sent *in the likeness of sinful flesh*, there was yet more love; and this he did for this end, that he might *for sin condemn sin in the flesh*, &c.; there was the very top and zenith of love. Now as there is a rise in these things in the setting off the love of God, so there is also a rise in them in their several engagements and encouragements to us to believe in Christ, and to believe in him yet more and more firmly and fiducially: he was *sent*, therefore we must believe; he was and is *God's own Son*, therefore we must the rather and the more strongly believe; he took *our flesh*, here is a higher argument for a higher faith; in that flesh he *condemned sin*, performed all that the law commanded, suffered all that the law threatened; what a faith doth this call for! Now if, notwithstanding all this, it shall yet be either no-believing or but faint-believing, both will be sad, though in a great disparity, for the faint-believing is unanswerable to what is revealed, and uncomfortable to the saint, but the no-believing is damnable to the sinner.

3. Thirdly, Is Christ God's own Son? How then should all honour and adore him! Certainly upon this Sonship the highest, yea, even divine adoration itself is due to him. Is he a Son?—such a Son?—the Son of such a Father? The greatness of his person, arising from that high and near relation wherein he stands to God, calls for the highest respect, reverence, veneration, which angels or men can possibly give unto him. Besides this, it is the absolute will of the Father that all should 'honour his Son even as they honour himself,' John v. 23; for he having the same nature and essence with the Father, the Father will have him have the same honour which he himself hath: which whosoever denies to him reflects dishonour upon the Father, who will not bear anything derogatory to the glory of his Son. It is a known story that of the carriage of Amphilochius to the Emperor Theodosius;[1] he had petitioned the emperor to be severe against the Arians, to discountenance and suppress them, because in their opinions they did so much disparage the Son of God; but could not prevail; whereupon he made use of this device: coming one day into the presence of the emperor, and of his son Arcadius, who now ruled jointly with his father, he made his humble obeisance to the emperor himself, and shewed him all reverence; but as for his son he passed him by, shewed him no respect at all, rather dealt derisorily with him, stroking him upon his head, and saying to him, in a way of contempt, *salve et tu, fili*. The emperor upon this was much offended, sharply reproves Amphilochius for his affront to his son, &c. Whereupon the good man vindicates his carriage, plainly telling the emperor he had given reverence enough to his son. And now the emperor was more incensed, commands him with great indignation to be thrust out of his presence, &c., which whilst some was doing, Amphilochius turned himself to the emperor and said thus: O emperor! thou being but a man canst not bear the contempt or disparagement of thy son; how dost thou think the great God can bear that contempt of his Son which the Arians cast upon him? The emperor was much affected at this, begged the bishop's pardon, commended his ingeny, and did that now which he refused to do before. The inference is undeniable, if great men stand so

[1] Nicephor., lib. xii. cap. 9. Sozom., lib. vii. cap. 6.

much upon the giving of all honour and due observance to their sons, much more will the great God stand upon the giving of all due honour and reverence to his own and only Son. Oh, therefore, let Christ be highly adored and honoured by you! If you ask me, how? I answer, every honouring of him is not sufficient, but it must be such as may suit with his infinite majesty and greatness; you must conceive of him as God, as the natural and eternal Son of God, and according to that honour which is due to him as such, so you must honour him. The apostle speaks of some who, ' when they knew God, they did not glorify him as God,' Rom. i. 21; so some pretend to give some glory to Christ, but they do not glorify him as God. Oh, this is that which you must come up to, to adore and reverence Christ in such a manner as may be suitable to his nature and relation, as he is the infinite God, and the eternal only-begotten Son of God; and what honour can be high enough for such a person?

But more particularly there is a twofold honour which you must all give to Christ.

1. The honour of worship: Heb. i. 6, ' When he bringeth in the first-born into the world, he saith, And let all the angels of God worship him.' God will have his only-begotten Son to be worshipped, though he be very tender to whom that honour is given. Divines do from hence strongly argue—yet I know some make but little of this argument—to prove the Godhead of Christ.[1] Thus, if religious worship be God's peculiar, if a God be the sole and adequate object of divine worship, if no creature be to share with him therein, it being that glory which he ' will not give to another,' Isa. xlii. 8; and Mat. iv. 10, ' Thou shalt worship the Lord thy God, and him only shalt thou serve;' and yet the Father will have Christ to be the proper object of divine worship; hence it follows, that then he is and must be more than mere man, that he is true and very God. And surely it would be no better than flat idolatry in us Christians to give proper and formal religious worship to Christ, was he not truly God as well as truly man. Therefore as to this Franciscus David and Christianus Franken, both Socinians, were in the right against Socinus, if Christ was but mere

man—the common principle in which they all agreed —then he could not be worshipped with religious worship without idolatry; whereupon they would not give any such worship to him. And as this worship proves Christ's Godhead, so his Godhead is the ground of it;[1] for the adequate, immediate, proper ground of divine worship, as attributed to Christ, is his divine nature, essence, and Sonship. True, he *as* man is to be worshipped, but not *because* he is man; the human nature of Christ is the object of worship, but it is only as it is taken into personal union with the divine. As he is mediator, and set in such an office, he is to be worshipped; but this is not the proper and fundamental reason thereof; for though he never had been mediator, yet worship would have been due to him, as the Father and Spirit are to be worshipped, though the office of mediator belongs not to them. Further, the Lord Jesus, as he in our nature hath done such great and excellent things for us, is to be worshipped; yet this is only a forcible motive and inducement thereunto, not the proper ground of it. It remains, then, that the alone reason of worship given or done to Christ is his being God, and the co-equal, co-essential Son of God. And he being so, what an obligation doth this lay upon you to worship him! There is inward worship, consisting in the trust, fear, reverence, adoration of the heart; there is outward worship, consisting in attendance upon, and due observance of, gospel institutions, as prayer, hearing the word, &c.; in both of these respects let Christ be worshipped by you, both are due to him as he is God's own Son. Well may you tender your homage to him in this way, when angels themselves bow before him and worship at his throne.

2. Secondly, There is the honour of obedience, which you must also give to Christ. This is annexed to the declaration of his Sonship; at the same time in which the Father attested that Christ was his Son, he enjoined obedience and subjection to him: Mat. xvii. 5, ' This is my beloved Son in whom I am well pleased;' what follows? 'hear ye him.'

---

[1] Remonstr. Apolog., cap. 2 and 16. Episcop. Inst. Theolog., lib. iv. sec. 2, cap. 34 and 35.

[1] Of this see *Zanch.*, De Tribus Elohim., lib. iii. cap. 12; *Junius*, Def. Trinit. contra Samosat., *Profess. Leid.*, Cens., cap. 16; *Voetius*, De Adorat. Christi; *Cheynel* on the Trinity, (very largely,) p. 334, &c.; *Dr Stillingfleet* on the Idolatry of the, &c., chap. ii. pp. 112-114.

This hearing of Christ is the creature's obeying of him in all his holy laws, commands, and institutions; and so it is as if God had said, Here is a person whom I own for my Son, in a special and peculiar way, whom therefore I have 'set as my king upon my holy hill of Zion,' Ps. ii. 6; into whose hands I have put 'all power,' Mat. xxviii. 18; upon whose shoulders I have laid 'the government,' Isa. ix. 7; therefore I charge you to hear him, and to yield all obedience and subjection to him. O sirs, it is God himself, and not such a poor worm as I, who requires this of you; it must be reverence and it must be obedience too, this high relation of Christ calls for both; and believe it, without this obedience he that is God's Son will never be your Saviour, for Heb. v. 9, 'Being made perfect, he became the author of eternal salvation unto all them,' and to none but them, 'that obey him.' I have spoken much to press believing on this Son upon you, but let me add, there must be obeying of him as well as believing on him. Obedience is not so of the very essence of faith, but that faith may very well be defined without it, yet it is an inseparable adjunct or consequent or fruit of faith; and these two do always concur in the subject, though they be different in themselves, and have a different influence upon justification and salvation. But that which I aim at is this, since Christ is the Son of God, and this is clearly revealed to you, since this Son hath made known to you in the holy gospel what his will and pleasure is, how he would have you to live, what to do, what to shun, I beseech you now hearken to him, comply with him in all his excellent commands, give up yourselves in a universal subjection to his blessed laws, let there be an obediential frame of heart to his whole will. This is indeed to honour him, and to honour him in such a way as best answers his Sonship to God and his lordship over you.

4. Fourthly, Is Christ no lower a person than God's own Son? What cause have we then to admire and wonder at the greatness of God's love in his sending of him! Here is a glass indeed to transmit and represent unto us the love of God; oh how shall we get our hearts affected with it! What thankfulness in us can bear any proportion to the mercy before us! For God to send, to send a Son,

such a Son, in such a manner, as follows in the words, here is the wonder of wonders; God never did the like before, and he will never do the like again; and, blessed be his name, there is no need he should! It would have been admirable mercy if God would have sent some other person upon this errand, to redeem and save undone sinners; if send he will, why did he not send an angel, or a body of angels, to try their skill and see what they could do? nay, why did he not send an angel, as he once did, with a flaming sword in his hand, to keep off sinners from the tree of life? Gen. iii. 24. Oh, this did not comport with his gracious designs, though it did too well with the creature's merit, therefore he would not do it; no, his own Son shall be pitched upon, he is the person whom God will send. And his end in sending this Son was as gracious as the person whom he sent was glorious. Surely here was love, great love, great even to the degree of infiniteness! Millions of angels were nothing to one Son, to one such Son. The nearer the relation was betwixt God and Christ, the greater was the affection shewn to us; Christ God's own Son, his first-born, his only-begotten Son, the Son of his love, who lay in his bosom, had been his delight for everlasting, for him to be sent to recover and save man, vile, sinful, wicked, undone man! the Son to be employed for the servant, the slave, the enemy! Oh astonishing mercy! Oh admirable goodness and condescension! How may we here cry out, 'Lord, what is man that thou art thus mindful of him? and the son of man that thou makest this account of him?' Ps. viii. 4, and cxliv. 3. Here was God so loving of the world, so as can never be expressed; he 'so loved the world as that he gave his only-begotten Son,' &c., John iii. 16. 'So loved the world.' What is there in this so? Why so inexpressibly, so unconceivably. 1 John iv. 9, 10, 'In this was manifested the love of God towards us, because that God sent his only-begotten Son into the world, that we might live through him; herein is love, not that we loved God, but that he loved us, and sent his Son to be the propitiation for our sins.' God owned it as a great discovery of Abraham's love to him, when upon his command he was willing to offer up his only-begotten son; but, alas! how infinitely short did that come of his own love in his sending and parting with his only-begotten Son for the good of sinners? Here he intended to give out the highest manifestation of his grace, and he hath done it to purpose. The heavens and the earth were once called upon to be filled with astonishment because of the ingratitude of a sinful people, Isa. i. 2; may not now heaven and earth, angels and men, all creatures whatsoever, be called upon to be filled with astonishment because of the stupendous love of God? O Christians! what influence hath this upon your dull and sluggish hearts? What are you made of that you are no more, in the sense of it, drawn out in the blessing, loving, admiring of God? Pray, if there be any holy ingenuity in you, take some pains with yourselves that you may be much more affected with it, and give not over till you have such thoughts and affections, upon God's sending his own Son, raised in you, as may in some measure answer to those thoughts and affections which you shall have about it when you shall be in heaven.

So much for exhortation. The third and last use shall be for comfort. And surely here is ground of strong consolation to believers, that which may highly conduce to the furthering of their joy, and the strengthening of their faith. You who are such, study this Sonship of Christ, dwell upon it often in your most serious thoughts, make the best of it, and then tell me whether you do not find that solid support and comfort from it which you desire and need.

Shall I broach this full vessel, and draw out a little of that heart-cheering liquor which is in it? Then know that,

1. As Christ is the Son of God, so are you. When I say *so* are you, you must understand me of the verity, not of the kind or manner of the sonship; you are not sons as Christ is, viz., by eternal generation; yet sons you are in another way, viz., by regeneration and adoption; and though herein you come short of Christ, you being but adopted sons, and he the natural Son, yet as you are but such, there is greater glory put upon you than if you were descended from, or adopted by, the greatest monarch of the world. May not this be matter of great comfort to you, to consider that whatever Christ is, that you are, according to your capacity and necessary subordination to him? that all that grace which fell upon him falls upon you likewise? And yet so it is. Is he the anointed of God? so are you; is he a Son? so are you; is he the beloved of God? so are you; is he the heir of God? so are you; in these respects also it is 'grace for grace,' John i. 16. I am upon your sonship in conformity to Christ's Sonship, the truth of which you have no reason to question, since the procuring of this for you was one thing that God in special aimed at in the sending of his great Son into the world: Gal. iv. 4, 5, 'When the fulness of time was come, God sent forth his Son, &c., that we might receive the adoption of sons,' and therefore in this relation Christ takes you in with himself: John xx. 17, 'Go to my brethren, and say unto them, I ascend unto my Father and your Father, and to my God and your God.'

2. You may now, upon this, confidently expect the bestowing of all good. For Christ being God's own Son, and he having given him to you, what can come after that can be too great, or too good, for him to give to you? What will God now deny after the gift of such a Son? 'He that spared not his own Son, but delivered him up for us all, how shall he not with him also freely give us all things?' Rom. viii. 32. Saints, let this be thought of; as all blessings come to you from God, as he is the God and Father of Christ, (for, Eph. i. 3, it is 'Blessed be the God and Father of our Lord Jesus Christ, who hath blessed us with all spiritual blessings in heavenly places in Christ;') so all blessings are assured to you from this relative consideration of God, viz., as he is first the God and Father of Christ, and then in him your God and Father too.

3. You may be sure that there is an infinite value, worth, and efficacy in Christ's obedience, and that he was a person able to accomplish your redemption. Christ being such a Son, this speaks him to be a person of great dignity; that dignity of his person gives the highest assurance to faith, both that he was every way able to go through what he undertook, and also that there must be an infinite virtue and merit in whatever he did or suffered. What can be so hard as that the power of the Son of God cannot effect it? And what can be so high as that the obedience of the Son of God cannot merit it? Had Christ been only the Son of man, then indeed faith could not have borne up with such confidence;

but he being the Son of God also, and having the nature, essence, attributes of God, how may faith triumph as to the efficacy and meritoriousness of his obedience. It was the blood of God which he shed, Acts xx. 28. Oh what a greatness and infiniteness of merit must needs result from the greatness and infiniteness of such a person![1] Heb. ix. 13, 14, 'If the blood of bulls and of goats, and the ashes of a heifer sprinkling the unclean, sanctifieth to the purifying of the flesh, how much more shall the blood of Christ, who through the eternal Spirit offered himself without spot to God, purge your conscience from dead works to serve the living God?'

4. You may go boldly to the throne of grace upon all occasions. For you have God's own Son to lead you thither and to make way for you; and not only so, but this own Son improves all his interest in and with the Father for your good. Why are you afraid to go to God? Heb. iv. 14-16, 'Seeing then that we have a great high priest that is passed into the heavens, (Jesus, the Son of God, &c.,) let us therefore come boldly unto the throne of grace, that we may obtain mercy, and find grace to help in time of need.'

5. You need not in the least question the prevalency of Christ's intercession. Doth Christ intercede, and shall he not prevail? Will not the Father hear such a Son? Suppose he may deny you, which he will not, yet surely he will not deny his own and only Son. Christ upon this relation may ask anything, and he shall have it. Mark the connexion, Ps. ii. 7, 'I will declare the decree: the Lord hath said unto me, Thou art my Son, this day have I begotten thee.' What follows now upon this? Why, ver. 8, 'Ask of me, and I shall give thee the heathen for thine inheritance, and the uttermost parts of the earth for thy possession.' God thinks nothing too much for this Son when he asks it of him; and it is the same when he asks for you as when he asks for himself. Therefore, fear not but that your prayers shall be graciously answered, Christ himself interceding for you. When the King's own Son carries the petition, doubtless it shall be granted.

[1] Superest, ut pœna illa Fidejussoris nostri pretio, dignitate, atque merito foret infinita, id quod aliter fieri non potuit, quam si persona patiens foret ipsa infinita. Nam ut peccati, &c. Vide *Thes. Salmur.* de Christo Mediat., part i. th. 13, p. 246.

6. This is the person to whom you are mystically united, and therefore his glory and greatness reflects a glory and greatness upon you. You are in Christ, not only as he is the Son of man, but as he is the Son of God also; for the union is terminated not in this or that nature, but in the whole person. The apostle, therefore, takes special notice of this, 1 John v. 20. 'We know that the Son of God is come, and hath given us an understanding that we may know him that is true; and we are in him that is true, even in his Son Jesus Christ.' Oh to be in this Son; there is the glory and safety of a believer!

I have done with this high and most evangelical truth, The Lord Jesus is God's own Son; upon which I have been somewhat large, partly because of the excellency of the argument itself, and partly because of the great opposition made against it: 2 John 3, 'Grace be with you, mercy, and peace from God the Father, and from the Lord Jesus Christ, the Son of the Father, in truth and love.'

CHAPTER XII.

OF CHRIST'S INCARNATION AND ABASEMENT IN FLESH.

In the likeness of sinful flesh.—ROM. viii. 3.

A fourth general in the words handled—Why the apostle is so express in the further adding of these words to the former—Five things laid down for the explication of them—Flesh not taken here in the same sense with flesh in what went before—A double synecdoche in the word flesh—Christ did not bring flesh from heaven with him, but assumed it here on earth—His sending in flesh was not his taking a mere human shape, &c. —Likeness to be joined not with flesh, but with sinful flesh—Two propositions raised from the words—Of the first, that Christ was sent in flesh—What his sending in flesh imports; this opened more strictly and more largely—Of Marcion, and others, who denied the verity of Christ's incarnation and body—That proved as to both, as also the verity of his whole manhood—Of his having a true soul—Of his submitting to the common adjuncts and infirmities of flesh—How the human nature in Christ and in us differ—His incarnation not impossible, not incredible—The reasons of it : 1. That the Old Testament prophecies, promises, types, might thereby receive their accomplishment ; 2. That Christ might be qualified for his office, as mediator, and the work of redemption ; 3. Because it was the fittest and the best way in order to the redeeming of man—Seven propositions laid down for the due stating and opening of Christ's incarnation : As, 1. That Christ, who before was the eternal Son of God, and had a previous existence, was made flesh : this made good against the Socinians ; 2. That the second person only was incarnate ; 3. That this was not done till the fulness of time ; 4. That it was not the divine essence absolutely considered which assumed flesh, but that essence considered as subsisting in the second person ; 5. That the nature assuming was the divine nature ; 6. That the human nature was so assumed as to subsist in the divine, and that both of these natures make but one person, where the hypostatical union is opened and proved ; 7. It is probable that if Adam had not fallen Christ had not been sent in the flesh—Of the second proposition, That Christ was sent in the likeness, yet but in the likeness, of sinful flesh—Of the sanctity of Christ's human nature—The grounds thereof —Use 1. To inform, 1. Of the excellency of the gospel and of the Christian religion ; as also, 2. Of the excellency of Christ's flesh or manhood—Use 2. Wherein several duties are urged upon Christians : as, namely, 1. To give a full and firm assent to the truth of Christ's incarnation, and also firmly to adhere to Christ as having assumed our flesh : where something is spoken against those who make little of a Christ in flesh, but are all for a Christ within ; 2. To be much in the study and contemplation of Christ incarnate ; 3. To adore the mystery itself, and also the Father and the Son in the mystery ; 4. To endeavour after the powerful influence of it upon heart and life : so as, 1. To be humble ; 2. Not to give way to sin ; 3. Especially not to those sins which do more directly disparage and debase the human nature ; 4. To love God and Christ ; 5. To be willing to do, to suffer, to be abased for Christ ; 6. To labour after a participation of the divine nature ; 7. To be highly thankful, both for the thing itself and also for the revelation of it—Use 3. Of comfort : as (1.) Christ in flesh must needs

be an effectual way for promoting God's glory and the sinner's good ; (2.) In this God hath given out a very high demonstration of his love ; (3.) By this all the promises are sealed, and all the great things of faith and hope made sure and credibel, particularly, 1. The mystical union ; 2. Communion with God, Christ's special presence, the inhabitation of the Spirit; 3. The communications of grace from God ; 4. Our sonship to God ; 5. The resurrection of our bodies ; 6. The future glory—(4.) God is now knowable and accessible ; (5.) The human nature highly dignified and advanced ; (6.) Christ upon this is the more compassionate ; (7.) There are few troubles of conscience wherein this may not afford matter of ease and relief.

THIS branch of the words contains a fourth head in it, which comes next to be opened. Our apostle having spoken of God's sending his own Son, he goes on to shew in what manner he sent him ; and, as to that, he saith God sent him in the likeness of sinful flesh. Here is nothing in the text but wonders, but the τὰ μεγαλεῖα, the great things of God ! The further we go the deeper the waters are, and still new matter offers itself to heighten our admiration. It was wonderful that God should send such a Son ; but that he should send such a Son in such a manner, in flesh, yea, in the likeness of sinful flesh, this is yet more wonderful. O Christian ! stay a little, pause upon these words, get thy thoughts up, thy heart elevated in the contemplation of what is here set before thee, and then read on.

In my entrance upon them, it may be inquired why the apostle is so particular and so express in this matter. Had it not been enough for him to have said, God sent his own Son, and so to have broke off, but he must also add that God sent him in the likeness, &c.[1] To which I answer, There was great reason for this amplification ; for the apostle being here treating of such great mysteries, of such high and glorious discoveries of the wisdom, grace, love of God towards lost sinners, he thought in these he could not be too full or too express ; and he being to set down in a little room the whole

[1] Nonne satis erat dicere, mittens Filium suum ? Hoc ipso verbo declaratum non fuisset istud magnum mysterium scituque dignissimum : quomodo videlicet peccatum peccati damnavit omnipotens, similitudine carnis peccati peccatores a peccato liberans, &c.—Corn. Mussus.

model and platform of man's salvation, the good Spirit of God directed him to put in enough, both for the setting forth of God's admirable love, mercy, &c., and also for the encouragement of the believer's faith with respect to the certainty, completeness, and fulness of his salvation. Now Christ's incarnation and abasement in man's nature being so pertinent and proper, and so necessary as to both of these ends, therefore our apostle will not pass that over without a particular mentioning of it. And elsewhere you find him, when he had spoken of Christ's mission, presently to subjoin Christ's incarnation also; as Gal. iv. 4, 'When the fulness of time was come, God sent his Son, made of a woman,' &c. It was not only God's sending of Christ, but his so sending of him, viz., in flesh, yea, in the likeness of sinful flesh, which puts such an emphasis and accent upon his own grace, and which doth give such full assurance to poor creatures that they shall be effectually redeemed and saved. Upon these considerations, therefore, besides the admirableness of the thing in itself, Paul, when he is upon such an argument, might very well superadd this to what preceded; and he is not satisfied with the once mentioning of it in the general, but he repeats it, and more particularly shews what use God made of Christ's flesh, or what good did by that redound to us: 'for sin he condemned sin in the flesh,' that is, in the flesh of Christ.

For the clearing up the true meaning of the words, and the vindicating of them from those false interpretations which some of the old heretics put upon them, I will lay down a few particulars.

1. First, That flesh, as here used concerning Christ, carries a quite other sense in it than what it did when it was spoken of before. You had it, ver. 1, 'Who walk not after the flesh,' &c.; in this verse, 'what the law could not do, in that it was weak through the flesh;' in which sense, as it is there used, it occurs in many following verses. Now flesh in these places is taken in a very different notion from flesh in this; for in them it is taken morally and accidentally, but here, where Christ is concerned in it, it is taken physically and substantially. In them it notes man's nature as corrupted, but here the very being and substance of the human nature, or the verity of the human nature itself,

abstracted from any such adjunct; and so it is twice taken in this verse.

2. That flesh in this application is not to be understood in its more narrow and limited sense, but in its more general and comprehensive sense. Here is a double synecdoche in the word, as it signifies, (1.) The whole body; (2.) The whole man, or the whole nature of man. Flesh in its strict acceptation is but a part of the body, and the body but a part of the man; but so you are not here to take it; for Christ had a perfect, entire, complete body, and everything, as well as mere flesh, which is proper to a body. For instance, he had blood as well as flesh, therefore both are named: Heb. ii. 14, 'He also took part of the same,' i.e., of flesh and blood; and he had bones as well as flesh: Luke xxiv. 39, 'A spirit hath not flesh and bones, as ye see me have.' Further, Christ was not only clothed with flesh, as that is limited but to one part of man, but he assumed the whole nature of man; he had a soul as well as a body, which two are the essential, constitutive part of man.[1] What more common in Scripture than by flesh to set forth man in his whole, entire, human nature? See Gen. vi. 12; Ps. lxv. 2; Isa. xl. 5; Joel ii. 28; Luke iii. 6; Rom. iii. 20; John xvii. 2; 1 Cor. i. 29. And so the word is frequently used there to represent the whole manhood of Christ. So John i. 14; 1 Tim. iii. 16; Heb. x. 20; 1 Pet. iii. 18, et passim. When, therefore, it is said God sent his Son in flesh, you are thus to conceive of it, that Christ did not only take flesh, but that with it he took the whole nature of man, that he was, as truly, so completely, man, consisting of flesh and spirit, body and soul; yea, that he assumed the entire human nature with whatever is proper to it, two things only being excepted, of which by and by. In this extent and latitude you are here to take the word flesh, a part being put for the whole.

3. Although it be said God sent his Son in the likeness of sinful flesh, yet we must distinguish between the mission and the incarnation. They differ in their order, Christ being first sent and then incarnate; as also in the place where each was done, for the mission was above, but the incarnation was here below. This I take notice of that I may the

---

[1] Ἐκ μέρους τὸ ὅλον συλλαβὼν ὑπο τῆς σαρκὸς ὀνομάζει τὸν ἄνθρωπον.—Cyrill. Alexandr. in John, p. 95.

better clear up that ambiguity which seems to be in the expression, which some among the ancients not understanding aright, runned themselves upon very erroneous opinions. For it being said that God sent his own Son in the likeness of sinful flesh, they from hence inferred that Christ came from heaven actually clothed with flesh, that his body was immediately created there, and that from thence he brought it down with him hither; and, to take in another of their heresies, that it was of such a nature as that it only passed through the Virgin's womb, ὡς δία σωλῆνος ὕδωρ, as water through a pipe, or as light through a glass.[1] But you are not to give way to these apprehensions, the true meaning of the words being this: Christ was sent in the likeness of flesh; not that he had it before he was on earth, but it was his Father's will, for the fulfilling of which he sent him, that he should descend and here below assume flesh. So that though the apostle expresses it by being sent in the likeness, &c., yet his meaning is rather to or for, or in order to, the likeness of sinful flesh: this was not done beforehand, just at his sending, but this was to be subsequent upon it, in its proper time and place. And earth was that place where this stupendous mystery of a Christ incarnate did commence; there was the attiring house where he put on his mean and mourning dress; it was in the Virgin where his body was so curiously and so wonderfully wrought. When he ascended he carried up his body from earth to heaven, but when he descended he did not bring down his body from heaven to earth; the foundation of his being incarnate was laid above, in the purpose and command of the Father, with respect to which he is said to be sent in the likeness, &c., but his actual assumption of flesh was done here below. True he saith, John. iii. 13, 'No man hath ascended up to heaven, but he that came down from heaven, even the Son of man which is in heaven;' and John vi. 62, 'What if you shall see the Son of man ascend up where he was before?' but this you are to understand as spoken only upon the κοινωνία των ἰδιωμάτων, communication of properties, that being here attributed to Christ in one nature, as the Son of

man, which was only proper to him in the other, as the Son of God. It is also said of him that the second man is the Lord from heaven, 1 Cor. xv. 47, but that you are to take not as referring to the matter and substance of his body, as if he brought that from heaven, but only as pointing to his descent from heaven, and the miraculous formation of his body here on earth. And whereas some speak, as you heard, of Christ's body being immediately created, and but passing through the Virgin as water through a pipe, the falsity of that opinion is very notorious; for the Scripture plainly tells us that it was produced in another way—that he was conceived and born of the Virgin, that the production of his substance was of hers, though in an extraordinary manner. Therefore it is said, Mat. i. 18, 'She was found with child of the Holy Ghost;' and ver. 20, 'That which is conceived in her is of the Holy Ghost;' and Luke i. 35, 'That holy thing which shall be born of thee, shall be called the Son of God;' and Elisabeth speaks of Christ as the fruit of her womb, Luke i. 42, and Paul says he was made of a woman, Gal. iv. 4, not made *in* a woman, but *of* a woman. From all which texts two things are evident: (1.) That though the formation of Christ's flesh was extraordinary and miraculous, yet it was not immediately created, especially not in heaven; (2.) That the Virgin Mary had a proper causality in the production of Christ's body, and therefore was not a mere pipe through which it did only pass.[1]

4. This sending of Christ in the likeness, &c., was not his assuming of a mere human shape, or his apparition only in the shape and form of a man, but it was the real assumption of the human nature consisting of soul and body. There is a vast difference betwixt Christ's incarnation and such apparitions as those which we have instances of in the Old Testament; and that, too, not only with respect to the apparitions of angels, but also of Christ himself; for it might easily be proved that it was he who appeared to Abraham, Gen. xviii. 13, 14, 17; to Jacob, Gen. xxxii. 24; to Moses, Exod. iii. 2, compared with Acts vii. 30–35. But now his incarnation was a quite other thing; for in that there was not the

---

[1] The first broachers of which were Apollinaris, Valentinus, &c. Of and against whom see Nazianz. ad Nectarium. Athan. de Incarn. Christi, tom. i. p. 619 et 1083.

[1] Of these things read Tertull. in his excellent Treatise de Carne Christi, p. 374.

taking of man's shape but of man's nature, not the taking of it so as to lay it down again after a short time, as was in apparitions, but so as to keep it and continue in it for ever. The apostle cries out, 1 Tim. iii. 16, 'Without controversy great is the mystery of godliness, God manifested in the flesh,' &c. ; but had there been in that nothing more than a mere apparition of Christ in flesh or in human shape, the thing had not been so strange that he should make such a mystery of it, for he knew this was very common ; therefore there must be more in it than so. To convince us of the truth and reality of Christ's flesh in opposition to all phantasms and mere apparitions, the Scripture speaks of him not only as appearing : Mal. iii. 2, 'Who shall stand when he appeareth?' 2 Tim. i. 10, 'But is now made manifest by the appearing of our Saviour Jesus Christ,' &c. ; Heb. ix. 26, 'Once in the end of the world hath he appeared,' &c. ; nor only as manifested, 1 John i. 2, and iii. 5, 8, ; 1 Tim. iii. 16 ; nor only as taking flesh, which expression to some might be more doubtful and general, as Heb. ii. 14, 16 ; but to put this out of all question, it says he was made flesh, John i. 14, which must be more than a bare appearance or manifestation in imaginary and fantastic flesh. It was enough for angels, when God had only some particular and ordinary message to send them upon, to assume an external shape and then lay it down again ;[1] but when Christ is to be born, to converse in the world a considerable time, to die, to make satisfaction in that nature in which the offence had been committed, here must be more than a spectrum, an apparition, here must be real flesh. And, indeed, the former Old Testament apparitions were but as so many præludiums of Christ's real incarnation ; in all these he did but *præludere humanitati suæ*, as Tertullian phraseth it.[2]

5. Therefore, as to the letter of the words, when it is said Christ was sent in the likeness of sinful flesh, this likeness is to be linked, not with flesh, but

with sinful flesh. He had true, real, very flesh, but he had only in appearance and likeness sinful flesh ; he had not a putative, imaginary body, but as to sin, though there was something like to that in his outward state and condition, yet it was but like to it, there was no such thing in truth and reality inhering in that nature which he assumed. This is that plain, genuine interpretation of the words against the old heretical pervertings of them which the orthodox, ancient and modern, put upon them ;[1] the truth of which I shall endeavour to make out in what will follow : at present I need say no more about it.

These things being thus premised, the whole matter will fall into these two propositions :

1. That Christ was sent in flesh.

2. That he was sent in the likeness, yet but in the likeness, of sinful flesh. Two very weighty and important truths ! therefore I hope the opening and confirming of them will not be judged tedious or unnecessary.

I begin with the first, where I shall consider the flesh in which Christ was sent, (1.) In its more strict ; (2.) In its more large notion. More strictly as it relates to the verity of Christ's incarnation and the reality of his body ; more largely as it relates to the verity of his whole manhood, which, as hath been already said, is made up and constituted of something more than flesh.

But before I enter upon either of these heads, I

---

[1] Nullus unquam angelus ideo descendit ut crucifigeretur, &c. Si nunquam ejusmodi fuit causa angelorum corporandorum, habes causam cur non acceperint carnem. Non venerant mori, ideo nec nasci. At vero Christus mori missus, nasci quoque necessario habuit ut mori posset.—*Tertull. de Carne Christi*, p. 363.

[2] *Vide* Irenæum advers. Hæres, lib. iv. cap. 37.

[1] Non in similitudine carnis, quasi caro non esset caro, sed in similitudine peccati carnis ; quia caro erat sed peccati caro non erat.—*Aug., vide* serm. 3 and 6, de verbis Apostoli. In similitudine carnis peccati fuisse Christum ait, non quod similitudinem carnis accepit, quasi imaginem corporis et non veritatem, sed similitudinem carnis peccatricis vult intelligi, quod ipsa non peccatrix caro Christi ejus fuit par cujus erat peccatum, genere non vitio Adæ, &c.—*Tertull. de Carne Christi*, p. 372. Similitudo ad peccati titulum pertinet, non ad substantiæ mendacium, &c.—*Idem adv. Marci.*, lib. v. cap. 14. Δία τοῦτο εἴρηται ἐν ὁμοιώματι γεγενῆσθαι σαρκὸς ἁμαρτίας οὐ γὰρ ἐν ὁμοιώματι σαρκὸς, ὡς τούτοις δοκεῖ, ἀλλ᾽ ἐν ὁμοιώματι σαρκὸς ἁμαρτίας.—*Basil.*, Ep. 65. Ἐπειδὰν εἶπεν ἁμαρτίας, διὰ τοῦτο καὶ τὸ ὁμοίωμα τέθεικεν, &c.—*Chrysost. in loc.* Οὐκ εἶπεν ἐν ὁμοιώματι, &c. φύσιν γὰρ ἀνθρωπείαν ἔλαβε, ἁμαρτίαν δὲ ἀνθρωπείαν οὐκ ἔλαβε.—*Theodoret.* Misit Deus, &c., ut in vera carnis susceptione agnosceretur veritas non fuisse peccati ; et quantum ad corpus veritas intelligeretur, quantum ad peccatum similitudo peccati.—*Cassian. de Incarn. Dom.*, lib. iv.

cannot but bewail, and oh that I could do it with the most inward and most intense sadness of spirit, that unworthy, wretched usage which our blessed Lord Jesus hath all along met withal ever since he was revealed to the world! He hath but two natures, and how hath he been impugned, opposed, struck at in both! First some attempted to undermine his Godhead, then others succeeded who attempted to undermine his manhood. It is very sad to consider, that he who is both God and man, if several men might have had their will, should have been long before this neither God nor man, but a very nothing. Ebion first comes upon the stage, and he denies him to be God; then come Marcion, Manes, &c., and they deny him to be man. The Arian ungods him, and the Manichee unmans him; what will they leave us of him who is our all? How was the primitive church fain to dispute, argue, contend to their utmost—and all little enough—for the defence of these natures of Christ! and God be blessed for their excellent zeal in such fundamental articles of the Christian faith. It is pity the church's zeal should ever run in any other channel. But Christ must be opposed some way or other, for he is ' set for a sign which shall be spoken against,' Luke ii. 34. The present contests of the world are now against him, chiefly with respect to his offices; but the past contests were against him chiefly with respect to his natures. I have, according to my poor ability, vindicated his natural and eternal Sonship, and consequently his Godhead; I am now to vindicate the truth of his incarnation and manhood.

This the forementioned heretics peremptorily denied, as appears by the ancients who wrote against them;[1] they asserted that Christ had no true flesh, it was only the likeness of flesh which he appeared in; that his body was only a fantastic, imaginary body.[2] And this pestilent opinion they did, in part, ground upon the words which we have at present before us.

[1] Athanas. tom. i. de Incarn. Christi; Tertull. de Præscrip. advers. Hæret., cap. 46, Hær. 3, et de carne Christi, et advers. Marcion., against whom he writes five books; Epiphan. tom. ii. lib. i., Hær. 24 et 80, et tom. iii. Hær. 42; August., tom. v. p. 925, &c.; Cyrill. Alexandr., tom. v. p. 678, &c.

[2] οὐ ὄντως ἀλλὰ κᾶτὰ δόκησιν.—*Ignat.* Hence they were called Δοκηταὶ. Valentinus carnem Christi putativam introduxit.—*Tertull. de Carne Christi.* They say Christ did but ψεύσασθαι ἐνἄνθρωπησιν, as Theophylact expresses it.

But as to them, by the giving of their true sense this weapon has been rescued out of the enemy's hand. And some expositors[1] (the more to weaken the objection of the adversaries as grounded upon this text) tell us, that the likeness here of sinful flesh is the sameness of sinful flesh; that Christ took that very flesh which was and is sinful, not that it was so in him, but that it is so in us; that he assumed that very flesh which in man is defiled by sin, yet not as defiled, but as true flesh. As when it is said concerning him that he was in the form of God, in the form of a servant, in the likeness and fashion of man, Phil. ii. 6–8, ἐν ὁμοιώματι, it is the same word with that in the text; the meaning is that Christ was truly God, truly a servant, truly man. And as it is said concerning Adam, he begat a son in his own likeness, Gen. v. 3, that is, he begat a son who was as truly a man and as truly a sinner as himself; so Christ was sent in the likeness, &c., viz., in just such flesh, or in the very self-same flesh which man hath made in himself sinful, and therefore passible and mortal. Now, though I cannot deny the truth of this exposition, as thus stated, nor that it may very well be grounded upon parallel places, yet because to some at the first hearing it may seem somewhat harsh, I rather incline to that which was laid down before in the opening of the words; it was the same flesh in Christ and in us in its physical consideration, but it being morally considered, it was but the likeness of sinful flesh.

But to come to that which I propounded, let us consider flesh in its strict acceptation, as it relates to the fleshly and bodily part; so I will lay down two things about it.

1. That Christ was indeed sent in flesh, was really incarnate, and did verily take flesh upon him. And what one thing is there in the whole gospel wherein it is plain and positive, if it be not so in this: John

[1] ὁμοίωμα σαρκὸς est ipsa caro, etiamsi non cum peccato, &c. Missus ergo Filius Dei ἐν ὁμοιώματι σαρκὸς ἁμαρτίας, i.e., in carne non peccatrice, eadem tamen, quæ in nobis peccarat, sive polluta, non in ipso, sed in nobis. Naturam peccati, h.e., peccatorum Dei Filius suscepit, puram quidem sed ut nostram, quæ peccarat expiaret. Cum notissimo Hebraismo ὁμοίωμα res ipsa dicatur, ut cum ὁμοίωμα ἀνθρώπου ipse homo dicitur, non video cur non et ὁμοίωμα σαρκὸς vera sit caro. Cum peccati non ab eo dicatur, qui assumsit atque hoc ipso expiavit, sed ab eo qui peccando corrupit.—*Heins.*

2 G

i. 14, 'And the word was made flesh.' 1 Tim. iii. 16, 'Without controversy great is the mystery of godliness; God manifested in the flesh.' Heb. ii. 14–16, 'Forasmuch then as the children are partakers of flesh and blood, he also himself likewise took part of the same, that through death he might destroy him that had the power of death, that is the devil; for verily he took not on him the nature of angels, but he took on him the seed of Abraham.' Rom. i. 3, 'Concerning his Son Jesus Christ our Lord, who was made of the seed of David according to the flesh.' Rom. ix. 5, 'Whose are the fathers, and of whom as concerning the flesh Christ came, who is over all, God blessed for ever, Amen.' Hence he is said to be 'made of a woman,' Gal. iv. 4. Many such places might be produced, to prove that Christ really assumed flesh; but these may suffice.[1]

And this flesh, wherein Christ was sent, was organised and formed into a perfect body. The apostle doth not only call it his flesh, but the body of his flesh: Col. i. 22, 'In the body of his flesh, through death,' &c. Heb. x. 5, 'Wherefore when he cometh into the world he saith, Sacrifice and offering thou wouldst not, but a body hast thou prepared me.' 1 Pet. i. 24, 'Who his own self bare our sins in his own body on the tree,' &c. Our Saviour did not assume a confused, indigested, and unshapen mass or lump of flesh—that was not his incarnation; but he assumed flesh cast into the very mould and form of our bodies, having the same several parts, members, lineaments, the same proportion which they have.

2. I add, not as a distinct head from the former, but only that I may more distinctly speak to it than as yet I have done, that as Christ was indeed sent in flesh, so the flesh in which he was sent was flesh indeed. He saith, 'My flesh is meat indeed,' John vi. 55; and I say his flesh was flesh indeed—as true, real, proper, very flesh as that is which any of us carry about with us. It was, as was said before, but the likeness of sinful flesh, but it was the reality of physical or substantial flesh. Christ's body was no spectrum or phantasm, no putative body, as if it had

no being but what was in appearance and from imagination, but as real, as solid a body as ever any was;[1] therefore the apostle, in the forecited place, Col. i. 22, calls it a 'body of flesh;' a body to shew the organisation of it, and a body of flesh to shew the reality of it, in opposition to all aërial and imaginary bodies. It had all the essential properties of a true body, such as are organicalness, extension, local presence, confinement, circumscription, penetrability, visibility, palpability, and the like: Luke xxiv. 39, 'Behold my hands and my feet, that it is I myself; handle me and see; for a spirit hath not flesh and bones, as ye see me have.'[2] 1 John i. 1, 'That which was from the beginning, which we have heard, which we have seen with our eyes, which we have looked upon, and our hands have handled of the word of life,' &c. He had also those natural affections, passions, infirmities which are proper to a body;[3] as hunger, Mat. iv. 2, 'When he had fasted forty days and forty nights, he was afterwards an hungered;' thirst, John iv. 7, and xix. 28, 'I thirst;' sleep, Mat. viii. 24; weariness, John iv. 6, 'Jesus, being wearied with his journey,' &c. He was conceived, retained so long in the Virgin's womb,[4] born, circumcised, lived about thirty years on earth, conversed all that time with men, suffered, died, was crucified, buried, rose again, ascended, sat down with his body at the right hand of God; with it will come again to judge the world. Doth not all this speak him to have a true body? Could all this be done in, and upon, and by an imaginary body? Had it been only such, then his conception, nativity, death, resurrection, ascension, are all too but imaginary things; his sufferings, crucifixion, but mere fancies;[5]

---

[1] See the strength of these, with other texts, drawn forth and vindicated against objections by Mr Tombes, in a little treatise called, Emmanuel or God-man, sect. 15, 16, &c., to the end of the book.

[1] *Vide* Aquin., p. iii. qu. 5, art. 1.

[2] Quomodo hanc vocem interpretaris.—*Marcion*, &c. Ecce fallit et decipit, &c. Ergo jam Christum non de cœlo deferre debueras, sed de aliquo circulatorio cœtu, nec salutis pontificem, sed spectaculi artificem, &c.—*Tertull. de Carne Christi*, p. 362.

[3] Esuriit sub diabolo, sitiit sub Samaritide, lacrymatus est supra Lazarum, trepidavit ad mortem, sanguinem fudit postremo; hæc sunt opinor signa cœlestia.—*Idem. ibid.*, p. 367.

[4] Marcion ut carnem Christi negaret, negavit etiam nativitatem; aut ut nativitatem negaret, negavit et carnem, scilicet ne invicem sibi testimonium redderent, et responderent nativitas et caro quia nec nativitas sine carne, nec caro sine nativitate.—*Tertull. de Carne Christi*, p. 358.

[5] Μὴ δύναται φαντασία τύπτεσθαι ἢ προσηλωθῆναι ἐν τῷ σταυρῷ.

and what then would become of us? Then all our faith, hope, yea, all our religion would vanish into a mere fancy also.[1] When Satan had him in the wilderness and was tempting of him, he thus assaulted him: Mat. iv. 3, 'If thou be the Son of God, command that these stones be made bread;' and ver. 6, 'If thou be the Son of God, cast thyself down.' Now what an absurd, ridiculous thing had it been for Satan thus to have tempted Christ, supposing that he had only had a fantastic body? What need would there have been of food for such a body? or what hurt could such a body have received by falling from the highest pinnacle? Nay, further, as Tertullian argues, what evil did his murderers do in the crucifying of him if he had not a true body?[2] for without that he could not have truly suffered; they then would have been excused, he suffering nothing at all by their means. The sacrament of the Lord's supper is a symbol and representation of his body: 1 Cor. xi. 24, 'This is my body, which is broken for you,' &c. Now what a pitiful thing would this sacramental representation thereof be, if in itself it was not a true body? Divers such considerations might be insisted upon if it was necessary.

So much for Christ's flesh in its stricter notion; I come now, in the second place, to consider it in its more large and extensive notion. So Christ was sent in flesh, that is, in the verity of man's nature; he verily took upon him the whole human nature, became true man, of the same make and substance with us, in all things like to us, some things excepted which do not in the least abolish or destroy the truth of his manhood. He is called 'the man Christ Jesus,' 1 Tim. ii. 5. 'Since by man came death, by man came also the resurrection of the dead,' 1 Cor. xv. 21. 'He was made in the likeness of men,' Phil. ii. 7. He is styled 'the Son of man,' Dan. vii. 13; John iii. 13; 'the seed of the woman,' Gen. iii. 15; 'the seed of Abraham,' Gen. xxii. 18; 'the seed of David,' Rom. i. 3; 'the Son of David,' Mat. i. 1; 'the branch of David,' Jer. xxiii. 5; he is said to be 'of the fruit of his loins,' Acts ii. 30.

The two essential or constitutive parts of man are soul and body; where these two are, there is the true man; Christ had both, therefore he was such. That he had a real body hath been already proved, I am only now to shew that he also had a real soul.[1] And indeed the former proves the latter; for if Christ would assume the body, which is but in a manner the bark, shell, or case of man, but the lowest and meanest part of him, but as the covering and garment of the soul,[2] לְבוּשׁ הַנֶּפֶשׁ, as the Jews call it, certainly he would assume the soul, the reasonable soul, that being the highest and the noblest part. This is that which principally makes the man, and hath the greatest influence into his being and essence; if therefore our Lord had only had a human body without a human soul, he had wanted that part which is most essential to man, and so could not have been looked upon as true and perfect man; but it was far otherwise. For indeed Christ redeemed and saved nothing but what he assumed, the redemption and salvation reach no farther than the assumption;[3] our soul then would have been never the better for Christ had he not taken that as well as our body; for τὸ ἀπρόσληπτον, ἀθεράπευτον, as Nazianzen expresses it, if he will save the whole man from sin he must assume the whole man without sin.[4] It is said of him, Luke ii. 52, he increased in wisdom and stature; here is stature

---

—Athan. de Incarn., p. 1083. Hæc quomodo in illo vera erant si ipse non fuit verus? Si non vere habuit in se quod figeretur, quod moreretur, quod sepeliretur, et resuscitaretur? Carnem scilicet sanguine suffusam, ossibus structam, nervis intextam, venis implexam, quæ nasci et mori novit?—Tertull. de Carne Christi, p. 361.

[1] Falsa est et fides nostra, et phantasma erit totum quod speramus a Christo.—Tertull., ibid.

[2] Scelestissime hominum, qui interemtores excusas Dei. Nihil enim ab eis passus est Christus, si nihil vere est passus. Parce unicæ spei totius orbis, quid destruis necessarium dedecus fidei?—Tertull.

[1] Vide Aquin. Sum., 3 p. quest. 5, art. 3. Suscepit non solum corpus humanum, ut quidam putant, sed et animam nostrarum animarum similem per naturam.—August. de Incarn. Verbi Dei, tom. iv. lib. ii. p. 243.

[2] ᾧ σπερ ἐνδεδυμένην σῶμα.—Nemes. de Nat. Hom., cap. 3, p. 94.

[3] Hoc Deus in nobis salvavit, quod pro nobis suscepit, et illam naturam participem fecit salutis quam sibi conjunxit.—Fulgent. ad Trasimund., &c.

[4] Totum hominem sine peccato suscepit, ut totum quo constabat homo a peccatorum peste sanaret.—August. de Civit. Dei., lib. x. cap. 17. Si totum debuerat liberare pietas, totum debuit suscipere divina majestas. Totus ergo fuit hominis a Deo suscipienda natura, quoniam in toto fuit captivitas captivanda, &c.—Fulgent. ad Trasimund. de Mysterio Mediat.

for his body and wisdom for his soul, his growth in that speaks the truth of the former, and his growth in this speaks the truth of the latter; his body properly could not grow in wisdom nor his soul in stature, therefore there must be both. There are three things in a reasonable soul, understanding, will, affections; now it is evident all these were in Christ. He had a human understanding, distinct from his divine understanding, otherwise how could he have been said to increase in wisdom? and how could he have been under the nescience of some things? as it is plain he was, for he knew not the precise time of the day of judgment,[1] Mark xiii. 32; as he was God he knew all things, so his understanding was infinite, he must therefore have some other understanding which was but finite, in reference to which there might be something which he did not know. He also had a human will, distinct from his divine will; for what could that will be which he did submit and subordinate to the will of his Father but this? Luke xxii. 42, 'Nevertheless not my will, but thine, be done.' Then for those affections which are proper to the soul, it is clear Christ had them; as namely, anger, Mark iii. 5, and x. 14; love, Mat. x. 21; sorrow, Mat. xxvi. 38, Luke xix. 41; fear, Heb. v. 7; joy, Luke x. 21, John xi. 15; pity, Mat. ix. 36, and xiii. 32. Now where these three things are, most certainly there is a true and real soul.

Yet here also our blessed Lord and Saviour is assaulted. He hath two natures which make up his person, his deity and his humanity, but both of them by several persons are taken away, as you heard but now; and there are two essential parts which make up one of his natures, his manhood, viz., soul and body, but both of these two by several persons are taken away also. Marcion divests him of a body and Apollinaris of a soul,[1] the Arians also are charged with this heresy;[2] these held that Christ had no soul, but that the deity was to him instead of a soul, and supplied the office thereof; that what the soul is to us and doth in our bodies, all that the divine nature was to Christ and did in his body.[3] Oh what light can be clear enough for

their conviction and guidance in the way of truth, whom God hath given up to 'strong delusions that they should believe lies'? 2 Thess. ii. 11. Are not the Scriptures clear enough in this matter that Christ had a real soul? What was the subject of his inexpressible sorrow and agonies in the garden, but his soul? Matt. xxvi. 38, 'My soul is exceeding sorrowful, even unto death,' &c. John xii. 27, 'Now is my soul troubled, and what shall I say?' What did he in special recommend to God when he was breathing out his last gasp, but his soul? Luke xxiii. 46, 'When Jesus had cried with a loud voice, he said, Father, into thy hands I commend my spirit, and having said thus he gave up the ghost.' What was the part affected in his sore desertion when he cried out, 'My God, my God, why hast thou forsaken me?' Surely his body could not be the immediate subject of a punishment purely spiritual; no, that must terminate in his spiritual part, the soul. By all this it appears then that Christ was as truly God, so also truly man, he having a true body and a true soul.

Yet a little further, that I may take in the whole truth, and leave out nothing which may tend to the heightening of Christ's incomparable love and condescension to sinners, he was not barely sent in flesh, so far as the verity of the human nature is concerned, in his assuming the essential parts thereof, but he also submitted to the common accidents, adjuncts, infirmities, miseries, calamities, which are incident to that nature. He lay so many weeks and months in the Virgin's womb, received nourishment and growth in the ordinary way, was brought forth and bred up just as common infants are, abating some special respects shown to him to discover the greatness of his person, had his life sustained by common food as ours is, was hungry, thirsty, weary, poor, reproached, tempted, deserted, &c.; lived an afflicted life, then died a miserable death; was a man of sorrows and acquainted with grief, Isa. liii. 3; made himself of no reputation, took upon him the form of a servant, was made in the likeness of man, Phil. ii. 7, not only in the taking of their nature, but also in submitting to those abasements and miseries which now that

[1] *Vide* Nazianz. Orat. 36, p. 588.
[2] See Epiphan., vol. i., p. 743, 771.
Ἄρειος, καὶ Εὐνόμιος σῶμα μὲν αὐτὸν ἐφασαν εἰληφέναι θεότητα δὲ ψυχῆς ἐνηργηκέναι τὴν χρείαν. — *Theodor.*, lib. 5, contra hæres., cap. 11.

nature is liable unto; his whole life was a life of sufferings, wherein as there was enough in his holiness, miracles, to shew him to be God, so there was also enough in his meanness, poverty, sufferings to shew him to be man.[1] In a word, he took all our infirmities upon him; take it with a double restriction, 1. To all our sinless infirmities:[2] such as are culpable and carry sin in them they must be excepted, for though he was made like to us in all things, yet without sin, Heb. iv. 15. 2. To all our natural infirmities: as to personal infirmities, such as are proper to this and that person, as blindness, deafness, lameness, &c., these Christ did not put himself under; for he did not assume this or that person, but the nature in common, and therefore was not liable to the particular infirmities of individuums, but only to those which properly belonged to the common nature. I would carry this a little higher; though I have said so much concerning the reality and sameness of Christ's human nature with ours, yet you are not in all respects to equalise that nature as it is in him and as it is in us; for substance and essence it is one and the same in both, yet in other considerations there is a great disparity; for

1. The human nature is solely and singly in us, in Christ it is conjunctly with the divine.

2. We have it in the way of common and ordinary generation, Christ had it in a special and extraordinary way.

3. It is tainted and defiled in us, in Christ it is perfectly pure and holy.

4. In us it hath its proper subsistence, in Christ it subsists only in his Godhead.

Thus I have shewn what this sending of Christ in the flesh is, and what it imports, viz., the truth of his incarnation, of his body, and his assumption of the whole, entire, and perfect nature of man; and also, as the several heads fell in my way, I have out of the word given you the proof of them: I say out of the word, for these mysteries are only to be

known and believed upon the light and authority thereof; if it asserts them, that certainly must be sufficient to command the belief of Christians, who profess in all things to make the Scriptures to be the rule of their faith. And as to the credibility of Christ's incarnation from rational considerations, in subserviency to and grounded upon gospel revelation, sundry authors, ancient and modern, have written very much, with great strength and evidence, to prove that it was neither impossible nor incongruous, neither absurd as to the thing nor unbecoming as to the person, for Christ to be made flesh;[1] but I will not engage so vast an argument, having to do with those who are sufficiently satisfied with what the word reveals.

Having thus explained and confirmed by Scripture authority the point in hand, I now proceed to a second thing—to give some short account of the grounds and reasons why Christ was thus sent in flesh. Paul puts an ὤφειλε before it: Heb. ii. 17, 'Wherefore in all things, it *behoved* him to be made like unto his brethren;' which behoving he brings down to one particular, 'that he might be a merciful and faithful high priest in things pertaining to God,' &c. But I must take in more.

1. Our Lord Jesus was incarnate that the Old Tes-

---

[1] Θεὸς νοούμενος τῇ τῶν τερα των ἐνεργείᾳ, ἄνθρωπος δε δεικνύμενος τῇ τῆς φύσεως ὁμοιοπαθεία.—*Justin Martyr,* Expos. Fidei.

[2] Ὁμολογοῦμεν ὅτι πάντα τὰ φυσικὰ καὶ ἀδιάβλητα πάθη ἀνθρώπου ἀνέλαβεν· ὅλον γὰρ τὸν ἄνθρωπον καὶ πάντα τὰ τοῦ ἀνθρώπου ἀνέλαβε, πλὴν τῆς ἁμαρτίας.—*Damascen.* de Orthod. Fid. lib. iii. c. 20.

[1] *Tertull. de Carne Christi.* Deo nihil impossibile nisi quod non vult.—Quodcunque Deo indignum est mihi expedit.— Quid magis erubescendum nasci an mori? Carnem gestare an crucem? circuncidi an suffigi? educari an sepeliri? in præsepe deponi an in monumento recondi?—Vide *Athanas.* de Incarn. Verbi Dei. tom. 1, p. 88, more fully, p. 95, &c. *Isidor. Pelus.* Epist. l. 1 Epist. 141. *Cyril. Hieros.* Catech. 12, 111. *Cyprian* de Bapt. Christi. p. 492. *Lactant.* de Vera Sapient. cap. 22. *Fulgent.* ad Regem *Trasim.* de Christo Mediat. *Anselm. cur Deus Homo.* lib. i. cap. 3, p. 92.—Hoc mysterium a recta ratione abhorrere ac tanquam impossibile rejici, nunquam probabit. Ratio quidem corrupta ac primæ philosophiæ ignara, futilia quædam argumenta contra illud fingit: verum ratio quæ infinitam divinæ essentiæ perfectionem agnoscit, ac Scripturam, ea qua par est modestia ac diligentia, consulit ac confert, mysterium hoc divinæ naturæ omnibusque ejus attributis quam convenientissimum esse fatetur. Incarnatio illa non solum fuit possibilis, sed ejusmodi, Patris consilio posito, quale in hominum salute exequi decrevit, simpliciter necessaria; tantumque abest ut a divina majestate abhorreat, ut nihil ejus omnipotentiam, omniscientiam, summam misericordiam ac justitiam, uno verbo, infinitam ejus perfectionem magis patefaciat ac illustret.—*Bisterfeld.* contra *Crellium,* lib. i. sect ii. cap. 32, pp. 341, 342.

tament promises, prophecies, types, might all be fulfilled and accomplished. The incarnation of Christ was no new thing, or that which was never spoken of before it was done. It was that very thing which the Spirit of God had testified beforehand, as the apostle speaks of his sufferings, 1 Pet. i. 11. It pleased God betimes, very early to give out some, though darker discoveries of it. You have it hinted in the πρωτοευαγγέλιον, the first gospel, or first gospel promise that ever God made: Gen. iii. 15, 'I will put enmity between thee and the woman, and between thy seed and her seed; it shall bruise thy head, and thou shalt bruise his heel.' Here is a Christ incarnate. Then it was more clearly intimated in the promise to Abraham: Gen. xxii. 18, 'In thy seed shall all the nations of the earth be blessed.' In process of time it was again held forth in the promise made to David, 2 Sam. vii. 12, which the apostle makes to point to Christ: Acts ii. 30, 'Therefore, being a prophet, and knowing that God had sworn with an oath to him, that of the fruit of his loins according to the flesh, he would raise up Christ to sit on his throne.' Afterwards this was most expressly promised and foretold; God would have it veiled and clouded no longer, but it shall shine forth more clearly: Isa. vii. 14, 'Behold a virgin shall conceive and bear a Son, and shall call his name Emmanuel;' Isa. ix. 6, 'Unto us a child is born, unto us a Son is given.' Yea, Moses, long before this, had given a plain prediction of it: Deut. xviii. 15, 'The Lord thy God will raise up unto thee a prophet from the midst of thee, of thy brethren, like unto me; unto him shall ye hearken;' ver. 18, 'I will raise them up a prophet from among their brethren, like unto thee,' &c. Now this prophecy Peter applies to Christ, Acts iii. 22, and pray mark those words in it, *from the midst of thee, of thy brethren, like unto me*, which clearly refers to his manhood and incarnation. And that prophecy of Balaam, Numb. xxiv. 17, had some reference to this also. You perceive I only meddle with those Scriptural predictions of it which are unquestionable, and which God would have fulfilled; as to the Sybilline predictions thereof, how far they are to be credited or valued, I concern not myself at all in that inquiry. But if any great stress could be laid upon them, one of these sybils went very far—so far that some learned persons do therefore

doubt whether its prediction was genuine, upon this very reason, because it was so express and clear.[1] But I have not to do with them, but with the sure oracles of God. Then as to types, which were nothing but real prophecies or promises wrapped up in visible representations, these also pointed to a Christ in our flesh. The Old Testament dispensation lay much in types, all of which pointed to Christ as the sum and substance of them; he was the kernel in those shells; all were but as so many *fasciæ* or swaddling bands in which the babe Jesus was wrapped, as Luther used to say. Christ, saith a reverend author,[2] was Abel's sacrifice, Noah's dove, Abraham's first fruits, Isaac's ram, Jacob's ladder, Moses' passover, Aaron's rod, the Israelites' rock, the patriarchs' manna, David's tabernacle, Solomon's temple; and all of these, saith he, prefigured his incarnation. But to wade into the several typical adumbrations of this would be a long work. In short, under the law, when persons or lands were to be redeemed, he that was next akin was to make the redemption; see Levit. xxv. 25, Ruth iii. 13, &c. Christ being to redeem sinners, he must take their flesh, that he may be akin to them, their *Goel*, (as he is sometimes styled,) and so be a fit person to be their Redeemer. The tabernacle seems to have a special reference to Christ's manhood, so the apostle brings it in Heb. viii. 2 : ·'A minister of the sanctuary, and of the true tabernacle, which the Lord pitched, and not man.' So again, Heb. ix. 11 : 'But Christ being come an high priest of good things to come, by a greater and more perfect tabernacle, not made with hands, that is to say, not of this building,' &c. By this tabernacle of the Lord's pitching, and not made with hands, he means the body or flesh of Christ, which was the true tabernacle, and of which the common tabernacle was but a type. And, indeed, there was so great a resemblance betwixt these two, as that the one might very well prefigure and typify

---

[1] Sybilla Cumæa in Virgil, Eclog. 4—

 'Ultima Cumæi venit jam carminis ætas :
 Magnus ab integro seclorum nascitur ordo :
 Jam redit et virgo, redeunt Saturnia regna :
 Jam nova progenies cœlo dimittitur alto,' &c.

Of this see Athanasius, tom. ii. p. 336 ; Dr Jackson on the Creed, book vii., sect. 2, chap. 8, p. 40, &c.

[2] Bishop Brownrigge, Serm. p. 115.

the other. For (1.) the outside of that tabernacle was but mean. It was made without of very ordinary and common things—within, it was rich and glorious, it being beautified with gold, silver, precious stones, &c.; but without all was plain, it being covered only with rams' skins and goats' skins, and such materials, Exod. xxv. 1, &c., and xxvi. 14, &c. So here, Christ's outside was, especially to some, but very mean: Isa. lii. 2, 'He hath no form nor comeliness, and when we shall see him, there is no beauty that we should desire him;' but yet he was exceeding glorious 'within,' as it is said of the church, Ps. xlv. 13. Such as had a discerning eye, they could see the inward glory of his Godhead shining through the cloud of his manhood: 'And the word was made flesh, and dwelt among us (and we beheld his glory, the glory as of the only begotten of the Father,) full of grace and truth,' John i. 14. (2.) God's special presence was in the tabernacle. There was the *Shechinah*, or habitation of God, wherein at first by an extraordinary cloud, he signified his glorious presence to be, as afterwards he did in the temple too; by which therefore Christ sets forth his body: John ii. 19–21, 'Jesus answered and said unto them, Destroy this temple, and in three days I will raise it up; but he spake of the temple of his body.' Both tabernacle and temple were types and resemblances of his flesh or manhood, in respect of the special presence and inhabitation of the divine nature in it.[1] Hence, some make all those great promises made to the people of Israel concerning God's presence with them, in special in the tabernacle and temple, to point to Christ's incarnation, and in that to receive their accomplishment;[2] (you may read them in Exod. xxv. 8; Exod. xxix. 44–46; Levit. xxvi. 11–13; Ezek. xxxvii. 26-28.) (3.) The tabernacle was a moveable thing.[3] Whilst Israel was in the wilderness in an itinerary posture, as they moved, the tabernacle moved with them—it was not fixed all that time, as afterwards it was. So it was with Christ: he was

here on earth with his body for some time, but neither he nor it were here long to abide. He ascended up to heaven, and thither he carried his body with him, and there it is fixed. This the evangelist alludes unto: John i. 14, 'The Word was made flesh, and dwelt amongst us,' &c.: ἐσκήνωσε, he *tented* or *tabernacled* it for a time amongst us, in respect of his short abode here; in reference to which our bodies too are set forth by tabernacles, 2 Cor. v. 1, 4; 2 Pet. i. 13, 14.

I might also instance in Melchisedech as a personal type of Christ; he was 'without father and mother,' &c., Heb. vii. 3, which is very applicable to Christ; for he, as the Son of God, was without mother, and as the Son of man, without father.[1] Well, then, that all these prophecies, promises, types, might be fulfilled, it was necessary that Christ should assume flesh. There is the first ground of it.

2. This was necessary in regard of Christ's office and work.

(1.) As to his office. He was to be the mediator betwixt God and man, and that was to be his great and standing office. Now in order to his administration thereof, it was requisite that he should be man and take our nature; for he who will be a mediator betwixt God and man must himself be both God and man. He must be God that he may be fit to transact, treat, negotiate with God; and he must be man that he may be fit to do the same with man. God alone was too high to deal with man, and man alone was too low to deal with God; and therefore Christ was a middle person betwixt both, that he might deal with both. He could not have been fit to be the mediator in respect of office, if he had not first been a middle person in respect of his natures; for, saith the apostle, Gal. iii. 20, 'A mediator is not of one, but God is one.' Not of one, that is, (1.) Not of one person; for mediation supposes more persons than one. Was there none besides God himself, Christ's mediatory work would be at an end; that necessarily implying different parties betwixt whom he doth mediate. (2.) Not of one nature; the mediator must necessarily have more natures than one. Observe it, God, saith the text, is one, viz., as he is *essentially* considered, and therefore as so he cannot be the mediator; but Christ, as *personally* con-

---

[1] Dr Cudworth on the True Notion of the Lord's Supper, p. 62.

[2] Dr Jackson on the Creed, book vii. sect. 3, ch. 20.

[3] Josephus calls it ναον μεταφερόμενον, templum portatile.—*Antiq. Jud.* lib. iii. cap. 5. And Augustine, Templum deambulatorium.

[1] ἀπάτωρ ἐντεῦθεν, ἀμήτωρ ἐκεῖθεν.—*Nazianz.*, tom. i. p. 375.

sidered, he is not of one, that is, not of one nature; for he is God and man too; whereupon he is the person who is qualified to be the mediator. And therefore when he is spoken of as mediator, his manhood is brought in, that nature being so necessary to that office : 1 Tim. ii. 5, 'For there is one God, and one mediator between God and man, the man Christ Jesus.'

(2.) Christ's incarnation and manhood was necessary in respect of that work which he was willing to undertake—I mean the work of redemption. If he will engage to redeem and save lost sinners, he must be so qualified as that he may first make satisfaction to an injured and offended God; for that God stood upon, and would not recede from;[1] he had decreed, as appears by the event, to save man that way, and what he decrees must accordingly be accomplished; he had threatened death to the sinner, which threatening therefore must be inflicted either upon the offender himself or his surety; and God, as *rector mundi*, will vindicate the honour of his government, and therefore will punish the transgression of his laws. Upon such considerations as these there must be satisfaction. Now, in order to that there must be suffering; yea, Christ himself must suffer, partly because he was pleased to substitute himself in the sinner's stead, and partly because his sufferings only could be satisfactory. But unless he be man, how can he suffer? So that the chain or link lies thus : without satisfaction, no redemption; without suffering, no satisfaction; without flesh, no suffering; therefore Christ must be incarnate. Look, as he must be more than man, that he may be able *so* to suffer, that his sufferings may be meritorious, that he may go through with his work and conquer all enemies, difficulties, discouragements whatsoever, all which could not have been done by a mere man; so he must be man that he may be in a capacity to suffer, die, and obey; for these are no works for one who is only God.[2] A God only cannot suffer, a man

only cannot merit; God cannot obey; man is bound to obey, whereupon his obedience will be but matter of debt, and therefore not meritorious; wherefore Christ, that he might obey and suffer, he was man; and that he might merit by his obedience and suffering, he was God-man. Just such a person did the work of redemption call for.

3. Christ must be made flesh because, as was said before concerning his sending, this was the best, the fittest, the most convenient way that God could pitch upon in order to the bringing about of his great designs. To make it the necessary way, especially with respect to satisfaction, that to some possibly may seem too high;[1] but surely none will deny but that this was the fittest and most convenient way; and had it not been so, the wise God would have taken some other way rather than it. But did he design to advance his own glory and the sinner's good; to give out the highest manifestation and utmost advancement of all his attributes; to promote and ascertain pardon, justification, salvation, all grace to believers; what way could have been thought of so proper, so effectual, as this of Christ's coming in our flesh? If God will punish sin, was it not meet that he should punish it in that nature in which it had been committed? What more congruous than, since man had been the sinner, that man should be the sufferer? By man we fell; God will therefore in wisdom so order it that by man too we shall rise again; that in the same nature wherein the τὸ τραῦμα, the wound, had been given, the τὸ φάρμακον, the cure and remedy, shall be pro-

---

[1] *Vide Anselm. Cur Deus Homo*, lib. i. cap. 11, 12, 19, 20.

[2] Suscipitur a virtute infirmitas, a majestate humilitas, ut quod nostris remediis congruebat, unus atque idem Dei et hominum mediator et mori ex uno et resurgere possit ex altero. Nisi enim esset verus Deus non adferret remedium, nisi esset verus homo non præberet exemplum.—*Leo de Nativ.* Quum mortem nec solus Deus sentire, nec solus homo supe-

rare posset, humanam naturam cum divina sociavit, ut alterius imbecillitatem morti subjiceret, ad expianda peccata; alterius virtute luctam cum morte suscipiens, nobis victoriam acquireret.—*Calvin Instit.*, lib. ii. cap. 12, &c. ἔπειδαν οὐκ ἐδύνατο ἡ θεότης, παθεῖν, &c.—Vide *Epiphan. adv. Hær.*, lib. ii. tom. ii. p. 748.

[1] De necessitate si quæritur, non simplex quidem et absoluta fuit, sed manavit ex cœlesti decreto unde pendebat hominum salus; cæterum quod nobis optimum erat statuit clementissimus Pater.—*Calvin. Instit.*, lib. ii. cap. 12. Licet Deus solo nutu voluntatis abolere potuisset peccatum, convenientius tamen ei visum fuit, si hac justitiæ via procederet ad destruendum regnum peccati.—*Estius in loc.* Poterat Deus suam incomprehensibilem misericordiæ largitatem patefacere, condonando noxam humano generi absque ullo actu perfectæ satisfactionis, &c.—Vide *Soto in Rom.* viii. 3; et *Aquin. Sum.,* p. 3, qu. 1, art. 2.

vided also, as one expresses it.[1] 1 Cor. xv. 21, 'For since by man came death, by man came also the resurrection of the dead: Rom. v. 12, 'As by one man sin entered into the world, and death by sin; and so death passed upon all men, for that all have sinned.' The human nature was to be redeemed, therefore it was fit that that nature should be assumed; that was corrupted and spoiled in us, therefore it was expedient that Christ, to heal this nature, should take it upon himself pure, unstained, and uncorrupted.[2] In short, Satan had foiled and baffled the first Adam in this nature; wherefore in it Christ, the second Adam, will foil and baffle him. To man was the law given, by man was the law broken; therefore by man also shall the law be fulfilled. So much for the grounds and reasons of Christ's incarnation.

Hitherto I have insisted upon what is more plain and easy, and have only in a more general way spoken to some things that concern the incarnation and manhood of Christ. I must now endeavour more particularly to open some other things about them, which are of a more mysterious and abstruse nature. I will reduce all to these seven propositions.

Prop. 1. That the Lord Jesus, who antecedently to his incarnation was the Son of God, and as such had a previous existence, even he was incarnate and made flesh. Here the Socinians again make their opposition; for though they acknowledge Christ's flesh and manhood,—they had not need to deny him that, it being all they grant him;[3]—yet that he, as pre-existing in the essence of God, and in the relation of God's natural Son, did assume the human

nature and unite it to the divine in one person, this they will by no means acknowledge; nay, this they fiercely and vehemently oppose. With what vile reflections and opprobrious speeches do they load this great article of our faith, as thus stated. Socinus is pleased to call it *merum humani ingenii commentum*, a mere fiction of the wit of man;[1] Smalcius, a very fable; yea, *Dogma in Christiana religione fere monstrosissimum*,[2] with many other such vile expressions which I either dread or disdain to mention. Only there is one, from this last-named author, which outstrips all the rest; it is this, 'We believe, saith he, that though it should be written not once or twice, but very often, and that too very plainly, that God was made man; yet it would be much better, (this being a thing very absurd, contrary to sound reason, blasphemous against God,) to find out some other sense of it which might suit with the nature of God, rather than to take it literally according to what such words do hold forth, thereby to expose religion to scorn.'[3] Oh the boldness and even blasphemy of the man! It is a vain thing to argue with these persons, either in this or any other point from the holy Scriptures; for let God say there what he will, if their reason, as the supreme judge of what is to be believed or not to be believed, doth not like it, the divine revelation, let it be never so plain, signifies nothing. Lord, whither will the pride of reason and the wickedness of the heart carry men who are given up to themselves? But if Scripture revelation must be thus subjected to human reason, let us bid adieu to all religion, saving what is natural. I thought this had been the highest reason in the world; that creatures should believe what

---

[1] Cyrill. Alexandr. Comment. in John, p. 95.

[2] Nascitur ut ipsam quam prius homo vitiaverat naturam melioraret.—*August. de. Temp.*, Serm. 20, p. 613, &c. Et quia ea natura pro nobis plecti debuit quæ peccaverat, quæque erat redimenda.—*Thes. Salmur.* de Christo Mediat., p. 244. Quoniam justitia et lex Dei ita flagitabant, ut caro humana quæ peccaverat, eadem pro peccato lueret.—*Pareus in loc.* Homo qui debuit, homo qui solvit, &c.—*Bern.* Ep. ad Innocent.

[3] Socin. in Explic. cap. 1 John, et in Disput. de Nat. Christi. Smalcius Homil. in 1 John, Hom. 8, refut. thes. Grawer et in refut. thes. Franzii. Crellius de uno Deo Patre., lib. ii. sec, 2, cap. 5, p. 562. Ostorod. instit., cap. 17. Catech. Racov., p. 89.

---

[1] Disp. de. Nat. Christi, p. 10. Humanationem merum humani ingenii fuisse commentum; p. 8, stupenda Dei metamorphosis.

[2] *Smalcius refut. thes. Franzii.* de Person. Christi, p. 67. Quod alicui persuaderi potuisse valde mirum esset, nisi homines vivi capti et dementati essent a Sathana, &c. Dogma tremendum.—*Id. Hom.* 8, in 1 cap. John, p. 87.

[3] Credimus etiamsi non semel atque iterum, sed satis crebro et apertissime scriptum extaret, Deum esse hominem factum, multo satius esse, quia hæc res sit absurda et sanæ rationi plane contraria, et in Deum blasphema, modum aliquem discendi comminisci, quo ista de Deo dici possint, quam ista simpliciter ita ut verba sonant intelligere, &c.—*Smalcius*, Homil. 8, in John, p. 89.

God reveals, because he reveals it, though they with their poor, dim, and shallow reason cannot comprehend what is so revealed by him. But I am fallen upon another controversy.

I hope to speak to those who bear a greater reverence to the sacred Scriptures; and surely if these may be believed, what can be more clear than this, that Christ is not only man, but that he who was before the Son of God was afterwards in time made the Son of man? Mark the text, 'God sent his own Son in the likeness of sinful flesh;' where Christ is supposed antecedently to be God's Son, then as such he was sent, and then incarnate. So Gal. iv. 4, 'When the fulness of the time was come, God sent forth his Son made of a woman, made under the law:' John i. 14, 'The Word was made flesh.' It is not only he, that is Christ the personal Word, *was* flesh, but he was *made* flesh; so the word ἐγίνετο is rendered elsewhere, John i. 12; 1 Cor. i. 30; Rom. vii. 13; Gal. iii. 13; Rom. i. 3; Gal. iv. 4; and the subject matter determines it to be so rendered here also. But how was Christ made flesh? Was this spoken of him only in respect of his mean, afflicted, calamitous state and condition here? Was that all that was meant by it? Surely no. That was so far from being all, that the evangelist had it not at all in his eye when he uttered these words; for he adds, 'And we saw his glory, the glory as of the only begotten of the Father;' he joins his being made flesh with the glory of his person, not with the meanness of his condition. And further, the substance must antecede the adjunct; the truth of the human nature must go before the abasement and miseries of it. So that when it is said, 'the Word was made flesh,' it can carry no other sense than that Christ took the very nature and substance of man upon him; I say Christ, for it is very evident, where men do not wilfully shut their eyes, that he is all along set forth by the *Word*, he being the personal, essential, and substantial *Word*. Now, observe he was the Word before he assumed flesh, and he who was so pre-existing he assumed flesh; for it is 'the Word was made flesh,' plainly implying the antecedency of his being in that notion to this his incarnation. Socinus is shrewdly pinched with this text, insomuch that he is fain to fall upon every word in it, with his usual criticisms and forced senses, there-

by to evade and elude the strength of it; but all his attempts are in vain. So also (for the word is not sparing in the revealing of this truth, though our adversaries are pleased to assert the contrary,)[1] Heb. ii. 14–16, 'Forasmuch then as the children are partakers of flesh and blood, he also himself likewise took part of the same, that through death he might destroy him that had the power of death, that is the devil: for verily he took not on him the nature of angels, but he took on him the seed of Abraham.' Here the apostle lays it down over and over by *taking:* 'he *took* part of the same,' 'he *took* not on him the nature of angels, but he *took* on him the seed of Abraham,' thereby to note Christ's assuming of the human nature, and joining of it to that other nature which he had before: 1 Tim. iii. 16, 'Without controversy great is the mystery of godliness; God was manifest in the flesh,' &c. A person here must be spoken of, and the Lord Jesus must be that person; for the following matter, 'justified in the Spirit, seen of angels, preached unto the Gentiles, believed on in the world, received up into glory,' is only applicable to a person, and to Christ as that person. By the way, they who alter the reading of the text, putting out θεὸς and putting in ὁ,[2] and so carrying it from the person of Christ to the gospel, have done no good service either to the truth in general, or in special to that particular truth which I am upon. Now it is not here said only that *Christ* was manifested in the flesh, but *God* was, &c., to shew that he who was incarnate (for that is the manifestation in the flesh here intended) was first God, or God before, and then he was incarnate. It is a mighty scripture that in Phil. ii. 6, 7, 'Who being in the form of God, thought it not robbery to be equal with God.' Here is Christ's pre-existing in the nature of the Godhead, and then after this comes his manhood. 'But made himself of no reputation, and took upon him the form of a servant, and was made in the likeness of men.'

It would be a long work to draw out the full strength of these and several other texts, in order to the more undeniable proving of the proposition before us; as also to answer the various replies, eva-

[1] Socin. de Nat. Christi, p. 7. Smalc. Hom. 8, in 1 c. John, p. 88.
[2] Erasmus, Grotius, &c.

sions, misinterpretations about them by such who dissent; and yet I could most willingly engage therein did I think such an undertaking would be proper in such a discourse as this, or tend to the advantage of any. But the truth is, I fear I should but perplex private Christians with things that possibly would be too high for them; and I am sure I should do that which is needless for others who know where this is done already.[1] And indeed the whole matter in this controversy is by Crellius himself brought into a narrow compass, wherein we are very willing to join issue with him, for he grants if Christ did pre-exist before he was incarnate, that then his incarnation must needs be believed and owned according to our stating of it; but I have already proved [2]—and others do it much more fully —that he did so pre-exist; therefore, upon that concession, the thing is clear, and I need say no more upon it. Only let me leave this one word with our opposers, their *homo Deus factus* is the greatest falsehood; but our *Deus homo factus* is the greatest truth.

Prop. 2. The second proposition is this: That Christ the Son of God, the second person in the ineffable Trinity, he only was incarnate. It is here said, ' God sending his own Son in the likeness,' &c.; the taking, then, of flesh was that personal act which was proper to the Son alone: and in that so often alleged text, John i. 14, it is said, ' The Word was made flesh;' which title, *the Word*, is never attributed to the Father, or to the Spirit, but always to the Son, and you see he is the person who was made flesh. It is true, incarnation was the act of the whole Trinity *approbativè*, but it was only the Son's act *terminativè;* all the persons approved of it and concurred to it, but it was terminated only in Christ, the second person.[3] The schoolmen compare Christ's flesh to a garment made by three virgin sisters, which yet but one of them only wears. A

question is commonly here started, Why the second person rather than the first or the third was thus incarnate?[1] Which some do venture to answer by assigning the reasons of it. I humbly conceive there is too much of curiosity in the question, and too much of boldness in the answer. Why Christ was incarnate, I can give several reasons; but why he rather than the other persons, there I must be silent. It is also queried, there being such an oneness betwixt all the persons, How the Son can be said to assume the human nature, and yet the Father and Spirit not assume it?[2] To which the answer is obvious: this difference might very well be upon that personal distinction which is betwixt them, for this assumption of flesh being not the act of the nature, which is common, but of the person, which is limited, the second person might so assume, and yet the other persons not.

Prop. 3. Thirdly, Christ's incarnation was in time, and not till the fulness of time. He was always God, for he that is not always God is never God, the divine essence admitting neither of beginning nor end; but he was not always man; there never was a time in which he was not God, but there was a time in which he was not man.[3] His generation as the Son of God was eternal; but his generation as the Son of man was but temporal. ' In the fulness of time God sent his Son, made of a woman,' &c., Gal. iv. 4. The evangelist sets him forth in his two natures, John i.; with respect to his divine nature, he shews that he was from everlasting: ' In the beginning was the Word,' &c.; ' the same was in the beginning with God,' &c.; then he comes to his human nature, and that he shews was in time, ' the Word was made flesh;' he was not so *ab æterno*, but he was made so in time. In such a sense Christ may be said to be incarnate from all eternity, viz., in regard of God's eternal purpose and decree, as in reference to that he is said to be ' the Lamb slain from the foundation of the world,' Rev. xiii. 8;

---

[1] *Arnold*. Catech. Racov. major, p. 271; *Calov*. Socin. Proflig., p. 285; *Cocceius* against *Socin.*, in cap. 1, John, cap. 15; *Bisterf.* against *Crellius*, p. 564; *Jacob. ad Portum* against *Ostorod.*, p. 166; *Owen* against *Biddle*, chap. xiii., p. 289, &c.

[2] See p. 179, &c.

[3] Sola persona filii incarnata est, operante tamen eandem incarnationem tota sancta Trinitate, cujus opera sunt inseparabilia.—*August. Quest. de Trinit.*, tom. iii. p. 1040. Vide *Anselm. de Incarn. Verbi*, cap. 3 et 4.

[1] See Lombard., lib. iii. dist. 1. Dr Jackson on the Creed, book vii. p. 255.

[2] Of this see *Zanchy de Tribus Elohim*, lib. v. cap. 6, p. 546, &c.; *Tilen. de Incarn. Filii Dei*, disp. 1, sec. 20; *Aug. Serm.* 3, *de Temp.*

[3] Neque enim caro illa quæ ex carne virginis nata est semper fuit, sed Deus, qui semper fuit, ex carne virginis in carne hominis advenit.—*Cassian. de Incarn. Dom.*, lib. 6.

but as to the actuality of his incarnation, that was but sixteen hundred and odd years ago.

A double inquiry here will be made. As (1.) If this was deferred so long, what then became of those who lived and died before Christ was incarnate? If that was so necessary as hath been shewn, what became of the patriarchs,—of all who lived under the law before that was in being? I answer, they had the merit, virtue, benefit of the thing, though they had not the thing itself; for God having decreed it, and Christ having covenanted and engaged to the Father, that in the fulness of time he would take flesh, the Father all along looked upon it as actually done, and accordingly dealt with believers under the law as though it had been actually done; insomuch that they had the same benefit by a Christ in flesh which we now have. Therefore, it is said, Rom. iii. 25, 'Whom God set forth to be a propitiation through faith in his blood, to declare his righteousness for the remission of sins that are past, through the forbearance of God:' Heb. ix. 15, 'For this cause he is the mediator of the new testament, that by means of death, for the redemption of the transgressions *that were under the first testament*, they which are called might receive the promise of eternal inheritance. Whatever our Lord is now, since the actual exhibition of him, he was the same before effectively and virtually, for it is 'Jesus Christ the same yesterday, and to day, and for ever,' Heb. xiii. 8. We read Mark xi. 9, 'They that went before, and they that followed, cried, saying, Hosanna: Blessed is he that cometh in the name of the Lord.' Believers who lived before Christ's incarnation, and they who follow since, both are equally obliged to magnify God for him, both receiving the same benefit by him.

(2.) It may be inquired why at this very *epocha*, or period of time, rather than at any other, was Christ incarnate? Why not either before or after, but just then? *Ans.*: Why, because it was that very time which God had set, therefore called 'the fulness of time,' Gal. iv. 4. He that is pleased to set the time for other things—as for the church's deliverances: 'Thou shalt arise and have mercy upon Zion, for the time to favour her, yea, the set time is come,' Psa. cii. 13; and so in several other cases—surely he was pleased to set the time for so

great a thing as the coming of his own Son in the flesh. He, in his eternal decree, had determined the precise time for this, which, therefore, when it was come, then Christ came. Now, I say, all must be resolved into this. True, there were some more immediate reasons why he came just when he did. He was to come before the sceptre was wholly departed from Judah, Gen. xlix. 10; whilst the second temple was standing, Hag. ii. 6-9; during the fourth monarchy, Dan. ii. 44; Daniel's seventy weeks were almost expired, Dan. ix. 24. There was a general expectation raised in the world of the coming of the Messiah, as might easily be made out. Now, with respect to these things, the Lord Jesus came at that very period of time whereat he did; but they all falling out but in compliance with and subordination to the decree of God, therefore the determination of the time of Christ's coming and incarnation must ultimately be resolved into that: Oh he just came when he did, neither sooner nor later, because the Father had appointed that very time.

Prop. 4. It was not the divine nature or essence, simply and absolutely considered, which assumed flesh, but it was that nature considered as subsisting in the second person.[1] If this restriction and stating of the point be not admitted, we cannot avoid our holding the incarnation was common to all the persons, contrary to what the church hath ever held, and to what was asserted but even now; therefore when it is said, 'God manifested in the flesh,' 1 Tim. iii. 16, you are to understand God in the personal, not in the essential notion.

Prop. 5. The nature assuming was the divine nature, that being considered as was laid down in the foregoing proposition. The manhood did not assume the Godhead, but the Godhead it; man did not be-

---

[1] Tota igitur natura divina fuit incarnata, sed non quatenus absolute et in se consideratur ut omnibus personis communis, sed quatenus personalibus proprietatibus seu τόπῳ ὑπάρξεως in persona filii determinata consideratur.—*Davenant. in Col.* ii. 9, p. 240. Solus Filius suscepit humanitatem in singularitatem personæ, non in unitatem naturæ divinæ.—*Concil. Tolet.* Neque enim divina natura, si proprie et accurate loqui velimus, sed persona divina assumsit naturam humanam. Divina quidem natura unitur humanæ, sed eam non assumsit, assumere enim non est naturæ sed suppositi.—*Bisterf. contra Crell.* p. 565. *Vide Alting. Theol. Problem.*, pp. 562, 577.

come God, but God became man.[1] It is not said that the flesh was made the Word, but the Word was made flesh.[2] This is a thing so unquestionable, that the very naming of it is enough.

Prop. 6. The Lord Jesus, the eternal Son of God, God blessed for ever, did so assume the human nature as in a most mysterious and inconceivable manner to unite it, upon the first framing or forming of it, to his divine nature, and to give that a subsistence in this, so as that both do make but one person; the essence, properties, operations of both natures yet remaining the same, without either conversion or confusion. Here the hypostatical union is both asserted and also described, for wherein doth the nature of that union consist, but in that which is here laid down? Of it you read, Col. ii. 9, 'In him dwelleth all the fulness of the Godhead bodily,' *i.e.*, personally and hypostatically. Rom. ix. 5, 'Whose are the fathers, and of whom as concerning the flesh Christ came, who is over all, God blessed for ever.' Here is both the natures of Christ, and both in him making but one person; upon the personal conjunction of which he is called 'Emmanuel, God with us,' Mat. i. 23.

But not to insist upon the proof of this union, which all but infidels and Socinians do believe, I will endeavour, as well as I can, rather to explain and open it; an undertaking which I enter upon, the Lord knows, with great fear and dread, because of the loftiness and mysteriousness of the thing to be opened. Oh it is a thing so sublime and mysterious as that it transcends the capacity of angels and men! How then shall I be able to speak of it or to it? Take whom you will, single out a person of the sharpest wit, the profoundest judgment, the most elevated reason, let all the most raised abilities concur in him, and then set the hypostatical union before this person. Alas! poor man, how will he be puzzled, nonplussed, unable to fathom so great a depth as this! And well he may, since it is the mystery of mysteries, one of the first magnitude, than which by a narrow intellect none more hard to be conceived of or understood. It is indeed sure

and certain to faith, which believes it because God reveals it; which readily answers all objections, and solves all difficulties about it by resting on divine revelation;[1] but if reason, beyond its proper bounds, will be prying into and judging of a thing so abstruse, its blindness as well as its boldness will soon appear. Its bucket will not go to the bottom of a well so deep; its line is too short to measure such heights, breadths, lengths, depths as are here to be found. I do not in the least wonder that they who make reason to be the supreme judge of matters of faith do throw off the belief of this mystery, for though it be not at all *contrary* to reason, that being supposed to be modest and rectified, yet it is infinitely *above* it. There are several unions in nature, but all come short of this; there is no resemblance in the whole compass of nature that doth exactly reach it. Some I know speak of a plant which hath no root of its own, only it grows and is sustained by a tree of another kind,[2] by which they would shadow out the subsistence of the human nature of Christ in the divine. Others tell us the union of the soul and body in man is of all resemblances the most fully expressive of this union.[3] Now it is granted these or some other such like resemblances may hold forth something of it; but, alas! it is but something—they go but a little way. Their discoveries are as imperfect as those which some travellers make of the world, who when they have seen and said all they can do, yet leave a vast *terra incognita* undiscovered. 'Without controversy great is the mystery of godliness, God manifested in the flesh,' &c. Christ's incarnation hath the precedency before all the other mysteries which are there mentioned about him. If that in itself be such a mystery, how must the mystery thereof be heightened, the hypostatical union being taken in and added to it? The mystical union is very mysterious, the hypostatical union much more. Well therefore might I in the proposition thus lay it down, that the uniting of the human nature in Christ to the divine is done in a most mysterious and inconceivable manner. Well, upon the due weighing of

---

[1] Διο οὐ ἄνθρωπον ἀποθεωθέντα, ἀλλὰ θεὸν ἐνανθρωπήσαντα.—*Damasc. de Orthod. Fide*, lib. iii. cap. ii., p. 167.

[2] Ὁ λόγος σάρξ γέγονεν, οὐχὶ ἡ σάρξ λόγος εἴρηται—*Athan. de Inc. Christi*, tom. i. p. 612.

[1] πρόφερε ἑτοίμην λύσιν, τὴν πίστιν.—*Justin. Martyr.*

[2] See Mr Perkins on Gal., p. 273.

[3] Yet there is a disparity in the union of these two in man, and of the two natures in Christ. Of which see Dr Jackson on the Creed, book vii., p. 333.

that which hath been said, it concerns me with all tenderness and humility to treat of this argument, and to fetch in all the light and direction that ever I may—for I shall need it all—from the word and Spirit.

(1.) I desire that this in the general may be taken notice of, that the hypostatical union is no common or ordinary union, but that which is special and extraordinary. Oh it is a union by itself, that which is of a very different and peculiar nature from all other unions, of which there is great diversity. For instance, there is a union by apposition, as in the several parts of a building; by mixtion, as in the several elements in a compound body; by alteration, as when water is turned into wine. There is a natural union, as in the soul and body in man; a moral union, as betwixt friend and friend; a relative union, as betwixt husband and wife; a mystical union, as betwixt Christ and believers; a union in respect of special presence or inhabitation, of special assistance, of special grace and favour, which was all that Nestorius would grant in the union of Christ's divine nature with his human; but most falsely, for then there would be no more, for substance, in the hypostatical union than what there is in that which belongs to all believers, Christ being in these respects united also to them, though in a lower degree.[1] Now some of these unions are not at all applicable to Christ; such as are so do yet come short of that high and glorious union that is betwixt his Godhead and his manhood; alas! take the highest of them, what is it when compared with the hypostatical union! You will ask me, why? or what is there in that more than in them? Let the following head be observed, and there will be the solution of this question. I add therefore,

(2.) The two natures are so united in Christ as that the human doth subsist in the divine, and that both do make up but one person. Herein lies the formal nature of the hypostatical union, that wherein it differs from and transcends all other unions whatsoever; the explication of this therefore I must a little insist upon.

[1.] First, The conjunction of the two natures in

Christ is so near, as that the Godhead imparts subsistence to the manhood; for the manhood as it is in Christ is ἀνυπόστατος, having no subsistence but what it hath in the personality of the eternal Word; so it subsists, and no otherwise. And here is one great difference betwixt the human nature as in us and as in Christ; in us it hath its proper personality and subsistence, in Christ it hath not so. But how comes this about? Take an answer to that from a judicious divine,[1] 'It is true, saith he, the essential parts of a man's body and soul being united, would have constituted a person, as they do in all other men, if they had been left to themselves; but it was prevented and stayed from subsisting in itself, and was drawn into the unity of the second person by divine and supernatural operation; whereby it was highly advanced, and subsists in a more eminent sort than it could have done if it had become a rational human person. And this may also prevent that objection which from hence so readily offers itself, viz., that if the human nature in Christ hath not a personal subsistence belonging to it, then it wants that perfection which that nature commonly hath in all men, which seems to make it less perfect and excellent in him than it is in them.[2] This is easily answered: the consequence is not good, because the want of this subsistence is compensated with advantage in that subsistence which the manhood hath in the Godhead; in which the human nature subsisting, it is so far from being depressed that it is highly advanced; as the sensitive soul in man, being joined with a nobler soul and subsisting in it, is thereupon more excellent than the sensitive soul in a beast, though there it hath a subsistence distinct from and independent upon the reasonable soul.

[2.] Secondly, Such is the union of the human with the divine nature in Christ, that it is taken into his person, and both make but one person.[3]

---

[1] οὐδὲν οὖν διαφέρει ἡμῶν, &c.—*Athan. de Inc. Verbi Dei.*, p. 593.

[1] Estwick against Biddle, p. 113.

[2] Incarnatio non est qualiscunque unio, sed est specialissima, proxima, et immediatissima unio, qua persona divina humanam naturam sua personalitate carentem ita terminat, ut eam personaliter sustentet, ipsique illud complementum, attamen longe eminentiori modo, communicet, quod a sua connaturali personalitate accepisset.—*Bisterf. contra Crell.*, p. 568. Vid. *Davenant. in Colos.*, p. 244.

[3] Deus in æternam personam Deitatis temporalem accepit

Here is the difference betwixt the essential union of the three persons, where there is but one nature yet three persons; as also betwixt the mystical union of believers, where there is the union of persons, yet not so as to make one person; and the hypostatic union of the two natures in Christ; for against the former, here is distinction of natures, yet but oneness of person; and against the latter, here is the union of natures, and so as to make but one person. And this follows upon the former head; for if the manhood hath not personality in itself, but only subsists in the Godhead, then it cannot cause any personal multiplication in him.   In short, in Christ there is nature and nature, but not person and person; *aliud et aliud*, but not *alius et alius*, for it is but one Christ; as soul and body make but one man, so God and man make, I say, but one Christ.[1] We call it the personal union, but how? Not because it is made up of persons, but because it centres in one person. Christ took the nature of man, but not the person of man; nature did not assume nature, nor did person assume person, but person assumed nature.[2] He was a person before incarnation, and his personality, or distinct personality, did not result from the unition of the two natures, only they are said to make one person, as the latter nature makes no personal addition to Christ. And he was a perfect person before the union, only *in ordine ad finem*, the redeeming of man, he was pleased to take the manhood into communion with the Godhead.[3] So much for these two things, wherein the nature of the hypostatical union mainly lies.

(3.) Though this union be thus close and intimous, yet notwithstanding, the essence, properties, operations of both natures are preserved entire, without any conversion or confusion. Nestorius multiplies the person; Eutyches errs upon another extreme, as it is usual when the staff is crooked and bends too much one way, they that would make it straight do often make it to bend as much the other way. He confounds the natures; to shun the plurality of persons he destroys the distinction of the natures; asserting that after the union the human nature was wholly swallowed up in the divine, and so leaving but one nature to Christ: both of these opinions were condemned by the primitive Church as equally false, heretical, and dangerous. Here is the admirableness of this union; though the Godhead and the manhood are brought into so near a conjunction, yet both retain that which is essential and proper to each; the one is not converted into the other, nor yet both confounded in one. 'The Word was made flesh,' but not so as to cease to be the Word still;[1] when Christ was incarnate he did not part with what he had, only he took what he had not; there was assumption, but no abolition, no conversion, no confusion.[2] Indeed the two natures stand at so great a distance, that though they may admit of union, yet they are not capable of any transmutation or commixtion; the Godhead can never be so

---

substantiam carnis.—*August.* Duas substantias accipimus in uno filio Dei, unam Deitatis, aliam humanitatis, non duas personas.—*Idem. de Trinit. et Unit. Dei.* Vid. *Anselm. de Incarn. Verbi.*, cap. 5, p. 87.

[1] In Deo non aliud et aliud, quia una natura; in Christo non alius et alius, quia una persona.

[2] Aquin. Sum., 3 part, quæst. 4, art 2.

[3] *Vide* Daven. in Colos., 242.

[1] Ὅ μὲν ἦν διέμεινεν, ὁ δὲ οὐκ ἦν προσέλαβεν.—*Nazianz.* Orat. 35, 375. Non potes dicere, nisi natus fuisset et hominem vere induisset, Deus esse desiisset, amittens quod erat, dum fit quod non erat. Periculum enim status sui Deo nullum est, &c.—*Tertull.* de Carn. Chr., p. 359. Quasi non valuerit Christus vere hominem indutus Deus perseverare.—*Idem.*, p. 360. Verbum caro factum est, &c., non in carnem mutatum, ut desisteret esse quod erat, sed cæpit esse quod non erat.—*August.* de Trin. et Unit., tom. iv. p. 947 and Ep. 174. Non mutando quod erat, sed assumendo quod non erat.

[2] Nemo credat Dei Filium coæternum et coæqualem conversum esse in hominis Filium, sed potius credamus, ut non consumpta divina, et perfecte assumpta humana substautia, manentem Dei Filium factum hominis Filium.—*August. de Temp.*, Serm. 23, p. 616, &c. Neutra tamen ex duabus naturis in aliam mutata est substantiam, unita quippe est, non confusa, verbi Dei hominisque substantia, ut in Deum quod ex nobis susceptum fuerat perveniret. O admirabile mysterium! O innarrabile commercium!—*Aug. Medit.*, cap. 16. οὐ τραπεὶς τὴν φύσιν· ἐνωθεὶς καθ᾽ ὑποστασιν ἀσυγχύτως καὶ ἀναλλοιώτως καὶ ἀδιαιρέτως, μὴ μεταβαλων τὴν τῆς θεότητος αὐτοῦ φύσιν εἰς τὴν τῆς σαρκὸς οὐσίαν, μήτε τὴν οὐσίαν τῆς σαρκὸς αὐτοῦ εἰς τὴν φύσιν τῆς αὐτοῦ θεότητος.—*Damasc. Orth. Fid.*, lib. iii. cap. 2, vide etiam ibid., cap. 3. οὐκ ὁ ἦν μεταβαλων, ἄτρεπτον γὰρ, ἀλλὰ ὁ οὐκ ἦν προσλαβων.—*Nazianz.* Orat. 39. λόγος καὶ πρὸ τῆς σαρκὸς καὶ μετὰ τὴν ἐν σαρκὶ οἰκονομίαν λόγος, καὶ ἦν καὶ ἐστι, καὶ ὁ θεὸς πρὸ τῆς τοῦ δούλου μορφῆς καὶ μετα τάυτήν ὁ θεὸς ἐστι, &c.—*Nyssen. contra Apollinar.*, lib. ii. p. 69. οὔτε ὁ ἦν τραπεὶς, καὶ ὁ οὐκ ἦν προσλαβων.—*Isidor. Pelus.*, lib. i. Ep. 323. τῇ ἑνώσει καὶ τῇ συναφείᾳ ἕν ἐστιν ὁ θεὸς λόγος καὶ ἡ σαρξ, οὐ συγχύσεως γενομένης, οὐδὲ ἀφανισμοῦ τῶν οὐσιῶν, ἀλλ᾽ ἐνωσεως

depressed as to be turned into the manhood, nor the manhood ever be so advanced as to be turned into the Godhead. The Athanasian creed thus sets it forth : 'Although Christ be God and man, yet he is but one Christ ; one, not by conversion of the Godhead into the flesh, but by taking of the manhood into God ; one altogether, not by confusion of substance, but by unity of person.' The Scriptures plainly hold forth the two natures of Christ to be distinct even after the union ; turn to Rom. i. 3, 4, and ix. 5 ; 1 Peter iii. 18 ; 2 Cor. xiii. 4. To which texts let me add a few considerations drawn out of some other texts. Christ says, John x. 30, 'I and my Father are one,' there is his Godhead ; but withal he says, John xiv. 28, 'My Father is greater than I,' there is his manhood too ; he says, John viii. 58, 'Before Abraham was, I am,' there is his being God ; and yet he was born but the other day, there is his being man too : he had the divine nature, for he was omniscient ; but he had the human also at the same time, for he is said to grow in wisdom, Luke ii. 52 ; and not to know the time of the last judgment, Mark xiii. 32, of which before. He was God, and so the Father's will and his were all one, but he was also man, and so he prayed, 'nevertheless not my will, but thine, be done,' Luke xxii. 42. He was the Lord of David and the Son of David, the branch of David and the root of David, Mat. xxii. 45 ; both root and offspring, Rev. xxii. 16 ; how could such different things be affirmed of him, but upon the distinction of his two natures ? That therefore is not in the least impeached by the hypostatical union. True, upon this union there is the communication of properties betwixt them, so as that that which is proper to one nature is applied to the other, as you see, John iii. 13 ; 1 Cor. ii. 8 ; Acts xx. 48, and so as that that which is predicated of the one may be also predicated of the other ; I mean in the concrete, for in the abstract this will not hold, as I cannot say the Deity is the humanity or the humanity is the Deity, yet I may truly say God is man and

ἀῤῥήτου.—*Chrysost.* in John i. 14. Vide *Athan. de Inc. Christi*, p. 624. See Leporius., his recantation in Cassian. de Incarn. Dom. lib. 1. Agit utraque forma cum alterius communione quod proprium est, verbo scil. operante quod verbi est, et carne exequente quod carnis est.— *Leo in Ep. ad Flav. Ep. Constantinop.*

man is God : a communication of properties, thus far or in this sense, we deny not ; it follows upon the union ; but that that which is essential to one nature should really, physically, be conveyed and made over to the other nature, as omnipresence, ubiquity, omniscience, &c., from the Godhead to the manhood, which is the popish and Lutheran communication ; this, as implying a contradiction, and carrying in it a perfect repugnancy to the nature of the thing, we cannot assent unto.

(4.) No sooner was the human nature framed or formed, but in that very instant of time it was united to the divine nature. This also I put down as another branch of the main proposition. It was taken as soon as it was made ; its first existence and its union were contemporary.[1] We distinguish betwixt the formation, sanctification, and assumption of the human nature, and we conceive of these as done successively in such an order, first that nature was formed, then sanctified, then assumed. But this is merely founded upon our conception, not that it was so indeed and really as to the things themselves ; for in truth there was no priority of time— priority of nature I deny not—betwixt the one and the other ; but at the very same moment wherein by the power of the Holy Ghost the manhood of Christ was formed, it was also sanctified and united to the Godhead. A question here is moved by some whether Christ's human nature was complete and perfect at the first ; that is, whether, as soon as ever his flesh was formed, his soul was infused and united to it ? or whether, as it is with us, there was not some space of time intervening betwixt the formation of the flesh and the infusion of the soul ? In the discussing of which there is a difference among them ; some being for the affirmative,[2] and others being for the negative.[3] But, which is to my purpose, all agree in this, that whether it was only flesh for some time, or whether both flesh and soul were formed together, yet still the union began at the first instant of the incarnation. There was a time before Christ's manhood did exist ; but as soon

[1] Ἅμᾶ σαρξ, ἅμα λογου σάρξ.—*Damasc. Orth. Fid.*, lib. iii. cap. 2. Vide *Lombard.*, lib. iii. dist. 2.

[2] Sharp. *Cursus Theol.*, p. 362.

[3] Lud. Capellus in *Thes. Salmur.*, part ii. p. 12, thes. 15 ; Dr Jackson on the Creed, book vii. sect. 3, cap. 29, p. 324.

as ever it did exist there was no time wherein it was under disunion and disjunction from his Godhead. Thus I have endeavoured by these four things to give you a little light concerning the hypostatical union of the two natures in Christ's person, which this sixth proposition led me unto; a point of such high importance, and so proper to the subject in hand, that I could not wholly pass it over, and yet withal so sublime and mysterious that I can neither speak nor conceive of it according to what is in it.

Prop. 7. Let me add but one thing further. It is probable, had there been no sin, that Christ had not been sent in flesh; or had not Adam fallen, and thereby involved his whole posterity in a state of sin and guilt, it is probable that Christ had not been incarnate. I express it modestly, going no higher than *it is probable;* because though the Scriptures make it *certain to me,* yet it is not so to others, nay, some are of a quite other opinion. The question is not, *de possibili,* what God by his absolute power and will might and could have done; but only *de facto,* whether, if man had not sinned, Christ should actually have assumed our nature; about which the schools, with other divines, are divided, some affirming it,[1] some denying it.[2]

The former affirm, though sin had not been, yet Christ would have come in flesh, not to have died or suffered, but only to have let the world see the glory and excellency of his human nature, that so great a work as his incarnation might not have been lost or not done, that God thereby might give out a singular demonstration of his love to man. The latter cannot lay so great a stress upon these things, and therefore assert, if man had not sinned, Christ had not been incarnate. And indeed their opinion seems to be more agreeable to the word; for that usually mentions saving from sin, and the taking away of sin, as the end and ground of Christ's taking

flesh. My text describes the state of the sinner to be desperate upon the terms of the law; and then upon that God sent his Son in flesh. It adds, further, he was thus sent to 'condemn sin in his flesh,' so that, had there been no sin to have been condemned, he had not been sent in flesh. So Mat. i. 21, 'She shall bring forth a son, and thou shalt call his name Jesus, for he shall save his people from their sins.' 1 Tim. i. 15, 'This is a faithful saying, and worthy of all acceptation, that Christ Jesus came into the world to save sinners,' &c. John i. 29, 'Behold the Lamb of God, which taketh away the sin of the world.' Dan. ix. 24, 'Seventy weeks are determined upon thy people, and upon the holy city, to finish the transgression, and to make an end of sins, and to make reconciliation for iniquity.' Tit. ii. 14, 'Who gave himself for us, that he might redeem us from all iniquity.' Mat. xviii. 11, 'For the Son of man is come to save that which was lost.' As soon as man fell Christ was promised as incarnate, Gen. iii. 15, but not before. The truth is, had we not been captives, what need would there have been of a redeemer? had we not been sick and wounded, what need of a physician? had there been no breach betwixt God and us, what need of a mediator in the way of reconciliation?[1] As to that which some allege, that Christ might have come though there had been no sin, for this end, that he might have secured man, though in innocency, from death, that is grounded upon a mere falsehood; for had there been no sinning, there would have been no danger of dying, and consequently no need of one to secure from death in a sinless state.[2]

I have done with the first thing observed in the words, Christ was sent in flesh, in the opening of which I have been somewhat large; but if that be all, I hope none will blame me for it; for the incarnation and manhood of the Son of God being the great foundation of our happiness, a thing wherein we have the very pith and marrow of the gospel, the

---

[1] Scotus in part iii. disput. 7, quest. 3 : Absque præjudicio concedi potest, etiamsi humana natura non peccasset, adhuc Christum carnem sumpturum fuisse. Alex. Alens., part iii. qu. 2, memb. 13 ; Catharinus de præd. Christi ; Pet. Galatinus de Arc. Cathol. ver., lib. vii. cap. 2 ; Osiander, &c.

[2] Aquinas, part iii. qu. 1, art. 3 ; Vasquez. in part iii. disp. 10, art. 3 ; Becan. Theol. Schol., part iii. cap. 1, qu. 7 ; Calvin. Instit., lib. ii. cap. 12, against Osiander ; Hoorneb. Socin. Confut., tom. ii. lib. i. cap. 2, p. 253 ; Stegm. Photin., disp. 15, p. 176 ; Alting. Theol. Probl., Loc. 12, Prob. 5, p. 564.

[1] Venit Filius hominis quærere et salvare quod perierat ; si homo non periisset, filius hominis non venisset.—*Aug.,* Serm. 8, de Verbis Apost. Nulla causa fuit veniendi Christo Domino, nisi peccatores salvos facere : tolle vulnera, tolle morbos, et nulla est medicinæ causa.—*Idem,* Serm. 9.

[2] Smalcius, disp. 12, contra Franzium. See Franzius's answer to him de Sacrif., disp. 15, th. 75, &c.

highest demonstration of the love of God, surely I could not stay too long upon it. It is an argument which very many have wrote upon, and some very fully ;[1] but that which I have said, as it was necessary, because the text led me to it, so it is sufficient with respect to my design in this work.

Before I fall upon the application of this head I must speak something to the second, namely, that Christ was sent 'in the likeness of sinful flesh ;' the apostle doth not say only God sent him in flesh, but he adds in the likeness of sinful flesh.

In the handling of this I have two things to open :
1. Christ was sent in the likeness of sinful flesh.
2. It was but in the *likeness* of sinful flesh.

Of the first. The apostle again uses his former Hebraism, for in the Greek it is ' in the likeness of the flesh of sin,' which is as much as, according to our rendering of it, ' in the likeness of sinful flesh.' The meaning of it is this, as Christ had *true* flesh, so he was under some appearance of having *sinful* flesh, there was some outward show, as if his human nature had been tainted with sin ; he externally appeared like a sinner, yea, as like a sinner as one could do who yet indeed and in truth was none ; such as looked upon him and saw how it was with him in his external condition, might be apt to conceive of him as they once did, John ix. 24, ' We know this man is a sinner.' There was something about Christ that had some resemblance of sin, otherwise Paul would not have called it ' the likeness of sinful flesh.' He saith, Heb. ix. 28, ' Christ was once offered to bear the sins of many ; and unto them that look for him shall he appear the second time *without sin* unto salvation ;' implying that Christ at his first coming was not without some appearance of sin. When he shall come the second time there shall not be the least show or appearance of it in him, nothing then but majesty and sanctity, but greatness and goodness, shall be seen in him ; but at his first coming it was otherwise.

[1] As Athanas. de Incarn. Verbi Dei, tom. i. p. 53, &c., et p. 591, &c., et de Hum. Nat., susc. 595, &c. ; Cyril. Alex., tom. v. p. 678, &c. ; Tertull. de Carne Christi, et contra Marcion, Cassian., Petav. Theol. Dogm., tom. iv. ; Ragusa in part iii. ; Aquin. with Vasquez., &c. ; Zanch. Oper. Theolog., tom. viii. ; Gerhard, Loc. Com., tom. i. de Pers. et Officio Christi, p. 312, &c., et in Uber. Exeg. Artic., tom. *ult.* lib. iv. p. 424, &c. ; Calvin. Instit., lib. ii. cap. 12, 13 ; with innumerable others.

But wherein was it the likeness of sinful flesh ?

I answer, If you take it in the restrained notion of the flesh or body of Christ, that was like to sinful flesh. How ? why, inasmuch as it was so far like to our flesh, which is really sinful, as to be passible and mortal ; passibility and mortality, the suffering of pain, anguish, &c., and dying, are shrewd signs and tokens of sin.[1] Had man continued in his innocent and sinless state, his body had not been liable to either of these ; but he sinning it became liable to both ; and it being so too with Christ's own body, here was the likeness of sinful flesh.

If you take it in the large notion, of the whole human nature or person of Christ as man, so it was the likeness of sinful flesh in several respects. He was truly man, and in appearance and likeness he was sinful man, for he was dealt with, handled, used just as guilty and sinful persons are, and that both by God and by men.[2] By God ; he charged upon Christ the sin of all the elect : ' The Lord laid on him the iniquity of us all,' Isa. liii. 6 ; he ' made him to be sin for us who knew no sin,' &c., 2 Cor. v. 21. He then let out his wrath upon him, demanded satisfaction of him, would have him to suffer, did not spare him in the least, Rom. viii. 32, yea, ' it pleased the Lord to bruise him,' Isa. liii. 10 ; though he prayed that the cup might pass from him, Mat. xxvi. 39, yet his Father would have him drink of it ; was not here the likeness of sinful flesh in God's dealing thus with him ? By men ; to them it was more than likeness, they charged him to be

[1] Carnem peccatrici similem in pœna, non in culpa. Habet tamen similitudinem carnis peccatricis per passibilitatem et mortalitatem.—*August.* In carnem suam non peccatum transtulit tanquam venenum serpentis, sed tamen transtulit mortem, ut esset in similitudine carnis peccati, pœna sine culpa ; unde in carne peccati et culpa solveretur, et pœna.—*Idem.* See him, lib xiv. cap. 5, contra Faustum Manich. Similem carni peccatrici in hoc quod erat passibilis, nam caro hominis ante peccatum passioni subjecta non erat.—*Aquin.* Si peccatum cum carne accepisset, dictus esset *missus in carnem peccati :* si etiam carnem immortalem et impassibilem sumpsisset, qualem modo habet, non diceretur missus in similitudinem carnis peccati ; at quia carnem accepit sine peccato, passibilem tamen et mortalem, qualis est peccatorum caro propter peccatum talis effecta, ideo dicitur missus in similitudinem carnis peccati.—*Tolet.*

[2] Ut tractaretur quomodo nocentes tractari solent.—*Grot. in Loc.*

really and actually guilty of sin, that he was a glutton, a wine-bibber, a friend of publicans and sinners, an impostor, a deceiver, a blasphemer, a breaker of the law, and what not, Mat. xi. 19, and xxvii. 63; John x. 36. Towards the close of his life they accused him of crimes of a very high and heinous nature, arraigned him as a malefactor, condemned him to die, executed him, crucified him betwixt two thieves, numbered him amongst transgressors, Isa. liii. 12; Mark xv. 28; he that had sin upon him by imputation was also a sinner by reputation; was not here the likeness of sinful flesh? Look upon him in his sorrows, afflictions, sufferings, he was 'a man of sorrows, acquainted with grief,' Isa. liii. 3; his whole life was but one continued passion; never was any sorrow like to his sorrow; afflicted without, afflicted within, he suffered from God, he suffered from man, drank such a cup as never any drank before him; was not here the likeness of sinful flesh? Did not the blind and sadly mistaken world judge Christ's own personal sin to be the proper cause of all his suffering? Isa. liii. 4, 'Surely he hath borne our griefs and carried our sorrows, yet we did esteem him stricken, smitten of God and afflicted.' Are not suffering and sin so conjoined and linked together, that where there is the one there is some appearance of the other also. I do not say that really and in truth where there is suffering there is also sin, yet I say apparently, and in the opinion and judgment of men, who take their measures in their judging of persons by their outward condition, wherever there is suffering there is sin; so that in our most holy and innocent Saviour it was the likeness of sinful flesh, because it was the reality of suffering flesh. Will you go on to his death, the worst and most exquisite part of his sufferings?[1] Did he die, did he so die, undergo a death so ignominious, so painful, yea, and so penal too, the punishment due for the sin of all believers being therein inflicted upon him?[2] Oh surely here was a very great likeness of sinful flesh! There

seemed to be much of mere man in Christ's low condition whilst he continued in the world, but there seemed to be much of sinful man in the manner of his going out of the world. What! so to suffer and so to die, and yet no sin? no, no sin for all that; but so to suffer and so to die, and yet no show or appearance of sin? yes, that there was, especially to them who could not look into things, and who were altogether ignorant of Christ's person, and of the great designs which he was carrying on. There was such a likeness of sin in these things as that it never yet failed, and was but a likeness, but only in this one great and unparalleled instance of our blessed Saviour.[1] As he submitted to the ordinary infirmities of the human nature, hunger, thirst, &c., in them there were some features and lineaments of sinful flesh; but as he submitted to death, to such a death, there was a more lively draught, a fuller resemblance of sinful flesh. As it was with the creatures which were offered in sacrifice, they in themselves were harmless and innocent, yet having the sins of the people laid upon them, and they dying for them, so they had the likeness of sinful flesh; and just so it was with Christ, upon his being offered up upon the cross as the sacrifice for our sins.

2. Here was much likeness, you see, of sinful flesh, yet it was but likeness and nothing more; some external appearance of sin there was, but that was all, yet no sin in truth and reality; it was the verity and sameness of natural flesh, it was but the likeness of sinful flesh. As it was with the brazen serpent, that was made in an exact resemblance of the fiery serpents, having that very shape and form which they had; yet it was but the likeness of them, for it had not that poison and venom in it which was in them; so here as to Christ, of whom the brazen serpent even in this was an excellent type; he seemed to have that very flesh which we have, and so he had in such a sense, but yet there was this difference, ours is envenomed, his not; it is truly sinful flesh in us, it was but like sinful flesh in him.

This, as before, may be understood either of

---

[1] In morte ejus potissimam causam sitam arbitramur, cur ei similitudo carnis peccati attributa sit ab apostolo.—*De Dieu.* Caro peccati habet mortem et peccatum, similitudo autem carnis peccati habuit mortem sine peccato. Si haberet peccatum caro esset peccati; si mortem non haberet, non esset similitudo carnis peccati.—*Anselm.*

[2] Tametsi nullis maculis inquinata fuit Christi caro, pecca-

trix tamen in specie visa est, quatenus debitam sceleribus nostris pœnam sustinuit.—*Calvin.*

[1] Christus induebat personam peccatum habentis, &c., cum caro passionibus mortique subjecta signum est communissimum hominis peccatum habentis, nec in aliquo fefellit nisi in Christo.—*Cajetan.*

Christ's fleshly part, or of his whole human nature. In the first respect, so his flesh was sinless. He had a true body, but there was no sin in that body. It was pure, holy, untainted flesh.[1] It was made, as to purity and sanctity, κατὰ τὴν ἀρχέτυπον πλᾶσιν,[2] according to the primitive and archetype formation of Adam's body in the state of innocency; that was created holy and spotless, and just such a body Christ did assume. It is true his body and Adam's differed in the manner of their production, but as to their purity and undefiledness by sin, so they did agree. He says his Father had 'prepared him a body,' Heb. x. 5. Now, if the holy God in such a wonderful and immediate manner, for such high and glorious ends, will prepare him a body, to be sure it shall be a holy body, and such an one as shall be proper for the attaining of those ends, which only a holy body was. It was, indeed, upon our account, and Christ's putting himself into our stead, a passible and mortal body, and so far like to sinful flesh; but had it not been for that, it had neither suffered nor died.

In the second respect, so the whole human nature in Christ was sinless.[3] He was true and very man, but not in the least sinful man. He was made man for the sin of man, but yet was man without the sin of man. That nature which is so sadly depraved, vitiated, corrupted in us, in him had its primitive, original purity and holiness. Sin was not so essential, or so inseparably twisted into it, but that God knew how to separate betwixt the nature itself and the deordination of it. Christ took the one, but not the other. The human nature is made up of soul and body; both of these in Christ were unstained,

not having the least *macula* or spot of sin cleaving to them. As it was an unpolluted, undefiled body, so it was also a pure, holy, spotless soul. The human nature, too, is attended with such affections[1] and such infirmities,[2] to all of which Christ submitted so far as they were sinless, but no further. As to the former, he had anger, sorrow, joy, compassion, love, but without the least stain or tincture of sin; as to the latter, he underwent hunger, thirst, pain, &c., but yet, under all, he was without sin. He could suffer; but he did not, nay, he could not, sin. Hence he is called God's 'holy one,' Ps. xvi. 10; 'the holy child Jesus,' Acts iv. 27; 'the most holy,' Dan. ix. 27; 'Jesus Christ, the righteous,' 1 John ii. 1; God's 'righteous servant,' Isa. liii. 11. He was 'a lamb without blemish and without spot,' 1 Pet. i. 19; 'holy, harmless, undefiled, separate from sinners,' Heb. vii. 26. It is said of him, 'he did no sin,' 1 Pet. ii. 22; 'he knew no sin,' 2 Cor. v. 21; he knew it in a way of imputation, for he was made sin, but as to any inhesion or commission, so he knew it not. The apostle saith he was 'tempted in all things as we are, yet without sin,' (that must always be excepted,) Heb. iv. 15. He challenged all his enemies: 'Which of you convinceth me of sin?' John viii. 14. He says of himself, he 'always did the things which pleased his Father,' John viii. 29; and now it is said of him, 'In him is no sin,' 1 John iii. 5. So that upon all this it appears that it was but the likeness of sinful flesh.

Christ, as man, had a threefold holiness—original, habitual, actual. (1.) He was originally holy. David bitterly lamented it, that he was 'shapen in iniquity, and in sin did his mother conceive him,' Ps. li. 5. And so it is with every man that comes into the world in the way of common generation. The very foundation of our being is laid in sin. But it was not so with our blessed Saviour; in his conception, the first framing and forming of his human nature, there was nothing of sin; for he was therefore conceived in the Virgin's womb in an extraordinary manner by the overshadowing of the Holy Ghost,[3]

---

[1] Τὸ σῶμα τοῦ Χριστοῦ οὐκ ἦν ἁμαρτίας σῶμα, ἀλλ᾽ ὁμοίωμα σαρκὸς ἁμαρτίας.—*Cyrill.*, lib. xv. contra Julian. Peccatricem carnem non assumpsit qualis est nostra, naturalem vero illam nostram assumpsit. Si caro Adæ erat vera caro antequam peccavit in paradiso, utique et Christi caro vera est humana caro, etiamsi peccati qualitatem non assumpserit.—*Muscul.* Nostram induens suam fecit, suam faciens non peccatricem eam fecit.—*Tertull.* de Car. Christi. Jerome's gloss upon the words, if those commentaries upon this Epistle be his, is liable to exception. Suscepta postea carne quæ ad peccandum esset proclivior, ipse tamen absque peccato eam suscepit. See Perer. upon this, Disp. 3, p. 850.

[2] Athan. de Incarnat. Christi, p. 620.

[3] Habuit natura humana quam Christus suscepit speciem peccati, non tamen ea revera peccato contaminari potuit.—*P. Martyr.*

[1] φαίνεται ὁ κύριος, &c.—*Vide* Oecum. *in loc.*, p. 301.

[2] Particeps factus est infirmitatis, non iniquitatis.—*Aug.* Trahens de homine mortalitatem, non iniquitatem.—*Id.* tom. iii. p. 1072.

[3] Hæc est similitudo carnis, quia cum eadem sit caro quæ et nostra, non tamen ita facta in utero est et nata sicut et caro

that he might be preserved pure from the common pollution ; so the angel told Mary, Luke i. 35, 'The Holy Ghost shall come upon thee, and the power of the Highest shall overshadow thee ; therefore, also, that holy thing which shall be born of thee shall be called the Son of God.' (2.) He was habitually holy. There was in his nature nothing but a universal rectitude and conformity to the rule and pattern of holiness ; he had therein grace, all grace, nothing but grace, without the least mixture of habitual corruption. We bring with us into the world natures most woefully depraved, such as are a very seed-plot and seminary of all evil ; but our Lord Jesus had a quite other nature, one that was perfectly sanctified, and not in the least tainted with sin. This also was brought about by his miraculous and extraordinary formation, for had he been begotten as we are, his nature had been tainted as well as ours is ; 'that which is begotten'—so I would read it rather than 'that which is born'—'of the flesh, is flesh,' John iii. 6 ; 'Who can bring a clean thing out of an unclean ? not one,' Job xiv. 4. The liquor will taste of the cask into which it is put. As water, when it comes from the fountain, may be very pure, yet if it runs through a dirty pipe, it will contract filth ; so let the soul as it comes out of God's hands be never so pure, yet upon union with the body begotten and propagated in the usual way, both it, and the nature of the person too, will be defiled. Therefore, to avoid this, Christ was begotten in another way ; by which means he was also freed from the imputation of Adam's sin ; for he not descending naturally and seminally from Adam, his sin was not imputed, nor imputable unto him. The apostle indeed saith, Heb. ii. 11, 'Both he that sanctifieth, and they who are sanctified, are all of one,' i.e., of one Adam as the common root ; but they are not both of this one Adam in the same manner, for they who are sanctified are of him and from him in a way of seminal propagation, but he who sanctifieth was not so. Whereupon, though Adam's sin be imputable and imputed to the former, it is not to the latter. As, according to the usual

illustration,[1] Levi being in the loins of Abraham paid tithes in him, Heb. vii. 9, 10 ; and yet Christ, who was also in the loins of Abraham, did not. So all men being in the loins of Adam, and carnally descended from him, sinned in him, and became partakers of his guilt ; but Christ, though in some sense he might be said to be in Adam's loins too—for his genealogy is carried up to Adam, Luke iii.—yet he not descending from him in the ordinary fleshly way, his person was exempted from the guilt of his sin, and his nature from the general depravation. (3.) Christ was actually holy ; there was nothing but holiness in whatever he did ; all his actings, inward and outward, did exactly correspond with the nature and will of his Father. He never was guilty of the least sin in thought, word, or deed. Sin was neither contracted nor committed by him ;[2] grace and holiness were advanced in him to the highest pitch, according to the utmost capacity of the human nature, without the least mixture of what is contrary thereunto. In a word, he lived in his whole course a most holy, innocent, spotless, sinless life, as the scriptures which have been alleged do abundantly testify.

This sanctity and sinlessness of Christ's human nature was necessary upon a double account.

1. To fit it for the personal union with his divine nature. Can it be imagined that ever the Lord Jesus would take a nature tainted with sin, and so nearly unite it to himself ? When the divine nature stood at so great a distance from sin, can we, without blasphemy, think that it would assume the human nature, had it been sinful, into so close a union as that both should make one person ? Oh such a thing was not possible ! God can take a sinning— if repenting—creature into his bosom, but he cannot take a sinning nature into his person. Christ might condescend to take flesh, and yet be God ; but he could not have taken sinful flesh, and yet be God. The human nature, simply considered, was not inconsistent with his Godhead ; but that nature, if sinful, was.

2. This was necessary in respect of Christ's office

---

nostra. Est enim sanctificata in utero et nata sine pecccato, et neque ipse in illa peccavit. Ideo enim Virginalis uterus electus est ad partum dominicum, ut in sanctitate differret caro domini a carne nostra.—*Ambrose.*

[1] Alting. Theol. Prob., prob. 8, p. 571 ; Dr Pearson on the Creed, p. 365.

[2] Eandem assumsit naturam Christus, sed in ea non peccavit. —*Ambrose.*

and undertaking for our good. In order to which, as he must be man, so he must be man perfectly holy and righteous; for he that is a sinner himself, cannot be a saviour to other sinners. Then it would be 'physician, heal thyself,' or 'saviour, save thyself;' all that such a one could do would be little enough for himself. Christ was both priest and sacrifice: with respect to both he must be without sin. As priest; for if sin had been chargeable upon him, he must then have offered for himself, and so have been in the same condition with the priests under the law, which the apostle shews he was not, Heb. vii. 26, 27. As sacrifice too; for whatever was offered up to God, it was to have no blemish in it. In allusion to which the apostle calls him 'a lamb without blemish and without spot,' 1 Peter i. 19; answerably to the paschal lamb, Exod. xii. 5, and to the two lambs in the fire offering, Num. xxviii. 3; and he is said to 'offer himself without spot to God,' Heb. ix. 14. How could Christ have taken off guilt from us had he had it lying upon himself? Or how could he have made us righteous had he not been righteous himself? Therefore, 2 Cor. v. 21, 'He hath made him to be sin for us, who knew no sin, that we might be made the righteousness of God in him;' and Isa. liii. 11, 'By his knowledge shall my righteous servant justify many.' Mark it, Christ being a righteous person himself, so he comes to justify and make others righteous. So 1 John iii. 5, 'And ye know that he was manifested to take away our sins, and in him is no sin.' The connexion is observable, he that will take away sin from others, must have no sin in himself;[1] Christ coming for that end, therefore in him there was no sin. Three things, as one observes from the words,[2] were requisite to him that should be the mediator; he must be God, he must be man, he must be perfectly and unmixedly holy. All these three qualifications you have in the text; Christ was God's own Son, there is his Godhead; he was sent in flesh, there is his manhood; he was sent but in the likeness of sinful flesh, there is his purity and holiness.

Use. 1. Having done with the explicatory part, I come now to what is applicatory. Where, in the

---

[1] Si esset in illo peccatum, auferendum esset illi, non ipse auferret.—*August.*

[2] Piscat.

first place, passing by other things, these two we are mainly informed of:

1. Of the excellency of the gospel and Christian religion.

2. Of the excellency of Christ's flesh or manhood.

1. First, That great truth which I have been upon informs us of the excellency of the gospel and Christian religion. The more raised and mysterious the things are which the one reveals and the other believes, the more excellent must both of them needs be; for this is a principle grounded upon reason, and strengthened by the consent of all who pretend to religion, whether it be true or false. What more common amongst men, when they would argue for the excellency either of that from which they fetch their religion, or of their religion itself, than to cry up the mysteries, and to tell us what high, sublime, mysterious things are contained in them. These make a great impression upon men's minds, and strongly induce them to believe that whatever hath in it such mysteries, must certainly be of God, and have a divine original. Therefore heathens themselves, as well as Christians, have much pleased themselves with this, and have been great pretenders to such and such mysteries, thereby to gain credit and reputation to their way. Now let us apply this principle or common test to the gospel-revelation and the Christian religion, and then I am sure their excellency above all other pretended revelations and religions will be evident. For look into all those admired and rare secrets, those high and raised mysteries, which they who know not the gospel did so much cry up and magnify; and do but compare them with this one mystery, God's own Son sent in flesh. Alas! what trifles, what shallow, contemptible, ridiculous things are they in comparison of it. A God incarnate shames all the little mysteries of the pagan religion, if so good a title may be given to so bad a thing; they all vanish before this, and are not able to stand in competition with it. Now where is this profound mystery revealed but in the gospel? And where is that revelation believed but in the Christian religion? Therefore how excellent must both needs be upon this account. The heathens knew nothing at all of this; they dreamt of men being made gods, but that he who was truly God should be made truly man, this they were alto-

gether ignorant of : in all their religion there was no such mystery. The apostle cries out, 1 Tim. iii. 16, 'Without controversy great is the mystery of godliness, God manifested in the flesh,' &c. His design in these, and in the following words, was to set forth the excellency of the gospel, which he calls godliness, because its main scope and tendency is to that. And how doth he do it ? Why, by the glorious mysteries held forth therein, of some of which he there gives a particular enumeration. As to the height and verity of which mysteries he saith, 'Without controversy,' &c., confessedly, beyond all dispute or denial, these are mysteries indeed. It is as if he had said, I know the poor heathens pretend to great and high mysteries, but indeed they are so far from being high mysteries, that they are no mysteries at all, they being but the fancies of deluded men. But, saith he, I will tell you of mysteries that are both real and sublime, which are so beyond all contradiction : 'Without controversy great is the mystery of godliness, &c. But how doth he make that appear ? He makes it out in some instances, and his first instance is in the incarnation of the Son of God : 'Without controversy great is the mystery of godliness ; God was manifested in the flesh,' &c. Oh there is a mystery indeed, a transcendent mystery, one which all the Gentiles cannot parallel. A very learned author,[1] in a very learned discourse upon this whole verse, proves that Paul therein throughout had his eye upon the Gentile rites, customs, pretensions to mysteries, &c., especially upon those amongst the Greeks, and amongst them especially upon those in their *Eleusinia sacra*, which above all others were in. highest repute at that time when the apostle wrote this epistle. Now, therefore, against them he sets down the great mysteries of the gospel and Christianity, which certainly were infinitely to be preferred before the other. The making out of this was our apostle's design, according to the opinion of the fore-named author, in every branch of the words ; but I will go no further than the first, that only suiting with the thing I am upon. And there are in it four things to prove the thing in hand : (1.) As to gospel mysteries, the true God was the object of them, and concerned in them ; but

[1] Jac. Gothofredus in 1 Tim. iii. 15, 16 ; in Critic, vol. vii. p. 3770, &c.

the Gentiles in their mysteries had to do with those which 'by nature were no gods,' which were but 'called gods,' as they are described, Gal. iv. 8 ; 1 Cor. viii. 5. (2.) In gospel mysteries one God only was the object of them, and Christians had to do with this one and only true God ; but the Gentiles in their mysteries had to do with variety and multiplicity of gods, and so indeed with no god, for many gods are no god : 1 Cor. viii. 5, 6, 'Though there may be that are called gods, whether in heaven or in earth, as there be gods many and lords many ; but to us there is but one God, the Father, of whom are all things, and we in him ; and one Lord Jesus Christ, by whom are all things, and we by him.' It is God (one God) manifested, &c. (3.) In gospel mysteries there is a God, as incarnate, commemorated and remembered in them ; in the Gentile mysteries it was not so. In them they had some notions, and made some commemorations of their gods ; but how ? only as common benefactors, as giving them bread and wine and corn, &c., but they went no higher ; but now Christians under the gospel, they commemorate God as taking flesh, and suffering in that flesh for their good. Oh there is mercy indeed, a mystery indeed ! (4.) Whereas the Gentiles in their mysteries pretended such and such apparitions of their gods, in opposition to these the apostle sets down the great and glorious appearance and manifestation of Christ. He was indeed manifested in the flesh, for he was so manifested in the flesh as to be made flesh ; his was not an appearance only, but a real assumption ; there is a mystery indeed. In these respects the apostle advances the mysteries of the gospel and of the Christian religion, above those which the blind Gentiles were such admirers of in their idolatrous way. Well ! we who know and believe these things, what high thoughts should we have of the gospel and of the Christian religion ! How should we adore and magnify God for his infinite mercy to us, in bringing of us under that revelation and that faith wherein this unparalleled mystery of a Christ incarnate is made known and embraced !

2. Secondly, This further informs us of the excellency and glory of Christ's flesh and manhood ; from the premises it clearly appears that that is, and needs must be, superlatively great. Was Christ himself

sent in flesh? Did God's own Son assume, and so assume, flesh? Oh what a lustre and glory must there be upon that flesh (or body) which such a person doth so assume! It is called, after its being glorified in him, ' a glorious body,' Phil. iii. 21, but it was a glorious body long before, even from the first moment of its formation and assumption. It is true, its glory whilst it was here on earth did not shine forth in its full brightness, there was a veil and covering upon it during the state of Christ's humiliation; but yet even then it was full of glory, though the fulness of its glory did not appear, as the sun is very glorious even when it is hid under a cloud. And, indeed, it was requisite, not only from the state of his abasement, but also from the weakness of those with whom he was to converse, that here he should very much keep in its glory, for we see when at his transfiguration he let it break forth in a more than ordinary manner, the beholders thereof could not well bear it, it filled them with consternation; read Mat. xvii. 1, &c. But yet, upon its miraculous framing, its unstained and unspotted sanctity, its near union with the Godhead, even here, I say, its glory was exceeding great. Oh what a sight will it be in heaven, to see this body of Christ in all its splendour, and to see him in this flesh sitting at the right hand of God! As he was at first sent in it, it was but mean in external appearance and to mere sense; but now he is ascended, and hath carried it up with him, and it is placed at the right hand of God: so it is an object so glorious that it is fit only for a glorified eye to behold.

And doth the body of Christ engross all this glory? Hath his soul no part or share therein? Yes, surely! It may rather be asked, Hath not that the greatest share, it being the better and nobler part, and capable of that of which the body is not? If God prepare so excellent a body, he will be sure answerably to prepare as excellent a soul to dwell in that body; as they that build stately houses will put in inhabitants that shall be answerable to them. Imagine a soul untouched and unblemished with sin, fully and perfectly sanctified, filled with grace to the utmost of its capacity, having nothing in its several faculties but truth in the understanding, holy conformity in the will, heavenliness in the affections; I say, represent to yourselves in your thoughts such

a soul, and then think what an excellent soul would that be? Just such a soul is in Christ. Indeed if we consider these constitutive parts of Christ's manhood as they stand apart and by themselves, they are excellent to a very high degree; but if we go further and consider them in the hypostatic union, then we are at a mighty loss, and cannot conceive what a glory is by that conferred upon them. As suppose a pearl was put into a glass of crystal, that would put a great radiancy upon it; but what if the sun itself could be put into this glass, how radiant then would it be? So here, the Lord Christ having so precious a soul dwelling in his flesh, even that, if there was nothing more, must make it very glorious; but when the Godhead itself dwells in it, how unspeakable must its glory and splendour needs be!

Leaving the parts, let me speak to the whole. The whole human nature in Christ is transcendently excellent. If the essential and eternal Son of God will so far condescend as to assume man's nature, certainly in him the manhood must have all that dignity, glory, perfection that ever it was capable of: and surely never was the human nature so advanced as in Christ. If you consider it as it is in us, so it hath its worth and excellency; for man is yet a glorious creature, though it is too true by the loss of God's image he hath lost very much of his glory. As he was at first created in the state of innocency, he was high indeed; by the fall the case is sadly altered, the human nature now is exceedingly debased and depressed; but yet even in its ruins, as it was with old Carthage, it may be seen what once it was. Much is lost, and the best is lost, but all is not lost; the glory of the saint is gone, but the glory of the man, in a great measure, yet remains. He is yet, as to his natural composition and endowments, very excellent, the top of the whole creation, God's masterpiece, and highest workmanship, endowed with a body curiously wrought, with a soul of divine original, excellent in its being and operations.[1] And besides this, which is general, it

---

[1] *Vide* Nyssen De Hom. Opis., cap. 3, p. 51. τὸ θήιον ἄνθρωπον πολυτελέστατον ζῶον εἰς τὸν κόσμον ἐσῴκισεν, ἀντίτιμον μὲν τὰς ἰδίας φύσεως, ὀφθαλμὸν δὲ τὰς τῶν ὄντων διακοσμάσιος.— *Euryphamus iu Stobœ.*, Ser. oi. p. 556. Theophrastus calls him ἀντίτιμον παρδδειγμα, as though God in him would vie with and outvie all that he had done besides in the whole visible creation. See Weems's Portrait, pp. 60, 61.

pleases God in some to restore the human nature, in part, to what it lost in Adam's fall, to advance it again by grace and regeneration ; yea, to take it up to heaven to the vision and fruition of himself. And now it is at its ἀκμή, here is its *non ultra*, its highest advancement ; it is not capable, as in us, of higher exaltation than what it hath by grace and glory. This dignity and glory the human nature hath in us ; but yet as it is so subjected, take it even at its highest elevation, it comes infinitely short of the dignity and excellency of the human nature of Christ ; the reason is, because in it there is all that hath been spoken in an eminent manner ; and besides, which is higher than all the former, it is taken into a near conjunction with the divine nature. How glorious must that manhood be, which subsists in the Godhead, and hath no subsistence but in that ! The nearer the union is with that, the greater is the perfection and glory of that which is admitted into that union. And hence it is that there is such a fulness of grace in Christ as man, over and above what is in the best of men, that he is ' anointed with the oil of gladness above his fellows,' Ps. xlv. 7 ; that his manhood bears a part in the mediatory office ; that it is to be worshipped with divine worship, as hath been proved before ; I say all this belongs to it by virtue of the hypostatical union, from which in all things it derives super-excellent glory. And yet I must tell you this human nature, as high as it is, is the lowest thing in Christ ; that which is the highest in us is but the lowest in him, *supremum infimi, infimum supremi.* As man he is glorious ; but what is he then as God ? What a person is Christ, take him altogether ! Oh let him be adored and reverenced by you as man ; but especially as he is God-man. So much for information.

Use 2. Secondly, Was Christ sent in flesh ? hence ariseth matter of exhortation to several duties.

1. I would exhort you to give a full and firm assent to the truth of Christ's incarnation, as also firmly to adhere to Christ as sent in flesh. Here are two things which I will speak to apart : first, See that you give a full and firm assent to the truth of Christ's incarnation. It is a thing which the Scripture lays a great stress upon : 1 John iv. 3, ' Every spirit that confesseth not that Jesus Christ s come in the flesh is not of God : and this is that

spirit of antichrist, whereof you have heard that it should come, and even now is it in the world.' 2 John 7, ' Many deceivers are entered into the world, who confess not that Jesus Christ is come in the flesh : this is a deceiver and an antichrist.' It seems the incarnation of Christ met with early opposition ; his flesh was no sooner translated to heaven but it was denied on earth. This apostle therefore, who in his Gospel had been a great asserter of it, in his epistles will be also a zealous defender of it ; and see how warm he was upon it. The denial of Christ's coming, and of his coming in the flesh, for there lies the main emphasis, he carries as high as antichristianism, and sets no lower a brand upon it. Antichristianism doth not only lie in the opposing of Christ in his offices, which is the latter and modern antichristianism, but also in the opposing of him in his natures as God and man, which was the first and ancient antichristianism. To deny Christ's manhood and assuming flesh, this is downright antichristian, the very spirit of antichrist, if the apostle here may be believed. Now there is a twofold denial of this ; one open, express, direct ; the other implicit, virtual, interpretative.[1] The former, I hope, is very rare, the latter, I fear, is too common ; he is no Christian who comes under the former, but there are too many Christians who come under the latter. As you read of some who ' profess that they know God, but in works they deny him,' Tit. i. 16 ; so here, all that own the gospel profess they believe Christ's incarnation, but yet virtually, interpretatively, consequentially, too many of them do no better than deny it. Now for you, my brethren, I assure myself I need not spend time in warning you against the denial—I mean the rank and gross denial—of our Lord's manhood and incarnation ; that antichristianism I hope you will never be guilty of ; yet two things I would say to you : (1.) Get such a firm and rooted belief of this fundamental doctrine, as that there may be no secret doubting about it ; no, not the least doubt stirring in the mind, for any doubting may by degrees, by little and little, work up to the full denial of it. (2.) That you will take heed not only of the open and

---

[1] Non attendamus ad linguam sed ad facta ; si enim omnes interrogantur, omnes uno ore confitentur Jesum esse Christum ; quiescat paullulum lingua, vitam interroga.—*Aug. in Ep. Joh.*, Tract. 3.

direct denial of it, but also of all those opinions and practices which may amount to a virtual, implicit denial of it.

This minds me of something, upon which I crave leave a little to digress, that passes betwixt papists and protestants : the former do greatly insult upon the forementioned texts, from which they think they have enough to free the pope, in whatever notion you consider him, from the charge of being antichrist ; and therefore thus they argue, He is antichrist who confesses not that Christ is come in the flesh ; but the pope doth confess this ; *ergo*, he is not antichrist ; this is one of Sanders's demonstrations.[1] To which it is answered,

1. That the apostle in these texts doth not define or describe 'the antichrist' by way of eminency, him who was to come afterwards, who is set forth 2 Thes. ii. 3–8 ; 1 Tim. iv. 1, but some lesser antichrists, who were already risen up in the apostles' days ; for he saith 'even now there are many antichrists,' 1 John ii. 18. 'This is that spirit of antichrist, whereof you have heard that it should come, and even now already it is in the world,' 1 John iv. 3, and 2 John 7. 'Many deceivers are entered into the world,' &c. ; 'this is a deceiver and an antichrist,' though not *the* antichrist. As to the grand antichrist, there was a τὸ κατέχον about him, a let and impediment in his way, to be removed before he could come, 2 Thes. ii. 7 ; but for the lesser antichrists, the precursors of the great one, they were already come. And it is probable that the apostle in these descriptions in special had his eye upon Simon Magus, who denied that Christ came in true flesh.[2] The argument then, so far as it is grounded upon these texts, only proves that his holiness is none of the little antichrists, of whom John spake as already come, which we readily grant, for we make him to be the great antichrist, of whom Paul spake as yet to come.[3]

2. Yet our divines will not wholly acquit him and his party as to this character of antichrist ; for though as to words and profession they confess that Christ is come in the flesh, yet implicitly and by consequence they plainly deny it, they maintaining

[1] *Vide* Whittak. ad Sanderi Demonstr. Resp., p. 765.
[2] Of him as to this see Cyrill., Catech. vi.
[3] *Vide* Antichrist. Demonstrat. per Rob. Abbat.

those opinions and practices which are interpretatively opposite to Christ's incarnation ;[1] as their burdening the church with such swarms of unnecessary ceremonies. If the substance be come indeed, and they believe it, why do they keep up the shadow ? Αἱ σκίαι παρατρέχουσι, ἡ ἀλήθεια ἐπισέρχεται, (*Nazianz.*,) under the gospel the shadows vanish, the truth and substance being come. Their doctrine of transubstantiation in effect denies Christ's body to be a true body ;[2] for can a true body exist *in puncto*, as they say Christ doth ? can it be a true body, and yet not extense ? Can it be a true body, and yet be present in a thousand places at once ? Can it be a body, and yet have none of those adjuncts which are inseparable from a body ? So, again, their invading of Christ's great offices, advancing of their own merits, satisfactions, &c., with many other things which might be instanced in, are all and each of them interpretative denials of our Saviour's being come in the flesh. Now, sirs, your religion doth not expose you to this guilt, but rather highly secures you from it ; but take heed you do not draw some opinion or practice into it, which may also make you guilty of denying implicitly the incarnation of the Son of God.

But I go further. It is not enough for you not to deny this great truth, no, nor just to believe it, but there must be a firm believing of it, a full and steady assent given to it. I would assure myself that you do believe the verity of Christ's manhood, the reality of his flesh, the truth of his incarnation ; but do you believe it steadily ? do you come up to a full assent to it ? are there no wavering, doubting thoughts about it ? are you rooted, stablished, confirmed in the belief of it ? This I pressed upon you before with respect to Christ's Sonship, and now I am to press it upon you with respect to his incarnation. Whence let me tell you, that though the belief of

[1] Quanquam P. R. et corde credit et ore confitetur Jesum esse Christum, hoc tamen non integre ac simpliciter, sed ex parte tantum facit, dum Jesu multa detrahit quæ Christo conveniunt : et Christum negat in carne venisse, non quidem totidem verbis atque aperte, sed per consequens et oblique, vere tamen et necessario.—*Whittak. resp. ad Sanderi Dem.*, p. 768.
[2] Pet. Molin. in Th. Sedan., vol. i. de Transub., p. ii. p. 831, where he proves ecclesiam Romanam destruere naturam humanam Christi, &c.

this be not the main, vital, essential act of faith, *qua* justifying, yet it is absolutely necessary to that which is so; for there will be no fiducial reliance upon Christ's person, which is the great act of faith as justifying, if antecedently there be not a firm belief of his being made flesh. Oh therefore, see that you be fully settled in your minds as to the unquestionable verity of this great article of the Christian religion. It would be sad if, in our circumstances, we should fluctuate about it; for did all the Old Testament prophecies point to it, as old Zacharias tells us they did: Luke i. 70–73, 'As he spake by the mouth of his holy prophets, which have been since the world began,' &c. 'To perform the mercy promised to our fathers, and to remember his holy covenant, the oath which he sware to our father Abraham,' &c.; in all which expressions his eye was chiefly upon the birth and incarnation of Christ. And have these prophecies received their full accomplishment? and have we lived to see this? and yet shall we doubt of the thing? Surely that would be sad. The patriarchs, and they who lived under the law, had but some dimmer discoveries of it; here and there an obscure promise, and that was all. To them, for a long time, this was revealed but in types and shadows. And it was, too, a great way off from them; yet they 'saw the promises afar off, and were persuaded of them,' as the apostle tells us, Heb. xi. 13. And now when Christ is come, when the thing is done, shall we be doubting and questioning in ourselves about it? When our light is so clear, shall our faith yet be weak? Our Lord's coming in flesh to redeem man was that great thing held forth in the Scriptures of the Old Testament, and they are full of it. Observe that passage, Heb. x. 5–7, 'Wherefore when he cometh into the world, he saith, Sacrifice and offering thou wouldst not, but a body hast thou prepared me: in burnt-offerings and sacrifices for sin thou hast had no pleasure. Then said I, Lo, I come (in the volume of the book it is written of me) to do thy will, O God.' What doth Christ mean by 'the volume of the book'? I answer, The whole body of the Old Testament Scriptures. This was not written only in this or that particular text, but you have it all along interwoven into the body of those Scriptures. Now when the whole stream and current of the Scripture runs to

this very thing, shall we yet give but a languid assent about it, especially when we have the New Testament revelation superadded to the former? the New Testament, I say, which gives us so full an account as to matter of fact in reference to the conception, nativity, life, death of Christ; which shews us how this and that prophecy, pointing to his incarnation, was fulfilled; which asserts it over and over again, telling us expressly that the word was made flesh, God was manifested in the flesh, &c.; shall we, notwithstanding all this, yet stagger in our faith about the truth of Christ's being sent in flesh? Oh believe it, and believe it steadily, so as to look upon it as a thing without controversy! Satan hath all along, more or less, made his assaults upon Christians in this as well as in other matters; and no question he will do the same to you, if it be possible to undermine and hinder your firm assent to it. But let him not prevail.

2. But under this branch of exhortation I am to urge, not only firmness of assent, but also firmness of adherence. I mean this: you must believe that Christ was sent in flesh, so as to cleave and stick to him as sent in flesh. There are some amongst us —whom therefore I cannot but look upon as most sadly deluded, and most dangerously erring in the very fundamentals of the Christian religion—who make little of a Christ in this notion. They are all for a Christ within them; but as to a Christ without them, or a Christ in flesh, as born of the Virgin Mary, crucified at Jerusalem, &c.—I say, a Christ thus stated, they decry and disregard. Oh that, from what I have heard and read, I had not too just occasion for this charge! It is highly necessary, therefore, that I should say something to antidote you against this venom, that under the pretence of a Christ within you, do not lose or overlook a Christ without. In a sober sense we are for a Christ within as much as any—viz., as he is formed in the soul at the new birth, Gal. iv. 19, as he is united to and dwells in believers, Col. i. 27; Rom. viii. 10; but yet it is a Christ without, as incarnate, whom we rely upon for life and salvation. As he is so considered, we eye him in the great acts of faith, and ground all our hope and confidence upon him. I have before told you (p. 194) that a Christ, as formed in the heart, is necessary to justification and salva-

tion, for he saves none but those who have this inward work; but yet it is a Christ as formed in the Virgin's womb, and as dying upon the cross, who is the proper, efficient, meritorious, procuring cause of justification and salvation. These two must by no means be parted, yet their efficiency or causal influence upon sinners' good is very different; for by the one mercy is procured, by the other it is only applied. The impetration is by the Christ without, the application only is by the Christ within. And therefore, though you are to put a high value upon the latter, and to endeavour to make sure of it as the way and condition of receiving benefit by Christ, yet you are to know it is the former by which all is merited, and therefore there the great stress of your faith must lie; it is a Christ as taking flesh, and dying in flesh, that you must stick unto: Mat. i. 21, 'She shall bring forth a son, and thou shalt call his name Jesus, for he shall save his people from their sins.' Christ the Son of Mary was to save: 1 Tim. i. 15, 'This is a faithful saying, and worthy of all acceptation, that Christ Jesus came into the world to save sinners,' &c. The apostle lays the meriting of salvation upon a Christ without, as coming into the world, and not as coming into the heart; he who died upon the cross, was slain, suffered at Jerusalem, he is the person whom God hath exalted to be Prince and Saviour: Acts v. 30, 31, 'The God of our fathers raised up Jesus, whom ye slew and hanged on a tree. Him hath God exalted with his right hand to be a Prince and a Saviour, for to give repentance to Israel, and forgiveness of sins.' Surely where persons have not forfeited the very principles of Christianity, this is a thing which needs no proof. Indeed Christ in the spirit will very little profit those who disregard him in the flesh.

But no more of this! Paul hath a passage which I would a little open: 2 Cor. v. 16, 'Henceforth,' saith he, 'know we no man after the flesh; yea, though we have known Christ after the flesh, yet now henceforth know we him no more.' How? Know Christ no more after the flesh? What doth he mean by this? Did he cast off all respects to him, all reliance upon him, as considered in his flesh? Oh no! All that he aims at is this; he knew Christ no more after the flesh, that is, so as to

have any further converse with him in a fleshly way; he did not expect again to eat and drink with him, as sometimes the apostles had done; all that external converse was now at an end. Or he means that he did not look for any fleshly advantages by him, as worldly honour, preferment, riches, &c. Or again, that he did not know him as in the state of his former abasement and humiliation, so the word flesh is somewhat taken more restrainedly, see Heb. v. 7. Thus you are to understand the apostle in these words, and not as if he laid aside all knowledge of, or respects unto, the Lord Jesus, as considered in his human nature.

In believing we must eye a whole Christ, Christ God and Christ man too; his whole person with both his natures is the proper object of faith. And certainly there is something in it that believing is so much set forth by its reference to his flesh; as John vi. 53, 54, 56, 'Verily, verily, I say unto you, Except ye eat the flesh of the Son of man, and drink his blood, ye have no life in you. Whoso eateth my flesh, and drinketh my blood, hath eternal life, and I will raise him up at the last day. He that eateth my flesh and drinketh my blood dwelleth in me, and I in him.' Take away this flesh, and Christ's fitness to be a mediator to God, and a Saviour to us, ceases; and consequently his fitness, too, to be the object of saving faith. It is Christ God-man whom in believing you have to do with; and you are neither so to eye his manhood as to overlook his Godhead, nor so to eye his Godhead as to overlook his manhood: both together do your work. Upon the whole, therefore, you are in the actings of faith to look upon Christ as having assumed your nature, and so to rest upon him.

2. Secondly, Be much in the study and contemplation of Christ as sent in flesh. What an object is a Christ incarnate for these! I have pressed you to study him as the Son of God; I would also press you to study him as the Son of man. To know him as God's own Son, and as having taken our own flesh, there is the τὸ ὑπερέχον, 'the excellency of the knowledge of him,' Phil. iii. 8. What dry, insipid, jejune knowledge is all other in comparison of the knowledge of Christ as God-man. One drachm of this, especially if saving, practical, and fiducial, is better than great heaps of mere natural and philo-

sophical knowledge. It cannot be enough lamented that Christ in his person, natures, offices, is so little known; as to that which I am treating of, his assuming man's nature, how little do the most understand of it. All hope to be saved by a Christ incarnate, but, alas! they know not what a Christ incarnate is. In the general, possibly they can tell you he was a man; but if you examine them about particulars, what woeful ignorance will you find in them! Is not this to be greatly bewailed! Nay, go even to saints themselves, how scant and dim is their light and knowledge about this! None can know it fully, some know nothing of it; they who know something, it is, God knows, but very little in comparison of what they might; they wade but ankle deep into this great depth. Is there not need, therefore, of this advice, to stir you up to the studying of Christ as sent in the flesh? Oh that you would study other things less, and this more! that you would every day, with all due sobriety, be prying, searching, diving into this mystery of a God manifested in the flesh! So the angels do. This is one of those things which they 'desire to look into,' 1 Pet. i. 12; and we being more concerned in it than they, shall not we be looking into it? David says, Ps. cxi. 2, 'The works of the Lord are great, sought out of all them that have pleasure therein.' Here is a great work indeed, the greatest that ever was done by God; many great and glorious things he hath done, but the sending of his own Son in our flesh exceeds them all. Now shall not this be sought out by us? Things are to be studied according to their excellency in themselves, and their influence upon the good of others. There are, in a very eminent manner, both of these inducements in the incarnation of Christ, to draw out our most serious endeavours after the knowledge of it; for what so excellent in itself, so beneficial to man, as that? It stands very high in the place and reference which it bears in and to the gospel; it is the soul and spirit, the marrow and kernel, of the whole gospel; one of the highest discoveries which the gospel makes; all the articles of faith, saith one, stoop and veil to it.[1] And if so, what a necessity doth this lay upon you to search as narrowly into it as ever you can? Pray do not object the mysteriousness of the thing, as if it

[1] Dr Sibbs on 1 Tim. iii. 16, p. 65.

was so much above you that you were not to meddle with it. For (1.) Though it be a great mystery, yet it is a mystery, in a great measure, revealed. (2.) The more mysterious it is, the more need there is of the most diligent inquisition into it. (3.) It is a mystery to curb curiosity and pride, but not to stifle sober and modest inquiries.

Further, be much in meditating upon and contemplating of Christ as sent in the flesh. You are to study him that you may know more of him; to meditate upon him that you may draw out and improve what you do know. O sirs! he that is in your nature in heaven, should he not be very much in your hearts here on earth? A Christ incarnate! How should our souls be swallowed up in thinking of him as such! What doth the whole world afford so deserving of our most fixed thoughts? Is there any flower in nature's garden out of which such sweetness may be sucked? What divine comfort, what heavenly delights, must needs flow from hence to the soul that is much in the contemplation of it? Is the foundation of our eternal happiness laid in it, and shall we not mind it? Is it a thing so rare, so unparalleled, and yet shall it be seldom in our thoughts? What fools are we to suffer ourselves to be so much taken up with trifles and shadows, when we might live in the daily view of Christ God-man! Why should an empty, perishing world engross our thoughts, when we have such an object as a Jesus incarnate to contemplate? Why do we dwell so much upon fleshly things of a deceiving and defiling nature, when the flesh-assuming Christ, the spotless and undefiled flesh of the Holy Jesus, is either not at all regarded, or very hastily passed over? It is said of Isaac, Gen. xxiv. 63, 'He went out to meditate in the field.' O Christians, what a spacious and delicious field is Christ's human nature for you to meditate in and upon! Oh that you would go out frequently and so do! You say, sometimes you would employ your thoughts in divine meditation and contemplation, but you cannot call to mind a proper object for it; or you are presently on ground, and want matter for your thoughts to work upon. Pray when it is so, fix upon the Word as made flesh; there is a fit and full object for these things, where, think and think as long as you will, yet fresh matter will offer itself; that is a well out of which the more you draw, the fuller you will find it to be : Ps. civ. 34, 'My meditation of him,' saith David, 'shall be sweet.' Surely the believer may say, My meditation of God, (who and as he was made man,) shall be sweet. Oh that you would live in the daily exercise of this heavenly duty upon this excellent object ! What a blessed thing would it be if we could lie down, rise up with a Christ, and especially a Christ incarnate, in our minds ! Methinks that which was the product and matter of God's thoughts from everlasting, should very much be the subject and matter of our thoughts in time.

3. Thirdly, Was Christ sent in flesh, yea, in the likeness of sinful flesh ? This should strike us all with amazement and astonishment. How should we admire and wonder at this dispensation ! Was it so indeed that such a person did become man— such a man ? Oh the wonder of wonders ! Here is nothing but wonders, a conflux and complication of wonders ; in this one thing there are many wonders, and those too not of the lowest rank, but the highest that ever were. Who can duly think of, weigh, ponder upon what is here laid down, without being transported and swallowed up in high and holy admiration ! The glorified ones in heaven are always wondering, and what is it which causeth them so to do ? It is the beholding of Christ in our flesh. They began betimes so to do, even as soon as ever Christ had assumed our nature, and they continue still to do the same, and so they will to all eternity. The angels were so full of joy and admiration upon the first breaking out of this, that they must come from heaven and give some vent to themselves, in singing, 'Glory to God in the highest, on earth peace, good will towards men,' Luke ii. 14. Now when there is such admiring and wondering in heaven, shall there be none in earth ? Things which are mysterious and strange affect us very much. Was there ever anything so mysterious and strange as the incarnation of the Son of God ? This is a mystery indeed, the first link in that chain of mysteries, 1 Tim. iii. 16. When little things make us wonder, it is an evidence of weakness ; when great things do not make us wonder, it is an evidence either of great inconsideracy or gross stupidity. The proud philosopher scorns to wonder at anything in nature, but the humble Christian, who hath things

before him far more sublime and unsearchable than any mysteries in nature, may well stand and wonder at those things in religion which it is not possible for him to comprehend. Amongst which, what more incomprehensible, (take it in all respects,) than the incarnation of God's own Son ? He that doth not wonder at this, pray what will he wonder at ?

To be more particular and distinct in the urging of this duty, of humble and thankful admiration, two things I would say :

1. Admire in reference to the thing itself.

2. Admire God and Christ, the persons who had the hand in it.

1. For the thing itself; Christ in our flesh. Pray pause and ruminate a while upon it, and then tell me what you think of it ; the more you look into it and consider it, the more you will admire it. A God to be made man ; a God to take dust—for flesh is but living or breathing dust—into intimate conjunction with himself ; a God to submit for some time to lie in the womb of a virgin. Oh wonderful ! Here is finite and infinite joined in one, eternity matched with time, the Creator and a creature making but one person ; here is the Lord and Sovereign of the world marrying into a mean and broken family ; the maker of the universe made himself ; here is two natures, which stood at an infinite distance each from the other, hypostatically united ; here is the verity of flesh, and yet but the similitude of sinful flesh ; here is a man begotten without man, a son without a father, for though Christ had more than a putative body, yet, as man, he had no more than a putative father :[1] Luke iii. 23, 'Jesus began to be about thirty years of age, being, *as was supposed*, the son of Joseph,' &c. ; here is a virgin conceiving and bringing forth a son, she remaining a virgin still : Jer. xxxi. 22, 'The Lord hath created a new thing in the earth, a woman shall compass a man ; are not all these stupendous, amazing, never enough to be admired things ? How do wonders here grow upon us ! No sooner doth one go off, but presently another succeeds in its room. Christ wrought many miracles in his flesh, but the greatest miracle of all was his assuming flesh. Let Jews and infidels scoff

---

[1] Filius Dei de Patre sine matre, Filius hominis de matre sine Patre.—*Aug. de temp.*, Serm. 23. Vide *Tertull. de carne Christi*, p. 373. Vacabat viri semen, &c.

and deride, the sincere Christian must admire and adore.

2. For the persons who had the great hand in this, they are to be admired too. I will instance, (1.) In God the Father; (2.) In God the Son.

(1.) God the Father he is to be admired; for it was he who 'sent his own Son in the likeness of sinful flesh;' he ordained and ordered all about this; he laid the foundation of it in his own purpose and will. It was 'the Lord's doing,' from first to last; should it not be 'marvellous in our eyes'? Ps. cxviii. 23. Ay! and, as was said before, it was the highest thing that ever he did; in this, with reverence be it spoken, he went to the utmost of all his attributes. 'In Christ's incarnation,' saith a reverend divine,[1] 'we may see God, as it were, resolving to do a work from himself to the uttermost, to manifest the uttermost of his glory in a work out of himself. The work of God within himself was his eternal generation, and the procession of the Holy Ghost; but now God would work out of himself, and that to the utmost extent. He had made a world, but there he had not manifested the uttermost of his glory; therefore God will, &c.; what is that? to take the nature of man into a personal union with his Son, that is the uttermost.' Now where God goes to the utmost of his attributes, it becomes us to go to the utmost of our thankfulness and admiration.

There are four attributes in God which upon the account of Christ's incarnation can never be enough admired. (1.) His wisdom, in finding out such a glorious way for the sinner's recovery. This was his invention and contrivance, and his only; the wisest creatures in the world, had they united all their wisdom, could never have thought of such a way for the redeeming of lost man. In so desperate a case God himself, to speak after the manner of men, was fain to set his own wisdom on work to find out a remedy; and this was that which he found out and pitched upon. Oh the infinite, unsearchable, incomprehensible wisdom of God! The apostle speaks of 'the deep things of God,' 1 Cor. ii. 10; of 'the manifold wisdom of God,' Eph. iii. 10; of his 'abounding in all wisdom and prudence,' Eph. i. 8. What may these expressions refer to, but to God's deep and most wise designs and

[1] Mr Burrough's Gosp. Conv., p. 89.

methods displayed in the work of man's redemption by a Christ incarnate? And, which was a great demonstration of his wisdom, see how the remedy was suited to the malady; man at first would be as God, and that ruined him; therefore now God shall be as man, and that shall restore him; man gave the wound, and man shall heal that wound; oh the wisdom of God! (2.) His power; for Christ, as he was 'the wisdom of God,' so also 'the power of God,' 1 Cor. i. 24, and as he was so in other respects, so eminently in that which I am upon. It was an act of mighty power for God so nearly to unite the Godhead and the manhood; the bringing of two natures so distant together in one person must needs be the product of infinite power. For God to make something out of nothing, that speaks the greatness of his power; but for God to be made man, there being, in some respects, a greater distance betwixt the Godhead and the manhood than betwixt something and nothing, this speaks a greater power. It is much that soul and body, two such different beings, should be so conjoined as to make a man, that such disagreeing elements should be reconciled *in corpore mixto*; but what are these to the joining of the Godhead and manhood in one *hypostasis*? (3.) His justice. Is sin committed? the holy law broken? Doth the creature lie under guilt? God stands upon the vindication of his honour, the making good of his threatenings, the satisfaction of his justice. Satisfaction he will have, and in that nature too in which the offence had been committed; and because the creature was altogether unable to make it, in order thereunto God will have his own Son to take flesh, that he may be in a capacity to obey, do, suffer what justice required; and when this Son had so assumed flesh God fell upon him, charged him with the guilt of all believers, exacted of him that punishment which was due to them, would not spare him in the least or abate him anything. Oh the severity and impartiality of God's justice! (4.) His mercy, goodness, and love. And doth not this attribute shine forth as brightly in our Saviour's being made flesh, as any of the former? Here was 'the tender mercy of our God,' Luke i. 78; God's so loving of the world, John iii. 16; the great manifestation of his love, 1 John iv. 9; his 'glorious grace,' and 'the riches of his grace,' Eph.

i. 6, 7. Did ever God give the world such a demonstration of his love and grace as in the incarnation of his Son? Oh matchless, infinite, unlimited love and grace! He had done exceeding well for man as he made him at first; for he put him into a very good state, stamped his own image upon him, made him above all other creatures to be his favourite; but he foolishly sinned, and fell from God, and thereby lost all his happiness. Well, what did God now do? Did he let man alone, shut up his bowels against him, fall upon him with his utmost wrath? Did he say, Nay, since it is thus, let him even rise as he has fallen; since he would be so foolish as for a trifle to break with me, let him rot and die and perish for ever, I will do no more for him? Oh no! Not such a word or thought did pass from the gracious God towards his miserable creature. He pitied undone man, found out help for him, yea, sent his own Son to restore him. And how did he send this Son? Why, in flesh. But in what flesh? Surely it shall be altogether glorious flesh, such as shall be of a quite other nature than that is which we poor mortals have! Ay! so it was in some respects, but in others but just like to sinful flesh. Put all this together, and was not here love? God will have sin to be punished, but then the punishment shall be laid upon his own Son, and the sinner himself shall be acquitted. Oh the height of justice, and yet oh the height of mercy too! There is more of mercy in God's sending Christ, and sending him in this way, than there would have been in his absolute pardoning of sin without any sending or any satisfaction; because always the more costly a mercy is, the more there is of mercy in that mercy. And mere pardon, nay, salvation itself, have not so much of mercy and love in them, as what was in Christ's assuming our nature; for, as to the first, it is more for a king to put himself into the traitor's stead, and himself to make satisfaction for his offence, than just to pardon him; and as to the second, in salvation there is our advancement, but in Christ's incarnation there was his abasement; now it is more for such a person as Christ to be abased, than it is for such a creature as man to be advanced. All which being considered, what an obligation doth there lie upon us to get our hearts raised up unto and drawn out in the highest admiration of God's mercy!

(2.) Secondly, God the Son, or Christ himself, the person who was incarnate, he, too, is greatly to be admired, with respect [1.] To his love; [2.] To his holiness; [3.] To his power.

[1.] For his love, which, indeed, was superlative and admirable, transcending the reach of the highest finite capacity. Christ knew what our flesh was, how much it was below him to take it; yet for our good he readily condescended to it, and was willing to debase and depress himself if he might but advance and exalt us.[1] Here was the mirror of love! The greatness of his person speaks the greatness of his love: Phil. ii. 6-8, 'Who being in the form of God, thought it not robbery to be equal with God, but made himself of no reputation,' &c. What a person was Christ before his incarnation! What a fall was here thereby for such a person! He who sate upon the throne was willing to lie in the manger.[2] He that was clothed with brightness and majesty disrobed himself, put off his own royal attire, and put on our coarse rags; he who filled the world confined himself to a womb; he who was the Maker of all owned a poor woman for his mother; he who was David's Lord became David's Son. What unsearchable mysteries of the grace of Christ are here! He had angels at his beck, and might have employed one of them upon this service; but he would not—he will come himself, and trust no creature in such an undertaking. Was not this love? God's first love, saith one,[3] to man, was in making man like himself, his second great love was in making himself like man. There is a *what manner of love* upon the sons of men being made the sons of God, 1 John iii. 1; but what manner of love was there in this, that the Son of God should be made the Son of man? I have nothing to say, but wonder, wonder. This great person vouchsafed to come so near to believers that he is 'not ashamed to call them brethren,' Heb. ii. 11. He was willing to be made like to

[1] ' Te propter vitamque tuam sum Virginis alvum
Ingressus, sum factus homo,' &c.
    —*Lactant de Benefic. Christi.*
[2] Jacet in pannis qui regnat in cœlis. Mundum implens, in præsepi jacens. Sidera regens, ubera lambens, &c. Conditor Mariæ natus ex Maria. Filius David Dominus David, semen Abrahæ qui est ante Abraham; factor terræ factus in terra.
—*August. de Temp.*, Serm. 20, and Serm. 23.
[3] Dr Reyn. on the Passions, cap. xi. p. 99.

them that they might be made like to him; he took of theirs that he might give them of his; and since they could not ascend to him, he was pleased to descend to them.[1] Oh inexpressible love! He did not only take flesh, but that very flesh and blood which we have; yea, he stooped to the likeness of our sinful flesh,[2] and how did he abase himself by and in this flesh! Phil. ii. 7, 8: 'But made himself of no reputation, (ἐκένωσε, he emptied himself, as it were, of all his former glory and fulness,) and took upon him the form of a servant, and was made in the likeness of men; and being found in fashion as a man he humbled himself, and became obedient unto death, even the death of the cross.' Christ's external state in our nature was so low and mean (which he yet never stuck at or regarded, his design being to do good, and not to appear in any worldly pomp or grandeur,[3]) that it seemed to be below him, not only as he was God, but even as he was man. He who before was equal to God, was now scarce equal to man. It was prophetically spoken in his person, Ps. xxii. 6, 'I am a worm and no man;' nay, he was scarce equal to the meanest of other creatures, for he saith, Mat. viii. 20, 'The foxes have holes, and the birds of the air have nests, but the Son of man hath not where to lay his head.' Now, surely, the lower Christ's condition was, the higher should be our admiration of his love. When the human nature, as in us, was at the worst, sadly tainted by Adam's fall, then Christ took it upon him. Though our stock was now sour and degenerate, yet he was willing to be ingrafted into it. When the noblest families are under an attainder of treason, persons are very shy of matching into them. It was no better than so with ours, and yet the Lord Jesus did not refuse to match into it. My brethren, had he assumed our nature before we had spoiled it, even that had been an admirable condescension; but to assume it when in us it was so spoiled and defaced, here was the highest condescension that was imaginable. The

angelical nature was pure and untainted; for though many angels had sinned, yet their nature was not touched, because they, not standing in a common head, as man did, the fall of some did not reach the whole order; and yet Christ meddled not with that nature, but with ours: Heb. ii. 16, 'Verily he took not on him the nature of angels, but he took on him the seed of Abraham.' Oh the grace and love of Christ to man! There are five expressions concerning him under the word *made*, every one of which holds forth the greatness of his humiliation, and consequently of his love. (1.) He was *made flesh*, John i. 14. (2.) He was *made of a woman*, Gal. iv. 4. He might have had flesh immediately created, but it was not so; there was the instrumental concurrence of a woman to it, which heightens his humiliation therein. Then (3.) he was *made under the law*, Gal. iv. 4; yea (4.) he was *made a curse* for us, Gal. iii. 13; yea, (5.) he was *made sin*, 2 Cor. v. 21. Now though there be some gradual rise, or rather fall, in all these, yet I conceive the first holds forth the greatest humiliation; the reason is, because there is a greater distance, and repugnancy betwixt God and flesh, than there is betwixt flesh and any of the other things which follow. But shall not all put together highly affect us, and fill our souls with high thoughts of the love of Christ? Blessed God! what hearts have we if such considerations as these will not work them up to a Christ-admiring frame? Dear Saviour! thou who didst once take our sinless flesh, be pleased to take away our lumpish, dull, sinful hearts; that there may be in us some such warm and raised affections as may, in some measure, answer to thine immense love in thy incarnation.

[2.] Admire the holiness of Christ. That he should take true flesh, and yet but the likeness of sinful flesh; be so like a sinner, and yet no sinner; come so near to sin, and yet be so far off from it; assume our nature, so woefully corrupted and vitiated, as it is in us, and live so long in that nature after it was assumed, and yet be perfectly free from sin; that so much sin should lie upon him, and yet not the least sin be committed by him; oh this is very strange and wonderful! Who can touch pitch and not be defiled? who can take a nature which, in its proper subject, was wholly depraved, and yet be holy? Why,

---

[1] Deplorata certe res erat, nisi majestas ipsa Dei ad nos descenderet, quando ascendere nostrum non erat.—*Calvin. Instit.*, lib. ii. cap. 12.

[2] οὐδὲ ἑτέραν ἔλαβε σαρκα, ἀλλ' αὐτὴν ταυτὴν τὴν καταπονουμένην.—*Chrysostom*.

[3] οὐκ ἐπιδείξασθαι ἦλθεν ὁ κύριος, ἀλλα θεραπεῦσαι καὶ διδάξαι τοὺς πασχοντας.—*Athan. de Inc. verbi.*, p. 96.

Christ did so, and yet was holy. And if he could not have so done without impeaching his holiness, as well as he loved man he would never have been made man. Oh let the holiness of Christ be adored by you!

[3.] Admire the power of Christ. That that nature which is so weak in us should be so strong in him; that he, even in our flesh, should be able to do and suffer as he did, this is admirable. Therein he baffled a tempting devil, bore up under the greatest pressures that ever lay upon any, did not sink under all his sufferings, wrought unquestionable miracles, pacified divine wrath, satisfied God's justice, fulfilled the law, condemned sin, subdued and conquered all the powers of hell, held it out till all was finished; all this was done in our flesh by Christ-man, though not as mere man. I say in our flesh; for had it not been so, the thing had not been so great; but that Christ in our very nature and flesh should be able to do such things, there is the wonder.[1] Doubtless he must be assisted and strengthened by a higher nature, otherwise it could not have been thus. Nay, that Christ-man should continue yet to do such strange and mighty things, oh stand and wonder at his power! It was the 'stone cut without hands'—by which you are to understand Christ in the miraculous production of his human nature—which 'smote the image,' &c., Dan. ii. 34. You read of 'one sitting upon the cloud, like unto the Son of man, having on his head a golden crown, and in his hand a sharp sickle' for the cutting down of his enemies, Rev. xiv. 14; and 'the Son of man is brought before the Ancient of days, and there was given him dominion and glory, and a kingdom, that all people, nations, and languages should serve him,' &c., Dan. vii. 13, 14. Now that Christ in the nature of man should be thus exalted, and also do such great and glorious things, is not this wonderful? Suppose you had seen Moses, when a child, in his ark of bulrushes, laid in the flags by the river's brink, Exod. ii. 3, and then afterwards had seen him, when grown up, at the head of the people of Israel, as their ruler and

deliverer, as he is styled, Acts vii. 35, subduing Pharaoh and all his host, would not this have struck you with admiration? What, then, shall we say and think of Christ? He that for some time was shut up in his mother's womb, lay as a weak infant on her lap, sucked at her breasts, &c., and when grown up suffered and died upon the cross, this very Christ is the Redeemer of the world, the Saviour of man, the king of all the earth, the universal conqueror over devils and all enemies whatsoever, exalted far above principalities, &c. What shall we say to these things? Verily they command adoring silence and wonderment.

I have been very long—yet not too long, I hope—upon this head. When the incarnation of the Son of God is before me, than which there never was a greater thing to be wondered at, could I say too much in order to the raising of your hearts to the highest adoration, both of the thing, and also of the persons concerned in it? What more proper and necessary to be urged upon such an argument than such a frame of spirit?

4. Fourthly, This great mystery of Christ's incarnation must have some powerful influence upon your hearts and lives. My brethren! it is not enough to believe it, to have an ineffective light in the head about it; no, nor sometimes to have the affections wrought upon in the admiration of it; but this must be attended with deep impressions upon the heart, and have a great efficacy upon the life. The apostle having spoke of the 'mystery of godliness,' 1 Tim. iii. 16, presently he falls upon Christ's being manifested in the flesh, as a great part of that mystery of godliness; and this in particular, as well as the whole gospel in general, is set forth thereby, because, where it is known and believed aright, it doth very much conduce and operate to the promoting of godliness. St John tells us, 1 John iv. 2, 'Every spirit that confesseth that Jesus Christ is come in the flesh is of God.' Is every spirit that confesseth this of God? Yes, so far as assent to the truth, and a faithful profession of that truth, will carry it. But such as would be said to be of God in a more special and saving way, they must not only assent and profess, but they must live suitably to what they do so believe and profess. This truth, of Christ's being come in the flesh, must have an

---

[1] Εἰ μὴ ἐν τῇ σαρκὶ νικὴ γέγονεν, οὐκ οὕτω θαυμαστὸν ἦν, &c.—*Chrysost.* Hæc erat Dei virtus, in substantia pari perficere salutem. Non enim magnum si Spiritus Dei carnem remediaret, sed si caro consimilis peccatrici, dum caro est sed non peccati.—*Tertull. adv. Marcion.*, lib. v.

efficacy upon them in what is practical, and then they will be of God indeed. A God incarnate is both the great encouragement to faith, and also the great incentive to duty.

Should I here fall upon the several particulars which offer themselves, and enlarge upon them, I should too much trespass. Briefly, therefore, let me but touch upon six or seven things.

1. Was Christ sent in flesh? And do you know and believe it? Oh how humble should you be! What an argument is here, from Christ's incarnation, for humility. In his assuming flesh he hath set before you the highest, the most glorious pattern of humility that ever was. Will you not follow it? 'Learn of me, for,' saith he, 'I am meek and lowly,' Mat. xi. 29. He gave sufficient evidence of his lowliness in becoming man. Now is it not better to learn of a humble God than of a proud man? O Christian! after such abasement of thy Lord and Saviour, wilt thou be haughty and proud? How unsuitable is a proud sinner to a humble Saviour! What, saith one, more mysterious than God humbled, more monstrous than man proud? Whenever pride, self-conceitedness, self-exalting, begin to rise in the heart, think of the humility of the Son of God, how he emptied himself, made himself of no reputation, took upon him the form of a servant, &c., and surely this will be an effectual antidote against pride. The apostle, when he would further lowliness of mind in the Philippians, this is the consideration which he sets before them, Phil. ii. 3, 6, 7, &c. We were undone by a proud devil and a proud heart; if ever we be saved it must be by a humble Saviour and a humble heart.[1]

2. Do not sin. Partly that there may be in you as full a conformity to Christ as here you can come up to. He took your nature and sinned not therein; you should be as like to him as ever you may. Partly that Christ may have his end in his coming in the flesh, for why did he so come, but 'that he might destroy the works of the devil,' 1 John iii. 8; that he might 'redeem you from all iniquity, and purify unto him-

self a peculiar people, zealous of good works,' Tit. ii. 14; that 'you being delivered out of the hands of your enemies, might serve him without fear, in holiness and righteousness before him all the days of your life,' Luke i. 74, 75. Partly, too, because upon Christ's sending in the flesh you have so full a demonstration of the evil of sin, how hateful it was to God, &c. For it having got into the world, nothing could expiate it unless God's own Son will take flesh, yea, and suffer and die in that flesh, and so bring about the expiation of it. Oh what an evil is sin! Now, notwithstanding and after all this, will you yet love it, and live in the commission of it? What will this be but, in effect, to say you regard not what Christ was or did? that you desire, as far as in you lies, to make this his great act, the taking of flesh, to be insignificant and to no purpose; as also to declare to the world by your practices that you have quite other thoughts of sin than what God himself hath.

3. Of all sins be sure you shun those which do most directly disparage and debase the human nature, such as drunkenness, intemperance, bodily uncleanness, &c. What a sad thing is it that ever such things should be done where there is such a nature! When Christ hath assumed that nature, and by assuming it hath so dignified and advanced it, nay, when he hath so highly glorified it as to carry it up with him to heaven, and there to sit with it at the right hand of God, shall we by such and such sinful courses, the gratifying of such base lusts, dishonour and disparage it?[1] God forbid! Sinners, let me entreat you, whenever the temptation comes to excite you to those evils which in special do intrench upon the glory of the human nature, as to drink to excess, to defile your bodies by fleshly lusts, &c., do but seriously think with yourselves that you are men, and shall such carry it as beasts? that your Saviour hath just such a body as you have, and doth he abuse it by the committing of such evils? that he hath your nature, and doth he so and so sin in it? that he hath restored it, as it is in himself, to its pristine glory, and will you, as it is in yourselves, keep it as vile as ever? Surely if such who are drowned

[1] Diabolus superbus hominem superbientem perduxit ad mortem, Christus humilis hominem obedientem reduxit ad vitam; quia sicut ille elatus cecidit et dejecit consentientem, sic iste humiliatus surrexit et erexit credentem.—*August.*, tom. iii. p. 1051.

[1] Agnosce, O Christiane, dignitatem tuam, et divinæ consors factus naturæ, noli in veterem vilitatem degeneri conversatione redire.—*Leo. de Nativ.*

in sensuality did but seriously think of this, they would abandon their base lusts, rather than by them debase their excellent nature.

4. Love God and Christ; yea, love them strongly, ardently, to a very intense degree of love. 1 John iv. 16, 'God is love,' (he hath made it to appear so in his sendingof Christ in flesh,) therefore he deserves love; he hath sufficiently acted and declared his love to you, how will you act and declare your love to him, &c. He loved, and *so loved* you, John iii. 16; will you not return love for love,[1] ay! and *so love* him too to the utmost of your capacity? What will fire the cold heart with love to God if this will not do it, viz., his sending his own Son in the likeness of sinful flesh? He that knows and considers, certainly he cannot but be full of divine love. And then love Christ. Was he willing to put on your rags, to clothe himself with your flesh? Did he take your nature, and that too under those circumstances which have been mentioned, doing this not for himself, but wholly for your good? Was he pleased so far to condescend as to become one of you, nay, to put himself not only into your nature but also into your stead—he might have been a man, and yet not a surety? Oh let him have your love, your most hearty and cordial love! Pray let it be your greatest grief that you have no more love for him who deserves so much. Alas! it is but a drop when it should be an ocean, but a poor spark when it should be a vehement flame. And I would have you to love Christ, who is incarnate, as well as because he was incarnate. What an alluring, attracting object of love is Christ, God-man! God loves him as he is in our flesh; the angels love him as in our flesh; the glorified saints love him too in that notion; will not you also love him as he is so considered? Christ in our nature is a person very amiable. What is there in mere man to draw our love to him, which is not in Christ, God and man, with great advantage? He indeed is the *deliciæ humani generis*, 'fairer than the children of men,' Ps. xlv. 2; the 'chiefest amongst ten thousand, altogether lovely,' Cant. v. 10, 16. Those excellencies which are but scattered in us, do all, like lines in the centre, concur in him. A Christ incarnate is the love of heaven; let him be the love of earth too.

5. So love Christ as to be willing, nay ambitious, to do, to suffer, to be abased for him. O sirs! what shall we do for him who hath done such inexpressible things for us?[1] Shall we be loath to take his cross who was so willing to take our nature? He had but the likeness of sinful flesh, and yet how willingly and patiently did he suffer! We have the reality of sinful flesh, shall we hang off from suffering, or be impatient under it? What abasement can be too much for the sons of men, when the Son of God was thus abased? What service can be too mean for us, when Christ stooped to the form of a servant? He that knows how much Christ's love was above him, will never think any work or service to be below him.

6. As Christ was pleased to partake with you in your nature, so let it be your desire and endeavour to partake with him in his. I mean that which the apostle speaks of when he saith, 'that by these you might be partakers of the divine nature,' 2 Pet. i. 4; even man, in such a sense, is capable of this, and therefore should pursue after it. It was part of Christ's humiliation to take our human nature, but it is our highest exaltation to be brought under the participation of his divine nature; of which, though we cannot be partakers as he was of the former, for then we should be properly and formally deified, which is high blasphemy, yet in the fruits and effects of it, and in regard of conformity and likeness to it, so we may. God may become very man, but man cannot become very God; he may be like to God by grace and holiness, but that is all,—thus we are to understand some passages of the ancients which seem to be very high.[2] Now this is that which I would have you to labour after; that as Christ hath taken of yours, so you may receive of his; as he was made like to you in what is proper to man, so you, according to your capacity, may be made like to him in what is proper to God.

7. Be thankful: not in a common, ordinary, formal

[1] Si amare pigebat, saltem reamare non pigeat.—*August. de Catech. Rud.*

[1] Deus homo factus est, quid facturus est homo, propter quem Deus factus est homo?—*Aug.*, tom. iii. p. 1070.

[2] Factus est Deus homo, ut homo fieret Deus.—*Aug. de Nativ.* Divinitas verbi æqualis Patri facta est particeps mortalitatis nostræ, non de suo sed de nostro, ut et nos efficeremur participes Deitatis ejus, non de nostro sed de ipsius.—*Aug.*, tom. iii. p. 1051. Αὐτὸς ἐνανθρώπησεν ἵνα ἡμεῖς θεοποιηθῶμεν.—*Athan. de Incarn. Verb.*, lib. i. p. 108.

manner, but in the most lively, enlarged, raised manner that is possible. Where the mercy is high and great, the thankfulness must bear some proportion to it. Did Christ condescend to take your flesh for such gracious ends? Oh, where is your praising and magnifying of God? Should not the whole soul be summoned in to give its most united acknowledgment of so signal a mercy? The angels never reaped that advantage by his incarnation which we do, and yet as soon as ever that took place they were at praising work: Luke ii. 13, 14, 'Suddenly there was with the angels a multitude of the heavenly host praising God, and saying, Glory to God in the highest,' &c. Good old Zacharias began his prophecy with thanksgiving: Luke i. 68, 69, 'Blessed be the Lord God of Israel, for he hath visited and redeemed his people,' &c. And Simeon, upon the sight of Christ in the flesh, was transported with joy: Luke ii. 29, &c., 'Then took he him up in his arms, and blessed God, and said, Lord, now lettest thou thy servant depart in peace, according to thy word: for mine eyes have seen thy salvation, which thou hast prepared before the face of all people; a light to lighten the Gentiles, and the glory of thy people Israel.' To move you to this thankfulness, I can say no more than what I have already said; let but that be considered, and you will daily, heartily, with the most raised affections, bless God for a Christ incarnate.

And as you should do this for the thing itself, so also for the revelation of it in the gospel; where 'the mystery which was kept secret since the world began is now made manifest,' as the apostle speaks, Rom. xvi. 25, 26. This we had never known if God had not there revealed it; and the deeper is the mystery, the higher is his mercy in the disclosing of it. 'To you it is given to know the mysteries of the kingdom of heaven; to others it is not so,' Mat. xiii. 11. How little doth the greatest part of the world know of a God in flesh! Nature may discover a God, but it is Scripture only which discovers God-man. Now, why is that revealed to you which is hid to so many? 'Even so Father, for so it seemed good in thy sight,' Mat. xi. 26. Nay, further, you have the clear revelation of this; what was hid in darker prophecies and types to the fathers under the Old Testament, is now under the New

made as evident to you as the light of the noon-day. You do 'with open face behold' the truth and glory of Christ's manhood, 2 Cor. iii. 18. You live under 'the days of the Son of man;' that which others expected and waited for, and saw but afar off, Heb. xi. 13, is now accomplished and made good to you. Under the law believers looked for the Son of God in flesh; you under the gospel look on the Son of God in flesh. Their language was, 'I shall see him, but not now; I shall behold him, but not nigh,' as Balaam prophesied, Num. xxiv. 17; but under the gospel the language is, 'That which was from the beginning, which we have heard, which we have seen with our eyes, which we have looked upon, and our hands have handled of the word of life: for the life was manifested, and we have seen it,' &c., 1 John i. 1, 2. I may say to you, what Christ once did to his disciples, Luke x. 23, 24, 'Blessed are the eyes which see the things which ye see: for I tell you, that many prophets and kings have desired to see those things which ye see, and have not seen them; and to hear those things which ye hear, and have not heard them.' Oh put the thing and the revelation thereof together, how should God for both be magnified by us! Had we as many tongues as members, was the whole body turned into this one member, yet we should not be able, for this high and glorious mercy, sufficiently to speak out and celebrate the praises of the most high God, as Augustine pathetically expresses it.[1] So much for this second use by way of exhortation.

Use 3. The third and last is for comfort. The point in hand is every way as fruitful for consolation as for exhortation. Christ sent in flesh! made flesh! what abundance of matter is wrapped up in this for the heightening of the true believer's joy! I have brought you to the very spring-head of divine consolation; oh that you might feel it flowing forth and running into your souls! 'Abraham rejoiced to see Christ's day,' the day of his incarnation; 'he saw it and was glad,' John viii. 56. Let me tell you, you see that about it which he never saw; will not you rejoice and be glad? 'Fear not,' said the angel to the shepherds, 'for behold I bring you good tidings

---

[1] Si certe omnia membra nostra verterentur in linguas, ad rependendum tibi debitas laudes nequaquam sufficeret exiguitas nostra.—*Aug. Medit.*, cap. 15.

of great joy, which shall be to all people.' What were these good tidings? why, 'Unto you is born this day in the city of David a Saviour, which is Christ the Lord,' Luke ii. 10, 11. Christ born! the Son of God incarnate! Good tidings indeed! blessed be God that they were ever brought to our ears! surely such tidings call for great joy. If God would please to open your eyes to let you see what there is in a Christ sent in flesh, to fix your thoughts upon it, to help you to make the best improvement of it, I cannot but assure myself that your hearts would be brimful of comfort, that your fears would vanish, like the dark cloud before the bright-shining sun; that instead of your sad despondencies of spirit you would triumph in Christ, and lift up your heads with joy. Oh how injurious are they to the saints in their heavenly glorying who would take away from them the manhood of Christ! since, as it is truly said, no man can glory in that head in which he believes there is not his own nature.[1] And how injurious are the saints unto themselves, who do so little meditate upon, improve, and draw comfort from Christ in this consideration!

If it be asked, What is there in a Christ incarnate for the strengthening of the faith, the heightening of the comfort of God's children? Give me leave to answer this question in several particulars.

1. There is this in it: certainly this must be an effectual, and the most effectual way imaginable, for the promoting of God's glory and the sinner's good. If Christ become man, that must be a very proper and powerful means in order to these ends; for, besides the greatness of the thing in itself, if it shall please God out of his abundant mercy to propound to himself the bringing about of such things, he out of his infinite wisdom will be sure to pitch upon such means as shall certainly reach them; and therefore he pitching upon this, unquestionably it shall attain what it was designed for. Is not this then ground of joy, and a great support to faith, to consider that there is a way, and such a way, found out, as shall infallibly and effectually promote your good?

2. In this you have a high demonstration of his love, yea, the highest that was possible; for there

was in it *ultimus divini amoris conatus;* infinite love itself could go no higher than a Christ in flesh.[1] Now this love of God is the strongest, the most heart-reviving cordial that can be given to a gracious person; and answerable to the degree of that, so is the degree of his comfort: for evermore where God displays his highest love, there he hath the highest comfort. You that are such, do you desire an evidence of this, and would that cheer you? Here you have one, the very highest that God could give, viz., his sending his own Son in the likeness of sinful flesh.

3. By this, as hath been already observed under a former head, all the promises are sealed, confirmed, and ratified. Christ's incarnation was not only one of the promises itself, yea, the grand Old Testament promise, but it was the seal and confirmation of all the rest. When God would give Ahaz a sign for the encouraging of his faith as to the making good of a particular mercy promised, what was that sign? Why, 'Behold a virgin shall conceive and bear a son, and shall call his name Immanuel,' Isa. vii. 14; and so it is in all other respects. The promises indeed are confirmed several ways, but there is not any one thing which gives a higher confirmation to them than this, Christ's being made flesh. Whatever God hath promised, it is all sure now to be made good. Why? because his great promise of the incarnation of his Son, than the which nothing could be more high and more improbable, is exactly accomplished. A Christ incarnate is faith's highest security. Saints, you have no reason now to question either God's power;—for what cannot he do who can unite the Godhead and the manhood? What can be too hard for him who can make a virgin to conceive—or his mercy and willingness to do anything for you;—for he that will send his own Son in the likeness of sinful flesh, what will he stick at? What can come after that can be so great as that? 'He that spared not his own Son, how shall he not with him give us all things?' Rom. viii. 32. Well, therefore, might the apostle say, 'All the promises of God in him (in Christ) are yea, and in him Amen,' &c., 2 Cor. i. 20.

---

[1] Nullus protest eo capite gloriari, in quo asserit naturam suam non haberi.—*Leo.*, Epist. xi.

[1] Nihil tam necessarium fuit ad erigendam spem nostram, quam ut demonstraretur nobis quantum nos diligeret Deus. Quid vero isto indicio manifestius quam quod Dei Filius naturæ nostra dignatus est inire consortium?—*Aug. de Trin.*, lib. xiii.

A very great and precious truth here lies before me, which therein I would fain speak more fully unto. It is this, that all the excellent objects of the Christian's faith and hope are made credible, nay, sure and certain, upon the incarnation of the Son of God. This I will endeavour to make out in some instances.

(1.) There is first the mystical union betwixt Christ and believers; a very great mystery, as you have heard. Christ in believers, and one with them, what can be more wonderful! Yet it is sure there is such a thing, and we may be assured of it, for it is made credible and certain by that which I am upon. The hypostatical union ascertains the mystical union. The union of persons is not so much as the personal union. He that hath thus united our manhood to his Godhead in one person, why may he not mystically unite our persons to his person, this latter union not being so high as the former? As it is said, Heb. vii. 7, 'the less is blessed of the better,' so I may here say, the less is confirmed by the greater. If Christ had not come so near us in the taking of our nature, the mystical union might have been more doubtful; but now there is no room for doubting. Observe that place, Heb. ii. 11, 'Both he that sanctifieth, and they who are sanctified, are all of one,'— there is the union in the same common nature; 'for which cause he is not ashamed to call them brethren,' —there is the near relation, or the mystical union, grounded upon the former.

(2.) There is communion with God, Christ's special presence in the soul, the inhabitation of the Spirit. All very high and glorious things, so high that the poor creature knows not how to believe them; yet they also are very credible and certain upon Christ's incarnation. It is more for God to be made man than it is for God to converse with man; God manifested in the flesh is more than God manifesting himself to flesh. Moreover, Christ in our flesh laid the foundation of the creature's communion with God, and removed that which hindered it, namely, distance and enmity. These two stood in the sinner's way as to this blessed communion, but Christ removed them both, and so brought it about. It is observable, the apostle having spoken of the incarnation of Christ, 1 John i. 1–3, presently he adds, 'and truly our fellowship is with the Father, and with his Son Jesus

Christ.' Oh if he had not condescended to take our flesh, there had been no such thing as our communion with God;[1] but now it is sure. And so it is in the other things which were mentioned. What is Christ's gracious presence in the soul, or the indwelling of the Spirit in a child of God, both of which are often spoken of in Scripture, to the personal presence and inhabitation of the Godhead in the manhood of Christ? 'In him dwelleth the fulness of the Godhead bodily,' Col. ii. 9.

(3.) There are such and such communications of grace from God to a gracious heart. These are very secret, yet very sure and credible. Upon communion of nature communications of grace do certainly follow. Christ having assumed flesh, there is now a way made through which God may convey his mercy and love to creatures as he pleases. The Godhead is the fountain from which all flows, and there is now a pipe to convey supplies from that fountain, viz., the manhood of Christ. 1 Cor. viii. 6, 'To us there is but one God, the Father, of whom are all things, and we in him; and one Lord Jesus Christ, by whom are all things, and we by him.' By Christ, in our flesh, all things come to us, and we by him go to God. He is the way, as he saith of himself, John xiv. 6; the way by which our duties are handed to God, and God's mercies to us. Oh, so long as Christ is mediator betwixt God and man as God-man, there may, and there shall be mutual intercourses and communications betwixt God and man.

(4.) The Scripture speaks much of the sonship and adoption of believers. A very great and glorious privilege! infinitely too great for such despicable worms as we are, considered in ourselves; yet through the grace of God in a Christ incarnate it is ours. This near relation to God upon the manhood of his own Son is now made very credible;[2] for if the Son of God was made the Son of man, why may not the sons of men be also made the sons of God?

[1] Alioqui nec satis propinqua vicinitas, nec affinitas satis firma, unde nobis spes fieret Deum nobiscum habitare; tantum erat inter nostras sordes et summam Dei munditiem dissidium. —*Calvin. Instit.*, lib. ii. cap. 12.

[2] Ἐγένετο υἱὸς ἀνθρώπου, θεοῦ γνήσιος ὢν υἱός, ἵνα τοὺς τῶν ἀνθρώπων υἱοὺς τέκνα ποιήσῃ τοῦ θεοῦ.—*Chrysost.* in 1 John. Si natura Dei Filius propter filios hominum factus est hominis filius, quanto est credibilius natura filios hominis gratia Dei filios fieri, &c.—*Aug. de Trinit.*, lib. xiii. cap. 9.

If the one was so abased, why may not the other be so advanced? especially if we consider that the bringing of believers into this new relation was one great and special end why Christ was incarnate: Gal. iv. 4, 5, 'When the fulness of the time was come, God sent forth his Son, made of a woman, made under the law, to redeem them that were under the law, that we might receive the adoption of sons.' When the evangelist had laid down the exaltation of believers to a state of sonship, John i. 12, and had shewn how that is brought about, ver. 13, immediately he falls upon Christ's being made flesh, ver. 14. Whether the latter carries any reference to the former, or is brought in upon this or that account with respect to the saints' sonship spoken of, I will not be positive in determining one way or another; only this I say as to the thing, it is not incredible that such who believe should become the sons of God, when the Word was made flesh.

(5.) There is the resurrection of the body. And what more incredible to us than that! Though the Scriptures are very express and plain in the asserting of it, though we know the power of God, and have many considerations for the assuring us of its truth and certainty, yet how apt are we to stagger and to be under doubtful thoughts about it! But saith the apostle, Acts xxvi. 8, 'Why should it be thought a thing incredible with you, that God should raise the dead?' Blessed Paul! is the resurrection of the dead a thing not incredible? What is there to take off the incredibility of it? why, enough and enough, especially to us Christians. Christ's incarnation, and that which followed upon it, is sufficient to remove the incredibility of this mystery; for he took our flesh, then died in our flesh, then rose again in our flesh—I say, *in our flesh*, for he rose not only with a true body, but with the self-same body that ours is, with that very body in which he died and was buried—and if so, why then should the resurrection of our flesh or bodies be incredible? This is nothing but what hath been done already to and in our flesh; and it is less to raise flesh than to take flesh; it was more strange for him who was God to die, than it is for him who is man, being dead, to live again. If it be said that Christ was an extraordinary person, and therefore that his resur-

rection is not to be bottomed upon for the making of ours sure and certain; I answer, But it is; because he did not rise as a single person, but as a common head; and therefore he rising, we may be assured that we shall rise too. 1 Cor. xv. 20–22, 'But now is Christ risen from the dead, and become the first-fruits of them that slept: for since by man came death, by man came also the resurrection of the dead. For as in Adam all die, even so in Christ shall all be made alive.' He that believes Christ's incarnation will upon that believe the resurrection. As it is well observed by some upon that passage betwixt Christ and Martha, which we read of, John xi., where he asked her, ver. 25, 26, 'I am the resurrection and the life: he that believeth in me, though he were dead, yet shall he live; and whosoever liveth, and believeth in me, shall never die; believest thou this?' Mark her answer: ver. 27, 'She said unto him, Yea, Lord: I believe that thou art the Christ, the Son of God, which should come into the world:' as if she had said, Yea, Lord, I do believe that thou canst raise the dead, since thou art the Son of God which wast to be, and now art, incarnate. He questions her about the resurrection; she professeth her faith in his incarnation; yet her answer was very pertinent, because she believing this could not but believe that also.

(6.) The possessing of the heavenly glory is the highest of all, and therefore of all the most incredible; for usually the higher the mercy is, the harder it is to believe it. What! saith the poor Christian, shall I in this flesh see God, and live with him for ever? Oh this is a thing very improbable, much too big for my hope and faith! but whoever thou art, if thou beest a sincere Christian, thou mayest believe it and be sure of it. For Christ took thy flesh, purchased heaven for thee in thy flesh, ascended up to heaven in thy flesh, and is there glorified in thy flesh; and therefore mayest not thou assuredly hope that thou also thyself in thine own flesh shalt go to God, and have it glorified in its measure, as well as the flesh of Christ is? What encouragement is here for faith! By Christ incarnate we do not only see that the human nature is capable of the future blessedness, but we have thereby ground of full assurance of it; for what could he aim at in his being so, short of heaven?

In our nature he both purchased it, and also took possession of it, and all for us: Heb. vi. 20, 'Whither the forerunner is *for us* entered, even Jesus, made an high priest for ever after the order of Melchisedec.' He being glorified, in him we are glorified;[1] as he rose as a public head, so he was glorified as a public head too. He who hath so advanced our nature, will in time advance our persons; his incarnation, which is past, secures our glorification, which is to come. It was more for Christ to come down to earth than it is for him to carry us up to heaven; if he will condescend to be like to us in his humiliation, he will have us to be like to him in his exaltation. What can be too high for man, when for him God was made man?[2] Well, believers, Christ being sent in flesh, what can now be too great for your faith? You have great and glorious things in your eye, but do not in the least question the accomplishment of them; all is made easy, credible, nay, certain, upon Christ's incarnation; that being done, all shall be done. This is the third thing for the comfort of God's people.

4. Fourthly, Was Christ sent in flesh? There is this in it for the strengthening of faith and the heightening of joy, that God is now knowable and accessible. It is beyond all contradiction, some may say, a blessed thing to know God; ay! but who can know him? can any see God and live? can a finite eye take a view of such an infinite majesty, the least ray of which outshines the sun in its greatest brightness? What! man to know God? alas! poor creature! his weak faculties will not bear the beholding of so glorious an object. To which I answer: All this, in such a sense, is very true, yet let not humble souls be discouraged; for this notwithstanding, they may yet know God savingly and comfortably, though not perfectly. In and by a Jesus in flesh the great God is knowable; partly as he by Christ, so considered, is most clearly manifested; in Christ God-man we have the brightest objective manifestation of God. The whole creation, though thereby much may be known of God, as you read,

Rom. i. 20, makes no such discoveries of him as Christ doth; therefore he is said, for this is one explication which the words will very well bear, to be 'the brightness of his Father's glory,' Heb. i. 3; and hence some style him *Speculum Patris*, the glass wherein the Father in the most clear and lively manner is represented: 'He that hath seen me hath seen the Father,' John xiv. 9; and the apostle speaks of 'the light of the knowledge of the glory of God in the face,' *i.e.*, in and by the manhood, 'of Jesus Christ,' 2 Cor. iv. 6. Partly too, as Christ in our flesh is a fit medium to transmit God as knowable to us; indeed God, as considered absolutely and in himself, is so infinitely above us, that we cannot here immediately behold him; so his glory, his immense and infinite perfections, should they be let out upon us, would soon reduce us to our first nothing. But he being considered in Christ, so mediately through Christ we can look upon him, see him and live; in this way the majesty of God is, as it were, so refracted, tempered, and qualified, that the poor dim eye of the creature may behold it. As we cannot immediately look upon the body of the sun, so its splendour and intense light presently dazzles us; yet we can look upon it in a pail of water; so here, we cannot immediately behold God in the brightness of his glory—a finite faculty must needs be dazzled by an infinite majesty—yet take him in the flesh and manhood of Christ, there his glory is so brought down to us that we can see him and know him to our comfort. Christ-man interposes not only between us and God's anger, to screen us from it, that we be not thereby consumed, but also between us and God's majesty, that we may not be overwhelmed by the infiniteness of it; he lets it out as our capacity will bear, and so by him God becomes knowable: he both carries us up to God, and also brings down God to us. Oh study God much! but then be sure you study him in Christ incarnate; in that way you may come to the knowledge of him. Augustine saith,[1] by the hypostatical union of the human nature with the divine, there is such a collyrium or eyesalve made for us, that we may with these very eyes almost see

---

[1] Est in ipso Jesu Christo unius cujusque nostrum portio, caro et sanguis. Ubi ergo portio mea regnat, ibi me regnare credo, ubi caro mea glorificatur, ibi gloriosum me esse cognosco, &c.—*Aug. Medit.*, cap. 15.

[2] Quid futurus est homo, propter quem Deus factus est homo?—*Prosper.*

[1] Per illam unionem hypostaticam, et assumptionem humanæ naturæ factum collyrium, per quod et oculis pene ipsis divinitas cerneretur.—*Aug. Tract.* iii. *in John.*

2 M

the Deity. How should we rejoice in the manhood of Christ! By that flesh in which the Godhead was sometimes hid it is now revealed; that which was once a veil to cover it, is now a glass to represent it. Do but know Christ, and you will know God.

I add, God is now accessible. Christians! Christ having taken your flesh, carried it up with him to heaven, sitting in it at the right hand of God, and therein interceding for you, through him you may now go to God, and that too with all holy boldness and confidence. You have not to do with a *Deus absolutus*, which Luther so much dreaded, but with God through a mediator; and, which may be a great encouragement to your faith, that mediator is 'the man Christ Jesus,' 1 Tim. ii. 5. You go to God, and you go by God, as clothed with your nature; it is *Deus qua itur, et Deus quo itur;* the God to whom you go commands your reverence, the God-man by whom you go encourages your confidence. Oh that you would more explicitly in duty revive upon your thoughts Christ's mediation and intercession in heaven in your nature! surely that would much embolden you in your addresses to God: Eph. iii. 12, 'In whom we have boldness and access with confidence by the faith of him.' Heb. iv. 14, 16, 'Seeing we have a great high priest, that is passed into the heavens, Jesus the Son of God, let us hold fast our profession. Let us come boldly unto the throne of grace, that we may obtain mercy, and find grace to help in time of need.' Heb. x. 19-22, 'Having therefore boldness to enter into the holiest by the blood of Jesus, by a new and living way, which he hath consecrated for us, through the veil, that is to say, his flesh; and having an high priest over the house of God; let us draw near with a true heart in full assurance of faith, having our hearts sprinkled from an evil conscience, and our bodies washed with pure water.' Had Joseph's brethren known that their own brother had been so near to Pharaoh, with what confidence would they have addressed themselves to him! Believers! Christ your brother, who is flesh of your flesh, is at God's right hand as the great master of requests, the great dispenser of mercies; why do you not more improve this for the emboldening of your spirits when in prayer you go to God?

It is a great thing for the saints' comfort to con-sider how things were formerly under the law, and how they are now under the gospel. Then God carried it in a way of greater state and majesty—then he kept a greater distance, and was more hardly accessible. See how the apostle sets it forth, Heb. ix. 1, &c., 'Then verily the first covenant had also ordinances of divine service, and a worldly sanctuary. For there was a tabernacle made; the first, wherein was the candlestick,' &c. 'And after the second veil, the tabernacle which is called the Holiest of all, which had the golden censer,' &c. Now when these things were thus ordained, the priests went always into the first tabernacle, accomplishing the service of God; but into the second went the high priest alone once every year, not without blood, which he offered for himself and for the errors of the people.' The apostle here takes notice of the partition or division of the tabernacle; for the *atrium*, or outer court, where the people used to be, that he speaks not of;[1] only he meddles with the first and second tabernacle, where the ordinary priests and the high priest did officiate. Now, he saith the first of these were to go no farther than the first tabernacle—the people might not go so far;—the high priest might go into the second tabernacle, the *Sanctum Sanctorum*. But how? With great restrictions. He must go alone, but 'once a year,'[2] and that too 'not without blood,' see Exod. xxx. 10; Lev. xvi.; and God was so strict about this, that it was as much as his life was worth, even for him at any other time to venture into the Holy of holies: Lev. xvi. 2, 'The Lord said unto Moses, Speak unto Aaron thy brother, that he come not at all times into the holy place within the veil, before the mercy-seat, which is upon the ark; *that he die not :* for I will appear in the cloud upon the mercy-seat.' Well, (not to instance in the re-

---

[1] Of this and of the whole tabernacle, see Joseph. Antiq. Jud., lib. iii. cap. 5.

[2] Augustine, whom Sigonius follows, differs in his interpretation of this : Quod autem scriptum est, Pontificem, semel in anno solum sancta esse ingressum, S. Augustinus interpretatur, eum quotidie quidem ingressum esse propter incensum, ac semel in anno propter expiationem cum sanguine purificationis. Verum possumus etiam dicere, eum quotidie quidem sanctuarium esse ingressum, sed sacerdotum comitatu stipatum, semel autem in anno solum, *i.e.,* sine sacerdotibus in die expiationum.—*Sigon. de Rep. Hebræ.,* lib. v. cap. 2. For this opinion he is severely taken up by *P. Cunæus de Rep. Heb.,* lib. i. cap. 4.

straints laid upon the priests, Levites, &c., which the word also mentions,) what might God's meaning be in this? See ver. 8, 'The Holy Ghost this signifying, that the way into the Holiest of all was not yet made manifest, while as the first tabernacle was yet standing.' As if the apostle had said, Let not any wonder that God then would keep men at such a distance; here was the reason of it, or the mystery which was at the bottom of it: Christ was not yet come—the true tabernacle was not as yet erected, the first tabernacle was only then standing. Christ had not assumed the nature of man, thereby to make way for man freely to go to God; therefore 'the way to the Holiest of all was not yet made manifest.' But now, under the gospel, Christ being incarnate and gone to heaven in our flesh, now all may go to God freely. The way to him is open; every believer in the world may now enter into the Holy of holies, all former restraints and distances are now taken away. Mark the scripture cited already, Heb. x. 19, 20, 'Having therefore, brethren, boldness to enter into the Holiest by the blood of Jesus, by a new and living way, which he hath consecrated for us, through the veil, that is to say, his flesh.' By this flesh, Christ's human nature, or Christ in the human nature, is unquestionably meant, which he calls the veil, in allusion to that in the tabernacle, wherein there was a twofold veil, one that covered the ark—Exod. xl. 3, 'And cover the ark with the veil;'—the other, which separated betwixt the *atrium* and the first tabernacle, as also betwixt the first tabernacle and the second—Exod. xxvi. 33, 'And the veil shall divide unto you between the holy place and the most holy.' So Heb. ix. 3, 'And after the second veil, the tabernacle which is called the Holiest of all:' to which also he alludes, Heb. vi. 19, 'which entereth into that which is within the veil.' Now with respect to these veils, Christ's flesh, or manhood, is set forth by the veil. (1.) As his Godhead for a time was hid and covered under it; (2.) As believers through this do go to God, as it is the way into the Holiest. And so it is here brought in, for he saith, 'by a new and living way, which he hath consecrated for us, through the veil, that is to say, his flesh.' You see what these texts drive at, and what the apostle draws from them, viz., that saints

now, upon the manhood of Christ, should with boldness enter into the Holiest, and draw near to God with full assurance of faith. This is their unspeakable privilege under the gospel, which they should improve and rejoice in. This is the fourth thing for comfort, God is now knowable and accessible.

5. Fifthy, This cannot but be exceedingly delightful to us, to consider the advancement and dignity of our nature. How is that nature advanced by Christ's assuming of it? That which was his abasement was its advancement. As a mean family is advanced when some person of eminency marries into it, so Christ having matched into our broken and decayed nature, what an honour did he thereby reflect upon it! God put a great deal of glory upon it in its first creation; Christ hath put much more glory upon it in the hypostatical union. The angelical nature, in some respects, is above ours, but in others ours is above it. The angels are not so concerned in the mystical conjunction to Christ as we are; their advantages by a Saviour are not so high as ours—they are confirmed by Christ in a state of happiness, and that is all; but we are confirmed and restored too. The great things which are done by Christ as mediator he doth them in our nature, and the great honour which is conferred upon him refers to him in our nature. It is the Son of man who 'stands on the right hand of God,' Acts vii. 56. 'Dominion, and glory, and the kingdom is given to the Son of man,' Dan. vii. 13, 14. He will judge the world as the Son of man, Mat. xxv. 31; John v. 27. But the main pre-eminence of the human nature above the angelical lies in the intimate uniting of it to the divine nature: Heb. ii. 16, 'Verily he took not on him the nature of angels, but he took on him the seed of Abraham.' Man was the creature that was to be redeemed, and therefore it was the nature of man that shall be assumed. Can we think of this without great joy? Christ himself as man is above us—'in all things he must have the pre-eminence,' Col. i. 18; but angels, who are of an other order, in several respects are below us.

6. A Christ incarnate is, and must needs be, very compassionate. This was one great reason why he took our nature upon him, and in that nature was exercised with such sorrows and sufferings, that he might the better know how to sympathise with his

members in all their sorrows and sufferings : Heb.
ii. 17, 18, 'In all things it behoved him to be made
like unto his brethren, that he might be a merciful
and faithful high priest, in things pertaining to
God, to make reconciliation for the sins of the
people. For in that he himself hath suffered being
tempted, he is able to succour them that are tempted.'
Heb. iv. 15, 'We have not an high priest which
cannot be touched with the feeling of our infirmities,
but was in all points tempted like as we are, yet
without sin.' He that hath felt what others undergo,
knows the better how to pity them ; sense and experience further compassion, where persons are not
made of flint ; none sympathise so much with those
who labour under gout, stone, &c., as those who have
been afflicted with those pains themselves. God
told the people of Israel, 'they knew the heart of a
stranger, seeing they themselves were strangers in
the land of Egypt,' Exod. xxiii. 9. How then must
the bowels of Christ work towards afflicted ones, he
himself having been afflicted just as they are. Besides the mercifulness and tenderness of his heart,
there is also his own former experience, which is
yet fresh in his memory, of their miseries, which
doth much draw out his compassion to them. Pray
what are your afflictions ? Let them be what they
will, Christ underwent the same. Are you poor ?
so was he. Are you tempted ? so was he. Are you
deserted ? so was he. Are you burdened under the
weight of sin ? so was he, though in a different way.
Do you suffer by men ? so did he. And if there be
any infirmities which he did not lie under, yet he
knows how to pity you ; for though he did not feel
those particular infirmities in kind, such as sickness,
blindness, &c., yet he had some others which were
equivalent to them, and so by proportion he knows
how to commiserate you ; so it comes in, Heb. v. 2,
'Who can have compassion on the ignorant, and on
them that are out of the way, for that he himself
also is compassed with infirmity.' It is some alle-
viation to our grief in our troubles when we know
we have some who sympathise with us under them.
O you that fear the Lord, know, in all your sorrows,
sufferings, troubles whatsoever, Christ in heaven
hath a fellow-feeling and sympathy with you ; he
suffers no more, but he sympathises still. Let this
be an allay to your grief, and a support to your faith.

7. Lastly, There is something in this which may
give ease and relief under all troubles of mind.
There is such a fulness in this truth for the comfort
of souls, that there is scarce any inward trouble or
discouragement which gracious persons here are exercised with, wherein they may not find considerable relief and satisfaction for conscience from this
incarnation of the Son of God. Christ's flesh is
precious balm for a wounded spirit, as it is meat
indeed to feed the hungry soul, so it is balm indeed
to heal the wounded soul ; it is a universal, catholic
cordial to revive and cheer under all faintings whatever. Do I speak to any who are under spiritual
darkness ? Oh that a Christ in flesh might be thought
of and improved by such !

To instance in the special fears, complaints, discouragements, burdens of troubled souls, and to
shew what there is in Christ as incarnate proper
for their support and comfort under all, would be
a vast work ; I must therefore only hint a few things.

Are you tempted to entertain hard thoughts of
God, to question on the mercifulness of his nature,
his goodness, &c. ? Do you conceive of him in some
hideous and frightful manner ? You greatly mistake
God, and think very much amiss of him. First
think of God in Christ, and then of Christ in flesh,
and surely you will have other apprehensions. A
Christ sent in flesh represents God as benign, good,
merciful, gracious, full of pity, tender-hearted, as
designing nothing but good to repenting sinners.
Did he thus send his own Son, and is he not all
this ? After he hath done such a thing, can you
imagine that he delights in the death of sinners, or
that he will not be gracious to all who fly to him ?

Are you afraid because of the justice and wrath
of God ? Pray remember therefore, Christ came in
flesh that he might satisfy the one and pacify the
other ; these were the very things which he undertook to accomplish ; and what he undertook, no question but he went through with.

Doth sin lie heavy upon your consciences ? Mark
the text, 'God sent his own Son in the likeness of
sinful flesh ;' for what end ? 'for sin to condemn sin
in the flesh ;' sin brought Christ from heaven, and
he would not return thither again till by a sacrifice offered in his flesh he had fully expiated it. Sin
itself could not stand before him as in our flesh

dying and suffering for it. If God will become man, the guilt of mere man shall not be so able to damn as the merit of God-man to save. O thou true penitent, be thy sins never so many, never so great, yet do not give way to despairing thoughts! Bring out thy sins, saith one,[1] weigh them to the utmost aggravation of them, and set but this in the other scale, God manifested in the flesh to take away sin, now will all thine iniquities seem lighter than vanity, yea, be as nothing in comparison of that which is laid down as a propitiation for them. And again, saith he, what temptation will not vanish as a cloud before the wind, when we see God's love in sending his Son, and Christ's love in taking our nature upon him, to reconcile us by the sacrifice of his blood?

But some may object, it is a great while since Christ took flesh, and in that flesh made satisfaction to God, is not the efficacy and merit thereof impaired by that? No, not in the least. Christ's merits are as fresh, and have as great an efficacy now, as they had at the first moment of his incarnation and passion. May not that of the apostle, Heb. ii. 16, have some reference to this, where he speaks of Christ's *taking* flesh in the present tense, as if it was done but now? for it is ἐπιλαμβάνεται, 'he *taketh* not on him the nature of angels, but he *taketh* on him the seed of Abraham.' I speak this for the comfort of Christians, but not so as to give advantage to the Socinian, who because the words run in this tense would therefore have them to be no proof of Christ's incarnation.

Do your many defects, the imperfections in your graces and duties, trouble you? you have Christ's perfect manhood, his perfect holiness and obedience in that nature to fly unto. The apostle, Col. ii., sets down the hypostatical union, ver. 9, 'In him dwelleth all the fulness of the Godhead bodily.' Well, suppose it doth so, what is this to believers? Why, it follows immediately, ver. 10, 'And ye are complete in him.' Christ being such a person, so full and perfect a mediator, in him every believer is and must be complete. So that though the sense of imperfections in yourselves must humble you, yet it must not overwhelm you, because in Christ you are perfect.

Are you afraid, notwithstanding all the calls, invitations, promises of the gospel, yet to close with

[1] Dr Sibbs on 1 Tim. iii. 16, p. 59.

Christ? Oh do not give way to such fears! If you come to him, cast yourselves upon him, will he cast you off? He hath assured you he will not: John vi. 37, 'Him that cometh to me I will in no wise cast off.' Besides his word you have this to secure you; he in his person came from heaven to you, and if you by faith shall go to him, do you think he will not give you kind reception? I am sure, and I will venture my soul upon it, that the gracious promises and encouragements of the gospel to draw sinners to Christ shall all be made good; for since he was pleased to take my flesh, I have not the least reason to doubt, but fully to be assured, that he is real, hearty, in good earnest in all of them. Many things of this nature might here be spoken unto, but it is full time to put an end to this subject.

CHAPTER XIII.

OF CHRIST'S BEING A SACRIFICE, AND EXPIATING SIN THEREBY.

And for sin condemned sin in the flesh; that the righteousness of the law might be fulfilled in us.—ROM. viii. 3, 4.

A fifth head in the words discussed, viz., the end of God in sending his own Son, or the effect thereof—How the wisdom of God is secured by this end—Of the placing of the words for sin—*The whole a little descanted upon—What the condemning of sin is, opened more generally, more particularly in three things—The condemning of sin* for sin *opened: a twofold interpretation given of it—Of the flesh in which sin is said to be condemned—The observation raised from the words: where, 1. Of Christ's being a sacrifice for sin—How he excels the old law sacrifices, and of their reference to him—Six things in those sacrifices which are all to be found in Christ, the true sacrifice. It is inquired, (1.) What kind of a sacrifice he was?—Proved that he was an expiatory sacrifice—Of the difference and distinction of the Jewish sacrifices—Four heads insisted upon for the confirming of the main truth: as, (1.) That our sins were the meritorious cause of Christ's sufferings; (2.) That he did substitute himself in the sinner's stead; where two questions are briefly answered, [1.] Whether he underwent the same punishment that was due to the sinner, or only that which was equivalent thereunto? [2.] Whether he took the guilt of sin upon himself, or only submitted to the punishment thereof? (3.) That he was killed and slain, and his blood shed, in correspondency with the Levitical expiatory sacrifices; (4.) This is proved from the ends and effects of his death, viz., atonement and expiation, both of which are opened— Of the concurrence of the heathens in their notions about sacrifices—It is inquired, (2.) When and where Christ was an expiatory sacrifice?—It is answered, when he died upon the cross. 2. Of the effect of his sacrifice, the condemning of sin—Parallel expressions cited—Of the nature of the expiation of sin—Of the extent of it with respect to the subject and object— Whether were all sins expiated by the law sacrifices? —Use 1. I infer from the premises, (1.) The verity of Christ's satisfaction; (2.) The true nature and principal ends of his death; (3.) The vanity and falsehood of all human satisfactions; (4.) The true notion of the Lord's supper; (5.) The happiness of believers under the gospel above theirs who lived under the law; (6.) The excellency of Christ's priesthood and sacrifice; (7.) The evil of sin; (8.) The severity of God's justice—Use 2. Several duties urged from hence: as holiness, the love of Christ, &c.—Use 3. This improved several ways for the comfort of believers.*

IN the preceding words, *God sending his own Son in the likeness of sinful flesh,* four things have been observed and opened. In these now read a fifth head offers itself to our consideration; and that is the effect of Christ's mission, incarnation, and of what followed thereupon, or God's end in all this. Did he pitch upon so admirable a way and method? Surely some high and glorious effect must be produced thereby. And so there was; for thereby sin was condemned. And surely, too, therein the wise God must propound to himself some great and very considerable end to be accomplished; and so he did; for he aimed at nothing lower than that the righteousness of the law might be fulfilled in believers.

In the words, then, we have both the effect, what God did by his own Son as first assuming and then

suffering in flesh; and also the end of God in his taking this strange and wonderful course; for these two, though they be distinct in themselves, and carry in them notions somewhat different, yet here in this place they both are alike applicable to the matter spoken of, and it to them. If it be considered with respect to God's intention, so it falls under the nature of an end; if with respect to his execution of what he intended, so it falls under the nature of an effect; therefore upon the oneness and coalition of these two, and the equal applicableness of the matter to each; whereas there are two branches in the text, each of which contains distinct matter in it—in the former the thing is expressed under the notion of an effect, ' and for sin, condemned sin in the flesh;' in the latter under the notion of an end, 'that the righteousness of the law might be fulfilled in us.'

It pleasing God to send his own Son, &c. His wisdom would have been liable to impeachment, if (1.) he had not effected some great thing thereby; if, (2.) which indeed should have been first mentioned, he had not designed some great thing therein. For the wisdom of an agent lies not only in his having an end in what he doth, but in his having such an end as shall be proportionable to the means which he pitches upon. If they be high, and the end but low, this speaks a defect in point of wisdom; for that ever shews itself, as in the fitting of the means to the end, so in the proportioning of the end to the means. If, therefore, the blessed God will single out such a medium as the sending of his own Son, &c., he then stands engaged, upon the account of his wisdom, to propound to himself such an end as may be answerable to that medium; which, therefore, accordingly he did, inasmuch as in that great act he had this great end or ends, the satisfying of his justice, the expiating of sin, the fulfilling of the law, &c., these were ends worthy of such means as the coming, incarnation, death of his own Son. Now all these are set down in the words before us, in which therefore you have that which is a full vindication, nay, the highest manifestation, of God's infinite wisdom.

I begin with the first effect or end here specified, 'And for sin, condemned sin in the flesh.' At my first entrance upon the whole paragraph I touched upon the reading of this clause, there being some difference amongst expositors about it ; therefore that I will not again insist upon ; only let me take notice of another difference among them which was not there mentioned. That refers to the placing of the words ; for whereas we take in *for sin* into this branch, some would have it placed in the former, thus : ' God sending for sin his own Son, in the likeness of sinful flesh, condemned sin in the flesh.'[1] But though this ranking of them may possibly seem to some to make the words run more smoothly, yet if it be admitted of, the conjunctive particle *and* must be quite expunged, which I should be loath to submit unto, because of its special significancy and emphasis in this place ; partly as it heightens the thing spoken of, and intimates the wonderfulness of the way in which it was brought about, and partly as it notes the joining together of that here mentioned with that which went before.[2] God did not only send his own Son in our flesh, but (which is to be superadded to that as an effect or consequent thereof) he also in that flesh for sin condemned sin. I will therefore keep to our methodising of the words, and if you take them as here they lie, there will be no necessity either of putting in or putting out. Yet if you will go by their sense, then you may read them with this addition, And by a sacrifice for sin, condemned sin in the flesh.

And for sin, condemned sin in the flesh. Good and blessed words ! No condemnation to them who are in Christ, ver. 1. Sin itself condemned, ver. 3. What could be spoken higher to raise the thankfulness, encourage the faith, heighten the joy of sincere Christians ! The word *condemned* is not so terrible when applied to the sinner, but it is as comfortable when applied to sin itself. That which had been the condemning is now the condemned thing ; how may a gracious soul rejoice at this ! The non-condemnation of persons spoken of in the first verse, is secured by and grounded upon the condemnation of sin in this, for both must not be condemned ; if sin be condemned, the sinner shall not. Observe here, sin

---

[1] Περὶ ἁμαρτίας pertinet ad participium πέμψας.—*Beza.* Omnino referendum puto περὶ ἁμαρτίας ad participium πέμψας.—*Justin.* So Cyril. reads them in John, lib. ix. cap. 47.

[2] Appositam siquidem intelligimus conjunctionem, ad significandam sequelam alterius beneficii ; ut scil. notemus, Deum non tantum misisse Filium suum in similitudine carnis peccati, sed et de peccato damnasse peccatum in carne.—*Cajetan.*

was the thing which God fell upon and dealt thus severely with. The apostle had told us ' the law was weak,' unable to help poor fallen man, whereupon he saith, ' God sent his own Son ;' but wherefore did he so do ? Was it that he might fall upon this law, and condemn the condemning law ? Oh no ! It was so far from that, that he would rather have it fulfilled, for so it follows, ver. 4. He had no evil eye at all upon his law, for that was good ; upon what then ? Why, upon sin, for that was evil, and very evil. Christ was sent that sin only might be condemned. And no wonder that God was so set against it, and resolved upon this severe process against it, it being the principal offender, the archtraitor and rebel against himself, the only object of his hatred, the bold opposer of his glory, the great obstructor of his grace, the cursed fomenter of breaches betwixt himself and his creatures, the murderer of souls, &c. Did not such a malefactor highly deserve to be condemned ? Yes, surely, and therefore so it shall be. Oh, saith God, I must take a course with this sin ; I must and will despatch it out of the way, and then my work is done. All my gracious designs will then be carried on without any let or impediment ; then the happiness of my people will be sure and full ; neither my own wrath, nor the curse of my law, nor the sting of death shall then be able to hurt them. Upon such grounds as these God would have sin condemned, and he was so set upon it, that in order thereunto he will on purpose ' send his own Son in the likeness of sinful flesh ;' yea, in that flesh to offer up himself as a sacrifice, and so to bring about sin's condemnation.

But to come to the close handling of the words. They being somewhat obscure, my first work must be to open them, that I may the better make way for the main observation which they resolve themselves into. There are three things in them to be explained.

1. The *condemning of sin.*
2. The condemning of sin *for sin.*
3. The condemning of sin *in the flesh.*

1. What doth the apostle mean by the condemning of sin ? ' And for sin *condemned sin,*' &c. The word in its usual acceptation is applied to persons rather than to things ; yet in such a sense it is properly enough applicable to them also, viz., as it sig-

nifies the disallowing, disapproving, sentencing, or judging of them to be so and so evil; according to which signification, sin may as truly be said to be condemned as the sinner himself in any other notion. But this will not reach the full scope and emphasis of the word in this place; for unquestionably there is a great deal more intended in God's condemning sin, than barely his sentencing or judging it to be a very evil thing; though Christ had never come in flesh, nor suffered in flesh, yet God would thus have condemned sin. Its condemnation is here brought in as a singular effect of the grace of God to sinners, but, according to this stating of it, it would only be an effect of his holiness, not at all of his grace; he may thus judge of sin, and yet the sinner perish by it. It is very true that God, in the death of his Son, did in this respect signally condemn sin. Oh, in that he made it to appear what thoughts he had of sin, what an evil thing he judged it to be, how he was set against it, &c.; but yet this is not the only thing, no, nor the main thing, held forth in this expression of God's condemning sin.

Well! for the right understanding of that, I conceive we must borrow our light from condemnation amongst men; for though sin be not a person, yet its being condemned will best be known by what is proper to condemned persons. Amongst us malefactors are seized upon, brought to trial, arraigned, proved guilty, sentenced to die, if their offence be capital; then the sentence is executed upon them, to cut them off, that they may do no more mischief; and this is their being condemned. Just so, so far as the nature of the thing would admit of, virtually and analogically all this was done by God in Christ's death against sin. It had been a heinous malefactor, guilty of high and notorious crimes, had done inexpressible mischiefs, for all which God will arraign, judge, sentence, cut it off, that it also may do no more mischief to his people; and this is its condemnation. Divers expositors, in their opening of the words, conceive of sin here as a person, and accordingly they open its being condemned by this allusive and analogical notion. Whatever is commonly done amongst men in their judicial processes against great offenders, all that, in effect, was done by God through Christ's death against sin; and so he condemned it.

But not to take up with generals, this may be more particularly opened in three things:

(1.) God by Christ condemned sin as he abolished its power. Sin's condemnation is its abolition; wherein doth that lie?[1] Why, partly in the taking away of its power, in the divesting it of that rule and command which it had over sinners for a long time: thus God condemned or abolished sin, he put an end to its reign and dominion, pulled it off from the throne, turned it out of office and authority, yea, adjudged it to die for all the evils of which it had been guilty. Thus it is with condemned men; upon the passing of the condemnatory sentence upon them they are *ipso facto* dispossessed of all their power and authority, and further than this too they must suffer the penalty of death for what they have done; so answerably it was with sin in God's dealings with it. It had acted the tyrant's part in and over the world a great while, had domineered and lorded it over its poor subjects at a strange rate, did with men what it pleased. Oh, but in the flesh of Christ God condemned it; that is, he broke it in its power, brought it down to some purpose, stripped it of that absolute, illimited dominion which it had before: Christ's cross was the ruin of sin's throne. And not only so, but there is a sentence of death too passed upon it; it shall not only lose its power, but its life also; God will have it killed, slain, put to death in all who have an interest in Christ's merits; he would not suffer such a malefactor to live, he will rid the world of it. This condemnatory sentence was passed upon it long ago, which though it be but gradually and in part executed whilst the saints are here below, yet when they shall once ascend to God then it shall be fully executed; insomuch that then sin shall quite be taken out of the way, and shall not have so much as a being in them in the glorified state. Thus many interpreters do open the condemning of sin;[2] and Socinus likes this interpreta-

[1] Secundum phrasin Hebraicam positum est *damnuvit* pro abolevit, extinxit, sustulit Deus.—*Perer.*

[2] Τὴν δύναμιν αὐτῆς ἐξέλυσε.—*Chrys.* Damnavit peccatum, *i.e.*, dominio suo mulctavit ne regnaret in carne.—*Staplet.* Ut ejus dominium et robur auferret.—*Tolet.* Damnavit, interfecit; κατακρίνειν est interficere sicut κατάκριμα pro morte, quia damnati interfici solent. Interfecit vero, *i.e.*, interficiendi vires nobis præstitit. Interficere est efficientiam adimere.—*Grot.* See Melanch., Bucer., P. Mart., De Dieu, Deodat.

tion so well that he contends for it, but fiercely opposes those which follow.[1]

(2.) Sin's condemnation lies in the abolition or expiation of its guilt. It here properly notes the taking away of that which was the hurtful, destructive, mischievous part of sin. Condemned men can do no hurt; let them be never so hurtful before, yet when once the sentence of condemnation is passed upon them they can be so no longer. Sin had been a very hurtful thing, and would have been so still, to precious souls, but God in the flesh of his Son, as suffering and satisfying, put a stop to it, took it out of the way, condemned it, that is, disabled it from doing the hurt it had done before, and removed that in it which was of so hurtful a nature. What was that? I answer, its guilt. Oh that is a hurtful thing indeed! it binds the sinner over to answer at God's tribunal for all the evils committed by him, exposes him to the wrath of the great God, renders him liable to a sentence of eternal death; but now it pleased God for sin to condemn sin, i.e., by Christ's being a sacrifice to expiate this guilt of sin, which in itself was so pernicious and hurtful, so that believers should not lie under it or eternally suffer for it. Now this is that explication of the word which is most commonly given by the best expositors, and I prefer it before the former upon these reasons:[2]

[1.] As to the abolishing of sin's power, that the apostle had spoken to already in the foregoing verse, 'the law of the Spirit,' &c., and he instances in the Spirit there as he doth in the Son here. Now, according to what was said before, as it is the proper act of the Spirit to free from sin's power, therefore that must be understood there; so it is the proper act of the Son to free from sin's guilt, therefore that must be understood here.

[2.] The word here used, κατέκρινε, all along in Scripture points to the guilt of sin and the punishment inflicted thereupon, never to its power or

dominion; for the proof of which several texts might be cited if it was denied. It is usually applied to the sinner; here only, if I well remember, it is applied to sin itself; and in this different application it carries a different sense: for as it is elsewhere applied to the sinner, it notes the imputation of guilt to him, and the passing of a condemnatory sentence upon him for that guilt; and as it is here applied to sin, it notes the expiation or abolition of its guilt; yet this doth not weaken what I have said, because in both references, though in a different sense, it still points to guilt and punishment, which is enough for my purpose.

[3.] The apostle speaks of that abolition of sin which was effected in Christ's flesh; therefore it must be understood of the abolition of its guilt rather than of its power, that being the thing which was most directly and immediately done in Christ's flesh.

[4.] It is that condemning sin which is for sin, i.e., by a sacrifice for sin; wherefore it must be taken in that sense which best suits with what was done in and by sacrifices. Now they abolished sin not so much by turning men from it, or by lessening its power, though that might follow as a consequent upon them, as by the expiating of its guilt;[1] this was the proper and primary effect of the Levitical sacrifices, in allusion to which when Christ, the true sacrifice, is said to purge away sin, to purify, &c., you are to understand those expressions as respecting the expiation of sin's guilt, as I shall have occasion further to prove in what will follow. For these reasons, though I would not exclude wholly the former sense, yet I prefer this before it.

(3.) There is a third interpretation put upon the word;[2] namely, God's condemning sin was his punishing of it in Christ's person, or his exacting of Christ that punishment which was due to the sinner himself. For this condemning must be joined with that which follows, in the flesh, and expounded by that; and then the meaning will be this, 'For

---

[1] Who renders it by exauctoravit, extinxit, abolevit, &c. De Servat., part ii. cap. 23.

[2] Damnatio peccati nos in justitiam asseruit, quia deleto reatu absolvimur, uti nos Deus justos reputet.—*Calvin*, with many others. Beza dissents, Non mihi facile persuaserim de peccatorum expiatione hic agi, est enim pars illa jam pridem ab apostolo explicata, adeo ut a ver. 12, cap. 5, aliud argumentum sit exorsus.

[1] This proved in Essenius de Satisf. Christi, cap. 8, p. 422; Turretin. de Sat., &c., part vi. p. 202; Dr Owen against Biddle, p. 574.

[2] See Pareus *in loc*, and in Dub. iii. p. 779. Condemnare perpetuo significat apostolo poenas peccati irrogare. Damnare peccatum est illud dignum poena judicare, poenasque pro eo exigere.—*Contzen*, his sense of the word justified by Calov. Socin. profl., p. 433.

sin God condemned sin in the flesh;' that is, he fell
upon sin, severely punished it, inflicted the curse and
punishment due to us for it in and upon the person
of his own Son; he 'laid the iniquities' of believers
upon Christ, Isa. liii. 6, and then punished them in
him, so that he bore that penalty which sinners themselves should have undergone. God did of him in
our nature *pœnas peccato debitas exigere*, or *maledictionem nobis debitam irrogare*. Man having sinned,
either he himself or his surety must suffer the
punishment thereby deserved; God will have sin
punished somewhere; therefore Christ having put
himself into the sinner's stead, he must bear the
punishment due to the sinner; for though God will
so far relax his law as to admit of a substitution or
commutation as to the person suffering, yet he will
have its penalty inflicted either upon the proper
offender himself, or upon the Saviour, who was willing to interpose for the offender, so as to suffer
what he should have suffered :[1] and God accordingly dealing with him and proceeding against him
in the laying of the punishment due for sin upon
him, this was his condemning sin in the flesh of
Christ. I am not now to prove the truth of the
thing—of that hereafter; at present I am only shewing how it is held forth in the word which I am
opening. So much for the first thing, what this condemning of sin is.

2. The second thing that needs explanation is the
condemning sin *for sin*; what may our apostle mean
by this for sin?

Augustine gives a threefold sense of it :[2] (1.) For
sin, that is, by that flesh which looked like to sinful
flesh; which therefore might be called sin, since, as
he saith, the resemblances of things do usually pass
under the names of the things which they resemble:
by that flesh sin was condemned. (2.) For sin he
makes to be as much as by a sacrifice for sin. (3.) He
expounds it of the sin of the Jews, not as heightening it, in which sense all the Greek expositors take
it, but as pointing to the effect of it; by that sin of
theirs in crucifying Christ eventually sin was condemned or expiated. But these things must be
further inquired into.

[1] See of God's relaxing his law and the threatening thereof,
Mr Baxter Aphor., p. 36, &c.; Mr Burgesse of Justif., p. 84.
[2] Contra duas Pelagian. Ep., lib. iii. cap. 6.

It is in our translation exactly as it is in the original—equally concise in both; and as the one is to
be filled up, so is the other also. The preposition
περί signifying *of* or *for*, accordingly it is rendered
both ways; some reading it *of sin*, as the old version, Anselm, the Greek interpreters generally, &c.,
they making the words to run thus: ' Of sin God
condemned sin.' Parallel to which περί ἁμαρτίας is
elsewhere so rendered; as John viii. 46, ' Which of
you convinceth me of sin?' John xvi. 8, 9, ' He
will convince the world of sin, &c. Of sin, because
they believe not on me.' In all it is περί ἁμαρτίας,
just as it is in the text. They who follow this reading make the sense of the words to be this: God
sending his own Son in the likeness of sinful flesh,
in that flesh of his Son, as suffering and dying, he
condemned sin of sin, inasmuch as by that strange
and wonderful course he made it to appear to the
world that sin was full of sin, highly guilty and criminal, ' exceeding sinful,' as the apostle speaks upon
another account, Rom. vii. 13.

Now though I shall not follow this exposition, yet
it containing nothing in it but what is true for the
matter of it, and it being given by some authors of
great repute, I will so far insist upon it as to give a
double illustration of it.

(1.) As it is applicable to sin in the general. Take
the whole body of sin, or sin in its utmost extent,
it was all condemned of sin in Christ's flesh, as first
assumed and then crucified. How? Why, by that
it was proved and judged to be a thing out of measure evil and faulty, thereby God let the world see
what sin is, what an excess of poison and malignity
there is in its nature. Did he send his own Son to
be incarnate; yea, to appear in the likeness of sinful flesh—so to be abased, suffer, and die? and was
sin the meritorious cause of all this? Was all this
done and suffered for the making of satisfaction for
the mischiefs and injuries which sin had been guilty
of? Oh what a condemnation was here of sin!
Never was there such a demonstration of sin's evil,
—what a heinous and capital offender it is,—as in
Christ's being made man and dying upon the cross.
The strangeness of the remedy shews the malignity
of the disease; the high terms of satisfaction the
greatness of the crime; God's severity laid upon the
flesh of his own Son in such unparalleled sufferings,

made it apparent to the world that sin is a quite other thing than what men generally take it to be. Had it not been evil, desperately evil, God had never dealt with Christ as he did, therefore in his flesh sin was condemned of sin.

(2.) This may more particularly be applied to that sin of killing and murdering the Lord Jesus. God did not only condemn sin of sin in the gross, but in special that sin which was committed against and upon the flesh of Christ in the crucifixion of him. Here it was the sin of sin ; here sin was sinful indeed. That it should so boldly, so injuriously, so wickedly fasten upon a person so near and dear to God, so inoffensive and innocent, so holy and gracious, what an aggregation of sins, and what an aggravation of sin's guilt was there in this ! Sin never was more sin than in this act ; here it was in its highest stature and fullest dimensions ; this was its masterpiece, the vilest thing that ever it did ; all its other crimes were but dwarfish things in comparison of this gigantic and overgrown crime. Well, according to its acting and carriage herein, so God judged it to be very guilty and sinful, and accordingly passed sentence upon it. And as to those that had a hand in this horrid fact, whether Satan, to whom some apply the words,[1] or the Jews, oh it was in all sin, full of sin ! Their offence was superlatively great in doing what they did to the flesh of God's own Son : sin in this act did rise exceeding high. Now the Greek expositors are very large upon this notion :[2] ‘ Of sin God condemned sin,’ &c. ; that is, say they, God judged the sin of the Jews according to what it was in its own nature, to be very great ;[3] it, or rather they, were guilty of a most unparalleled offence, high injustice, prodigious cruelty, inexpressible ingratitude, strange impudency, upon their crucifying of the holy Jesus, the Lord of glory.[4] And in the pursuance of this explication, these

expositors bring in sin as a person—as a person arraigned by God for this particular crime—after trial and process sentenced to be highly guilty, and accordingly to be dealt with. And they also insist upon God's way and method in his dealing with sin, which was not in the way of power, but of justice ; he did not downright subdue it by plain force, but he condemned it after the hearing of that plea it could make for itself : as also upon God's order, first he condemned it, and then he punished it.[1]

This interpretation some later writers do fall in with, and much applaud.[2] Bucer himself at first was taken with it, but afterwards he altered his thoughts. Beza passes a severe censure upon it.[3] The truth is, the apostle in the words seems to look at another thing ; this was not the condemnation of sin which he had mainly in his eye, viz., the heightening, or aggravating, or proving of its guilt, and then passing sentence upon it according to that ; no, but there was another condemnation which he drove at, viz., the abolition and expiation of its guilt. God so condemned sin as that it might never condemn the sinner. That is the apostle's proper and principal scope, as I humbly conceive. Augustine, though he reads it, too, *de peccato condemnavit*, &c.,[4] yet he opens it in a different sense, he making this *of sin* to be as much as *by sin ;* and so he thus glosses upon it : By the sin of the Jews, in their putting of Christ to death, God abolished and took out of the way all the sin of all the elect. He so overruled the matter that even by sin sin was destroyed. By the greatest sin that ever was committed, sin itself was condemned. Had not the blood of Christ been spilt, though that in itself was a most wicked act, there had been to believers no remission, no expiation. As death was destroyed by death, so sin by sin ; it condemned Christ, but by so doing it was condemned itself. So much for the first reading of the words.

---

[1] Damnavit peccatum, *i.e.*, Satanam de peccato, quod nempe Christum innocentem in cruce interfeciset.—*Ambros.* So also *Hilarius in Ps.* lxvii.

[2] *Vide* Chrysost. *in loc.* (very largely insisting upon this.)

[3] —, τὰ μέγιστα πτↄιουσαν καὶ ἁμαρτάνουσαν. τοῦτο δηλↄ̂ι τὸ καὶ περὶ ἁμαρτίας, δείξας ἀναιδῶς ἁμαρτάνουσαν τὴν ἁμαρτίαν.—*Œcum.*

[4] τὸν τῶν ἁμαρτωλῶν ὡς ἁμαρτωλὸς θάνατον ὑπομείνας ἤλεγξε τῆς ἁμαρτίας τὴν ἀδικίαν, ὅτι καὶ μὴ ὑποκείμενον θανάτῳ σῶμα θανάτῳ παρέδωκεν.—*Theodoret.*

[1] Μέγα ἡμαρτηκεῖαν ἤλεγξε καὶ τοτὲ αὐτὴν κατεδίκασεν.—*Chrysost.*

[2] Hæc Chrysostomi expositio convenientissima et inter omnes accommodatissima videtur.—*Tolet.* Hæc Græcorum expositio ita placet ut eam cæteris anteponendam cum Toleto censeam.—*Estius.* Vide *Alap. Catharin.*, &c.

[3] Hæc expositio nihil aliud est quam subtilis argutia.—*Beza.*

[4] *In loco prius citato.*

2. Secondly, The preposition is rendered by *for*, and that rendering of it our translators, according to other versions and the general current of interpreters, follow ; 'and for sin condemned sin,' &c.[1] If we take it so, the words then may carry a threefold sense in them.

(1.) That sin was the procuring, meritorious cause of all that which God the Father did in a way of severity upon and against Christ. He condemned sin in Christ's flesh, fell very severely upon him, testified great anger and displeasure against him, inflicted sharp and dreadful punishments upon him. Why did such a Father so deal with such a Son ? What might be the cause that a person so innocent should suffer as he did ? Why, it was sin, not his, but ours, which brought all this upon him. Had it not been for that God had never sent his Son in flesh into the world, and then have punished him in that flesh as he did. Christ might thank sin for all his sufferings, and lay all the evils which he sustained in soul and body at its doors ; that set his Father against him, that laid the foundation of all his sorrows, that brewed that bitter cup which he was to drink ; that was the meritorious cause of all the miseries that ever befell him. It was for sin that God so condemned sin in his flesh. The preposition $\pi\epsilon\rho\iota$ is sometimes used in this sense : so John x. 33, 'For a good work we stone thee not, but ($\pi\epsilon\rho\iota$ $\beta\lambda\alpha\sigma\phi\eta\mu\iota\alpha\varsigma$) for blasphemy, and because that thou being a man makest thyself equal with God.' 1 Peter iii. 18, 'For Christ also hath once suffered ($\pi\epsilon\rho\iota$ $\dot\alpha\mu\alpha\rho\tau\iota\tilde\omega\nu$) for sins,' &c., which is as much as $\dot\upsilon\pi\dot\epsilon\rho$ $\dot\alpha\mu\alpha\rho\tau\iota\tilde\omega\nu$; Gal. i. 4 ; Heb. x. 12.

(2.) The *for sin* may be taken finally. Wherefore did God thus condemn sin in his Son's flesh? Wherefore was it with Christ as it was ? Oh, it was for sin! namely, that he might take it away, acquit the sinner from its guilt, make satisfaction for it, overrule it in all its pleas and power, quite destroy it. God would deal with sin in the person of his own Son, he having submitted to take the guilt of it upon himself, that thereby he might give a thorough despatch to it, and thoroughly rid believers of its hurtfulness : 1 John iii. 5, 'And ye know that he was manifested to take away our sins ; and in him is

no sin.' Ver. 8, ',For this purpose the Son of God was manifested, that he might destroy the works of the devil.' In this final notion $\pi\epsilon\rho\iota$ is taken Mat. xxvi. 28 ; 1 Cor. xv. 3.

(3.) It may be understood materially, with respect to Christ's being a sacrifice for sin. For sin God condemned sin. How? Why, as Christ submitting to be a sin-offering, was and did that by which this effect was produced. According to this interpretation we must read the words, as is noted in the margin, thus :[1] 'By a sacrifice for sin God condemned sin.' Whatever there is in this condemning of sin, and there is abundance in it, it was all brought about by that sin-offering or sacrifice which Christ in his flesh offered up to God. It was cut off, expiated, disabled as to its destructive and damning nature, &c. All this was effected by Christ's being a sacrifice. So that the words are elliptical, there being in them something cut off and left out, which must be supplied by the inserting or adding of *by a sacrifice*, or some other such word. Which ellipsis is very usual and common in holy writ, especially when it is treating of sacrifices. Lev. x. 17, 'Wherefore have ye not eaten the sin-offering?' So we read it, but in the Hebrew it is only 'the sin,' 'in the holy place,' &c. It would be tedious to cite the very many places of this nature which do occur in that book, Lev. iv. 3, xxix. 33, v. 6, 7, ix. 11, 22, xii. 6–8, xiv. 13, and xvi. 16. Isa. liii. 10, 'When thou shalt make his soul sin ;' we fill it up by 'an offering for sin.' Hosea iv. 8, 'They eat up the sin of my people ;' that is, the sacrifices which were to be offered up for the people. Ezek. xlv. 19, 'The priest shall take of the blood of the sin ;' we read it ' of the sin-offering.' Nothing more usual in the Old Testament than to make the words *Chattaath* and *Ascham* to be expressive both of sin, and of the sacrifice too by which that sin was to be expiated ;[2] answerably to which is $\dot\alpha\mu\alpha\rho\tau\iota\alpha$, used in the New : 2 Cor. v. 21, 'He that knew no sin was made sin,' &c. ; that is, a sacrifice for sin. An ellipsis like to this in the text, you have, Heb. x. 6, 'In burnt-offerings

---

[1] Propter peccatum.—*V. Syr.* Propter ipsum peccatum.— *Tremell.*

[1] Phrasi Hebræa peccatum vocat sacrificium pro peccato.— *Franz. Schola Sacrif.*, disp. vii. th. 56.

[2] Sicut hostias quæ pro peccato offerebant in lege, peccati nomine vocabant cum ipsæ delicta nescirent, sic et Christi caro, quæ pro peccati nostris oblata est, peccati nomen accepit.— *Hieron.* See *Grotius de Sat. Christi*, cap. 1, p. 16.

and for sin thou hadst no pleasure,' where sacrifices is left out, but must be put in ; so here in the words which I am upon. This, now, is that interpretation which is most generally pitched upon, which seems best to correspond with other parallel texts, and with the matter and scope of this which we have in hand, and therefore that only I shall insist upon.[1] And indeed the two former senses are included in this, and do most naturally incorporate with it, as you will perceive in the following discourse.

3. There is a third thing to be opened, which in a very few words shall be despatched. It is said here, 'For sin God condemned sin *in the flesh;*' now this being indefinitely propounded, it may be asked, Of what or of whose flesh doth the apostle speak? I answer, Of the flesh of Christ. God sent him in the likeness of sinful flesh, and in that very flesh sin was condemned. I know some interpret it of our flesh;[2] but the most apply it to Christ's flesh. There is in different respects a truth in both; for in our flesh sin is condemned as to the effect and benefit thereof, but in Christ's flesh it was condemned meritoriously and causally. The Syriac, therefore, (to make this the more express,) turns it, 'and for sin condemned sin in *his* flesh.' Sin shall be punished and expiated in that nature wherein it had been committed. Man in the flesh had committed sin, and God in the flesh (of him who was man) will condemn sin, *ut caro humana quæ peccaverat eadem*

---

[1] Per hostiam carnis suæ quam obtulit pro peccante damnavit peccatum in carne sua.—*Orig.* Hostia pro peccato damnavit peccatum in carne.—*Melanch.* Per hostiam pro peccato Christum, Deus abolevit peccatum in hominibus.—*Vatabl.* Sed quid si, mittens filium, &c., vult dicere, et quidem hostiam pro peccato, sive ut esset hostia pro peccato.—*Drus.* Ego adduci nequeo ut nomen peccati alio sensu hic positum esse existimem, quam pro expiatrice victima, quæ אשם dicitur Hebræis, sicuti Græci καθαρμα vocunt sacrificium cui maledictio injungitur.—*Calv.* For sin, that he might be a sacrifice for sin.—*Dr Ham.* To be a propitiatory sacrifice for sin.—*Deod.* To the same purpose *P. Martyr, Heming., Piscat., Vorst., Lud. de Dieu,* &c., whom I need not cite ; yet *Beza* will not admit of this exposition : Præpositio περι nulla ratione potest hanc interpretationem admittere; neque nunc apostolus agit de Christi morte et nostrorum peccatorum expiatione, sed de Christi incarnatione et naturæ nostræ corruptione per eam sublata.—*Beza.*

[2] Augustinus exponit de nostra carne in qua peccatum tyrannidem possidet extra Christum.—*Muscul.* Sed melius est ut dicamus, debilitavit fomitem peccati in carne nostra.—*Aquin.*

---

pro peccato lueret. Our Saviour's being a sacrifice pointed to his flesh;[1] it was the human nature wherein he offered up himself, and therefore in that God is said to condemn sin. And as sin shall be expiated in that nature wherein it had been committed, so Satan too shall be baffled in that nature over which he had been victorious. Christ will beat him upon his own ground; he had overcome man, and man shall overcome him. Oh the wisdom, mercy, power of God! But these things were, under the former head, much enlarged upon. I will only further take notice of two things :

1. This condemning of sin is here brought in as God's act : 'God sent his own Son, &c., and for sin condemned,' &c. But is not this applicable to Christ also? Yes, if you consider him as God and as the eternal Son of God;[2] so it was and is his act as well as the Father's to abolish, acquit, and absolve from sin's guilt in an authoritative way. But in the clause which I am opening Christ is not spoken of in that notion as he was God, only as he was man, and as a victim and sacrifice for sin, and so he acquits from sin, not authoritatively, but as the way and means which God made use of for the bringing about of this mercy for sinners.

2. The flesh of Christ here is not to be considered simply and absolutely, but under this restriction or special consideration as dying, and thereby satisfying divine justice.[3] I would take in his whole humiliation, but this being the highest degree thereof, therefore eminently by it sin was condemned. Oh when this flesh of Christ hung upon the cross, then sin received its condemnatory sentence, its mortal wound ; then when Christ was condemned, sin, in another sense, was condemned also. This, I say,

---

[1] Sacerdos noster a nobis accepit quod pro nobis offerret, accepit enim a nobis carnem, in ipsa carne victima factus est.—*August. in Ps. cxxix.*

[2] Quamvis de Christo ut est Filius Dei posset vere dici eum expiare authoritative et judicialiter, quatenus ipse cum Patre potestatem habet remittendi peccata, quia tamen hic consideratur non ut Deus sed ut Mediator, ut sacerdos et victima—non potest aliter expiatio quam per pœnæ lationem succedaneam et vicariam mortem explicari.—*Turret. de Sat. Christi,* pars. vi. p. 204.

[3] Hoc factum est per carnem, *i.e.,* per mortem quam in carne et juxta humanam naturam passus est.—*Zuingl.* In carne, *i.e.,* per carnem Filii sui suspensam et mortificatam in cruce. —*Estius.*

was brought about in his flesh, as suffering the penalty of death, so the apostle puts it in Col. i. 22, 'In the body of his flesh through death.' I will add nothing further upon this.

The words being thus explained, it is high time that I come to that doctrinal truth which they mainly hold forth, that is this, The Lord Jesus submitting to be a sacrifice for sin, and offering up himself as such to God, he did thereby take away, abolish, expiate all sin in all its guilt, so as that it shall never be charged upon believers to their eternal ruin. In the language of the text it is, in short, 'For sin, sin was condemned.' You heard but now in the opening of the condemning of sin, that that admits of more senses than that one which I now instance in the observation; yet, however, this being most agreeable to the nature of a sacrifice, in reference to which Christ is here set forth, I therefore only mention it.

In the handling of this point, which carries me again into the very midst of the Socinians' camp, where I should not choose to be, but I must follow the word whithersoever it leads me, there are two things to be spoken to:

1. To Christ's being a sacrifice for sin.

2. To the blessed effect of that blessed sacrifice, viz., the condemnation or expiation of sin.

1. I begin with the first, Christ was a sacrifice for sin; which though in the general none deny, yet when we come to particulars about it, as, namely, the true notion of his being so, the efficacy, ends, effects of his sacrifice, the time when and the place where it was offered, with several other things which are incident about it, there many differences do arise. Certainly there are none who believe the Scriptures, but in some sense or other they must grant Christ to be a sacrifice, because they are so plain and express about it: Isa. liii. 10, 'When thou shalt make his soul an offering for sins.' 1 Cor. v. 7, 'For even Christ our passover is sacrificed for us.' 2 Cor. v. 21, 'He that knew no sin, was made sin,' a sacrifice for sin, &c. Eph. v. 2, 'Walk in love, as Christ also hath loved us, and hath given himself for us, an offering and a sacrifice to God for a sweet smelling savour;' where the apostle seems to allude (1.) To the *Mincah* and *Zebach* amongst the Jews,[1] the

[1] *Cloppenb. Schola Sacrif.*, p. 3. *Franzius*, disp. 13, thes. 2, 3.

former of which did refer to their oblations of the fruits of the earth, set forth here by προσφορὰ, the latter to the sacrificing and offering of living creatures, set forth here by θυσία. (2.) He alludes to the pleasingness and gratefulness of the primitive sacrifices to God: Gen. viii. 21, 'And the Lord smelled a sweet savour,' &c. Noah's sacrifices (spoken of ver. 20) were highly pleasing to God; the like you have of the Levitical sacrifices: Lev. i. 9, 'An offering made by fire, of a sweet savour unto the Lord;' so ver. 13, 17. Answerably to which, yea, far above them, Christ was 'a sacrifice of a sweet smelling savour to God.' Heb. vii. 27, 'This he did once when he offered up himself.' Heb. ix. 14, 'Who through the eternal Spirit offered up himself to God: ver. 26, 'But now once in the end of the world hath he appeared to put away sin by the sacrifice of himself:' ver. 28, 'So Christ was once offered to bear the sins of many.' Indeed the great business of the apostle, in his excellent epistle to the Hebrews, is both to assert and also to illustrate Christ's being a sacrifice for sin, which he doth so fully and plainly as that one would think there should be no doubts or differences amongst any that bear the name of Christians, about either the thing, or the true nature and notion thereof.

Yea, Christ was not only *a* sacrifice, a true, real, proper sacrifice, in opposition to those who would make him but an improper, figurative, metaphorical sacrifice, but he was *the* sacrifice in a way of eminency; unto which therefore all the law sacrifices did bear a special reference; for,

1. Those were the types of this, all of them typifying and prefiguring Christ the grand sacrifice, and like the gnomon in the dial pointing to him in this consideration.[1] I say, all were typical adumbrations of him; therefore we find they are, not only in the body and lump of them, but as taken severally and apart, applied and brought down to him; yea, he was shadowed out by them not only with respect to

[1] *Propter hoc etiam omnia sacrificia veteris testamenti leguntur, ut hoc unum sacrificium designarent, per quod vera est remissio peccatorum, et mundatio animæ in eternum.—Ambros. in Ep. ad Heb.*, cap. 9. *Fuit apud veteres oblatio holocausti concio quædam de morte Christi, qua nos a peccatis per fidem purgati sumus. Quin omnia sacrificia legis in unum Christum respiciunt, atque unicum ejus sacrificium adumbrant.—Munster. in Lev. i. 1.*

matter, but also with respect to the several rites and modes used about them; both of which assertions are sufficiently made out in the forenamed epistle. And whereas some affirm that the annual expiatory sacrifices, of which you read Lev. xvi., only did prefigure Christ and his being a sacrifice;[1] it is a very great falsity. Those indeed might so prefigure him eminently, but not solely; for we find others applied to him as well as those, as, namely, the lamb in the daily offering, the paschal lamb, which was partly a sacrifice and partly a sacrament, John i. 29; 1 Pet. i. 19; 1 Cor. v. 7; Rev. v. 6, &c., and xiii. 8; the red heifer, to be sacrificed upon occasion for the expiating of the guilt of unknown murder, Num. xix.; Heb. ix. 13; the daily sacrifices, Heb. vii. 27, and x. 11. But, passing by these things, I say Christ was typified by the old sacrifices; and probably that might be one end of God in his instituting of them. For that they were of divine and positive institution,[2] and not taken up upon the light or law of nature, is to me, though I know others[3] think otherwise, a truth clear enough. But why did God institute them? to appoint the slaying of so many poor creatures, such various and costly sacrifices to be offered, so often to be repeated, such for every day, such for every Sabbath, such for every new moon, such every year at the solemn and anniversary expiation, besides what were offered at the passover, at several feasts, at the lesser and greater jubilee, upon particular and special occasions, as dedications, &c.? Pray, what might be God's end or ends in all this? Was it that he might shew his dominion over the creatures? was it that he might by this demonstrate the evil of sin, and what the sinner deserved upon it? was it to gratify the

---

[1] Socin. de Servat., part ii. cap. 9. Against him in this, see Grotius de Sat. Christi, pp. 126, 127; Turretin. de Satis., p. 216; Franz., disp. 6, thes. 34, &c.; Essen. Tri. Crucis, p. 226; Hoornb. Socin. Conf., 597, 599.

[2] For this *vide* Suarez. in 3 part. Sum. Aquin., quest. 83, art. 1, disp. 71; Rivet in Gen., exerc. 42, p. 170, &c., et p. 222; Franz. de Sacrif., disp. 2, thes. 76, disp. 3, thes. 76, disp. 16, thes. 33; Cloppenb. Scho. Sacrif., probl. 2, p. 51, &c.; Dr Owen de Theologia Adamica, lib. ii. cap. 1, pp. 133, 134.

[3] The Papists generally: Bellarm. de Missa., lib. i. cap. 29; Valentia de Missæ Sacrificio, lib. i. cap. 4. Others are of this opinion also: the author of Eccles. Policy, p. 100, &c., Defence, &c., p. 421, &c., who yet grants expiatory sacrifices to be of divine institution, p. 427, &c.

Jews, who having been amongst the Egyptians, where sacrifices did abound, might therefore be taken with them and fond of them, and thereby to prevent their idolatry?[1] Several such ends and reasons are assigned, but surely that which I am upon must not be left out, if not preferred before any other, viz., therefore God did ordain and institute sacrifices, that by them he might typify and prefigure that great sacrifice which was to come;[2] thereby the better to prepare and inform the world about it. But how, or in what measure, and in what extent God did clear up this notion, use, and end of sacrifices, I shall not be too forward to determine.

2. As the law sacrifices were types, so they were but types. There was little in them, take away the typical nature of them; what poor things were they further than as they did point to Christ! The apostle calls them but 'shadows of good things to come,' Heb. x. 1; 'figures for the time then present,' chap. ix. 9; 'patterns of things in the heavens,' ver. 23; 'examples and shadows of heavenly things,' chap. viii. 5.

3. Nay, thirdly, all that virtue and efficacy which was in them was all derived from, and did all depend upon, this great sacrifice, the Lord Jesus.[3] Alas! what could they do by any inherent virtue in themselves for the expiating of sin and pacifying of God? Heb. x. 4, 'It is not possible that the blood of bulls and goats should take away sins.' How often doth the apostle go over this, viz., the weakness of the Levitical sacrifices with respect to expia-

---

[1] Theodoret for this, vol. iv. de curandis Græc. affectionibus, cap. 7, p. 584.

[2] Fagius in Lev. i. 2 gives two reasons of them. Ut populus in idololatriam pronus ab idolis averteretur et in cultu Dei retineretur. Deinde ut typos haberet populus Dei sacrificii Christi, quem oportebat aliquando in crucem agi pro peccatis suorum.—*Rivet. in Gen.*, p. 222. Præcipue quia voluit adumbrari sacrificiis passionem futuram mediatoris et, &c.

[3] Hujus sacrificii a Christo peragendi sacrificia cætera typi erant; quia ut pecus moriebatur pro homine Levit. xvii. 11, ita et Jesus Christus esset sanguinem suum effusurus pro nobis. Utraque igitur auferebant reatum; hoc tamen discrimine, quod sacrificium Christi id præstabat virtute sua, illa vero legalia proprie et directe solum tollebant reatum ratione poenæ temporalis; in figura tantum promitterent piis effectum spiritualem et æternum, puta ablationem reatus æterni sive poenæ infernalis.—*Vossius de Idolol.*, lib. i. p. 297.

tion and atonement! Doubtless whatever virtue or efficacy was in them in order to the production of these effects, it wholly depended upon Christ the sacrifice that was to come.

Yet here I would not be misunderstood. In such a sense I do not make the law sacrifices to be mere types or altogether weak; for as to that which the apostle calls 'the purifying of the flesh,' Heb. ix. 13, they were more than types, and had more than a typical expiation;[1] and with respect to that by virtue of God's institution they were able to effect it. But besides this there was 'the making of persons perfect as pertaining to the conscience,' the 'purging of the conscience,' &c., Heb. ix. 9, 14; now as to this their strength was wholly derived, and their use wholly typical. By the purifying of the flesh is meant exemption from those civil and ecclesiastical penalties which upon such transgressions of the law the Jews were liable to. God gave them, with respect to their polity, such and such laws, which if any did break they were so and so to be punished; yet he was so gracious to them as to allow in several cases the offering of sacrifices, in order to the expiating of their guilt, and the preventing of the punishment threatened to them, as they stood in such a politic capacity; therefore as to this sacrifices had a real efficiency and also a full efficacy. By the making perfect, as pertaining to the conscience, is meant the doing away of sin's guilt in the sight of God, the setting of things right betwixt God and the sinner, the pacifying of his wrath, securing from eternal punishment. Now as to this the Mosaical sacrifices could do nothing; here they were mere types and altogether weak; this was to be done by the alone sacrifice of Christ. So that whereas some do argue against the sacrifices under the law as not prefiguring Christ, because they had no power or virtue in them to take away sin, I answer (1.) As to the taking away of external guilt and obligation to external punishment, so far they had a power; (2.) Suppose they had had none at all, yet for all that they might have had this use;[2] as, I hope, the brazen serpent was a real type and

prefiguration of Christ, in reference to his spiritual healing of the poor sin-stung soul, and yet that of itself had no virtue at all to bring about that effect, which should bear any analogy unto the thing typified.

4. That those old sacrifices had a special reference to Christ, the great sacrifice, is evident from this, because with him they began, and with him they ended.[1] For as soon as ever Christ had been exhibited in that primitive promise, Gen. iii. 15, that 'the seed of the woman should bruise the serpent's head,' &c., immediately upon this, as divines do not only conjecture but prove, sacrifices did commence; and as soon as he himself came and had offered himself upon the cross, as the true sacrifice, within a very little while the Jewish sacrifices ceased. Within a few years after their temple was destroyed, and with that all their sacrifices expired; yea, in process of time, though Julian gave them encouragement to re-edify the temple,[2] for this very end that sacrifices might again be used, and the Jews thereupon endeavoured to their utmost so to do, yet God from heaven blasted them in all their attempts in a miraculous and extraordinary manner. Oh, the true sacrifice was come, therefore there shall be no more use of what was but typical thereof, as the dark shades of the night vanish when the sun itself arises.[3] The heathen oracles intrenched too much upon Christ's prophetical office, and therefore at his coming they must cease;[4] and sacrifices did as much intrench upon his priestly office and the oblation of himself, and therefore after his death they shall and did cease too. It was prophesied of the Messiah that he should 'cause the sacrifice and the oblation to cease,' Dan. ix. 27; and Heb. x. 8, 9, 'Above when he said, Sacrifice and offering and burnt-offerings and offering for sin thou wouldst not, neither hadst pleasure therein; which are offered by the law: then said he, Lo, I come to do thy will, O God. He taketh away the first, that he may establish the

---

[1] See Dr Stillingfleet in his discourse concerning the True Reason of Christ's Sufferings, p. 423, &c.

[2] This made good by Jacob. ad Portum contra Ostorod., p. 468; Turretin. de Sat. Christi, p. 237.

[1] Cum promisso Messiæ inceperunt sacrificia, cum Messia defuncto defuncta sunt, &c.—Franzius, disp. 10, thes. 98. See him also disp. 21, p. 757.

[2] The full story in Socrates, lib. iii. cap. 20; Sozom., lib. v. cap. 22.

[3] Vide Cyprian. adversus Judæos, lib. i. cap. 16; Tertull. contra Marcion., lib. ii.

[4] Read Plutarch, de Oraculorum Defectu, p. 409.

second;' that is the observation which the apostle makes upon it. And this very thing, the ceasing of sacrifices, was revealed to some amongst the Jews themselves; for in the age before Christ's coming they had got this prophecy amongst them, *Omnes oblationes cessabunt in futuro sæculo,* In the age that is next to come all sacrifices shall cease.[1] And if there be not something extraordinary in the case, why do the modern Jews, they knowing how express and positive God's institution and command is about sacrifices, live in the omission of them? for as to that which some speak of, as to their annual sacrificing even now at the time of the great expiation, I cannot give any great credit to it.[2]

Let not any think that all this discourse, concerning the reference of the ancient sacrifices to Christ the true sacrifice, is unnecessary; for I have gained two things by it: (1.) That the Lord Jesus is the great sacrifice; all former sacrifices pointing to him as the end, matter, substance, accomplishment of them.[3] (2.) That he is also a true and real sacrifice; for was there reality in the type, and shall there not be the same, with advantage, in the antitype? or shall they be shadows of a shadow? Shall there be such a shell and no kernel, such a bone and no marrow in it?

But to go on. In the old sacrifices there were these six things:

1. The person who did institute, ordain, and appoint the use of them; who was God himself, whose institution of them, though it be not expressed in the Scriptures, yet it may very strongly be inferred from them.

2. The person unto whom they were offered; and he also was God himself.

3. The persons offering, viz., the priests, to whom by divine appointment this work was committed, and it was a great part of their work, and one great end of their office: 'For every high priest taken from among men is ordained for men in things pertaining to God, that he may offer both gifts and sacrifices for sins,' Heb. v. 1.

4. The matter of the sacrifice, or the thing offered; which was very various, according to what God was pleased to specify and appoint, oxen, bulls, heifers, sheep, rams, goats, &c.

5. The oblation itself. When the beast was slain it was to be offered up, and then part of the blood thereof was to be carried into the Holy of holies, there to be presented before the Lord; and the main stress of the expiation lay not upon the presentation, which followed after, but upon the mactation and solemn oblation of the sacrifice.[1]

6. The altar upon which all was to be offered.

Now answerably and in correspondency to all these:

1. God instituted, appointed, ordained Christ to be the sacrifice. It was his will and ordination that his Son should offer up himself a propitiatory or expiatory sacrifice: Rom. iii. 25, 'Whom God hath set forth to be a propitiation through faith in his blood.' 2 Cor. v. 19, 'God was in Christ reconciling the world to himself,' &c. 1 Pet. i. 20, 'Who verily was foreordained before the foundation of the world,' &c. It was as much the appointment of God that Christ, the true sacrifice, should die, be slain, offered up, as that under the law any of those sacrifices should be so used. And as from all eternity he decreed and appointed Christ to be the sacrifice, so in time he fitted and prepared him for his being so; therefore, saith Christ, 'But a body hast thou prepared me,' Heb. x. 5, without which he could not have been a sacrifice.

2. Christ offered up himself to God. He had to do with God as he stood in the quality and respect of a sacrifice, for this was a part of his priestly office which primarily refers to God;[2] as king and prophet he hath to do with us, but as priest he had to do with God, that he might propitiate and atone him. So it was with the Aaronical priests; they were 'ordained for men in things pertaining to God,' Heb. v. 1, and surely so it must be too with the great priest whom they did typify. Heb. ii. 17, 'That he might be a merciful and faithful high priest in things pertaining to God.' The apostle

---

[1] Vorstius ex Jalcutt ad finem Ezræ, &c. Sic consentiunt in abolitionem sacrificiorum.—*Alting. Shiloh.,* p. 423.

[2] Buxtorf. Synag. Judaica, cap. 20, p. 357.

[3] Omnia hæc suo modo in typo facta, perfectissime in Christo præstita sunt in veritate et reipsa, &c. Utpote qui mortis suæ sacrificio peccata nostra delevit, ab ira Dei nobis est umbraculum, et sacrificio suo apud Deum nos reconciliavit. —*Zarnov. de Sat. Christi,* p. 38.

[1] See Dr Stillingfl. against Crellius, chap. v. p. 451.

[2] Grot. de Sat. Christi, cap. 10, p. 121.

speaks it expressly : ' And hath given himself for us, an offering and a sacrifice to God for a sweet smelling savour.'

3. Here was the person offering, and that was Christ himself. He as mediator, as God-man, was the priest to offer up himself. They under the law had variety of sacrifices and variety of priests ; we under the gospel have but one sacrifice and one priest, who first offered up himself, and now continues, in another way, to offer up our duties and services to God.

4. As Christ was the priest offering, so he was the sacrifice offered ; for he was both, which was unusual and extraordinary. The Levitical priests and the sacrifices which they offered were distinct— they were not bound to offer themselves ; but our Lord Jesus was priest and sacrifice too ; in his person he was the offerer, in his human nature he was the thing offered.[1] It was necessary that he should offer something, ' For every high priest is ordained to offer gifts and sacrifices ; wherefore it is of necessity that this man have also somewhat to offer,' Heb. viii. 3. What then did he offer ? such things as had been offered before ? the blood of bulls and goats ? No, he offered ' his own blood,' Heb. ix. 12 ; his own body : Heb. x. 4–7, 10, ' Through the offering of the body of Jesus Christ once for all ;' that very body which was so miraculously framed, with which he lived here on earth, which he carried up with him afterwards to heaven ; that very body, I say, he freely offered up upon the cross as a sacrifice to God. His soul comes in too, but that is himself : Isa. liii. 10, ' When thou shalt make his soul an offering for sin.' His whole self in his whole human nature was the matter of this sacrifice : Eph. v. 2, ' And hath given himself for us an offering,' &c. Heb. i. 3, ' When he had by himself purged our sins.' Heb. ix. 14, ' Who through the eternal Spirit offered himself without spot to God.' So Heb. vii. 27. The text saith, ' For sin God condemned

sin in the flesh ;' by which *flesh* the apostle understands the whole manhood of Christ, and that was the sacrifice for sin by which sin was condemned.

5. There was Christ's formal and proper oblation performed upon the cross, by and upon which the sins of believers were to be expiated. That there was in Christ an oblation none deny, but that this was done at his death, or here on earth, and was expiatory in that sense which we put upon it, both of these are vehemently denied by the Socinians ; but I shall have occasion to vindicate both by and by.

6. In Christ's sacrifice there was an altar too, namely, his Godhead : ' The altar sanctified the gift,' Mat. xxiii. 19 ; so it was here. The deity of Christ did not only sustain and strengthen his human nature in his being a sacrifice therein, but it also gave merit and efficacy to his sacrifice ; for how did that come to be so meritorious and effectual for the good of sinners, but from this, that he who offered up himself was God as well as man ? Therefore the apostle, speaking of the efficacy of this sacrifice above the Levitical sacrifices, lays it upon Christ's Godhead : Heb. ix. 14, ' How much more shall the blood of Christ, who through the eternal Spirit (his deity) offered himself,' &c.

The chiefest difficulties not lying in these things, I do not, you see, make any long stay upon them ; but there being a twofold inquiry which will carry us into the very bowels of the main truth, and take in what is most struck at by our adversaries, that I would rather spend my time upon. The Lord Jesus being a sacrifice, it will be asked—

1. What kind of a sacrifice he was ?

2. When and where he was that sacrifice ?

1. To the first I answer, He was a propitiatory or expiatory sacrifice, answering unto, yet infinitely exceeding, the Jewish expiatory sacrifices, by which he was shadowed out and typified. The proof and illustration of this very thing is the design and business of the apostle in that epistle, I mean that written to the Hebrews, which gives us more light into it than all the books that ever were written before or besides. Pray read, again and again, the 5th, 7th, 8th, 9th, 10th chapters thereof, and you will find the apostle there doing these three things : (1.) He proves that Christ was not only a sacrifice,

---

[1] Ut quoniam quatuor considerantur in omni sacrificio, Cui offeratur, a quo offeratur, quid offeratur, pro quibus offeratur : idem ipse unus verusque mediator, per sacrificium pacis reconcilians nos, unum cum illo maneret cui offerebatur, unum in se faceret pro quibus offerebat, unus ipse esset qui offerebat et quod offerebat.—*August. de Trinit.* Utrum Christus simul fuerit sacerdos et hostia ?—*Aquin.* in 3 p., qu. 22, art. 2.

but that he was, truly and really, an expiatory sacrifice ; for he instances in all, the proper constitutive ingredients into and effects of the law-expiatory sacrifices, all of which he applies and brings down to Christ. (2.) He shews the analogy and resemblance betwixt those expiatory sacrifices and this of Christ, and what respect they all carried to this. (3.) He shews wherein and how far the latter exceeded the former. The discussing of these three heads takes up the greatest part of that most excellent commentary upon the law sacrifices ; the particular texts in it I will not at present cite, as they are proper to what I have now laid down, but that will be done in what will follow.

For our better procedure in speaking to this important truth, before I can well fall upon the close handling of it, it will not be amiss for us a little to cast our eye upon and to take a short view of the Jewish sacrifices,[1] with the general nature whereof I intend not at all to meddle ; only give me leave— that being proper to the business in hand, and indeed necessary for the better understanding of it— to shew how these were diversified and distinguished : concerning which several divisions and distinctions are given of them ; but the best and shortest is this, viz., some were gratulatory and some propitiatory, or some eucharistical and some expiatory.

Eucharistical were those that were designed for the expressing of gratitude, for the giving of thanks and praise to the Lord upon the receiving of mercy, of which you read, Lev. vii. 15, and xxii. 29 ; Ps. l. 14 ; Hosea xiv. 2 ; but these I am not concerned about.

Expiatory were those that were designed for the atoning and pacifying of God, the averting of his anger, the doing away the guilt of sin, and the preventing or removing of the punishment of it. These were the sacrifices which took up the greatest room in the body of Mosaical sacrifices, and which did in special point to the grand sacrifice of our Lord Jesus, and to that too as expiatory.

Now these expiatory sacrifices were many and various, all of them carrying something in them whereby they differed and were distinguished each

[1] Of which, in particular, see Philo. Jud. de Victimis; Joseph. Antiq. Jud., lib. iii. cap. 10; Sigon. de Repub. Hebr.; lib. iii. cap. 2, with very many others ; Dr Owen on the Hebr. in Proleg. Exercit., 24; Dr Stillingfl. Answer to Crellius, p. 473.

from the other ; which differences, with the grounds and reasons of them, if we could exactly hit upon, it would be of marvellous great use to us in many things ; but, alas ! excepting where the gospel itself opens this for us, we are much in the dark about it. The Jewish writers, that should help therein, contribute but very little help, as they tell us who are most conversant in them. If we take a brief and general scheme of them, this is clear : the old expiatory sacrifices differed in the matter of them ; for in some it was living creatures, in others it was what grew from the earth ; and often these two were joined, the *Zebach* and the *Mincah* going together in the same sacrifice, as in the daily sacrifice, Exod. xxix. 39, 40, and in divers others. They differed in the rites used about them, all of which were prescribed by God himself. Some were to be poured out, some burnt ; some to be slain and offered by the ordinary priests, some by the high priest himself ; the blood of some to be carried into the Holy of holies, of others not so ; some to be wholly consumed ; and God to have all, as in the holocausts ; some but in part consumed, in which of what was left, one part was to go to the priests, as in the sin and trespass offering, and the other to the persons who brought the sacrifice, as in the peace-offering, provided that that which was offered was for private persons ; for if it was offered for the whole congregation, then no private person might share in the residue, Lev. xxiii. 19, 20. They differed in the time which was appointed for them : for some were to be offered every day, morning and evening, called the daily sacrifice, Exod. xxix. 38–40 ; Num. xxviii. 3–5 ; 2 Chron. viii. 13 ; 1 Chron. xvi. 40 ; Ezek. xlvi. 13, 14 ; Dan. viii. 11, ix. 21, xi. 31, and xii. 11 ; Neh. x. 33 ; Ezra ix. 4, 5 ; some to be offered but every Sabbath-day, Num. xxviii. 9, 10 ; some at the new moons, Num. xxviii. 11 ; some at the revolution of the sabbatical year, Lev. xxv. 2, &c. ; some at the great jubilee, Lev. xxv. 8, &c. ; some at the solemn feasts, as that of the passover, Exod. xii. ; Num. xxviii. 26 ; of pentecost, Lev. xxiii. 17, &c. ; of tabernacles, Num. xxix. 12 ; some but once a-year at the great anniversary expiation, Lev. xvi., *per tot.* They differed in the rise of them ; some being purely from the will of the offerer, the free-will offerings,[1] Lev.

[1] *Vide* L'Empreur de Leg. Hebr., p. 264.

vii. 16, and xxii. 21 ; others occasioned by some special emergency of providence, when some eminent
mercy was received, or some great judgment to be
removed, &c., 2 Sam. vi. 13, 17 ; 1 Chron. xv. 26 ;
2 Chron. xxix. 21, &c. ; 2 Sam. xxiv. 25 ; others
were constant, being set and stated by God himself,
as those that have been already mentioned. They
differed according to the persons for whom they
were appointed ; some for the prince, some for the
priests, some for private men, some for the whole
community, for each of which directions are given,
Lev. iv. And then as to the kinds or species of
them, there were the burnt-offerings, about which
rules are set down Lev. i. ; meat-offerings, of which
Lev. ii.; peace-offerings, Lev. iii. ; the sin-offering,
Lev. iv. ; the trespass-offering, Lev. v. and vi. Some
reduce all to three : the burnt-offering, the peace-
offering, the sin-offering ;[1] some to two, the holocaust
and the thank-offering ;[2] but of such different apprehensions there is no end.

Now, though these sacrifices were thus diversified
amongst themselves, yet the most, if not all of them,
agreed in this, that they were in their use, end, and
effects of an expiatory nature. I say all, for unquestionably it belonged not only to the sacrifices used
at the anniversary expiation, nor only to the sin-
offering and trespass-offering, to expiate sin, but all
the rest, more or less, were designed for this end,
and accordingly did produce this effect. Agreeably
to which Christ, the true and great sacrifice, in the
offering up of himself to God, did truly, properly
expiate sin ; for if they did so, he then much more ;
because they in their expiation were types of him in
his expiation. Now, whatever is in the type must
needs be in the thing typified ; as also because their
expiation was done in the strength and virtue of
Christ's sacrifice. Now, surely that which gives
expiatory virtue to other things must needs have
such virtue in itself.

For the better opening and proving of Christ's
being an expiatory sacrifice, by making a collation
or parallel between him and the expiatory sacrifices
under the law, there are these four things which I
shall endeavour to make good :

[1] Philo. Jud. de Vict., p. 648: τὸ ὁλοκαυστὸν, τὸ σωτήριον, τό
περὶ ἁμαρτίας.
[2] Joseph. Ant., lib. iii. cap. 10 : Δυὸ εἰσιν ἱερουργίαι, &c.

1. That in those expiatory sacrifices, whatever
was laid upon them it was for the sin of the people,
as the impulsive and meritorious cause thereof ; and
that so it was with Christ in his sufferings.

2. That those sacrifices were substituted in the
place and stead of the offenders themselves, bearing
their punishments ; and that so it was with Christ
in reference to sinners.

3. That those sacrifices were to be offered up,
killed, slain, consumed, and in that way they became
expiatory ; and that so it was with Christ.

4. That by those sacrifices God was actually
atoned and propitiated, the expiation and remission
of sin procured ; and that so it was by Christ.
These things being cleared and proved, it will be
evident that Christ was a true expiatory sacrifice.
I will go over them as briefly as the nature of the
thing will admit of.

1. First, I say in those expiatory sacrifices, whatever was laid upon them it was for the sin of the
people, as the impulsive and meritorious cause
thereof. For wherefore were the poor innocent
beasts and living creatures killed and slain as they
were? what had they done that so many of them
must be put to death from day to day? Did God
delight in making his temple a slaughter-house?
was it his pleasure to have it thus that he might
shew his dominion and sovereignty over the creature?
Surely that was not the great thing which he designed therein! he had other ways, which might
seem more suitable to his goodness and pity to his
creatures, wherein he might have made known his
dominion over them. And, besides, if this was the
only thing aimed at, why must the people lay their
hands upon the cattle when they were sacrificed?
why must they confess their sins over them, as you
will see under the next head they were to do?
These rites evidently declare that God did not here
proceed in the way of absolute dominion, but that
there was sin in the case as the procuring cause of
all this ; and if so, they having no sin of their own
for which they could thus suffer, their suffering
must be resolved into the sin of the people as that
which brought it upon them. So it was with Christ
our sacrifice ; his sufferings were exceeding sharp,
his precious life was taken from him, he died upon
the cross, endured hard usage indeed. Whence

did all this befall him? Was there not some special cause why it should be thus with God's own Son? Yes. What was that? Why, sin; sin was that cause. But whose sin? not his own, for he was perfectly free from all sin—'he knew no sin,' 2 Cor. v. 21; he was 'holy, harmless, undefiled, separate from sinners,' Heb. vii. 26; 'a lamb without blemish and without spot,' 1 Pet. i. 19. It must be our sin, then, that was the meritorious cause of all Christ's sufferings: Dan. ix. 26, 'After threescore and two weeks shall Messiah be cut off, but not for himself.' Isa. liii. 4–6, 'Surely he hath borne our griefs, and carried our sorrows: yet we did esteem him stricken, smitten of God, and afflicted. But he was wounded for our transgressions, he was bruised for our iniquities; the chastisement of our peace was upon him, and with his stripes we are healed. All we like sheep have gone astray; we have turned every one to his own way; and the Lord hath laid on him the iniquity of us all.' Rom. iv. 25, 'Who was delivered for our offences, (διὰ τὰ παραπτώματα,) and raised again for our justification.' It is the same preposition in both branches, but its sense is different, which difference rises from the different nature of the matter spoken of; for when it is joined with sins or offences it imports that they were the meritorious cause of Christ's sufferings; but when it is joined with Christ's resurrection and the sinner's justification, there its signification and import is final; yet too in such a sense the διὰ may be taken meritoriously in the latter as well as in the former branch. Socinus tells us that this, with some other parallel expressions, only notes our sins to be the occasion, but not the impulsive cause of Christ's sufferings;[1] as also that the particle διὰ is, both here, and elsewhere, always taken in a final, never in any meritorious sense. But most untruly; for it is said, Eph. v. 6, 'Because of these things the wrath of God comes upon the children of disobedience;'[2] διὰ ταῦτα, for these things, as those which merit and bring down the wrath of God upon sinners. But I will not stay

upon the refuting of the usual cavils and false assertions about this, because I conceive this head may not be so proper to that which I am upon; for I am not now speaking to the sufferings or death of Christ under the consideration of a punishment, to which a meritorious cause doth point, but of a sacrifice. The expiatory sacrifices, it is very true, were punished for the sins of men; but yet that wherein they were expiatory, and as they were expiatory, more immediately pointed to something else, namely, to that which will follow in the succeeding particulars; and so it is here too with respect to Christ, whose death, as is usually observed, falls under a threefold consideration; it was a punishment, a sacrifice, a ransom. With respect to the first, the effect thereof was satisfaction; to the second, the effect thereof was atonement; to the third, the effect thereof was redemption. Now I, at present considering it in the second notion, as it is a sacrifice, have not so much to do with that which refers to it in the notion of a punishment; therefore this first particular I pass over.

2. Secondly, In the Levitical expiatory sacrifices there was the substitution of them in the place and stead of the offenders themselves. The people's sin, and the punishment due to them thereupon, was laid upon the thing sacrificed; insomuch that whereas they should have died, by surrogation and commutation the poor beasts died for them. This was the great thing intended and designed in those sacrifices;[1] and that it was really so done in them the Scripture is very clear. Take that one place, Lev. xvii. 11, 'For the life of the flesh is in the blood: and I have given it to you upon the altar to make an atonement for your souls: for it is the blood that maketh an atonement for the soul.' In all the four books of Moses, which treat so much upon sacrifices, there is not a more pithy and plain account given of their use and end than here in this place. The Lord, in the 10th verse, severely prohibits the eating of blood. In this verse he backs his prohibition with a double argument: (1.) Because the life of the flesh was in the blood; (2.) Because he had set that apart for a

---

[1] De Servat., part ii. cap. 7, and part iii. cap. 7.

[2] Ubi est διὰ cum accusativo; quæ apud Græcæ linguæ authores sacros et profanos usitatissima est nota causæ impulsivæ. Ut cum dicitur διὰ ταῦτα propter hæc, venit ira Dei in filios contumaciæ, Eph. v. 6.—Grot. de Sat. Christi, cap. 1, in Rom. iv. 25.

[1] Nequaquam sacra Scriptura admittit alium finem sacrificiorum quam hunc ipsum, quod nimirum vice hominum sunt passa pecora sacrificialia.—Franzius in Præfat. ad. Schol. Sacrif. Patriarch.

high and sacred use, viz., to be used in sacrifices in order to atonement : 'And I have given it you upon the altar to make atonement,' &c. For this great effect mainly lay upon the blood : 'It is the blood that maketh atonement for the soul.' Now mark it, it is to make atonement *for your soul*, and it makes atonement *for the soul*, that is, *in the stead of your soul*,[1] (he speaking to the people of Israel ;) so that in the blood sacrificed there was soul for soul, life for life ; the soul and life of the sacrifice for the more precious soul and life of the sinner. Was not here substitution of the one in the room of the other? Hence it is that the sacrifices were said to 'bear the iniquities of the people,' because of the transferring of the guilt and punishment of sin over to them ; so you read Lev. xvi. 22, and x. 17. Hence also was the laying on of hands upon the sacrifice, sometimes by the priests, sometimes by the people. You have it prescribed in the burnt-offering, Lev. i. 4 ; in the peace-offering, Lev. iii. 2, and viii. 13 ; in the sin-offering, Lev. iv. 15, 24, 29, 33. At the great expiation Aaron was to 'lay both his hands upon the head of the live goat, and to confess over him all the iniquities of the children of Israel,' &c., Lev. xvi. 21. Now what might be the meaning of this rite? Was it to signify that the thing offered was now *Deo sacrum*, as being set apart for God and consecrated for his use, upon which account imposition of hands was used in other cases? or was it expressive of obtestation, to hold forth the people's praying to God, *Quicquid a nobis peccatum est, sit in hujus victimæ caput*, Whereinsoever we have offended, let all be laid upon the head of this victim? or did they by this testify the sense of their deserts to die themselves? These things, I grant, may very well be taken in ; but the main thing held forth in it was the translation of the sinner's guilt to the sacrifice, and the substitution of it in his stead. Whenever the people thus laid their hands upon the sacrifice they did in effect say, Upon this beast we lay all our sins ; and this was the primary intendment of that rite.[2] And had there not been a strange conveyance or imputa-

tion of something of this nature to the things sacrificed, I would fain know a reason why the messenger that only went with the scape-goat into the wilderness, as also why he who only burnt the residue of the bullock, whose blood had been carried into the Holy of holies, I say why both of these should be accounted unclean, so unclean, as that before they had been purified and washed they were not to be admitted into the congregation ; for so God enjoined, Lev. xvi. 26-28. And now, after all this, when the great Lord and sovereign was pleased to have it thus, hath given out so full a declaration of himself about it, when Scripture is so clear, yea, and when nature too, as you will hear, hath given such a confirmation of it ; I say, after and notwithstanding all this, for any yet to deny it, to bring their little objections against it, (as that because there was no communion of nature and species betwixt men and beasts, therefore there could be no substitution,[1] &c.,) this must needs discover excess of pride and folly. The thing possibly, in some respects, may seem somewhat strange, but it becomes us to acquiesce in what God himself was pleased to determine upon, and then to order and reveal in his law.

From these sacrifices I proceed to the much higher sacrifice, Christ himself ; where we shall find an exact correspondency between the type and the antitype, the one fully answering to the other. Did they carry substitution in them? that eminently was in Christ. He indeed substituted himself in the sinner's room, took our guilt upon him, and put himself in our place ; died not only for our good, but in our stead ; did undergo what we should have undergone ; vouchsafed to die that we might not die ; bare himself in his soul and body as our ἀντίψυχος, the punishment due to us. Here was substitution far above what was in the law sacrifices. But this Socinus and his followers cannot endure to hear of.[2] Oh they rally all their force, unite all their strength, set themselves with all their might to oppose and beat down this great truth! There are but few of the evangelical mysteries which these pernicious gospel-destroyers do not assault, some way or other ;

---

[1] So it is rendered in several versions of the words, set down in Franz., p. 446. See this text improved and vindicated in Dr Stillingfl. against Crell., p. 429, &c.

[2] Hoc ritu qui offerebat, significabat se scelera sua conjicere n caput bovis qui propterea mactabatur. — *Drusius in Lev*. i. 4.

[1] That objection answered in Grotius de Sat., cap. 10, p. 123 ; Essenius Tri. Crucis, p. 218 ; Turretin. de Sat., p. 246.

[2] De Servat., p. ii. cap. 4 (et passim). In Prælect., cap. 18. With him concur Crellius, Smalcius, &c., and all of that party.

but as to that which is now before us, Christ's suffering, dying, satisfying in our stead, the sum of gospel revelation, the great article of the Christian faith, the main prop and foundation of the believer's hope, this they make their fiercest assaults upon; whatever stands, if they may have their will, this shall not. But alas, poor men! when they have done their worst, it will stand firm upon its sure basis as an eternal, unmoveable truth. It is so established in the word, and so rooted in the hearts of Christians, that, in spite of the most subtle and fierce oppositions of all gainsayers, it shall abide for ever. Well, however, let us see what ground we have for our belief of it, and surely upon inquiry it will appear we have enough and enough. If the gospel be not clear in this, it is clear in nothing; and blessed be the Lord, who, in a point of such vast importance to souls, hath given the world a revelation of it so plain and full! Substitution in the case of the old sacrifices is not so evidently held forth in the law, but substitution with respect to Christ and his sacrifice is more evidently held forth in the gospel: Rom. v. 6, 'For when we were yet without strength, in due time Christ died *for the ungodly;*' ver. 8, 'But God commendeth his love towards us, in that while we were yet sinners Christ died *for us.*' 1 Peter iii. 18, 'For Christ also hath once suffered for sins, *the just for the unjust.*' 1 Peter iv. 1, 'Forasmuch then as Christ hath suffered *for us* in the flesh,' &c. 1 Peter ii. 21, 'Because Christ also suffered *for us,*' &c. John x. 15, 'I lay down my life *for the sheep.*' John xi. 50, 'Nor consider that it is expedient for us that one man should die *for the people,* and that the whole nation perish not.' Heb. ii. 9, 'That he by the grace of God should taste death *for every man.*' 2 Cor. v. 14, 15, 'If one died *for all,* then were all dead: and that he died *for all,* that they which live should not henceforth live unto themselves, but unto him which died *for them,* and rose again.' In all these places the preposition ὑπὲρ is used, which, though not always, yet most frequently, notes substitution—the doing or suffering of something by one in the stead and place of others;[1] see Rom. ix. 3; 2 Cor. v. 20. And so it is all along

[1] Of this and the other prepositions, Grot. de Sat., cap. 10, p. 3, and cap. 9, p. 115; Hoorneb, p. 566–568; Calov., p. 421, &c., and p. 453.

here to be taken, where it being used of persons, the nature of the matter spoken of, the use of the word in parallel texts, as also in Greek authors, gives this sense the preference before any other. But suppose this may be eluded, the other preposition ἀντὶ proves the thing undeniably. Mat. xx. 28, 'Even as the Son of man came not to be ministered unto, but to minister, and to give his life a ransom *for many,*' λύτρον ἀντὶ πολλῶν. 1 Tim. ii. 6, 'Who gave himself a ransom (ἀντίλυτρον) for all.' Christ did not barely deliver poor captive souls, but he delivered them in the way of a ransom, which ransom he paid down for them in their stead; so as that what they themselves should have paid, that he was pleased to pay for them. This is and must be the sense and import of the word, for every one knows that ἀντὶ in composition (out of that I know it hath other senses, see Heb. xii. 2; 1 Cor. xi. 15) signifies but two things, either opposition and contrariety, 1 John ii. 18; or substitution and commutation, Rom. xii. 17; Mat. v. 38; 1 Peter iii. 9; Luke xi. 11; so that the matter will come to this, we must either carry it thus, that Christ gave himself a ransom against sinners, than which nothing more absurd; or else thus, that he gave himself a ransom in the stead and place of sinners, than which nothing more true.

I might further prove it by 2 Cor. v. 21, 'He hath made him to be sin for us, who knew no sin; that we might be made the righteousness of God in him.' Gal. iii. 13, 'Christ hath redeemed us from the curse of the law, being made a curse for us.' If he had not so been in his own person, woe to poor sinners! they must then have lain under it themselves to all eternity. What a full and convincing chapter is that of Isa. liii. for the proof of that which I am upon! It would take up a great deal of time to go over it, and to draw out the strength and emphasis of the several expressions in it.[1] I must not engage so far. But surely the tongue of man could not utter, nor the head of man invent, any words or phrases more plain and apposite for the set-

[1] This is done by very many anti-Socinian writers. Particularly see Grot de Sat., p. 111, &c. (Oh that he had not afterwards spoiled in his commentaries upon Isa. liii. what he had before, in this excellent treatise, so nervously and orthodoxly asserted! but there he is as weak as here is strong.) Dr Owen against Biddle, p. 499, &c.; his vindication of the true sense of it against Grotius, p. 521, &c.

ting forth of Christ's substitution than what you have there. The truth is, its edge is every way as sharp against the Socinian who denies this, as it is against the Jew who denies Christ's Messiahship. Ver. 4, 'Surely he hath borne our griefs and carried our sorrows,' &c. ; ver. 5, 'The chastisement of our peace was upon him, and with his stripes we are healed ;' ver. 6, 'The Lord hath laid on him the iniquity of us all,' or 'the Lord hath made the iniquities of us all to meet on him ;' ver. 7, 'He was oppressed and he was afflicted,' &c, or, as the words are rendered by some, 'it was exacted and he answered;'[1] ver. 8, 'For the transgression of my people was he stricken ;' ver. 11, 'For he shall bear their iniquities ;' ver. 12, 'And he bare the sin of many.' Is not all this spoken of our Lord Christ, and is there not in it sufficient proof of his susception of the sinner's guilt, and bearing the punishment due for it ? It runs much in the style of the old sacrifices ; they had the sins of the people 'laid upon them,' Lev. xvi. 21. And the priests, too, are said to 'bear their iniquity,' Lev. x. 17 ; 'that Aaron may bear the iniquity of the holy things,' Exod. xxviii. 38. Answerably to which the prophet tells us that Christ, our sacrifice and priest too, had the iniquities of all believers laid upon him, and that he bare them in his own person. So the apostle, Heb. ix. 28, 'So Christ was once offered to bear the sins of many,' &c. And that is a great scripture, 1 Peter ii. 24, 'Who his own self bare our sins in his own body on the tree ;' ἀνήνεγκεν, he 'took them up' with him when he ascended the cross. The apostle uses the word, Heb. vii. 27, 'Who needeth not daily, as those high priests, to offer up (ἀναφέρειν, to carry up) sacrifice, first for his own sins, and then for the people's. For this he did once when he offered up himself,' (ἀνενέγκας, when he carried up himself.) So in the place cited but now, 'Christ was once offered to bear the sins of many,' ἀνενέγκειν ἁμαρτίας. It is an allusion to the priests, who carried up the sacrifice, and with it the sins of the people, to the altar. Christ did the same with respect to his cross, whither he first carried up sin, and then he carried or bore it away.

I have but just mentioned these scriptures to prove the thing in hand, to which should I have spoken as largely as the matter in them would have borne, or should I now fall upon the refutation of the adversaries' replies, such as they are, by which they endeavour to weaken them, I should certainly run myself upon unpardonable prolixity.

To back this notion of these expiatory sacrifices, which were of God's own appointment and institution, I thought, though it would have been but as the holding of a candle to the sun, to have shewn that it was the very notion of the heathens themselves in their idolatrous sacrifices ; which, whether persons or things, they always looked upon as substituted in the room and stead of the offenders themselves ; but I have altered my purpose, because I conceive it will be most proper, at the close of the four heads which I am upon, to bring in altogether of what I have to say upon those pagan sacrifices, by way of parallel with the true sacrifices.

It is no time for us to divide amongst ourselves, or unnecessarily to run into parties, when the common enemy is in the field, yea, making fierce assaults upon us ; to defend ourselves against whom all our united strength will be little enough. Otherwise two things should here be further inquired into ; as,

1. It having been said that Christ did so far substitute himself in our stead as to undergo the punishment due to us, it may be queried, Whether he underwent the idem, the very self-same punishment that we should have undergone, or only the tantundem, that which did amount and was equivalent thereunto ? To which I answer, though I am very loath to meddle in points wherein persons eminent for learning and piety seem to differ, that in different respects both may be affirmed : the punishment which Christ endured, if it be considered in its substance, kind, or nature, so it was the same with what the sinner himself should have undergone ;[1] but if it be considered with respect to certain circumstances, adjuncts or accidents, which attend that punishment, as inflicted upon the sinner, so it was but equivalent, and not the same.[2] The

[1] So the word Nagas is taken, 2 Kings xxiii. 35; Zech. ix. 8. Significat adigere ad solutionem debiti.—Forer. Opprimi et ad solvendum adigi ab exactore.—Morus in loc.

[1] Mr A. Burg. of Justif., pp. 73, 74 ; Turret. de Sat., p. ix. p. 281.
[2] Non quidem idem Deo solutum quod debebatur ab iisdem,

punishment due to the sinner was death, the curse of the law, upon the breach of the first covenant; now this Christ underwent, for he was 'made a curse for us,' Gal. iii. 13; the adjuncts or circumstances attending this death were the eternity of it, desperation going along with it, &c.; these Christ was freed from, the dignity of his person supplying the former, the sanctity of his person securing him against the latter; therefore, with reference to these, and to some other things which might be mentioned, it was but the *tantundem*, not the *idem*. But suppose there had been nothing of sameness, nothing beyond equivalency in what Christ suffered, yet that, say some,[1] would be enough for the making good of the main truth against the adversary; for it was not necessary to his substitution that he should undergo in every respect the same punishment which the offender himself was liable unto, but if he shall undergo so much as may satisfy the law's threatening, and vindicate the lawgiver in his truth, justice, and righteous government, that was enough. Now that was unquestionably done by Christ.

2. Secondly, It having also been said that our Saviour took upon him the guilt of our sins, it may further be queried, Whether he took the guilt itself of them, or whether he did anything more than bear the punishment due for them? *Ans.* He first took the guilt upon him, and then he bare the punishment. Far be it from me to assert anything which may reflect the least dishonour upon Christ—I dread with my soul such a thing—but I see nothing, in the asserting of his voluntary susception of our guilt, which hath any tendency to that, therefore I hope I may affirm it safely and confidently; it is so far from that, that it was the highest manifestation of his love, and that which was necessary for our justification. There is in sin the *macula* and the *reatus*, the stain, or filth, and the guilt of it; or there is in it the fact, the fault, and the guilt; the two former are solely ours,[2] but the third and last Christ was pleased to

nos etenim debebamus æternas pœnas exsolvere, verum, pependit æquivalens Christus, &c.—*Hoornb. Socin. Conf.*, p. 253; V. Stegm. Photin., p. 260; Mr Baxter's Aphor., p. 26; Life of Faith, p. 325; also the author of *The Great Propitiation*, p. 71, &c.

[1] Dr Stillingfl. against Crellius, p. 441.

[2] Suscipiendo pœnam et non suscipiendo culpam, et culpam delevit et pœnam.—*Augast. de Serm. Dom.* in Luc., Serm. 37.

take upon himself. What is guilt but obligation to punishment? If the holy Jesus will freely put himself under that obligation, what can be said against it? certainly that he might do, and yet in himself be as holy and innocent as ever he was, and neither be the committer of sin, nor in the least be defiled by it, for the *macula* and the *reatus* are two different things. And indeed I do not well see how he could be said to bear the punishment of sin, that being strictly taken, if first he should not take its guilt. We all grant Christ's sufferings to be penal, but how could they have been so without guilt? therefore having no guilt of his own, he must be looked upon as assuming ours, upon which he might be said properly to undergo punishment. Had no guilt lain upon him he might have suffered, but he could not have been punished, punishment always necessarily presupposing guilt. I would not stretch too far allusive and metaphorical descriptions of Christ; but yet in all such that which is the first and most natural import of them must be improved and made use of. Now such a description of Christ is his being a surety; of which what is the first and natural import? surely this, a surety is one who takes the debt of another upon himself, and so, in case of the debtor's insufficiency, becomes liable to the payment of it; as to the consequences and inconveniences that follow, if he submits to them, that is but more remote, but the first and proper thing in his suretyship is his making of the debt to be his own; the application of this to the thing in hand is plain enough. 2 Cor. v. 21, 'He hath made him to be sin for us, who knew no sin, that we might be made the righteousness of God in him;' what is this being made sin? is it Christ's being a sacrifice for sin? Yes, but that is not all; it notes also, I am sure I am not singular in this interpretation, his being under the guilt of sin. Where Christ is said to 'bear sin,' that may possibly signify no more than the bearing of the punishment thereof, as the phrase is used, Lev. v. 1, and xx. 17; 2 Kings vii. 9; but when it is said he 'was made sin,' that implies his voluntary susception of the sinner's guilt; and that this is the sense of the words in this place is evident from what follows, 'that we might be made the righteousness of God in him.' It is not said he bare the punishment of sin, that we thereupon might not

2 P

be punished, but he was made sin, under the guilt of it, for it is opposed to righteousness, that we might be made the righteousness of God in him, *i.e.*, that he taking our guilt, and so taking it away, as that was made over to him, so his righteousness might be made over to us, upon which we might be made guiltless and righteous before God. For my part, unless this sense be admitted, I do not understand what tolerable interpretation can be put upon the words. He is said to ' carry up our sins in his own body,' &c., 1 Pet. ii. 24; did he carry up the punishment of them? that is somewhat harsh; it was their guilt that he carried up with him when he ascended the cross. This was the very way wherein he must justify and save; for as he could not have saved us if first he had not taken our nature, so he could not have justified us or taken away our guilt, if first he had not taken it upon himself. For the *macula peccati*, that he was not capable of, therefore that shall be removed another way; but for guilt, it being not contracted but assumed, that he was capable of, and that was the thing for which satisfaction was to be made; therefore that he must take upon him and so take it away. Oh the transcendent love of Christ in this submission! his righteousness made over to us, and our sin made over to him; we made righteous and he made guilty, by imputation and in a law sense, what grace can be higher than this!

I have done with the second thing, Christ's substituting himself in our stead, in correspondency with what was done in the old Jewish sacrifices. The third follows, viz., Those sacrifices were to be consumed and slain, their blood to be shed and offered, and so they became expiatory. Such as consisted or were made up of inanimate things were to be consumed; others that consisted of living creatures were to be killed. As for instance, the meat-offering, that was to be burnt, Lev. ii. 1, 2; it follows, indeed, ver. 12, the oblation of the first fruits was not to be burnt, they being to be kept for the priests' use, Num. xviii. 13; but the meat-offering offered by and for the priests was to be burnt, vers. 14–16. The sacrifices of this kind and nature were to be consumed as well as others; for where their materials were liquid, those were to be poured out; where solid, those were to be bruised and burnt; still in every sacrifice some way or other there was *destructio rei oblatæ*. But eminently this was true in those wherein living creatures were to be sacrificed, they were to be destroyed or consumed indeed. And it is observable, the higher the sacrifice was, the greater was the destruction or consumption of it; for in such as were more ordinary, as those that were offered for private persons, there commonly but part of the sacrifice was consumed, and part reserved for the priests; but in the higher and more extraordinary, such as were designed for the priests and the whole community, especially those whose blood was carried into the Holy of holies at the solemn anniversary expiation, in them all was to be consumed; read Lev. vi. 30, and xvi. 27. The scape-goat seems to be an exception against this destroying, even of the great expiatory sacrifices, it being not to be slain, but sent into the wilderness by some fit messenger, Lev. xvi. 21, &c.; but the truth is, though that, for some typical reasons, was not presently and downright destroyed, yet virtually and in effect it was; for upon the sending of it into the wilderness it would in a little time be either starved to death, or devoured by wild beasts. But to come more closely to the business: the living creatures in sacrifices were to be killed, and then after that their blood in a special manner was to be offered upon the altar, it being that upon which the expiation did mainly depend. So the Lord himself tells us, Lev. xvii. 11, ' For the life of the flesh is in the blood, and I have given it to you upon the altar to make an atonement for your souls : for it is the blood that maketh an atonement for the soul;' where the first words, *for the life of the flesh is in the blood*, come in not only as a reason to back the prohibition that went before, ver. 10, in which notion I considered them before; but also as a reason of that which follows, viz., why God appointed the use of blood in sacrifices for atonement. It was upon this ground, because therein was the life of the creature. Now he designing life for life, therefore he pitched upon blood, wherein the life did lie. The apostle tells us, Heb. ix. 22, ' And almost all things are by the law purged with blood, and without shedding of blood is no remission.' And if you look into the Levitical sacrifices you will find what he saith to be true. In the burnt-offering for private persons there was killing and blood, Lev. i. 5 ; the same in the peace-offerings, Lev. iii. 2, 8, 13 ; the same in the sin-offerings, Lev. iv. 7, 16–18 ; and so in the rest. And the observation of these commands, which run so much upon blood, was so necessary, that should any of the priests have dared to have entered into God's presence in any other way than by sacrifices, and the blood thereof, he would not have taken it well at their hands ; yea, should they have brought into the temple never so many bullocks, rams, goats, &c., and not have slain them, or having slain them had not presented their blood before him according to his institution, they would have done no good either to themselves or others ; for God, to shew his justice, hatred of sin, &c., stood upon blood, and blood he would have. From all this we may infer, that those old sacrifices did not expiate as bare antecedents or conditions, without which God would not pardon, or as the offering of them carried in it some obedience to God's commands, both of which were common to many other things as well as to them. Surely there was more in it than so ;[1] for can we reasonably think that God would have been so positive and so express in his injunctions about so many sacrifices, so severe in the punishing the neglect of them, have ordered the taking away the lives of so many creatures, and have so much insisted upon their death and blood in order to expiation, had he looked upon them only as prerequisite and remoter conditions of pardon, or common acts of obedience, and that as such only they should be expiatory? Certainly had there been nothing in them more than this, the merciful Creator would have spared the blood of the poor creatures, and would have pitched upon some other course, which might have seemed, at least, more consistent with his wisdom and goodness. We may conclude them therefore to be means instituted by God in order to atonement and expiation, to the effecting of which, by virtue of his own institution and the merit of the great sacrifice to come, they had a direct and effectual tendency.

This foundation I have laid for the better understanding of the destroying, killing, shedding of blood that was in the typical sacrifices. I come now to build upon it with respect to the real sacrifice, Christ Jesus. In conformity to them, therefore,

[1] Dr Stillingfleet against Crellius, p. 516, &c.

Christ was slain, died upon the cross, his body broken, his blood spilt, &c.—all which speaks him to be a true expiatory sacrifice. Had he not died and suffered he could not have been such ; but upon that he is not only such a sacrifice really but eminently, the dignity of his person putting a superlative worth and efficacy upon his death and sacrifice. Oh what was the death of creatures to the death of God's Son ? What was the blood of beasts to the blood of him who was God? Acts xx. 28 —for such a person to die, to shed his blood for the expiation of sin ? Here was a sacrifice indeed ! And surely one great end of God in ordering the death of the old sacrifices, was to convince the world of the necessity of the death of this far greater sacrifice. By them he designed, in ways best known to himself, to lead men to a dying and bleeding Christ. How much doth the Scripture speak of his blood ! and though his whole humiliation must be taken in as making up his sacrifice, yet in special what a stress and emphasis doth it put upon his death and blood, wherein his greatest humiliation lay, with respect to their influence upon the good of sinners ! Eph. i. 7, 'In whom we have redemption through his blood, the forgiveness of sins.' Rom. iii. 25, 'Whom God hath set forth to be a propitiation through faith in his blood,' &c. Rom. v. 9, 'Much more then, being now justified by his blood, we shall be saved from wrath through him.' 1 John i. 7, ' And the blood of Jesus Christ his Son cleanseth us from all sin.' Rev. i. 5, 'Unto him that loved us, and washed us from our sins in his own blood.' 1 Pet. i. 19, 'But with the precious blood of Christ, as of a lamb without blemish and without spot.' Mat. xxvi. 28, 'This is my blood of the New Testament which is shed for many, for the remission of sins.' Heb. ix. 12, &c., 'Neither by the blood of goats and calves, but by his own blood, he entered in once into the holy place, having obtained eternal redemption for us. For if the blood of bulls and of goats,' &c. Col. i. 14, 'Having made peace through the blood of his cross.' Surely there must be some special reason why this blood of Christ is so often mentioned, and why the great benefits which sinners receive by him are in such a way of eminency ascribed to it, of which some account will be given in the following particular. Oh the severity of God's justice, which nothing could satisfy but the blood of his own Son ! Oh the love of Christ, who thought not the best blood in his veins too good for sinners ! Oh the truth of his satisfaction ! for what could such blood be spilt but for that ? what end could be proportionable to such a medium but satisfaction ? Oh the admirable harmony between type and antitype, the shadow and the substance, sacrifice and sacrifice ! Under the law it was blood, under the gospel it was blood too ; only that was common blood, but this excellent and precious.

4. Fourthly, If we compare Christ with the Jewish sacrifices in their ends and effects, that will further demonstrate him to be a true expiatory sacrifice. What were they ? Atonement and expiation. By them God was to be atoned and sin to be expiated. Now both of these were designed and admirably effected in and by Christ ; therefore he was what I am proving.

That those sacrifices were of an atoning nature, and appointed for that end, what can be more plain ? Here the so often cited text, which indeed is the key to the whole body of the Levitical sacrifices, doth recur : Lev. xvii. 11, ' I have given it to you upon the altar ;' for what end? 'to make an atonement for your souls ;' where the word used, as in very many other places, is *caphar*, which signfies to pacify, appease, or assuage the anger of one that is incensed.[1] So it is taken, Gen. xxxii. 20, ' I will,' saith Jacob concerning his brother Esau, ' appease him with the present that goeth before me.' So 2 Sam. xxi. 3. It signifies also to cover, Ps. xxxii. 1 ; to redeem, &c., Ps. xlix. 7, 8 ; but this of atoning, or pacifying, is most usual. Now in order to this atoning, God appointed sacrifices, the shedding of whose blood was to make an atonement, saith the Lord here, and he goes over it again, ' for it is the blood that maketh an atonement for the soul.' All along in the several kinds of sacrifices it runs, ' It shall be accepted for him to make an atonement for him ;' ' The priest shall make an atonement for them,' &c. This always comes in as the great end or effect of the law sacrifices ; whence they are said to be ' of a sweet savour unto

the Lord,' not only because of their pleasingness to God, but also because they made him propitious to, and well pleased with, such as had offended him ; so Lev. i. 9, 13, 17. It is the same word, but sometimes it rendered by reconciling : as Lev. vi. 30, ' No sin-offering . . . to reconcile withal in the holy place ;' Lev. viii. 15, ' To make reconciliation upon it.' We find when at any time in some particular judgments the anger of God did break forth, either against the people or against particular persons, presently they betook themselves to sacrifices, thereby to atone and propitiate him : Num. xvi. 46, ' And Moses said unto Aaron, Take a censer, and put fire therein from off the altar, and put on incense, and go quickly unto the congregation, and make an atonement for them : for there is wrath gone out from the Lord ; the plague is begun.' 2 Sam. xxiv. 25, ' And David built there an altar unto the Lord, and offered burnt-offerings and peace-offerings. So the Lord was entreated for the land, and the plague was stayed from Israel.'

As to the other end or effect, viz., expiation, that also belonged to sacrifices ; they had a power or virtue in them to cleanse and purify from sin's guilt, to procure pardon and remission, whence they were called expiatory ; and had it not been for this effect they could not have passed under that denomination. A full proof of it you have in that one sacrifice, the heifer, which was to be offered for the cleansing of the people, when murder had been committed, but the actor of it was concealed : Deut. xxi. 7, 8, ' And they shall answer and say, Our hands have not shed this blood, neither have our eyes seen it. Be merciful, O Lord, unto thy people Israel, and lay not innocent blood unto thy people of Israel's charge : and the blood shall be forgiven them. So shalt thou put away the guilt of innocent blood from amongst you,' &c. Was not here expiation ? And wherein did that lie, but in the putting away of the guilt of innocent blood, and in the obtaining of pardon ? for it is said, ' And the blood shall be forgiven them.' This is that which is set forth by cleansing from sin : Lev. xvi. 30, ' For on that day shall the priest make an atonement for you, to cleanse you, that you may be clean from all your sin before the Lord.' Num. iii. 5, ' For blood defileth the land, and the land cannot be cleansed

---

[1] This sense of the word justified by all anti-Socinian writers. Franz., disp. 15, th. 38 ; Turretin. de Satisf., p. 208 ; Grot. de Sat., p. 39 ; Hoorneb, Socin. Confut., p. 607 ; Dr Stillingfl., p. 509, &c.

of the blood that is shed therein, but by the blood of him that shed it.' The apostle sets it forth by 'purifying of the flesh,' Heb. ix. 13, by which he means the taking away of that ceremonial, ritual, or civil guilt which any did lie under. And he puts it out of all doubt, that expiation in the old sacrifices did not point to the abolition of sin's power, but to the ablation of sin's guilt; for having said, Heb. ix. 22, that 'almost all things are by the law purged with blood,' he tells you what he meant by that purging, adding, 'without shedding of blood is no *remission*,' or *expiation of sin's guilt*. And this is the notion which always he drives at in that epistle, in those several words which he there uses, viz., sanctifying, purifying, purging, &c. Indeed this was the chief and most proper effect of sacrifices;[1] other things might be done by them, but this was the main, therefore it so often comes in upon this account, 'And the priest shall make an atonement for them, and it shall be forgiven them,' Lev. iv. 20; so verses 26, 31, 35. And this might be one reason why God prohibited the offering of sacrifices to any but to himself, because the end of them being the forgiveness of sin, and none being able to reach that end but himself, therefore none should be sacrificed unto but himself.[2]

For the better understanding of this double effect of the law sacrifices, I desire four things may be considered:

1. That the atonement and expiation effected by those sacrifices must be conceived of as done by them in that notion which was proper to them as sacrifices. None can deny but that they did atone and expiate; but how did they so do? There is the question. I answer, this was done by them as they were substituted in the place of offenders, and were slain in their stead and for their sake. Other accounts I know by some are given of this, but that now set down is the true, as appears by what hath been already spoken under the two foregoing heads.

2. That this atoning and expiating virtue was not limited only to the sacrifices used at the anni-

versary great expiation, but it belonged to the other sacrifices. For instance, to burnt-offerings, (I take in those that were made use of before the giving of the law about sacrifices;) see Job i. 5; xlii. 8; after the giving of the law to free-will offerings, Lev. i. 3, 4, &c.; to the meat-offering and drink-offering, Lev. ii. *per tot.*; and xxiii. 13; Num. xv. 7, 10, 13, 14; to the peace-offering, Lev. iii. 15, 16; to the sin-offering and trespass-offering, Lev. iv. 6; to the ram, which was therefore called the ram of atonement, Num. v. 8. There is no end of such instances.

3. That yet the atonement and expiation proper to those sacrifices is to be limited according to the bounds which God himself was pleased to set; for it was but in such cases, and for such sins, wherein he did admit of them in order to these effects, of which more by and by.

4. That these effects were not produced by any inherent or innate virtue in the sacrifices themselves, but only as they were instituted by God, and as they derived efficacy from the sacrifice to come, Christ himself. Take away these two things, and what could these sacrifices have done? What could there be in them to pacify an angry God, or to purify a guilty sinner? What was the blood of a beast, as considered in itself, to expiate the sin of a man? The apostle plainly tells us, Heb. x. 4, 'It is not possible that the blood of bulls and goats should take away sin.' Therefore he says there was 'no perfection by the Levitical priesthood,' Heb. vii. 11; and 'the law made nothing perfect,' Heb. vii. 19; 'in which were offered gifts and sacrifices, that could not make him that did the service perfect, as pertaining to the conscience,' Heb. ix. 9. So that whatever virtue those sacrifices had, further than the taking away of civil guilt, ritual uncleanness, securing from church and state penalties, it wholly depended upon the institution of God and the merit of Christ. The brazen serpent healed such as were stung, yet not from any intrinsic power in itself, but only as God was pleased to give that power and efficacy to it; and so it was here in the case of the old sacrifices. These four things I have laid down, both to clear up the sacrifices themselves, and also because they are of great use to set us right in our conceptions about Christ the great sacrifice, which must be opened by them.

---

[1] *Vide* Essen. Tri. Crucis, lib. i. sec. 4, cap. 8, p. 6.

[2] Causa cur noluerit Deus alteri sacrificari quam sibi, ea potissimum videtur, quod sacrificia imprimis fierent ad expianda peccata, solus vero Deus jus habeat ea condonandi.—*Vossius de Idol.*, lib. i. p. 977.

Answerably now to these two great ends and effects of the Mosaical sacrifices, the same were designed to be done, and were actually done, by the Lord Jesus, when he offered up himself to God upon the cross; whereby he also, (1.) Atoned God; (2.) Expiated the sin of the elect. As God was angry and offended with the sinner, so Christ by his death procured atonement, pacification, reconciliation; as the sinner lay under guilt, so Christ brought about the purgation or expiation of his guilt. Both of these were done by him, and that too not only really, but in a much higher way than what was done by the old sacrifices, therefore he was a true proper expiatory sacrifice, yea, the most eminent expiatory sacrifice.

1. For atonement or reconciliation. By Adam's fall a sad breach had been made betwixt God and man; sin had greatly incensed the holy God against his sinful creatures, nay, there was a mutual and reciprocal enmity contracted between them. Things being in this dismal state, the blessed Jesus interposed himself in order to the appeasing of an offended God, and the reconciling of him and the sinner, the two parties that were at variance. For the effecting of which, he did not only as a bare *internuntius* treat with both, or only offer up prayers to the one, (in which respect Moses atoned God, Exod. xxxiv. 10–14,) and entreaties to the other, 2 Cor. v. 20, and so proceed by some verbal interposures; but, when nothing else would do it, he was willing even to lay down his own life, to die as a sacrifice upon the cross, by this means to bring God and man together again in amity and love. By which death of Christ the offended God was perfectly atoned and reconciled to the sinner; so as that now, upon the satisfaction made to him therein, he could without any injury to his justice and holiness receive the sinner into his favour, and not inflict upon him that wrath and punishment which he had made himself obnoxious unto. This is the true notion of atonement and reconciliation by Christ, and all that we mean by it.[1] But that this was thus done by him, what one thing is there in all the matters of faith wherein the gospel is more clear and full? 1 John ii. 2,

'And he is the propitiation for our sins.' 1 John iv. 10, 'Herein is love, not that we loved God, but that he loved us, and sent his Son to be the propitiation for our sins.' Rom. iii. 25, 'Whom God hath set forth to be a propitiation through faith in his blood,' &c. Rom. v. 10, 11, 'For if when we were enemies we were reconciled to God by the death of his Son, much more being reconciled we shall be saved by his life: and not only so, but we also joy in God, through our Lord Jesus Christ, by whom we have now received the atonement.' 2 Cor. v. 18, 19, 'All things are of God, who hath reconciled us to himself by Jesus Christ.' 'God was in Christ reconciling the world to himself.' Col. i. 20, 21, 'And, having made peace through the blood of his cross, by him to reconcile all things unto himself,' &c. 'And you that were sometimes alienated and enemies in your mind by wicked works, yet now hath he reconciled, in the body of his flesh through death.' So Eph. ii. 13, 14, &c. Isa. liii. 6, 'The chastisement of our peace was upon him,' *i.e.*, by his penal sufferings our peace was made with God. It is true, which our adversaries would fain improve to their purpose,[1] that all along in these scriptures the reconciliation is said to be on man's part, as if sinners were reconciled to God, not God to them; but there is a special reason for that, viz., because they were the first in the breach, they fell out with God before he fell out with them;[2] as also because the averseness to reconciliation is on their part; wherefore if they be willing to be reconciled to God, and are actually reconciled to him, there is no question of it but that he is willing to be reconciled to them, and is so actually. Some would have the reconciliation, as on God's part, to be spoken of: Heb. ii. 17, 'That he might be a merciful and faithful high priest, in things pertaining to God, to make reconciliation for the sins of the people;' where ἱλάσκεσθαι τὰς ἁμαρτίας is, according to the Hebrew *enallage*, as much as ἱλάσκεσθαι θεὸν περὶ τῶν ἁμαρτιῶν, as Grotius well observes.[3] However, supposing that this text doth not so expressly hold forth the thing, yet there is enough in those convincing reasons, arguments, and consequences, which

---

[1] Non statuimus Deum ex irato proprie factum esse propitium, sed Christi satisfactione causas iræ divinæ obliteratas esse, ut salva justitia sua possit gratiam exhibere.—*Essenius*, p. 253.

[1] Socin. de Serv., p. i. cap. 8.
[2] Baxter's Life of Faith, p. 189.
[3] De Satisf., p. 93.

the word elsewhere affords, to prove the reconciliation to be mutual, as is fully proved by divers.
Which reconciliation, you see, was accomplished by
Jesus Christ, yea, by his death and blood; so that
he exactly answers to the first effect of the Jewish
sacrifices.

2. Then for the second, the expiation of sin, that
also was done, with great advantage, by Christ; his
death carried indeed a sin-expiating virtue in it,
and was most truly of an expiatory nature. Let us
a little look into the Scripture and see what it saith
about this; and that we shall find not only to assert
the thing, but so to assert it as withal to set down
and determine the nature and true notion of it. I
mean this, the Scripture doth not only in general
speak of Christ's taking away or expiating of sin,
but it shews in what manner he did it, and wherein
the nature of that expiation did consist; as, namely,
that he did expiate it in that way which was agreeable to what was done in and by the old sacrifices,
and that according to the notion proper to their
expiation, so his must be understood. For in speaking thereof it uses those expressions which point
to those sacrifices and to their expiation; thereby
noting, (1.) That Christ did expiate in that very
way wherein they did; and (2.) That therefore his
expiation, in the nature of it, must run parallel with
theirs. Take a few instances: Heb. ix. 13, 14, 'For
if the blood of bulls and goats, and the ashes of an
heifer sprinkling the unclean, sanctifieth (ἁγιάζει)
to the purifying of the flesh: How much more shall
the blood of Christ, who through the eternal Spirit
offered himself without spot to God, purge (καθαριεῖ)
your conscience from dead works to serve the living
God?' Ver. 22, 23, 'And almost all things are by
the law purged with blood; and without shedding
blood is no remission. It was therefore necessary
that the patterns of things in the heavens should
be purified (καθαρίζεσθαι) with these; but the heavenly
things themselves with better sacrifices than these.'
Heb. i. 3, 'When he had by himself purged our
sins,' or as it is in the Greek, he having by himself
made purgation or expiation (καθαρισμὸν ποιησάμενος)
of our sins. 1 John i. 7, 'And the blood of Jesus
Christ his Son cleanseth (καθαρίζει) us from all sin;'
by which cleansing the apostle meant the expiation
or remission of sin; for ver. 9, he puts them together,

'He is faithful and just to forgive us our sins, and
to cleanse us from all unrighteousness.' Heb. x. 22,
'Having our hearts sprinkled (ἐῤῥαντισμένοι) from an
evil conscience, and our bodies washed (λελουμένοι) with
pure water.' Rev. i. 5, 'Unto him that loved us and
washed (λούσαντι) us from our sins in his own blood.'

Now pray observe from these scriptures—

1. That the expiating of sin, under the terms of
purifying, purging, cleansing, washing, sprinkling,
is expressly attributed to Christ.

2. That he, as being a sacrifice, by dying and
shedding his blood, so did expiate sin.

3. That the proper and primary effect of his death
and blood was the expiation of sin's guilt, and as
a consequent thereof its remission: Mat. xxvi. 28,
'This is my blood of the New Testament which is
shed for many *for the remission of sins.*' Eph. i. 7,
'In whom we have redemption through his blood,
the forgiveness of sins.' So Rom. iii. 25.

4. That as the Jewish sacrifices were truly expiatory, they, in their way, taking off sin's guilt
and the punishment due thereupon, wherein the
formal nature of their expiation did consist; so
answerably Christ Jesus was a true expiatory sacrifice, he, in his way too, taking off sin's guilt, &c.,
wherein the formal nature of his expiation did and
must consist also.

This I ground upon a twofold consideration: (1.)
Because by those very words which were proper to
those sacrifices, and by which their expiation of sin
was set forth, I say by those very words the sacrifice
of Christ, and the efficacy thereof, is described; therefore it must be as truly expiatory of sin as they
were: this is sufficiently proved in the places that
have been cited. And I might further add, that the
words there used are the very same with those which
the Greek profane authors do always use, when they
are speaking of their expiatory sacrifices, and of the
effect of them, of which many instances are given by
the learned.[1] (2.) Because the apostle, who most
uses these words, and in the place too where he
most uses them, I mean in his Epistle to the
Hebrews, doth professedly draw a parallel betwixt
Christ and the law sacrifices, shewing there was a
great analogy and resemblance betwixt them. True,

[1] Stuck. de Sacrif., fol. 148; Grot. de Sat., pp. 128, 129,
with many others.

he asserts a greater excellency and efficacy in the one than in the other, and as to the manner of working he shews there was a vast difference between them; but yet as to the great effect of a sacrifice, expiation of sin, in that, so far as the nature of the things would admit of, they did agree. Well then, if they did purify and expiate, so must Christ; and as they did purify and expiate, in taking away guilt by death and blood, so must Christ; otherwise where would the analogy be between them? Was it not thus, there would be expiation in the type, and none in the antitype; and one way of expiation in the type, and another in the antitype, both of which are directly contrary to the apostle's scope and design in the forenamed epistle.

Some possibly will ask why I multiply so many words, and stay so long upon this point? I will tell them; I do it to vindicate both the reality, and also the true notion, of our Saviour's expiatory sacrifice. For the Socinians, who have not left us one fountain of evangelical comfort unpoisoned, herein deal with their usual subtlety.[1] Very fair words are spoken by them, as though they were for and did own Christ's expiation of sin; but when they come to open it, and to shew what they mean by it, they make it a quite other thing than what indeed it is; they keep the word, but quit the Scripture-sense thereof. Christ, say they, did expiate sin; but how? Why, by begetting faith in the sinner, by working repentance in him, by turning and drawing him off from sin, by delivering from the effects of it, by declaring the will of God about remission and the way thereunto, as his death was an antecedent to his exaltation in heaven, where, say they, he only expiates sin, &c. In such things as these, but not in Christ's undergoing the punishment due to the sinner and dying in his stead, they make his expiation of sin to lie. Now though much might be, and is, said against each of these particularly,[2] yet that which I have in the general insisted upon is a sufficient confutation of them all, viz., Christ must expiate sin in that way and sense wherein the sacri-

fices under the law did. Now did they expiate any other way than as they were substituted in the offender's room, and as they died in his stead? Therefore that must be the way wherein Christ our sacrifice doth expiate also. Thus I have gone over the four heads propounded for the proving of Christ to be a true, proper, expiatory sacrifice.

Only for the further clearing and confirming of what hath been said, it will not be amiss, before I go off from this, to shew how the heathens themselves, in their notions about their sacrifices, did exactly agree with what I have now delivered concerning the Jewish sacrifices, and also concerning Christ, the far greater sacrifice. The business of sacrificing was not a thing used and practised only amongst the Jews, but amongst Gentiles and heathens also; yea, even amongst those this practice in ancient times was so catholic and universal, as that there was scarce any considerable nation or people in the world of whose using of sacrifices we have not some account. Whence this came about I am not now to inquire; only, in a word, it proceeded partly from the instigation and delusion of the devil,[1] who loves to ape it after God, and to stir up his blind and deluded followers to do that to false gods which should only be done to the true God. Partly from the practice and example of the patriarchs,[2] the knowledge of whose sacrificing, according to divine institution, being diffused and spread over the world by tradition, (which commenced first from Adam to Seth; then continued from Seth to Noah; then from Noah to his sons; and they peopling the world transmitted the use of sacrifices to their posterity,) it had this effect, to draw men universally to conform unto and imitate the example of these patriarchs in this matter. And though they soon degenerated from the primitive and right use of sacrifices, in their departing from the true object of them, and in their sacrificing to them that were no gods, Gal. iv. 8, yet, in their idolatrous way, they continued and kept up the observation of them from one generation to another. In process of time when

---

[1] Socin. de Serv., p. ii. cap. 11, 13, 14, 16, 17; Crellius *contra* Grot., cap. 10, sec. 2.

[2] Grot. de Sat., p. 136; Hoorneb, p. 581, &c.; Franz., p. 207 and 450; Dr Stillingfl. against Crell., cap. 6, p. 507, &c.; Turret., p. 202, &c.; Jacob. ad Portum., p. 464, &c.

[1] See Rivet. in Gen., Exerc. 42; Dr Owen Theol. Nat., i. cap. 8, p. 89.

[2] Prima victimarum Gentilium origo est ex divina institutione patriarchis facta, urgente insuper conscientia.—*Essen.*, p. 237.

the Jews, after their coming out of Egypt, were formed into a distinct polity, and sacrifices were re-instituted by God, and all things in special laws made by him precisely ordered about them. It is probable that from thence the Gentiles did receive further light, which accordingly they in a great measure complied with; for do but bate the difference in the object, and in some other things, and there was a great agreement betwixt the sacrifices of the one and of the other, as also in the conceptions of both about them. This being the thing which falls in with what I design, I must be more particular about it; for instance therefore thus: In the Jewish expiatory sacrifices there was a surrogation or substitution of the things sacrificed in the room and stead of the offenders themselves, as hath been shewn; the same was also done in the Gentile sacrifices, and this was that very notion which they in them went upon.[1] Nothing more usual amongst them than for one to die for another, especially for the community;[2] and if they apprehended their gods by the inflicting of such and such evils upon them to be angry, presently they substituted some (whom they called *Viri piaculares*, περικαθάρματα, περίψηματα [3]) to die in the stead of all the people, so to make expiation. And as the Jews testified their designing and believing of this by their laying on of hands upon the sacrifices, so did the Gentiles also.[4] In the Jewish sacrifices there was the killing of them, the shedding of their blood, &c.; the Gentiles in theirs, too, were for death and blood.[5] The Jews

[1] Which, therefore, they called *Hostiæ succedaneæ.* Men' piaculum oportet fieri propter stultitiam tuam, ut meum tergum stultitiæ tuæ subdas succedaneum ?—*Plaut.*

[2] As the Decii amongst the Romans; Codrus amongst the Athenians; Menecæus amongst the Thebans, &c.

Hanc tibi Eryx meliorem animam pro morte Daretis
Persolvo.—*Virgil.*

[3] In allusion to whom, some think, the apostle uses these words, 1 Cor. iv. 13; *Suidas* in V., περίψημα; *Dr Hammond* in loc. In the lustration or purgation of their cities they used to put to death some malefactor, and at the execution of him to say, περίψημα ἡμῶν γενοῦ, be thou a victim in our stead.

[4] See Dr Stillingfl. against Crellius, p. 444.

[5] Et culpam hanc miserorum morte piabunt.—*Virg.*

Date gaudia Thebis
Quæ pepigi, et toto quæ sanguine prodigus emi.
                                        —*Statius.*

Upon this, Porphyry wrote much against these sacrifices, περὶ ἀποχ., lib. ii. p. 59.

hoped by their sacrifices to propitiate and atone God when offended; the Gentiles by theirs designed and hoped the same, for they had their *sacrificia ἱλαστικὰ*, too.[1] The Jews had their burnt-offerings, whole burnt-offerings, their sin-offerings, their solemn and annual expiations, and all for purging, purifying, expiating of sin; the Gentiles in all these concurred with them.[2] Nay, because they would be sure to do this effectually, by the sacrificing of their best to their gods, and conceiving that the life of man was most proper to expiate for the life of man; therefore, though this was their great sin, in order to the pacifying of their gods and the expiating of guilt, they stuck not at the sacrificing of men themselves, yea, of their dearest children;[3] instances of which, with commands against it, frequently occur in Scripture, 2 Kings iii. 27, xvii. 31, and xxiii. 10; 2 Chron. xxviii. 3; Jer. vii. 31, xix. 5, and xxxii. 35; Ps. cvi. 37, 38; Lev. xviii. 21, and xx. 2. In other things the heathens borrowed from the Jews; in this the Jews from the heathens. Upon the whole then it appears, that Scripture and nature do both concur in that notion of expiatory sacrifices which I have insisted upon; and surely in

[1] V. Stuckium de Sacrif., fol. 146; Gyrald. Synt. 17, p. 491. Placuit ad averruncandam Deorum iram victimus cœdi. —*Liv.*, lib. viii. Mactata veniet mitior hostia—*Horat.*

[2] Et solida imponit taurorum viscera flammis—*Virgil.* See Grot. on Lev. i. 9.

Sæpe Deos aliquis peccando fecit iniquos,
Et pro delictis hostia blanda fuit.—*Ovid.*
Annua quæ differre nefas celebrate faventes
Nobiscum.—*Virgil.*

They called these sacrifices, ἁγνιστικὰ καθαρτικὰ, from their purging and purifying from guilt. See instances in Grot. de Sat., p. 124.

Teque piacula nulla resolvent.—*Horat.*

[3] Pro vita hominum nisi vita hominis redattur, non posse Deorum immortalium numen placari arbitrantur—*Cæsar de Bel. Gallico.*

Sanguine quærendi reditus animaque litandum
Argolica.—*Virg.*
Sanguine placastis ventos et virgine cæsa.—*Idem.*
Omnis et humanis lustrata cruoribus arbor.—*Lucan.*

This ἀνθρωποθυσία prevailed so much, that the senate of Rome was fain to make a decree against it.—*Plin. Nat. Hist.*, lib. iii. cap. 1. See of it *Euseb. de Præpar. Evang.*, lib. iv. cap. 16; *Tertull. Apol.*, cap. 9; *Theodoret*, vol. iv. p. 589; *Porphyr.*, περὶ ἀποχ., lib. ii. sec. 27; *Saubertus de Sacrif.*, cap. 21, p. 517; *Stuck.*, fol. 41; *Grot. de Sat.*, p. 132; *Cloppenb. Spicileg.*, p. 212.

the applying of it to Christ—the grand expiatory sacrifice—the gospel is exceeding clear. So that when we assert his substitution in the stead of sinners, his dying for them, his atoning God, and expiating sin by his death and blood, we say nothing but what Jews and heathens in their expiatory sacrifices apprehended, believed, and acted upon. They then who differ in these things, (as to the general nature, use, and end of such sacrifices,) they differ not only from us, but from all mankind; of whom it might be expected they would better agree with heathens, since they do so ill agree with Christians.

I have despatched the first inquiry, What a kind of sacrifice Christ was? The second follows, When and where he was such a sacrifice? To which I answer, When he was here on earth, and especially when he died upon the cross, then and there he was this expiatory sacrifice. All are not of my mind herein. The enemy, who waylays me in every step I take in these great truths, is upon me again, and forces me to defend myself, or rather the truth I have laid down. He saith, Christ's being thus a sacrifice points to his being in heaven, and to what he there doth; that his death here was but a preparation to his sacrifice as there to be made, or but an antecedent condition to his having of power there to expiate sin, with much more to that purpose.[1] Here, then, lies the difference between us and Socinians. We say Christ's being the expiatory sacrifice belongs to that part of his priestly office which he executed here upon earth; they make it to refer to that part of his priestly office which he now executes in heaven. We time it in Christ's dying upon the cross; they in his sitting upon the throne.

Now that I may at once prove what is true, and also confute what is false, I argue thus:

1. It appears that here Christ's sacrifice was exhibited, or that here he made his expiatory offering, because the Scriptures speaks of it as a thing that is past, and antecedent to his exaltation and glory, and therefore it must be done here on earth, and not in heaven: Eph. v. 2, 'And *hath given* him-

[1] Socin. de Serv., part ii. cap. 12, 15; Smalc. de Divin. Christi, cap. 23; Catech. Racov. de Mun. Christi. Sacerd., quæst. 2.

self for us an offering, a sacrifice to God for a sweet-smelling savour.' Heb. i. 3, 'When he *had* by himself purged our sins, he sat down on the right hand of the Majesty on high.' Mark it, the sacrifice-purgation or expiation of sin was over and done, and then Christ's exaltation in heaven followed after: Heb. ix. 12, 'Neither by the blood of goats and calves, but by his own blood, he entered in once into the holy place, *having obtained* (not to obtain) eternal redemption for us.' Heb. x. 12, 'But this man, *after he had offered* one sacrifice for sins for ever, sat down on the right hand of God.' He did not first sit down on the right hand of God, and then offer up his sacrifice for sins; but he first offered, and then he sat down on the right hand of God.

2. When the Scripture speaks of Christ's expiation of sin by the sacrifice of himself, it speaks of it as a thing done but once; therefore it must refer to his death, which was but once, not to his intercession, or any other act in heaven, which is a continued, repeated, and reiterated act: Heb. ix. 26, 'For then must he often have suffered since the foundation of the world; but now *once* in the end of the world hath he appeared to put away sin by the sacrifice of himself:' ver. 28, 'Christ was *once* offered to bear the sins of many.' Heb. vii. 27, 'This he did *once* when he offered up himself.' Heb. x. 10, 'By the which will we are sanctified, through the offering of the body of Jesus Christ once for all.' Doth this *once* agree with anything that he now doth in heaven?

3. If Christ had not despatched his expiatory work at his death, why did he then say, 'It is finished'? John xix. 30. If his expiating of sin was yet to come and to be done in heaven, how could he with truth have spoken these words, that all was finished, when the great thing was yet undone?

4. That of the apostle is pertinent to our purpose: Heb. x. 5, 'Wherefore when he *cometh into the world*, he saith, Sacrifice and offering thou wouldst not, but a body hast thou prepared me,' &c. Wherefore did Christ come into the world? Why, to be a sacrifice, and to do that which the old sacrifices could not. God was even weary of them, could no longer 'take pleasure' in them, Heb. x. 8; he will have Christ, the better sacrifice, to come into the world, which accordingly he did. Ay! but what

was the world into which he came? Surely it must
be this lower world; for it must be understood of
that world into which he came to do the will of
God, as appears ver. 7–9. Now that was this world
below rather than that above; for where do we
read that Christ ascended into the upper world to
do the will of God, especially this will of God referring to his assuming a body, and offering up that
body? ver. 5, 10. These were things to be done
only on this lower stage of earth; whence, then, it
follows that here his sacrifice was made.

5. There was, as hath been observed, to be an
analogy and resemblance betwixt Christ's sacrifice
and the Levitical sacrifices, and he was to expiate
in that way wherein they did expiate; but if you
do not place his sacrifice in his death, where will
that analogy be? or how will he expiate in that
way wherein they did? What is there in Christ as
in heaven that carries any resemblance to the killing, slaying, shedding the blood, offering of the
Levitical sacrifices? There he sits in great glory,
puts forth his regal power, is head of his church, &c.;
but what is all this to suffering, dying, pouring out
his blood, wherein he was to answer to those sacrifices? Doth the Scripture lay so much upon his
death and blood for expiation, and yet shall that be
done where there is none of these?

It will be said, there is this in Christ in heaven to
carry resemblance to the old sacrifices: their blood
was carried by the high priest into the Holy of holies,
and there sprinkled by him towards the mercy-seat,
upon which expiation and atonement followed. Now
parallel to this Christ himself, our high priest, is
entered into heaven, the sanctuary not made with
hands, and there he executes his priestly office, after
a sort, for expiation and atonement also. To which
I reply, Christ's entrance into heaven cannot be
denied, nor that that doth much resemble what was
done by the high priest under the law, all that being
but typical of this: Heb. ix. 24, 'For Christ is not
entered into the holy places made with hands, which
are the figures of the true; but into heaven itself,
now to appear in the presence of God for us.' And
therein we have the second part of his priesthood,
the oblation of himself here on earth being the first,
and his intercession in heaven the second; which
two must not be divided, but conjoined; the former

must not jostle out the latter, nor the latter the
former. Which second part of his priesthood was
necessary, partly in respect of Christ himself, for the
completing and consummating of his priesthood, the
perfection and excellency of which depended upon
it; for, saith the apostle, Heb. viii. 4, 'If he were
on earth he should not be a priest,' i.e., not a priest
of the highest rank; he would come short of the
high priest, and be but as one of the ordinary
priests, if he should only offer without, and after
that not enter into the sanctuary as the high priest
did, and he only. And partly too in respect of
believers, that he might not only make his oblation
for them in order to impetration, which he had done
on earth, but that he might further present and
plead the merit of that oblation in order to application, and the actual giving out the benefits purchased and merited thereby, which was to be done
in heaven. Therefore this we readily grant and
firmly believe. But that our Lord's whole priesthood doth lie in this, or that he only in this place
and state doth expiate sin, or that his resemblance
herein to the high priest is sufficient, that we utterly
deny. For,

1. The Scripture, as hath been proved, in drawing
the parallel betwixt Christ and the law sacrifices,
doth not instance only in what was done by the high
priest in the Holy of holies, but also in what was
done by the other priests in the temple, and in those
sacrificial acts which were proper to them as well as
to him; nay,

2. It mainly instances in these; making the resemblance chiefly to lie in the mactation and oblation of those sacrifices, which was done without;
and therefore it must be Christ's death on the cross,
and not his intercession in heaven, which must be
meant by them.

3. As that which is asserted by our opposers
would utterly destroy all analogy betwixt Christ
and those priests, and the far greatest part of sin-
expiating sacrifices, so it would in truth leave Christ
no sacrifice or oblation at all; inasmuch as what he
doth in heaven cannot, in any strictness or propriety
of speaking, come under the notion of an oblation
or sacrifice. There indeed is the presenting, commemorating, pleading of the sacrifice which he
offered here on earth, but that is all; he improves

the sacrifice there upon the throne, but he made it here upon the cross; he applies the expiation there, but he wrought it here.

4. It is true the high priest entered into the sanctuary and there expiated sin, but it was with the blood which had been shed and offered without: some of that blood, before offered upon the priest's altar, he carried into the Holy of holies, and there presented it before the Lord, and so made atonement. Had he gone in thither without this blood, and only have shewn himself before God, it would have signified nothing; what he there did was grounded upon the virtue of the preceding oblation, which was only now in a more solemn manner represented before the Lord. Just so it is with our Lord Jesus; he entered into heaven, and there intercedes as our high priest to his Father, but the efficacy of this his intercession is founded upon his blood shed when he was here on earth: take away his oblation here and take away his intercession there, for it is that which gives the efficacy and prevalency to this. Therefore he is said 'to enter into the holy place,' but how? why, 'by his own blood,' Heb. ix. 11; he must first shed his blood here upon earth, and then carry the virtue and merit of it with him into heaven, and so he may expect to do something which upon his mere appearance in heaven he could not have done. So that there must be something in Christ's priesthood and sacrifice more than what is proper to him now he is above, in correspondency to what was done by the high priest in his entering into the Holy of holies and there expiating sin. I think if all be put together which hath been spoken upon this account, the truth, which I contend for, is written as with the beams of the sun, therefore I will say no more.

Thus I have finished the first thing propounded for the clearing of the observation, namely, Christ's being a sacrifice for sin; where I have shewn that he was a sacrifice, what a kind of sacrifice he was, and when or where he was such a sacrifice. The second thing propounded to be opened was the effect or efficacy of this sacrifice, viz., the condemning of sin: 'And for sin condemned sin in the flesh.' In this I will be but very brief, because it falls in with what hath been already insisted upon.

Here was a strange and wonderful sacrifice, the most costly one that ever was offered up to God; therefore surely something that is extraordinary and great must be effected by it; and so there was. What was that? why, sin was cut off, taken out of the way, as condemned persons use to be, its guilt abolished or expiated, wherein you have heard the condemning of it doth mainly consist. How this is set forth by such terms as answer to the law sacrifices, I have already shewn: Heb. i. 3, 'When he had by himself *purged* our sins.' 1 John i. 7, 'And the blood of Jesus Christ his Son *cleanseth* us from all sin.' Rev. i. 5, 'Unto him that loved us, and *washed* us from our sins in his own blood;' but there are some other terms by which it is set forth which have not as yet been mentioned; as, namely, the *taking away* of sin: John i. 29, 'Behold the Lamb of God, that taketh away the sin of the world.' 1 John iii. 5, 'And ye know that he was manifested to take away our sins,' which taking away of sin was a thing far above the power of the Levitical sacrifices. Heb. x. 4, 'For it is not possible that the blood of bulls and of goats should take away sins.' So also the *finishing* and *making an end* of sin: Dan. ix. 24, 'To finish the transgression, and to make an end of sins:' where the finishing of transgression is not the filling up of its full measure, of of which you read Gen. xv. 16; 1 Thes. ii. 16; neither is it the completing or perfecting of it, as we commonly take the word, in which respect Christ is said to be 'the author and finisher of our faith,' Heb. xii. 2, and to finish what he had to do and suffer, John xvii. 4, and xix. 30; but it is as follows, the making an end of sin, such a finishing as is destructive, not perfective. By Christ's sacrifice sin was destroyed, he thereby made an end of it, or sealed it up, as the word signifies, so as that it should never be seen or come forth again to the hurt of God's people. Again, it is set forth by the *putting away* of sin: Heb. ix. 26, 'But now once in the end of the world hath he appeared (εἰς ἀθέτησιν) to put away sin by the sacrifice of himself;' the word is rendered by *disannulling*, Heb. vii. 18, by *making void* or *abrogating*, Mark vii. 9. Set it as high as you will, the virtue and efficacy of Christ's sacrifice will reach it; by the oblation of himself he hath quite disannulled or abrogated and put away the guilt of sin. Put all together, here is purging, cleansing, washing, taking away, putting away, finishing, making an end of sin, all of which are the same with the condemning of sin in the text; do not all prove the real expiation of the sin of believers as the result and issue of the sacrifice of Christ?

I having in what goes before said enough for the opening of the true notion of our Saviour's expiating of sin, under the present head I have but two things further to speak unto—the one referring to the nature of the act, the other to the extent of the act.

1. As to the nature of the act, know that Christ hath so expiated sin's guilt as that it shall never be imputed to the believing sinner, in order to the inflicting of eternal punishment upon him. This must be rightly apprehended, or else we shall run ourselves upon great mistakes. When you read of the expiating, condemning, taking away of sin, (and so on in the other expressions named but now,) you are not only to understand them as pointing to the removal of sin's guilt, in their proper and primary intention, but also as holding forth no more about that removal of guilt than the non-imputation thereof to punishment. Christ indeed, by the sacrifice of himself, hath done all that which I am speaking of; but how? Not but that believers have yet guilt upon them; that that guilt, as considered in itself, makes them liable to the penalty threatened; that the formal intrinsic nature of guilt, viz., obligation to punishment, doth yet remain, and is the same in them which it is in 'others. All, therefore, which it amounts unto is only this, that this guilt shall not be charged upon such, or imputed to them for eternal condemnation. Sin is sin in the godly as well as in the ungodly; thereupon there is guilt upon them as well as on the other, and upon this guilt they are equally obnoxious to the law's sentence. But now here comes in the expiation by the obedience, death, satisfaction of Christ, by which things are brought to this happy issue, that though this be so, yet these persons shall be exempted from wrath and hell, and the punishment deserved shall not be inflicted. Thus far we may safely go, but beyond this we cannot; we may, for the encouraging of faith, the heightening of comfort, set this sin-expiatory act of Christ very high, but we must not set it so high as to assert contradictions. But these things

will be more fully stated when I shall come to the handling of the main doctrine of justification.

2. For the extent of the act, that must be considered two ways; either as it respects the *subject* for which this expiation was wrought, or as it respects the *object*, the thing expiated.

1. As to its extent in reference to the subject. And so Christ's expiatory sacrifice reaches, (1.) both to Jew and Gentile; not to the one or to the other exclusively, but to both: 1 John ii. 2, 'And he is the propitiation for our sins, and not for ours only, but also for the sins of the whole world.' (2.) To those who lived under the law, as well as to those who now live under the gospel. The former had the benefit of Christ's expiation of sin as well as the latter: Rom. iii. 25, 'Whom God hath set forth to be a propitiation through faith in his blood, to declare his righteousness, *for the remission of sins that are past*, through the forbearance of God'—where by *sins past* you are to understand those that were committed under the first testament, before Christ's coming in flesh. So the apostle opens it: Heb. ix. 15, 'And for this cause he is the mediator of the New Testament, that by means of death, for the redemption of the transgressions that were *under the first testament*, they which are called might receive the promise of eternal inheritance.' Nay (3.) there is a sufficiency of virtue and merit in Christ's sacrifice to expiate the sins of all men in the world. Yet (4.) in point of efficacy it extends no further than to true believers. Others may receive some benefits by a dying Christ; but this of the full and actual expiation of sin belongs only to those who have saving faith wrought in them. As this which I here assert is matter of controversy, I have no mind to engage in it. As it is practically to be improved and enlarged upon, so I shall speak to it in the use; therefore at present I will say no more to it.

2. As to its extent in reference to the object or the thing expiated, it reaches to all and every sin. Christ is such a sin-offering as doth take off from those who believe in him all guilt whatsoever. By his sacrifice for sin he condemned sin, that is, all sins whatsoever; it is indefinitely expressed, and to be understood universally. Take sin collectively in the whole heap or mass of it, or

take it distributively for this or that particular sin, all is expiated and done away by Christ's blood. The expiation is so full and complete that there is not the guilt of any one sin, little or great, left unremoved : 1 John i. 7, 'The blood of Jesus Christ his Son cleanseth us from *all sin.*' Acts xiii. 39, 'And by him all that believe are justified from *all things*, from which ye could not be justified by the law of Moses.'

Whether the Levitical sacrifices did thus universally expiate sin is a controverted point ; wherein the Socinians hold the negative, the orthodox the affirmative. The former say those sacrifices did free from the guilt of lesser sins, such as were sins of ignorance, committed through incogitancy, inadvertency, human infirmity ; but for great and grievous sins, such as were committed against knowledge, or willingly and wilfully, they did not free from their guilt. The latter assert and defend the contrary ;[1] and not without very good and weighty reasons ; for if we look into the annual expiatory sacrifice, we find that all sins were expiated by it : Lev. xvi. 21, 'Aaron shall lay his hands upon the head of the live goat, and confess over him *all the iniquities* of the children of Israel, and *all their transgressions in all their sins*, putting them upon the head of the goat, &c. And the goat shall bear upon him *all their iniquities*, unto a land not inhabited.' Ver. 30, 'On that day shall the priest make an atonement for you, to cleanse you, that ye may be clean from *all your sin* before the Lord.' Ver. 34, 'And this shall be an everlasting statute unto you, to make an atonement for the children of Israel *for all their sins*, once a year.' And as it was thus in the public sacrifices for all the people, so also in the private sacrifices for particular persons. Therefore as you read of the *chataath*,[2] the sin-offering which was appointed for sins of ignorance, Lev. iv. 2, xiii. xxii. xxvii. ; so of the *asham*, the trespass-offering, which was appointed for sins committed knowingly and willingly, such as

[1] *Vide* Calov. Socin. Proflig., p. 625 ; Lubert. *contra* Socin. ; Hoorneb. Socin. Confut., p. 602 ; Turretin. de Sat. Christi, p. 226 ; Stegm. Photin., p. 282 ; Owen against Biddle, p. 474, and p. 469.

[2] Of the difference of these two (*chataath* and *asham*) much is written. Fagius makes the one to refer to sins of omission, the other to sins of commission.—In Lev. iv. 2. Others make *asham* to point to sins particularly enumerated, *chataath* to

were of a more high and heinous nature ; as falsehood in the detaining of what was deposited, lying, violence, perjury, &c., Lev. vi. 2, 3, &c. Were not these great and horrid sins ? And yet God appointed sacrifices for the expiation of them : Num. v. 6, 'When a man or woman shall commit *any sin* that men commit, to do a trespass against the Lord, and that person be guilty, then they shall confess their sin,' &c. The priest is said, Heb. v. 1, to be 'ordained in things pertaining to God, that he may offer both gifts and sacrifices *for sins*.' It is set down without any exception or limitation ; so Heb. vii. 27. It is true, which the adversaries make great use of, the apostle sets it forth by 'the errors of the people :' Heb. ix. 7, 'Into the second went the high priest alone once every year, not without blood, which he offered for himself and for the errors of the people.' But then you must know that by these errors he means not only smaller sins, but all whatsoever, even such as were of a very crimson dye. And the Greek word ἀγνοήματα, here rendered by errors, with the Hebrew word *scagag*, do often point to great and grievous sins,[1] Acts iii. 17, and xiii. 27 ; 1 Tim. i. 13 ; 2 Pet. ii. 12 ; 1 Sam. xxvi. 21 ; John vi. 24 ; Ps. cxix. 21. Therefore why should we limit it to sins of a lower size and stature, especially if we consider that in that sacrifice, to which the apostle here plainly refers, the expiation was general of all sins, as you heard but now out of Lev. xvi. ? And it is very true too, that for sins which were committed with a high hand, contumaciously, in open defiance of God, &c., there he would not admit of a sacrifice for the expiating of sins so circumstantiated : Num. xv. 27, &c., 'If any soul sin through ignorance, then he shall bring a she-goat. And the priest shall make an atonement for the soul that sinneth ignorantly, when he sinneth by ignorance before the Lord, to make an atonement for him, &c. But the soul that doth aught presumptuously, the same reproacheth the Lord, and that soul shall be cut off from among his people : because he hath despised the word of the

sins in general.—See Dr Owen, Exerc. 24, on the Heb., p. 317 ; Dr Stillingfl. against Crellius, p. 474. But the most distinguish them as one was for sins of ignorance, the other for sins knowingly and willingly committed.—*Vide* Petit. Var. Lect., lib. ii. cap. 8 ; Saubert. de Sacrif., cap. iii. p. 65.

[1] See Franz. Schol. Sacrif., disp. 6, th. 60.

Lord, that soul shall utterly be cut off, his iniquity shall be upon him.' Heb. x. 26, 'For if we sin wilfully after that we have received the knowledge of the truth, there remaineth no more sacrifice for sins, but a certain fearful looking for of judgment,' &c. But this doth not weaken the truth of what I have said, viz., that even great offences were expiated by sacrifices, because they might be such and yet not come up to this sinning with a high hand and wilfully against the Lord, and thereupon might be expiable. Were there no sins of a middle nature betwixt such as were of mere infirmity and such as were committed perversely and obstinately, out of open contempt and defiance of God? Surely there were, (you have had instances of such ;) and was there no expiation for such? The contrary hath been proved.

To clear up this whole matter I would lay down three things :

1. When we say that the law sacrifices did take off the guilt of all sins, yea, of great sins, we always except such as God himself did except; where he was pleased to make a limitation, there we must do the same, but not otherwise.

2. It is evident that, as to some sins, God did make an exception. For the case stood thus : it pleased the Lord to give excellent laws to the people of Israel, those laws he backed with a severe penalty, that penalty was death, which was due upon every violation of the law.[1] It being so, yet out of his great compassion, he who, being the lawgiver, might therefore relax and alter his laws and the penalties annexed to them as seemed good to him, would not proceed in the utmost rigour, but he would graciously moderate and mitigate his threatenings. And therefore though death was incurred by every sin, yet it shall not accordingly be inflicted, but a substitution shall be admitted of, the beast shall die, but the sinner himself shall live. Upon this God appointed sacrifices, wherein the punishment due to the offender should be laid upon the thing sacrificed, and thereby his sin expiated. Well, but though he will be so gracious as thus to admit of the expiation of sin, yet, partly out of respect to his own honour, and partly out of respect to the Jewish polity, civil and ecclesiastical, he will do this with some kind of restriction; that is, he will admit of sacrifices for

[1] See Grotius de Sat. Christi, p. 122.

the expiating of some sins, but not of all. The murderer was to die, and no sacrifice to be accepted of on his behalf, Num. xxxv. 30–32, with reference to which some understand that of David, Ps. li. 16, 'Thou desirest not sacrifice, else would I give it,' &c. ; so the adulterer, Lev. xx. 10, the idolater, and so in several other cases. Here now was a limitation set by God himself, and therefore here could be no expiation, in the external and ordinary way. Indeed upon repentance there might be the doing away of the moral guilt, which made the offender liable to God and to eternal death; but as to political guilt, which made the offender liable to temporal death, that, if public and known, could not by sacrifices be taken off. When therefore you hear so much spoken of the virtue and efficacy of the old sacrifices as expiatory, you must always understand it according to this stating of it.

3. Those sacrifices may be considered absolutely or relatively. Absolutely and in themselves, and so their expiation reached only to some sins, and to the removal of some guilt, viz., that which was ritual and ceremonial. Relatively with respect to Christ, who was typified by them, and so by virtue of his great sacrifice to come, which they prefigured ; to persons duly qualified their expiation was general of all sins and of all guilt—I mean of all moral guilt before God, though not of all political guilt before men.

But though there be this difficulty as to the type, as to the antitype there is none. By Christ's offering up of himself to be sure all sins are expiated, even the greatest are washed away by his blood; none can stand before his infinite merit and satisfaction. Former sacrifices were weak, but Christ the grand sacrifice he is strong, 'able to save to the utmost all that come to God through him,' Heb. vii. 25. He is not only a sin-offering to remove the guilt of lesser sins, but a trespass-offering to remove the guilt of the greatest sins ; therefore as he is set forth by the former in the text, so by the latter in Isa. liii. 10. Where final impenitency and unbelief do not hinder, the death of Christ is sufficient to acquit from all guilt; by it all who perform the gospel-conditions have a full and universal discharge.

I have now gone through the several things necessary to be spoken unto for the explaining and confirming of the point; the use follows.

Use 1. Was Christ a sacrifice for sin? and did he thereby condemn sin? I shall from hence infer something, (1.) By way of information; (2.) Of exhortation; (3.) Of consolation.

First for information; and so this great truth may be useful in the informing of our judgments in sundry particulars. As,

1. We learn from it the truth of Christ's satisfaction. Here, amongst many others, is a very considerable argument to prove that Christ did really satisfy God's justice for man's sin; which therefore all who write upon, and for the verity of his satisfaction, do in special insist upon, with great evidence and advantage to the cause which they defend. And indeed it carries such light and conviction in it, as that the grand opposer of this satisfaction was more troubled to get off from it than from any other argument whatsoever; for when he came to answer Covetus's arguing for it from the legal sacrifices as prefiguring Christ, he was forced to say, &c., *in quo major vis esse videtur*,[1] in which (head of testimonies) there seems to be greater strength than in any of the former. And the annual great expiation being urged, as to that he saith, *difficilis sane nodus solvendus restat*,[2] one hard knot remains to be untied; it was a hard knot indeed, which he might endeavour to loose, but could not. The word *satisfaction*, it is very true, we have not ῥητῶς, expressly, in so many letters and syllables in the whole Bible, but the thing we have; yea, as to that the Scripture is so copious and full that it is not in any one other thing more copious and full. But suppose we had there the word as well as the thing, what would that signify to those with whom I have now to do? when Socinus is so bold as to say, For my part, although I should find that, meaning Christ's satisfaction, asserted in Scripture, not once but often, yet I should not therefore believe the thing to be as dissenters do hold;[3] wherein he comes but little short of what his friend Smalcius dared to speak

concerning the incarnation of the Son of God, of which you had an account before.

It is not for me here to launch out into that vast controversy of Christ's satisfaction, in the opening, stating, proving, defending of which so many volumes have been written; I must confine myself to that one thing which lies before me. And there is enough in it to stablish you in the belief of what we contend for; for was Christ, truly and properly, a sacrifice for sin? Were our sins the meritorious cause of his sufferings? Did he put himself into the sinner's stead, taking his guilt upon him, and undergoing that punishment which he should have undergone? Did he die, shed his blood, that he might thereby atone God and expiate sin, all of which have been proved out of the unerring word? And doth not all this amount to a demonstration of the truth of Christ's satisfying the justice of God for sin? Do we mean anything by his satisfaction but these things? And are not they clear enough from scripture light? The truth is, all the other arguments brought for the proof of Christ's satisfaction—I say all of them do either run into or fall under this one, of his being a sacrifice for sin. If God would pardon sin, be appeased towards the creature, &c., absolutely and without the intervention of any satisfaction, why did he appoint sacrifices under the law? Why must so many creatures die? Why must so much blood be spilt? *Quorsum perditio hæc?* He whose tender mercies are over all his works, Ps. cxlv. 9, who hath pity and goodness for all that he hath made, would he unnecessarily, or merely to shew his absolute dominion, have ordered so many creatures to be killed, slaughtered, destroyed from day to day? Why did he so peremptorily stand upon this, that 'without shedding of blood there should be no remission'? Heb. ix. 22. But I go higher, if God had not required satisfaction, why must Christ himself be made a sacrifice for sin?[1] Why must he take flesh, and then die in that flesh? Why must his precious blood be poured

[1] Socin. de Servat., p. ii. cap. 9.

[2] *Ibid.*, cap. 12.

[3] De Servat., p. iii. cap. 6. Ego quidem etiamsi non semel, sed sæpe id in sacris monumentis scriptum extaret, non idcirco tamen ita rem prorsus se habere crederem, ut vos opinamini.

[1] Si non fuisset peccatum, non necesse fuerat Filium Dei agnum fieri, nec opus fuerat eum in carne positum jugulari, sed mansisset hoc quod erat in principio, Deus verbum. Verum quoniam introiit peccatum in mundum, peccati autem necessitas propitiationem requirit, et propitiatio non sit nisi per hostiam, necessarium fuit provideri hostiam pro peccato.— *Orig in Num.*, Hom. 4.

out? Why must he feel the wrath of his Father? be under a necessity of suffering, and of such suffering too? Was there not a cause for this? Yes, surely. And what could that be but satisfaction? God had great and weighty reasons which made him to insist upon this, so as that he would in this, and in no other way, let out his love and mercy to sinners. For instance, he must vindicate his truth, make good his threatenings, maintain his own honour, as also the honour of his laws, make known his holiness, let the world see what sin was, what an extreme hatred he had to it, keep up and assert his rectoral righteousness, &c.; for though, as *pars offensa* and creditor, he might have done what he pleased, yet, as *rector mundi*, he must do that which shall speak him to be just and righteous in his government.[1] Now were not these great and weighty reasons for God to do what he did, and could these high ends have been attained without satisfaction? All his attributes were equally dear to him, and thereupon shall all be advanced alike; he was not for the advancing of mercy only, but of justice also; and therefore he will so carry it in his dealings with man as that he may glorify the one as well as the other. If he justify the sinner, wherein he displays so much of mercy, he will do it in such a way as that he may display his justice too; wherefore Christ must be a sacrifice, first, to expiate sin by his blood, and then God will not charge it upon the sinner: Rom. iii. 25, 26, 'Whom God hath set forth to be a propitiation through faith in his blood, to declare his righteousness for the remission of sins that are past,' &c.; he goes over it again, 'To declare, I say, at this time his righteousness;' wherein or for what end? 'that he might be just, and the justifier of him which believeth in Jesus.' What could the apostle have spoken fuller and plainer to determine the business in hand? How can the deniers of Christ's satisfaction, and of the necessity thereof, stand before the light of this scripture? Propitiation must be made by blood, by the blood of Christ, that thereby God might declare his righteousness; that he might be just, not so much in himself and in the general, as in this special act of the justifying of a sinner. Had we no other text in

[1] *Vide* Hulsium in Theol. Jud., p. 473; Grot. de Sat., cap. 2.

all the sacred records but this one, methinks it should be enough to silence and convince gainsayers; it is a bulwark for faith, which will stand firm in spite of all the little batteries that men can make against it. But the truth of Christ's satisfying divine justice will yet more fully appear from what follows in the next head, therefore I go on to that.

2. Secondly, This may help us to right notions concerning the nature and ends of Christ's death. For if it be asked, How or in what manner he died? we see he died as a sacrifice; if it be further asked, Wherefore did he die, or what were the main ends of his dying? I answer, He died chiefly for such ends as are most proper to sacrifices. If God's own Son die, undoubtedly there must be something special in his death, and some great ends must be designed to be promoted thereby—'died Abner as a fool dieth?' 2 Sam. iii. 33—but what were they? *Ans.* Such as may best comport and suit with the common ends of all sacrifices, especially of those by which he was more directly typified, and therefore the pacifying of an angry God, the purifying of a guilty sinner, being the principal ends in the death of the typical sacrifices, as you have heard, answerably these must also be the principal ends of the death of Christ, the real sacrifice.

The Socinians, in this matter, run into two dangerous errors: (1.) They make that in Christ's death to be supreme and principal which was indeed but subordinate; nay (2.) They make that which was but subordinate to be the sole thing therein, altogether excluding and denying what was supreme and principal. Now this one thing which I am upon, viz., Christ's being and dying as a sacrifice, in correspondency with the ends of the Levitical sacrifices, was it rightly understood and firmly believed, would be a sufficient confutation of, and antidote against, their pernicious tenets. For do they say that the main end of the death of Christ was to turn men from sin? The contrary appears, because that was not the main end in the law sacrifices. Or do they say that Christ died only for our good? It was not so, because that doth not agree with the law sacrifices, which were offered not only for the sinner's good, but in the sinner's stead. Or do they say that he died only as a witness of the truth, as an example?

2 R

&c. It was not so neither, because it shuts out that which was the principal intendment of the law sacrifices.

But besides this there are some other things of considerable strength, which, that we may the better take in, we must more particularly inquire into those causes or ends of Christ's death which they assign; that by the removal of false causes and ends—I mean in their exclusive sense—the true ones may the better appear.[1]

They say, therefore, (1.) Christ died for this end, that he might bear witness to the truth, confirm the evangelical doctrine, and give assurance to the world of the verity of what he had taught. To which we reply, The question is not whether these were true and proper ends—that we readily grant—but whether they were the principal, much more the sole ends of Christ's death—that we utterly deny. And our denial is grounded upon these reasons.

1. All along in Scripture the confirmation of the doctrine of the gospel is laid upon Christ's works and miracles, not upon his death, read Acts ii. 22; John x. 25, *et passim*. And he, having by these given a sufficient proof or evidence of the truth of what he had taught, it cannot be imagined that he died only or chiefly for this, that by his death he might give a further proof or evidence thereof. Besides, if this was the main thing designed and effected thereby, then, in the remission of sin, reconciliation with God, &c., we should owe as much to Christ's miracles as to his death; than which nothing can be more repugnant to the whole tenor of the word.

2. This would take away the peculiarity or speciality of Christ's death. For if there was nothing in it more than bearing witness to the truth, or confirmation of the gospel doctrine, then all the apostles and martyrs who ever died did the same, inasmuch as they by dying bore witness also to the truth, and confirmed the gospel doctrine. Then, as he saith to us, Mat. v. 47, 'What do ye more than others?' we

[1] Socin. de Serv., p. i. cap. 3, &c., et de Officio Christi; Crellius de Caus. Mortis Christi, with all the rest. Against them see Grot. de Sat., p. 26, &c.; Franz. de Sacrif., p. 400, &c., and 606, &c.; Hoornb. Socin. Conf., lib. iii. p. 492, &c.; Portus *contra* Ostorod., p. 447, &c.; Turret., p. vii. p. 247, &c.; Dr Stillingfl. discourse concerning the true reasons of the sufferings of Christ, with many others.

may say the same to him, What, blessed Jesus, dost thou more than others? And would not this be a fine question? Certainly the death of the mediator and the death of the martyr are two different things, not only *quoad gradum*, but *quoad speciem;* but if it was as this sort of men would have it, there might be a gradual difference betwixt them, but nothing more. Must Christ's dying for us amount only to his dying as a martyr for the truth? Here is the μαρτύριον, but where is the λυτρὸν? Paul laid down his life upon this account, and yet saith he, 'Was Paul crucified for you?' 1 Cor. i. 13.

3. Nay, thirdly, If Christ had died only upon this ground and for this end, then several of the martyrs had gone beyond him. How readily and cheerfully did many of them die! How desirous were they of laying down their lives for the gospel! They did not fear death; all their fear was that God would not so far honour them as to call them out to suffer it for his sake. And when they came to die, what abundance of inward peace and comfort had they! how were their souls brimful of heavenly consolation! They had as much thereof as ever heart could hold; so much that all their outward torments were nothing to them. But was it thus with Christ? True, he was very ready and willing to die, yet there was a time when he prayed, again and again, that the cup might pass from him: 'Father, if it be possible, let this cup pass from me,' Mat. xxvi. 39, 42, 44; and he had an innocent, sinless fear of death, for he 'was heard in what he feared,' Heb. v. 7. And had he such raptures and ecstasies of joy at his death as several of the martyrs had? Oh no! His soul was 'exceeding sorrowful;' he was under bitter agonies and conflicts, had great terrors in his spirit, &c., Mat. xxvi. 38; Luke xxii. 44. Now, had he died only as they did, merely to have borne his testimony to the truth, and for the confirmation of the doctrine of the gospel, would it have been thus? What! saints so full of joy, and God's own Son so full of sorrow? Saints in their sufferings to have such a mighty presence of God with them, and God's own Son to cry out, 'My God, my God, why hast thou forsaken me?' Surely there must be something special and extraordinary in his death above theirs. And so there was, for he had the guilt of all believers upon him, lay under the wrath of God, bare the

punishment due to sinners, was under the curse of the law, &c. These were the sad ingredients in his death which put such a bitterness into it. Had there been nothing more in it than bare martyrdom, or what is proper to that, how would he have been said to be 'a curse for us'? Gal. iii. 13 ; what singular thing would there have been in his being 'obedient to death, even the death of the cross'? Phil. iii. 8.

2. Secondly, It is said Christ died for this end, that he might set before men an example of obedience, patience, submission to God's will, zeal, and the like. I answer, that this was one end is very true, but that this was the only end is very false. Christ did not design his death to be only exemplary to us, but that it should also be satisfactory to God. He had in his eye the expiation of our sin, as well as our imitation of his example. 'Christ,' saith the apostle, 'also suffered for us, leaving us an example that we should follow his steps,' 1 Pet. ii. 21. But was that all? No. Ver. 24, 'Who his own self bare our sins in his own body on the tree.' Here was substitution in our stead, susception of our guilt, as well as the propounding of an example. If Christ should further the happiness of sinners only in this exemplary way, what then would become of the fathers, and of all those who lived before he came and died in the flesh, who therefore could reap no benefit by his example? And this would make the effects of his death to terminate wholly in us, and not at all to reach to God ; whereas he is 'a priest in things pertaining to God,' Heb. ii. 17.

3. They say Christ died for this end, that by his death he might strengthen and encourage faith, and thereby raise up men to the assurance of the remission of sin, freedom from eternal death, the possession of eternal life, &c. *Ans.* We grant that faith receives eminent support and encouragement from this, that it gives the highest satisfaction that is possible as to the certainty of gospel blessings ; yet this must not be looked upon as the primary, much less as the only end of Christ's death. For (1.) The blessing must be procured before there can be any assurance of it ; the thing must be supposed to be before persons can be sure of it. Now how was that brought about but by the death of Christ? and if so, then the only end thereof was not assurance ; but there must be another antecedent end, viz., the purchasing or effect-

ing of the thing which was to be the matter of that assurance ; and by that the Scripture mainly represents Christ's death : Mat. xxvi. 28, 'This is my blood of the New Testament, which is shed for many for the remission of sins.' Mark it, it was shed for the procuring of this great blessing, not for the assuring persons of it. (2.) This assurance is as much, if not more, the effect of Christ's resurrection as of his death. Indeed for him to die, that contributes very much, but it is his dying and rising again that hath the greatest influence upon it : 1 Pet. i. 3, 'Blessed be the God and Father of our Lord Jesus Christ, which, according to his abundant mercy, hath begotten us again unto a lively hope ;' by what? 'by the resurrection of Jesus Christ from the dead.' As to purchase and impetration we owe more to Christ's death than to his resurrection ; but as to assurance and subjective certainty, we owe more to his resurrection than to his death ; therefore the apostle brings this in with a *rather :* Rom. viii. 34, 'It is Christ that died, yea rather, that is risen again.' He is said to be 'delivered for our offences, and to be raised again for our justification,' Rom. iv. 25. The sinner's justification was merited by his death, but it was manifested by his resurrection ; thence, therefore, faith in its being assured of that privilege, must fetch its main encouragement ; so that this cannot be the only thing aimed at in his death, since it more properly belongs to another head. (3.) The Old Testament saints were high in their assurance, and yet they lived before the death of Christ. (4.) His death, simply considered, gives no such encouragement to faith, or ground of assurance. Consider it, indeed, as we state it, that is, as he died in our stead, to satisfy God's justice, appease his Father's wrath, expiate our sin, &c., and so it is highly strengthening to faith ; but if you take it in itself, and as our adversaries state it, so there is but little in it for faith's advantage. What inducement or encouragement would this be to sinners to believe, to set before them the death of Christ, unless those ends and considerations about it be taken in which our antagonists oppose? Without which it would rather draw out men's fear than their faith, rather drive them from God than to God ; for so more of his justice and severity would therein appear to deter them, than of his mercy to allure and encourage them. Oh, did God deal so with his own Son, who too was innocent and blameless? what, then, will he do to such vile, wretched, guilty creatures as we are? Must Christ so die? would not God spare him in the least? what, then, will become of such as we? Upon the whole matter, the Socinians say Christ's death was not at all intended to be satisfactory to God. I am sure, according to their stating of it, it is not at all consolatory to sinners.

4. They say Christ died for this end, that he might have a right and power after his death, when he should be in heaven, to forgive sin. *Ans.* Whilst he was here on earth, before his death, he had that right or power, therefore that could not be any end thereof : Mat. ix. 2, 'Son, be of good cheer; thy sins be forgiven thee;' and when some murmured at this, see how he stood upon the asserting of it : ver. 6, 'That ye may know that the Son of man hath power *on earth* to forgive sins,' &c.

5. It is said Christ died for this end, that he might procure for himself such and such power, dignity, and glory. But to this we say, it was so far from being the main end, that it was indeed no end at all; it being but the consequent, not the end of his death. See Phil. ii. 8, 9.

These defective causes and ends being removed, it remains that I set down those which were the chief and principal. And they were such as these : Christ died to be a sacrifice for sin, Heb. ix. 26, and x. 12; a ransom, 1 Tim. ii. 6; Mat. xx. 28; a propitiation, 1 John ii. 2; to reconcile God to us, and us to God, Rom. v. 10; 2 Cor. v. 19; Eph. ii. 13, 14; Col. i. 20, &c.; to deliver us from the curse of the law by his being made a curse for us, Gal. iii. 13; to save from wrath to come, 2 Thes. i. 10; to justify and make righteous, 2 Cor. v. 21; Rom. v. 9; to procure remission of sin by his blood, 1 John i. 7; Eph. i. 7; Mat. xxvi. 28; to overcome death by death, Heb. ii. 14; to purchase eternal life, John vi. 51; Heb. ix. 12. As he died in our place and stead, taking our guilt and bearing our punishment, so he died for these ends, that he might restore us to God's love and favour, and expiate all our sins by his making satisfaction for them. These were not only ends, but the supreme and primary ends of his death. I do not exclude the former, provided that, (1.) They be taken in conjunction with these;

nay (2.) In subordination to them. Christ in his dying might intend this and that, as his bearing witness, &c., but his main and principal intendments were satisfaction, reconciliation, forgiveness of sin, &c.; in the revealing of which the Holy Scriptures are so express and plain that to me it is very strange that any opposition, much more that so vehement opposition, should be made against it. Good Lord! how are opposers fain to strain their wit, to summon in all their invention and subtlety, for the finding out of some forced and pitiful interpretations of the texts alleged, thereby to evade the true sense and meaning of them! how do they set these scriptures, and themselves too, upon the rack, that they may seem to reconcile them with their hypotheses! but all in vain, as is abundantly proved.

3. Thirdly, From hence I infer the vanity and falsehood of all human satisfactions. Was the Lord Jesus himself a sacrifice for sin? and did he thereby condemn, abolish, expiate all sin for his members? Then what needs to be done, or can be done, further by any creatures in the way of satisfaction? 'What can the man do that cometh after the king?' Eccles. ii. 12. I cannot but take notice, how whoever will engage in these weighty points he must tread upon thorns and briers every step he takes; no sooner shall he have got off from one enemy, but there will be some other at hand with whom he must encounter also. I find it, I am sure, to be so; for no sooner have I quit myself of the Socinians, but the papists, in a full body, make head against me. The former would wholly take away Christ's satisfaction, the latter would add man's to it; the one denies the verity, the other the perfection of it. For they tell us, it is very true that Christ did fully satisfy the justice of God by his being a sacrifice for sin, and fully expiate the sins of believers, in respect of their guilt and of the eternal punishment due thereupon; but not in respect of temporal punishments : these, they say, they are yet liable unto, notwithstanding all that Christ hath done and suffered, and that, too, not only in the present, but for some time in the future state; for the preventing or removing of which, satisfaction must be made to God, either by themselves or by others. This is the Romish doctrine; in which, so far as I have gone, we have falsities enough; but should we go farther to their particular explication

and stating of the latter branch—men's satisfying by themselves or by others—what a mass and heap of ungrounded, unscriptural, absurd opinions should we there meet with : for there come in their penances, fastings, pilgrimages, corporal punishments, voluntary poverty, masses and prayers for them who are in purgatory, indulgences, &c. Oh what a big-bellied error is this of human satisfactions ! What a numerous train of falsities is it attended with ! Contrary to this we hold that Christ, by the once offering up of himself to God, did so fully free from all guilt and from all punishment too whatsoever, as that there is no need of any satisfaction at all to be added to his.[1]

The truth of ours, the falsehood of their opinion, might very largely be made out from these following considerations :

1. In the Jewish sacrifices, with which our Lord's doth correspond, there was no satisfaction or compensation, but only what was in and by the sacrifices themselves. Indeed in them God ordered, in case any private person had been injured, that satisfaction should be made to him by the sacrificer, Lev. vi. 5 ; but otherwise, as to the expiation of all guilt before God, and exemption from all punishment, the sacrifices themselves—their absolute and relative notion too being taken in—were sufficient. Respect being had to Christ, and moral conditions being performed, they alone did acquit from guilt and from eternal punishment, and they too of themselves did acquit from temporal punishment, without the intervention of any other satisfaction.[2] If the guilty person did offer up his sacrifice, that was judged enough to free him from all the penalties which otherwise he was obnoxious unto. And shall more be done by the type than by the antitype ? must they not agree in this as well as in other things ?

2. All punishment, in order to satisfaction, is inconsistent with the nature and tenor of the remission of sin. This gracious act is set forth by ' blotting out' of sin, Isa. xliii. 25 ; by ' covering' it, Ps. xxxii. 1 ; ' not imputing' it, Rom. iv. 8 ; ' not re-membering' it, Isa. xliii. 25 ; ' casting it into the depths of the sea,' Micah vii. 19. It goes so high in its degree as that God promises upon the sinner's repentance his sin should not be so much as mentioned, Ezek. xviii. 22 ; if it should be sought for it should not be found, Jer. l. 20 ; and it is so universal in its extent, that where one sin is pardoned every sin is pardoned, Isa. xxxviii. 17 ; Micah vii. 19 ; Col. ii. 13. Now how is punition reconcilable with this ? For God to do all this, and yet to punish in a vindictive way, or in order to satisfaction,—for I only speak of punishment in that notion,—is a contradiction. I know what our adversaries say, that in remission God acquits from the guilt, but not from the temporal punishment. I reply, this is their πρῶτον ψεῦδος, that rotten foundation upon which their whole superstructure is built. I am not afraid, notwithstanding the decree and anathema of the Council of Trent,[1] to aver it to be an utter falsehood ; for if the guilt be done away, as they affirm, what room is there then for punishment ? that being the ground of this, if it be removed, this must be removed also. Pray let me ask, a person by pardoning grace being made guiltless, whence should the punishment of this person arise ? That common maxim which our writers so much insist upon, viz., *Sublata culpa tollitur pœna*, is of most unquestionable truth, and backed with the concurrent suffrages of the ancients. The guilt being taken away, the punishment is taken away also, saith Tertullian ;[2] and where there is pardon there is no punishment, saith Chrysostom.[3] And indeed to affirm the contrary is to make the remission of sin little better than a ludicrous thing ; it would then be as if the creditor should say to his debtor, I freely forgive thee all thou owest me, only I must throw thee into prison, there to lie all thy days ; or as if the judge should say to the offender, I acquit thee from all thy crimes, only thou must die for them : just so it would be here, if God should remit the fault and yet exact the punishment. I do not deny but that he may lay many evils even upon pardoned persons, but then I deny them to be, properly

---

[1] See the thirty-first article of our church.

[2] Dominus qui exactissime omnes expiandi ritus per Mosem exsequitur, nuspiam tamen hanc aut illam satisfaciendi rationem constituit, sed totam in sacrificiis compensationem requirit.—*Turret. de Sat.*, p. 329.

[1] Sess. iv. cap. 8, can. 13.

[2] Exempto reatu eximitur et pœna.—*Tertul. de Bapt.*, cap. 5.

[3] Ὅπου συγχώρησις, οὐδημία κόλασις.—*Chrysost.*, Hom. viii. ad Rom.

and strictly, punishments; for the matter of them they may be so, but formally they are not so; chastisements they are, but not punishments; medicinal, but not penal; they do not come from God's vindictive wrath, nor doth he design them for the satisfaction of his justice, but they proceed from other causes, and are designed for other ends;[1] as, namely, to quicken them to repentance, to make them more sensible of the evil of sin, to refine them more from their dross, to heighten their graces, to draw out their patience, to make themselves and others to fear, &c. For God thus to afflict or correct is very well consistent with pardoning grace; but to punish, under any notion of satisfaction, save only that of Christ's, is not. In different respects we may and do both affirm and deny punishment to be incident to God's people; for when we have to do with the Antinomian, in such a sense we affirm it; but when with the papists, who would have it to be satisfactory to divine justice, we utterly deny it.

3. Thirdly, Human satisfactions are but mere human inventions, groundless, unnecessary, because Christ himself hath made satisfaction, yea, full and plenary satisfaction; his expiatory sacrifice being complete and perfect, why should anything be added to it? Heb. x. 10, 'By the which will we are sanctified, through the offering of the body of Jesus Christ once for all:' ver. 14, 'For by one offering he hath perfected for ever them that are sanctified;' for by that he procured remission of sins. 'Now,' saith the apostle, ver. 18, 'where remission of these is, there is no more offering for sin,' that is, no need of any further expiatory sacrifice. Hath the Lord Jesus, by the sacrifice of himself, satisfied or not? If he hath, for that our opposers dare not deny, then I argue, Shall he satisfy and the sinner too? will God have the debt twice paid? shall the surety pay it and the debtor too? This double satisfaction would

impeach both the justice and also the grace of God.[1] I ask further, hath Christ fully satisfied, or not? if he hath, for this is not denied neither, then I ask, what need is there of any additional or supplemental satisfaction? If he hath paid the utmost farthing, what hath the creature then left to pay, but only duty, love, thankfulness? &c. The papists speak very high concerning this satisfaction of our Saviour, for they say it is not only sufficient and full, but redundant and overflowing; they talk of a περίσσευμα, a superfluity or pleonasm and overplus, there is enough in it and to spare; and this overplus they make to be the matter of that treasure which is deposited in the church's hands, out of which the pope fetches his indulgences. That speech of Clement the Sixth is famous, One drop of Christ's blood was sufficient for the redemption of all mankind; as if all the rest might have been spared, which in effect speaks the Father to be too profuse and prodigal of his Son's blood. But notwithstanding all these high words, they are not contented with Christ's satisfaction alone, but there must be some *assumenta*, some of their own satisfactions to piece with it. We do not greatly fancy such high expressions, yet as to the thing we go higher than they; for we fully acquiesce in our Lord's most perfect satisfaction, without adding anything, under the notion of satisfaction, thereunto.

All that they say is this, Christ hath fully satisfied with respect to guilt and to eternal condemnation, but not with respect to temporal punishments. *Ans.* The vanity and unsoundness of this distinction hath been already refuted; all punishment resulting from guilt, if there be a full expiation of that, the punishment ceases, let the kind of it be what it will. But where do we find in the word any such restriction or limitation, that Christ satisfied for eternal, not for temporal punishments? did he not bear the one as well as the other? Isa. liii. 4, 'Surely he hath borne our griefs, and carried our sorrows,' &c.; and did he not take off from the sinner whatever he bare in his own person, so far as satisfaction is concerned? As to that question of Bellarmine, If Christ hath satisfied for our whole guilt and punishment, why after

[1] Ad demonstrationem debitæ miseriæ, vel ad emendationem labilis vitæ, vel ad exercitationem necessariæ patientiæ, temporaliter hominem detinet pœna, etiam quem jam ad damnationem sempiternam reum non detinet culpa.—*Aug. tr. postr. in Joh.* Pœnæ ante remissionem peccatorum sunt supplicia peccatorum, post remissionem sunt certamina, exercitationesque justorum.—*Id.*, lib. ii. De Peccat. Mer. et Rem., cap. 34. Νουθεσίας μᾶλλον ἢ καταδίκης τὸ γινόμενον, ἰατρείας ἢ τιμωρίας, διορθώσεως ἢ κολάσεως. — *Chrysost.*, Hom. xli. in Mat.

[1] Non patitur justitia Dei ut duas exigat satisfactiones propter unum debitum, cum una ei abundantissime est satisfactum.—*Thes. Sedan.*, vol. ii. p. 357.

the remission of the guilt do we suffer so many evils ?[1] It hath been already answered, they are but chastisements, not punishments ; corrections to us, not satisfactions to God.

4. Take one thing further. To satisfy an offended God is Christ's peculiar, an act wherein no creature must share with him. Human satisfactions do not only derogate from the perfection of his satisfaction, in which the strength of the former head did lie, but they also intrench upon the confinement of it to himself ; it is for man to sin, but it is only for the Son of God to satisfy ; this carries glory in it, wherein there must be no partner or co-rival with Christ : Heb. i. 3, 'When he had *by himself* purged our sins ;' mark that *by himself*, he and he alone could do such a thing as this. What can creatures do in God-satisfying work ? can they do anything for themselves that shall amount to a compensation for faults committed ? it is not satisfaction unless it be the payment of the whole debt, but, alas ! they cannot pay so much as a farthing ; they who when they have done and suffered all they can must say they are unprofitable, Luke xvii. 10, are very unfit persons to compensate injuries done to God. And if they cannot satisfy for themselves, much less can they do it for others,[2] as he that cannot pay his own debts is very unfit to pay the debts of others. The wise virgins had but just oil enough for their own lamps ; they could spare none for the supply of the foolish virgins, Mat. xxv. 8, 9. There is a great difference betwixt suffering for the good of others, and satisfying for the fault of others ; a Paul may do the former, 2 Tim. ii. 10 ; Col. i. 24, a Christ only can do the latter.

Obj. But Christ satisfied that the saints might satisfy.[3] *Ans.* We desire a Scripture proof of that ; otherwise our negation is as authentic as their affirmation.

Obj. But Christ's satisfaction is applied by the saints' satisfactions. *Ans.* We find no means of applying his satisfaction, but only the word and sacraments without, and the Spirit working faith and repentance within.

Obj. But we, say they, make the saints only subordinate, not co-ordinate agents with Christ in the matter of satisfaction. *Ans.* 1. Even that is too much. 2. They go higher ; for their great writers maintain,[1] that the saints apart, by and of themselves, without being beholden to Christ's merit or satisfaction, may as to temporal punishments make full satisfaction. These are but very weak pretensions to build an opinion upon, which doth so much intrench upon the glory of Christ's person, and the perfection of his sacrifice. There is but one argument for human satisfactions which is considerable, and that is that vast profit, those large incomes and revenues, which this brings in to the dispensers of them ; and this I confess I cannot answer. Were but these taken away, I assure myself this controversy would soon be at an end ; it is the satisfying of corrupt men in their pride, avarice, filthy lucre, rather than the satisfying of a punishing God, that is at the bottom of these disputes. I look upon this point, with its appurtenances, to have as much of the core and venom of popery in it as any one point whatsoever ; therefore I could not omit to speak a little about it. But for those who desire to look further into it, to see the things which I have but touched upon fully made out and vindicated, the arguments to the contrary answered, they may peruse the authors cited in the margin.[2]

4. Fourthly, Hence ariseth matter of information concerning the true nature and ends of the sacrament of the Lord's supper. . When I have spoken something to this, I hope I shall be off of all briers. The difference betwixt papists and protestants was not so great about the foregoing head, but it is every way as great about this. They hold,[3] that in the sacrament of the Lord's supper, (or mass, as they are pleased to call it,) under the elements of bread and

---

[1] *De Purgat.*, lib. i. cap. 10 : Si Christus satisfecit pro omni culpa et pœna, cur adhuc tam multa mala patimur ?

[2] Ὃς οὐδὲ περὶ τῶν ἰδίων ἁμαρτημάτων διος ἐστιν ἐξίλασμα δοῦναι τῷ θεῷ, πῶς ἰσχύσει τοῦτο ὑπὲρ ἑτέρου πρᾶξαι.—*Basil. in* Ps. xlviii.

[3] Bellarm. de Pœn., lib. iv. cap. 15.

[1] Amongst others see Vasquez in iii. part ; Thom., qu. 94, art. 2 and 3.

[2] Dallæus de Pœnis et Sat. ; Sudeel Adversus Humanas Satisfactiones ; Rivet. Sum. Controv., tract 3, qu. 12 and 13 ; Thes. Salmur., p. ii. p. 61, &c. ; Thes. Sedan., vol. i. p. 594, &c. ; Chamier, t. iii. lib. xxiii. ; Chemnit. Exam., lib. ii. sess. 4, cap. 8 ; Calvin. Inst., lib. iii. cap. 4 ; Turretin. de Satisf., Disp. 11, p. 305, &c.

[3] Concil. Trident., sess. 22, cap. 1, &c.

wine, as broken and poured out, the body and blood of Christ are offered up to God as a true and proper propitiatory sacrifice, and that too not only for the living, but also for the dead. The other hold that the sacrament neither is, nor ever was, designed to be a propitiatory sacrifice, but only a commemoration and application of that one and only sacrifice which the Lord Jesus, when he died upon the cross, offered up to God.[1] Now which of them in these different opinions have truth on their side, it is our present work to inquire after.

In order to which I have two things to do: (1.) To shew what the sacrament is not; (2.) To shew what it is.

For the first, it is not a sacrifice, I mean it is not a propitiatory sacrifice, as if there was any proper oblation of Christ's body and blood in it (further than what is done in a symbolical and sacramental manner) for propitiation and expiation. There is in it indeed, in a sacramental way, that body and blood which was really offered up to God upon the cross, but not as so offered up in this ordinance. I say it is not a sacrifice; for it is a sacrament, therefore not a sacrifice. These two carry a great difference in them: there is giving in the one, receiving in the other; in the one we offer to God, in the other God offers to us.[2] Accordingly with respect to Christ; as a sacrifice he was offered for us, in the sacrament he is offered to us, which are two things of such different notions as must needs be the ground of an inconsistency betwixt them; for can he at the same time be offered for us and to us too? If the Lord's supper be a sacrifice, it must cease to be a sacrament, for it cannot be both. True, the passover was both; it was a sacrament, (as it was a sign or token of Israel's deliverance in Egypt, Exod. xii. 13, and as it was to be eaten,) and it was also, in respect of the mactation and killing of the paschal lamb, a sacrifice;[3] therefore we read of sacrificing the passover: Deut. xvi. 5, 6, 'Thou mayest

not sacrifice the passover,' &c. 'There thou shalt sacrifice the passover at even,' &c. But the reason of its being a propitiatory sacrifice as well as a commemorative sacrament was this, because it was a special type of Christ, the great propitiatory sacrifice; whereupon it is said, 1 Cor. v. 7, 'Christ our passover is sanctified[1] for us.' Had it not been for this—its typical nature and reference—it could not have been both. Now in the Lord's supper there being nothing of this—it being wholly a representation of what is past, not at all a type of what is to come—it is not capable of being a sacrifice and a sacrament too; so that if we give to it the nature and notion of the former, we take from it and destroy the nature and notion of the latter.

But to argue more closely. That the eucharist is no propitiatory sacrifice, I prove by these arguments.

1. As Isaac once to his father, Gen. xxii. 7, 'Behold the fire and the wood, but where is the lamb for a burnt-offering?' So I would say, Behold the bread and the wine, the body and the blood, but where is the priest to turn these into, and to offer them as a sacrifice? Are there priests now under the gospel entrusted with an office, and invested with a power of sacrificing? It was always thought that with the ceasing of the old law sacrifices the sacrificing priesthood ceased also. I know it is very usual to give the title of priests to gospel ministers, which if taken in such a sense may be admitted; but if by priests you understand persons in office to whom it should appertain to offer up new expiatory sacrifices, in that sense all protestants deny any such now to have a being. Whence it follows, that as where there are no sacrifices, there there is no priesthood, so where there is no priesthood, there there are no sacrifices, for these two mutually depend each upon the other; and consequently that the Lord's supper is no sacrifice, upon the defect of this priesthood. We are told, indeed, that our Saviour, when this ordinance was instituted by him, did authorise and empower his apostles, and after them all ministers successively, at the consecration of the elements to turn them into a sacrifice, whereupon they may strictly and properly be looked upon as priests. Which if it be so, (as it is not,) they must then be priests either according to the

---

[1] Of this controversy see Phil. Mornæus de Euch., lib. iii. cap. 1, &c.; Hospin. Hist. Sacram., lib. v. cap. 13, p. 548, &c.; Camer. Opusc. Misc., p. 522, in 4to; Masonus de Min. Anglic., lib. v. cap. 1; Forb. Instr. Historico-Theol., lib. xi. cap. 20.

[2] Sunt proprie sacrificia populi ad Deum, ut sacramenta Dei ad populum.—*Morn. de Euch.*, lib. i. cap. 1.

[3] See this proved in Cloppenb. Scho. Sacrif., p. 142, &c.

[1] Qu. 'Sacrificed?'—ED.

Aaronical order, or according to that of Melchisedec, those being the two orders to which the sacrificing priesthood did belong.   But neither of these can be true : not the first, the Aaronical priesthood being abrogated ; not the second, the priesthood of Melchisedec being incommunicable to any but to Christ himself, as the apostle strongly proves, Heb. vii. It is observable amongst the Levitical priests, whilst the high priest himself was ministering in the Holy of holies, such as were of a lower rank were not at that time to sacrifice without; and why not so here? Christ our high priest is now in heaven, presenting the merit of his great sacrifice offered upon the cross ; and he himself being so employed, it is not for any ordinary priests to be sacrificing, in an expiatory way, here on earth.   And further, those priests, so long as they lived, were to execute their office themselves, into which none were to intrude till by their death room was made for others' succession ; so that if they had lived for ever, none had meddled with sacrificing but they.   Christ therefore living for ever to manage the business of what is propitiatory, none without great intrusion can pretend in a thing of that nature to join with him : Heb. vii. 23, 24, 'And they truly were many priests, because they were not suffered to continue by reason of death ; but this man, because he continueth ever, hath an unchangeable (ἀπαρ-άβατον,) priesthood,' or that priesthood which passeth not from him to another.   When Christ was here on earth he offered up himself as a propitiatory sacrifice ; if any now after him should pretend in that way to offer up his body and blood, as to the matter of the sacrifice, they would, in part, do that which he himself did ; and so there would be a passing of his priesthood in some way of equality, though not of cessation, to others.

2. It hath been observed, that in every expiatory sacrifice there was the destruction or consumption of the thing sacrificed, either in part or in the whole ; there being, therefore, no such thing in the Lord's supper, it cannot be looked upon as a true and proper expiatory sacrifice.   Pray what is destroyed therein ?   Doth Christ's body and blood cease to be what they were ?   In his sacrifice upon the cross there was a destruction, in the separation of his soul and body for a time, but what is there like to this in the sacrament ?   Bellarmine having

taken notice of this argument,[1] thinks to elude it with a very pretty distinction, viz., that Christ's body in itself is untouched in the sacrament, it losing nothing of its *esse naturale* when it is eaten there ; yet it doth lose its *esse sacramentale*, the bread being eaten by which it was signified and made visible.[2] *Ans.* As if the ceasing of something which was but external, visible, and representative, the thing itself remaining untouched, and the same that it was before, would amount to that destruction which was in the Levitical sacrifices, and which was necessary to be made upon the body of Christ at his death, in order to his being an expiatory sacrifice ! Surely either we are a sort of men so weak and sottish as that we will believe anything, or they are a sort of men so wedded to their opinions as that they will say anything that will but suit with their purpose, otherwise so great a man had never given so pitiful an answer to so considerable an objection.

3. Thirdly, If the sacrament be a real, propitiatory sacrifice, then so many sacraments, so many propitiatory sacrifices ; and as oft as that is administered, so oft there is a real, substantial oblation of Christ's body and blood in a propitiatory way.   But this is directly contrary to what the word saith ; therefore it is by no means to be admitted.   For that speaks but of one only propitiatory sacrifice, of Christ's once offering himself, namely, when he died upon the cross ; which one offering was so full and perfect, so effectual to all intents and purposes for redemption, propitiation, &c., as that it is not in anywise to be repeated or reiterated : Heb. vii. 27, 'Who needeth not daily, as those high priests, to offer up sacrifice, first for his own sins, and then for the people's ; for this he did *once* when he offered up himself.' Heb. ix. 12, 'By his own blood he entered in *once* into the holy place, having obtained eternal redemption for us.' Ver. 26–28, 'For then must he often have suffered since the foundation of the world ; but now *once* in the end of the world hath he appeared to put away sin by the sacrifice of himself.   And as it is appointed unto men once to die, but after this the judgment; so Christ was *once* offered to bear the sins of many,' &c.   Heb. x. 10, 12, 14, 'By the which will we are sanctified through the offering of the body of Jesus Christ *once* for all.   But this man,

[1] De Missa., lib. i. cap. 2.   [2] De Missa., lib. i. cap. 27.

2 s

after he had offered *one* sacrifice for sins for ever, sat down on the right hand of God. For by *one* offering he hath perfected for ever them that are sanctified.' Now how shall we reconcile the multiplication of propitiatory sacrifices, the reiteration of Christ's offering, with these texts? There is, saith the apostle, but one only propitiatory sacrifice, that which our Saviour offered upon the cross. Nay, say our adversaries, but there is; the mass is a propitiatory sacrifice also. The true propitiatory sacrifice, saith he, was made but once; nay but, say they, it is not so; it is renewed, repeated, and made over and over again. Christ, says he, did once, and but once, offer up himself; nay, say they, but he is offered again and again, as often as the mass is celebrated, in which his body and blood are as really offered as they were when he died upon the cross. Christ, saith he, by the one oblation of himself, hath obtained eternal redemption, put away sin, perfected for ever them that are sanctified; nay, say they, but he hath not; for besides that there must be the propitiatory oblation of him in the sacrament. Now let every person judge whether these things be not flat contradictions to the word of God, according to what we charge them with.

For the solving of this, therefore, they give us another pretty distinction, viz., of our Saviour's bloody and unbloody sacrifice, of that which was offered on the cross, and that which is offered at the mass. That, they say, it is very true, was but once, and is not to be iterated; but it is not so with the latter; wherefore the apostle, in all that hath been cited, must be understood as designing to exclude only the multiplying and repeating of the bloody, but not of the unbloody sacrifice; and so the mass is not at all concerned therein.

To which I answer, In shunning one contradiction they run upon another; for what can be more contradictory to the word, as also to the nature of the thing, than an unbloody, propitiatory sacrifice? It says, Heb. ix. 22, 'Without shedding of blood there is no remission.' Yes, say they, but there is; in the sacrament there is no shedding of blood, and yet thereby there is remission. Do they not still maintain that which plainly contradicts the Scripture? and instead of stopping one gap, do they not make another? The apostle, after he had been speaking

so fully of Christ's sacrifice upon the cross, in the perfection and unrepeatableness thereof, draws an inference universally to exclude all other propitiatory sacrifices: Heb. x. 18, 'Now where remission of these is, there is no more offering for sin.' They then must be highly bold who will presume to except and limit where the Spirit of God doth not, and where the matter spoken of doth not require any such exception or limitation; nay, where indeed the matter will not bear any such thing, as here it will not; for if by Christ's oblation sin be fully remitted, how can any further sacrifice be joined with it in order to remission? To me this is a most necessary principle, viz., when men will distinguish upon the letter of the Scripture, so as to affirm what that denies, or to deny what that affirms, or so as to enlarge what that straitens, and to straiten what that enlarges. It highly concerns them to look to this, that their distinctions be well grounded upon other scriptures, and consonant thereunto; for otherwise they must run themselves into dangerous errors without all possibility of being convinced; and without this all religion will be undermined, and the word of God made wholly insignificant. Now to apply this rule. Our dissenters, when we urge the forementioned places, which are so clear and cogent for what we hold, would put off all by distinguishing of a bloody and unbloody sacrifice. I desire to know what Scripture ground or warrant they have for this distinction, in the sense wherein they use it? what is there to be found there to justify such a thing as an unbloody propitiatory sacrifice?

Something I know they offer at, but, alas! it is that which will not satisfy or command the faith of such who are serious and considerative. For instance, Gen. xiv. 18, 'And Melchisedec king of Salem brought forth bread and wine; and he was the priest of the most high God.' Whence they thus argue: Melchisedec did sacrifice bread and wine; there, say they, was an unbloody sacrifice, and that which was typical of Christ's sacrifice, and of his being offered at the sacrament *modo incruento*, under the species of bread and wine; therefore there was such a sacrifice thereat to be offered, which accordingly was done first by Christ himself, and yet is done successively by his ministers. Yea, they tell us that this unbloody sacrifice was the great thing in respect of which he is said to be a priest 'after the order of Melchisedec,' Heb. vi. 20; Ps. cx. 4. *Ans.* All this is denied with the same, but better grounded, confidence with which it is affirmed. It is sad that any should build so great an article of faith as this is amongst the Romanists, upon so weak and sandy a bottom; but how much more sad is it, that men's zeal should be so fierce upon it as to make it a matter of life or death, accordingly as it is believed or not believed? for the truth is, that which they call the unbloody sacrifice hath occasionally been made bloody enough in the death of thousands of martyrs, who could not look upon it as others do. But as to the argument, our divines reply, (1.) It is not evident that what Melchisedec here did was done in the way of a sacrifice to God. It is said he brought bread and wine; it is not said that he offered bread or wine to God. There is a great difference betwixt *protulit* and *obtulit*, betwixt a civil gift to men and a religious offering to God. Josephus[1] carries this bringing of bread and wine no higher than Melchisedec's kindness or hospitality to Abraham and his weary soldiers.[1] (2.) Suppose this was done in the way of a sacrifice, how will it be proved that it was done in the way of a propitiatory sacrifice, since it is only said that 'he blessed Abraham,' ver. 19. Nay, (3.) Suppose that too, yet what will it be to those who cannot justly pretend to be priests according to the order of Melchisedec, that being an incommunicable order? And (4.) The apostle, Heb. vii., opening this Melchisedec, in his priesthood, and in this very act, shewing how he was the type of Christ, and wherein Christ, the antitype, suited with him, doth not at all instance in his bringing of bread and wine, or in his offering any unbloody sacrifice, which surely he would have done had the resemblance or analogy betwixt Christ and him lain in that. But he instances in the oneness of Melchisedec's priesthood, in his eternity, in his authoritative benediction even of Abraham himself, in Abraham's paying tithes to him, &c. These are the things wherein all along in that chapter he illustrates Christ's agreement with Melchisedec. So that for any to infer, from his bringing of bread and

wine, that Christ at the sacrament, (for I do not love the word mass,) is offered up to God by every ordinary priest, as an unbloody propitiatory sacrifice; I say, for any to make such an inference from such premises, it argues them to be either injudicious, or over-credulous, or too much devoted to a party. The paschal lamb also is alleged for the making good of this distinction, with some other things; but neither barrel better herrings, as is fully made out by our protestant writers, where persons are not resolved to shut their eyes upon the clearest light.

4. Fourthly, In the present contest it will be best to have recourse to the institution of the sacrament. Now if that, with the whole administration about it, be consulted, what shall we find to give it the notion of a sacrifice? *Obj.* It is said, this we find: Christ there saith, 'Do this in remembrance of me,' Luke xxii. 19; 1 Cor. xi. 24. Now this *hoc facite* is as much as *hoc sacrificate*. *Ans.* What is it to play with the Scripture if this be not so? A few things being considered, the vanity of this criticism will soon appear. If *this do* was as much as *this sacrifice*, certainly that would have been a thing of such high import, as that of the three evangelists which set down the sacramental institution, two of them would not have wholly omitted it; and yet so it is. Luke recites it, but Matthew and Mark make no mention at all of it. And if that was the sense of the word, then the sacrificing act would lie upon the people as well as upon the priests; for as the *Do this* was spoken by Christ to the disciples, Luke xxii. 19, so it was also spoken by Paul to the body of the saints at Corinth, 1 Cor. xi. 24. When there is nothing spoken in the whole institution of the Lord's supper as referring to a sacrifice, it is somewhat strange that this word should come in by itself and carry such a sacrificial sense in it.[1] Besides, doth not that which follows sufficiently clear it up? *Do this.* How? or for what end? To be a sacrifice? No, but 'in remembrance of me.' We deny not but that *facere* doth sometimes signify to sacrifice,[2] answerably to the Hebrew word עשׂה, Num. vi. 16; Ps. lxvi.

---

[1] Antiq. Jud., lib. i. cap. 11. Ἐχόρησε ὁ Μελχισιδέχης τῷ Ἀβραμου στρατῷ ξένια, &c.

[1] Ineptum est interpretari verbum *facere* sensu sacrificatorio, ubi nulla in tota reliqua narratione fit sacrificii aut oblationis mentio.—*Forbes. Instruct. Historico-Theol.*, p. 616.

[2] Cum faciam vitula, &c.—*Virgil.*

15, and the Greek ῥέζειν.[1] But where hath ποιεῖτ, which is here used, that signification? Nay, where have the other words that signification, but when they are joined with a noun setting forth a thing that is usually designed and set apart for sacrifices? whereas the word here is joined with a bare pronoun.

Obj. But they have a stronger plea than this, grounded upon the words of the institution, where Christ saith, 'This is my body which is given for you,' Luke xxii. 19; and 'broken for you,' &c., 1 Cor. xi. 24; 'This cup is the New Testament in my blood which is shed for you,' &c., Luke xxii. 20; Mat. xxvi. 28. Now doth not this body as *given* and *broken*, and this blood as *shed*, prove a sacrifice? yea, that under the bread and wine there was a real oblation of Christ's body and blood?

Ans. No; unless it be understood, as it ought to be, of his oblation upon the cross, and not at the table. When he saith, 'This is my body which is given for you,' &c., 'This is my blood which is shed,' &c., did he mean that giving of his body or that shedding of his blood which was done just at the sacrament? That we utterly deny. What then did he mean? Why, that which would shortly be when he should die on the cross; then his body should be broken and his blood poured out in a real and substantial manner, but not till then. And this interpretation is not at all weakened by Christ's expressing himself in the present tense, (which *is given*, which *is shed*,) it being usual in the Scripture to put that tense for the *paulo-post futurum*; and I hope this answer will not be either opposed or slighted by our adversaries, since the vulgar translation itself renders the words in the future tense, which shall be given, shall be shed; yea, in their *Canon Missæ*, too, they are so rendered.

2. But, secondly, Having shewn what the Lord's supper is not, I am now to shew what it is. As to that, in brief, it is a lively representation and solemn commemoration of that sacrifice which the Lord Jesus offered up to God when he died upon the cross. It is not a sacrifice, but a memorial of a sacrifice. Herein lies the nature of this ordinance, and this was the great end of Christ in the institut-

ing of it. 'Do this,' saith he, 'in remembrance of me,' Luke xxii. 19.' As oft as ye eat this bread and drink this cup, ye do shew the Lord's death till he come,' 1 Cor. xi. 26. This, too, was the great end of the passover, unto which the sacrament of the Lord's supper succeeds: Exod. xii. 14, 'And this shall be unto you for a memorial.' Great mercies have always had their memorials, that they might not be forgotten;[1] what a mercy was Christ's dying and sacrificing himself! What glorious and unspeakable benefits do believers receive thereby! Therefore, lest this should wither and decay in their memories, this ordinance was appointed to be a standing memorial thereof. And this is that notion which the fathers had of the sacrament,[2] though some would fain draw them to be of another opinion, than which nothing more false. It is not to be denied but that they very often did call it a sacrifice; yea, sometimes they speak of unbloody sacrifices;[3] but did they thereby mean any real, propitiatory, and unbloody sacrifice, in the popish sense? No; they explain themselves by the commemorating of Christ's sacrifice, by the offering up of praises, thanksgivings, penitential tears to God, and the like, in which respects only they did so speak of it.[4]

To this also we may add, the Lord's supper is not only a memorial of, but a feast upon, Christ's sacrifice.[5] The believing soul doth therein by faith feed and feast itself upon a crucified Saviour. Anciently sacrifices were attended with feasts,

[1] See Vines on the Sacrament, pp. 143, 144.

[2] This proved by Morn. de Euch., lib. iii. cap. 4 and 5, with divers others.

[3] Euseb. Demonstrat. Evang., lib. i. cap. *ult.*

[4] Τὴν αὐτὴν ἀεὶ ποιοῦμεν, μᾶλλον δὲ ἀνάμνησιν θυσίας ἐργαζόμεθα.—*Chrysost. Hom.* 17 in *Ep. ad Heb.* Quid ergo nos? Nonne per singulos dies offerimus? offerimus quidem, sed recordationem facientes mortis ejus.—*Ambros in Ep. ad Heb.*, cap. 10. Illud quod ab hominibus appellatur sacrificium signum est veri sacrificii, in quo caro Christi post ascensionem per sacramentum memoriæ celebratur.—*August. de Civit. Dei*, lib. x. cap. 15. Vide etiam *contra Faustum Manichæum*, lib. xx. cap. 21. *Theodoret* in cap. 8 Ep. ad Heb. Sacrificium quod quotidie in ecclesia offertur, non est aliud a sacrificio quod ipse Christus obtulit, sed ejus commemoratio.—*Aquin.* in iii. p., qu. 22, art. 3, resp. ad. 2. Illud quod offertur et consecratur, vocatur sacrificium et oblatio, quia memoria est et repræsentatio veri sacrificii et sanctæ immolationis factæ in ara crucis, &c.—*Lombard.*, lib. iv. dist. 12.

[5] See Dr Cudworth's True Notion of the Lord's Supper, ch. 5.

[1] Ῥέζειν ἐστὶ τὸ θύειν.—*Casaub. in Athen.*, lib. xv. cap. 23.

nullum sacrificium sine epulo.[1] As soon as the sacrifice was over, men used to have a feast, to eat and drink together ; and this custom prevailed both amongst Jews and Gentiles.[2] Gen. xiii. 54, 'Then Jacob offered sacrifice upon the mount, and called his brethren to eat bread,' &c. ; Exod. xviii. 12, 'And Jethro, Moses' father-in-law, took burnt-offerings and sacrifices for God : and Aaron came, and all the elders of Israel, to eat bread with Moses' father-in-law before God.' See also Exod. xxxiv. 15 ; Num. xxv. 2 ; 1 Cor. x. 18, &c. Now parallel to this, after Christ's sacrifice, there is the sacramental feast, wherein the communicant doth spiritually feed upon the body and blood of the Lord Jesus, eats and drinks of the bread and water of life. Here is not *oblatio,* but *participatio sacrificii.* The apostle having spoken to the sacrifice, 'Christ our passover is sacrificed for us,' he presently subjoins the feast which was to go along with that sacrifice, 'Therefore let us keep the feast, not with old leaven,' &c. 1 Cor. v. 7, 8. At the sacrament there is not only a commemoration of Christ's death, but there is the Christian's fetching out of the sweet and comfort thereof for inward strength and nourishment.

Yet further, the Lord's supper is a seal of all those blessings which Christ, by his death and sacrifice, did purchase for his. But this I must pass over. I have been very long upon this fourth inference, but no longer than what the nature of the thing and our present state did make to be necessary. It is highly requisite that we should all have right apprehensions concerning the blessed sacrament ; therefore to help you therein, and to obviate all popish delusions, I have been thus large upon this head.

5. Fifthly, I infer the happiness of such who live under the gospel above those who lived under the law. It is none of the least of our mercies that we are cast under the evangelical, rather than under the legal administration. Old Testament believers were the elder brethren, but the younger, those who live under the New Testament, are the best provided for. For the making out of this I shall not insist upon the comparing of sacraments and sacraments,

priesthood and priesthood, privileges and privileges, but only touch upon the matter of sacrifices. In reference to which we have the advantage in sundry respects ; for they, in a manner, had but the shell, it is we that have the kernel ; they had but the shadow, it is we that have the substance ; they had but the type, it is we that have the antitype. All their sacrifices were but darker adumbrations of that great sacrifice which is now fully revealed to us, and actually exhibited for us. They had variety and multiplicity of them, we have all in one ; theirs were costly and burdensome, ours costs us nothing but thankful application ; theirs, of themselves, could only cleanse from ritual and civil guilt, ours from all guilt whatsoever ; they had the blood of beasts, we the blood of God's own Son. One of the great differences betwixt the covenant of grace, as then and as now dispensed, lies in the difference of the sacrifices.[1] To them it was testified and ratified by the blood of ordinary creatures, to us it is so by the blood of Christ ; compare Exod. xxiv. 8 with Mat. xxvi. 28. Surely we have the advantage over them, 'God having provided some better things for us, that they without us should not be made perfect,' as it is Heb. xi. 40. Oh what degree of thankfulness can be high enough for that knowledge of, interest in, benefit by Christ's sacrifice which we now have under the gospel, above what they had who lived under the Jewish sacrifice?

And if our state be better than theirs, how much more is it better than the state of the poor Gentiles ! As to Jews and Christians, it is happiness and happiness compared together ; but as to Gentiles and Christians, it is happiness and misery. The Jews had their sacrifices from God himself, to whom they were offered, and by whom they were owned, but in the pagan sacrifices there were none of these ; they were neither instituted by God nor directed to him, therefore it could not be expected that ever they should be blessed by him. And besides this, there was nothing of Christ in their sacrifices. Men sacrifices they had, but as to the sacrifice of Christ, God-man, that they knew nothing of; without which what could all their sacrifices signify for the purging away of guilt? They had great variety of them ;

---

[1] Stuckius de Sacrif., p. 145 ; Rosin. Antiq. Rom., lib. iii. cap. 33. Ubi quod diis tributum erat conflagrassent, ad epulas ipsi et convivia vertebantur, &c.

[2] Dr Cudworth, ch. 2.

[1] *Vide* Alting. Shiloh, lib. v. cap. 17. In hoc sacrificio vertitur omnis ratio et variatio fœderis, &c.

some blind notions of expiation, purgation, atonement by them, but, alas! not being offered to the true God, nor backed with the true and only propitiatory sacrifice of Christ, they were all in vain. They used to twit Christians with their want of temples, altars, sacrifices, &c.; [1] but we can easily answer them, We have all in Christ, whose one sacrifice upon the cross was more than all their hecatombs and sacrifices whatsoever. We may be the objects of their derision, but surely they should be the objects of our compassion; and whilst we pity them, let us be highly thankful for ourselves that ever this one, only, perfect sacrifice was made known to us, as well as offered for us.[2]

6. Sixthly, We may from hence take notice of the excellency of Christ's priesthood and sacrifice. I put them together, because they do mutually prove the excellency each of the other; his priesthood must needs be excellent, because he offered up such an excellent sacrifice, and his sacrifice must needs be excellent, because it was offered by such an excellent priest. The setting forth of the excellency of both is the main scope and business of the apostle in his Epistle to the Hebrews, that full and most evangelical commentary upon the Levitical sacrifices; but he reduces the latter under the former, proving the glory and excellency of the priesthood of Christ from the excellency of his sacrifice. Indeed in the making out of that he makes use of several other mediums or arguments: as, (1.) The greatness and dignity of Christ's person, Heb. iv. 14; (2.) The extraordinariness of his call, Heb. v. 4, 5; (3.) The pre-eminence of the order, according to which he was priest, above the Aaronical order, he being priest after the order of Melchisedec, Heb. v. 6, 10, and vi. 20; (4.) His oneness and singleness in this office, Heb. vii. 23, 24; (5.) His solemn inauguration into it, Heb. vii. 20, 21; (6.) Its perpetuity and everlastingness, Heb. v. 6, and vii. 16, 24; (7.) The excellency of the sanctuary where it is discharged, Heb. viii. 1, &c., and ix. 11, 12, 24; (8.) The betterness of the covenant to which it refers, Heb. viii. 6, &c. All these heads the apostle doth distinctly insist upon; but that medium or argument which he is most large

[1] Origen. *contra* Celsum., lib. viii.
[2] See the grounds of this fully set forth by Stuckius de Sacrif., f. 154, &c., in his *Antithesis Ethnicismi et Christianismi.*

upon to prove the excellency of Christ's priesthood, is the excellency of his sacrifice above all the law sacrifices. And that he makes out, (1.) From the matter of it. The priests under the law offered such and such things only, not themselves, but Christ offered himself; they the blood of creatures, he his own blood: Heb. ix. 12, 'Neither by the blood of goats and calves, but by his own blood he entered in once into the holy place,' &c.; ver. 14, 'How much more shall the blood of Christ, who through the eternal Spirit offered himself,' &c.; ver. 23, 'It was therefore necessary that the patterns of things in the heavens should be purified with these, (*i.e.*, the blood of beasts,) but the heavenly things themselves with better sacrifices than these.' Heb. i. 3, 'When he had by himself purged our sins;' so Heb. vii. 27, and ix. 26. (2.) From the virtue and efficacy of it. The law sacrifices were weak and unprofitable, could 'make nothing perfect,' Heb. vii. 18, 19; 'could not make him that did the service perfect, as pertaining to the conscience;' they only 'sanctified as to the purifying of the flesh,' Heb. ix. 9, 13. 'It is not possible that the blood of bulls and of goats should take away sins,' Heb. x. 4. But Christ by his sacrifice hath 'obtained eternal redemption,' Heb. ix. 12, that reaches the conscience to 'purge it from dead works,' &c., Heb. ix. 14. (3.) Those sacrifices being thus weak were many, and often to be repeated; but this of Christ, having such an efficacy in it, was but one, and but once offered, never any more to be repeated. Heb. vii. 27, 'Who needeth not daily, as those high priests, to offer up sacrifice, for this he did once when he offered up himself;' Heb. ix. 12, 'By his own blood he entered once into the holy place;' ver. 25, &c., 'Nor yet that he should offer himself often, as the high priest entereth into the holy place every year with the blood of others; for then must he often have suffered since the foundation of the world: but now once in the end of the world hath he appeared to put away sin by the sacrifice of himself.' Heb. x. 1, &c., 'The law having a shadow of good things to come, and not the very image of the things, can never with those sacrifices which they offered year by year continually make the comers thereunto perfect. For then would they not have ceased to be offered? because that the worshippers once purged, should have had no more conscience of sins,' &c. To these now the apostle opposes Christ's sacrifice, ver. 5, 6, &c. ; and of that he saith, ver. 10, 'By the which will we are sanctified, through the offering of the body of Jesus Christ once for all ; ' ver. 11, 12, 'And every priest standeth daily ministering, and offering oftentimes the same sacrifices, which can never take away sins. But this man, after he had offered one sacrifice for sins for ever, sat down on the right hand of God ; ' ver. 14, 'For by one offering he hath perfected for ever them that are sanctified.' The heathens had their sacrifices, which they called *hostiæ succedaneæ*,[1] which they offered up to their gods in case those which they had offered before did not succeed. The Lord Jesus, by his one sacrifice, did so effectually do what he designed and the sinner needed, as that there is no room for or need of any *hostia succedanea*. (4.) The apostle makes it out from the sanctity of Christ's person and the perfection of his sacrifice. The law priests offered 'first for their own sins, and then for the sins of the people,' Heb. vii. 27. 'They ought, as for the people, so also for themselves, to offer for sins,' Heb. v. 3. 'The high priest went once every year into the second tabernacle, not without blood, which he offered for himself (Lev. xvi. 11) and for the errors of the people,' Heb. ix. 7. But now as to Christ, he was 'holy, harmless, undefiled, separate from sinners,' Heb. vii. 26. He had no sin of his own to expiate by his sacrifice. He was 'made sin,' but yet he 'knew no sin,' 2 Cor. v. 21. Under the law both priest and sacrifice were to be perfect, *i.e.*, without any open and external blemish. As to the first, read Lev. xxi. 17 to the end ; as to the second, God gave several precepts about it. The paschal lamb was to be without blemish, Exod. xii. 5 ; the oblation for vows and for freewill-offerings, the sacrifice of peace-offerings, were to be without blemish, perfect, otherwise they should not be accepted, Lev. xxii. 18–25. So the red heifer was to be without spot, and wherein there was no blemish, Num. xix. 2 ; so the firstlings of the cattle, Deut. xv. 21, and all sacrifices whatsoever, Deut. xvii. 1. And this the heathens[2] themselves

made conscience of in their sacrifices. In correspondency to all this, in a moral and spiritual sense, our Lord's sacrifice was perfect, without the least blemish. He offered himself without spot to God, Heb. ix. 14 ; he was a lamb without blemish and without spot, 1 Peter i. 19. (5.) The excellency of Christ's sacrifice appears from the great effects of it. He 'put away sin by the sacrifice of himself,' Heb. ix. 26. So that 'there is no more offering for sin,' Heb. x. 18. 'Being made perfect, he became the author of eternal salvation unto all them that obey him,' Heb. v. 9. By this sacrifice sin was condemned, abolished, expiated, God appeased, the law satisfied, eternal redemption obtained, Heb. ix. 12. Oh what an excellent sacrifice was Christ's sacrifice, and, consequently, what an excellent priesthood was Christ's priesthood !

7. Seventhly, Was Christ a sacrifice for sin in order to the condemning of it ? and could it be condemned by nothing short of that ? hence we are informed that sin is a very evil thing, and of a very heinous nature. Had it not been a notorious and capital offender, would God have condemned, and thus condemned it ? Would he so severely have punished it in the flesh of his own Son ? Must even this Son be offered up upon the cross as a sacrifice for the expiation of it ? Oh what a cursed heinous thing is sin ! that had made such a breach between God and his creatures, that Christ must die or else no reconciliation ; that had so highly struck at the honour of the great God, that nothing below the sharpest sufferings of his dearest Son could make satisfaction for it ; its poison and venom was such that there was no cure for the sinner, into whom that poison had got, but only the precious blood of Christ himself. God had such a hatred and abhorring of it, as that for the testifying thereof, even he whom he loved from all eternity must be made a curse,[1] Gal. iii. 13 ; what a demonstration was this of the transcendency of the evil of sin ! Would you take a full view thereof ? Pray look upon it in and through this glass ; a sacrificed Christ gives the clearest, the fullest representation of sin's

---

[1] Succedaneæ dictæ, si primis hostiis litatum non erat aliæ post easdem ductæ hostiæ cædebantur, quæ quasi prioribus jam cæsis luendi piaculi gratia subdebantur et succedebant.— *Gyrald. Synt.*, xvii. p. 465 ; *Saubert. de Sacrif.*, cap. 19, p. 477.

[2] Οὐδὲν κολοβὸν προσφέρομεν πρὸς τοὺς θεούς, ἀλλὰ πάντα

τέλεια καὶ ὅλα.—*Athen. Deipn.*, lib. xv. cap. 5. &c., quas cum immolabant, nisi puræ integræque fuissent, minus proficere putabant.—*Gyrald.*, p. 491.

[1] Grot. de Sat. Christi, p. 67.

heinousness. True, we may see much of that in sin's own nature, as it is the transgression of God's most holy and most excellent law; as also in the threatenings which are denounced against it; and further in the dreadful effects of it, both here and hereafter, the loss of God's image and favour, and eternal damnation; is it not a very evil thing? What a mischievous thing hath this sin been! It cast the falling angels out of heaven into hell, and turned them into devils; it thrust Adam out of paradise, made God to be an enemy to him who but now was his favourite, cut off the entail of happiness, and instead thereof entailed misery and a curse upon all his posterity: it made God at once to drown a whole world, it laid Sodom in ashes, levelled Jerusalem itself to the ground, caused God to forsake his own people the Jews, &c.; it would be endless to enumerate all the sad mischiefs of sin.

Now, I say, in these things we may see much of the evil of it, but not so much as what we see in the death and sufferings of the Lord Christ; there, there is the highest discovery and fullest representation of it. He to be 'a man of sorrows and acquainted with grief,' Isa. liii. 3; he to be bruised and broken, yea, and his Father to be pleased in the bruising of him, Isa. liii. 10; he in his own person to undergo the law's penalty, to tread the winepress of the wrath of God, Isa. lxiii. 3; he to be obedient to death, even the death of the cross, Phil. ii. 8; he to cry out, 'My God, my God, why hast thou forsaken me?' he to be killed, and slain, and hanged upon a tree, Acts v. 30; and all this for sin. Oh what an excess of evil doth this hold forth to be in it! Indeed that the poor creatures should be so destroyed in the law sacrifices, that so many millions of them, they in themselves being harmless and innocent, should die and be sacrificed for man's sin, this represents very much of its cursed nature; but yet that comes infinitely short of that representation thereof which we have in a dying, crucified, sacrificed Christ. The death of all those sacrifices was nothing to the death of this one sacrifice, whereby sin eminently appears in its own colours. What a sad thing is it that men generally make so little a thing of it, as though there was not much evil either in it or by it; but in so doing how do their thoughts differ from God's thoughts,

for surely if he had not judged it to be very heinous, he had never carried it towards his Son as he did. I would desire sinners to take their prospect of it through this medium, of Christ's being a sacrifice for it; if anything in the world will bring them to the sight of its malignity, this will do it. It pleases God to look upon believers through a dying Christ, and so he loves them; but could we but look upon sin, a thing never to be loved, through a dying Christ, how should we hate it!

8. Eighthly, This demonstrates also the severity, impartiality, terribleness of God's justice. By Christ's death and sacrifice we have not only a declaration of the justice of God in itself, in that he would not remit sin without blood for satisfaction, Rom. iii. 25, but a declaration also of the adjuncts and properties of his justice, viz., that it is very severe, impartial, and terrible. He was inflexibly set upon the punishment of sin; such was his hatred of it and his respect to the honour of his law, that sin shall not by any means escape his punishing hand; and every punishment too shall not suffice, but it shall be such as may fully answer the heinousness of the offence. Ay! and if his own Son shall interpose in the sinner's stead, and take his guilt upon him, and become his surety, even he, be he never so dear to God, must undergo the utmost punishment that ever he was capable of, both for matter and degree. God will fall upon him and 'not spare' him, Rom. viii. 32, no, not in the least. Oh how severe and impartial is his justice! Never was there such an instance or demonstration of these, as in the sufferings of the Lord Jesus. For pray consider what it was that he suffered; besides all the sufferings of his life, at last he suffered death; and that not a common or ordinary death, but the very worst of deaths; a death that had all ingredients into it to make it bitter, wherein was all that bitterness which either the wrath of man, or, which was much worse, of God himself, could squeeze into it. And though Christ, foreseeing what this death was, prayed again and again that he might be saved from it, John xii. 27, that this cup might pass from him, Mat. xxvi. 39, 42, 44, yet his Father was inexorable and would not hear him; but die he must, and so die too; surely here was divine justice under the highest severity and impartiality, yet without

the least mixture of injustice. And when the thoughts and sense of this were upon Christ, they made his soul exceeding sorrowful, Mat. xxvi. 38; cast him into most bitter agonies, insomuch that he sweat, as it were great drops of blood falling to the ground, Luke xxii. 44. How dreadful and terrible is punitive justice! what a 'fearful thing is it to fall into the hands of the living God!' Heb. x. 31; this we see and know in our Saviour's case. Oh that we may never know and feel it in our own experience!

I might further infer from the premises, (9.) The unsearchable wisdom of God; (10.) Also his unconceivable love and grace; (11.) The preciousness of souls; (12.) The costliness of salvation; (13.) The great dignity of Christ's person, from which his sacrifice derived all its virtue and efficacy; but I must not speak to all that this vast subject would lead me to. So much for the inferences drawn from the main point.

Use 2. The next use shall be exhortation, in which I would press some of those duties which do best suit with the truth before us. Hitherto I have chiefly been upon the informing of the judgment; I now come to matters of practice.

1. And first, as Christ's Sonship and incarnation, (of which before,) so his being a sacrifice, and thereby condemning sin, should be very much the object of your study and meditation. This you are to study, that you may know more of it; to meditate upon, that you may draw out and improve what you already know about it; for so I would at present distinguish betwixt these two, supposing the one to be like the filling of the vessel, the other like the drawing out of that vessel. As to the first, I would be earnest with you to be much in studying a sacrificed, crucified Christ. If the knowledge of him as taking flesh is to be laboured after, as you have heard it is, surely the knowledge of him as dying in flesh, and as condemning sin in his flesh, is also to be laboured after. In this sacrifice of Christ you have the very mirror of the grace of God, the masterpiece and highest elevation of his love, the glorious product of his infinite wisdom, the great basis and foundation of man's happiness; should it not, therefore, with the greatest diligence be looked into? Our excellent apostle determined to 'know nothing

save Jesus Christ, and him crucified,' 1 Cor. ii. 2. The preaching of this was the great matter of his ministry: 1 Cor. i. 23, 'We preach Christ crucified;' and he makes the gospel in its revelation mainly to point to this, which therefore he calls τὸν λόγον τοῦ σταυροῦ, 'the word of the cross,' 1 Cor. i. 18. It being so, how should the consideration hereof heighten our endeavours after a full and distinct knowledge of it! God's own Son to be offered up as a sacrifice for the sin of man! Oh admirable and wonderful dispensation! what a mystery is this! how should all be prying into it! Here we have Christ at his worst; now the knowledge of him as at the worst is the best knowledge for Christians; for they having their best by his worst, the knowledge of him under that notion must needs be the best knowledge for them. If Christ, as a sacrifice, in the full import thereof, was but better understood by sinners, oh what benefit and advantage would thereby accrue to them! How steadily would they believe! how ardently would they love! how patiently would they suffer! how thankfully would they adore! how cheerfully would they walk! Should not these be prevailing inducements to such to labour after a fuller knowledge of him, as so considered? But in the enforcing of this duty let me not be mistaken; it is not a notional, historical knowledge only of Christ as sacrificed that I would have you to pursue after, but I would state it as practical, as operative and powerful: this, this is that knowledge which is to be desired. When Paul had spoken so high of the knowledge of Christ —Phil. iii. 8, 'Yea, doubtless and I count all things but loss for the excellency of the knowledge of Christ Jesus my Lord'—see how he opens that knowledge of him which he looked upon as so excellent: ver. 10, 'That I may know him, and the power of his resurrection, and the fellowship of his sufferings, being made conformable unto his death.' It is a poor thing to have light about this in the head, if that light be not attended with power and efficacy upon the heart and life; the clearest notions concerning Christ's death, without suitable impressions within, and that which in the sinner himself may bear some analogy and conformity thereunto, do not profit. Oh therefore so study a crucified Saviour as to be crucified with him, Gal. ii. 20, dead

2 T

with him, Rom. vi. 8, so as to feel the energy of his death in the heavenliness of your affections, and holiness of your conversations : this is the knowledge which we should study, and pray for, and aspire after.

For the second, Christ as a sacrifice is also much to be meditated upon. Oh how frequent, how serious and fixed should our thoughts be upon this ! How should we be often reviving this upon our minds, never suffering it to decay or wither in our memories ! This is so great and necessary a duty, that we have an ordinance instituted by Christ on purpose, and for this very end, often to inmind us of his dying as our sacrifice, and to keep it fresh upon our memories for ever : 'Do this in remembrance of me.' 'As oft as ye eat this bread, and drink this cup, ye do shew the Lord's death till he come,' 1 Cor. xi. 24, 26. But it is not enough to think of this just before or at the sacrament, but we should live in daily, frequent meditation upon it. I say we should do so ; but, alas ! it is to be feared we do not so. Oh how little is a dying, crucified Christ thought of ! The dying friend or relation is remembered, but the dying Saviour is forgotten. This proclaims to the world that we have but a low sense of his great love, that we see but little in his oblation ; for surely if we did, we should think oftener of it, and after another manner than now we do. Christians ! pray be sensible of former neglects, and let it be better for the future ; let not a day pass over you wherein some time shall not be spent in remembering and considering what Christ your sacrifice upon the cross suffered for you. Upon this also you would reap great advantages ; for certainly, was Christ's death but duly thought of and improved, oh, it would highly embitter sin, effectually wean from the world and the sensual delights thereof, mightily encourage and strengthen hope and faith, strongly engage the soul to obedience. Therefore, pray be persuaded to think less of other things, and more of this. And do not barely think of it, but think what there is in it ; yea, labour to go to the very bottom of it, and by serious meditation to press out all that juice and sweetness which is in it. The believer should be always sitting upon this flower, and sucking comfort from it. What is the full breast to the child that doth not draw it ?

Christ as a sacrifice for sin is a full breast, but yet if sinners by faith, prayer, and meditation do not draw from this breast, they will be little the better for it. He was indeed but once offered, but that one oblation is often to be remembered and continually to be improved, with respect both to duty and comfort. How that is to be done, the following particulars will shew.

2. This should have a very powerful influence upon you to break your hearts *for* sin and *from* sin. First *for* sin. Was Christ indeed made a sacrifice ? as such was his body broken and his precious blood poured forth ? did he undergo such sufferings in his life, and then complete all in his dying on the cross? and all for sin ? How can this be thought of with any seriousness, and the heart not be kindly and thoroughly broken ! What will cause the hard heart to melt and thaw into godly sorrow for sin, if the consideration of Christ's sacrifice and death will not do it ? Oh methinks his blood, as shed for sinners, should soften the most adamantine heart that is ! Did we but consider our Saviour's passion in the matter and quality of it, in its bitter ingredients and heightening circumstances, and then also consider that our sins were the meritorious cause of it, that they brought him to the cross, and laid the foundation of all his sorrows; did we, I say, but consider this, certainly we should be more deeply afflicted for sin than now we are. What ! that I should be accessory to the death of the Son of God ! that I should bring the nails and spears which should pierce him ! that I should be the occasion of all his sufferings in soul and body ! What a cutting, heart-breaking consideration is this ! Zech. xii. 10, 'They shall look upon me whom they have pierced ;' what follows ? 'And they shall mourn for him as one mourneth for his only son ; and shall be in bitterness for him as one that is in bitterness for his first-born.' The true penitent cannot look upon a crucified Saviour, especially when he considers what he hath done to further his Saviour's crucifixion, without the highest degree of holy grief. But especially this heart-brokenness should be in us when we are at the sacrament, where we have such a sensible and lively representation of Christ's death and sacrifice. Oh shall we there see his broken body, and yet our hearts be unbroken ? Shall we view

him there shedding his blood, and we shed no penitential tears? Shall we there behold what he endured and felt for sin, and we yet have no pain, no contrition for it? How unsuitable is such a frame to such an object, under such a representation! What was the temper, think you, of the women who were spectators of Christ when he was hanging upon the cross? Mat. xxvii. 55. Unquestionably they were filled with inexpressible sorrow. Why, sirs, when you are at the Lord's table, in a spiritual way you see him also as dying upon the cross; he is there before your eyes, evidently set forth and crucified among you, Gal. iii. 1. Oh how should your eye affect your heart, Lam. iii. 51, even to fill you with evangelical sorrow!

But this is not enough; therefore, (2.) There must be brokenness *from* sin as well as *for* sin. Surely after such a thing as Christ's death sin must be loved and lived no more; the heart must eternally be broken off from it. Pray look into the text, and see what pressing motives there are in it for this. (1.) Here is Christ dying as a sacrifice, making his soul an offering for sin. Now, sinners, shall that live in you, or will you live in that, which made your Saviour to die? shall he die for sin, and will you yet live in sin? shall his death, as to you, be in vain?[1] will you continue sin upon the throne when Christ was upon the cross? do you desire to have him there again, crucified afresh? as the apostle speaks, Heb. vi. 6; would you renew his wounds, and cause them to bleed again? was it not enough for such a person to be once sacrificed? can you wade even through his precious blood to the gratifying of your base lusts? Oh dreadful! I remember that passage of David, 2 Sam. xxiii. 15, &c., where you find him longing for the waters of Bethlehem: 'Oh that one would give me drink of the water of the well of Bethlehem which is by the gate!' Upon this his earnest desire, 'three of his mighty men brake through the host of the Philistines and brought him some of this water; but,' saith the story, 'he would not drink thereof, but poured it

out unto the Lord.' Why so? Oh, saith he, 'be it far from me that I should do this; is not this the blood of the men that went in jeopardy of their lives?' So here; sometimes your desires and inclinations are strongly carried out to such and such sins; but pray consider there is blood in the case. Those sins cost Jesus Christ his blood; he did not only jeopard, but actually lose his life; will you, then, meddle with them, be they never so sweet or pleasing to the flesh? I hope you will not; I am sure you should not. To strengthen this further, pray consider what Christ's end or ends were in his being thus a sacrifice: they refer either to God or to you; to God, as he designed to satisfy his justice, appease his wrath, vindicate his honour, &c.; to you, as he designed your sanctification, holiness, the abolition of sin's power, &c.—I say, the abolition of sin's power; for though the primary end, and the most immediate effect of Christ's sacrifice was the expiation of its guilt, yet in subordination to this, however in conjunction with it, the breaking of its power and freedom from its evil acts were by him also aimed at therein: Gal. i. 4, 'Who gave himself for our sins, that he might deliver us from this present evil world, according to the will of God and our Father.' Tit. ii. 14, 'Who gave himself for us, that he might redeem us from all iniquity, and purify unto himself a peculiar people, zealous of good works.' 1 Pet. ii. 24, 'Who his own self bare our sins in his own body on the tree, that we, being dead to sin, should live unto righteousness: by whose stripes ye were healed.' Now was this one of Christ's great ends in his sacrificing of himself, and shall he not have it? Hath he accomplished his ends with respect to God, and shall he not accomplish his ends with respect to you? Would you divide and compound with him to let him have half of what he designed and purchased, but no more? would you separate between justification and sanctification? That will not be allowed. How smartly doth the apostle argue for the death of sin from the death of Christ! Rom. vi. 3–11, 'Know ye not, that so many of us as were baptized into Jesus Christ were baptized into his death? Therefore we are buried with him by baptism into death: that like as Christ was raised up from the dead by the glory of the Father, even so we also should walk in newness of life. For

[1] Ergo et tu dignum te gere tali pretio, ne veniat Christus qui te mundavit, qui te redemit, et si te in peccato invenerit dicat tibi, quæ utilitas in sanguine meo? quid profeci tibi dum descendo in corruptionem, &c.—*Ambros. de Virgin.*, lib. iii.

if we have been planted together in the likeness of his death, we shall be also in the likeness of his resurrection : knowing this, that our old man is crucified with him, that the body of sin might be destroyed, that henceforth we should not serve sin. For he that is dead is freed from sin. Now if we be dead with Christ, we believe that we shall also live with him: knowing that Christ being raised from the dead dieth no more ; death hath no more dominion over him. For in that he died, he died unto sin once ; but in that he liveth, he liveth unto God.' Sirs, was Christ sacrificed for sin ? I will tell you what we should now do : let us sacrifice our sins for Christ. There is a great difference in the sense of the one and of the other ; yet take but that aright, and both are true. Christ was a blessed person, and he was sacrificed out of love ; but sin is a cursed thing, which therefore must be sacrificed out of hatred. It was pity that Christ should die ; it is pity that sin should live. He was sacrificed for our sin that he might take that away which was injurious to us ; we must sacrifice our sins for him that we may take that away which is so injurious and offensive to him. But to go on in the text. (2.) God condemned sin. There is very much in this also to set us against sin, in whatever notion the word *condemning* be taken. Did God condemn it, and shall we approve of it ? Hath he passed a sentence of death upon it, and shall we yet be for the life of it, as if we would reverse or contradict his sentence, or hinder the execution of it ? Did he look upon it as a traitor, rebel, capital offender, and shall we look upon it as a harmless and innocent thing ? Hath he in the death of his Son given out such a declaration of his hatred of it, and shall we yet love it, and like it, and live in it ? Yea, (3.) God ' condemned sin in the flesh' of Christ ; now shall it be judged, punished, abolished in Christ's flesh, and yet reign in ours ? Rom. vi. 12 ; shall he in his flesh suffer for it, and we in ours commit it ? What an absurd, incongruous thing would this be ! Upon the whole matter, therefore, how do we all stand engaged by the strongest obligations that are possible to be holy, and not to sin ! Let it be condemned in our flesh, as, in a different respect, it was condemned in Christ's. As God hath condemned it so as that we shall not die for it, so let us condemn

it so as not to live in it. And in special, whenever it shall come to tempt you to what is evil, pray remember that Christ was made a sacrifice for it ; and let it appear by your holy and circumspect walking that you have a due sense thereof, and that you do not from thence fetch any encouragement to sin against God, which was one of Porphyry's objections against sacrifices in general, viz., they would encourage men to be wicked.[1]

3. Thirdly, I would excite you to labour after, and to make sure of a personal interest in this great sacrifice, and in the benefits resulting from it. For it is a thing to be resented with the greatest sadness imaginable, that where there is such a sacrifice, so at first offered up to God, and now so revealed to men, that yet so many millions of souls should perish, and, as to their spiritual and eternal state, be little the better for it ; because they regard not, as to themselves, either the thing, or the good that flows from it. My brethren, I beseech you, if you have any love for your souls, let it not be so with you ; but let it be your greatest care to secure an interest in this sacrifice, and to partake of the blessings procured by it ; be often considering and questioning with yourselves, Here is a sacrifice for expiation and atonement, but what is this to us ? here is a dying Christ, but did he die for us ? shall we be ever the better for his death ? if this propitiatory oblation be not ours, what will become of us ? Under the law the Gentile strangers were to offer sacrifices as well as the born Jews, see Num. xv. 14, 15 ; Lev. xvii. 8 ; and amongst the Jews the poor as well as the rich ; with respect to which difference in men's outward condition God accordingly appointed different sacrifices, Lev. xiv. 21 ; but yet something or other both were to sacrifice ; and in their offerings for the ransom of their souls all were to give alike : Exod. xxx. 15, 'The rich shall not give more, the poor shall not give less, than half a shekel.' Now all this was to shadow out two things about Christ's sacrifice : 1. Its equal extent to all men, notwithstanding all national or civil differences ; be they Jews or Gentiles, rich or poor, it is the same Christ to all, if they believe, for

---

[1] Πῶς κεχαρισμένα θύειν ἡγούμενος τοῖς θεοῖς ταῦτα, οὐκ ἐξεῖναι, ἀδικεῖν οἰήσεται αὐτῷ, μέλλοντι διὰ τῶν θυσιῶν ἐξωνεῖσθαι τὴν ἁμαρτίαν.—Porphyr., περὶ ἀποχ., lib. ii. p. 97.

'there is no difference,' Rom. iii. 22. (2.) The equal obligation lying upon all men to look after, make sure of, and rest in this one and the same all-sufficient sacrifice. None, in order to remission, justification, atonement, eternal life, need to carry more to God, by faith and prayers, and none must carry less. Sirs, let us all put in for a share in Christ's offering, and in the benefits purchased thereby; for if we should come short of that, we are lost eternally. Are not reconciliation with God, the expiation of sin, eternal redemption, &c., things most necessary and most desirable? If so, where can we hope to have them but in a sacrificed Redeemer—but in the imputation of the merit of his death and sacrifice? And I add, do not only make sure of the thing, objectively considered, but labour also after the subjective assurance of it. Oh when a Christian can say, Christ died for me, 'gave himself for me,' Gal. ii. 20; his body was broken and his blood shed for me; he took my guilt and bare my punishment; how is he filled with 'joy unspeakable,' 1 Pet. i. 8, with 'peace that passes all understanding,' Phil. iv. 7; what a full tide of comfort is there in his soul! This is the receiving of the atonement, as some open it, and that is very sweet: Rom. v. 11, 'And not only so, but we also joy in God, through our Lord Jesus Christ, by whom we have now received the atonement.'

4. In the actings of faith eye Christ as a sacrifice for sin, and there let all your hope and confidence be bottomed. I say, in the actings of faith eye Christ as a sacrifice; for indeed this grace hath to do with him mainly and principally as dying and sacrificed. The apostle speaks of 'faith in his blood,' Rom. iii. 25; it is a bleeding, crucified Saviour that is the great and most proper object of faith: true, it takes in a whole Christ, all of Christ, his nativity, holy life, resurrection, ascension, intercession, &c., but that which it primarily and chiefly fixes upon is his death and passion. When a soul is brought into Christ to close with him in the way of believing, what of him is first in its eye in that act? is it a Christ as ascending, as sitting at the right hand of God, as interceding? no, thus it beholds him for the after-encouragement and support of faith; but that which it first considers is a Christ as dying upon the cross, and so it lays hold upon him. And

no wonder that it is so, since all the great blessings of the gospel do mainly flow from Christ's death; they are assured and applied by his resurrection, ascension, and intercession, but they were procured and purchased by his death, as the Scriptures abundantly shew, Rom. v. 9, 10; Eph. i. 7, *et passim.* Now that which hath the most causal and most immediate influence upon these, that deserves to be first and most eyed by faith. Here is the difference betwixt faith and love; this chiefly looks to the excellencies of Christ's person, but that to the merit and efficacy of his sacrifice. When the apostle, Gal. ii. 20, had spoken so high of his 'faith in the Son of God,' he tells you in what notion he did therein consider him, by adding, 'who loved me and gave himself for me.' The stung Israelite was to look upon the brazen serpent *as lifted up*, and so he was healed; do you desire to find healing, redemption, salvation by Christ? Oh look upon him *as lifted up upon the cross*, so all good shall come to you.

Further, I say, let all your hope and confidence be bottomed here; this is that firm rock which you must only build upon for pardon, peace with God, salvation, for all. Oh take heed of relying upon anything besides this sacrifice! Gal. vi. 14, 'God forbid that I should glory, save in the cross of our Lord Jesus Christ;' he that glories or trusts in anything besides that, his glorying is vain. The forlorn undone sinner should be always clasping and clinging about this cross, resting upon the merit of Christ thereon, and upon that only; for all that hope will be but dying hope which is not solely bottomed upon a dying Saviour. The heathens could not believe that ever the death of sacrifices should do the guilty person good;[1] they looked upon it as folly to hope for life by another's death; but, blessed be God, we see that which they did not! we firmly believe and steadily hope for expiation and salvation by Christ's one offering of himself, and lay the sole stress of our faith and happiness upon that which they counted folly. But let us be sure we do not mistake here— I mean, let us indeed place our whole confidence in Christ's meritorious death, for if we rely partly upon that, and partly upon something else, we spoil all.

5. Fifthly, You must so confide and rely upon

---

[1] Quum sis ipse nocens, moritur cur victima pro te? Stultitia est morte alterius sperare salutem.

Christ's one, most perfect, and all-sufficient sacrifice, as yet withal to be careful that you, on your part, do perform those gospel conditions which God enjoins and requires of you, in order to remission, justification, glorification. This word of advice is so necessary that it is by no means to be passed over. Christians, it is a thing of very high importance for you rightly to understand yourselves in this matter; therefore take it thus: All your trust and reliance is solely to be bottomed upon the death and sacrifice of the Lord Jesus; but yet you cannot regularly and warrantably act this trust and reliance upon this only ground or foundation, unless in your own persons you perform those conditions which God prescribes in his word. The whole business of merit and satisfaction lies upon Christ—that is wholly out of your hands and only in his; but as to believing and repenting, the two grand gospel conditions, they lie upon yourselves—I speak with respect to the act, not to the power—and must be done by yourselves; yea, and the doing of these is as necessary on your part under the notion of conditions, as suffering and dying was on Christ's part under the notion of merit. And it is most certain that the latter without the former will not profit you, because Christ never designed to impute or make over his merit to any, further than as they should make good these conditions of faith and repentance. We have here two dangerous rocks before us, and it must be our care and skill to shun both of them; the one is the setting of inherent grace or duty too high, as when we make it to share with Christ in merit and trust; the other is the setting of inherent grace or duty too low, as when upon the pretence of Christ's alone merit and full satisfaction we quite throw it off, and are altogether careless about it, as supposing it now to be a thing wholly unnecessary. Now we are exceedingly prone to dash upon the one or the other of these rocks; either we run ourselves upon popery in the former, or upon antinomism and libertinism in the latter. Oh what need have all to beg the guidance of the unerring Spirit, that thereby they may evenly steer betwixt both, and avoid each extreme! which they shall most happily do, if Christ and his sacrifice be only eyed by them in the way of reliance, and yet holiness, obedience, faith, repentance have also that respect which is due to

them as means and conditions. Much hath been said concerning the perfection and sufficiency of Christ's sacrifice, that he hath thereby put away all sin, fully expiated its guilt, perfected for ever them that are sanctified, &c.; shall any now from hence infer that all is done by Christ, that the creature hath nothing to do but only to receive the benefits prepared and purchased? God forbid. True, Christ's sacrifice was perfect *in suo genere* but not *in omni genere;* it was perfect as to what was meritorious and satisfactory, so as to exclude all other sacrifices and supplements whatsoever upon that account, but not so as to exclude all conditions which God will have the creature to perform; which though they can add nothing to the perfecting of the believer's great sacrifice, yet they do prepare and fit sinners for the participation of the benefits merited thereby.

To instance in all these conditions, or to enlarge upon any one of them, would be a long work; briefly therefore, as ever you desire to be the better for a dying Saviour, to share in the great and blessed effects of his sacrifice, look to it that you repent and believe. Oh if you be found at last in the number of the impenitent and unbelieving, all that Christ hath done or suffered will be a very nothing to you! notwithstanding all that you will eternally perish. Here is indeed an expiatory sacrifice; ay! but yet, as to you, no repentance, no expiation: here is sin condemned by Christ's oblation of himself; ay! but yet if the sinner doth not penitentially condemn sin in himself, and himself for sin, for all this he will be judicially condemned at the great day. The Scripture everywhere makes repentance the way to and condition of remission of sin: Acts ii. 38, 'Repent and be baptized every one of you in the name of Jesus Christ, for the remission of sins.' Acts v. 31, 'Him hath God exalted with his right hand to be a Prince and a Saviour, for to give repentance to Israel, and forgiveness of sins;' with very many other places to this purpose. The apostle having said, 1 John i. 7, 'The blood of Jesus Christ his Son cleanseth us from all sin;' presently subjoins, ver. 9, 'If we confess our sins, he is faithful and just to forgive us our sins, and to cleanse us from all unrighteousness.' Great is the efficacy of Christ's blood, but it is upon condition of the sinner's repentance: 'if we confess our sins,' &c. At the Jewish anniversary expiation all the sins of the people were by the sacrifices done away, yet God would have them then to 'afflict their souls,' Lev. xvi. 29 ; and the high priest was in their stead to 'confess their iniquities and all their transgressions in all their sins,' ver. 21 ; we under the gospel have our great expiation by the death of Christ, but this also must be attended with penitential abasement and humiliation. So likewise as to faith ; this too is a grace or condition indispensably necessary to the partaking of the benefits of Christ's propitiatory sacrifice. Therefore the apostle, speaking of propitiation, brings in our faith as well as Christ's blood, *it* having an instrumental as well as *that* a meritorious influence thereupon : Rom. iii. 25, 'Whom God hath set forth to be a propitiation through faith in his blood,' &c. To the blessings of the new covenant as the blood of Christ was necessary, that thereby there might be impetration ; so faith also is necessary, that thereby there may be application.[1] Our Lord's sacrifice is every way sufficient for atonement, yet 'he that believeth not, the wrath of God abideth on him,' John iii. 36 ; so also it is sufficient for expiation, yet it is only 'whosoever believeth on him shall receive remission of sins,' Acts x. 43. Under the law the blood of the sacrifice was to be so and so sprinkled with a bunch of hyssop, Exod. xii. 22 ; Heb. ix. 19, to which custom David alludes, Ps. li. 7, 'Purge me with hyssop and I shall be clean.' Now answerably to this, Paul speaks of 'the blood of sprinkling,' Heb. xii. 24 ; it was not enough for Christ only to shed his blood, but that must be sprinkled upon the sinner ; how ? why by faith, which under the gospel answers to the hyssop under the law. Well, after our Saviour's being an offering for sin, as we have nothing further to do but only, through grace enabling of us, to perform these evangelical conditions, so nothing less than that will serve our turn for a share and interest in the great effects and fruits thereof.[2]

6. Sixthly, You are not to rest in some one single application of yourselves, or in the first application of yourselves at your first believing, to this great sacrifice, for expiation and remission ; but you are

[1] Grotius de Sat., p. 141.
[2] *Vide* Cameron Misc., p. 529.

to repeat and renew it daily. For though, it is true, all the guilt of believers is removed thereby, yet that is done in this method ; it is removed as it is contracted, and as the benefit of it is accordingly drawn forth by the fresh applications of it. Oh do not rest in what you did at your first conversion, but be you every day applying yourselves to a sacrificed Christ ! New guilt must have new pardons, and daily sins call for daily expiations. It is observable that Christ is set forth not only by the yearly expiatory sacrifices, or by those that were but seldom offered ; but also by the daily sacrifices : John i. 29, 'Behold the Lamb of God,' &c. We should not lie down in our beds at night before we have applied ourselves to a dying Christ for the cleansing of our persons from the guilt of the sins of the day past ; yea, we should never go to God in duty, but we should revive upon our thoughts, and make use of this sacrifice. Under the law the blood was to be sprinkled even upon the mercy-seat, Lev. xvi. 14. God sits upon a throne of mercy, but even that requires the blood of Christ ; no mercy from him, no acceptance with him, can be expected, but upon the intervention of this sacrifice.

7. Seventhly, Upon this sacrifice, and what followed thereupon, God and Christ are highly to be admired and adored by you. This holy admiration hath been already again and again pressed upon you, under the foregoing gracious acts mentioned in the text ; but surely that which is now before us doth as much deserve and call for it as they or any other whatsoever. Is God to be admired because he sent his own Son, because he sent this Son in flesh, yea, in the likeness of sinful flesh ? And is he not to be admired also for his making of him to be a sacrifice for sin, and for the condemning of sin in his flesh ? Doubtless he is. What ! Christ a sacrifice ? a sacrifice for such as we ? such great things brought about thereby ? Oh what matter is here to draw out admiration ! What so great, so wonderful as this ! How much are the highest thoughts, the most raised affections, below the greatness of this mystery ! It hath, my brethren, been largely set before you ; now I would ask, How are your hearts affected with it ? It is very sad, if we can hear of such stupendous mercy, and yet be but little wrought upon under the hearing of it. Pray

fancy to yourselves what the angels thought of this, what frame they were in when they saw the Son of God hanging and dying upon the cross as an expiatory sacrifice. Oh you may well suppose that it filled them with astonishment; they were even amazed at this strange and wonderful spectacle. Never such wondering in heaven as when the Lord Jesus was thus suffering on earth. Now, shall that be little to you which was so great to them? Shall they thus admire, and will you, who were most concerned in the thing, and the greatest gainers by it, be stupid and unaffected? In Christ's being a sacrifice God on his part hath displayed and advanced all his attributes, yea, they by this have received their utmost advancement; infinite wisdom, justice, holiness, mercy, could go no higher than a Christ crucified. And, on your part, by this your work is done, your happiness being every way secured and your misery fully prevented; by this you are reconciled to God, and God to you; condemning sin is condemned itself, all its guilt expiated, the righteousness of the law fulfilled, &c.; by a strange and unthought-of method God hath fetched the greatest good out of the greatest evil; by Christ's dying you live. All which being considered, is there not sufficient ground why you, and all, should admire and adore God? And, amongst other things, pray in special admire his love, his transcendent, superlative, matchless love. What manner of love was this, that God should give his Son to be a sacrifice for you! 1 John iv. 10, 'Herein is love, not that we loved God, but that he loved us, and sent his Son to be the propitiation for our sins.' Rom. v. 8, 'But God commendeth his love towards us, in that while we were yet sinners, Christ died for us.' Had not Christ been a person infinitely dear to God, the thing had not been so much; but that he should devote him to be sacrificed whom he so dearly loved, there is the incomprehensibleness of his love. It is reported of the Phœnicians that in their sacrifices they did not use to sacrifice an enemy or a stranger, but τῶν φιλτάτων τίνα,[1] some one that they had a special love for. This I am sure was done by God in his giving of the Son of his love to be a sacrifice for us; therefore what admiration can be high enough for him! When Abraham had the

[1] Porphyr. de Abstin., lib. ii.

knife in his hand, and was just going to offer his son Isaac, Gen. xxii. 10, &c., God stopped his hand, and provided a cheaper sacrifice for him. This was more than what he did for his own Son; him he would have to be offered up, and would admit of no other sacrifice; and when the hand of justice was lifted up, ready to destroy us, then God, to secure us, interposed and found out a sacrifice of propitiation, not a ram, but his only-begotten Son. Oh the heights, breadths, lengths, depths of his love!

And must not Christ be admired also? Surely yes. Was not his love, too, admirable as well as the Father's? Oh well might the apostle say, Gal. ii. 20, 'Who loved me, and gave himself for me.' Eph. v. 2, 'And walk in love, as Christ also hath loved us, and hath given himself for us, an offering and a sacrifice to God for a sweet smelling savour.' Ver. 25, 'As Christ also loved the church, and gave himself for it.' Rev. i. 5, 'Unto him that loved us, and washed us from our sins in his own blood.' This was loving indeed! When the Jews saw Jesus weeping over Lazarus, they said, 'Behold how he loved him!' John xi. 36; but, alas! what was Christ's weeping over him to his dying for us! What was the shedding of a few tears to the shedding of his blood! How may we come with a more emphatical, 'Behold, behold how he loved us!' He that 'knew no sin' was willing to be 'made sin,' 2 Cor. v. 21; to 'bear our sins in his own body upon the tree,' 1 Pet. ii. 24; to put himself in our stead, yea, to die in our stead, for our sakes to be 'obedient to death, even the death of the cross,' Phil. ii. 8; to let out his precious blood for the expiation of sin, when nothing else would do it; and when all Mosaical sacrifices were weak, he, by a far higher sacrifice, undertook the work: 'Lo, I come to do thy will, O God,' Heb. x. 7. Was not here love, even love 'passing knowledge'? Eph. iii. 19. Such high affection on his part should draw out high admiration on our part.

Let me here add, we should so admire God and Christ as to love them and to be thankful. Have they 'so loved' us, John iii. 16, and shall not we return love for love? What monsters and prodigies shall we be, if, after such a manifestation of their love to us, there be not reciprocation of our love to them! God designed and prepared the sacrifice,

therefore he must have our love ; Christ was the
sacrifice, therefore he must have our love too. Both
deserve it, both must have it : John x. 17, ' Therefore doth my Father love me, because I lay down
my life.' Now doth the Father love him for this,
and shall not we much more ? Did we but think of
this sacrifice, and hold our hearts close to it in
holy meditation, surely it would cause them to love
Christ !

Then, I say, be thankful ; yea, let your whole
soul upon this go out in thankfulness ; be ever
praising, magnifying God for his unspeakable mercy
in Christ your sacrifice, your Redeemer, your Saviour.
Often call upon your sluggish hearts and say, ' Bless
the Lord, O my soul, and all that is within me bless
his holy name.' Did God ' set forth Christ to be a
propitiation' ? Rom. iii. 25. Did he ' lay upon him
the iniquities of you all' ? Was the chastisement
of your peace upon him, and by his stripes are you
healed ? Isa. liii. 5, 6. That guilt and wrath which
would have ruined you for ever, are they now both
done away, so as that they shall never hurt you ?
Did Christ die that you might not die, but live for
ever ?[1] Did you sin and he suffer ? Was the innocent person punished that the guilty might be acquitted ?[2] Was sin condemned for you who deserved
to be condemned for it ? What praise and admiration can be high enough for such things as these !
The Jews in the day of atonement were to make the
trumpet sound throughout their land, Lev. xxv. 9 ;
so we, having received the atonement by Christ's
sacrifice, should evermore be sounding forth the
praises of the Most High. You read of the elders,
Rev. v. 8, &c., they ' fell down before the Lamb,
having every one of them harps, and golden vials
full of odours, which are the prayers of saints. And

they sang a new song, saying, Thou art worthy to
take the book, and to open the seals thereof, for
thou wast slain, and hast redeemed us to God by
thy blood,' &c. Christians ! why are not your
harps always in your hands ? Why are not your
souls always full of holy affections, as the golden
vials full of odours, in the remembrance of him who
was slain and sacrificed for you ?

8. Lastly, Do you offer to God the sacrifices
proper to you, as Christ offered to God the sacrifice
proper to him ? For expiatory sacrifices, as you
need them not, Christ's one sacrifice being every
way sufficient for that end, so you are not able to
come up to them, for you can present nothing to
God properly and formally expiatory ; yet there are
other sacrifices which you may offer up to him.
And though the external and fleshly sacrifices of the
law are out of date, yet there are the internal and
spiritual sacrifices of the gospel, which you now are
as much obliged to observe and offer as ever the
Jews were the former. What are they ? Why, you
are to present yourselves, your bodies, souls, the
whole man, ' a living sacrifice, holy, and acceptable
to God,' Rom. xii. 1. You are to dedicate your
persons to Christ, so as to ' live to him who died
for you,' 2 Cor. v. 15 ; yea, so as to be ' ready to be
offered' in sacrifice, by dying for him, to allude to
that, Phil. ii. 17. You are, as ' an holy priesthood,
to offer up spiritual sacrifices, acceptable to God by
Jesus Christ,' 1 Pet. ii. 5—which spiritual sacrifices
are spiritual duties and evangelical worship, prophesied of Mal. i. 11, ' In every place incense shall be
offered unto my name, and a pure offering'—here
come in prayer and praise, those two eminent sacrifices under the gospel :[1] Ps. cxli. 2, ' Let my prayer
be set forth before thee as incense : and the lifting
up of my hands as the evening sacrifice.' Ps. cxvi.
17, ' I will offer to thee the sacrifice of thanksgiving : and will call upon the name of the Lord ;' so
Ps. cvii. 22, and liv. 6 ; Heb. xiii. 15, ' By him
therefore let us offer the sacrifice of praise to God
continually, that is, the fruit of our lips, giving
thanks to his name.' This is set forth, as here by
' the fruit of the lips,' so elsewhere by the ' free-
will offerings of the mouth,' Ps. cxix. 108 ; by ' ren-

---

[1] Mediator noster puniri pro seipso non debuit, quia nullum
culpæ contagium perpetravit. Sed si ipse indebitam mortem
non susciperet, nunquam nos a debita morte liberaret.—*Gregor.*, lib. iii. *Moral.*, cap. 13.

[2] Peccat iniquus et punitur justus ; delinquit reus et vapu-
lat innocens ; offendit impius et damnatur pius ; quod mere-
tur malus patitur bonus, &c. Quo nate Dei, quo tua descendit
humilitas ? quo tua flagravit charitas ? &c. Ego inique egi, tu
pœna mulctaris ; ego facinus admisi, tu ultione plecteris, &c.
Me ad illicitam concupiscentiam rapuit arbor, te perfecta charitas duxit ad crucem ; ego præsumsi vetitum, tu subiisti acu-
leum, &c.—*August. in Quest. in V. and N. Testam.*, Qu. 55.

[1] Oratio pure directa de corde fideli, tanquam de ara sancta
surgit incensum.—*August.* in Ps. cxli.

2 U

dering the calves of our lips,' Hosea xiv. 2. And for the pleasingness of this to God above all the Levitical sacrifices, see Ps. l. 13, 14, and lxix. 30, 31. Oh this is a sacrifice which we should often be offering up to God through Christ Jesus. Another evangelical sacrifice is a broken spirit, than which, next to a broken Christ, nothing more acceptable to God : Ps. li. 16, 17, ' For thou desirest not sacrifice ; else would I give it : thou delightest not in burnt-offering. The sacrifices of God are a broken spirit ; a broken and a contrite heart, O God, thou wilt not despise.' So also bounty to the poor distressed saints, this is ' an odour of sweet smell, a sacrifice acceptable, well-pleasing to God,' Phil. iv. 18. ' But to do good and to communicate forget not, for with such sacrifices God is well pleased,' Heb. xiii. 16. And, to sum up all, holiness of heart and life, that is an excellent sacrifice, excelling all the old law sacrifices whatsoever : 1 Sam. xv. 22, ' Hath the Lord as great delight in burnt-offerings and sacrifices, as in obeying the voice of the Lord ? Behold, to obey is better than sacrifice ; and to hearken, than the fat of rams.' Micah vi. 6–8, ' Wherewith shall I come before the Lord, and bow myself before the high God ? shall I come before him with burnt offerings, with calves of a year old ? Will the Lord be pleased with thousands of rams, or with ten thousands of rivers of oil ? shall I give my firstborn for my transgression, the fruit of my body for the sin of my soul ? He hath shewed thee, O man, what is good ; and what doth the Lord require of thee, but to do justly, and to love mercy, and to walk humbly with thy God ?' The heathens themselves, upon the light of nature, looked upon moral goodness as the best and most acceptable sacrifice.[1] I am sure evangelical holiness is so. The wickedness of the Jews made God even to abhor and slight the sacrifices which were instituted by himself ; as we find, Isa. i. 11, &c., and lxvi. 3 ; Jer. vi. 20, and vii. 21, &c. ; Amos v. 21, 22. If we live in

sin, we may offer this and that to God, but it is all nothing ; nay, that makes all our sacrifices an abomination to him, Prov. xv. 8. Oh live the holy life, keep the heart pure, mortify whatever is evil, do good, shun all excesses, be heavenly in your affections, in all things act in compliance with God's nature and will, &c., this will please him more than the most costly oblations which you can bring to him. These are the sacrifices which now under the gospel we are to offer ; and surely we should offer them with all readiness and faithfulness. Our Lord having submitted to the bloody sacrifice of himself on the cross, and left us none but these easy and delightful sacrifices, how readily should we close with them ! But so much for this use.

Use 3. A third shall put an end to this subject, and that is of comfort. Was Christ a sacrifice for sin ? Did he thereby condemn sin ? What doth this truth drop but honey and sweetness to them who are in Christ ? I say, to them who are in Christ ; for they are the persons only who can lay hold upon the grace contained in it : as the non-condemnation of the person in the first verse, so the condemnation of sin in this, belongs only to such. You that are in the number of these, to you I bring glad tidings, matter of great joy. Out of the bitter comes sweet ; for Christ to die as a sacrifice, this was bitter to him, but it is sweet to you. His death, passion, and whole humiliation speak nothing to you but consolation. Oh did believers, especially such as are under a troubled spirit, but better understand and better improve this sin-condemning sacrifice, they would certainly have more of inward peace and comfort than now they have. I must not insist upon the particular and full drawing out of that consolatory matter which it affords ; therefore shall conclude with a brief review only of what the text offers.

And so, 1. Here is a sacrifice for sin. All men in Adam having ' sinned wilfully, after that they had received the knowledge of the truth,' there might have been ' no sacrifice for their sin,' (to allude to that, Heb. x. 26 ;) but the gracious God, notwithstanding all this, was pleased to admit of a sacrifice ; yea, himself to find out and ordain that sacrifice. Here is matter of comfort.

2. Christ himself was this sacrifice. And if so,

---

[1] Vis Deos propitiare ? bonus esto. Satis illos coluit quisquis imitatus est.—*Senec.*, Ep. ix. 5. Non immolationibus et sanguine multo colendus est Deus ; sed mente pura, bono honestoque proposito.—*Idem.* Μᾶλλον' τὸ δαιμόνιον πρὸς τὸ τῶν θυόντων ἦθος ἢ πρὸς τῶν θυομένων πλῆθος βλέπει.— *Porphyr.*, περὶ ἀποχ., lib. ii. p. 62. Οὐκ εἰκὸς τοὺς θεοὺς χαίρειν ταῖς δαπάναις τῶν θυομένων ἀλλὰ ταῖς εὐσεβείαις τῶν θυόντων.—*Arist.* Rhet., lib. iii. With many more in *Stuck.* de Sacrif., p. 153, col. 2 ; *Saubert.* de Sac., cap. 1, p. 4.

how pleasing must it needs be to God! Eph. v. 2, 'And hath given himself for us, an offering and a sacrifice to God for a sweet-smelling savour.' I tell you, there was infinitely more in this one sacrifice to please God than there is in all your sins, put them all together, to displease God. If Christ be the sacrifice, there must be an infinite efficacy and merit in it. From the dignity of his person an infiniteness of merit must needs result. If he will die and shed his blood, what can be too high for you? Surely, too, there is more in his offering to save you than there is in sin to damn you. If he be the sacrifice, no question but the Father did accept of it. And indeed of this he hath given sufficient evidence to the world, not only by his carriage towards the saints, but also, and chiefly, by his carriage towards Christ himself; for whereas of old he was wont to testify his acceptation of the sacrifices by consuming them by fire from heaven, Gen. xv. 17; Lev. ix. 24; Judges vi. 21; 2 Chron. vii. 1; here, with respect to Christ's sacrifice, he testified his acceptance in a higher way, viz., by raising him from the dead, taking him up to heaven, re-admitting him into his presence, and setting him at his own right hand; for would the Father have done all this to his Son had he not been well pleased with his person and oblation? Oh there is a convincing evidence of this in his going to the Father, John xvi. 8–10. By this sacrifice, thus accepted, you are made perfect, as you have often heard out of Heb. x. 14, 18; there is nothing now to be done by Christ or by you, but only to apply and improve what he hath already done. Is not this ground of strong consolation? And know, further, for your comfort, that the virtue of Christ's offering is as great now as it was at the first; his blood is as effectual with God for your good now as it was when it was just running warm from his veins, and so it shall be to the end of the world.[1] And that he may make the best of it, he is entered into the holy place, where it is his business to present and plead the merit thereof. He backs his oblation on earth with his intercession in heaven, and what can be spoken higher for your support and comfort! he that was the sacrifice here is the advocate there.

3. By this sacrifice sin was condemned. Sin con-

[1] Adeo magnum est hoc sacrificium, ut quamvis unum sit et semel oblatum, sufficiat ad æternitatem.—*Anselm.*

demned! What a word is that! That which would have condemned you, and which only can condemn you, that is by Christ condemned itself: condemning sin is condemned by a condemned Saviour. And shall it be condemned, and you too? Shall Christ suffer the penalty due to it, and you too? Oh no! As God was just to punish it once, so he is gracious, and just too, not to punish it twice. What this condemning of sin is you have heard. If you follow the word the comfort lies thus: a condemnatory sentence is by God, upon Christ's account, passed upon it; he hath adjudged it to die for all the mischiefs done by it, both against himself and against you too. This cursed tyrant, this heinous malefactor, is under a sentence to be cut off, that it may no longer either dishonour God or hurt you. And should not you rejoice in this? Who fears a condemned person? What do the accusations of a condemned man signify? Sin is a condemned thing; fear it not. If you leave the word, and come to the main import of it, then the comfort lies thus: the guilt of all your sins is fully done away and expiated by Christ's sacrifice. This lamb of God, as offered, hath taken it all away; his blood hath cleansed you from all sin; your scape-goat hath carried all your iniquities into the land of forgetfulness. Oh, your guilt was charged upon Christ, and it shall not be charged upon you too; you are to mourn over it, but yet know he hath fully satisfied for it. What would you have more? You have in the former verse the power of sin abolished by the law of the Spirit; in this, the guilt of sin abolished by the sacrifice of Christ. Oh how complete is your redemption! The plaster is every way as large as the sore. What holy triumphs may you now make over all which may seem to endanger you! Rom. viii. 34, 'Who is he that condemneth? it is Christ that died,'[1] &c.

4. Observe, it is sin that was condemned. The apostle speaks of it in the lump and mass; and so he saith it is expiated. Our Lord's sacrifice did not take off the guilt of this or that particular sin, but of all sin; his expiation was total and universal. Under the law sacrifices the blood was to be sprinkled seven times, Lev. xvi. 19, thereby to prefigure the

[1] Mortuum Cæsarem quis metuat? sed morte Christi quid efficacius?—*Cyprian.* de Dupl. Martyrio.

thoroughness and perfection of the expiation of sin by Christ's sacrifice.

5. This is brought in as God's act: 'God sent his own Son, and for sin condemned sin.' He that was the *persona læsa*, the injured person, the just judge, against whom sin was committed, and who therefore was to punish it, he who is the supreme and authoritative agent in and about the great concerns of souls, he appointed Christ to be a sacrifice, owned and accepted his sacrifice, and upon that acquits sinners from all guilt. Oh there is much in this to encourage the drooping Christian! Rom. viii. 33, 'Who shall lay anything to the charge of God's elect? it is God that justifieth.' The Father cannot but be well pleased with Christ's propitiatory sacrifice, since this was of himself: Rom. iii. 25, 'Whom God hath set forth to be a propitiation,' &c.

6. This was done too in Christ's flesh, which also hath great sweetness in it. It is added, saith one,[1] for our further assurance, to the end that we may not doubt of the forgiveness of our sins, which are destroyed in our proper nature which the Son of God took upon him. Had Christ done and suffered what he did in the nature of angels, we might have questioned whether any good would thereby have accrued to us; but all being done in our nature, surely he did it for us, and we shall reap the benefit thereof.[2]

7. To all this let me add one thing further, and it is a great one, namely, that by this sacrifice of Christ you have not only the bare condemnation or expiation of sin, but with that you also have a right and title unto, and collation of all gospel blessings and privileges whatsoever. Was it only the taking off of guilt, and the appeasing of divine wrath, that would be very much; but over and beyond these there is, Christ's active fulfilling the law being taken in, a positive righteousness made over to you, an interest in God's fatherly love, the purchase of heaven; and in this sense we are for a redundancy of Christ's merit. The benefits of Christ's sacrifice to believers are not only those which are privative, such wherein they are freed from all evil;

but there are also those which are positive, such wherein they are entitled to and instated in the possession of all good; yea, even of the heavenly blessedness itself: Heb. v. 9, 'And being made perfect, he became the author of eternal salvation unto all them that obey him.' Heb. ix. 12, 'Having obtained eternal redemption for us;' it comes in as the effect of Christ's blood and sacrifice. In his great undertaking to redeem and save sinners, we may suppose him to have two things in his eye: the one was that he should have a people in the world; the other was that through him this people should partake of all blessings requisite to their happiness. Now both of these were effected and secured by his sacrifice. As to the first, that was made sure by this, according to that promise or prediction: Isa. liii. 10, 11, 'When thou shalt make his soul an offering for sin, he shall see his seed, &c. He shall see of the travail of his soul, and shall be satisfied;' in reliance upon which he himself said, 'And I, if I be lifted up from the earth, will draw all men unto me,' John xii. 32; and that upon his death and sacrifice he had a people, and a numerous people too, the evangelical history doth abundantly testify. Then as to the second, that also was promoted and secured by his sacrifice, inasmuch as thereby the covenant of grace, the summary of all blessings, was ratified and confirmed. It was an ancient custom,[1] used amongst men at the sanction and ratification of their covenants, to make use of sacrifices, as we find, Gen. xxi. 22-24, &c.; Jer. xxxiv. 18; Exod. xxxiv. 7, 8; in allusion to which custom it is said, Ps. l. 5, 'Gather my saints together unto me; those that have made a covenant with me by sacrifice.' Answerably now to this, Christ by his sacrifice confirmed and ratified the covenant of grace betwixt God and believers; wherefore he said, 'This cup is the New Testament in my blood,' *i.e.*, the seal and ratification of the new covenant, Mat. xxvi. 28; 1 Cor. xi. 25; and the apostle doth in special insist upon this in Heb. ix. 15, 16, &c. Well, then, by Christ's sacrifice—the blood of the covenant, as it is called, Zech. ix. 11— all blessings whatsoever are insured and made over to God's people; and if so, is not that a sufficient

---

[1] Deodat. *in loc.*

[2] Addit Paulus in carne, quo certior sit nostra fiducia, dum videmus peccatum in ipsa natura nostra fuisse devictum et abolitum; sic enim sequitur, naturam nostram vere fieri participem ejus victoriæ.—*Calvin.*

[1] Et cæsa jungebant fœdera porca.—*Virgil.* See Mr Mede on Mal. i. 11.

ground of comfort to such? What shall I say? If the atoning of an angry God, the washing away of all sin, the fulfilling of a righteous law, the satisfying of infinite justice, the ratification of the covenant of grace, the purchase of heaven; if there be anything in all these things (as surely there is) to promote spiritual joy, you have them all by this great sacrifice; therefore rejoice, and again I say rejoice. So much for this head, which I very well know I might have despatched with much more brevity; but it containing that matter in it which is not commonly so fully opened, and which is of so high concern to us, therefore I have been thus large upon it.

CHAPTER XIV.

OF THE FULFILLING OF THE LAW'S RIGHTEOUSNESS IN BELIEVERS.

That the righteousness of the law might be fulfilled in us. —ROM. viii. 4.

Of the second end or effect of Christ's being sent in flesh, viz., the fulfilling of the law's righteousness—A general explication of the main scope of the words, and of the principal matter contained in them—More particularly it is inquired, 1. Of what law doth the apostle here speak? 2. What is the δικαίωμα *or righteousness of the law? 3. What is it to fulfil the law's righteousness? 4. How the righteousness of the law is fulfilled in us?—Four interpretations given of it: 1. That it is perfectly and personally fulfilled by the saints themselves; 2. That it is personally fulfilled in them, though not perfectly, yet inchoately, and in respect of God's acceptation; 3. That it is perfectly but not personally fulfilled in them, Christ's obedience and perfect fulfilling of the law being imputed to them; 4. That it is fulfilled in them in respect of the remission of sin—Three propositions laid down to clear up the third interpretation and the main truth: as, 1. That Christ was made under the law; that opened in some particulars; 2. That Christ perfectly fulfilled the law; 3. That his fulfilling of it is imputed and reckoned to believers—Two questions raised and answered: Whether Christ's active and passive obedi-*

ence, or his passive only, be imputed?—In what sense may it be said to be imputed?—Use 1. First, To shew upon what terms believers are justified and saved; secondly, What a respect God hath for his law—Use 2. To exhort persons (1.) To get an interest in this privilege; (2.) Such as have an interest in it are exhorted [1.] To go as far as ever they may in the personal fulfilling of the law; [2.] To look after the fulfilling of the evangelical law in themselves; [3.] To admire the love of Christ—Use 3. The comfort of this drawn forth to believers.

THESE words hold forth another end or effect of Christ's being sent in the likeness of sinful flesh; for I do not understand them to refer to the clause immediately foregoing, 'and for sin condemned sin in the flesh,' as if they were an assignation of the end or effect of Christ's condemning sin by the sacrifice of himself; but I take them as referring to that which is before spoken of, 'God sent his own Son in the likeness of sinful flesh,' and as they do represent God's end in that. Wherefore did God so do? What did he design or aim at therein? Why, at this, 'that the righteousness of the law might be fulfilled in us.'

The conjunctive particle, ἵνα, may be taken either τελικῶς or εἰδικῶς. In the first notion, which is most usual and common, it carries a final sense, and notes the end why God sent his Son in flesh; namely, that he might fulfil, in his own person, the law's righteousness, and so imputatively, or in a law-sense, believers in him. I say this was God's end; for it doth not come in as a bare event or consequent upon Christ's taking our nature, and doing in that nature what he did; but it was the very end which God designed and propounded to himself therein;[1] viz., that Christ might perfectly fulfil the law, which to do to the saints themselves in their own persons was altogether impossible; and yet upon which, it being accepted of by God on their behalf and made over to them, they should be accounted just and righteous, even as if they had fulfilled it in their own persons. This is the first import of the word. Then it may be taken εἰδικῶς, or by way of apposition; and

---

[1] Idque totum hoc consilio fecit, ut nos perfecte justi coram ipso perficeremur, non secus atque illi habiti fuissent qui omnia divinæ legis præcepta conservassent.—*Vorst.*

so it notes the superadding of some further matter, and that which is distinct from what went before.[1] In this appositive sense it is used, John xv. 12, and xvii. 3. And so the apostle's meaning is this : God sent his Son into the world not only to be a sacrifice for sin, and thereby to condemn sin, by his bearing the law's penalty due to it ; but also, by his active obedience and conformity to the law's commands, to bring things to this, that the righteousness of the law should be fulfilled in believers. Christ's being a sacrifice for sin was not sufficient to answer all the ends and demands of the law ; there must be the doing of what it commanded as well as the suffering of what it threatened ; therefore Christ was sent for both, and both were accomplished by him. Man in his lapsed state stood in need of two things, satisfaction and merit :[2] satisfaction, with respect to God's punitive justice, the expiation of sin by the undergoing of the punishment incurred by it, &c. ; merit, with respect to eternal life and the possession of the heavenly blessedness ; the measure and foundation of which merit was the fulfilling of the law in active obedience. Now both of these are here distinctly spoken unto ; Christ for sin condemned sin in the flesh ; there is satisfaction ; and he also fulfilled the righteousness of the law in the stead, at leastwise for the good, of believers ; there is merit. So that in the words we have a further account of that full benefit and complete salvation which sinners have by the Lord Jesus ; and so much for their main scope, and the general explication of the matter contained in them.

In the more particular opening of them four things are to be inquired into :

1. Of what *law* doth Paul here speak ?

2. What he means by the *righteousness* of the law.

[1] See Burg. of Justif., 2 part, p. 361.

[2] Cum duo nobis peperisse Christum dixerimus, impunitatem et præmium, illud satisfactioni, hoc merito Christi distincte tribuit vetus ecclesia. Satisfactio consistit in peccatorum tralatione, meritum in perfectissima obedientiæ pro nobis præstitæ imputatione.—*G. Vossius in Prefat. ad Grotium de Sat. Christi.* In homine lapso duo consideranda, quod pro peccatis ejus solvendum fuit, ut liberaretur ; tum ut vitæ insuper fieret particeps, quod præstari debuit id ad quod vita promissa erat, &c. Utrumque apostolus docet et conjungit, Rom. viii. 3, 4, &c.—*Hoornb. Socin. Confut.*, lib. iii. cap. 1, p. 657.

3. How this righteousness of the law is said to be *fulfilled.*

4. In what sense is it said to be fulfilled *in us?*

To the first of these inquiries I shall answer very briefly : It is the moral law which is here chiefly spoken of. That which is called 'the law of works,' Rom. iii. 27, in contradistinction to the evangelical law, or the law of faith ; the law which God at first made with Adam in the state of innocency, and afterwards, for the matter of it, renewed and copied out again to the people of Israel, abridging it in the ten commandments ; the law which called for universal, perfect, constant obedience, and promised life thereupon, which was a draught, or model and summary, of all that duty which God required of man ; this is that law which the apostle here had mainly in his eye. It is the same with the law spoken of in the foregoing verse, 'What the law could not do in that it was weak,' &c., (where I had occasion to speak something about it, to which I refer you.[1]) It is here said, that 'the righteousness of the law,' &c. Now the law to which righteousness is annexed is commonly the moral law ; see Rom. x. 5 ; Phil. iii. 9, *et passim ;* and that is the law which Christ in special fulfilled. Therefore he having said, 'Think not that I am come to destroy the law or the prophets ; I am not come to destroy, but to fulfil,' Mat. v. 17, he explains himself, vers. 21, 27, &c., what law he meant, by instancing in some branches of the moral law. And the apostle having styled Christ 'the end of the law,' Rom. x. 4, 5, shows that he also by this meant the same law, as appears by what he immediately adds, 'For Moses describeth the righteousness which is of the law, that the man which doth those things shall live by them.' I add further, it is that law, the righteousness whereof is fulfilled in us, that is, by imputation. Now, it is the righteousness of the moral law, as fulfilled by Christ, which is most eminently imputed to us ; therefore that law must here chiefly be understood. I deny not but that there are other laws besides this with which righteousness is coupled ; as those particular and positive laws laid upon Christ with respect to the management of his office. When the business of his baptism was before him, he would have it done ; for, saith he, 'thus it be-

[1] See page 164, &c.

cometh us to fulfil all righteousness,' Mat. iii. 15. Yea, the ceremonial law itself had its δικαιώματα, for that is the word, Heb. ix. 1; and it is said of Zacharias and Elisabeth, Luke i. 6, 'They were both righteous before God, walking, ἐν πάσαις ταῖς ἐντολαῖς καὶ δικαιώμασι, in all the commandments and ordinances of the Lord blameless;' where some distinguish, making the ἐντολαὶ to refer to the commands of the moral law, and the δικαιώματα to the rites and ordinances of the ceremonial law.[1] Neither do I deny but that other laws besides the moral law were fulfilled by Christ, for he fulfilled all, and that his fulfilling of them also was for our good; but yet it was the moral law with which especially righteousness is joined, which Christ eminently fulfilled, and which fulfilling is in a higher notion imputed to us. Therefore I interpret the word *law* here as mainly pointing to that; and in so doing I have the concurrent suffrages of all the expositors that I have looked into, one or two only excepted.

2. What is here meant by the δικαίωμα, or *righteousness of the law?* The Vulgate, Ambrose, Erasmus, Tremellius, &c., read it, 'the justification of the law,' as the word δικαίωμα is translated, Rom. v. 16; and the Greek interpreters pitch upon the sense as to the thing, 'that the righteousness of the law,' &c., that is, say they, that the primary end and scope of the law, (viz., to justify, for that was the end of the law as given at first,) might be fulfilled in us.[2] Beza, with divers others, render it, 'that the right of the law,' &c. The law had a right to lay its commands upon the creature, and to exact his obedience thereunto; it being God's own law, the declaration of his will, it having his authority stamped upon it; and it enjoining nothing but what was righteous, just, and good, it was its right to command, and to be obeyed when it did so command. And in case it was not so, it had a further right, viz., to demand satisfaction in the enduring of its penalty; for it had a double right—one as it did and might require active obedience, the other as it did and might require satisfaction by suffering in case of disobedience; and these two put together make up its

[1] See Dr Hammond on Rom. viii. 4, in Annot.

, Τὸ δικαίωμα τοῦ νόμου, τουτέστι τὸ τέλος, ὁ σκοπὸς (σκοπὸν γὰρ εἶχε τὸ δικαιοῦν τὸν ἄνθρωπον) πληροῦται ἐν ἡμῖν.—*Theoph.*

righteousness.[1] Some make this to lie in the law's threatenings or damnatory sentence against sinners, in that curse which it denounces against the transgressors of it, Gal. iii. 10;[2] as the δικαίωμα τοῦ Θεοῦ spoken of, Rom. i. 32, is God's punishing and avenging justice, and that dreadful sentence passed by him, that they who do such things are worthy of death, so the δικαίωμα τοῦ νόμου is the penal or maledictory part of the law. But this is only a part of its righteousness, and the secondary part thereof too; its preceptive righteousness, in its demanding of active obedience, must be taken in, and that too as that which is primarily and principally intended by it; therefore it is generally opened by that.[3] The Scripture speaks of 'the law of righteousness,' Rom. ix. 31; of 'righteousness by the law,' Gal. iii. 21; of 'the righteousness of the law,' Rom. ii. 26, and in the text. Some difference there is betwixt these, but that I shall not stand upon. The latter is all that duty, righteousness, obedience which the law requires, with the penalty which it threatens, and will have inflicted upon disobedience.

3. We are to inquire what this *fulfilling* of the law's righteousness is? *Ans.* The former head

[1] Δικαίωμα τοῦ νόμου duplex, condemnandi peccatores et rursus exigendi obedientiam perfectam.—*Pareus.* Jus legis ut qui peccaverant punirentur, et qui ad vitam intrare volebant servarent mandata.—*Streso.* Δικαίωμα illud quod requirit lex; nempe tum plenam pœnæ reatibus nostris debitam luitionem, ut a condemnatione liberemur; tum plenam legis præstationem, ut ad æternam vitam ἱκανοὶ inveniamur, ex illa promissione, hoc fac et vives, &c.—*Beza*; see Burg. of Justif. part ii. p. 358.

[2] Δικαίωμα seu jus legis nihil aliud est quam κατάκριμα et damnatoria sententia legis, qua maledictionis et mortis æternæ supplicio, &c.—*Jacob. ad Portum* Fid. Orthod. Defens., cap. 34, p. 975; *vide* Pareum *in loc.* ὅπερ ἦν δικαίωμα τοῦ νόμου, τὸ μὴ γίνεσθαι ὑπεύθυνον τῇ ἀρᾷ.—*Chrysost.*

[3] Significat eam rectitudinem quæ præcipitur in lege.—*P. Martyr.* Justitia quam lex exigebat.—*Vatabl.* Totum quod lex præcipit.—*Alap.* Δικαίωμα ipsa legis præcepta, &c—*Perer.* Justitia legis est justitia quam præcipit lex.—*Estius.* Implere justum legis est totum quod lex precipit efficere.—*Tolet.* Ut justificatio legis, *i.e.*, justitia quam lex prescribit et exigit impleretur, &c.—*Staplet.* Antidot., p. 627. Ut ad impleret opus præceptorum legis.—*Ver. Æthiop.* Ut nos præstaremus omnia quæ in lege Mosis per se honesta sunt.—*Grot.* Jus, justitia, justificatio legis in eo consistit, ut per omnimodam cum lege conformitatem justi atque inculpati habeamur coram Deo.—*De Dieu.* Δικαίωμα is anything that God hath thought meet to appoint or command his people.—*Dr Hammond.*

being rightly apprehended, there will be little or no difficulty in this. To fulfil the righteousness of the law, it is fully to answer all its demands, to come up to perfect and universal conformity to it, to do whatever it enjoins, or to suffer whatever it threatens, or both. For so it was fulfilled by Christ—in his active obedience as to the one, in his passive obedience as to the other; as he was perfectly holy he did what the law commanded, and besides this, as he was made a curse, Gal. iii. 13, he underwent what the law threatened. It is questioned whether one of these be not enough for us, either to obey or to suffer; but all grant that both were necessary on Christ's part, and that both were done by him, and so he fulfilled the law's righteousness. This is the genuine and plain notion of the word, yet I know other interpretations are given of it. The righteousness of the law was fulfilled, inasmuch, say some,[1] as that righteousness which it did foretell was actually accomplished in Christ: Rom. iii. 21, 'But now the righteousness of God without the law is manifested, being witnessed by the law and the prophets;' that righteousness, which before was witnessed, promised, foretold in the law, received in Christ its full accomplishment, and therein lies the fulfilling of its righteousness. But this exposition of the word is, I conceive, not so proper to the thing here spoken of; it is another fulfilling which is here intended; not so much that which is the bringing into act what was foretold, or which is the verifying of a prophecy or prediction, in which sense it hath usually joined with it τὸ ῥηθέν, as Mat. xiii. 35; or ἡ γραφὴ, as James ii. 23; or τὰ γεγραμμένα, as Luke xxiv. 44; or ἡ προφητεία, as Mat. xiii. 14; as the perfect obeying of what was enjoined in the command, and the doing to the full what the law as preceptive did require, rather than what the law as predictive did foretell.

Again, some make this fulfilling of the law to be no more than *adeptio finis*,[2] the bringing about of that

[1] This interpretation noted and confuted by Burg. of Justific., pp. 361, 362.

[2] Bodius in Eph. v. 28, p. 799, who yet afterwards sets down that notion which I close with: Impleri quoque dicitur cum perfecte præstatur et observatur, quod a Christo pro nobis factum est, etsi ea præstatione vitam æternam non dicatur nobis acquisivisse.

which was the great end of it. What was that? why, to drive sinners to Christ. By its discovering sin and guilt, for 'the law was added because of transgressions,' Gal. iii. 21, and wrath, the consequent thereof, and the sinner's utter inability to help himself, eventually it was a means to bring such to look out for help in Christ. Therefore, Gal. iii. 24, it is said, 'The law was our schoolmaster, to bring us unto Christ;' and in this sense some take that passage, Rom. x. 4, 'Christ is the end of the law for righteousness;' *i.e.*, that which God mainly designed in the law, and which was the great end that he aimed at therein, it was to drive sinners to Christ, to obtain righteousness in and through him. This explication I do not close with neither, for I suppose the apostle is not here speaking so much of the fulfilling of the end of the law as of the fulfilling of the matter of the law; for he speaks of that which is imputable to us, as you will hear: now it is Christ's performing the matter of the law, and not the end of the law in itself, which comes under imputation.

'That the righteousness of the law might be fulfilled,' that is, say others,[1] that it might not be commanded in vain, nor without effect, as it is in respect of unbelievers. But this exposition will carry us to that fulfilling of the law which is in our own persons, which is not here intended; and this will better suit with the τὸν νόμον φυλάττειν, Rom. ii. 26, and the τὸν νόμον τελεῖσθαι, Rom. ii. 27, rather than with the τὸ δικαίωμα τοῦ νόμου πληρῶσαι in the text. These and such like explications of the word therefore being rejected, I stick to that which was first laid down; to fulfil the law's righteousness, it is fully, exactly, to do and to suffer whatever that righteous law demanded.

4. The resolution of the fourth inquiry will take me up more time: How are we to understand the fulfilling of the law's righteousness in the saints? 'That the righteousness of the law might be fulfilled *in us*;' he means in such who are in Christ Jesus, and who do believe on him. Every true believer is a fulfiller of the law; but how or in what sense he is so, there is the difficulty: in one sense nothing more true, in another nothing more false.

In the resolving of this a fourfold answer is given, and a fourfold interpretation put upon the words.

[1] Deodate *in loc.*

(1.) First, say some, the righteousness of the law is perfectly and personally fulfilled by the saints themselves. This the popish writers, in their polemical discourses, and also in their commentaries upon the text, do assert; wherein yet, to give every one their due, they differ from the old Pelagians;[1] for whereas they held that a man by the mere power of nature might perfectly keep the whole law, these hold that a man cannot do this without the assisting grace of God; but that being vouchsafed, they say, regenerate persons may keep the whole law. Thus they expound the words, and then from them they endeavour to prove, against us, a possibility of perfect obedience to the law of God by the saints in this life; insomuch that, say they, saints may here live without all sin, venial sins only excepted, which break no squares betwixt God and the creature; that they may do all the good which the law requires; nay, that this perfect conformity to the law is not only possible but easy; nay, that such who are high in grace, may not only do just what the law demands, but that they may supererogate and do more than what it demands. This is the doctrine which they of the Romish church teach and maintain with great zeal.[2]

We are not ashamed to declare our dissent from them in this proud opinion, which, in a great measure, owns its descent from the old pharisees.[3] We believe that since Adam's fall no man, Christ only excepted, did ever thus in himself fulfil the law's

[1] Hinc patet per solam naturam et legem sine gratia Christi, hominem in hac corruptione non posse totam legem totumque decalogum implere.—*A Lapide.*

[2] Concil Trident., Sess. 6, cap. 18; Bellarm. de Justif., lib. iv. cap. 10, &c.; Becan. Man. Controv., lib. i. cap. 17; Perer. Disp. iii. in cap. 8 ad Rom. Ut justificatio legis, &c., *i.e.*, ut nos legem impleremus, idque faciendo justi essemus, quia factores legis justificabuntur.—*Estius.* Peccato in nobis per redemptionis Christi gratiam abolito, factaque cum Deo reconciliatione, legem implere nobis est jam possibile, et facile.—*Tolet. Vide* Justinian., Catharin., Staplet., Rhemists *in loc.,* &c. Nemo miretur quod dixerim posse nos absque omni culpa absolute esse. Nam et iterum dico, posse per Dei gratiam et liberum arbitrium, hominem perfectam assequi justitiam coram Deo, immunitatem scilicet ab omni peccato, modo voluntas ejus non desit, adjuvante divina ope.—*C. Mussus.*

[3] See Calvin. Instit., lib. ii. cap. 7, sec. 5; Chemnit. Exam. De Bonis Operibus, 3 qu., p. 181; Chamier. tom. iii. lib. xi.; Whittak. *contra* Duræum. de Parad., lib. viii. pp. 201, 202; Bradsh. de Justif., cap. 11.

righteousness. Indeed, in the state of innocency, man had a power to do this, but not since; and to hold the contrary is to confound the two states, and to make little difference between man as standing and man as fallen. The law's righteousness is a draught or copy of man's primitive holiness, so that to say that he can now in himself come up to that righteousness is in effect to say he is as holy and righteous as ever he was, and no ways impaired by Adam's fall. By that we are all made unrighteous, and such as are unrighteous can never perfectly fulfil a righteous law. He must be sinless, do no evil, who will exactly reach the law's righteousness; but are any such here on earth?[1] 1 Kings viii. 46, 'There is no man that sinneth not;' Eccles. vii. 20, 'For there is not a just man upon earth, that doeth good and sinneth not;' James iii. 2, 'In many things we offend all;' 1 John i. 8, 'If we say that we have no sin we deceive ourselves, and the truth is not in us;' Prov. xx. 9, 'Who can say, I have made my heart clean, I am pure from my sin?' Read Ps. cxxx. 3, and cxlii. 2; Job ix. 2, 3, and xv. 15, &c.; Rom. iii. 19; Gal. iii. 22. Further, he must not only do good, all good, but he must do it in the most intense and highest degree that he is capable of, or else he doth not fulfil the law's righteousness: Mat. xxii. 37, 'Thou shalt love the Lord thy God with all thy heart, and with all thy soul, and with all thy mind;' but where is the man who thus loves God? Now if there be but a gradual defect, the law is not fulfilled.[2] Its righteousness extends to the inward man, and to the inward acts of the soul. As to external acts, if evil, especially if grossly and scandalously evil, it is possible for one to refrain from them; if good, it is possible for one to come up to them; but this will not amount to the perfect keeping of the law unless there be an abstaining from heart-evils, from evil thoughts and concupiscence within—so Christ, the maker and expounder of the law, opens it against the pharisees, Mat. v.—and unless also there be the doing of what is good from a right principle to a right end. If the righteousness of the law did lie only in external acts, something might be said; but when

[1] Ἀναμάρτητος ανθρώπων οὐδεὶς πάρεξ τοῦ γινομένουδι' ἡμᾶς ἀνθρώπου.—*Clem. Constit.,* lib. ii. cap. 18.

[2] Peccatum est cum non est charitas quæ esse debet, vel minor est quam esse debet.—*Aug. de Perfect. Justitiæ.*

it reaches to internal acts, who can say that there all is right? Oh how great is the law's strictness! Deut. v. 32, 'Ye shall observe to do therefore as the Lord your God hath commanded you: you shall not turn aside to the right hand or to the left.' And its demands are so severe, that if you fail in any one point, you are gone, you fail in all: Gal. iii. 10, 'Cursed is every one that continueth not in all things which are written in the book of the law to do them.' James ii. 10, 'For whosoever shall keep the whole law, and yet offend in one point, he is guilty of all,' and if so, he must be strangely arrogant and ignorant too that will pretend to come up in himself to the law's righteousness. If any could so do, to him the reward would be reckoned not of grace, but of debt, Rom. iv. 4; his justification would be by works, whereas the Scripture excludes any from being justified that way, Rom. iii. 19, 20; Gal. ii. 16. His righteousness would be of the law, and so, as to him, Christ 'died in vain,' Gal. ii. 21. If the law's righteousness was fulfillable in this sense, why did the apostle in the verse foregoing speak of the law's ἀδυναμία, or weakness? Whence doth that proceed but from our weakness, and utter inability perfectly to obey it? If it be said, as it is, that Christ came in flesh for this very end, to take off this weakness, that we might be able fully to keep it in our own persons, that we peremptorily deny. He came that the righteousness of the law should be fulfilled for us and in us imputatively, but not personally. Had he designed the latter, it is strange that we should not have one instance in all the New Testament of any one person who ever did so fulfil the law. I know some are mentioned, but all that is said of them doth amount only to integrity of parts, not to perfection of degrees; to eminency in grace and obedience, but not to law exactness; to evangelical, but not to legal perfection.

Obj. But doth God enjoin the creature that which is impossible?[1]

Ans. Just thus the Pelagians of old argued for the possibility of men's keeping the law; and Augustine, writing against them, was fain again and again to answer this very objection.[2] We say, what is simply

and absolutely impossible God doth not impose upon the creature;[1] but what he himself hath made impossible voluntarily and by his own default, that the great lawgiver may and doth impose. This impossibility doth no way intrench upon the goodness of God, because the sinner hath contracted and wilfully brought it upon himself. I hope the creditor may demand his debt, though the debtor cannot pay it, if through sloth, prodigality, bad husbandry, he hath disabled himself thereunto. That is the sinner's case with respect to perfect obedience to the law. God may demand his right, though the creature hath lost his power. This objection at the first hearing seems to have something in it, and it is very plausible to put an ugliness upon the protestants' doctrine; but when it is looked into and duly weighed, there is nothing at all of strength in it. Others, for brevity sake, I must omit. It appears, then, that the fulfilling of the law's righteousness in this sense, viz., of the saints' perfect and personal fulfilling thereof in themselves, is not according to truth, and therefore must be rejected.

(2.) Secondly, It is said that the law is fulfilled in and by the saints inherently and personally, but not perfectly. Thus some of our own divines do expound the words; they making them to refer to that obedience which belongs to sanctification, and which sanctified persons in themselves come unto; who though in the high and rigid notion they do not fulfil the law, yet in a soft and mild notion they do.[2] There is a begun, inchoate obedience in them thereunto, which is continued and carried on higher and higher till it be consummate. They do not only love and like the law, and consent to it that it is good, but they obey it in part; which, though it be but in part, yet they being sincere therein, and desiring to arrive at what is perfect, God accepts of them as though they did perfectly fulfil it. Thus evangelically, though not legally, the law's righteousness is fulfilled in them. It is not unusual in Scripture to set forth inchoate, partial, imperfect obedience, by the fulfilling of the law: Rom. ii. 27, 'And shall not uncircumcision

[1] Bellarm. de Lib. Arb., lib. v. cap. 18.
[2] De Nat. et Grat., cap. 43; De Peccat. Mer. et Rem., lib. ii. cap. 6, 7, 9.

[1] *Vide* Chamier., tom. iii. lib. xi. p. 328; Thes. Sedan., vol. i. p. 479; Pet. Martyr (in loc): Quanquam si quis recte, &c.
[2] Lex data est ut gratia quæreretur, gratia data est ut lex impleretur.—*August. de Spir. et Lit.*, lib i. cap. 19.

which is by nature, if it fulfil the law, judge thee,' &c. Rom. xiii. 8, 'He that loveth another hath fulfilled the law;' ver. 10, 'Love is the fulfilling of the law.' Gal. v. 14, 'All the law is fulfilled in one word, even in this; Thou shalt love thy neighbour as thyself.' Gal. vi. 2, 'Bear ye one another's burdens, and so fulfil the law of Christ.' Now in this sense the saints in themselves, in this life, may be said to fulfil the law's righteousness. They who go this way differ in this. Some interpret the words solely of inherent and personal obedience;[1] others take in that also which is by imputation.[2]

I cannot deny the truth of what is here said as to the thing; but whether it be the proper interpretation of the text, that I question: I think not. My reasons why I so think are these: (1.) The apostle speaking of that obedience, or fulfilling of the law, which was one of the great ends of God in sending his Son, it must be most proper here to understand that obedience and that fulfilling of the law which was first effected in the person of this Son, and then made over to believers by imputation. (2.) This law-fulfilling coming in as the high product of the love and wisdom of God, it may very probably be conjectured that if there be one fulfilling of the law higher than another, the highest here must be taken; and therefore it must not be that which is but inchoate and imperfect in us, but rather that which was complete, full, perfect in Christ. (3.) Though the fulfilling of the law be sometimes taken in that lower sense which hath been mentioned, yet the law-righteousness more usually notes that exact, universal obedience which the law requires; which notion, therefore, we may the rather be induced here to follow. (4.) The interpretation given by these worthy persons will not so well suit with what the apostle is now upon; he is, in short, summing up the grand benefits that saints have by Christ, shewing how they are secured from condemnation, and restored to a state of happiness. In order to which, he first sets down the expiation of sin, the satisfaction of

God's justice, &c., which were done by Christ's sacrifice or passive obedience in dying. Then he goes on to that which was further to be done; the holiness of God and of his law must be satisfied also, eternal life must be merited, &c. Now these must be done by Christ's active obedience or fulfilling the law's righteousness; therefore that he adds, that the righteousness of the law, &c. Wherefore we must here understand Christ's obedience as imputed, not our own as inherent, if that word be proper; otherwise we shall leave out one of the great benefits which we have by Christ, viz., that which results from his active obedience, and one of the ways wherein he did promote our salvation; whereas the apostle designs to set down both distinctly.

(3.) Thirdly, Others open it thus: the righteousness of the law is fulfilled in believers perfectly, yet not personally, but imputatively. Their meaning is this: the Lord Jesus in his own person, whilst he was here on earth, did fully obey the law, perfectly conforming to it in all its holy commands; now this his most perfect obedience to the law is made over, reckoned, imputed to his members, as if they themselves in their own persons had performed it. The law's righteousness is not fulfilled in them formally, subjectively, inherently, or personally, but legally; they being in Christ as their head and surety, and imputatively, so it is. This is the fulfilling which suits with the words, for it is said that the righteousness of the law might be fulfilled *in us;* not *by us,* but *in us:* in us, that is, not only for our sake and for our good, but as Christ's obedience is ours by imputation. If the former senses be rejected, this must be received; for since the law's righteousness must be fulfilled in the saints, (otherwise what the apostle here affirms would not be true,) and since there are but two ways wherein it can be fulfilled, either by themselves or by some other, it necessarily follows, if they do not fulfil it the first way, that the second must take place; and so it must be fulfilled by Christ for them, and his obedience be imputed to them. And this is that exposition of the words which our protestant divines,[1] so far as imputation

---

[1] Id quod nonnulli de justificatione interpretantur, &c., ideoque de sanctificatione vitæ intelligitur. Nam quod objici potest, nos non esse perfectos, ideoque, &c. Illud non sequitur, quia etsi legem non compleamus simpliciter ac simul, complemus tamen secundum quid, secundum omnia præcepta, inchoata obedientia, et successive.—*Gomar.* in loc.; Balduin, Deodat, &c.

[2] Pareus in Dub., p. 780; P. Martyr.

[1] Obedientia Christi, quæ in carne nostra exhibita nobis imputatur, ut eo beneficio pro justis censeamur.—*Calvin.* Quomodo justitia Christi in nobis impleta est per Christum? Duplici nomine, 1. Imputative, aliena justitia, quæ Christi est,

in general is concerned, do commonly give. But about it many things are necessary to be spoken unto, both for the explaining and also for the vindicating of it, which, therefore, shall be done by and by.

(4.) Fourthly, The fulfilling of the law's righteousness, say some, is no more than the remission of sin. He that hath his sins pardoned is a fulfiller of the law. Christ by his death having procured for us the remission of all our sins, upon that we are looked upon by God as if we had done or kept the whole law; thus Piscator opens the words.[1] And before him Ambrose speaks the same: *Quomodo impletur in nobis justificatio legis, nisi cum datur remissio omnium peccatorum?* How is the righteousness of the law fulfilled in us, unless it be in the remission of all our sins? To which we may add that of Augustine:[2] *Omnia mandata Dei facta deputantur, quando quicquid non fit ignoscitur;* all the commands of God are deemed to be done, when that is pardoned which is not done, (if it be good, or which should not have been done if it be evil.)

Two things I would say against this interpretation: (1.) It sounds very harsh to say we fulfil the law, when God is pleased to pardon the violation of it; nay, the thing is not true. God's remitting the breach of the law, and our actual fulfilling of the duties of the law, are not equipollent, but distinct and different things. Upon remission the sinner is exempted from the law's penalty, but he cannot upon that alone be said to fulfil it. If the prince

adeoque et nostra, &c.   2. Quod per Spiritum Christi regenerati, pro mensura gratiæ Dei vitam et justitiam eam exprimimus quam lex Dei exigit.   Magis placet prior sententia hoc loco.—*Muscul.   Vide* Bezam *in loc.*; Vorstium *in loc.* Justificatio legis, quæ requirit vel opera vel pœnam, impleta est in Christo per se, et ut sic dicam inhæsive, quia ipse præterquam quod passus est, etiam operatus est perfectissime; in nobis vero impleta est per fidem, et ut sic dicam applicative, nam per fidem fit ut Christi justitia, nostra quodammodo evadat.—*Rolloc.*   See Fulke and Cartwright against the Rhemists; Elton upon Rom. viii. p. 97, &c.

[1] Christus sua morte nobis acquisivit remissionem omnium peccatorum, ac proinde effecit, ut habeamur pro iis qui perfectam legi obedientiam præstiterint.—*In Paraphr.* The righteousness, &c., quatenus Christus sua morte eis acquisivit omnium peccatorum remissionem, quod perinde est ac si perfectam legi obedientiam præstitissent; æquipollent enim hæc nihil pecavisse, et perfectam legi obedientiam præstitisse.—*In Observ.*

[2] Retract., lib. i. cap. 19.

be pleased to pardon the breaker of the laws, will that amount to the making such a one to be a keeper of the laws? There is enough upon his pardon for non-punition, but nothing more. (2.) In the justification of sinners there is not only the remission of sin, but also the imputation of Christ's righteousness; these are the two parts of justification, and which take in the whole nature of it; it is not complete in the one or in the other part, but in both conjunct. I know some very learned persons make remission of sin to be the whole of justification;[1] I humbly differ from them. When God justifies, he doth not only pardon, and so look upon the sinner as not guilty; but he doth also impute Christ's righteousness, upon which he looks upon him as positively righteous;[2] this will hereafter be made out more fully, if God give leave. Thus it is in the justification or righteousness of the law; to the making up of which it is not enough only to be pardoned, and so not to be judged a breaker of the law, but there must be the doing of what the law enjoins, otherwise its righteousness is not fulfilled. It is one thing to be innocent, in the taking off of guilt, and another thing to be righteous in the way of positive obedience;[3] both are necessary as to that which I am upon, and included in it. *Not guilty* is not a sufficient plea or answer to the law's demands; there must be something, either in the sinner himself or in his surety, which may be looked upon as a formal and actual obeying of it.

Thus I have given a fourfold explication of the fulfilling of the law's righteousness in the saints. The third is that which seems to me to be the best, viz., this righteousness of the law is fulfilled in the saints, as Christ for them in his own person did perfectly obey the law, and as that his perfect obedience is imputed and reckoned to them, upon which it is theirs to all intents as if they had so obeyed in

[1] Wotton de Reconc. Pec., part 1, lib. ii. cap. 3, &c.

[2] *Vide* Zanch. ad Eph., cap. 5, p. 249, et quam plures alios. Uti Christus nobis factus et δικαιοσύνη et ἀπολύτρωσις, ita ad salutem atque justificationem requiritur, præter remissionem peccatorum, etiam justitiæ Christi imputatio, qua vitæ jus nobis addicitur, &c.—*Hoorneb. Socin. Confut.,* lib. iii. p. 658.

[3] Justus dicatur cui peccata omnia remittuntur justitia innocentiæ, quia posita hac remissione innocens censetur, &c., sed non justitia obedientiæ cui præmium vitæ debetur, &c.—*Turretin. de Sat. Christi,* p. 273.

their own persons. But there being many difficulties about this, and it leading me to the main truth which the words hold forth, I must endeavour further to open it.

Which I shall do in the discussing of these three propositions:

1. That our Lord Christ was made under the law.

2. That being made under the law he fulfilled it.

3. That his fulfilling of the law is imputed to believers; so as that in him they fulfilled the law also.

Prop. 1. Christ was made under the law. The apostle is express in this: 'When the fulness of the time was come, God sent forth his Son made of a woman, made under the law,' Gal. iv. 4; made under the law, that is, made subject to the law, so as that he was under the obligation thereof, and bound in all things to conform to its righteousness. And this subjection of Christ to the law did result partly from his nature, partly from his office. From his nature, as he was man, and so a creature, for his manhood was a created thing; now every creature as such is indispensably subject to the law of God, a creature necessarily must be under the law of his Creator and sovereign. So far therefore as Christ was such he was indispensably obliged to the law; so far his subjection was natural, and thereupon necessary. From his office, or that economy and dispensation which he had submitted unto as mediator, redeemer, surety, &c., with respect to this he was to be subject too, yet in it his subjection was purely free and voluntary. It is a nice question which some discuss,[1] Whether Christ's subjection to the law did arise from the natural necessity of his being, as he was man and a creature, or whether it did arise only from that mediatory office which he had submitted to? I think, things being rightly stated, both may be taken in; both nature and office did require that Christ should be subject to the law, though in different ways.[2]

For the better understanding of Christ's being made under the law, I desire you to take notice of four or five things.

(1.) This must be understood of him with respect to his human nature. This was the nature which only was capable of subjection; Christ as man

only could be obedient. As to his divine nature he made the law, so he was the lawgiver, and so he was in all acts of power and authority equal with the Father; it was solely in respect of his human nature that he was made under the law, which was part of that form of a servant which he took upon him, Phil. ii. 7. As he was God it was proper to him to command, as he was man only it was proper to him to obey; in the former notion he was 'Lord of the Sabbath,' Mat. xii. 8; in the latter he was bound to keep the Sabbath. Christ as man, and because man, was subject; but then it was only as such.

(2.) Christ, as being made under the law, is to be considered not merely as a creature, upon which he was subject to it, but as a creature in the state of his humiliation and suretyship, during which state only his subjection to the law was to continue. For his human nature now in heaven is a creature, and yet there it is not, if we speak strictly, under the law; for though Christ there doth materially the things which the law requires, as to be holy, to love God, &c., yet he doth not do them formally as acts of obedience to the law, but as things which spring from the perfection of his nature and state; therefore, I say, when we are speaking of Christ's being subject to the law, we must not consider him only as man, but as man in such a way or state, in the carrying on of such an undertaking, which when he had effected, his subjection was to cease. Some say, that though the subjection which Christ was under in reference to his office as mediator be at an end, yet his subjection to the law, which was natural, and did arise from his being a creature, that yet remains. I answer, If by this natural subjection they mean only that which results from his being, or that obligation which results from the intrinsic goodness of things, so we grant him even in heaven to be under it; but if they mean that subjection or that obligation which relates to and results from an external law, so we deny Christ there to be under it; in his glorified state he doth the things which the law commands, but not as or because they are commanded by the law.

(3.) The principal law that Christ was made under, and which he was principally obliged to fulfil, was the moral law.[1] This was the law which

---

[1] See Bodius on Eph., cap. 5, p. 812, &c.

[2] This opened in *Turretin. de Sat. Christi*, pp. 277, 278.

[1] *Vide* Bradsh. de Justif., cap. 18.

at first was made to Adam, which he brake, and so entailed the curse upon all his posterity; therefore Christ, the second Adam, was also made under this law, that he might fulfil it, and so restore man to his primitive happiness. This was the law which was the rule and standard of righteousness; wherefore if Christ will convey a righteousness to the creature, he must be made under and fulfil this law. He is said to be 'a curse for us;' now that curse doth mainly refer to the moral law, though it is very true, by way of allusion it is set forth by that which was proper to the judicial law, Gal. iii. 13. And he is also said to 'redeem us from the law,' that is, from the curse of the law; now it is the curse annexed to the moral law that he redeemed us from; therefore that was the law which he was made under. This was the law most excellent; if Christ would submit to put himself under the obligation of a law less excellent, surely he would not refuse to submit to put himself under the obligation of this, which was the most excellent law. Especially considering how necessary this was for the good of sinners; for since God stood upon the performance of this law as the way wherein he would justify, it was most necessary that Christ should be subject to it and perform it, or else there would have been no justification. Had he been made only under the ceremonial law, then the benefits of his obedience would have reached no further than that people who were concerned in that law; and so the Jews would have had all, and the poor Gentiles nothing. If Christ will redeem and save both, he must make good that law which did equally oblige both; now that was the moral law: Gal. iv. 4, &c., 'God sent forth his Son made of a woman, made under the law, to redeem them that were under the law, that we (Gentiles as well as Jews) might receive the adoption of sons.' Christ came not to save this or that nation or people, but mankind; wherefore he must be subject unto and fulfil that law in order thereunto, in which not any particular people, but all mankind were concerned; which, I say, was the moral law.

(4.) Yet besides this general law, which concerned all mankind,[1] (which therefore the Saviour of mankind subjected himself unto,) there were other particular and special laws to whose obligation he sub-

[1] Bradsh. of Justif., cap. 19.

mitted, and unto which he was obedient. As he was a man, he was subject to the moral law; as he was of the seed of Abraham, of the stock of Israel, so he was subject to the ceremonial law; as he was mediator, there were some particular and positive laws laid upon him, to which he was subject also. In obedience to the ceremonial law he was circumcised, Luke ii. 21, presented in the temple, with the usual offering of the poor and mean, Luke ii. 22, kept the passover, Mat. xxvi. 17, and the like. In obedience to the special laws laid upon him as mediator, the chiefest of which was that he should so and so suffer, yea, lay down his life, he did according to the will of his Father; therefore he is said to be 'obedient to death, even the death of the cross,' Phil. ii. 8, and to 'learn obedience by the things he suffered,' Heb. v. 7; and John x. 18, 'No man taketh it (his life he speaks of) from me, but I lay it down of myself; I have power to lay it down, and I have power to take it again. This commandment have I received of the Father;' so John xiv. 31. We commonly distinguish between the moral law, under which, as being general, Christ was, and that special law which was laid upon him as mediator. But some I find do not very well approve of this distinction;[1] their reason is, because it seems to assert that something was imposed upon Christ by the latter law, unto which he was not obliged by the former, which, say they, was not so. For there was nothing enjoined in the mediatory and positive law, unto which Christ was not obliged by the moral law; there was, indeed, in it a more particular application and determination of Christ's duty in his circumstances, but the thing itself was pre-enjoined, and he pre-engaged thereunto from the moral law. But this I will not concern myself about. He that would see a particular draught of Christ's obedience to the severals laws which he was made under, and the several capacities in which he all along obeyed, may find it done to his hand by others largely and distinctly, as particularly by Zanchy on Phil. ii. 8, p. 114, &c.

(5.) Though Christ was thus made under the law, and so obliged to keep it, yet this notwithstanding, his obedience thereunto was meritorious for us, and

[1] Burg. of Justif., p. ii. p. 396, &c.; Bodius on the Eph., pp. 386, 387.

imputable to us. For this is usually objected by the Socinian opposers of the imputation and merit of his obedience ;[1] for if Christ, say they, was subject to the law, as he was, and so bound for himself to do what he did, how can his obedience be made over to others, or merit for others ? for *debitum tollit meritum.*

For answer to this several things are said, but I will instance only in three.

[1.] In the business before us, Christ is not to be considered only as man, but as God-man. Had he obeyed as mere man, his obedience could not have been meritorious, for so all would have been but a due debt and for himself ; but he obeying who was God-man, so it became meritorious for others.[2] His obedience and subjection was indeed terminated in his human nature, but that must not be abstracted from his divine, both being now united in one person ; which union, though it did not make Christ incapable of obeying, yet it did put a singular virtue, and worth, and merit into his obeying. And as to his obeying for himself, take the explication of that in the words of a reverend divine :[3] ' It is, saith he, alleged that Christ as man fulfilled the law for himself, and therefore not for us. *Ans.* The flesh or manhood of Christ considered by itself, apart from the Godhead of the Son, is a creature that owes homage unto God. Yet if it be considered as it is received into the unity of the second person, and is become a part thereof, it is exempted from the common condition of all other men, and is not bound to perform subjection as all men are ; for if the Son of man be Lord of the Sabbath, then also is he Lord of the whole law.'

[2.] Though Christ, when he had submitted to assume man's nature, was bound to keep the law, yet his keeping thereof was in effect free and voluntary, and so imputable and meritorious, inasmuch as he, for the sake of man, freely consented to the tak-

ing of that nature, without which he had not been under any obligation to the law.[1] When he was man he was bound to obey ; but he was not at all, but by his own consent, bound to be man, and therefore his obedience was free, because his incarnation was free and without any obligation. A worthy person thus expresses it :[2] ' Even Christ's obedience to the moral law was not his duty, till he voluntarily undertook it ; it being, therefore, upon his consent and choice, and not due before consent, must needs be meritorious. And though when he was once a servant, he was bound to do the work of a servant, yet when he voluntarily put himself in the state of a servant, and under the law, not for his own sake, but for ours, his work is nevertheless meritorious.' As it is with a surety, he having engaged with and for the debtor, is thereby bound to pay the debt ; yet he pays it freely, inasmuch as it was his own free act to bring himself under such an obligation ; and so it was here in what Christ did.

[3.] It is further added, that though Christ, considered simply and absolutely as man, might be obliged by the law, yet as our surety, and undertaking for us in a fide-jussorial manner, so his obligation was wholly voluntary and free.[3] My author goes on and opens himself thus : ' Suppose Christ to be made a man, and thereby absolutely obliged to fulfil the law for himself, yet that he should enter into agreement with the Father to obey it as a surety, for such a term of years upon earth, thereby to procure salvation for a sinner undone otherwise, this was wholly gracious and voluntary, and Christ was not obliged to it as man.' Upon the whole, these three things being well weighed, the objection is sufficiently answered ; for suppose that Christ in such a sense

---

[1] Quocirca nec pro aliis magis quam quilibet alius homo, legem divinam conservando satisfacere potuit, quippe qui ipse eam servare omnino deberet.—*Socin. de Servat.*, p. iii. cap. 5. Against him see *Calov. Socin. Proflig.*, sect. 5, controv. 1, p. 642.

[2] Obediens factus fuit ad mortem Patri, non necessum id habuit natura sed œconomia nostræ redemptionis. Ut etiam meriti vis non naturæ humanæ qua natura, sed qua Deo unita, est adscribenda.—*Stegman.*, disp. 23, p. 266.

[3] Mr Perkins on Gal. iv. 4, p. 274.

---

[1] Quicunque pro se et suo loco vel Adæ vel Abrahæ factus est filius, is quoque pro se et suo nomine ad legem implendam tenebatur ; qui vero non pro se sed pro aliis vel homo fieri vel Israelita nasci voluit, is quoque non pro se sed pro aliis ad legem quamlibet implendam obligatus est. At Christus, &c. —*Turret. de Sat.*, p. 276. *Vide* Polanum in Dan. ix. p. 196 ; Bodium on Eph., pp. 811, 812 ; Hoorneb. Socin. Confut., lib. iii. p. 627. Quamvis humana natura, ut creatura quævis, Deo sublex observantiam debuit, attamen quia nec eam assumere tenebatur, neque simplicis creaturæ obedientia fuit sed θεανδρικὴ, ideo pro quibus hoc et istud factum, quidni et pro iisdem satisfecisse dicatur ?

[2] Mr Baxt. Aphor., p. 58.

[3] Burg. of Justif., p. ii. p. 409.

was bound to keep the law, yet there were other respects, peculiar to his person and obedience, which made it so voluntary and for us, as that it may truly be looked upon as meritorious and imputable. So much of the first proposition.

Prop. 2. The second is this, Christ being thus made under the law, he fulfilled it. Mat. iii. 15, 'Thus it becometh us to fulfil all righteousness;' chap. v. 17, 18, 'Think not that I am come to destroy the law, or the prophets; I am not come to destroy, but to fulfil. For verily I say unto you, Till heaven and earth pass, one iota or one tittle shall in no wise pass from the law, till all be fulfilled.' Rom. x. 4, 'Christ is the end of the law for righteousness to every one that believeth;' the end of the law, viz., as the law in him received its full and final accomplishment. Two things, as you have heard, were contained in its righteousness—the duty it commanded, the penalty it threatened; in both respects Christ fulfilled it. For in his active obedience he did the former, and in his passive obedience he underwent the latter. The preceptive and mandatory part of the law he fulfilled actively, both as he shunned whatever evil that prohibited, and also as he did whatever good that enjoined. He was originally and actually holy, acted all along in exact and universal conformity to the law's commands; so he fulfilled it actively, John viii. 46; 2 Cor. v. 21; 1 Peter ii. 22, and i. 19; Acts iii. 14; Dan. ix. 24; 1 John ii. 2; Heb. vii. 26. The penal and minatory part he fulfilled passively, by his bearing of its curse when he died upon the cross. With respect to both, Christ's obedience was so full and perfect, so adequate to all the law's demands, that it could not but say, I have enough, I am fully satisfied, I can ask no more.

And this fulfilling of the law was the foundation upon which his satisfaction and merit was built; without which he could neither have satisfied nor merited. Oh, saith God, Son! if thou wilt satisfy me, there is my holy and just law, satisfy it; unless that be satisfied I cannot be satisfied; by its violation I was offended, by its fulfilling I must be appeased. Well, Christ accepts of the terms. 'Lo, (saith he,) I come: in the volume of the book it is written of me, I delight to do thy will, oh my God: yea, thy law is within my heart,' Ps. xl. 7, 8. And what he undertook he made good; he went so far

that neither the righteous God nor the righteous law could tax him with any defect. If it had not been thus, though he had obeyed never so much for us, though his obedience had been never so free and voluntary, yet it would not have been either satisfactory or meritorious; for all satisfaction and merit are founded upon the fulfilling of the law's righteousness. The gracious God is pleased to accept of an imperfect obedience, if sincere, *from us*, but the just God would have a perfect obedience *for us*. He can accept of a mite from us, but from our surety he would have the whole debt paid down.

Whether Christ's active fulfilling of the law, as considered in itself, in its intrinsic worth and value, could properly and formally merit of God, as some hold;[1] or whether it did merit, respect being had to God's ordination, covenant, and promise, as others,[2] is a nicety that I have no mind to engage in. That was the way wherein he merited, which is the thing that I only design to speak unto.

Prop. 3. The third proposition: Christ having thus fulfilled the law, this his obedience is made over and imputed to believers. For otherwise how doth the apostle here say, 'that the righteousness of the law might be fulfilled *in us?*' This is that imputed righteousness which is so often spoken of in that one chapter of Rom. iv. In reference to this, Christ is said to be 'made righteousness to us,' 1 Cor. i. 30; to be 'the Lord our righteousness,' Jer. xxiii. 6; and we are said to be 'the righteousness of God in him,' 2 Cor v. 21; to be 'accepted in him,' Eph. i. 6; to be 'presented' to God as 'not

---

[1] Opera Christi absolute considerata meriti proprie dicti rationem habent; non respectu promissionis alicujus, sed insita sua vi, tanquam opera θεανδρικὰ absolute indebita. Eadem autem benigna promissione Dei niti, quatenus meritum illud ad nos refertur, omnino concedimus.—*Essen. Tri. Crucis*, p. 294.

[2] Equidem fateor, si quis simpliciter et per se Christum opponere vellet judicio Dei, non fore merito locum, quia non reperiretur in homine dignitas quæ possit Deum promereri.—*Calvin. Instit.*, lib. ii. cap. 17, sec. 1. *Vide Chamier.*, tom. iii. lib. ix. cap. 1, sec. 7. Nec aliter Christi meritum accipimus, quam quod legi plenissime satisfecit, non solius obedientiæ insita vi ac dignitate ad divini juris rigorem appensa, sed ad legem satisfactoriæ, sic meritus ex divina promissione fuit, non absque ea. Meritum ad fœdus non extra illud æstimatur, non ad merum Dei jus, quasi ulla cujusquam actione in rationem debiti trahi posset.—*Hoornb. Socin. Conf.*, p. 627.

having spot, or wrinkle, or any such thing,' Eph. v. 27; by his obedience to be 'made righteous,' Rom. v. 19. Many other scriptures might be cited which hold forth this great evangelical truth, and also these that I have cited might be much enlarged upon; but the difficulty lying not so much in the general as in the particular stating and explication of it—where indeed there is enough of difficulty—therefore I shall rather direct myself to that.

And here two weighty questions must be discussed.

1. Whether Christ's active fulfilling the law, or his active as well as his passive obedience, be imputed to believers?

2. In what sense may it be said to be imputed to them?

My text, and the subject which I am upon from it, lay a necessity upon me of speaking something to these points; otherwise I should most gladly have passed them by. It is much against my spirit, God knows, to revive and keep up those controversies, which I could wish with all my soul had never been started, but being started, that they might now be buried. And further, it grieves me exceedingly to meddle in those matters wherein I must unavoidably differ from some or other of those who, for their piety and learning, are of great eminency and repute in the church of God, and for whose names and persons I have a very high veneration. Yet for all this I dare not, to please myself, and to avoid what is ungrateful to me, go out of my way. It is merely sense of duty, as I apprehend it, which makes me to engage in this unwelcome province. These controversies, as they are managed by some in their utmost latitude, are grown to a great vastness; but it would be highly inconvenient for me, now I am upon the close of this work, which is already grown above its due proportion, to be prolix about them. I shall contract myself, therefore, and only in short speak to that which I conceive is absolutely necessary for the clearing up of the things in question.

1. As to the first question, Whether Christ's active fulfilling the law, or whether his active as well as his passive obedience, be imputed to believers? I shall not spend any time about the terms, in inquiring whether they be proper or not, or whether the things be rightly distinguished or not, since there

was action in Christ's passive obedience, and passion in his active. All understand the thing which we intend in the use of the words; therefore, without any further debate, I will take them as they are commonly used and understood.

In answer to this question, I find four opinions about it:

1. That neither the active nor the passive obedience of Christ are properly and really imputed to believers.

2. That the passive obedience of Christ only is imputed.

3. That both active and passive are imputed.

4. That the active obedience of Christ is imputed as well as the passive, but not in the same way; not *quatenus* active, but as it was a part of Christ's satisfaction and merit.

For those who espouse the first opinion, Socinians and papists, I will not at present meddle with them. One of their great arguments against the imputation of Christ's obedience, particularly his active obedience, about which only I would contend, viz., that he being a creature was under an obligation to obey, that he obeying for himself, his obedience could not be imputed to others; this argument, I say, hath been already answered. And as to the other arguments which they use, they will fall in with those which shall be presently spoken unto, as they are urged by others, who yet are far from being Socinians or papists, against the imputation of Christ's active obedience.

Secondly, There are others, much more orthodox and sound in the faith than the former, who, though they hold the imputation of Christ's obedience, yet they limit that imputation to his passive obedience; asserting that that only is imputed to believers. They deny not but that his active obedience was necessary for his person and office, for the qualifying of him for his mediatorship; but that it is formally imputed to them who believe, that they deny. They say, God did accept of the death and sufferings of his Son as a full satisfaction for his violated law; that the righteousness thereof is fulfilled by his bearing its penalty; that upon the alone bearing of that penalty sin is remitted, and the sinner completely justified; that this passive obedience is sufficient, to all intents and purposes, for satisfaction and merit too, without any further imputation of his active obedience; so that if the sinner do but perform the conditions on his part, of believing and repenting, in Christ's death alone there is every way enough for him. The grounds they go upon in the defence of this opinion are many. One is, that when the Scripture speaks of reconciliation with God, remission of sin, justification, &c., still it lays the stress of all upon Christ's passive obedience, or upon his death and blood. So Mat. xx. 28, and xxvi. 28; John vi. 51, &c.; Acts xx. 28; Rom. iii. 25, and v. 9; Gal. iii. 13; Eph. i. 7, and ii. 13, &c.; Col. i. 20–22; 1 Pet. i. 19; Heb. ix. 12, and x. 14. Besides this they prove it by several reasons, which are chiefly drawn from the sufficiency of Christ's passive obedience for the sinner's relief in his lost condition, and also from the great difficulties, if not absurdities, as they judge, which attend the other opinion for the imputation of his active obedience. This opinion hath the more prevailed since the first broaching of it—which was not very long ago; for it was not made matter of controversy till these latter ages of the church—not only from the strength and weightiness of the arguments with which it is backed, which cannot be denied, but also from the assertors of it, they being many, and some of them persons deservedly of very great reputation in the church of Christ; such as Piscator, Pareus, Scultetus, Capellus, Camero, Forbes, with divers others.

The third opinion is, that Christ's whole obedience, active as well as passive, is imputed to us; his obeying the law to the full, perfect conforming to its commands, his doing as well as his dying obedience, is, say these, made over and reckoned to believers in order to their justification and salvation. This also is asserted by several divines of great note;[1]

[1] Cum Christus descenderit de cœlis, omniaque egerit et passus sit propter nos homines, et propter nostram salutem (nobis enim natus est, nobis vixit, pro nobis factus est sub lege, ut eos qui sub lege erant redimeret) idcirco utraque pars obedientiæ Christi, i.e., tota ejus obedientia nostra facta est, cessitque in salutem nostram.—*Zanch. in Phil.*, cap. 2, 8, p. 115. See Calvin Instit., lib. ii. cap. 16, sect. 5. This way goes Junius in Thes. de Justif.; Polanus in Syntag., lib. vi. cap. 36; and in Comment in Dan., p. 186, &c.; Brocmand. de Servat. Jesu Christo, art. 16, sect. 12, qu. 4; Gomarus de Justif. against Kargius; Rivet against Camero; Lucius against Piscator and Gataker; Downeham of Justif., lib. i. cap. 4, p. 24, &c.; Burgess of Justif., part ii. serm. 34, p. 338.

and that not only by some of them by the by, ὡς ἐν παρόδω, but also by others who do largely insist upon the proof and making of it good against those who think otherwise.

The reasons upon which they ground this opinion are such as these:

1. As the disobedience of the first Adam, in which he brake the law, is imputed to men, upon which they become guilty; so the obedience of Christ, the second Adam, even that in which he kept the law, must be imputed also to them, that thereby they may be made righteous. For their guilt and righteousness must not only be conveyed in the same way or manner, viz., by imputation; but these, being opposites, must proceed from like opposite causes; and therefore if their guilt arises from Adam's breach of the law, which is imputed to them, answerably their righteousness must arise from Christ's obedience to the law, which therefore must also be imputed to them. So the apostle draws the parallel or comparison: Rom. v. 19, 'As by one man's disobedience many were made sinners, so by the obedience of one shall many be made righteous.' Where observe, (1.) He speaks of Christ's obedience in the general—'by the obedience of one,' &c.— wherefore to limit this to one branch of his obedience, his passive obedience, as though by it alone sinners were made righteous, is neither safe nor warrantable. (2.) If we will proceed in that way, so as to single out this or that part of Christ's obedience, and ascribe righteousness to it, then the antithesis will carry it for his active rather than for his passive obedience; for that being the obedience which stands in direct opposition to Adam's disobedience, it must, by the rules of opposition, most properly here be understood. (3.) The apostle makes the imputation of both to run parallel, according to the acts and effects which are proper to each: 'As by the disobedience of one many were made sinners, so by the obedience of one shall many be made righteous.' So that as the one act is imputed for guilt, so the other is imputed for righteousness; and as in the one person, he being a public person and head, we broke the law, so in the other, he being a public person and head too, we perform the law. If it be said that Adam's disobedience did not lie in the transgression of the moral law, but only of that

particular positive law which God gave him of not eating of the tree of knowledge; and so that Christ's obedience did not lie in the keeping of the moral law, but in his obeying of that positive law which God laid upon him, namely, of laying down his life; —which if so, then the text proves nothing of that for which it is alleged, but rather the quite contrary;—I answer: Though it is very true that in Adam's disobedience, immediately and proximately, there was only the transgressing of that positive law, yet in the transgressing thereof there was virtually and collaterally the breach of the whole moral law, all this law being summed up in and guarded by that *lex primordialis*, as Tertullian calls it.[1] The argument then from the comparison holds good: As Adam violating the moral law, his active disobedience is imputed for guilt; so our Lord Jesus obeying the moral law, his active obedience thereunto is imputed for righteousness, which is the thing to be proved.

2. That obedience of Christ must be imputed, without the imputation of which the righteousness of the law is not, or could not be fulfilled in believers; this cannot be denied, for it is brought in here expressly as the end of God's sending his Son, ' that the righteousness of the law might be fulfilled in us.' Now I assume, but without the imputation of Christ's active obedience, the law's righteousness is not and could not be fulfilled in believers, *ergo.* This I prove from what hath been already said; the law's righteousness consists in two things: (1.) In its requiring perfect conformity to its commands; (2.) In its demanding satisfaction, or the undergoing of its penalty upon the violation of it. This being so, how can the law's righteousness be fulfilled in saints either by the active or by the passive obedience of Christ apart and alone? Put them both together and the thing is done; there is that in both which is fully adequate to the law's demands; but divide them, and it is not so. The passive obedience satisfies as to the law's penalty, and secures from the law's curse, but where is our performing of the duty which

the law requires, if the active obedience be not imputed also? And it is conceived that this righteousness of the law doth mainly and primarily refer to the preceptive and mandatory part of the law, and but secondarily to the penal and minatory part of the law; for in all laws, civil or sacred, that which is first intended in them is active obedience—the bearing the penalty is annexed but to further and secure that; so that he who only bears the penalty doth not answer the first end and the main intention of the law. Whence I infer, since the righteousness of the law is fulfilled in believers, as the apostle here saith it is, that therefore the commanding part of the law must be fulfilled in them, that being the main branch of its righteousness, and that which is principally designed by it; but that cannot be, unless the active obedience of Christ be imputed to them. This argument, with submission to better judgments, is to me of great weight; and I desire the words may be well observed. It is not said that the righteousness of the law might be *endured*, suffered, or undergone by us, as if it did relate to the penalty of the law; but that the righteousness of the law might be *fulfilled* in us, which surely most properly must relate to the doing part of the law. Doth he fulfil who suffers?[1] that is very harsh. To say that one of the things that have been spoken of was or is sufficient, viz., the undergoing of the punishment without the doing of the duty, and that therefore the imputation of Christ's death and sufferings is enough; I say, for any to assert this, they do, in my thoughts, offer some violence to the text in hand, which tells us the righteousness, the whole righteousness, of the law, was to be and is fulfilled in believers.

3. It is urged, thirdly, It is necessary, not only in respect of the law, but of ourselves also, that Christ's active obedience should be imputed, inasmuch as our righteousness and title to eternal life do indispensably depend upon it. The law is the measure and standard of righteousness; let that be fulfilled and a person is righteous, otherwise not; without this none can stand before the great God as being such. Well then, the sinner himself being altogether un-

[1] In hac lege data Adæ omnia præcepta condita recognoscimus, quæ postea pullulaverunt data per Mosen, &c. Igitur hac generali et primordiali Dei lege, omnia præcepta legis posterioris specialiter indita fuisse cognoscimus, quæ suis temporibus edita germinaverunt.—*Tertull. adv. Jud.*, cap. 2.

[1] Qui maledictionem legis perpetitur, per hoc non implet mandata legis, aut operatur justitiam, &c.—*Wegelin. de Obed. Christi.*

able thus to fulfil the law, thereby to be made righteous, Christ's fulfilling of it must be imputed to him in order to righteousness. Guilt and righteousness do both carry in them a reference to the holy law: when that is broken, it is guilt; when that is kept, it is righteousness; therefore as, supposing that law had not been transgressed, we had not been guilty, so unless that law be fully conformed to, we cannot be righteous, Deut. vi. 25. Now where shall we find this full conformity to the law but in Christ? and what will that in Christ avail us if it be not imputed and made over to us? So as to eternal life, unto which, without fulfilling the law, we can have no claim or title; for the old law condition or covenant being yet in force, *Hoc fac et vives*, 'Do and live,' Lev. xviii. 5; Rom. x. 5; Gal. iii. 12; Luke x. 28; unless this condition be performed we cannot hope for life. True indeed, under the covenant of grace God accepts of what is done by the surety, and he doth not exact of the sinner in his own person the perfect obeying of the law as the condition of life, but yet he will have the thing done either by or for the sinner, either by himself or by his surety, or else no life; doth not this then evince the necessity of the imputation of Christ's active obedience?

But it is queried, Was not Christ's passive obedience, without the active, sufficient for both of these—for righteousness and for life? To which they of this opinion answer, No; they say upon Christ's death and suffering we are freed from guilt, but upon that, abstractly from his active obeying of the law, we are not strictly and positively made righteous; so also, upon his death and suffering, they say, we are saved from wrath and hell, but yet upon that alone we are not entitled to heaven. They grant in Christ's death a fulness and sufficiency of satisfaction, but as to merit, for that they must take in the holiness and obedience of his life. I do but recite, not undertaking, at present, to defend what is here asserted; only let me close this head with one thing which to me is observable. Our Lord being both to do and to suffer, to obey actively and passively, that he might fully answer the law's demands for the justification and salvation of sinners, it is considerable how the New Testament, in two eminent places, speaks distinctly to both these

parts of his obedience, in their distinct reference to both the parts of the law under the Old Testament, and in their distinct influence upon the sinner's good: Gal. iii. 13, 'Christ hath redeemed us from the curse of the law, being made a curse for us: for it is written, Cursed is every one,' &c.; or as it is, ver. 10, 'Cursed is every one that continueth not in all things,' &c. Here is Christ's passive obedience, with respect to the old curse or penal part of the law here mentioned, and the benefits which we reap thereby, viz., deliverance from the law's curse. That is one place; the other is Rom. x. 5, 'Christ is the end of the law for righteousness to every one that believeth. For Moses describeth the righteousness which is of the law, That the man which doeth these things shall live by them.' Here is Christ's active obedience, with respect to the mandatory part or doing righteousness of the law here mentioned also, and the imputation and benefit of this to believers, viz., righteousness and life. 'Christ is the end of the law for righteousness,' that is, to convey that righteousness which the law could not, or to perform the law in order to righteousness, which the sinner could not; take it as you will, it must have reference to the moral law and to the preceptive part thereof, for so the apostle opens it in that which follows, ver. 5. Now Christ's active obedience thereunto is imputed to believers, otherwise why is it said that he is the end of the law for righteousness to every one that believeth? All that I drive at is (1.) That the imputation of the passive obedience in Gal. iii. 13 must not jostle out the imputation of the active obedience in Rom. x. 5. (2.) That as the imputation of the one is necessary to free from the law's curse, so the imputation of the other is necessary for the having of righteousness and life.

4. If Christ actively fulfilled the law for us, then his active fulfilling thereof must be imputed to us, but so he did, *ergo*. The consequence I judge to be good and strong; for surely whatever Christ did on our behalf, in our stead, as designing and aiming at our good as his main end, that must needs be imputed to us; otherwise he and we too might lose that which he principally designed in his obedience, which is not to be imagined. As to the assumption that Christ actively fulfilled the law for us, that is generally asserted and defended by divines against

Socinians and others. For whereas these affirm that Christ fulfilled the law for himself, he as a creature being under the obligation of it, they prove the contrary, of which before; shewing that Christ was not, in that way wherein he fulfilled the law, at all obliged so to fulfil it for himself; but that all was done by him purely upon our account: he obeyed not merely as a subject but as a surety, therefore his obedience must be for us, and so imputable and imputed to us. And whereas others affirm, that Christ actively fulfilled the law, that he might thereby be fitted and qualified for his mediatory office, two things are answered: (1.) The Scripture, when it speaks of Christ's subjection to the law and accomplishment of it, doth not lay it upon this end or upon what refers to Christ himself, but upon that which refers to us as the proper end thereof. He was 'the end of the law for righteousness to them that believe,' &c., 'made under the law, to redeem them that were under the law, that we might receive the adoption of sons.' (2.) They say that Christ's fitness for his mediatory office did result from his person, from the personal union of the divine and human natures in him, rather than from his active obedience to the law; for else he could not have been looked upon as one fit to be a mediator till he had finished his whole obedience to the law; whereas from the first instant of the personal union he was fit for that work and office. It was fit, nay necessary, that Christ the Mediator should conform to the law; but these are two different things—what was fit for the mediator to do, and what must fit him to be the mediator. These ends therefore respecting Christ himself being removed, it follows that it was wholly for us that he fulfilled the law: whence then I infer that that must be imputed to us, otherwise the end of it would not be attained; for without the imputation of it we should neither be the persons designed in it, nor profited by it. To prevent mistakes, and to give this argument its full strength, I would state it thus: Whatever Christ did, that we were obliged to do, and which was to be our righteousness before God, that certainly must be imputed to us. I do not say that all which Christ did is strictly and properly imputed to us, but whatever he did, if we were bound to do it, and if the doing of that was to be our righteousness, that

must be imputed, or else we are in a sad case. He was incarnate for us, yet that is not formally imputed. Why? because sinners were not under any obligation to any such thing; so I might instance in his working of miracles, intercession, &c. But now if our Lord will be pleased to put himself under the law, and to fulfil the law, that must be made over to us, because that was a thing which we ourselves, according to the capacity of creatures, were bound unto, and this was to be our righteousness before God. What is so circumstantiated must be imputed; therefore this being taken in, the argument is good.

Several other arguments are produced for the imputation of the active as well as the passive obedience. As that both together make most for the glory of Christ,[1] and for the ease and comfort of burdened souls.[2] That it is a mighty loss for Christians to lose Christ's active obedience; and why should it be the active only, or the passive only, if they may have both? *Quidni utraque?* saith Pareus himself, can we have too much of Christ? Is not all of him precious? And do not we need all? Surely the safest way is to take in as much of him as ever we warrantably may.[3] They who go this way also urge the consent of the reformed churches, the suffrages of several famous divines, as concurring with them; that their opinion hath the advantage of being judged the more ancient and orthodox, which that excellent person Mr Bradshaw, though he somewhat dissents about the thing, doth ingeniously confess.[4] But these things I shall pass over; if the foregoing arguments will not convince and satisfy, I shall hope for less from these. So much for this third opinion.

[1] See Bodius in Eph., p. 796.

[2] Neque conscientias pacaret aliqua justitiæ portio; sed perpetuo illas trepidare necesse esset, nisi firmiter persuasæ forent totam justitiam legis sibi imputari.—*Polan. in Dan.,* p. 187.

[3] Certe tutius ibit ille, qui plus Christo ad majorem gloriam ascribit quod in eo quærat, quam qui ei quicquam adimit. Et qui totam salvatoris et sponsoris nostri obedientiam legi divinæ præstitam amplectitur, quam qui præcipuam ejus partem pro justitia coram Deo sibi imputari non credit.—*Wegelin Disp. de Obed. Christi.*

[4] Noram probe, sententiam priorem antiquiorem et orthodoxam magis passim audire. Sed et re apud me accuratius perpensa penitusque perspecta, suo merito ea id audire visa est.—*In Præfat. ad Tract. de Justif.,* p. 6.

4. There is a fourth. Say some,[1] the active as well as the passive obedience of Christ is imputed, yet not in the sense of the promoters of the former opinion, but only thus, as it was a part of Christ's satisfaction for the violation of the law ;[2] as it is so considered, they say, it is imputed, but not in any other notion. They say Christ's active obeying was satisfactory and meritorious as well as his passive, than which nothing more certain ; and indeed the passive without the active had not been satisfactory or meritorious. It was Christ's voluntary subjection to the will of his Father, which was an active thing, even in his dying, which put such an efficacy into his death.[3] Now his active obedience being thus taken, is, they grant, made over and reckoned to believers. Others, to the same purpose, consider Christ's active obedience two ways ;[4] either strictly as active, as it lay in conformity to what the law commanded, or as there was humiliation and abasement attending that obedience : in the former respect they deny it to be imputed, in the latter they say it is. This middle and reconciliatory opinion is somewhat new and modern, and owned, as yet, but by very few, but in those few, for their worth and eminency, there are very many. I shall not set myself to argue or object anything against it, though something might be said upon that account ; I rejoice with all my heart that we may have the active obedience of Christ upon any terms or under any considerations. I am so far from arguing against it that I keep it by me as a reserve ; that if there be not solid and satisfactory answers to be given to the weighty objections made against the imputation of Christ's active obedience as commonly asserted, which is to be tried by and by, I may fall in and close with it. No more at present therefore about the first question.

[1] Bradshaw de Justif. in Præfat., p. 10.

[2] Thus Grotius de Sat., cap. 6, p. 89; Bradshaw de Justif., cap. 18, sec. 5, 6 ; Mr Baxter's Aphor., p. 54 ; Great Propit., pp. 92, 93.

[3] Neque tamen excluditur reliqua pars obedientiæ qua defunctus est in vita, &c. Et sane in ipsa, (i.e., in morte crucis, for that he is speaking of and doth immediately go before,) primum gradum occupat voluntaria subjectio ; quia ad justitiam nihil profuisset sacrificium nisi sponte oblatum.—*Calvin. Instit.*, lib. ii. cap. 16, sec. 5.

[4] Gataker. Animadv. in Lucium., p. i. sec. 1, p. 2 ; Bodius in Eph., p. 798.

I go on to the second. The imputation of Christ's fulfilling the law, or of his active obedience being granted, it is further to be inquired in what sense this imputation is to be taken, and how far it is to be carried ? This question hath its difficulties as well as the former. The learned differ not only about the matter of imputation, or what is imputed, but also about the nature and the right stating of the act. Even they who agree in the imputation of Christ's active obedience, do yet differ in the stating of that imputation.

For it is the opinion of some that Christ's active obedience is so imputed to believers as that God reckons it to them as done in their stead ; that in his obeying and fulfilling the law, they legally, and in God's estimation, obeyed and fulfilled the law also ; that his obedience is accepted for them, and made over to them, even as if they had so obeyed in their own persons. Others cannot close with this high and rigid imputation, as they are pleased to call it. They say the imputation is to be carried no higher than thus : That Christ's obedience is imputed to believers, that is, it is reckoned to them for their good, but not as done in their stead ; that it is theirs in the effects and benefits of it, but not as to the thing itself, so as that they in their persons should be looked upon as having in Christ fulfilled the law. They are for Christ's obeying *propter nos*, but not *pro nobis*.

This latter stating of imputation is that which some follow, whom, upon many accounts, I am bound to respect and reverence ; and I acknowledge, as before, the former stating of it to lie open to very weighty and considerable objections. Yet, in compliance with my present light, I must crave leave to differ from them, though I do it with all modesty and submission ; and the objections made against the high and strict imputation will, as I judge, admit of fair and satisfactory answers. Therefore I believe and affirm that our Saviour's active obedience is imputed, reckoned, made over to us, as being done in our stead, and not only finally for our good ; that it is ours, not only as to such and such effects, but that the thing itself is ours, in a law sense ; that God reckons it to us as if we had done it in our own persons, and that therein, in part, consists our righteousness before God.

The arguments upon which I build this position are these :

1. If the imputation of Christ's righteousness or obedience be not taken for the imputing thereof to us as done in our stead, but only as done for our good, then whatever he did, or doth, may as properly be said to be imputed to us as his righteousness and obedience. The reason of the consequence is plain, because that all which Christ did or doth is for our good; his incarnation, nativity, ascension, intercession, &c., all are for the good of those who love God. If therefore there be nothing more in the imputation of his obedience than the reckoning of it to us for our good, then the forementioned things may equally and as properly be said to be imputed to us as it, which I suppose will not be affirmed; if it be, it will admit of a very easy confutation.

2. That must be the right stating of the imputation of Christ's obedience which best suits with his suretyship, but that which I plead for doth so, *ergo.* A surety doth not pay the debt only for the debtor's good, but as standing in the debtor's stead, and so his payment is reckoned to the debtor; the same we must hold with respect to Christ and sinners, or else we quit the main notion of his being a surety. Take away Christ's obeying in our stead, and make it to be only for our good, and so imputed, and you may then suppose him to be a loving and compassionate Saviour, but not strictly a surety; for to that it is requisite that he pay our very debt, and that that payment be accepted of as made in our stead.

3. Christ's obedience is imputed as Adam's disobedience was imputed. This is grounded upon the apostle's parallel between them in Rom. v., of which before. Now how is Adam's disobedience imputed to us? *Ans.* Not only for our hurt, or in the mischievous effects of it, but the guilt itself of his disobedience is imputed, insomuch that in his sinning we all sinned. Answerably, *ex opposito,* Christ's obedience is, and must be, imputed to us; viz., not only for our good, and in the happy effects of it, but the thing itself is ours, insomuch that in his obeying, reputatively and legally, we obeyed also. I cannot understand the analogy betwixt the two Adams, wherein the apostle is so clear, unless this imputation, as here stated, be granted; and I humbly conceive he who grants we disobeyed in Adam, must grant we also obeyed in Christ.

4. Christ's righteousness is imputed to us in that way wherein our sin was imputed to him; this is grounded upon 2 Cor. v. 21. Now our sin was imputed to Christ, not only in the bitter effects of it, but he took the guilt of it upon himself,[1] as hath been already proved. So then his righteousness, or active obedience itself, must be proportionably imputed to us, and not only in the effects thereof.

5. The proper *terminus* of imputation is righteousness. It is, according to its notion in Scripture, the reckoning or making over of a thing to a person for righteousness: 'Abraham believed God, and it was imputed to him for righteousness,' Rom. iv. 3. If therefore Christ's obedience be imputed to us, it must be so imputed as to be our righteousness before God; no imputation lower than this will serve our turn, nor suit with the Scripture notion of the word.

6. They who dissent bring in the imputation of Christ's active obedience as a part of his satisfaction, whence I argue he satisfied in our stead; as he obeyed he satisfied, therefore he obeyed in our stead. Christ's active obedience being satisfactory as well as his passive, why should not that *eo nomine* come under the same imputation which the passive doth?

7. If this be all in the imputation of Christ's obedience, that it is reckoned to the sinner for his good, then we are all agreed, all controversies are at an end. For who, even amongst the rankest deniers of imputation, do not assent to this, that all was done and suffered by Christ for our good, and is so far reckoned to us? Wherefore either our protestant divines have been grossly mistaken in disputing for that which was not denied, or else they had other apprehensions about imputation.

These, in short, are the arguments which incline, yea command me, to believe the high and strict imputation of Christ's active obedience or fulfilling the law. But I have as yet done but half of my work; the objections which are made against what hath been asserted must be answered. It hath been affirmed that Christ's active as well as passive obedience is imputed to believers; now that is objected against. It hath been affirmed also that the imputation of Christ's obedience is to be taken as hath been stated; that, too, is objected against: both, therefore, must be defended. The objectors do not

[1] See Mr Bradshaw de Justif., cap. 16, p. 77.

all concur in their opinions about these two heads; yet in their main objections about them in a great measure they do; wherefore I shall take them as they lie before me promiscuously and in common, and so endeavour to answer them.

Obj. 1. First, It is objected that in the Scripture remission of sin, justification, reconciliation with God, eternal life, are wholly and solely ascribed to Christ's passive obedience, to his death on the cross, under which yet is included the whole humiliation and abasement of Christ. The particular scriptures cited for the proof of this have been already set down.

Ans. They who are for the active obedience as a part of Christ's humiliation, and as such do hold the imputation of it, making it and the passive to be but one and the same obedience, only diversified in its acts, all of which do yet meet and concur in his humiliation—these, I say, are not at all concerned in this argument; and they who take them as distinct parts of his obedience, and as such hold the imputation of them, are very little pinched by it; for the answer is easy and obvious. These great effects are attributed to Christ's death and blood, not exclusively and solely, as to jostle out the influence of his holy life and active obedience, but eminently only. In his dying there was the highest piece, the consummation of all his obedience; therefore the main stress is laid upon that, the chiefest part being, by a usual synecdoche, put for the whole; but yet the obedience of his life is to be taken in in conjunction with the obedience of his death, and so the sinner's happiness is completed. It is not only here said that God for sin condemned sin, which refers to Christ's death, but also 'that the righteousness of the law might be fulfilled in us,' which refers to his life. As we read of being justified by his blood, and the like, so we read of his being 'made under the law, to redeem them who were under the law, that we might receive the adoption of sons,' and of his being 'the end of the law for righteousness to every one that believeth.'

Obj. 2. If Christ's active obedience be imputed, and in such a manner, too, so that in his obeying and fulfilling the law believers did obey and fulfil it, thence it will follow that his passive obedience, his death itself, was in vain, and needless; for this being so, the saints must be perfectly righteous, as

having done what the law required, and so there would be no need of Christ's suffering or satisfaction, for that supposes guilt and the non-performance of the law.

Ans. This objection is very considerable, yet I conceive the consequence is not so pressing. The reason is, because, though upon the imputation of Christ's active obedience one part of the law is satisfied, yet there being another part of the law to be satisfied also, for that his passive obedience was necessary. Suppose that believers upon the former might be looked upon as now fulfilling the law's commands, yet guilt being before contracted, the penalty of death thereupon incurred, that the one might be expiated by the undergoing of the other, it was necessary that Christ should die and suffer. The law requiring both of these, in both it must be satisfied; insomuch, saith one,[1] that if we could have a perfect righteousness conformable to the law, *de novo*, and not have satisfied the punishment, our debt would not have been discharged—we had still been in our sins. The twofold obedience, or double righteousness of Christ, do not destroy or undermine each other. It was necessary that he should obey actively for the doing of what the law enjoined; it was necessary also that he should obey passively for the suffering of what the law threatened, for both of these were necessary to reach the law's righteousness, and so to lay the foundation of a complete righteousness for the creature—in order to which, therefore, both must be imputed to him. I know what is objected against this, but all cannot be spoke unto at once.

For the better answering of the objection in hand, it is said by some that the imputation of Christ's passive obedience must be supposed to antecede in order of nature, though not of time, the imputation of his active; for in the justifying of believers, God dealing with them as sinners, we must suppose him first to take off guilt and punishment due for what was past, before he makes over a positive righteousness to them for the time to come. If this be so, we shall easily get off from what is objected; wherein dissenters go upon this, that a person being judged righteous upon his imputative, active fulfilling of the law, to him no further or subsequent

---

[1] Mr Burg. of Justif., part ii. p. 411.

imputation is necessary. We say so too ; but then we suppose an antecedent imputation of that obedience which was proper to free from guilt and wrath, viz., Christ's passive obedience. So that the matter comes to this : Though Christ's active obedience being imputed, a child of God is righteous, and a fulfiller of the law, and so nothing further is necessary for him ; yet it doth not hence follow that Christ's passive obedience was in vain, or needless, because in the methods of divine grace that is first imputed for freedom from guilt and hell, before the active is imputed in order to righteousness and heaven. Very large discourses there are abroad in the world about these things. I only design to set down in short what is satisfactory to myself, but how far it may be so to others, that I must leave with God.

Obj. 3. Christ's passive obedience was sufficient ; for thereby the justice of God was fully satisfied, the sinner's guilt fully expiated, full payment made of all that he owed, &c. What need, therefore, is there of any imputation of his active obedience to be superadded to the imputation of the former ?

Ans. If the passive obedience be taken in conjunction with the active, we grant the sufficiency of it to all intents and purposes ; but if it be taken disjunctly from the active, then we grant its sufficiency for such and such ends or effects, but not for all. For the removal of guilt, the satisfying of the penal part of the law, the freeing from hell and death, so it was sufficient ; but besides this, the preceptive part of the law was to be fulfilled, the condition of life was to be performed, the sinner was to be made positively righteous, heaven was to be merited. Now as to these, abstractly from the active obedience of Christ, the passive was not sufficient. Upon his dying, believers shall not die or be damned, or be looked upon as guilty ; but for their being righteous and entitled to eternal life, Christ must actively fulfil the law ; for the promise of life is annexed to doing : 'Do this and live,' Lev. xviii. 5 ; Rom. x. 5. 'There needs no more,' saith a reverend person,[1] 'than innocency, not to die ; and when guilt is taken away we stand as innocent, no crime then can be charged upon us. But to reign in life, as the apostle speaks, to inherit a crown, there

[1] Blake on the Covenant, cap. xii. p. 77.

further is expected, which we not reaching, Christ's active obedience supplied to us, not adding to ours, but being in itself complete, is accounted ours, and imputed to us.'

Obj. 4. But it is said the law requires no more than either doing or suffering. If one of these be done, it is enough ; both of them the law neither doth nor can demand. Wherefore, if we suffered in Christ, and that be reckoned to us, it is not required that we should also obey in Christ.

Ans. The truth of the antecedent is not only questioned, but flatly denied ; and the contrary thereunto is proved, viz., that *in statu lapso* the law's obligation is not disjunctive, *ad alterutrum*, either to do or suffer ; but it is conjunctive or copulative, *ad utrumque*, both to do and suffer.[1] Indeed, say they of this opinion, if man had continued in the state of innocency, one of these had been enough, namely, the active obeying of the law ; for he being then without sin could not lie under any obligation to suffer. But he being fallen, stands obliged to both —to obey, as he is a creature, to suffer, as he is an offender. So that it was not enough for Christ in suffering to answer the one obligation, but he must also by doing answer the other also. In the laws of men one of these is enough, but in the laws of God, there being a vast disparity betwixt the creature's subjection to him and to men, it is not so ; and, as I apprehend it, they who differ in this point do too much run themselves upon that absurdity which they would fasten upon those from whom they differ : for whereas they charge the opinion of these that it acquits us from all obeying on our part, this principle which they maintain seems to do it much more ; for if either obeying or suffering be as much as the law requires, then, Christ having suffered the utmost of the law's penalty, we are not under any obligation to obey too.

Obj. 5. It having been said that Christ's passive obedience was necessary to free from guilt and eternal death, and his active necessary for righteousness and eternal life, against this it is objected that it supposes a medium betwixt being freed from guilt and being made righteous, and so betwixt being

[2] See Advers. inter Piscat. et Lucium., p. i. sec. 4 ; Polan. in Dan., p. 191, &c.; Turret. de Sat. par. viii. p. 271, &c. ; Bodius, in Eph., p. 805.

freed from eternal death and the having of eternal life, which is a great mistake. For these are such contraries as do admit of no medium between them, and therefore upon the negation of the one, the affirmation of the other, in a fit subject, must needs follow; and so *vice versâ*. As if it be not night, it is day; if it be not darkness, it is light; if it be not crookedness, it is straightness, &c. So here, if it be not guilt, it is righteousness; and if it be not eternal death, it is eternal life; these being contraries, ὧν οὐκ ἐστι μεταξὺ. Therefore they who grant freedom from guilt and hell upon Christ's death, and yet assert the necessity of the obedience of his life for righteousness and heaven, build upon a false hypothesis.

Ans. To this it is answered, what is here alleged holds true in natural and physical contraries, but not in moral or law contraries. The malefactor, upon his prince's or the judge's pardon, is acquitted from his guilt, and with respect to that he is innocent; but yet he cannot upon this be looked upon as being righteous, or as having done what the law required of him: so it is in that which I am upon. It is one thing for the sinner not to be unjust, and another thing for him to be just; upon the non-imputation of sin he is the former, but the latter he cannot be without a positive righteousness. Not to be judged as a transgressor of the law, and to be judged as a fulfiller of the law, are two distinct things. And so as to the other; although there be no medium betwixt natural life and death, so that upon the negation of the one there is always the position of the other, yet between eternal life and eternal death there is a medium. For we may suppose a person to be freed from the one, and yet not presently admitted into the other; he may be saved from hell, and yet not be taken up to heaven; for he may be annihilated, or continued in some state of happiness here below, this notwithstanding. I only speak of the possibility of the thing, not asserting that ever *de facto* it is so. The traitor may be freed from death, and yet not restored to all those high dignities and privileges which he had before. And why not so here? It is true, whoever is freed from hell is admitted into heaven; but this is not necessary from the nature of the thing, as though there might not be a *status intermedius*, but only from the

will and ordination of God. The necessity therefore of the imputation of Christ's active obedience for righteousness and life is not weakened or nulled by this objection.

Obj. 6. To put more strength into it, it is further urged that the opinion argued against makes justification to consist of different parts, viz., remission of sin and imputation of righteousness; also it makes these different parts to proceed from different causes, as the remission of sin from Christ's bearing the penalty of the law, and the imputation of righteousness from his fulfilling the precepts of the law. Whereas, say some, the whole nature of justification lies in the remission of sin; to be pardoned and to be made righteous, are in Scripture terms equipollent and synonymous. And, say others, all in justification is but one act, proceeding from one and the same cause; that very act which makes the sinner not guilty makes him also at the same time to be righteous; as that which takes away crookedness at the same time makes straight, that which expels darkness at the same time introduces light. The putting on of the garment, and the removal of the nakedness, are but one and the same thing, and done together.

Ans. Many things are here mentioned which cannot so distinctly be spoken to in the answering of an objection. What place remission of sin hath in justification, whether of being the form of it, or but an integral part, or only an effect and consequent, is a thing that divines are not very well agreed about. Whether the whole of justification doth lie in remission is a point wherein also they differ. But I must not at present engage in these debates; I will defer the discussing of them till I come to open the doctrine of justification, which the 30th verse of this chapter will lead me to. I shall now only suggest what is proper for the answering of the objection before us.

And 1. What if the opinion argued against doth make remission of sin and imputed righteousness to be different parts of justification, they both as integral parts concurring to the completing and perfecting of it?[1] I say, what if it so doth? is it the worse for that? Is this a novel tenet, or that which but few or none do own? Have not several with

[1] See Burg. of Justif., part ii. serm. 27.

great solidity and judgment defended it? As to any error in it, or any absurdities that will follow upon it, I must confess I do not, as yet, understand either the one or the other. A difference of parts in sanctification is commonly granted, viz., mortification and vivification; the abolition of the power of sin, and the implantation of the divine nature; the putting off the old man, and the putting on the new man, Eph. iv. 22. Now, why may not justification have its parts as well as sanctification? If the believer's righteousness doth lie in the fulfilling of the law, and there be different parts in that law, its commanding and its punishing part, then that righteousness which results from the fulfilling of it must admit of different parts too. So that remission of sin is one part, that being grounded upon the satisfying of one part of the law, and imputation of righteousness is another part, that being grounded upon the satisfying of the other part of the law. The Scripture speaks of these not as one and the same, but as distinct: Rom. iv. 25, 'Who was delivered for our offences,' there is remission; 'and was raised again for our justification,' or righteousness, there is the other part. How the latter is attributed to Christ's resurrection is not my business now to inquire, I only cite the words as holding forth a distinction betwixt remission and righteousness. So Rom. v. 9, compared with Rom. v. 19; and Dan. ix. 24, 'To make reconciliation for iniquity, and to bring in everlasting righteousness;' here are the two parts of justification set forth as different and distinct. It is true, the apostle, Rom. iv. 6–8, speaking of the sinner's righteousness, instances only in the forgiveness or non-imputation of sin; but he doth not do it as if that was the all in that righteousness; but, 1st, Because that being one eminent part thereof, he puts it for the whole; 2d, Because that remission of sin and the imputation of a positive righteousness being never parted, in naming the one he included the other, not as if they were one and the same in their nature, but because they are never separated in the subject. I cannot yet be convinced but that the removal of sin's guilt, and the introducing of a positive righteousness, are things of a different nature and carry distinct notions in them; for, besides what hath been already said, though in God's dealing with fallen sinners

they are never parted, yet as they are considered in themselves they may be parted. Amongst us sometimes sin is remitted when yet the offender is not justified: as we see in the case of Joseph's brethren, Shimei, Abiathar, &c. And it is possible for a person to be justified though he hath no sin to be remitted, as it would have been with Adam had he stood, he was then capable of justification, but not of remission. Now this their separableness evinces a difference or distinction betwixt them. To object, therefore, against the imputation of Christ's active obedience, as well as of his passive, one being supposed to free us from guilt, the other to make us righteous, that this would infer two different parts of justification; this is so far from being an objection, that it is but a plain asserting of what is so indeed.

2. Whereas it is said that this doth also make different causes of justification, I say, as before, what if it doth? Provided that by those ye understand only the different grounds or matter of justification according to its different parts; that is, as Christ died and shed his blood, there is the ground of the sinner's discharge from guilt, that which is imputed to him in order to that effect; then, as he in all things actively conformed to the law, there is the ground of the sinner's positive righteousness, or that which is imputed to him in order to that effect. Such a multiplication of causes, which are not so of a diverse nature but that they do unite and concur in some one as the general cause, as these do in Christ's righteousness or obedience, carries in it nothing repugnant to Scripture or reason. This righteousness of Christ is the one only material cause of the sinner's righteousness; but that dividing itself into his active and passive righteousness, accordingly the causes of the sinner's righteousness are diversified.

3. The allusions brought against the truth in question seem to fasten some absurdity upon it. For they tend to this, that for any to say upon one act sin is remitted, and upon another the person is made righteous, it is as if one should say that by one act the crookedness of a thing is removed, and that by another it is made straight, and so as to light and darkness.

To which I reply, I except against these similitudes as not suiting with the thing in hand; they are proper for things of another nature, not for that which we are upon, for that being a law act, is not to be judged of by things of a physical nature. Suppose the effects mentioned are produced by one and the same act, yet they are not so pertinently alleged, because what we are speaking of falls under another consideration. We are not concerned about crookedness and straightness, but about guilt and righteousness. All allusions which suit not with these, as things of a legal nature, are insignificative. Will they say that that which frees the offender from guilt, when he stands arraigned before the judge, doth also make him a true and exact keeper of the law? that at the same time, and by the same sentence, wherein he is acquitted from the violation of the law, that he is also thereupon to be looked upon as a person that hath really kept the law? Such an instance as this would be pertinent; but then we should determine it in the negative. And, indeed, I could humbly desire that in these points we might be very sparing in argumentative similitudes of this nature, for it is very well known how by them some endeavour to decry and undermine all imputation of Christ's righteousness. To be made righteous by the righteousness of another, it is, say they, as if a man should see with another's eyes, or be learned with another's learning, or wise with another's wisdom, &c. There is similitude for similitude, though upon a far more pestilent and mischievous design. Therefore in law acts, such as we all grant justification to be, let us keep to those allusions which are proper to such acts; or else, upon the disparity of physical and law acts, we shall run ourselves and others upon great mistakes.

Obj. 7. This seems to reflect upon God some error or mistake in his judging, as if he should esteem the sinner to do that in Christ which he did not do, and which he knows the sinner did not do. And it is said that it is not possible that we, by any estimation, can be the subjects of those acts, qualities, accidents, which belong to another subject.

Ans. Though the debtor himself doth not pay the debt, but the surety in truth pays it, yet without any mistake the creditor may in a law sense look upon the debtor as having paid it, inasmuch as his surety paid it for him; and what his surety doth he doth; they being in law but one person. The appli-cation of this, as to God's judging with respect to Christ and sinners, is plain and obvious. But I ask, Why should this be thought a mistake in God to look upon us as obeying in Christ, when, I hope, it is not made a mistake in him to look upon us as disobeying in Adam? Wherein is the truth of God more impeached in the one than in the other? We did not personally eat of the forbidden fruit, and yet I presume it will not be denied but that, in Adam's eating of it, legally we did eat it too, and that God doth most truly and righteously reckon us guilty of it as though we had done the fact in our own persons. Grant, then, that there is no mistake there, and it will follow that there is none here. Nay, further, Why may we not as well be said to obey in Christ as to suffer in Christ? His sufferings were as remote and alien from our persons as his active obeying, and yet it is granted that they are so reckoned to us as that in them even we may be said to suffer and satisfy; and if the passive obedience of Christ be thus imputed without any mistake, why may not the active without any mistake be imputed also? Clear God in the one, and you must likewise clear him in the other. And whereas it is said that those acts, qualities, or accidents which belong to one subject cannot be made over to another; this strikes at all imputation, though I suppose it is not so designed, for that which is imputed must be out of that subject unto which it is imputed, otherwise it is inhesion and not imputation. Adam's disobedience was his own personal and subjective act, and yet it is ours imputatively and legally. But of this I will say no more.

Obj. 8. If Christ actively obeyed and fulfilled the law, as in our stead, so that his obedience be imputed to us, hence it will follow that we are not at all obliged ourselves to obey or keep the law, Christ having done that in his person for us.[1] For as he, bearing the curse and penalty of the law in our stead, we are thereupon freed from that curse; so if he did obey the law's commands in our stead, we must also thereupon be freed from any obligation to obedience on our part thereunto.

Ans. All that follows from hence is this, that Christ obeying the law for us and in our stead, we are not bound to obey it for those ends and upon

[1] Mr Bradsh. of Justif., p. 85.

those accounts upon which he obeyed it, as, namely, for satisfaction and for righteousness before God ;[1] but as to other ends, and upon other accounts, we are yet, and must be so, under an obligation to obey it. For being creatures, we are indispensably bound to keep that law which our Creator and Lord is pleased to lay upon us, so as that nothing can absolve us from that obligation. And, besides, not only love and gratitude to God do call for this obedience from us, but it is the way wherein we can only hope for benefit by Christ's satisfactory and meritorious obedience. We must not carry our Saviour's fulfilling the law for us beyond what he intended. Now, it appears by the whole tenor of the gospel that he never intended it to exempt believers from obedience as it speaks duty, but only as it was the condition of the first covenant. I therefore think that it may as well be argued that saints should not die, or bear any punishment for sin, because Christ died for them, and bore the penalty of the law for them, as that they should not obey actively because Christ obeyed the law for them. It is true, upon the imputation of his passive obedience they are freed from suffering in order to satisfaction, yet in other respects suffer they shall. And so upon the imputation of his active obedience they are freed from obeying, so as that their righteousness before God should not lie in that, yet upon other accounts obey they must, notwithstanding all that Christ hath done. In short, we may as well argue against others, that upon their principles God's people are not liable to any punishment, as they do against us, that upon our principles, God's people are not under any obligation to obey the law. And that explication or distinction which will clear and justify their opinion in the consistency of the saints' sufferings with Christ's passive obedience, will do the same for ours in the consistency of the saints' obedience with Christ's active obedience.

Obj. 9. It is objected, that the imputation of Christ's obedience, as thus stated, makes believers to be no sinners, yea, as righteous as Christ himself was. They in him fulfilling the law, where is their sin? and his righteousness being made over to them, are they not as righteous as he was?

Ans. This is one of the beaten, threadbare arguments with which the Romanists impugn in gene-

[1] *Vide* Luciam in Advers., p. i., sec. 5.

ral the imputation of Christ's righteousness. Our protestant writers thus answer them : Though Christ's righteousness be imputed to believers, yet for all that they are sinners, and may justly be so denominated, inasmuch as the denomination is taken from what is inherent in them, notwithstanding what is imputed to them. Saints may be considered either as they are in themselves, (and so who can deny them to be sinners? so the best must cry out, Unclean unclean,) or as they are in Christ, they being justified through the imputation of his righteousness, and accepted in him as their head and surety, and so who will deny them to be righteous? He fulfilled the law for them, which obedience of his being reckoned to them in God's account, and imputatively, they may be said to be without sin— there is no Antinomism in this if it be rightly understood;—yet, as they are in themselves, and as to what is inherent and done by them, there is, God knows, too much of sin in them. It is no absurdity for the same subject, under diverse considerations, to be looked upon as sinless, and yet as sinful : Cant. i. 5, ' I am black, but comely.' Oh what a pure, spotless, righteous person is the believer in respect of imputation ; and yet what an impure, defiled, sinful person is he in respect of inhering corruption !

As to the other part of the objection, I deny the consequence. May we not be righteous but upon this we must be as righteous as Christ himself was? As the former I would be loath to deny, so the latter I would be as loath to affirm. It doth not follow, if Christ's obedience and righteousness be imputed to us, that therefore we must be as righteous as he was ; because it is made over to us, not in the fulness and infiniteness of it, but only so far as our case and necessity doth require ;[1] or not absolutely in the utmost extent and degree of it, but *in tantum quod hoc*, that we may be looked upon as fulfillers of the law, and as partakers of that righteousness which we need and are capable of. And pray wherein doth the imputation of Christ's passive obedience come short as

[1] Per justitiam Christi nobis imputatam non possumus dici absolute sive omnimodo justi, &c.; sed—eatenus nos justos factos æstimat Deus, quatenus legis divinæ transgressores exterimus. Ut in tantum ex illa Christi justitia justi facti dicamur, in quantum ex inobedientia nostra injusti constituti simus.—*Bradsh. de Justif.*, c. 24, sec. 27.

to what is here charged upon the imputation of his active? Will not the argument lie as much against that as against this? For upon that, it is said, the law was fully satisfied, and received from Christ, in our stead, its full accomplishment. Upon that we are looked upon as having committed no evil and omitted no good, that Christ's infinite merit and satisfaction is ours, &c. Wherefore may it not with equal strength be inferred from the imputation of this that we are not sinners, and that we are righteous as Christ was, as it may from the imputation of the other?

Obj. 10. This makes Christ to have done that very thing, for matter, which we ourselves should—that he paid that very debt of obedience in kind, and not in value only, which the law required, and which we should have paid; which if so, and that that be reckoned to us, we are then justified by works, and our righteousness is legal rather than evangelical.

Ans. I have had occasion, in what went before, to speak a little of the *idem* and *tantundem*, as they refer to Christ's sufferings, in answer to that question, whether he suffered the self-same penalty which the law threatened, and the sinner himself should have endured; or whether he suffered only that which was equivalent thereunto?—in the deciding of which I closed with the common determination, that Christ's sufferings, for kind and substance, were the same which the law threatened; but as to some certain circumstances and accidents, they were but equivalent. The same resolution I shall give concerning the *idem* and *tantundem* with respect to his active obedience. As to the substantial duties required by the moral law, to them in kind he submitted, and to that very obedience which we were obliged unto; so it was the *idem*. But then there were some circumstances arising from some special considerations about his person, which in other things made a difference, with respect to which it was but the *tantundem*. What all were bound to do in the great and indispensable duties of the law, as holiness, love to God, &c., that Christ did; but what some only are bound to do, upon certain special obligations lying upon them, as they stand in such and such relations, as magistrates, husbands, &c., that was not done by Christ *in specie*, he not standing in those relations. In the substantial duties of the law, and in those

acts of obedience which were in general necessary, Christ did just that which we should have done, (understand me that I speak of legal, not of evangelical obedience; for though Christ did that for us which the law demanded, yet he did not do that for us which the gospel demands.) But as to some particular duties of the law proper to such persons in such circumstances, those he, not being under those circumstances, did not do; and yet there is no defect in his obedience, the want of this particular being supplied and made up by his general obedience. The text saith ' that the righteousness of the law might be fulfilled in us.' Now why may we not content ourselves with this, that Christ fulfilled the law's righteousness, without running of ourselves upon perplexing debates about the *idem* and the *tantundem?* The case, in brief, stands thus: the law must be obeyed. In ourselves we neither did nor could obey it: our surety, therefore, must do it for us; he doing it for us, his obedience must be imputed to us. This imputation must be of that very obedience which we were bound unto; otherwise, (this, and not something else in the lieu of it, being demanded by the law,) we are yet debtors to the law. Therefore it follows that Christ did the *idem* which we should have done. For as he delivered us from the curse of the law by bearing that very curse in his own person which we should have borne, so he fulfilled the righteousness of the law for us by conforming to that very righteousness in his own person which we should have come up to.

As to our justification by works, which is pleaded against this imputation, to that I shall speak immediately in the use.

And thus I have,—with no small grief and trouble, the Lord knows, to see in this point differences amongst persons so godly, so learned; and as to myself, that I should so unavoidably be concerned in these unhappy controversies,—gone over and answered the most material objections that I have met with against the imputation of Christ's active obedience. I would not be so fond or weak as to hope, that what I have said should have any influence upon those learned and judicious persons from whom I differ, so as to alter their opinion; they knew it all before, and had it from others with great advantage, and yet could not be thereby convinced. However, I thought

I could not do less than what I have done. Possibly thereby weaker Christians may come to some clearer insight into these matters; if there, too, I be disappointed, yet I have laid down the grounds of my own persuasion, which this subject made necessary. Whether the answers I have given to the objections will be satisfactory to others, I know not; but I seriously profess, as to the main, they are so to me. I must acknowledge in some of them there are those difficulties which it is not an easy thing to get over; yet upon the whole matter I must say that, after the most serious thoughts, I, as to myself, can with more ease and satisfaction answer the arguments brought against the imputation of the active obedience, than I can those which are brought for it, otherwise I had not embraced an opinion which some knowing men oppose with scorn and derision.

I come to the application, wherein I must be very short.

Use 1. From the truth I am upon we learn, (1.) In what way or upon what terms a believer is justified. What are they? why, the fulfilling of the law's righteousness; which though it could not be done by the believer himself, yet by Christ it is done for him. In the justifying of sinners God proceeds upon the perfect righteousness and full demands of the law; and being justified, they are righteous according to that strict and exact righteousness which the law itself holds forth.[1] You read much of legal and of evangelical righteousness, of justification by works and by faith; there seems to be a contrariety between these two—and so there is in some respects —but if you consider them materially and fundamentally, they are one and the same. The righteousness by which we are justified, it is both legal or the righteousness of works, and also evangelical or the righteousness of faith; in reference to Christ it is legal, as he exactly fulfilled the law; in reference to us it is evangelical, (that righteousness which was never performed in our own persons, being graciously made over to us, and accepted for us.) And so as to ourselves we are justified by faith, but as to

our head and surety we are justified by works. God deals with us in our own persons upon the terms of the covenant of grace, but he dealt with us in Christ upon the terms of the covenant of works; and, indeed, in the justification and salvation of a sinner all these concur. The Scripture, it is true, sets them in opposition one to the other, and makes them incompatible; but that is only in reference to the same subject, under the same personal consideration. The same person as considered in himself, and by himself, cannot be justified by works and by faith too, by the covenant of works and by the covenant of grace too. But let Christ be taken in, and so these things are reconcilable. As Christ in his person did all which the law or covenant of works required, so in him our justification is by the law of works, &c.; but as that his righteousness is imputed to us and applied by us, so our justification is of grace, by faith, &c. That very righteousness which is legal in the head, is evangelical in the members, in respect of the application of it. Blessed be God for the sweet harmony and concurrence of both covenants; of law and gospel, works and faith, in the sinner's justification and salvation! It is admirably brought about by this great thing which the text speaks of, Christ's fulfilling the righteousness of the law for us.

2. Secondly, It shews us what great respect and value the great God had for his holy law, and what a high honour he put upon it. Which appears from this; the apostle here setting down God's high and glorious ends in the sending of his Son into the world, he makes them all to centre in the satisfaction and accomplishment of his law. That it might be satisfied in its penalty, Christ shall be a sacrifice, as you had it before; that it might be satisfied in its commands, Christ in his own person shall fulfil the righteousness of it, as you have it here. Here was by both plenary satisfaction made to the law, which was the very thing which God stood upon and would have done. And rather than it should not be done, his own Son must come from heaven, and put on flesh, and be himself made under the law; he must live a holy life, and die a cursed death, and all to satisfy the law. And this was a thing so great in God's eye, as that he looked upon the fulfilling and answering of the law's demands as a valuable compensation for all the abasement and humiliation of

---

[1] *Justi sumus coram Deo ex illa etiam absolutissima legis formula.—Beza.* If with our justification from sin there be joined that active obedience of Christ which is imputed to us, we are just before God according to that perfect form which the law requireth.—*Engl. Annot.*

his dearest Son. Oh let us think honourably of the law, for surely God did so! The apostle had seemed to speak somewhat diminutively of it before, 'What the law could not do in that it was weak;' but here he puts a great deal of glory upon it, in making this the end of the incarnation of the Son of God, 'that the righteousness of the law might be fulfilled in us.' God never designed by the sending of Christ to have his law abolished or abrogated;[1] no, but rather to have it accomplished and fully satisfied. 'Think not that I am come to destroy the law or the prophets; I am not come to destroy, but to fulfil,' Mat. v. 17. In Christ's obedience, active and passive, we have a high demonstration of that singular respect which God bare to his law. Sin was a base thing, therefore that shall be condemned; but the law was good, therefore that shall be satisfied.

Use 2. Secondly, From hence, by way of exhortation, I would urge a few things upon you. As (1.) Make sure of an interest in the privilege here spoken of. To have the righteousness of the law fulfilled in us! Oh what a privilege is this! Is it yours? Are you in the number of the *us* in the text? Is Christ's obeying the law so made over to you, as that, in God's estimation, the righteousness thereof is fulfilled in you? Sirs, this is a thing that must be done either *by you* or *for you*. The former being impossible, what relief have you from the latter? If you cannot plead this fulfilling of the law's righteousness, either by yourselves or by your surety, you are lost for ever; you are under that debt to the law which you will never be able to pay, Gal. v. 3; you are yet 'in your sins,' unjustified persons; you lie open to the wrath of that God whose law you have violated; can make no good claim of life, (for the law is not done, its condition of life is not performed;) and, which is very dreadful, if the law's righteousness be not fulfilled in you, the law's curse will most certainly be inflicted upon you. God will have a perfect righteousness and obedience somewhere, or he will not justify and save. If, therefore, the perfect righteousness and obedience of Christ be not imputed to you, what will you do? what will become of you? Woe to that man who,

when he shall come at the great day to stand before God's tribunal, shall not be judged in and through Christ, a fulfiller of the law! that shall then be found without the garment of Christ's imputed righteousness! how will the law fall upon him for non-obedience, and thereupon demand satisfaction of him in the suffering of eternal torments! Pray think of this in time, so as to get an interest in Christ's fulfilling the law's righteousness. Some dispute whether his righteousness be imputed to any; let your inquiries (you taking the thing *in thesi*, for granted) be about something else, viz., whether in particular it be imputed to you? and what you may be and do that it may be imputed to you?

For your direction and help in both of these inquiries, look to three things, union with Christ, faith, the spiritual conversation; these are the evidences of the privilege, and also (especially the two former) the grounds and means of obtaining it. The *us* of whom the apostle speaks, in whom the law's righteousness is fulfilled, are, (1.) Such who are in Christ, 1 Cor. i. 30; (2.) Such who believe, Rom. iii. 22, and iv. 24; Phil. iii. 9. (3.) Such who live the spiritual life; for so they are here characterised, 'that the righteousness of the law might be fulfilled *in us, who walk not after the flesh, but after the Spirit.*' So that would you either know whether Christ obeyed the law for you, and that his obedience be imputed to you, or would you take some course in order to the securing of this grace to yourselves, these are the things which your eye must be upon, that you be in Christ, that you be true believers, that you be holy and spiritual in your walking. God never intended that his Son's obedience should be imputed to any but only to such as these.

2. You who pretend to the having an interest in this glorious privilege, I would with the greatest earnestness exhort you to go as far in your own persons as is possible in the fulfilling of the law's righteousness. And this I would with the more vehemency press upon you, because of those ugly aspersions and calumnies which some do cast upon this precious truth, and the worthy assertors of it. How do papists let fly whole volleys of bitter invectives against protestants, because they assert the imputation of Christ's obedience, and so expound these

[1] Nota per Christum non abolitam esse legis justitiam, non respectu quidem nostri; verum impletam eam etiam respectu nostri et in nobis.—*Rolloc.*

words! [1] And there are some others who are high enough in their censuring and calumniating of this doctrine, as if it tended to nothing but to make men careless and loose and profane; as if it opened a wide door to all licentiousness, and did cut the sinews of all piety and godliness. Oh therefore I would entreat you to be the more strict, exact, holy, obedient in your course, that you may live down all these scandals, and that your conversation may be a visible confutation of them. It is no new thing for the doctrines of imputed righteousness, of not resting on the law for justification, the decrying of works for righteousness, the crying up of faith as the great condition of righteousness and life—I say, it is no new thing for these evangelical truths to be reviled by some and perverted by others. Therefore, as to the latter, the apostle, when he was speaking of them, was fain ever and anon to interpose something by way of caution, that he might obviate these misinterpretations, perversions, abuses which some might make of what he had said. 'Do we,' saith he, 'make void the law?' Rom. iii. 31. 'Is Christ the minister of sin?' Gal. ii. 17. And surely we have need to do the same as to that which I am upon. Oh, say some, did Christ in our stead obey the law? is his fulfilling the law made over to us? Then we have nothing to do; we are under no obligation on our part to obey too; is not Christ's perfect fulfilling the law enough? what can be further required of us? what need we trouble ourselves about any obedience or holy walking? But God forbid that any of you should thus reason! We are indeed too prone to such reasonings; it is very natural to us to catch at anything that may comply with the gratifying of the flesh, and with the easing of us as to the severities of a holy, obediential course; and hence it is that we suck poison out of the sweetest flowers, 'turning the grace of God into wantonness.' But, I assure you, there is nothing in Christ's obedience, and in the imputation thereof, that hath any tendency or gives

any encouragement or patronage to any such loose inferences; for though he obeyed the law for us, yet we ourselves must obey it too; his obedience must not jostle out ours; both together, upon different accounts, do very well agree. Indeed, he having obeyed the law, we are not bound to obey it for such an end as for satisfaction and merit, for righteousness and life; yet in other respects, and for other ends, as that we may conform to the will of God, and so please him; that we may in our sphere imitate our holy Saviour; that we may testify our love and gratitude to God, &c., so we are as much bound to keep and obey the law as ever. Oh it is such an excellent law, in the commands and injunctions of it, that all should delight in conforming to it! As it is the law of works, calling for perfect and personal obedience, and giving no strength thereunto, so it is burdensome; but as it puts the creature upon works, and is the rule and matter of obedience, so the gracious soul will delight in it. Wherefore, though Christ hath fulfilled it for you, yet it becomes you too to live in all obediential compliance with it, and subjection to it.

And, I say, herein go as far as is possible. You cannot perfectly fulfil it, (blessed be God that is not required of you,) but yet you should do as much as ever you can; you should endeavour after perfect obedience, though you cannot arrive at it. Our Saviour's perfect obedience may encourage us in our lamented defects, but we must not thereupon stint or limit ourselves in our obedience. A gracious man's will is always above his power; he can do but little, but he would do all. It was a high commendation given to Caleb, Num. xiv. 24; saith God of him, 'He followed me fully,' or, as it is in the Hebrew, *vajemalle achari*, he 'fulfilled after me;' and thus it is with every Caleb, one that is after God's own heart, as the word signifies, he is for fulfilling after God. The apostle speaks of πλήρωσις της ὑπακοῆς, the fulness or fulfilling of obedience, 2 Cor. x. 6. Epaphras prayed for the Colossians, chap iv. 12, that they 'might be complete in all the will of God;' and it is said of Zacharias and Elisabeth, Luke i. 6, 'they were righteous in all the commandments and ordinances of God.' Oh that it might be thus with you! If straight bodies be put together there is a universal contiguity betwixt them; they

[1] Ita nunc juxta hujus bestiæ sanctimoniam, (he means Beza,) renatus in Christo et credens in eum, Christique justitiam forti fide apprehendens, fornicetur, inebrietur, omni spurcitia contaminetur, peccatum pro nihilo habetur, utcunque supersint reliquiæ ejus in nobis.—*Staplet. Antidot.*, p. 630. Hæc σοφὰ φάρμακα sunt et dæmonum præstigiæ, quibus legem Dei eludere, &c.—*Vide Contzen. in loc.*, qu. 1.

3 A

will meet and touch each the other throughout; and so where the heart is sincere it will close with every part of God's law. Christians, pray rejoice in Christ's fulfilling the law's righteousness, and rest upon that only; but yet in the way of duty and obedience aspire in yourselves at the highest fulfilling of the law which here you are capable of.

3. Thirdly, The law righteousness Christ hath fulfilled for you, but the gospel righteousness you must perform yourselves. The moral law, as it was strictly and properly the covenant of works, Christ hath satisfied in his doing of what it required, but the evangelical law, requiring faith and repentance, you yourselves must satisfy; Christ's obedience to the former is made yours by imputation, but as to the latter there must be your own personal and inherent obedience. We read of Christ's being 'made under the law,' and of his 'fulfilling the law,' but we never read of his being made under the gospel, or fulfilling the conditions thereof; no, you must repent yourselves, believe yourselves, or else all that Christ hath done upon the account of the law will not profit you. I would not be mistaken in this; therefore (1.) I do not mean that you are to perform the gospel conditions in your own strength; was it so, you might as well do what the law as what the gospel requires, it being as easy in your own strength to obey the one as the other: you yourselves are to repent and believe, but it is not of yourselves; these are the gift of God. Nor (2.) do I mean that the performing of the gospel conditions is left to the lubricity of your wills, so as that it should be uncertain and undetermined whether you should perform them or not; for, upon the election of God, and the purchase of Christ, all that do belong to him shall certainly believe and repent. Nor (3.) do I mean, that upon the fulfilling of the gospel law you should have another formal righteousness before God distinct from that which results from Christ's obeying the moral law, which is imputed to you; but only that upon your performing of the gospel conditions way may be made for the application of Christ's legal obedience to you, as the only thing wherein stands your righteousness. These are things which might be very much enlarged upon, but I am now in haste. All therefore that I drive at is this, Christ fulfilled the moral law for you, but he never fulfilled the

gospel law for you; you must repent and believe yourselves, or else you cannot rely upon the imputation of Christ's obedience to the law; if you be impenitent and unbelieving, both law and gospel are unfulfilled and in full force against you. It will be an insignificant plea at the great day, when the law's righteousness shall plead against you, for you to say, Lord, Christ fulfilled that righteousness; true, will God say, he did so, but the gospel righteousness was not fulfilled by you; therefore what my Son did as to the other is nothing to you.

4. One thing more, you that are believers take a further view of the great love of God and Christ, and let the sense of it work up your hearts to the highest thankfulness. Was God pleased to send his own Son in flesh, for this very end, that he might fulfil the law? and when his Son had so done, doth he reckon that obedience to you as if you had done it yourselves? Oh incomprehensible, infinite, amazing love! Was Christ willing to submit to this, on these terms to take flesh? Oh the transcendent, superlative love of Christ! He who made the law to be made under the law! he who was the Lord and Sovereign to be willing to become a subject! he to undertake to do that which you could never have done, and without the doing of which you must have eternally perished! he to condescend to do what the law demanded, to suffer what the law threatened! What shall we say to this love? surely we can never enough adore it, or sufficiently bless God for it. Saints, did you but consider what humiliation this was in the Son of God, what a dreadful enemy this law would have been had not its righteousness been fulfilled, into what a blessed state things are now brought; it would certainly highly affect you with the love of Christ, and engage you to love, serve, praise him eternally.

Use 3. The third use is comfort to the people of God; and indeed to such here is not a little matter of rejoicing. The righteousness of the law fulfilled in us? great and blessed words! Did God employ such a person, in such a way, for such an end? That end must needs then be attained; and if so, what shall hurt them for whom it was attained? You who believe do often fear that the law's righteousness is ready to rise up against you; you tremble at the thoughts of it when you consider how short you come of it; but fear it not, for in Christ it is exactly, perfectly fulfilled; and that for you too, in your stead, that it is as well as if you had obeyed it fully in your own persons; is not here ground of comfort? You eye the imperfection of your own obedience, and you do well; but pray eye too the perfect obedience of the Lord Jesus, which is yours by imputation. 'There is now no condemnation to them who are in Christ.' Why *now* no condemnation? because now Christ hath fulfilled the law's righteousness for such; and thereupon who or what shall condemn them? You are troubled because of the law of sin, but that the Spirit hath freed you from; you are troubled because of the law of God, inasmuch as you come so much short of its righteousness, but that by Christ is fulfilled for you. You desire a righteousness, such a one as will bear you out before God; here it is for you, Christ's own righteousness is yours; oh you may say, 'In the Lord we have righteousness,' Isa. xlv. 24. When you had none of your own, God provided another and a better for you; *Assignata est ei aliena justitia, qui caruit sua,* Bernard. Epist. 190, ad Innoc.; Christ was willing to be made sin that you might be made the righteousness of God in him.[1] You may with holy confidence say, Law! thou demandest much of me, and that very justly, and I cannot myself answer thee in these demands; but there is my Saviour, my surety, he hath paid the full debt for me, he hath in my room and place done and suffered all that thou canst require, to his satisfaction I appeal. A good appeal! the Lord give you more and more of the comfort of it! That which often causes a gracious soul to be troubled, is the consideration not only of the law's penalty, but also of the law's purity. Oh it is a righteous law, and it calls for an exact doing righteousness in the creature; what will become of me, who cannot answer it herein? Now under this trouble, the belief of the imputation of Christ's active obedience may be of great use. And this is one reason why I would be the more loath to part with the imputation of that obedience, because under troubles of conscience it is so proper, so necessary, so sovereign a cordial for many fainting Christians. To shut up all: believers, Christ's

[1] *Delicta nostra sua delicta fecit, ut justitiam suam nostram justitiam faceret.*—*August.*

whole obedience, active and passive, is yours; what would you have more? What can sin, or Satan, or conscience, or the law itself now object against you? Be humble and mourn in the sense of the imperfection of your own inherent righteousness, yet withal rejoice and glory in the fulness, perfection, everlastingness of that righteousness which is imputed to you. It is a terrible word to sinners, the righteousness of the law must be fulfilled *on* them, it is a comfortable word to the saints; the righteousness of the law is fulfilled *in* them.

CHAPTER XV.

SPIRITUAL WALKERS THE SUBJECTS OF THE FORE GOING PRIVILEGE.

Who walk not after the flesh, but after the Spirit.—
ROM. viii. 4.

The sixth head in the words, viz., the description of the persons to whom the privilege belongs—Some short animadversions upon the words—The main doctrine raised from them, but not handled—A brief survey of these four verses, and recapitulation of the principal matter in them—The conclusion of this volume.

IN the opening of the matter which the apostle is upon in this and in the preceding verse, I have taken notice of,

1. The act itself, viz., the *sending* of Christ.

2. The person whose act this was; *God* sent, &c.

3. The person who was sent, as he stands in a very near relation to God; God sent his *own Son,* &c.

4. The way or manner in which this Son was sent; *in the likeness of sinful flesh.*

5. The great ends of God in all this, or the great effects produced thereby; namely, the *condemning of sin,* &c., and the *fulfilling of the law's righteousness* in and for believers. These several heads have all, more or less, been opened.

6. The apostle having appropriated the last end or effect, the fulfilling of the law's righteousness, to

such a sort of persons, that the righteousness of the law might be fulfilled *in us*, he goes on to describe those persons by their qualification and course; they are such *who walk not after the flesh, but after the Spirit*.

This description or character we had before, with respect to union with Christ, or exemption from condemnation: 'There is no condemnation to them which are in Christ Jesus, who walk not after the flesh, but after the Spirit.' Here it is repeated with respect to Christ's fulfilling of the law, and the imputation of that his obedience. Who are the persons who have a share also in this, and who shall be the better for it? why, such 'who walk not after the flesh, but after the Spirit.' As the mystical union and freedom from condemnation, so the imputation of Christ's righteousness is attended, in every subject that is a real partaker thereof, with a spiritual and holy conversation. These are different privileges, but for the evidence of them the apostle makes use of the same character or description.

Who walk not after the flesh, &c. The words are not descriptive of the nature of the thing spoken of before, as if the righteousness of the law was fulfilled in believers in their not walking after the flesh, &c., as some would have it;[1] but they are descriptive of the persons for whom and in whom that thing was done. There is a vast difference betwixt these two; our holiness is not the fulfilling of the law, but whoever is a holy man, Christ's fulfilling of the law is imputed to him; and so he doth fulfil it.[2]

In the bringing in of this description three things might be designed by the apostle:

1. To assert the happiness of all who live the spiritual life; in them by Christ the righteousness of the law is fulfilled.

2. To stave off all others from laying claim to this grace;[3] none but holy livers can warrantably apply Christ's satisfying of the law to themselves.

3. To obviate all abuses of this precious truth, all misinterpretations of it,[1] as also all security and carelessness in them who have an interest in the privilege.[2] Hath Christ fulfilled the law for us? Some from hence might be apt to infer, Then we may live as we list, there is nothing now for us to do; no, not so, saith the apostle, for though Christ hath fully satisfied the law, yet all for whom he hath done this do and must walk 'not after the flesh, but after the Spirit.'

Who walk not, &c. Faith being the proper and immediate condition of the imputation of Christ's righteousness or obedience to the law, why doth not the apostle instance in that, rather than in spiritual walking? *Ans.* Because he is not here so much shewing how Christ's righteousness is imputed, as who they are, (or how they carry it,) to whom it is so imputed.[3] He that would have Christ's righteousness to be his, must believe, for that is the proper act in order thereunto. But he that would know himself, or would manifest to others, that he is righteous in Christ's righteousness, that must be brought about by the heavenliness of his conversation.

The observation which lies plainly before us from these words is this, That all such who have Christ's righteousness imputed to them, they are not fleshly but spiritual walkers; they do not live the carnal and sinful, but the holy and the heavenly life. Or thus, None can warrantably pretend to an interest in Christ's obedience, (active or passive,) but only such who in their course are acted by the Spirit, and not by the flesh. But I shall not say anything upon this point; both because this walking not after the flesh, but after the Spirit, hath been already fully opened; and also because as to the inseparable connexion betwixt this imputation and this conversation, I may hereafter have occasion to speak more concarnem, ambulant; Christus enim iis duntaxat justitia et legis satisfactio est, qui crucifixo jam vetere homine Spiritui obtemperant, h.e., solis fidelibus.—*Zuingl.*

[1] Quia suam justitiam nullis communicat Christus, nisi quos Spiritus sui vinculo sibi conjungit, additur iterum regeneratio, ne putetur Christus esse peccati minister, sicuti proclive est multis ad carnis lasciviam rapere quicquid de paterna Dei indulgentia traditur.—*Calvin.*

[2] *Vide* Chrysost. et Œcum. *in loc.*

[3] Etsi fides principalis conditio sit, quia tamen interna est, &c. Ideo addit illam externam, de qua nemo gloriari possit, nisi se habere foris demonstret.—*Pareus.*

---

[1] Pererius, Disp. 3 in cap. 8 ad Rom.

[2] Apostolus non affirmat justificationem legis a nobis impleri, sed in nobis; nec quia incedimus secundum Spiritum ut hæc causa sit, sed ut hoc testimonio et judicio intelligamus legis justificationem in nobis impleri qui secundum Spiritum incedimus.—*Whittak. contra Duræum. de Patad.*, lib. viii. fol. 203.

[3] Ideo apostolus admodum apposite, &c.—Vide *Bezam. in loc.* Christus est illis justitia qui juxta Spiritum, non juxta

veniently to it, when I shall have more room for it than here I have.

I will close all with a brief survey of the verses which I have gone over, that we may the better understand the apostle's method in them, and also what progress we have made in the thing which he is upon.

He first lays down his main foundation, in this proposition, 'There is no condemnation to them who are in Christ Jesus,' ver. 1. Then he amplifies himself about this proposition: where (1.) He characterises the proper subject of the privilege, (viz., of non-condemnation,) 'who walk not after the flesh, but after the Spirit.' This only he names in the general, ver. 1 and 4; but then ver. 5 he falls upon a more full and particular illustration of it, which he continues in several verses. The second thing he doth about the proposition is to prove the truth of the predicate, that there is no condemnation, &c. And this he doth by these mediums: They who are freed by the regenerating Spirit from the power of sin, and by Christ's death and sacrifice from the guilt of sin, as also who have Christ's full obedience and satisfaction of the law imputed to them, to them there is no condemnation. But thus it is with all in Christ Jesus: 'By the law of the Spirit of life in Christ' they are 'freed from the law of sin and death,' (there is deliverance from the power of sin;) God, by Christ's being a sacrifice, hath condemned sin, (there is deliverance from the guilt of sin;) and the righteousness of the law is fulfilled in them,

(there is Christ's obedience imputed to them;) upon all this it must needs follow that to them there is no condemnation, (which was the thing to be proved.)

Now these being things of great weight and importance, wherein the very vitals and spirit of the gospel do lie, the due and distinct opening of them, with other truths interwoven in the words, hath made this volume grow to a far greater bigness than what I expected. Wherein I have been unnecessarily prolix, I humbly beg the reader's pardon; but truly in speaking to the saint's exemption from condemnation, the mystical union of believers with Christ, the spiritual life, the Spirit's agency in freeing souls from the bondage of sin, the law's inability to justify and save, Christ's mission, eternal Sonship, sacrifice, active fulfilling the law, &c.; I say, in these weighty and fundamental points, so little understood by the most, so much oppugned by some, I thought I could scarce say too much. Yet if such who are judicious shall tell me this is a fault, I will endeavour to mend it in what shall follow, wishing that I could as easily mend other faults as that. Well! I have begun, and having so done I purpose, with God's grace and leave, to go on till I shall come to the end of this excellent chapter; with this proviso, if I may have some encouragement that these past labours may, in some measure, be useful and profitable. Without that, why should I proceed to trouble others and myself too? The good Lord give a blessing to what is done, and assist in what is yet further to be done!

THE END.

THE INDEX,

DIRECTING TO THE PRINCIPAL THINGS INSISTED UPON IN THIS BOOK.

Reader, in the drawing up of this index many
things occasionally spoken unto have slipped me ;
but thou wilt find them under those main heads
which I chiefly insist upon, to each of which thou
art here directed.